Equity Valuation
Fourth Edition

Materials Coordinated by
Roger M. Edelen
The Wharton School of the
University of Pennsylvania

The McGraw-Hill Companies, Inc.
Primis Custom Publishing

New York St. Louis San Francisco Auckland Bogotá
Caracas Lisbon London Madrid Mexico Milan Montreal
New Delhi Paris San Juan Singapore Sydney Tokyo Toronto

McGraw·Hill

A Division of The McGraw·Hill Companies

Equity Valuation

This book contains select materials from

The Analysis and Use of Financial Statements by Gerald I. White, CFA, Ashwinpaul C. Sondhi, Ph.D., Dov Fried, Ph.D. Copyright © 1998, 1994 by John Wiley & Sons, Inc.
Reprinted with permission of the publisher.

Valuation: Measuring and Managing the Value of Companies, Second Edition by Tom Copeland, Tim Koller, Jack Murrin. Copyright © 1995, 1994 by by John Wiley & Sons, Inc.
Reprinted with permission of the publisher.

Damodaran on Valuation: Security Analysis for Investment and Corporate Finance by Aswath Damodaran. Copyright © 1994 by John Wiley & Sons, Inc. Reprinted with permission of the publisher.

McGraw-Hill's Primis Custom Publishing Series consists of products that are produced from camera-ready copy. Peer review, class testing, and accuracy are primarily the responsibility of the author(s).

567890 XRC XRC 9098

ISBN 0-07-234138-6

Editor: J. D. Ice
Cover Design: Maggie Lytle
Printer/Binder: Xerographic Reproduction Center

Table of Contents

Section I
Discounted Cash Flow Models

Section II
Price Multiple Valuation

Discounted Cash Flow Models

Security Analysis: How to Analyze Accounting and Market Data to Value Securities

Robert W. Holthausen and Mark E. Zmijewski

Chapter 2

Interest Tax Shields, the Cost of Capital, and Valuation

1. Recall our alternative techniques for *valuing the firm*.

Adjusted Cost of Capital Method (WACC).

The first technique discounts the free cash flows of the unlevered firm (i.e., ignores financing) using an adjusted cost of capital, such as the weighted average cost of capital (WACC), which explicitly incorporates the value of the interest tax shield in the discount rate. This is referred to as the *adjusted cost of capital* method (ACC). In practice, this is the technique most commonly used.

This method requires forecasts of the free cash flows of the unlevered firm and the WACC for every period.

This method is most useful if the firm adopts a "constant" debt to value capital structure strategy.

Adjusted Present Value Method.

The second technique discounts the same free cash flows of the unlevered firm at the cost of capital for the unlevered firm (i.e., the equity cost of capital assuming the firm is 100% equity financed) and adds the present value of the tax shield. This technique is often referred to as the *adjusted present value* method (APV). The cost of capital for the unlevered firm used in this technique is higher than the adjusted cost of capital used in the first technique, because it doesn't incorporate the value of the interest tax shield.

This method requires forecasts of the free cash flows of the unlevered firm, the unlevered cost of capital, forecasts of interest tax shields, and a discount rate for valuing the interest tax shield.

This method is most useful if you have forecasts of future interest tax shields for all periods which implies that you have forecasts of explicit levels of future debt.

While we discuss the adjusted cost of capital method and adjusted present value method as alternative methods, in truth, we often use both methods in the same valuation situation. For example, you may use the adjusted present value method for near term cash flows (because you believe the debt amounts are not related to firm value in the short term) and the adjusted cost of capital method for flows that are further off in the future (because you believe the firm will follow a constant debt/value strategy in the long run).

Security Analysis: How to Analyze Accounting and Market Data to Value Securities
  Robert W. Holthausen and Mark E. Zmijewski
  \CH2.W51

Do not reproduce without permission.
July 29, 1998

3

2.   Discounting equity flows to value common equity.

We also discussed valuing the equity directly by discounting the free cash flows to the equity at the equity cost of capital. Implementing this technique is not possible unless you first value the firm using either the ACC or APV methods, which ever is appropriate; therefore; we do not recommend using this approach as it does not provide an independent valuation.

A.   In these notes we:

(1)   review the value of the interest tax shield;

(2)   review the adjusted cost of capital method (weighted average cost of capital) and adjusted present value method and make clear when each alternative is most easily implemented;

(3)   discuss conceptually, how one obtains estimates of the unlevered cost of capital from estimates of the cost of equity capital and cost of debt capital or alternatively, how to obtain estimates of the equity cost of capital from estimates of the unlevered cost of capital and the debt cost of capital;

(4)   review valuing a firm's common equity by discounting the free cash flows to the equity at the equity cost of capital and discuss why this technique is always difficult to implement; and

(5)   discuss recent theoretical extensions concerning the value of the interest tax shield.

3.   **Interest Tax Shields - Background.**

In this section we discuss some of the theoretical underpinnings of the effect of the capital structure strategy on the value of the firm.

A.   Modigliani & Miller (M&M) -- With No Taxes.

M&M show that with perfect capital markets (i.e., no taxes, no transactions costs, no information processing or acquisition costs, assets infinitely divisible, market participants act as price takers) that the weighted average cost of capital and the value of the firm is not affected by capital structure, holding investment policy fixed.

Simple idea -- Holding investment policy fixed, the value of the assets of the unlevered firm is unchanged by how you split up the cash flows (i.e., by what claims you issue against the cash flows). This is a restatement of the value additivity principle in reverse.

Assuming no taxes implies that the firm's weighted average cost of capital is unaffected by leverage; therefore, the value of the firm is unaffected by the firm's financing decisions.

Security Analysis: How to Analyze Accounting and Market Data to Value Securities
Robert W. Holthausen and Mark E. Zmijewski
\CH2.W51

B.   M&M -- With Corporate Taxes

The introduction of corporate taxes affects M&M's proposition because of the value of the interest tax shield. Interest expense is a tax-deductible expense for the corporation whereas dividends are not; thus, payments made to debtholders escape taxation at the corporate level. Based on this preferential treatment of interest payments, many academics and practitioners argue that there is a tax advantage to debt. While there is not unanimity on the issue of the tax advantages of debt in the capital structure, we hold off on that until later in the Chapter. Since payments to debtholders are tax-deductible,

Value of Firm   =   Value of Firm if 100% Equity Financed

                       + Present Value of the Interest Tax Shield.

Thus, adding debt to the capital structure increases the value of the firm by the present value of the interest tax shield. The present value of the tax shield is the present value of the tax savings on the interest associated with the debt.

Example 2.1:

Assume a firm has $100,000 of debt at a coupon rate of 10%, and that it plans to retire $20,000 of debt per year at the end of each of the following five years. Assume the interest is paid at the end of each year based on the debt outstanding at the beginning of the year. After 5 years the debt will be fully retired and the firm does not plan to ever issue debt again. Further assume that the tax rate was 40% and that the appropriate discount rate for valuing the interest tax shield is 10%.

Solution:

Year	Debt O/S at Begin	Interest	Interest Tax Shield	Discount Factor	Present Value
1	100,000	10,000	4,000	0.90909	3,636.36
2	80,000	8,000	3,200	0.82645	2,644.64
3	60,000	6,000	2,400	0.75131	1,803.14
4	40,000	4,000	1,600	0.68301	1,092.82
5	20,000	2,000	800	0.62092	496.74
	Total				9,673.70

Often you will see the present value of the tax shield calculated as the product of the corporate tax rate and the amount of debt. This is a shortcut formulation and it is correct only assuming that the required rate of return for the risk of the tax shield is equal to the

Security Analysis: How to Analyze Accounting and Market Data to Value Securities
Robert W. Holthausen and Mark E. Zmijewski
\CH2.W51

Do not reproduce without permission.
July 29, 1998

5

cost of debt capital, that the *level* of debt of the firm is permanent and that the firm is not expected to grow or decline over time.

Why is the present value of the tax shield just to the corporate tax rate times the amount of debt given the assumptions?

$$\text{PV Tax Shield} = \frac{\text{corporate tax rate x interest rate x amount of debt}}{\text{appropriate discount rate for valuing the tax shield}}$$

Since the interest rate on debt is assumed to be equal to the appropriate discount rate for valuing the interest tax shield, the PV of the tax shield is equal to the corporate tax rate multiplied by the amount of debt. This formulation is not appropriate for a growing or declining firm which anticipates holding constant the dollar amount of debt, since the appropriate discount rate for valuing the interest tax shield would change over time.

There are some empirical regularities that cannot be explained by M&M's view of the world (that the value of the levered firm equals the value of the unlevered firm plus the value of interest tax shields. First, we do not observe most firms financing 100 percent of the firm with debt. Second, we do not observe large changes in firms' capital structures when we there are large changes in corporate tax rates. We discuss these issues at the end of this chapter.

C.   Choice of Interest Rate for Valuing Interest Tax Shields.

The choice of the discount rate appropriate for valuing the interest tax shield is an important issue that is not completely settled in finance. The debate regarding the appropriate discount rate for interest tax shields revolves around the risk associated with the interest tax shield. Interest tax shields are risky because of variation in the amount of debt outstanding which will be related to the return the firm earns on its operating assets, variation in statutory tax rates, and variation in the firm's marginal tax bracket because of changes in profitability.

At present, there is some consensus in academe regarding the appropriate discount rate for interest tax shields under certain assumptions. The problem is that firms probably don't behave strictly in accordance with either of the two most common assumptions.

One view is that for a firm that has a fixed schedule of debt financing that is *not related to the value of the firm*, the cost of debt is an appropriate discount rate for valuing the interest tax shields. In other words, for a firm for which you have a forecast of all future interest tax shields that is independent of firm value, the cost of debt is the appropriate discount rate. The rational for this conclusion is that the amount of the debt does not depend on the value of the firm, and only depends on the risk of changes in statutory tax rates and the risk that the firm may not be able to get an interest deduction because it isn't profitable. Further, the riskiness of the firm's ability to obtain a tax deduction based on its profitability is well-approximated by the cost of debt.

Security Analysis: How to Analyze Accounting and Market Data to Value Securities
  Robert W. Holthausen and Mark E. Zmijewski
\CH2.W51

Do not reproduce without permission.
July 29, 1998

6

The other view of the world is that for a firm that manages its capital structure with a fixed debt/value ratio, the amount of the interest tax shield for a year is only known one year in advance (this assumes that the firm adjusts its capital structure at annual intervals which is the typical assumption). Thus, the amount of the interest tax shields beyond one year depends on the value of the firm. Given this capital structure strategy, the discount rate for a year in which the interest tax shield is known is the cost of debt, and the discount rate for years in which the interest tax shield is not known is the cost of capital for the unlevered firm. The rational for using the cost of capital for the unlevered firm is that the amount of the interest tax shield depends on the value of the firm.

In truth, probably neither of these working assumptions is strictly correct. Managers would not literally adjust their debt for every change in the firm's market value (or even annually), hence discounting the interest tax shield at the cost of capital for the unlevered firm could conceivably be slightly too high. Of course, managers cannot literally pursue a debt policy which is independent of the value of the firm. Thus, valuing the interest tax shield at the cost of debt may be too low a discount rate. The true discount rate for valuing interest tax shields probably lies between the two extremes. Which assumption one should use depends on which of the two alternative policies is closest to management's capital structure policy. The two alternatives would certainly bound the value of the interest tax shields.

Consider an LBO transaction in which there is a fixed repayment schedule for the debt down to some long run capital structure. Many argue that the discount rate for valuing the interest tax shield during the period in which the debt is paid down to a constant capital structure is well approximated by the cost of debt. The explanation for this conclusion is that the amount of debt is not tied to the value of the firm because the firm has agreed to a set pay down schedule, and the cost of debt reflects the risk associated with non-payment.[1]

For our purposes in this chapter, we assume that interest tax shields are valued using either the cost of debt or the unlevered cost of capital. The cost of debt is used whenever you have forecasts for interest tax shields that do not depend on the value of the firm, i.e., management is managing to a fixed dollar amount of debt at each point in time, regardless of the value of the firm. The unlevered cost of capital is used whenever the amount of debt is assumed to vary with the value of the firm, in particular when management is assumed to manage to a constant debt/value ratio.

---

[1]Note, the cost of debt is not necessarily equal to the stated interest rate on the debt because the relevant variable, the expected return on the debt, is typically lower than the stated interest rate in very highly leveraged transactions (or with any speculative grade debt) because of the default probability. An alternative way to say this is that promised yields to maturity do not equal expected yields on speculative grade debt. On the other hand, in some LBO transactions, the expected return on the debt is actually higher than the stated interest rate because the debt has some equity kickers attached to it.

Security Analysis: How to Analyze Accounting and Market Data to Value Securities
  Robert W. Holthausen and Mark E. Zmijewski
\CH2.W51

While we discuss this further in chapter 4, it is inconceivable that the amount of debt in the firm's capital structure is completely independent of the firm's value. As such, at least in the long-run, we recommend that ultimately the amount of debt in the capital structure be tied to firm value.

4.   The Adjusted Present Value and Adjusted Cost of Capital Valuation Methods Revisited.

    A.   The Adjusted Present Value Method (APV).

The adjusted present value (APV) method discounts the free cash flows of the firm ignoring financing at the cost of capital for the unlevered firm, and then adds the present value of the interest tax shields.[2] We discuss obtaining estimates of the cost of capital for the unlevered firm in a later section. The interest tax shield can be discounted using whatever discount rate is appropriate, whether that be the cost of debt capital, the cost of capital of the unlevered firm, or some other discount rate.

    (1)   Several advantages of the APV method are

        (a)   It is completely general so that you can apply it to a firm whose capital structure is changing through time or whose cost of capital for the unlevered firm is changing through time.

        (b)   It is the more easily implemented method for valuing a firm whose capital structure is changing through time. However, it is very difficult to implement if the debt is assumed to be a constant proportion of the value of the firm.

        (c)   The APV makes it obvious how much of the firm's value is based on the value of the interest tax shield.

The APV method always works, but it is not necessarily the easiest method to use.

    (2)   The APV method requires the following information

        (a)   An estimate of the unlevered cost of capital for a firm, which is typically assumed to be constant overtime unless there is a forecast for the purchase or sale of assets with different risk than the firm. Estimates of the unlevered cost of capital for a firm are derived from knowledge of the value of the equity, value of the debt, cost of equity capital, cost of debt capital and value of the interest tax shield. Since all of these are not typically known for a firm you wish to value, the unlevered cost of capital is typically estimated from publicly traded comparable firms.

---

[2]It is important to recognize that it is also necessary to subtract any expected costs of financial distress from the value of the interest tax shields; we discuss this issue at the end of the chapter.

Security Analysis: How to Analyze Accounting and Market Data to Value Securities
  Robert W. Holthausen and Mark E. Zmijewski
  \CH2.W51

(b)   Free cash flows of the unlevered firm for every year.

(c)   The interest tax shields for every year. Note that for a firm that maintains a constant capital structure strategy (constant debt/value ratio where debt is adjusted annually to maintain the constant debt/value ratio), the value of the firm in year t-1 must be known to calculate the amount of debt outstanding in year t-1 and the interest tax shield in year t.

(d)   A terminal value for the unlevered firm and the interest tax shields.

For firms that follow a constant capital structure strategy, it is the need to measure the amount of the interest tax shields in each year, which is determined by the value of the firm in the previous year, that makes the APV method impractical to implement.

B.   The Adjusted Cost of Capital Method (Weighted Average Cost of Capital).

The adjusted cost of capital method values the free cash flows of the firm (assuming it is 100% equity financed) at the weighted average cost of capital. This adjusted cost of capital is lower than the cost of capital for the unlevered firm, because the value of the interest tax shield is imbedded in the discount rate. Rather than adding the value of the interest tax shield as a separate amount, the value of the interest tax shield is obtained through a reduction in the discount rate used to discount the free cash flows of the unlevered firm.

(1)   This method requires the following information

(a)   An estimate of the adjusted cost of capital for a firm, e.g., WACC. Estimates of the adjusted cost of capital for a firm are derived from knowledge of the debt to value ratio, the tax rate applicable to the interest deduction, the cost of equity capital, the cost of debt capital and an adjustment for the value of the interest tax shield. The cost of equity capital for a private firm is usually derived from knowledge about the cost of capital of the unlevered firm for a publicly traded company.

(b)   Free cash flows of the unlevered firm for every year.

(c)   A terminal value for the (levered) firm and the interest tax shields.

The adjusted cost of capital method is most easily implemented when a firm manages its capital structure to have a constant debt/value ratio, and if we assume that interest tax shields that depend on the value of the firm are discounted at the unlevered cost of capital.[3] This method is not easily implemented when the debt/value ratio is unknown[4]

---

[3]The WACC method is also easily implemented if the dollar amount of debt in the capital structure is constant and perpetual.

Security Analysis: How to Analyze Accounting and Market Data to Value Securities
Robert W. Holthausen and Mark E. Zmijewski
\CH2.W51

July 29, 1998

or changes through time which is the case when a firm follows a capital structure strategy that focuses on particular dollar amounts of debt outstanding over time. For a firm for which you do not know the debt/value ratio, you must first calculate the value of the firm given the expected free cash flows and interest tax shields, and then you can calculate the debt/value ratio and WACC. In this situation, however, you must know the value of the firm to calculate the WACC which defeats the purpose of using WACC.

For a simple capital structure, the weighted average cost of capital is defined as

$$WACC_t = k_{E_t} (E_t/V_t) + k_{D_t} (1-T) (D_t/V_t)$$

where:

$WACC_t$	=	the weighted average cost of capital at time t (adjusted cost of capital rate)
k_{E_t}	=	cost of equity capital at time t
k_{D_t}	=	cost of debt capital at time t
E_t	=	market value of the equity at time t
D_t	=	market value of the debt at time t
V_t	=	market value of the levered firm at time t = $E_t + D_t$
T	=	the appropriate tax rate for calculating the value of the interest tax shield

The weighted average cost of capital is the average cost of capital for the firm given a capital structure. It is a weighted average of the cost of equity and debt capital. The cost of debt capital is multiplied by one minus the tax rate (1-T) in order to reduce the effective cost of debt capital because of the tax deductibility of interest.

If other forms of financing exist, such as preferred stock, then the WACC calculation includes the cost of capital of the preferred, weighted appropriately, as well.

It is important to always keep in mind that both k_{E_t} and k_{D_t} change with changes in the underlying risk of the assets and the capital structure of the firm; therefore, if the debt/value ratio changes over time, the cost of equity and the cost of debt changes over time. In other words, if you are using a constant weighted average cost of capital over time, then the weighted average cost of capital presumes that the firm will always keep

---

[4]This situation arises because many investments are financed with a dollar amount of debt before the value of the investment is known. For example, assume you are starting a firm with an initial investment of $20,000, one-half of which you expect to finance with debt. You expect this firm to generate sufficient cash flows to avoid any need for additional debt financing. The original financing decision is made on the basis on the initial investment in this case, without regard to the subsequent value of the firm. In this case, the value of the firm, and hence, the debt/value ratio is unknown. Of course over time, management may choose to adapt the debt policy to pursue a fairly constant debt/value ratio.

Security Analysis: How to Analyze Accounting and Market Data to Value Securities
Robert W. Holthausen and Mark E. Zmijewski
\CH2.W51

the proportion of the market values of the debt and equity constant. Thus, if the value of the equity unexpectedly increases or decreases, management is assumed to make appropriate adjustments in the capital structure to keep the debt/equity proportions constant.

C.   When is the weighted average cost of capital useful?

The weighted average cost of capital is the discount rate appropriate for valuing "scale expansions" or projects that have the "average" risk of the existing operating assets (unlevered firm), assuming the firm's debt/equity ratio is unchanged.

The weighted average cost of capital is appropriate for valuing the entire firm (i.e., when discounting the cash flows to the firm) assuming the assumptions required for the weighted average cost of capital are met.

The weighted average cost of capital is not an appropriate discount rate for all of the firm's projects. For example it is not appropriate for projects which are either riskier or safer than the average risk of the firm's existing operating assets (unlevered firm), or for projects which will induce changes in the capital structure of the firm.

5.   **Estimating the Cost of Capital.**

In this section we present formulae for estimating the equity cost of capital, weighted average cost of capital, and unlevered cost of capital based on the underlying assumption of a firm's capital structure strategy.

In the typical valuation analysis you perform the following steps to obtain an estimate of the cost of capital for the firm you are interested in valuing (assume that firm is not currently publicly traded):

(1)   Use the financial data of publicly traded comparable firms to estimate the unlevered cost of capital for the firm you are valuing.[5] In order to obtain an estimate of the unlevered cost of capital you must calculate the unlevered cost of capital for each of your comparable companies from estimates of the debt and equity cost of capital for each of your companies and assumptions about the value of their interest tax shields.

But how do you obtain the unlevered cost of capital from the equity and debt cost of capital? You must use the appropriate formula for determining the unlevered cost of capital from knowledge of the equity and debt cost of capital and knowledge of the comparable firm's capital structure policy.

---

[5]You may also use some historic financial data for the firm you are valuing for this purpose.

Security Analysis: How to Analyze Accounting and Market Data to Value Securities
Robert W. Holthausen and Mark E. Zmijewski
\CH2.W51

Do not reproduce without permission.
July 29, 1998

11

(2)   If you have all of the information required to implement the adjusted present value method for the firm you are interested in valuing (specifically, forecasts of all interest tax shields), then you use the estimate of the unlevered cost of capital from the comparable firms to value the unlevered cash flows of the firm you are valuing and add on the value of the interest tax shields for the firm of interest.

(3)   Alternatively, if you do not know the expected interest tax shields because the firm you are valuing is going to follow a constant debt/value capital structure strategy, then you need to use the unlevered cost of capital derived from the comparable firms, to calculate the equity cost of capital for the firm you are valuing. The weighted average cost of capital for the firm you are valuing can then be estimated from the equity cost of capital, debt cost of capital, the debt to value ratio and the firm's marginal tax rate.

But how do you obtain the equity cost of capital for the firm you are valuing from the unlevered cost of capital for the comparable firms? You must use the appropriate formula for determining the equity cost of capital from knowledge of the unlevered cost of capital for the comparable firms and from knowledge of the debt cost of capital and capital structure of the firm you are valuing.

It is typically the case that you do not observe the unlevered cost of capital for a publicly traded firm, rather, you observe the equity cost of capital and the debt cost of capital and calculate the cost of capital for the unlevered firm from this and other information. In what circumstance do you observed the unlevered cost of capital for a publicly traded firm? When the firm has an all equity financed capital structure.

As we shall see, exactly how one performs these calculations depends on the capital structure strategy of the firm. Different assumptions lead to different calculations and different costs of capital.

An Important Caveat: The material which follows attempts to provide an understandable and consistent view of the valuation process. In practice, many valuation experts do not maintain consistency in the valuation process (i.e., they may inadvertently perform calculations which actually make different assumptions about the value of the interest tax shields). We think using inconsistent assumptions is inappropriate valuation practice, but in reality the size of the errors induced in by these practices is likely to be small. While we recommend not making inconsistent assumptions (it never looks very good when you are asked to support your valuation work -- for example in court), you may ultimately choose to make some of these inconsistent assumptions. If nothing else, these notes should allow you to make an informed choice.

These formulations assume that the firm has only debt and equity in its capital structure and that interest tax shields are valued using the either cost of debt capital or the cost of capital of the unlevered firm. In addition, some (but not all) of these formulas assume that the cost

Security Analysis: How to Analyze Accounting and Market Data to Value Securities
Robert W. Holthausen and Mark E. Zmijewski
\CH2.W51

Do not reproduce without permission.
July 29, 1998

12

of debt and the coupon rates on the debt are identical. For now, assume that the cost of debt and coupon rates are the same. The appendix to Chapter 4 will revisit this issue. Moreover, financial distress costs are assumed to be zero. We introduce more complicated capital structures in a later chapter.

We begin our discussion by examining how the equity cost of capital is determined from the cost of capital for the unlevered firm, the debt cost of capital, and the capital structure strategy, but first we put these issues in the context of the economic balance sheet we presented in Chapter 1.

A. The Economic Balance Sheet.

Below we present an economic balance sheet for the market value of the firm. It is important to know that the economic balance sheet differs from the accounting balance sheet in two ways. First, the market value, not the accounting (historic cost) value of the assets are relevant to this balance sheet. Second, all assets and liabilities, not only the assets and liabilities recorded by accountants, are relevant to this balance sheet. We assume for simplicity that the firm is financed only with debt and equity. The economic balance sheet makes a simple point.

Security Analysis: How to Analyze Accounting and Market Data to Value Securities
Robert W. Holthausen and Mark E. Zmijewski
\CH2.W51

Do not reproduce without permission.
July 29, 1998

13

Assets (at market value):

MV of Assets of the 100% Equity Financed Firm	V_{Ut}	@ k_U
MV of Tax Shelters from Financing = $DVTS_{t,all}$		
MV of Tax Shelters discounted at k_{Dt} this period	$DVTS_{t,k(Dt)}$	@ k_{Dt}
MV of Tax Shelters discounted at k_U this period	$DVTS_{t,k(U)}$	@ k_U
MV of the Assets/Equities of the Firm	V_{Lt}	

Equities (at market value):

MV of Debt Financing	D_t	@ k_{Dt}
MV of Common Equity	E_t	@ k_{Et}
MV of the Assets/Equities of the Firm	V_{Lt}	

where:

k_U	=	cost of capital for the unlevered firm assumed constant
k_{Et}	=	cost of equity capital for the equity at time t
k_{Dt}	=	cost of debt capital at time t
$WACC_t$	=	weighted average cost of capital at time t
E_t	=	market value of the equity at time t
D_t	=	market value of the debt at time t
$DVTS_{t,k(Dt)}$	=	present value of the interest tax shield at time t discounted at discount rate k_{Dt} in period t.
$DVTS_{t,k(U)}$	=	present value of the interest tax shield at time t discounted at discount rate k_U in period t.
T	=	the appropriate tax rate for calculating the value of the interest tax shield.

The assets of the firm can be divided into the assets of the firm if 100 percent equity financed and the assets of the firm associated with its financing decisions, in particular, the interest tax shield. The assets of the 100 percent equity financed firm have a value and a discount rate that is independent of the firm's capital structure. The value of the firm is equal to the value of the unlevered firm plus the discounted value of the interest tax shields.

The discount rate for the cash flows from the unlevered firm is the unlevered cost of capital, the discount rate for the interest tax shields is either the unlevered cost of capital or the debt cost of capital (depending on the capital structure strategy of the firm), and the discount rate for the firm is equal to its weighted average cost of capital. There are two claims on the value of the firm, the fixed debt claims and the residual equity claims. The discount rate for debt is the cost of debt and the discount rate for equity is the cost of equity.

Security Analysis: How to Analyze Accounting and Market Data to Value Securities
  Robert W. Holthausen and Mark E. Zmijewski
\CH2.W51

Do not reproduce without permission.
July 29, 1998

14

The important relation to glean from the economic balance sheet is that the unlevered cost of capital is given by the operating (not financing) decisions of the firm. The equity cost of capital is determined from the unlevered cost of capital, the capital structure, the effect of the interest tax shields on the value of the firm, and the debt cost of capital. Further, the weighted average cost of capital is related to the equity cost of capital, the after-tax debt cost of capital, and financial leverage.

B.   The equity cost of capital for a firm.

In this section we discuss how the equity cost of capital is determined from the unlevered cost of capital, the debt cost of capital, and the capital structure strategy. The intuition underlying each of the cases we discuss below is that the equity cost of capital is equal to the unlevered cost of capital plus some additional amount that depends on the debt/equity ratio and the value of the interest tax shields. Remember that the unlevered cost of capital is taken as given based on the firm's operating decisions.

First, we derive the general case for the equity cost of capital, and then we discuss four cases which make simplifying assumptions regarding the value of the interest tax shelters.

General Case.

Given the economic balance sheet, it must be the case that the required rate of return on the (economic) assets of the firm is equal to the required rate of return on the securities financing those assets; in other words,

$$V_{Ut}*k_U + DVTS_{t,k(Dt)}*k_{Dt} + DVTS_{t,k(U)}*k_U = D_t*k_{Dt} + E_t*k_{Et}.$$

Therefore,

$$k_{Et} = V_{Ut}/E_t*k_U + DVTS_{t,k(Dt)}/E_t*k_{Dt} + DVTS_{t,k(U)}/E_t*k_U - D_t/E_t*k_{Dt}.$$

Since, $V_{Lt} = D_t + E_t = V_{Ut} + DVTS_{t,k(Dt)} + DVTS_{t,k(U)}$,

and $V_{Ut} = D_t + E_t - DVTS_{t,k(Dt)} - DVTS_{t,k(U)}$,

$$k_{Et} = (D_t+E_t-DVTS_{t,k(Dt)}-DVTS_{t,k(U)})/E_t*k_U + DVTS_{t,k(Dt)}/E_t*k_{Dt} + DVTS_{t,k(U)}/E_t*k_U - D_t/E_t*k_{Dt}.$$

$$k_{Et} = k_U + (D_t-DVTS_{t,k(Dt)})/E_t*k_U + DVTS_{t,k(Dt)}/E_t*k_{Dt} - D_t/E_t*k_{Dt}.$$

$$k_{Et} = k_U + (D_t-DVTS_{t,k(Dt)})/E_t*k_U - (D_t-DVTS_{t,k(Dt)})/E_t*k_{Dt}.$$

$$k_{Et} = k_U + (k_U - k_{Dt})*(D_t-DVTS_{t,k(Dt)})/E_t.$$

The intuition underpinning this general case is that the equity cost of capital is equal to the unlevered cost of capital plus a premium for the financial risk due to financial leverage. Since interest is tax deductible, and since the risk of some of this tax shelter is less than the unlevered cost of capital, the risk premium is reduced.

Security Analysis: How to Analyze Accounting and Market Data to Value Securities
Robert W. Holthausen and Mark E. Zmijewski
\CH2.W51

Do not reproduce without permission.
July 29, 1998

15

Next, we discuss four cases which make assumptions that simplify the general case. Case I is the case in which there is no tax deduction for interest or the discount rate for all tax shields is the unlevered cost of capital. Case II is the case in which you have a forecast of all interest tax shields that do not depend on the value of the firm and you discount the interest tax shields at the debt cost of capital. Case III is the case in which the firm follows a fixed debt/value ratio so that future interest tax shields depend on the value of the firm.

Case I - No tax deduction for interest

If there is no tax deduction for interest, issuing debt does not increase the value of the firm. Though you may believe this case is irrelevant, that is not the case since interest is not tax deductible in all countries. In this case, $DVTS_{t,k(Dt)}=0$. Therefore, the equity cost of capital in terms of an the unlevered cost of capital and debt cost of capital is equal to

$$k_{Et} = k_U + (k_U-k_{Dt})*D_t/E_t.$$

Thus, the equity cost of capital is equal to the unlevered cost of capital plus an increase to compensate for equityholders for the risk resulting from the capital structure strategy of the firm. Intuition is that there is now a fixed claim which must be satisfied (payment to the debtholder) before the equity holders obtain anything.

This is a formulation that you may have seen before. It is the standard treatment for levering and unlevering betas (a very closely related topic which discuss in the next chapter). Note, that it critically hinges on the assumption of no tax deduction for interest (or equivalently, no taxes).

The above formula is also appropriate for calculating the equity cost of capital from the unlevered cost of capital if all interest tax shields are discounted at k_U. In this case, $DVTS_{t,k(Dt)}=0$ again. Note however, that interest tax shields will add value, but not through any change in the discount rate of the equity since the interest tax shields are assumed to be as risky as the unlevered cash flows.

Case II - Interest tax shelters do not depend on the value of the levered firm.

In this case, we assume that the interest tax shelters are known and do not depend on the value of the firm (i.e., there is a fixed schedule for the maintenance, growth or decline of debt which is not affected by variation in firm value. Under this assumption, all interest tax shields are discounted at the debt cost of capital.

The equity cost of capital is equal to the general case unless some assumptions can be made about $DVTS_{t,k(Dt)}$

$$k_{Et} = k_U + (k_U - k_{Dt})*(D_t-DVTS_{t,k(Dt)})/E_t.$$

Security Analysis: How to Analyze Accounting and Market Data to Value Securities
Robert W. Holthausen and Mark E. Zmijewski
\CH2.W51

Do not reproduce without permission.
July 29, 1998

16

In case II the increase in the equity cost of capital required to compensate equityholders for the capital structure risk is reduced (relative to the no tax deduction case) because of the value of the interest tax shields. The larger the value of the interest tax shields, the lower the required premium. Another way of saying this is to note that the equity holders have a claim to the cash flows from operating assets with a discount rate k_U which becomes more risky because of the leverage effect. Simultaneously with increases in leverage, however, the equity holders lay title to another asset, interest tax shields, which are discounted at k_{Dt}, a lower discount rate.

We sometimes make simplifying perpetuity assumptions regarding the present value of the interest tax shields. If so, case II can be simplified even further. One simplifying assumption is that the firm is going to have a fixed dollar amount of debt and that the firm is expected to generate the same cash flow in perpetuity. Given this assumption, the value of the interest tax shields ($DVTS_{t,k(Dt)}$) is equal to T*D. Substituting T*D into the above formula yields another formula you may have seen before:

$$k_{Et} = k_U + (k_U - k_{Dt})*(1-T)*D_t/E_t.$$

Alternatively, assume that the firm's debt is going to grow at some rate, g, and that the firm is expected to grow at approximately the same rate as the debt. Given this assumption, the value of the interest tax shields ($DVTS_{t,k(Dt)}$) is equal to $(k_{Dt}*T*D)/(k_{Dt}-g)$. Substituting this result into the above formula yields

$$k_{Et} = k_U + (k_U - k_{Dt})*[1-(Tk_{Dt}/(k_{Dt}-g))]*D_t/E_t.$$

Case III - Constant debt/value capital structure strategy.

In this case, the firm can grow in any manner, constant or otherwise but it manages its capital structure to have a fixed debt to firm value ratio. Debt is assumed to be fixed at the end of each year, dependent on the value of the firm and then held constant until the end of the next year. Thus, there are no midyear adjustments to hold debt to value constant. The interest tax shield is discounted at the cost of debt for the last period (because the debt for the last year is always fixed at the beginning of the year) and is discounted at the cost of capital for the unlevered firm for all other years because the amount of debt outstanding varies with the value of the firm.

This is often referred to as the Miles and Ezzell formulation (see Miles and Ezzell [1980]; also discussions by Brealey and Myers, Chapter 19.

Make sure you understand what's being assumed. Suppose the D/V ratio is 40% and the value of the firm right now (the end of the year) is 500. Management arranges to have 200 of debt so that D/V = 40%. Assume the interest rate is 10% and the tax rate is 30%. Management only revisits the capital structure decision at the end of every year.

Under these assumptions the interest expense (assumed to be paid at the end of the year) will be 20 and the interest tax shield will be 6. Notice, that at the beginning of this year, we knew the interest tax shield for the end of the year, because we knew the amount of debt outstanding, except for the potential risk of non-payment or non-deductibility. **Give the only risk involved in the first year's interest tax shield is non-deductibility and non-payment, the appropriate discount rate for this tax shield is Kd.**

In valuing the firm, our cash flow forecasts will yield *expected values* of the firm at each future point in time. Assume that given our cash flows, we expect that the value of the firm at the end of the first year will be 1000. Our expectation is, that management will now have to have issue more debt so that 400 of debt is outstanding, because their capital structure policy is to maintain a D/V ratio of 40%. The interest tax shield for year 2 is expected to be 12.

But notice we do not know what the interest tax shield for year 2 will actually be until the end of year 1 when we observe the value of the firm at the end of year 1. For example, if at the end of year 1, the value of the firm is only 750, management will only want 300 of debt outstanding the interest tax shield will only turn out to be 9 for the second year? So what is the riskiness of the second year's interest tax shield?

The risk of the second year's interest tax shield varies between the first and second year. During the first year there is risk because we do not know what the value of the firm will be at the end of the first year. What is the risk associated with variation in firm value? It is as risky as the underlying assets of the unlevered firm. The appropriate discount rate is thus Ku for the first of the two years.

However, after the first year the only risk remaining is that of non--payment or non-deductibility? There is no risk about the amount of debt? Thus, the second year's tax shield is discounted by Kd in the second period.

- **Thus, to discount the second year's tax shield we discount it by Ku for the first period and Kd for the second period.**

Thus, ITS_2 (the interest tax shield for year 2) is discounted by $1/(1+K_u)(1+K_d)$.

ITS_3 is discounted by $1/(1+K_u)^2(1+K_d)$.

Using this logic how is ITS_4 discounted?

More formally --

The assumptions in this approach suggests that the value of the interest tax shields is

$$DVTS_{t,all} = D_t T k_{Dt}/(1+k_{Dt}) + DVTS_{t+1,all}/(1+k_U), \text{ and}$$

Security Analysis: How to Analyze Accounting and Market Data to Value Securities
Robert W. Holthausen and Mark E. Zmijewski
\CH2.W51

$$DVTS_{t,k(Dt)} = D_tTk_{Dt}/(1+k_{Dt}).$$

Substituting this formulation of $DVTS_{t,k(Dt)}$ in the general case results in the following equity cost of capital

$$k_E = k_U + (k_U - k_{Dt})*[D_t-(D_tTk_{Dt}/(1+k_{Dt}))]/E_t$$

$$k_E = k_U + (k_U - k_{Dt})*[1-(Tk_{Dt}/(1+k_{Dt}))]*D_t/E_t.$$

Note, this is very close to the value for k_E we obtained in case I where we assumed no tax deduction for interest. WHY? Because most of the tax shield is discounted at the cost of capital of the unlevered firm in case III, and little is discounted at the cost of debt. Hence, the differences in the discount rates between case I and case III are small. However, applying the logic of case I and case III would yield very different valuations, because in one case we value the interest tax shields and in the other we do not value them.

Some notes on discounting interest tax shields under these assumptions.

It is useful to truly understand what is being assumed about discounting the cash flows in this case. Note what the assumption that the discount rate for a tax shield is the cost of debt in the last period and the cost of capital for the unlevered firm for all prior years implies about the valuation of the interest tax shields.

$$DVTS_{t,all} = D_tTk_{Dt}/(1+k_{Dt}) + DVTS_{t+1,all}/(1+k_U), \text{ and}$$

$$DVTS_{t+1,all} = D_{t+1}Tk_{Dt+1}/(1+k_{Dt+1}) + DVTS_{t+2,all}/(1+k_U), \text{ and}$$

$$DVTS_{t+2,all} = D_{t+2}Tk_{Dt+2}/(1+k_{Dt+2}) + DVTS_{t+3,all}/(1+k_U), \text{ and}$$

$$\vdots \quad \vdots \quad \vdots \quad \vdots \quad \vdots \quad \vdots \quad \vdots$$

$$DVTS_{t+N,all} = D_{t+N}Tk_{Dt+N}/(1+k_{Dt+N}) + DVTS_{t+N+1,all}/(1+k_U).$$

$$\vdots \quad \vdots \quad \vdots \quad \vdots \quad \vdots \quad \vdots \quad \vdots$$

Substituting $DVTS_{t+1,all}$ to $DVTS_{t+\infty,all}$ into $DVTS_{t,all}$, results in

$$DVTS_{t,all} = D_tTk_{Dt}/(1+k_{Dt}) + D_{t+1}Tk_{Dt+1}/((1+k_{Dt+1})*(1+k_U))$$

$$+ D_{t+2}Tk_{Dt+2}/((1+k_{Dt+2})*(1+K_U)^2)$$

$$+ .... + D_{t+N}Tk_{Dt+N}/((1+k_{Dt+N})*(1+k_U)^N) + ...$$

Security Analysis: How to Analyze Accounting and Market Data to Value Securities
Robert W. Holthausen and Mark E. Zmijewski
\CH2.W51

If you assume that the firm (all value relevant characteristics) will infinitely grow at some rate g and that K_{Dt} and K_U are constant through time, then the above formula can be rewritten as

$$DVTS_{t,all} = D_t Tk_{Dt}/(1+k_{Dt}) * \{1 + (1+g)/(1+k_U) + (1+g)^2/(1+K_U)^2 + ... + (1+g)^N/(1+k_U)^N + ... \}$$

This infinite series can be rewritten as

$$DVTS_{t,all} = D_t Tk_{Dt}/(k_U-g)*[(1+k_U)/(1+k_{Dt})].$$

Case IV - Interest Tax Shields All Discounted at K_U

If interest tax shields are all discounted at the unlevered cost of capital, then the formula for calculating the equity cost of capital from the unlevered cost of capital is identical to Case I because $DVTS_{t,k(Dt)}=0$. Therefore, the equity cost of capital in terms of an the unlevered cost of capital and debt cost of capital is equal to

$$k_{Et} = k_U + (k_U-k_{Dt})*D_t/E_t.$$

The difference between this and Case I is that interest tax shields will add value, but not through any change in the discount rate of the equity since the interest tax shields are assumed to be as risky as the unlevered cash flows.

Example 2.2:

The following example is somewhat tedious and represents mindnumbing repetition. However, it is included to help assure students that they understand the mechanical application of the formulas.

Assume that you collected the following information for the COE Company for the following independent situations. For all situations assume that the cost of capital for the unlevered firm is 20.0 percent (fixed by the operating decisions of the firm). Assume further that the cost of debt capital is 10.0 percent for all periods. For each example which follows, it is assumed that the firm currently has $200 of debt outstanding and that the free cash flows of the unlevered firm are equal to $100. Calculate the equity cost of capital under the following different assumptions.

(1)   There is no tax deduction for interest, COE Company's debt is expected to grow at 4% per year in perpetuity, COE's free cash flows to the unlevered firm are expected to grow at 4% per year, and COE Company's debt/equity ratio is .47.

In this situation, the correct formula for the cost of equity capital is

$$k_{Et} = k_U + (k_U-k_{Dt})*D_t/E_t, \text{ and the solution is}$$

$$.2470 = .20 + (.20-.10)*.47.$$

Security Analysis: How to Analyze Accounting and Market Data to Value Securities
Robert W. Holthausen and Mark E. Zmijewski
\CH2.W51

This would be the answer for a Case IV problem as well (i.e., where there was a tax deduction for interest but it was valued at the unlevered cost of capital.

(2)   The tax rate for interest deductions is 40.0 percent, COE Company has debt that will grow at a rate of 4 percent in perpetuity, COE's free cash flows to the unlevered firm are expected to grow at 4% per year, and COE Company's debt/equity ratio is .36.

In this situation, the correct formula for the cost of equity capital is

$k_{Et} = k_U + (k_U-k_{Dt})*[1-(Tk_{Dt}/(k_{Dt}-g))]*D_t/E_t$, and the solution to the problem is

$.2120 = .20 + (.20-.10)*[1-(.40*.10/(.10-.04))]*.36$

The reduction in the equity cost of capital from the previous situation results from the value of the interest tax shields. The larger the value of the interest tax shields, the lower the capital structure required risk premium.

Why did the debt/equity ratio change from the situation in which there was no tax deduction for interest?

NOTE: **In problems (1), (2) and (3), the debt/equity ratio provided was unnecessary, because you were provided enough information to calculate the debt/equity ratio. While that is generally not the case in the application of these formulas, convince yourself that you understand the valuation scenarios sufficiently to independently calculate the debt/equity ratios.**

(3)   In problems (2) and (3) you can not use the general form of the formula, unless you calculate the value of E_t, and $DVTS_t$, where the general form is:

$k_{Et} = k_U + (k_U-k_{Dt})*(D_t-DVTS_{t,kd})/E_t$,

To use the general formula you must know k_U, k_{Dt}, T, D_t, E_t, and $DVTS_t$. For the previous situation, assume that the tax rate for interest deductions is 40.0 percent, COE Company has debt that will grow at a rate of 4 percent in perpetuity, and COE Company's debt/equity ratio is .36; further, assume that you have been able to observe the current value of the equity, $558, and the current value of the debt, $200.

In this situation, the general formula for the cost of equity capital can be used. First, you must calculate the value of the interest tax shields, which is

$\$133 = .40*.10*200/(.10-.04)$; next you can calculate k_E using the general formula

$.2120 = .20 + (.20-.10)*(200-133)/558$

Security Analysis: How to Analyze Accounting and Market Data to Value Securities
Robert W. Holthausen and Mark E. Zmijewski
\CH2.W51

(4)   The tax rate for interest deductions is 40.0 percent and the COE Company's capital structure strategy is to have a constant debt/value ratio equal to .29. (equivalent to a debt equity ratio of .408)

In this situation, the correct formula for the cost of equity capital is

$k_{Et} = k_U + (k_U-k_{Dt})*[1-(Tk_{Dt}/(1+k_{Dt}))]*D_t/E_t$, and the solution to the problem is

$.2394 = .20 + (.20-.10)*[1-(.40*.10/(1.10))]*(.29/(1-.29))$.

(5)   The tax rate for interest deductions is 40.0 percent, COE Company will have a fixed dollar amount of debt in perpetuity, COE's free cash flows to the unlevered firm are not expected to change, and COE Company's debt/equity ratio is .53.

In this situation, the correct formula for the cost of equity capital is

$k_{Et} = k_U + (k_U-k_{Dt})*(1-T)*D_t/E_t$, and the solution to this problem is

$.2318 = .20 + (.20-.10)*(1-.40)*.53$

The reduction in the equity cost of capital from the previous situation results from the value of the interest tax shields which effectively changes the leverage ratio, even though the free cash flows of the unlevered firm and amount of debt issued are the same as in problem (1). The larger the value of the interest tax shields, the lower the risk premium added on because of changes in capital structure.

C.   The weighted average cost of capital (WACC) for a firm.

The weighted average cost of capital is a weighted average of the equity and debt cost of capital, however, in this section we discuss how the weighted average cost of capital is determined from the unlevered cost of capital, the debt cost of capital, and the capital structure strategy. The intuition underlying this calculations is that the equity cost of capital is equal to the unlevered cost of capital plus some additional amount that depends on the debt/equity ratio and the value of the interest tax shields; thus, the weighted average cost of capital can be calculated from the equity and debt costs of capital. The weighted average cost of capital as a function of the equity and debt costs of capital is

$$WACC_t = k_{Et}*(E_t/V_t) + k_{Dt}*(1-T)*(D_t/V_t)$$

We discuss four specific cases below. In truth, one need not read the following material. One need only insert the actual estimate of the cost of equity capital from any of the cases discussed previously to obtain the WACC. Below however, we solve for the WACC in terms of the cost of equity capital from the various cases discussed previously. We do

Security Analysis: How to Analyze Accounting and Market Data to Value Securities
Robert W. Holthausen and Mark E. Zmijewski
\CH2.W51

Do not reproduce without permission.
July 29, 1998

22

this only because students often see the WACC written in terms of the unlevered cost of capital and it is use to know what case those formulas are derived from.

Case I is the case in which there is no tax deduction for interest. Case II is the case in which you have a forecast of all interest tax shields that do not depend on the value of the firm and you discount the interest tax shields at the debt cost of capital. Case III is the case in which the firm follows a fixed debt/value ratio so that future interest tax shields depend on the value of the firm. The cost of equity capital from the previous section is substituted in the weighted average cost of capital formula to restate the weighted average cost of capital to be a function of the unlevered and debt costs of capital.

Case I - No tax deduction for interest.

In this case, issuing debt does not increase the value of the firm (i.e., interest is not tax deductible). Though you may believe this case is irrelevant, that is not the case since interest is not tax deductible in all countries. The weighted average cost of capital is equal to

$$WACC_t = k_U.$$

Note this is not the correct formula for the weighted average cost of capital if interest is tax deductible and all tax shields are discounted at the unlevered cost of capital.

Case II - Interest tax shelters do not depend on the value of the levered firm.

In this case, the interest tax shelters are known and do not depend on the value of the firm; therefore, they are discounted at the debt cost of capital. The weighted average cost of capital for the firm is

$$WACC_t = k_U*(1-DVTS_{t,k(Dt)}/V_t) + k_{Dt}*(DVTS_{t,k(Dt)}-TD)/V_t$$

This formulation is not used that often because if the debt/value ratio varies from period the period, the WACC varies from period to period as well. As discussed previously, in such cases, the adjusted present value method is typically used.

If you can make some simplifying perpetuity assumptions regarding the interest tax shields, the case II can be simplified even further. Assume that the firm is going to have a fixed dollar amount of debt and that the firm is a perpetuity. Given this assumption, the value of the interest tax shields ($DVTS_{t,k(Dt)}$) is equal to T*D. Substituting T*D into the above formula yields

$$WACC_t = k_U*(1-T*D_t/V_t)$$

Alternatively, assume that the firm's debt is going to grow at some rate, g, and that the firm is a perpetuity. Given this assumption, the value of the interest tax shields ($DVTS_{t,kd}$) is equal to $(k_{Dt}*T*D)/(k_{Dt}-g)$. Substituting this result into the above formula yields

Security Analysis: How to Analyze Accounting and Market Data to Value Securities
Robert W. Holthausen and Mark E. Zmijewski
\CH2.W51

Do not reproduce without permission.
July 29, 1998

23

$$WACC_t = k_U*(1-Tk_{Dt}/(k_{Dt}-g)*D_t/V_t) + k_{Dt}*(Tk_{Dt}/(k_{Dt}-g)-T)*D_t/V_t$$

Case III - Constant debt/value capital structure strategy.

In this case, the firm can grow in any manner, constant or otherwise but it manages its capital structure to have a fixed debt to firm value ratio. Debt is assumed to be fixed at the end of each year, dependent on the value of the firm and then held constant until the end of the next year. Thus, there are no midyear adjustments to hold debt to value constant. The interest tax shield is discounted at the cost of debt for the last period (because the debt for the last year is always fixed at the beginning of the year) and is discounted at the cost of capital for the unlevered firm for all other years because the amount of debt outstanding varies with the value of the firm.

The assumptions in this approach suggests that the value of the interest tax shields is

$$DVTS_{t,all} = D_tTk_{Dt}/(1+k_{Dt}) + DVTS_{t+1,all}/(1+k_U), \text{ and}$$

$$DVTS_{t,k(Dt)} = D_tTk_{Dt}/(1+k_{Dt}).$$

The weighted average cost of capital for this case is

$$WACC_t = k_U*(1-Tk_{Dt}/(1+k_{Dt})*D_t/V_t) + k_{Dt}*(Tk_{Dt}/(1+k_{Dt})-T)*D_t/V_t$$

which can be simplified to

$$WACC_t = k_U - k_{Dt}*(T*D_t/V_t*(1+k_U)/(1+k_{Dt}))$$

Case IV - Tax Shields Discounted at K_U

In this case we assume that all tax shields are discounted at the unlevered cost of capital. But remember we assume that interest is tax deductible. The resulting formula is

$$WACC_t = k_U - [k_{Dt}*T*(D_t/V_t)]$$

Example 2.3:

As before, the following example is somewhat tedious and represents mindnumbing repetition. However, it is included to help assure students that they understand the mechanical application of the formulas.

Use the information in example 2.2 for each part of this example to calculate the weighted average cost of capital for the COE Company. Use the formula that uses k_E and k_{Dt} [$WACC_t =$

Security Analysis: How to Analyze Accounting and Market Data to Value Securities
Robert W. Holthausen and Mark E. Zmijewski
\CH2.W51

Do not reproduce without permission.
July 29, 1998

24

$k_{Et}*(E_t/V_t)+k_{Dt}*(1-T)*(D_t/V_t)]$ <u>and</u> the formula that use k_U and k_{Dt} for each situation below.

(1)   There is no tax deduction for interest and COE Company's debt/equity ratio is .47. The weighted average cost of capital based on k_E and k_{Dt} is

$.2000 = .2470*(1-(.47/(1+.47))) + .10*(.47/(1+.47))$

The WACC formula based on k_U and k_{Dt} is

$WACC_t = k_U,$

$.2000 = .2000$ (This is not the correct answer for a case IV situation)

(2)   The tax rate for interest deductions is 40.0 percent, COE Company will have fixed dollar amount of debt in perpetuity, and COE Company's debt/equity ratio is .53. The weighted average cost of capital based on k_E and k_{Dt} is

$.1723 = .2318*(1-(.53/(1+.53))) + (1-.40)*.10*(.53/(1+.53))$

The WACC formula based on k_U and k_{Dt} is

$WACC_t = k_U*(1-T*D_t/V_t)$

$.1723 = .20*(1-.40*(.53/(1+.53)))$

(3)   The tax rate for interest deductions is 40.0 percent, COE Company has debt that will grow at a rate of 4 percent in perpetuity, and COE Company's debt/equity ratio is .36. The weighted average cost of capital based on k_E and k_{Dt} is

$.1718 = .2120*(1-(.36/(1+.36))) + (1-.40)*.10*(.36/(1+.36))$

The WACC formula based on k_U and k_{Dt} is

$WACC_t = k_U*(1-Tk_{Dt}/(k_{Dt}-g)*D_t/V_t) + k_{Dt}*(Tk_{Dt}/(k_{Dt}-g)-T)D_t/V_t$

$.1718 = .20*(1-.40*.10/(.10-.04)*.36/(1+.36))$

$+ .10*(.40*.10/(.10-.04)-.40)*(.36/(1+.36))$

(4)   To use the general formula you must know k_U, k_{Dt}, T, D_t, E_t, and $DVTS_{t,k(Dt)}$. For the previous situation, assume that the tax rate for interest deductions is 40.0 percent, COE Company has debt that will grow at a rate of 4 percent in perpetuity, and COE Company's debt/equity ratio is .36; further, assume that you have been able to observe the value of the equity, $558, and the value of the debt, $200. The value of the interest tax shields is $133. The weighted average cost of capital based on k_E and k_{Dt} is

Security Analysis: How to Analyze Accounting and Market Data to Value Securities
Robert W. Holthausen and Mark E. Zmijewski
\CH2.W51

$$.1718 = .2120*(1-(.36/(1+.36))) + (1-.40)*.10*(.36/(1+.36))$$

The WACC formula based on k_U and k_{Dt} is

$$WACC_t = k_U*(1-DVTS_{t,k(Dt)}/V_t) + k_{Dt}*(DVTS_{t,k(Dt)}-TD)/V_t$$

$$.1719 = .20*(1-133/(200+558)) + .10*(133-.40*200)/(200+558)^6$$

(5)   The tax rate for interest deductions is 40.0 percent and the COE Company capital structure strategy is to have a constant debt/value ratio equal to .29. The weighted average cost of capital based on k_E and k_{Dt} is

$$.1873 = .2394*(1-.29) + (1-.40)*.10*.29$$

The WACC formula based on k_U and k_{Dt} is

$$WACC_t = k_U*(1-Tk_{Dt}/(1+k_{Dt})*D_t/V_t) + k_{Dt}*(Tk_{Dt}/(1+k_{Dt})-T)D_t/V_t$$

$$.1873 = .20*(1-.40*.10/1.10*.29) + .10*(.40*.10/1.10-.40)*.29$$

which can be simplified to

$$WACC_t = k_U - k_{Dt}(T*D_t/V_t*(1+k_U)/(1+k_{Dt}))$$

$$.1873 = .20 - .10*.40*.29*(1.20)/(1.10)$$

D.   The unlevered cost of capital.

As we discussed in the introduction to this chapter, it is most often the case that the cost of capital for the unlevered firm is not observable, although the cost of equity capital and the cost of debt capital are observable. In these situations you can use the equity cost of capital formulae we present above to calculate the unlevered cost of capital. In this section we restate the above equity cost of capital formulae to solve for the unlevered cost of capital.

We discuss four cases. Case I is the case in which there is no tax deduction for interest. Case II is the case in which you have a forecast of all interest tax shields that do not depend on the value of the firm and you discount the interest tax shields at the debt cost of capital. Case III is the case in which the firm follows a fixed debt/value ratio so that future interest tax shields depend on the value of the firm. Case IV assumes interest tax shields are discounted at the unlevered cost of capital.

---

[6]Rounding the market value of equity in the information provided in this problem results in the .0001 rounding error.

Security Analysis: How to Analyze Accounting and Market Data to Value Securities
Robert W. Holthausen and Mark E. Zmijewski
\CH2.W51

Case I - No tax deduction for interest

In this case, issuing debt does not increase the value of the firm (i.e., interest is not tax deductible). Though you may believe this case is irrelevant, that is not the case since interest is not tax deductible in all countries. The unlevered cost of capital is equal to

$$k_U = k_{Et}*E_t/(E_t+D_t) + k_{Dt}*D_t/(E_t+D_t).$$

Case II - Interest tax shelters do not depend on the value of the levered firm.

In this case, the interest tax shelters are known and do not depend on the value of the firm; therefore, they are discounted at the debt cost of capital. The unlevered cost of capital is

$$k_U = k_E*E_t/(E_t+D_t-DVTS_{t,k(Dt)}) + k_{Dt}*(D_t-DVTS_{t,k(Dt)})/(E_t+D_t-DVTS_{t,k(Dt)})$$

If you can make some simplifying perpetuity assumptions regarding the interest tax shields, the case II can be simplified even further. Assume that the firm is going to have a fixed dollar amount of debt and that the firm is a perpetuity. Given this assumption, the value of the interest tax shields ($DVTS_{t,kd}$) is equal to $T*D$. Substituting $T*D$ into the above formula yields

$$k_U = k_E*E_t/(E_t+D_t*(1-T)) + k_{Dt}*(D_t*(1-T))/(E_t+D_t*(1-T)).$$

To implement this formula, however, you need to observe E_t and D_t which may not be observable. The above formula can be restated to avoid this problem

$$k_U = (k_E+k_{Dt}*((1-T)*D_t/E_t))/(1+(1-T)*D_t/E_t).$$

Alternatively, assume that the firm's debt is going to grow at some rate, g, and that the firm is a perpetuity. Given this assumption, the value of the interest tax shields ($DVTS_{t,k(Dt)}$) is equal to $(k_{Dt}*T*D)/(k_{Dt}-g)$. Substituting this result into the above formula yields

$$k_U = k_E*E_t/(E_t+D_t*(1-Tk_{Dt}/(k_{Dt}-g))) + k_{Dt}*(D_t*(1-Tk_{Dt}/(k_{Dt}-g)))/(E_t+D_t*(1-Tk_{Dt}/(k_{Dt}-g)))$$

To implement this formula, however, you need to observe E_t and D_t which may not be observable. The above formula can be restated to avoid this problem

$$k_U = (k_E+k_{Dt}*((1-Tk_{Dt}/(k_{Dt}-g))*D_t/E_t))/(1+(1-Tk_{Dt}/(k_{Dt}-g))*D_t/E_t).$$

Security Analysis: How to Analyze Accounting and Market Data to Value Securities
Robert W. Holthausen and Mark E. Zmijewski
\CH2.W51

Case III - Constant debt/value capital structure strategy.

In this case, the firm can grow in any manner, constant or otherwise but it manages its capital structure to have a fixed debt to firm value ratio. Debt is assumed to be fixed at the end of each year, dependent on the value of the firm and then held constant until the end of the next year. Thus, there are no midyear adjustments to hold debt to value constant. The interest tax shield is discounted at the cost of debt for the last period (because the debt for the last year is always fixed at the beginning of the year) and is discounted at the cost of capital for the unlevered firm for all other years because the amount of debt outstanding varies with the value of the firm.

The assumptions in this approach suggests that the value of the interest tax shields is

$$DVTS_{t,all} = D_t Tk_{Dt}/(1+k_{Dt}) + DVTS_{t+1,all}/(1+k_U), \text{ and}$$

$$DVTS_{t,k(Dt)} = D_t Tk_{Dt}/(1+k_{Dt}).$$

The unlevered cost of capital for this case is

$$k_U = k_E * E_t/(E_t + D_t * (1-Tk_{Dt}/(1+k_{Dt}))) + k_{Dt} * D_t * (1-Tk_{Dt}/(1+k_{Dt}))/(E_t + D_t * (1-Tk_{Dt}/(1+k_{Dt})))$$

Note, this is close to the value for the unlevered cost of capital we obtained in case I. WHY? Because more of the tax shield is discounted at the cost of capital of the unlevered firm in case III, and little is discounted at the cost of debt. Hence, the differences in the discount rates between case I and III are small. This doesn't mean case I and case III wouldn't give you very different valuations, because in one case we value the interest tax shields and in the other we don't value them.

To implement this formula, however, you need to observe E_t and D_t which may not be observable. The above formula can be restated to avoid this problem

$$k_U = (k_E + k_{Dt} * ((1-Tk_{Dt}/(1+k_{Dt})) * D_t/E_t))/(1 + (1-Tk_{Dt}/(1+k_{Dt})) * D_t/E_t).$$

Case IV - Interest Tax Shields Discounted at K_U

In this case, issuing debt increases the value of the firm, but the riskiness of the tax shield is the same as the underlying asset (i.e., interest is not tax deductible). Though you may believe this case is irrelevant, that is not the case since interest is not tax deductible in all countries. The unlevered cost of capital is equal to

$$k_U = k_{Et} * E_t/(E_t + D_t) + k_{Dt} * D_t/(E_t + D_t).$$

Security Analysis: How to Analyze Accounting and Market Data to Value Securities
Robert W. Holthausen and Mark E. Zmijewski
\CH2.W51

Do not reproduce without permission.
July 29, 1998

28

Example 2.4:

As before, the following example is somewhat tedious and represents mindnumbing repetition. However, it is included to help assure students that they understand the mechanical application of the formulas.

Assume that you collected the following information for firms that are comparable to the COE Company (see examples 2.3 and 2.4). Calculate the cost of capital of the unlevered firm.

(1) Comparable firm 1: There is no tax deduction for interest, the cost of debt is 10 percent, the equity cost of capital is .2470, and debt/equity ratio is .47.

In this situation, the correct formula for the cost of capital for the unlevered firm is

$k_U = k_{Et}*E_t/(E_t+D_t) + k_{Dt}*D_t/(E_t+D_t)$, and the solution is

$.2000 = .2470*(1-.47/(1+.47)) + .10*.47/(1+.47)$

Note this would be the solution for a Case IV problem as well -- interest tax shields discounted at the unlevered cost of capital.

(2) Comparable firm 2: The tax rate for interest deductions is 40.0 percent, the cost of debt is 10 percent, COE Company will have fixed dollar amount of debt in perpetuity, the cost of equity capital is .2318, and the debt/equity ratio is .53.

In this situation, the correct formula for the cost of capital for the unlevered firm is

$k_U = (k_E+k_{Dt}*((1-T)*D_t/E_t))/(1+(1-T)*D_t/E_t)$, and the solution is

$.2000 = (.2318+.10*(1-.40)*.53)/(1+(1-.40)*.53)$

(3) Comparable firm 3: The tax rate for interest deductions is 40.0 percent, the cost of debt is 10 percent, debt will grow at a rate of 4 percent in perpetuity, the equity cost of capital is .2120, and the debt/equity ratio is .36.

In this situation, the correct formula for the cost of capital for the unlevered firm is

$k_U = (k_E+k_{Dt}*((1-Tk_{Dt}/(k_{Dt}-g))*D_t/E_t))/(1+(1-Tk_{Dt}/(k_{Dt}-g))*D_t/E_t)$,

and the solution is

$.2000 = (.2120+.10*((1-.40*.10/(.10-.04))*.36))/(1+(1-.40*.10/(.10-.04))*.36)$

Security Analysis: How to Analyze Accounting and Market Data to Value Securities
Robert W. Holthausen and Mark E. Zmijewski
\CH2.W51

(4)   You could not use the general form of formula for the above situations,

$$k_U = k_E * E_t/(E_t + D_t - DVTS_{t,k(Dt)}) + k_{Dt} * (D_t - DVTS_{t,k(Dt)})/(E_t + D_t - DVTS_{t,k(Dt)})$$

because you did not have any information about the value of the debt, the value of the equity, or the value of the interest tax shelters. That is the good news for these formulae, however, the bad news is that you must make explicit assumptions regarding the value of the interest tax shield (no value, $T*D$, or $D*(Tk_{Dt}/(k_{Dt}-g))$), which may be inconsistent with the actual value of the interest tax shields.

To use the general formula you must know k_U, k_{Dt}, T, D_t, E_t, and $DVTS_t$. For comparable firm 3, assume that the tax rate for interest deductions is 40.0 percent, the cost of debt is 10 percent, debt will grow at a rate of 4 percent in perpetuity, the cost of equity capital is .2120, and the debt/equity ratio is .36; further, assume that you have been able to observe the value of the equity, $558, and the value of the debt, $200.

In this situation, the general formula for the cost of equity capital can be used. First, you must calculate the value of the interest tax shields, which is

$133 = .40*.10*200/(.10-.04)$; next you can calculate k_U using the general formula

$.2000 = .2120*558/(200+558-133) + .10*(200-133)/(200+558-133)$.

(5)   Comparable firm 4: The tax rate for interest deductions is 40.0 percent, the cost of debt is 10 percent, the cost of equity capital is .2394, and the capital structure strategy is to have a constant debt/value ratio equal to .29.

In this situation, the correct formula for the cost of capital for the unlevered firm is

$$k_U = (k_E + k_{Dt} * ((1-Tk_{Dt}/(1+k_{Dt}))*D_t/E_t))/(1 + (1-Tk_{Dt}/(1+k_{Dt}))*D_t/E_t)$$

$$.2000 = (.2394 + .10*((1-.40*.10/1.10)*(.29/(1-.29)))) /$$

$$(1 + (1-.40*.10/1.10)*(.29/(1-.29)))$$

Security Analysis: How to Analyze Accounting and Market Data to Value Securities
Robert W. Holthausen and Mark E. Zmijewski
\CH2.W51

Do not reproduce without permission.
July 29, 1998

30

E.   Summary.

Of the four cases, the third or fourth case is the relevant one when you assume that the firm is going to use a target debt/value ratio. Note however, to the extent that the firm's capital structure policy is "sticky," then we begin to move away from this case because in fact the debt will not change exactly as the value of the firm changes. Case I typically provides a number which is very close to case III and may be a useful approximation to case III. In Chapter 4, we provide a detailed examples of how the adjusted present value method and the adjusted cost of capital method provide equivalent results for these cases.

F.   Levering and Unlevering in Practice

Most practitioners do not know about all of this formulas and rely on one almost exclusively. While that is not correct theoretically, it is probably what you will observe. Also, most practitioners lever and unlever betas, not costs of capital, though the process is identical. The formulas that you are most likely to see used are

Case II with the value of interest tax shields written as T*D

$$k_{Et} = k_U + (k_U-k_{Dt})*(1-T)*D_t/E_t.$$

$$k_U = k_E*E_t/(E_t+D_t*(1-T)) + k_{Dt}*(D_t*(1-T))/(E_t+D_t*(1-T)).$$

$$WACC_t = k_U*(1-T*D_t/V_t)$$

Case III -- Miles/Ezzell Formulation

$$k_E = k_U + (k_U - k_{Dt})*[1-(Tk_{Dt}/(1+k_{Dt}))]*D_t/E_t.$$

$$k_U = (k_E+k_{Dt}*((1-Tk_{Dt}/(1+k_{Dt}))*D_t/E_t))/(1+(1-Tk_{Dt}/(1+k_{Dt}))*D_t/E_t).$$

$$WACC_t = k_U - k_{Dt}*(T*D_t/V_t*(1+k_U)/(1+k_{Dt}))$$

Case IV -- Tax Shields Discounted at Unlevered Cost of Capital

$$k_{Et} = k_U + (k_U-k_{Dt})*D_t/E_t.$$

$$k_U = k_{Et}*E_t/(E_t+D_t) + k_{Dt}*D_t/(E_t+D_t).$$

$$WACC_t = k_U - [k_{Dt}*T*(D_t/V_t)]$$

Also remember, that you do not need these formulas for WACC, you can always substitute your estimate of K_E into the textbook WACC formula

$$WACC_t = k_{Et}(E_t/V_t) + k_{Dt}(1-T)(D_t/V_t)$$

Security Analysis: How to Analyze Accounting and Market Data to Value Securities
Robert W. Holthausen and Mark E. Zmijewski
\CH2.W51

6. The Value of the Interest Tax Shield -- Extensions.

A. M&M with Corporate Taxes and Financial Distress Costs.

Question--If M&M with taxes is correct why aren't firms almost entirely debt financed? What is the cost of high leverage? For one thing, the present value of the interest tax shields may not increase very much after leverage becomes quite high. If firms have large amounts of debt, the probability that they can use all of the interest deductions fall and the expected marginal tax rates may also be lower. Graham (1996, *Journal of Financial Economics*) indicates that a non-trivial proportion of publicly traded U.S. firms have expected future marginal tax rates approximating 0% (almost 30% in 1992). (See HZ Figures 1 and 2).

In addition, when costs of financial distress are introduced, the firm faces tradeoffs in determining its capital structure. Interest tax shields reduce the WACC with increases in leverage. Financial distress costs increase the WACC with increases in leverage. The typical scenario described is that the WACC decreases as leverage is increased from zero until some point, call it L*. Increases in leverage beyond L* increase the WACC.

Thus, L* is assumed to be the optimal debt/equity ratio because it minimizes WACC.

Therefore, with financial distress costs, we conclude:

Value of Firm =   Value of firm if 100% Equity Financed

+ Present Value of the Interest Tax Shields

- Present Value of Financial Distress Costs

What are financial distress costs? Here are a few of them:

(1)   loss of customers, employees, and suppliers when they become worried that the firm may go out of business (Unisys, Harnischfeger, Chrysler (remember their birthday party ads?));

(2)   costs of being denied access to the capital markets during some periods (particularly for growth firms) (are we limiting our ability to take certain opportunities);

(3)   costs of conflicts of interest between stockholders and debtholders which increase with leverage (conflicts arise over changes in the risk of the firm's investments, the payment of dividends or share repurchases to shareholders and increases in leverage senior to existing debt);

(4)   indirect costs of bankruptcy (i.e., the costs of inefficient operations while in bankruptcy proceedings); and

Security Analysis: How to Analyze Accounting and Market Data to Value Securities
Robert W. Holthausen and Mark E. Zmijewski
\CH2.W51

Do not reproduce without permission.
July 30, 1998

32

(5)   direct costs of bankruptcy (i.e, the legal costs associated with bankruptcy proceedings determining how the assets are to be split among the claimants).

The present value of financial distress costs increase with increases in leverage. Adding financial distress to the model may explain why firms are not almost 100% financed. However, the revised view of the world does not explain why we don't observe changes in firms's capital structures when we have changes in corporate tax rates.

B.   Taxes and Interest Tax Shields -- Extensions.

The following material is quite controversial and is based on Millers "Debt and Taxes" paper (See Brealey & Myers, Chapter 18). It has caused us to reflect on the "true" value of the interest tax shield. The arguments in the following material have caused some financial managers to reduce their valuation of the interest tax shield.

With the introduction of personal taxes, we assume that investors are interested in their after tax wealth. Hence, the corporation is interested in structuring its capital structure to maximize the after tax returns to its claimants.

We now address questions regarding how much is left over at the claimholder level after either a debt or equity holder receives a pre-corporate-tax distribution from the corporate level.

Since interest is deductible at the corporate level, debt holders receive the following for a given distribution from the corporate level.

$$(1 - \text{personal tax rate on interest})$$

Since an equity flow is first taxable at the corporate level, equity holders receive the following for a given flow of cash at the corporate level.

$$(1 - \text{personal tax rate on equity}) \times (1 - \text{corporate tax rate}).$$

If $(1 - \text{personal tax rate on interest}) >$

$(1 - \text{personal tax rate on equity}) \times (1 - \text{corporate tax rate})$

then corporate debt should be issued. If the inequality is reversed, corporate debt should not be issued. If the two are equal then capital structure is irrelevant again.

The value of the interest tax shield is calculated by determining the increase in the after tax wealth of the bondholders and stockholders when we lever the firm. The after tax wealth is calculated by valuing the after tax cash flows at the after tax cost of capital.

Security Analysis: How to Analyze Accounting and Market Data to Value Securities
   Robert W. Holthausen and Mark E. Zmijewski
\CH2.W51

Assume that all personal income is taxed at the same rate

Assume that all personal income is taxed at the same rate. This would be the case if all equity income came as dividends or if all capital gains are immediately realized and the tax rate on capital gains and dividends are the same.

If we assume that all personal income is taxed at the same rate then the value of the interest tax shield is left intact. Why?

$$(1 - \text{personal tax rate on interest}) >$$

$$(1 - \text{personal tax rate on equity}) \times (1 - \text{corporate tax rate})$$

Thus, the after all taxes amount of cash is greater for a $1 paid out in the form of interest than in the form of equity return.

PV Tax Shield (assuming constant debt level) =

$$\frac{\text{corporate tax rate} \times \text{interest rate} \times \text{debt} \times (1 - \text{personal tax rate})}{\text{discount rate for tax shield} \times (1 - \text{personal tax rate})}$$

Thus, introducing personal taxes decreased both the after tax payments to the bondholders and stockholders as well as the after tax cost of capital. But there is still a tax advantage to debt.

Under these assumptions, the M&M view with taxes still stands.

Assume that dividends and interest are taxed more heavily than capital gains at the personal level

Under this assumption, the effective tax on the flows to equity holders are less than the tax to debt holders if the equity holders receive some of their return in the form of capital gains and capital gains are taxed at a different rate or if the realization of capital gains is optional. The flows to debtholders escape corporate taxation, but the flows to equity holders are taxed at the corporate and personal level.

If $\quad (1 - \text{personal tax rate on interest}) >$

$$(1 - \text{personal tax rate on equity}) \times (1 - \text{corporate tax rate})$$

then corporate debt should be issued. But the unresolved question is what is the effective personal tax on equity. If the corporation paid no dividends and equity flows were obtained only through capital gains, then it is possible that the inequality will reverse because for a long-term buy-and-hold investor, the capital gains tax is effectively zero.

If the inequality is reversed, corporate debt should not be issued. If the two are equal then capital structure is irrelevant again.

Security Analysis: How to Analyze Accounting and Market Data to Value Securities
Robert W. Holthausen and Mark E. Zmijewski
\CH2.W51

Do not reproduce without permission.
July 29, 1998

34

So far so good----

BUT -- <u>What happens if their is variation in the tax rates faced by equity holders and</u>
<u>debtholders?????</u>

With progressivity introduced into the personal tax rate structure, the question posed is much less obvious.

For simplicity, assume that the tax on all equity holders is zero (it doesn't have to be) and that debtholders have personal tax rates between 0% and 50% and that the corporate tax rate is 46%.

Also assume that no firms have debt in their capital structure.

Does that make sense? No! As a financial manager you should issue some debt because you can issue the debt to tax exempt investors and the formula above says that makes sense (i.e. 0% < 46%).

But all corporations will do that. Once the tax exempts have purchased as much debt as they can we turn to investors in the very low tax brackets. To entice them to hold debt instead of equity we have to pay them enough that after tax, they are made better off.

Corporations as a whole can continue doing this as long as the corporate tax savings is greater than the personal tax loss an investor would suffer from being a debt holder instead of an equity holder.

Once corporations have enticed all investors to hold debt whose personal tax on interest is 46% or less (given the example), no more debt can be issued. Why? The enticement corporations would have to pay to the next group of investors exceeds the corporate tax savings.

Thus, Miller's model implies there is an equilibrium debt/equity ratio for the economy (i.e., for corporations considered as a whole). But in equilibrium, all debtholders receive the same interest rate (assume equal risks), and it is set at the margin.

Now consider what the model implies for an individual corporation. To see this most easily, consider a new corporation. Its debt/equity ratio is a matter of indifference, because it will have to entice an investor with a 46% personal tax rate to invest.

IMPLICATION: Once the economy is in equilibrium, capital structure for the
                     individual firm is a matter of irrelevance.

                     Hence, there is no value to the interest tax shield, because the before tax
                     interest rate has already been grossed up to compensate individuals for
                     the tax they will bear.

Security Analysis: How to Analyze Accounting and Market Data to Value Securities
    Robert W. Holthausen and Mark E. Zmijewski
\CH2.W51

Where does that leave us?

These predictions rely on the assumption that the tax on equity flows are less than the tax on interest. Since capital gains are only taxed when realized in the United States (i.e., when the asset is actually sold), the effective tax on equity flows are still less than the tax on interest income.

Consider the effect of the 1986 Tax Reform Act. The corporate tax rate is 34% and assume that the personal tax rate on income is 28% (its more complicated than this at the margin for wealthy individuals). Interest, dividends and realized capital gains are all taxed at 28%. Lets assume, however, that because capital gains can be postponed, that the effective tax rate on equity is 14%. In that case $1 sent from the corporation leaves $0.72 in the debt holder's pocket (no tax at the corporate level and 28% at the personal level). However $1 from the corporation to the equity holder is taxed $0.34 at the corporate level. The remaining $0.66 is taxed at the assumed 14% rate (a tax of $0.09) leaving $0.57. Under this scenario, the tax advantage of debt is $0.15 ($0.72-$0.57) for a $1.00 flow, or only 15% (not 34% which is the corporate tax rate).

• Now consider more recent changes in the U.S. tax code:

Top corporate tax rate is 35%.

Top marginal tax bracket for individuals is 39.6% (interest and dividends). Assume top bracket individuals were induced to hold taxable debt.

Top marginal tax rate on capital gains is 28%. Lets assume, however, that because capital gains can be postponed, that the effective tax rate on equity is 14%.

In that case $1 sent from the corporation leaves $0.604 in the debt holder's pocket for the wealthiest individuals (no tax at the corporate level and 39.6% at the personal level). However $1 from the corporation to the equity holder is taxed $0.35 at the corporate level. The remaining $0.65 is taxed at the assumed 14% rate (a tax of $0.091 leaving $0.559. Under this scenario, the tax advantage of debt is $0.045 ($0.604-$0.559) for a $1.00 flow, or only 4.5% (not 35% which is the corporate tax rate).

If the effective tax on equity is only 7.08%, then we would be indifferent between debt and equity (from a tax perspective only) assuming that Miller's argument holds. If the effective tax on equity is less than 7.08%, then there is no tax advantage of debt.

Security Analysis: How to Analyze Accounting and Market Data to Value Securities
Robert W. Holthausen and Mark E. Zmijewski
\CH2.W51

IN PRACTICE: Most financial managers believe there is a tax advantage associated with borrowing (assuming that the corporation's expected tax rate is non-zero.

The value of the interest tax shield is likely to be less than the present value of the marginal corporate tax rate times the interest expense because of the existence of differential personal tax rates between bondholders and stockholders.

The value associated with issuing debt is likely to be less than the value of the interest tax shield because of the costs of financial distress.

Security Analysis: How to Analyze Accounting and Market Data to Value Securities
Robert W. Holthausen and Mark E. Zmijewski
\CH2.W51

Do not reproduce without permission.
July 29, 1998

37

HZ Figure 1 and 2

Some Evidence on the Distribution of U.S. Marginal Tax Rates

Source: John R. Graham, "Debt and the Marginal Tax Rate," *Journal of Financial Economics* (May, 1996), pp. 41-74

Security Analysis: How to Analyze Accounting and Market Data to Value Securities
Robert W. Holthausen and Mark E. Zmijewski
\CH2.W51

Do not reproduce without permission.
July 30, 1998

38

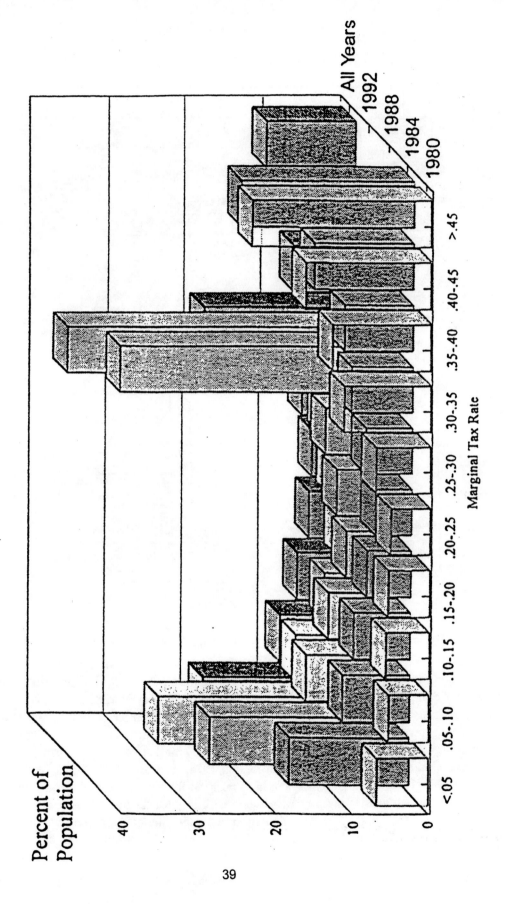

Fig. 2. The empirical distribution of the marginal tax rate.

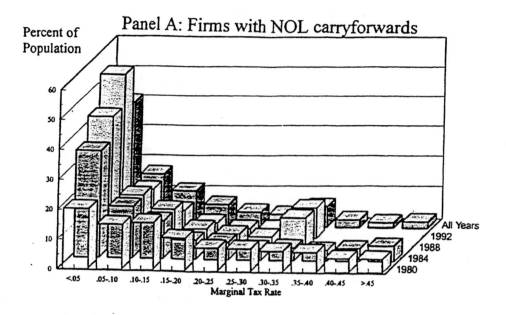

Panel A: Firms with NOL carryforwards

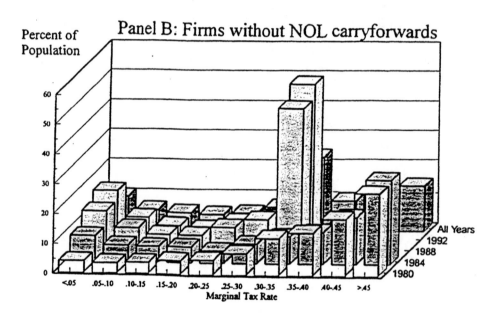

Panel B: Firms without NOL carryforwards

Fig. 3. The empirical distribution of the marginal tax rate given *NOL* carryforward status or firm size.

Panel A (B) shows the distribution of the marginal tax rate for all Compustat firms with nonmissing taxable income data which have (do not have) net operating loss carryforwards; firms with (without) *NOL* carryforwards comprise approximately 25% (75%) of the sample. Panel C (D) shows the distribution of the marginal tax rate for all Compustat firms with nonmissing taxable income data in the smallest (largest) quartile of firms, where size is defined by market value of the firm. The data are presented for the years 1980 (1981 for size conditioning), 1984, 1988, and 1992, and aggregated across all years from 1980–1992. The total sample contains tax rates for 10,240 firms. The marginal tax rate is calculated for a given year as the present value of additional taxes owed from earning an extra dollar of income in that year. The tax calculation considers the effect of net operating losses, the investment tax credit, the alternative minimum tax, and other nondebt tax shields such as depreciation.

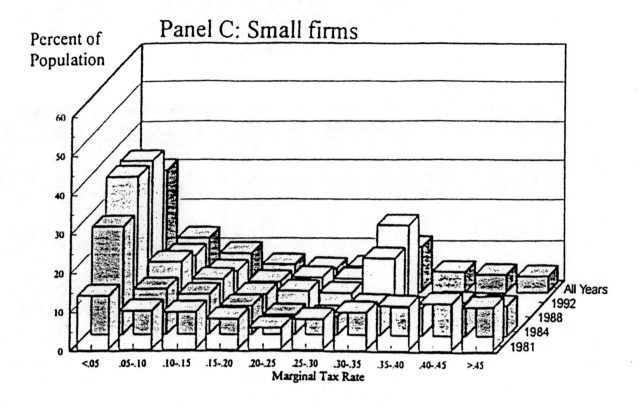

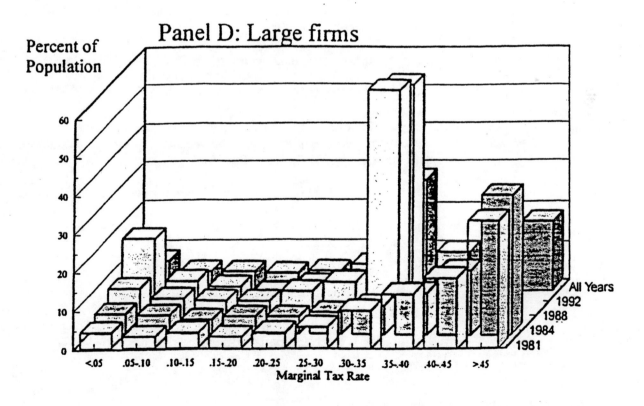

Fig. 3 (continued)

Chapter 2

Problems for Review ·

Like the examples in the chapter, these questions are mechanical and are intended to familiarize students with the mechanical applications of the formulas.

1. Assume that you collected the following information for the COC Company for the following independent situations. For all situations assume that the cost of capital for the unlevered firm is 22.0 percent and the cost of debt capital is 12.0 percent for all periods. Calculate the equity cost of capital.

    (1) There is no tax deduction for interest and COC Company's debt/equity ratio is 1.14. (Ans = 33.43%)

    (2) The tax rate for interest deductions is 40.0 percent, COC Company will have fixed dollar amount of debt in perpetuity, and COC Company's debt/equity ratio is .91. (Ans = 27.43%)

    (3) The tax rate for interest deductions is 40.0 percent, COC Company has debt that will grow at a rate of 2 percent in perpetuity, and COC Company's debt/equity ratio is .74. (Ans = 25.84%)

    Why did the debt/equity ratio change from the situation in which there was no tax deduction for interest?

    (4) In the above situations you could not use the general form of formula,

    $$k_{Et} = k_U + (k_U - k_{Dt}) * (D_t - DVTS_{t,kd})/E_t,$$

    because you did not have any information about the value of the debt, the value of the equity, or the value of the interest tax shelters. To use the general formula you must know k_U, k_{Dt}, T, D_t, E_t, and $DVTS_t$.

    For the previous situation, assume that the tax rate for interest deductions is 40.0 percent, COC Company has debt that will grow at a rate of 2 percent in perpetuity, and COC Company's debt/equity ratio is .74; further, assume that you have been able to observe the value of the equity, $542, and the value of the debt, $400.

    Use the general formula to calculate the cost of equity capital. (Ans = 25.84%)

    (5) The tax rate for interest deductions is 40.0 percent and the COC Company capital structure strategy is to have a constant debt/value ratio equal to .47. (Ans = 30.42%)

Security Analysis: How to Analyze Accounting and Market Data to Value Securities
Robert W. Holthausen and Mark E. Zmijewski
\CH2.W51

2.	Use the information in problem 2.1 for each part of this example to calculate the weighted average cost of capital for the COC Company. For all situations assume that the cost of capital for the unlevered firm is 22.0 percent and the cost of debt capital is 12.0 percent for all periods. Use the formula that uses k_E and k_{Dt} [WACC$_t$ = $k_{Et}*(E_t/V_t)+k_{Dt}*(1-T)*(D_t/V_t)$] and the formula that use k_U and k_{Dt} for each situation below.

(1)	There is no tax deduction for interest and COC Company's debt/equity ratio is 1.14. (Ans = 22.0%)

(2)	The tax rate for interest deductions is 40.0 percent, COC Company will have fixed dollar amount of debt in perpetuity, and COC Company's debt/equity ratio is .91. (Ans = 17.82%)

(3)	The tax rate for interest deductions is 40.0 percent, COC Company has debt that will grow at a rate of 2 percent in perpetuity, and COC Company's debt/equity ratio is .74. (Ans = 17.92%)

(4)	To use the general formula you must know k_U, k_{Dt}, T, D_t, E_t, and DVTS$_t$. For the previous situation, assume that the tax rate for interest deductions is 40.0 percent, COC Company has debt that will grow at a rate of 2 percent in perpetuity, and COC Company's debt/equity ratio is .74; further, assume that you have been able to observe the value of the equity, $542, and the value of the debt, $400. (Ans = 17.92%)

(5)	The tax rate for interest deductions is 40.0 percent and the COC Company capital structure strategy is to have a constant debt/value ratio equal to .47. (Ans = 19.55%)

3.	Assume that you collected the following information for firms that are comparable to the COC Company (see problems 2.1 and 2.2). Calculate the cost of capital of the unlevered firm.

(1)	Comparable firm 1: There is no tax deduction for interest, the cost of debt is 12 percent, the equity cost of capital is .3343, and debt/equity ratio is 1.14. (Ans = 22.0%)

(2)	Comparable firm 2: The tax rate for interest deductions is 40.0 percent, the cost of debt is 12 percent, COC Company will have fixed dollar amount of debt in perpetuity, the cost of equity capital is .2743, and the debt/equity ratio is .91. (Ans = 22.0%)

(3)	Comparable firm 3: The tax rate for interest deductions is 40.0 percent, the cost of debt is 12 percent, debt will grow at a rate of 2 percent in perpetuity, the equity cost of capital is .2584, and the debt/equity ratio is .74. (Ans = 22%)

Security Analysis: How to Analyze Accounting and Market Data to Value Securities
Robert W. Holthausen and Mark E. Zmijewski
\CH2.W51

(4)   You could not use the general form of formula for the above situations,

$$k_U = k_E * E_t/(E_t + D_t - DVTS_{t,k(Dt)}) + k_{Dt}*(D_t - DVTS_{t,k(Dt)})/(E_t + D_t - DVTS_{t,k(Dt)})$$

because you did not have any information about the value of the debt, the value of the equity, or the value of the interest tax shelters. To use the general formula you must know k_U, k_{Dt}, T, D_t, E_t, and $DVTS_{t,k(Dt)}$.

For comparable firm 3, assume that the tax rate for interest deductions is 40.0 percent, the cost of debt is 12 percent, debt will grow at a rate of 2 percent in perpetuity, the cost of equity capital is .2584, and the debt/equity ratio is .74; further, assume that you have been able to observe the value of the equity, $542, and the value of the debt, $400.

Use the general formula to calculate the cost of capital of the unlevered comparable firm 3. (Ans = 22%)

(5)   Comparable firm 4: The tax rate for interest deductions is 40.0 percent, the cost of debt is 12 percent, the cost of equity capital is .3042, and the capital structure strategy is to have a constant debt/value ratio equal to .47. (Ans = 22%).

Security Analysis: How to Analyze Accounting and Market Data to Value Securities
   Robert W. Holthausen and Mark E. Zmijewski
   \CH2.W51

Do not reproduce without permission.
July 30, 1998

44

Robert W. Holthausen and Mark E. Zmijewski

Chapter 5A

Measuring and Understanding Free Cash Flows - Basic Concepts

---

1. Introduction.

Why Examine the Statement of Cash Flows? Ultimately our objective in this and the next chapter is to estimate and analyze the future free cash flows of the firm in order to conduct financial analysis and perform a valuation analysis. Forecasting free cash flows requires an understanding of the firm in its present state, as well as understanding likely future changes. The balance sheet and income statement are two widely used and understood financial statements for this purpose. The statement of cash flows, however, is not well understood. To aid in estimating the future free cash flows, we discuss the preparation and usefulness of the statement of cash flows. The statement of cash flows is often used as the basis for calculating free cash flows, especially when measuring historic free cash flows.

What Is a Cash Flow? Cash flow can have many definitions, most of which are useless to an analyst interested in valuation. For example, presenting the net change in the cash holdings of a firm can be called the net cash flow, but who cares? A naive (and useless) cash flow definition is an inflow or outflow in a firm's "checkbook." The cash flow statement reconciles the change in the cash balance of the firm with changes in the other items on the balance sheet. The present form of the cash flow statement partitions this reconciliation into four parts; cash flows from operations, investing activities, financing activities, and foreign currency translation adjustments.

The important characteristic of the cash flow concept in security analysis is the relevance of the cash flow to a particular security holder.[1] We use the term "free cash flow" with respect to a particular security (e.g., common equity) to represent the cash flow relevant for analysis of that security.

2. The Algebra of the Cash Flow Statement.

Like all accounting financial statements, the cash flow statement is merely a particular restatement of the "one and only" accounting equation,

Assets = Liabilities + Shareholders' Equity.

In this section of the chapter we review the algebra the underpins the statement of cash flows. Understanding this algebra is key to understanding the preparation of the cash flow statement, and it will provide you with a conceptual framework for analyzing the cash flow effects any type of transaction. Before we begin the algebra, here are some variable definitions.

---

[1]For example, assume you hold a firm's long-term bond (not due to mature for, say, 20 years) as an investment. An important factor in analyzing the riskiness of the bond is estimating the expected cash flows from the firm's current operations available for interest payments. (Other factors are important as well, e.g., the solvency of the firm's balance sheet.)

Security Analysis: How to Analyze Accounting and Market Data to Value Securities
  Robert W. Holthausen and Mark E. Zmijewski
\CH5A.W51

Do not reproduce without permission.
July 29, 1998 - 2:10 pm

45

Variable definitions.

C	-	cash balance.
NCCA	-	non-cash current assets.
NCA	-	non-current assets.
TA	-	total assets.
CL	-	current liabilities.
LTL	-	long-term liabilities.
SE	-	shareholders' equity.
PIC	-	paid-in-capital.
RE	-	retained earnings.
NI	-	net income.
R	-	revenues.
E	-	all expenses.
DIV	-	dividends.
OI/XX	-	other adjustments for XX.

The Equation.

$$TA = CL + LTL + SE$$

$$C + NCCA + NCA = CL + LTL + PIC + RE$$

Let $\Delta X = X_t - X_{t-1}$.

The cash flow statement merely reconciles the change in the cash balance with the changes in the other balance sheet accounts.

$$\Delta C + \Delta NCCA + \Delta NCA = \Delta CL + \Delta LTL + \Delta PIC + \Delta RE$$

$$\Delta C + \Delta NCCA + \Delta NCA = \Delta CL + \Delta LTL + \Delta PIC + NI - DIV + OI/RE$$

$$\Delta C = \Delta CL + \Delta LTL + \Delta PIC + NI - DIV + OI/RE - \Delta NCCA - \Delta NCA$$

$$\Delta C = \Delta CL + \Delta LTL + \Delta PIC + R - E - DIV + OI/RE - \Delta NCCA - \Delta NCA$$

Notice that the algebra of the accounting equation guarantees the preparation of a statement of cash flows from comparative balance sheets, an income statement, a statement of shareholders' equity, and a statement of retained earnings. Partitioning the above equation into informative relations is the key to financial analysis. That is, partitioning cash flows into,

$$\Delta C = \{CFs \text{ relevant for valuation}\} + \{CFs \text{ reconciling the change in cash balance}\}.$$

Accountants attempt to provide useful information that partitions the cash flows into cash flows from operations, investing activities, financing activities, and foreign currency translation. We discuss how accountants partition the statement of cash flow equation next.

Security Analysis: How to Analyze Accounting and Market Data to Value Securities
  Robert W. Holthausen and Mark E. Zmijewski
\CH5A.W51

Do not reproduce without permission.
July 29, 1998 - 12:00 pm

46

3.   Information Accountants Provide in the Cash Flow Statement.

Prior to FASB Statement 95, firms were required to present a statement of changes in financial position (SCFP). The SCFP would reconcile the change in "funds" on the statement of financial position to changes in other accounts on that statement. Firms could define funds in a variety of ways, the most popular of which were working capital and cash (plus cash equivalents). In the 1970s most firms used a working capital definition of funds but cash became the more dominate definition for large firms in the 1980s.

FASB Statement 95 became effective for annual periods ending after July 15, 1988. It provides rigid guidelines for the following items. Focus on cash receipts and expenditures. The firm must reconcile the change in cash and cash equivalents. Cash flows must be classified into cash flows from operations, cash flows relevant to investing activities, cash flows relevant to financing activities, and the effect of foreign currency translations. Operating cash flows can be presented via the direct or indirect methods (details below) but sufficient information should be available to convert one method to the other. Investing and financing activities should emphasize gross cash flows rather than net cash flows (e.g., the statement discloses debt issued and debt retired separately). Noncash transactions (e.g., debt for assets) must be presented in separate disclosures. Cash interest payments and cash income tax payments must be disclosed in the statement or separate disclosure.

FASB Statement 95 is not perfect, however. FASB Statement 95 does not require firms to provide the details of the cash flow effects from discontinued operations, extraordinary items, special items, or from mergers that are accounted via the purchase method (pooling-of-interest method mergers must retroactively restate all financial statement presented). FASB Statement 95 also does not require firms to follow specific rules regarding the definition of cash and cash equivalents or what cash flows are operating cash flows versus non-operating cash flows.

A primary source of data for measuring free cash flows is the accounting statement of cash flows. In years prior to FASB Statement 95 (pre 1988), the statement of changes in financial position was one of the primary sources of data, supplemented with information from the other financial statement and footnotes. These data, however, are not as useful as the FASB Statement 95 statement of cash flow data and they should be used with caution.

The general form of the statement of cash flows is

Operating Cash Flow (see calculation below)
Plus Net Cash Flows from Investing Activities
Plus Net Cash Flows from Financing Activities
Plus Foreign Currency Translation Adjustment
Change in Cash and Cash Equivalents

Security Analysis: How to Analyze Accounting and Market Data to Value Securities
Robert W. Holthausen and Mark E. Zmijewski
\CH5A.W51

4.   Measuring After-Tax Cash Flow from Operations.

In this section of the chapter we present the two generally accepted methods of measuring cash flow from operations, the direct and indirect methods. FASB Statement 95 allows operating cash flows to be measured either by the indirect method (adjusting net income) or the direct method (converting all revenues and expenses to cash flows). If a firm uses the direct method, then the firm must provide a reconciliation of net income to operating cash flow in a footnote. Both methods, if applied properly, result in the same operating cash flow. Below we provide a general method for calculating cash flow from operations using the indirect method.

Calculation of Cash Flow From Operations (CFO):

	Net Income from the Statement of Income	**[1]**
+	Expenses and Losses Not Decreasing Working Capital	+[2]

> Depreciation, Depletion, and Amortization of Intangibles
> Amortization of Non-current Prepaid Expenses
> Loss on the Sale of Non-Operating Assets or Retirement or Conversion of Debt
> Minority Interest Deductions (subsidiary's net income)
> Loss on the equity accrual of Subsidiary's Net Income plus Dividends Received
> Unrealized Losses (Price Declines of Mkt Securities)

-	Revenues, Gains, and Additions not Increasing Working Capital	-[3]

> Gain on the Sale of Non-operating Assets or Retirement or Conversion of Debt
> Minority Interest Additions (subsidiary's net loss)
> Gain on the equity accrual of Subsidiary's Net Income less Dividends Received
> Unrealized Gains from Price Increases of Marketable Securities
> (up to previous Unrealized Losses)

+	Decreases in Operating Current Assets (other than Cash) and Increases in Operating Current Liabilities	+[4]
-	Increases in Operating Current Assets (other than Cash) and Decreases in Operating Current Liabilities	-[5]
+/-	Adjustments for Discontinued Operations	+/-[6]
+/-	Adjustments for Extraordinary Items	+/-[7]
+/-	Adjustments for Cumulative Affect of Change in Accounting Principles	+/-[8]
	After-tax Cash Flow From Operations	**=[CFO]**

Security Analysis: How to Analyze Accounting and Market Data to Value Securities
Robert W. Holthausen and Mark E. Zmijewski
\CH5A.W51

Below we provide a general method of measuring cash flow from operations using the direct method.

	Cash Operating Revenues	-[1]
-	Cost of Goods Sold Paid in Cash	-[2]
-	Selling, General and Administrative Expenses Paid in Cash	-[3]
-	Interest Expense Paid in Cash	-[4]
-	Income Taxes Paid in Cash	-[5]
	After-tax Cash Flow From Operations	**=[CFO]**

+	Net Revenues	
-	Change in Current Trade Receivables	
-	Change in Non-Current Trade Receivables	
	Cash Operating Revenues	**-[1]**

+	Cost of Goods Sold	
+	Change in Inventory	
-	Change in Accounts Payable (to Suppliers)	
	Cost of Goods Sold Paid in Cash	**-[2]**

+	Selling, General and Administrative Expenses	
+	Change in Pre-Paid Assets	
-	Change in Accrued Expenses and Wages	
	Selling, General and Administrative Expenses Paid in Cash	**-[3]**

+	Interest Expense (excludes capitalized interest)	
-	Change in Interest Payable	
	Interest Expense Paid in Cash	**-[4]**

+	Income Tax Expense	
-	Change in Income Taxes Payable	
-	Change in Net Deferred Taxes on the Balance Sheet	
	Income Taxes Paid in Cash	**-[5]**

Security Analysis: How to Analyze Accounting and Market Data to Value Securities
Robert W. Holthausen and Mark E. Zmijewski
\CH5A.W51

An Example of the Direct Method of Calculating Cash Flows From Operations.

Below we present the Statement of Cash Flows of CRAY RESEARCH, INC. AND SUBSIDIARIES, who uses the direct method of calculating cash flow from operations. Cray also provides the indirect method of calculating cash flow from operations as supplemental information (required by GAAP).

CRAY RESEARCH, INC. AND SUBSIDIARIES
CONSOLIDATED STATEMENTS OF CASH FLOWS

| | Years ended December 31 | | |
	1992	1991	1990
	(In thousands)		
Cash flows provided by (used in) operations:			
Receipts from customers	$904,266	$765,836	$838,715
Payments to suppliers/employees	(690,693)	(650,858)	(494,707)
Income taxes paid	(27,686)	(53,812)	(89,348)
Interest received	11,104	12,879	20,309
Interest paid	(9,336)	(7,800)	(8,167)
Other, net	(839)	(544)	2,491
Total cash flows provided by operations	186,816	65,701	269,293
Cash flows provided by (used in) investing:			
Expenditures for property, plant and equipment	(90,035)	(73,341)	(81,811)
Expenditures for leased systems and spares	(37,227)	(57,854)	(58,267)
Acquisitions, net of cash acquired	-	(4,122)	(30,089)
Decrease (increase) in long-term investments	(30,000)	60,000	20,000
Other, net	9,870	871	3,136
Total cash flows used in investing	(147,392)	(74,446)	(147,031)
Cash flows provided by (used in) financing:			
Proceeds from borrowings	13,250	10,469	3,698
Proceeds from purchase of common stock by employees	11,225	12,971	10,444
Repayments of debt	(15,014)	(40,889)	(53,203)
Repurchases of common stock	(30,041)	-	(89,422)
Total cash flows used in financing	(20,580)	(17,449)	(128,483)
Effect of exchange rate on cash	(854)	(3,508)	4,463
Increase (decrease) in cash and equivalents	17,990	(29,702)	(1,758)
Cash and equivalents at beginning of year	36,963	66,665	68,423
Cash and equivalents at end of year	$54,953	$36,963	$66,665

Security Analysis: How to Analyze Accounting and Market Data to Value Securities
Robert W. Holthausen and Mark E. Zmijewski
\CH5A.W51

Supplemental Cash Flow Information

	1992	1991	1990
		(In Thousands)	
Reconciliation of net earnings (loss) to cash flows provided by operations:			
Net earnings (loss)	$(14,875)	$113,047	$112,994
Items which do not use (provide) operating cash flow:			
Depreciation and amortization	126,850	119,382	111,996
Loss on sale or retirement of fixed assets	4,500	995	160
Loss (gain) on sale of investments, net of writedowns to market	1,298	(3,405)	-
Accrual of costs under university research and development grants	1,572	644	7,322
Income tax benefit from stock option plans	654	961	919
(Increase) decrease in operating assets:			
Receivables	102,082	(125,650)	45,015
Inventories	(18,760)	(59,572)	25,620
Other	5,560	(14,279)	(10,892)
Increase (decrease) in operating liabilities:			
Accounts payable and accrued expenses	2,488	(2,950)	7,746
Income taxes payable	(28,419)	9,636	(28,545)
Deferred income and customer advances	4,017	27,029	(293)
Other	(151)	(137)	2,749
Cash flows provided by operations	$186,816	$65,701	$269,293
Noncash investing and financing activities:			
Liabilities assumed in acquisition	$-	$1,515	$3,024
Investment valuation allowance	-	(6,338)	6,338

Security Analysis: How to Analyze Accounting and Market Data to Value Securities
Robert W. Holthausen and Mark E. Zmijewski
\CH5A.W51

5.   Free Cash Flows (FCF): The Concept.

Free cash flows are cash flows available for distribution to a specified group of security holders. The free cash flows of the unlevered firm are the cash flows available to all security holders; the free cash flows of the common equity are the cash flows available to the common equity holders. The free cash flow for a period may not be the cash flows that are distributed to the security holders, but they are available for distribution. Our purpose for calculating historic cash flows is to understand past cash flows to forecast future cash flows. Thus, it is important to partition cash flows into cash flows pertaining to existing operations (and expected expansion of existing operations) and cash flows from "one-time" investment decisions (e.g., mergers).

A useful cash flow measure is a measure indicating the amount of cash that has been generated by the firm and is available for distribution to security holders, even though the firm may choose not to distribute some of that cash flow; hence, the term "Free Cash Flow." In other words, how much cash can be distributed to the security holders at the end of the period and leave the firm with the same productive capacity (or an expanded productive capacity as per internal growth expectations) as it had in the beginning of the period.

Do we measure free cash flows before or after income taxes, before or after capital expenditures, before or after interest expense, before or after capitalized interest, before or after dividends, before or after changes in financing? Since all security holders receive cash flows from the firm only after the firm pays its income taxes, we calculate free cash flows after income taxes. However, historical taxes may not be the relevant taxes for the analysis, and your analysis should always based on expected taxes. Similarly, capital expenditures must be made for the firm to continue to operate; therefore, all free cash flows are calculated after capital expenditures.

Interest expense, however, is only relevant to measuring the free cash flows to common equity holders. The free cash flows of the firm are not affected by interest expense. Interest payments that are capitalized are no different from interest payments that are expensed when calculating free cash flows, although differences in the tax effects (capitalized vs. expensed) exist. Dividends are not the same as interest, however. First, the type of dividend effects the calculation. Only cash dividends affect the free cash flows. Neither common stock or preferred stock dividends affect the free cash flows of the unlevered firm, but preferred stock dividends must be deducted to calculate the free cash flows of the common equity. Changes in financing do not affect the free cash flows of the unlevered firm. Changes in non-common equity financing, however, increase the free cash flows of the common equity.

6.   The General Schedule for Calculating the Free-Cash Flow Statement.

Recall the two general free cash flow schedules from chapter 1. The operating cash flow schedule begins with cash flows from operations, the earnings before interest and taxes schedule begins with earnings before interest and taxes. The schedule you use depends only on the information you have available. The free cash flows are the same for both methods.

Security Analysis: How to Analyze Accounting and Market Data to Value Securities
  Robert W. Holthausen and Mark E. Zmijewski
\CH5A.W51

The operating cash flow method is

	After-tax Cash Flow from Operations (Cash Flow Statement)	[CFO]
-	Change in Required Cash Balance[2]	-[1]
+	Interest Expense Paid in Cash	+[2]
-	Tax Shelter from Financing Charges (interest tax shield)	-[3]
	Cash Flow from Operations of the Unlevered Firm	=[CFOUN]
-	Net Capital Expenditures (includes non-cash transactions)	-[4]
	Free Cash Flows of the Unlevered Firm	=[FCFUN]
-	All Cash Interest and Non-Common Stock Dividends Paid in Cash	-[5]
+	Tax Shelter from Financing Charges (interest tax shield)	+[3]
+	Change in the Financing from Non-Common Equity (includes non-cash transactions)	+[6]
	Free Cash Flows of the Common Equity	=[FCFCE]
	Items to Reconcile to the Statement of Cash Flows:	
+	Change in Common Equity Financing	+[7]
-	Common Stock Cash Dividends	-[8]
+/-	Other Adjustments (e.g., changes in accounting principle, errors and prior period adjustments affecting cash, etc.)	+/-[9]
+	Change in Required Cash Balance	+[10]
	Change in Cash Balance	=[CHGCB]

The earnings before interest and taxes method is

+	Earnings Before Interest and Taxes (EBIT)	+[1]
+	Non-Cash Expenses (depreciation)	+[2]
-	Non-Cash Revenues (gains)	-[3]
-	Cash Tax Payments without Any Interest Tax Shield[3]	-[4]
-	Net Cash Capital Expenditures (includes non-cash transactions)	-[5]
-	Change in Required Working Capital[4]	-[6]
-	Cash Operating Expenditures not in EBIT (exploration expense)	-[7]
	Free Cash Flows of the Unlevered Firm	=[FCFUN]

---

[2]We define the "Change in X" as the change in account X during the period; that is, the ending balance in account X minus its beginning balance, $X_t - X_{t-1}$.

[3]You can estimate this number as Income tax expense plus the tax shelter from financing. This approach assumes that there would be no change in deferred income taxes or income taxes payable if the firm had no financial leverage. You can estimate the tax shelter from financing as the tax rate multiplied by interest expense, keeping in mind that the IRS may require interest capitalization that is not the same as the interest capitalized on the financial statement records.

[4]Includes the required change in the cash balance.

Security Analysis: How to Analyze Accounting and Market Data to Value Securities
Robert W. Holthausen and Mark E. Zmijewski
\CH5A.W51

The calculation of the free cash flow of the common equity and the reconciliation of the free cash flow of the common equity to the change in the cash balance (on the statement of cash flows) is the same as for the cash flow from operations method. We do not repeat that part of the schedule here. Current accounting standards require supplemental disclosures for all significant non-cash transactions; non-cash transactions are not recorded in the statement of cash flows. Examples of such transactions are the purchase of non-current assets by assuming liabilities (which includes capitalizing leased assets), conversions of debt and preferred stock, and debt refinancing.

7.   Cash Flow Measures and Financial Analysis.

Potentially useful cash flow measures for financial analysis are after-tax operating cash flow, free cash flow of the unlevered firm, and free cash flow available to common shareholders. Less useful but widely used cash flow measures are income plus depreciation, income plus depreciation plus change in deferred income taxes, and income plus depreciation plus deferred income taxes, minus preferred stock dividends. The limitation of these cash flow measures is that ignore the required investment in capital assets and working capital.

What do analysts say about cash flows? An article in the *Institutional Investor*, 1988, "Go with the (cash) flow" indicates that most analysts use earnings rather than cash flows. Most analysts agree that cash flows are a useful check on the "quality of earnings," and they are not very useful for high growth firms. They disagree as to how to measure cash flows for financial analysis, and they seem to think that cash flow numbers may be more comparable for cross-country comparisons.

Here is a list of questions to ask when analyzing cash flows.

1.   What cash flows are generated by operations for all investors, all stockholders, and common stockholders?

2.   Are the cash flows generated by operations expected to continue or is there some "one-time" events on the cash flow statement? For example, if a firm's operating cash flow came from a large decrease (or increase) in inventory (or accounts receivable), is this good or bad news?

3.   Is the firm able to cover its fixed costs from operations?

4.   Are accruals in income, increasing, decreasing, or remaining the same?

5.   Are earnings increases associated with operating cash flow increases (quality of earnings)? If not, is it because of growth or accounting manipulation?

6.   Will the firm be able to meet short-term commitments and does the firm have a sufficient safety margin?

7.   How are asset replacement and expansion financed?

8.   Is the firm dependent on outside financing to maintain operations?

9.   Is the firm dependent on outside financing to expand?

Security Analysis: How to Analyze Accounting and Market Data to Value Securities
Robert W. Holthausen and Mark E. Zmijewski
\CH5A.W51

Do not reproduce without permission.
July 29, 1998 - 12:00 pm

54

10.   Have cash sales as a percent of total sales changed significantly?

11.   What is the cash flow (CFO, FCFUN, and FCFCE) rate of return? CFO and FCFCE are usually deflated by stockholders equity and FCFUN is usually deflated by total assets.

Income vs Cash Flows - are they complements or substitutes? Income and cash flows are not substitutes. Neither earnings nor cash flow individually reveal the true performance of a firm. Both metrics are useful. Earnings provide some information on the earning power of the firm, but you cannot spend earnings. Free cash flows provide information on the consumable resources and they are less easily manipulated. They suffer, however, from poor matching of revenues and expenses (e.g., capital expenditures). We know little about the time-series properties of free cash flows other than they are typically more variable than earnings, usually due to "lumpy" capital expenditures.

The bottom line is, however, if you could predict either earnings or cash flows over the long run more accurately than the implicit forecast in the market price, you could engage in a very profitable investment strategy. The ratio of earnings to cash flows from operations indicates the magnitude of accruals in earnings, although this calculation is not informative when some denominators are negative or very close to zero. Examine this ratio over time to indicate if earnings growth is also resulting in cash flow growth. If not, where are the cash flows going? Possibly to fund needed current asset growth. Possibly from accounting manipulations.

What do we know about the distribution of cash flows? There is little cash flow research in the literature and much of the literature that exists is deficient. Cash flows must be measured (estimated) by examining financial statement data carefully. Even with a careful analysis of financial statements, one can only estimate cash flows. Much of the data needed to prepare accurate cash flow statements are not public. It is difficult to rely on existing published work in journals because most studies use naive cash flow measures that may not reflect cash flow.

The degree of correlation between income and cash flow measures depends on the definition of cash flows. Naive definitions are highly correlated with net income and there is little data (possibly none) on more realistic cash flow measures. Most studies show that cash flow relations do not provide superior ability to predict events, such as bankruptcy, relative to historical cost accounting earnings, but all such studies use naive cash flow measures. Some recent studies show that cash flows are useful when making portfolio decisions, but again, very little research has been conducted on this topic to date.

8.   **Preparing the Statements of Cash Flows and Free Cash Flows - The BCF-A Company.**

Below we provide the financial statements of BCF-A Company (comparative balance sheets, an income statement, and statement of retained earnings). In this example we prepare a statement of cash flows and two statements of free cash flows (using the cash flow from operations and the earnings before interest and taxes methods).

Here are some additional notes for this problem.

1.   The income tax rate for BCF-A is 40%.
2.   BCF-A needs an increase in cash of $1,000 to operate in next year.

Security Analysis: How to Analyze Accounting and Market Data to Value Securities
Robert W. Holthausen and Mark E. Zmijewski
\CH5A.W51

90 THE BCF-A COMPANY - Income Statement	2000	2001	Ref#
91 -------			
92 Net Revenues	30,000	80,000	
93			
94 Cost of Goods Sold (w/o Depreciation)	(15,000)	(48,000)	
95 Selling, General & Administrative	(1,500)	(16,000)	
96 Depreciation Expense	(4,000)	(5,000)	8
97			
98 Total Expenses	(20,500)	(69,000)	
99			
100 Income Before Interest and Taxes	9,500	11,000	
101 Interest Expense	(500)	(3,000)	
102			
103 Income Before Taxes	9,000	8,000	
104 Income Tax Expense	(1,200)	(3,200)	
105			
106 Net Income	7,800	4,800	1
107 Beginning Retained Earnings	0	7,800	
108 Dividends	0	(1,000)	2
109			
110 Ending Retained Earnings	7,800	11,600	
111			

112					
113 THE BCF-A COMPANY - Balance Sheet	2000	2001		CHANGE	Ref#
114 -------				-------	
115 ASSETS					
116 Cash and short-term investments	23,000	33,900		10,900	balance
117 Accounts receivable	5,000	7,000		2,000	3
118 Inventories	7,000	6,900		(100)	4
119					
120 Total current assets	35,000	47,800		12,800	
121					
122 PROPERTY, PLANT, AND EQUIPMENT	40,000	50,000		10,000	9
123 Less accumulated depreciation	(4,000)	(9,000)		(5,000)	8
124					
125 Net Property, plant, and equipment	36,000	41,000		5,000	
126					
127 TOTAL	71,000	88,800		17,800	
128					
129					
130 LIABILITIES AND SHAREHOLDERS' EQUITY					
131 Accounts payable -- trade	2,200	6,200		4,000	5
132 Interest Payable	500	500		0	
133 Income Taxes Payable	500	2,500		2,000	6
134					
135 Total current liabilities	3,200	9,200		6,000	
136 Long-term Debt	10,000	13,000		3,000	10
137					
138 Total liabilities	13,200	22,200		9,000	
139					
140 Common Stock at Par	50,000	55,000		5,000	7
141 Retained earnings	7,800	11,600		3,800	1&2
142					
143 Total shareholders, equity	57,800	66,600		8,800	
144					
145 TOTAL	71,000	88,800		17,800	
146					
147					

Security Analysis: How to Analyze Accounting and Market Data to Value Securities
Robert W. Holthausen and Mark E. Zmijewski
\CH5A.W51

	ACCOUNT	REF #	DEBIT	CREDIT
149				
150	--------			
152	Cash Flow From Operations	1	4,800	
153	Retained Earnings (Income)			4,800
154				
155	Retained Earnings (Dividends)	2	1,000	
156	Cash Flow From Financing			1,000
157				
158	Accounts receivable	3	2,000	
159	Cash Flow From Operations			2,000
160				
161	Cash Flow From Operations	4	100	
162	Inventories			100
163				
164	Cash Flow From Operations	5	4,000	
165	Accounts payable			4,000
166				
167	Cash Flow From Operations	6	2,000	
168	Income Taxes Payable			2,000
169				
170	Cash Flow From Financing	7	5,000	
171	Common Stock			5,000
172				
173	Cash Flow From Operations	8	5,000	
174	Accumulated Depreciation			5,000
175				
176	Property, Plant, and Equipment - Cost	9	10,000	
177	Cash Flow From Investing			10,000
178				
179	Cash Flow From Financing	10	3,000	
180	Long Term Debt			3,000

	THE BCF-A COMPANY - Cash Flow Statement	2001	REF #
181	--------		
182	Net Income	4,800	1
183			
184	Adjustments:		
185	Depreciation Expense	5,000	8
186	Change in Accounts Receivable	(2,000)	3
187	Change in Inventories	100	4
188	Change in Account Payable	4,000	5
189	Change in Income Taxes Payable	2,000	6
190		--------	
191	Cash Flow from Operations	13,900	
192		--------	
193	Investing Activities:		
194	Purchase of Property, Plant and Equipment	(10,000)	9
195		--------	
196		(10,000)	
197		--------	
198	Financing Activities:		
199	Increase in Long Term Debt	3,000	10
200	Change in Common Stock	5,000	7
201	Dividends	(1,000)	2
202		--------	
203		7,000	
204		--------	
205	Change in Cash Balance	10,900	
206		========	
207			
208	Additional Schedules		
210	Interest Expense	3,000	
211		--------	
212	Amount Paid	3,000	
213		========	
215	Income Tax Expense	3,200	
216	Change in Income Taxes Payable	(2,000)	
217		--------	
218	Amount Paid	1,200	
219		========	

Security Analysis: How to Analyze Accounting and Market Data to Value Securities
Robert W. Holthausen and Mark E. Zmijewski
\CH5A.W51

```
220 THE BCF-A COMPANY - Statement of Free Cash Flows          2001
221 ----------------------------------------------------------------
222 Marginal Tax Rate                                         40.0%
223
224                                                           ======
225 Operating Activities - Net Cash Flow                      13,900
226 Less - Change in Required Cash Balance                   (1,000)
227                                                           --------
228 Adjusted Operating Cash Flow                              12,900
229                                                           --------
230 Plus - Interest Expense                                    3,000
231 Less - Income Tax Shelter from Debt Financing            (1,200)
232                                                           --------
233 Effects of Interest and the Interest Tax Shield            1,800
234                                                           --------
235 Cash Flow From Operations of the Unlevered Firm           14,700
236 Less - Purchases of Property, Plant and Equipment        (10,000)
237                                                           --------
238 Free Cash Flow of the Unlevered Firm                       4,700
239 Less - Total Effects of Financial Leverage               (1,800)
240 Cash Flows to (from) Non-Equity Security Holders           3,000
241                                                           --------
242 Free Cash Flow of the Common Equity                        5,900
243 Items to Reconcile to the Statement of Cash Flows:
244 Cash Dividends - Common                                  (1,000)
245 Change in Common Stock                                     5,000
246                                                           --------
247 Change in Excess Cash                                      9,900
248 Plus - Change in Required Cash Balance                     1,000
249                                                           --------
250 Change in Cash Balance - FCF Statement                    10,900
251                                                           ======
252 Change in Cash Balance - B/S                              10,900
253                                                           ======
254


255 EBIT Calculation of Free Cash Flows                       2001
256 ----------------------------------------------------------------
257 Net Income (Loss)                                          4,800
258 Plus - Interest Expense                                    3,000
259 Plus - Income Taxes - Total                                3,200
260                                                           --------
261 Earnings Before Interest and Taxes                        11,000
262
263 Required Changes in Working Capital:
264 Required Change in Cash Balance                           (1,000)
265 Change in  Accounts Receivable                            (2,000)
266 Change in Inventories                                        100
267 Change in Account Payable                                  4,000
268 Change in Income Taxes Payable                                NA
269
270 Depreciation Expense                                       5,000
271                                                           --------
272 Subtotal                                                  17,100
273 Less - Cash Tax Payments without any Interest Tax Shield  (2,400)  Cash Taxes Paid 1200 + ITS 1200
274 Less - Net Capital Expenditures                          (10,000)
275                                                           --------
276 Free Cash Flow of the Unlevered Firm                       4,700
277                                                           ======
278
```

Security Analysis: How to Analyze Accounting and Market Data to Value Securities
Robert W. Holthausen and Mark E. Zmijewski
\CH5A.W51

9.   Non-U.S. Cash Flow Statements

In theory the statement of cash flows can be created from the accounts of a company, assuming the disclosures are sufficient. In the U.S., it is not always possible to perfectly derive the statement of cash flows from the information disclosed in the annual report or 10-K of the company.

Outside the U.S., there are many countries where no cash flow statement is required. Virtually every country requires the disclosure of an income statement and balance sheet. Germany and the Netherlands do not require a statement of cash flows. Listed companies in Japan are required to disclose a statement of cash flows, but it is unaudited.

In countries where a cash flow like statement is required, it may have a different form than provided in the U.S. For example, in the United Kingdom, interest and dividends pain are grouped in separate category and thus are neither part of cash flows from operations (interest in the U.S.) or cash flows from financing (dividends in the U.S.). This does not cause any problems, as long as you know the various rules in countries and understand what you required. Therefore, if you were to start with CFO for a U.K. firm, the algorithm to free cash flow of the unlevered firm would be different than in the U.S., but you should be able to figure out how, with no problem (assuming you familiarize yourself with the disclosure rules).

In many South American companies it is still common to present a statement of changes in funds, where funds is defined as working capital (current assets - current liabilities). This was the standard reporting format in the U.S. until the early 1980's. The major differences are that changes in current operating accounts (e.g., inventory, receivables, payables, etc.) are not included in the changes in funds. Moreover, short term debt is considered part of working capital and is not considered financing. Again, however, if you know the disclosure rules, this should pose no particular problem to your ability to capture the firm's free cash flows.

Security Analysis: How to Analyze Accounting and Market Data to Value Securities
Robert W. Holthausen and Mark E. Zmijewski
\CH5A.W51

Do not reproduce without permission.
July 29, 1998 - 12:00 pm

59

Chapter 5A

Problems for Review

1.   Preparing the Statements of Cash Flows and Free Cash Flows - The BCF-B Company.

Below we provide the financial statements of BCF-B (comparative balance sheets, an income statement, and statement of retained earnings). Prepare the following for the year ended December 31, 2001:

    A.   Statement of Cash Flows.
    B.   Statement of Free Cash Flows using the Cash Flow From Operations method.
    C.   Statement of Free Cash Flows using with Earnings Before Interest and Taxes method.

Here are some additional notes for this problem.

    1.   During 2001 BCF-B sold property, plant, and equipment that had an acquisition cost of $5,000.
    2.   The income tax rate for BCF-B is 40%.
    3.   BCF-B needs an increase in cash of $1,000 to operate in next year.

	2000	2001
104 THE BCF-B COMPANY - Income Statement		
105 --		
106 Net Revenues	80,000	100,000
107 Gain on Sale (Other Revenues)	0	700
108		
109 Total Revenues	80,000	100,700
110		
111 Cost of Goods Sold (w/o Depreciation)	(40,000)	(50,000)
112 Selling, General & Administrative	(20,000)	(20,000)
113 Depreciation Expense	(10,000)	(13,000)
114		
115 Total Expenses	(70,000)	(83,000)
116		
117 Income Before Interest and Taxes	10,000	17,700
118 Interest Expense	(1,000)	(3,000)
119		
120 Income Before Taxes	9,000	14,700
121 Income Tax Expense	(1,200)	(5,880)
122		
123 Net Income	7,800	8,820
124 Beginning Retained Earnings	0	7,800
125 Dividends	0	(4,000)
126		
127 Ending Retained Earnings	7,800	12,620
128		
129		

Security Analysis: How to Analyze Accounting and Market Data to Value Securities
  Robert W. Holthausen and Mark E. Zmijewski
\CH5A.W51

		2000	2001	CHANGE
130	THE BCF-B COMPANY - Balance Sheet			
131	-----------------------------------			----------
132	ASSETS			
133	Cash and short-term investments	19,500	22,420	2,920
134	Accounts receivable	8,000	18,000	10,000
135	Inventories	2,000	1,500	(500)
136				
137	Total current assets	29,500	41,920	12,420
138				
139	PROPERTY, PLANT, AND EQUIPMENT	100,000	125,000	25,000
140	Less accumulated depreciation	(10,000)	(22,000)	(12,000)
141				
142	Net Property, plant, and equipment	90,000	103,000	13,000
143				
144	Pre-Paid Expenses (Non-Current)	0	3,000	3,000
145				
146	TOTAL	119,500	147,920	28,420
147				
148				
149	LIABILITIES AND SHAREHOLDERS' EQUITY			
150	Accounts payable -- trade	4,200	8,200	4,000
151	Accrued Liabilities (Expenses)	6,000	3,500	(2,500)
152	Interest Payable	1,000	1,100	100
153	Income Taxes Payable	500	2,500	2,000
154	Dividends Payable	0	1,000	1,000
155				
156	Total current liabilities	11,700	16,300	4,600
157				
158	Long-term Debt-A	20,000	20,000	0
159	Long-term Debt-B	0	15,000	15,000
160				
161	Long-term liabilities	20,000	35,000	15,000
162				
163	Total liabilities	31,700	51,300	19,600
164				
165	Common Stock at Par	80,000	85,000	5,000
166	Additional paid-in capital	0	0	0
167	Foreign currency translation adj	0	0	0
168	Retained earnings	7,800	12,620	4,820
169				
170		87,800	97,620	9,820
171	Treasury Stock, at cost	0	(1,000)	(1,000)
172				
173	Total shareholders, equity	87,800	96,620	8,820
174				
175	TOTAL	119,500	147,920	28,420
176				
177				

Security Analysis: How to Analyze Accounting and Market Data to Value Securities
Robert W. Holthausen and Mark E. Zmijewski
\CH5A.W51

2.   Understanding how events affect the statements of cash flows and free cash flows.

Schedules to calculate cash flow from operations and the statement of free cash flows appear below. For each part of this problem indicate each line number (on both schedules) that are affected by the information in that part of the problem. Indicate the amount of the effect and if the effect represents an increase or decrease. Ignore income taxes unless otherwise instructed. If instructed to include income tax effects, assume the marginal tax rate is 40% and that income taxes are paid in cash by year-end. Also assume each part of the problem is independent unless stated otherwise.

Calculation of Cash Flow From Operations (CFO):

	Net Income from the Statement of Income	**[1]**
+	Expenses and Losses Not Decreasing Working Capital	+[2]
-	Revenues, Gains, and Additions not Increasing Working Capital	-[3]
+	Decreases in Operating Current Assets (other than Cash) and Increases in Operating Current Liabilities	+[4]
-	Increases in Operating Current Assets (other than Cash) and Decreases in Operating Current Liabilities	-[5]
+/-	Adjustments for Discontinued Operations	+/-[6]
+/-	Adjustments for Extraordinary Items	+/-[7]
+/-	Adjustments for Cumulative Affect of Change in Accounting Principles	+/-[8]
	After-tax Cash Flow From Operations	**=[CFO]**

Calculation of Statement of Free Cash Flows:

	After-tax Cash Flow from Operations (Cash Flow Statement)	**[CFO]**
-	Change in Required Cash Balance	-[1]
+	Interest Expense Paid in Cash	+[2]
-	Tax Shelter from Financing Charges (interest tax shield)	-[3]
	Cash Flow from Operations of the Unlevered Firm	**=[CFOUN]**
-	Net Capital Expenditures (includes non-cash transactions)	-[4]
	Free Cash Flows of the Unlevered Firm	**=[FCFUN]**
-	All Cash Interest and Non-Common Stock Dividends Paid in Cash	-[5]
+	Tax Shelter from Financing Charges (interest tax shield)	+[3]
+	Change in the Financing from Non-Common Equity (includes non-cash transactions)	+[6]
	Free Cash Flows of the Common Equity	**=[FCFCE]**
	Items to Reconcile to the Statement of Cash Flows:	
+	Change in Common Equity Financing	+[7]
-	Common Stock Cash Dividends	-[8]
+/-	Other Adjustments (e.g., changes in accounting principle, errors and prior period adjustments affecting cash, etc.)	+/-[9]
+	Change in Required Cash Balance	+[10]
	Change in Cash Balance	**=[CHGCB]**

Security Analysis: How to Analyze Accounting and Market Data to Value Securities
  Robert W. Holthausen and Mark E. Zmijewski
  \CH5A.W51

A.   A firm sells inventory for $1,000 (on account); the inventory has a book value of $600.

B.   A firm collects an account receivable of $100.

C.   A firm orders inventory; the inventory will be shipped in 30 days which has a cost of $500.

D.   A firm receives inventory that was ordered previously which has a cost of $500.

E.   A firm writes off an account receivable of $700; the firm uses the allowance method.

F.   A firm sells land that is not required for its operations on December 31, 19X1 for $6,000. The land was purchased ten years earlier for $2,000. The gain is taxable.

G.   A firm sells some old equipment for $3,000. The acquisition cost of the equipment was $6,000 and the depreciation taken to date is $2,000; the accounting book value is also equal to its taxable basis.

H.   A firm sells some old equipment for $5,000. The acquisition cost of the equipment was $6,000 and the depreciation taken to date is $2,000; the accounting book value is also equal to its taxable basis.

I.   A firm declares and pays a special dividend of $1,000 to its common shareholders.

J.   A firm declares but does not pay a dividend of $1,000 to its common shareholders.

K.   A firm issues additional common stock of $3,000.

L.   A firm issues additional preferred stock on January 1, 19X1. The preferred stock has a par value of $1,000 and an annual dividend equal to $100 due on December 31 of each year. Assume the dividend was declared and paid on December 31, 19X1. Indicate the effect for the year ended December 31, 19X1.

M.   A firm issues preferred stock on January 1, 19X1. The preferred stock has a par value of $1,000 and an annual dividend equal to $100 due on December 31 of each year. Assume the dividend was declared and but not paid on December 31, 19X1. Indicate the effect for the year ended December 31, 19X1.

N.   A firm buys land and a building for $50,000. The seller of the building financed 80 percent of the sale with a mortgage.

O.   A firm pays $5,000 interest and $2,000 principal on a mortgage that it purchased.

Security Analysis: How to Analyze Accounting and Market Data to Value Securities
Robert W. Holthausen and Mark E. Zmijewski
\CH5A.W51

Do not reproduce without permission.
July 29, 1998 - 2:09 pm

63

3

ANALYSIS OF CASH FLOWS

STATEMENT OF CASH FLOWS

Cash flow data supplement the information provided by the income statement as both link consecutive balance sheets. The statement of cash flows is intended to report all the cash inflows and outflows (classified among operating, investing, and financing activities) of the firm for a specified period. It also provides disclosures about that period's noncash investing and financing activities.

The classification of cash flows among operating, financing, and investing activities is essential to the analysis of cash flow data. Net cash flow (the change in cash and equivalents during the period) has little informational content by itself; it is the classification and individual components that are informative.

Cash flow from operating activities (cash from operations or CFO) measures the amount of cash generated or used by the firm as a result of its production and sales of goods and services. Although deficits or negative cash flows from operations are expected in some circumstances (e.g., rapid growth), for most firms positive operating cash flows are essential for long-run survival. Internally generated funds can be used to pay dividends or repurchase equity, repay loans, replace existing capacity, or invest in acquisitions and growth.

Investing cash flow (CFI) reports the amount of cash used to acquire assets such as plant and equipment as well as investments and entire businesses. These outlays are necessary to maintain a firm's current operating capacity and to provide capacity for future growth. CFI also includes cash received from the sale or disposal of assets or segments of the business.

Financing cash flow (CFF) includes cash flows related to the firm's capital structure (debt and equity), including proceeds from the issuance of equity, returns to shareholders in the form of dividends and repurchase of equity, and the incurrence and repayment of debt.

Direct and Indirect Method Cash Flow Statements

SFAS 95, Statement of Cash Flows (1987), permits firms to report cash from operations either *directly,* using major categories of gross cash receipts and payments, or *indirectly* by providing a reconciliation from accrual-based net income to CFO.

Exhibit 3-1 contrasts the direct and indirect cash flow statements of the WSF Company. These statements are generated from the company's balance sheet (Exhibit 3-2) and income statement (Exhibit 3-3).

65

EXHIBIT 3-1. THE WSF COMPANY
Statement of Cash Flows for Year Ended December 31, 1997

A. Direct Method

Cash collections		$ 2,675,000
Less: Cash inputs	$(1,750,000)	
Cash expenses (rent, operating)	(430,000)	
Cash interest	(125,000)	(2,305,000)
Cash flow from operations		**$370,000**
Capital expenditures	(500,000)	
Investment in affiliate	(710,000)	
Cash flow from investments		**(1,210,000)**
Short-term borrowing	500,000	
Dividends paid	(35,000)	
Cash flow from financing		**465,000**
Net cash flow		**$ (375,000)**
Cash balance, as of December 31		
1997	$ 3,625,000	
1996	4,000,000	
Net change		**$ (375,000)**

B. Indirect Method

Net income		78,870
Add: Noncash expenses		
Depreciation expense		175,000
		$ 253,870
Changes in operating accounts		
(Increase) in receivables	(224,500)	
Decrease in inventories	425,000	
(Decrease) in accounts payable	(475,000)	
Increase in accrued liabilities	50,000	
Increase in interest payable	125,000	
Increase in taxes payable	40,630	
Increase in advances from customers	175,000	116,130
Cash flows from operations		**$ 370,000**

Note: Cash flow from investing and financing identical to that shown on direct method. The firm would also provide a separate footnote on cash payments for interest and taxes. The WSF Company paid $125,000 in interest, but it made no tax payments during the year ended December 31, 1997.

Under the indirect method, CFO is computed by adjusting net income for all:

1. Noncash revenues and expenses
2. Nonoperating items included in net income
3. Noncash changes in operating assets and liabilities

Enterprises using the direct method must also provide such a reconciliation. Firms using both methods must disclose the cash outflows for income taxes and interest within the statement or elsewhere in the financial statements (e.g., in the footnotes).[1]

[1]Required by para. 29 of SFAS 95.

EXHIBIT 3-2. THE WSF COMPANY
Balance Sheets at December 31, 1996 and 1997

	1996	1997
Assets		
Cash	$4,000,000	$3,625,000
Accounts receivable	0	224,500
Inventory	850,000	425,000
Current assets	$4,850,000	$4,274,500
Investment in affiliates	0	710,000
Buildings	3,500,000	4,000,000
Less: Accumulated depreciation	0	(175,000)
Long-term assets	$3,500,000	$4,535,000
Total assets	$8,350,000	$8,809,500
Liabilities		
Short-term debt	$0	$500,000
Advances from customers	0	175,000
Accounts payable	850,000	375,000
Accrued liabilities	0	50,000
Interest payable	0	125,000
Taxes payable	0	40,630
Dividends payable	0	35,000
Current liabilities	$ 850,000	$1,300,630
Bonds payable	2,500,000	2,500,000
Total liabilities	$3,350,000	$3,800,630
Common stock	1,000,000	1,000,000
Additional paid-in capital	4,000,000	4,000,000
Retained earnings	0	8,870
Stockholders' equity	$5,000,000	$5,008,870
Total liabilities and equities	$8,350,000	$8,809,500

Cash flow statements prepared using the indirect method have a significant draw-back. Because of the *indirect format, it is not possible to compare operating cash inflows and outflows by function with the revenue and expense activities that generated them, as is possible from cash flow statements prepared using the direct method.* In the absence of acquisitions, divestitures, and significant foreign operations, the indirect method simply recasts the income statement and the balance sheet, providing little new information on or insight into a firm's cash-generating ability. As a majority of firms prepare the SoCF using the indirect method,[2] it is often necessary to convert an indirect statement into a direct one.

[2]Of the 600 firms surveyed by the AICPA in the 1994 *Accounting Trends and Techniques,* only 14 report using the direct method.

EXHIBIT 3-3. THE WSF COMPANY
Income Statement for Year Ended December 31, 1997

Net sales		$ 2,724,500
Less: Cost of goods sold		(1,700,000)
Gross margin		$ 1,024,500
Less: Operating expense	$360,000	
Depreciation expense	175,000	
Rent expense	120,000	
Interest expense	250,000	(905,000)
Income before taxes		119,500
Tax expense		(40,630)
Net income		$ 78,870

Statement of Retained Earnings

Beginning balance, January 1, 1997	$ 0	
Net income	78,870	
Dividends declared	(70,000)	
Ending balance, December 31, 1997	$ 8,870	

The Preparation of a Statement of Cash Flows

The cash flow statement combines cash flows for events that are reported on the balance sheet (e.g., purchases of assets) and the income statement (e.g., the sale of goods). The process is complicated by differences between the time cash flows occur and when they are recognized as revenues, expenses, assets, or liabilities. The next section discusses methods used to prepare direct and indirect method cash flow statements.

Transactional Analysis

Transactional analysis[3] is a technique that can be used to create a cash flow statement for firms that do not prepare such statements in accordance with SFAS 95 and IAS 7.[4] It can also be used to convert indirect method cash flow from operations to the direct method.

One objective of transactional analysis is to understand the relationship between the accrual of revenues, expenses, assets, and liabilities and their cash flow consequences. Another goal is to classify cash flows among operating, financing, and investing activities as required by SFAS 95.

---

[3]See Ashwinpaul C. Sondhi, George H. Sorter, and Gerald I. White, "Transactional Analysis," *Financial Analysts Journal,* Sept./Oct. 1987, pp. 57–64. "Cash Flow Redefined: FAS 95 and Security Analysis," *Financial Analysts Journal,* Nov./Dec. 1988, pp. 19–20 by the same authors links the transactional analysis method of preparing cash flow statements to those required by SFAS 95.

[4]The number of non-U.S. companies preparing statements of cash flows is on the increase. IAS 7, Cash Flow Statements, was issued a few years after SFAS 95; foreign firms using IAS 7 are not required to reconcile their cash flow statements to U.S. GAAP. Despite these trends, many foreign firms do not report any cash flow statement or report changes in funds (see "Cash Flow Statements: An International Perspective," near the end of this chapter).

The method reconciles line-item changes in the balance sheet with their related income statement components to derive the cash flow consequences of the reported transactions and events. These changes are grouped according to whether they are operating, investing, or financing in nature. The classification and cash flow description for a typical firm follow:

Changes Included in Cash Flow from *Operating* Activities (CFO)

Balance Sheet Account	Cash Flow Description
Accounts receivable	Cash received from customers
Inventories	Cash paid for inputs (materials)
Prepaid expenses	Cash expenses
Accounts payable	Cash paid for inputs/expenses
Advances from customers	Cash received from customers
Rent payable	Cash expenses
Interest payable	Interest paid
Income tax payable	Income taxes paid
Deferred income taxes	Income taxes paid

Changes Included in Cash Flow from *Investing* Activities (CFI)

Balance Sheet Account	Cash Flow Description
Property, plant, and equipment	Capital expenditures
	Proceeds from property sales
Investment in affiliates	Cash paid for acquisitions and investments

Changes Included in Cash Flow from *Financing* Activities (CFF)

Balance Sheet Account	Cash Flow Description
Notes payable	Increase or decrease in debt
Short-term debt	Increase or decrease in debt
Long-term debt	Increase or decrease in debt
Bonds payable	Increase or decrease in debt
Common stock	Equity financing or repurchase
Retained earnings	Dividends paid

The relationship between balance sheet changes and cash flows can be summarized as follows:

- Increases (decreases) in assets represent net cash outflows (inflows). If an asset increases, the firm must have paid cash in exchange.
- Increases (decreases) in liabilities represent net cash inflows (outflows). When a liability increases, the firm must have received cash in exchange.

While these points are simplistic (they ignore payments or receipts other than cash), they are useful in practice.

Two examples clarify the application of these points to transactional analysis:

1. When accounts receivable increase, the period's sales revenues must have exceeded cash collections. Thus, the increase in receivables must be deducted from the accrued sales revenue to derive the cash collected from customers during the period.

2. When interest payable increases, that means the firm did not pay all the interest expense accrued during the period. Hence, the increase in interest payable must be deducted from the interest expense to compute the amount of interest paid during the period.

Preparation of a Direct Method Statement of Cash Flows

Exhibit 3-4 illustrates the use of transactional analysis to prepare a direct method statement of cash flows for the WSF Company. This simplified example allows us to explain the method without the complications present in most actual financial statements.

We use the data from Exhibits 3-2 and 3-3. A brief discussion of the most critical problems in the preparation of cash flow statements is provided later.

Cash Flows from Operations

Cash Collections. The principal component of CFO is the cash collections for the period. To derive this amount, we start with WSF net sales of $2,724,500 in 1997. The increase of $224,500 in the balance of accounts receivable means that cash has not yet been collected for all the sales recognized. In addition, the firm received cash advances ($175,000) for which revenue has not yet been recognized.

We modify net sales by deducting the increase in accounts receivable and adding the increase in advances, to arrive at cash collections. This is the amount of cash actually received during the period as a result of sales activities, regardless of when the related revenues were recognized.

Cash Outflows. The next stage involves the computation of operating cash outflows incurred to generate the cash collections. The first component is the cash outflow for inputs into the manufacturing or retailing process. The decrease in inventory balances[5] (cash outflow occurred in the prior period) is subtracted from, and the decrease in accounts payable (cash outflow in the current period for goods received in a prior period) is added to the cost of goods sold to determine the cash inputs or outflow for the manufacturing process.

The remaining income statement accounts and their related balance sheet accounts are similarly modified to their cash analogs to determine the cash outflows for operating expenses, interest, and taxes. In each case, the goal is to link the income statement account with related balance sheet accounts. By related, we mean that the balance sheet account contains cash flows that either have been recognized in that income statement category (accruals and payables) or will be recognized in the future (prepayments).

---

[5]The cash outflow for inputs is not affected by the inventory valuation method used by the firm, facilitating comparison across firms.

EXHIBIT 3-4. THE WSF COMPANY
Transactional Analysis ($ 000)

	Income Statement	Balance Sheet			Cash Effect	Cash	
		12/31/96	12/31/97	Change			
Cash Collections							
Net sales	2,724.5				Increase	2,724.5	
Accounts receivable		—	224.5	224.5	(Decrease)	(224.5)	
Advances		—	175.0	175.0	Increase	175.0	**2,675.0**
Cash Inputs							
COGS	(1,700.0)				(Decrease)	(1,700.0)	
Inventory		850.0	425.0	(425.0)	Increase	425.0	
Accounts payable		850.0	375.0	(475.0)	(Decrease)	(475.0)	**(1,750.0)**
Cash Expenses							
Operating expense	(360.0)				(Decrease)	(360.0)	
Rent expense	(120.0)				(Decrease)	(120.0)	
Accrued liabilities		—	50.0	50.0	Increase	50.0	**(430.0)**
Cash Taxes Paid							
Tax expense	(40.63)				(Decrease)	(40.63)	
Taxes payable		0	40.63	40.63	Increase	40.63	—
Cash Interest Paid							
Interest expense	(250.0)				(Decrease)	(250.0)	
Interest payable		0	125	125	Increase	125.0	**(125.0)**
							370.0
Operating Cash Flow							
Capital Expenditures							
Depreciation	(175.0)				(Decrease)	(175.0)	
Buildings—Net		3,500	3,825	325.0	(Decrease)	(325.0)	**(500.0)**
Cash Invested in Affiliates							
Investment in affiliates		—	710.0	710.0	(Decrease)		**(710.0)**
							(1,210.0)
Investing Cash Flow							
Cash from Borrowing							
Short-term debt		—	500.0	500.0	Increase	500.0	
Bonds payable		2,500	2,500	—		—	**500.0**

EXHIBIT 3-4. (*continued*)

	Income Statement	Balance Sheet			Cash Effect	Cash
		12/31/96	12/31/97	Change		
Equity Financing						
Common stock		1,000	1,000	—		
Additional paid-in capital		4,000	4,000	—		—
Dividends						
Net income	78.87					
Dividends declared					(Decrease)	(70.0)
Dividends payable		—	35.0		Increase	35.0	**(35.0)**
						465.0
Financing Cash Flow						
Change in cash						**(375.0)**

In many cases, disclosures are inadequate to do this precisely. Educated guesses and approximations may be necessary. For example, we assume that accounts payable reported by WSF relate only to the purchase of inventory for operating purposes although they may also be related to other operating expenses.

A careful reading of footnote data is necessary to obtain additional information on aggregated balance sheet accounts, permitting finer breakdowns of assets and liabilities. For example, in addition to trade accounts receivable, the amounts reported on the balance sheet may include notes and loans receivable, which either belong to the miscellaneous category of operating cash flows or represent investment cash flows.

Additionally, balance sheet and income statement accounts may require reallocation of some components. For example, when depreciation expense is not reported separately in the income statement, we must reduce COGS by the amount of depreciation expense to accurately reflect cash inputs and create a "depreciation expense" account to correctly estimate cash invested in property. The depreciation expense may be disclosed separately in footnotes, or in the indirect cash flow statement.

Cash flows that are considered nonrecurring[6] or peripheral to the basic activities of the firm are combined in the miscellaneous category, which also includes the cash impact of transactions for which the financial statements and the footnotes do not provide information enabling more precise classification.

Investing Cash Flow

Capital expenditures for long-term assets such as plant and machinery are usually the primary component of investing cash flow. As depreciation changes (net) property, plant, and equipment, the calculation of capital expenditures requires the amount of

---

[6]However, the transaction should be analyzed to determine whether it is best classified as operating, investing, or financing.

depreciation, depletion, and amortization expense in addition to the changes in all related long-term asset accounts.[7]

Capital expenditures may be calculated net or gross of proceeds on the sales of these assets. The cash flows from such sales are considered investment cash flows, regardless of whether they are netted in capital expenditures. Trends in gross capital expenditures contain useful insights into management plans. Segment disclosures should be monitored for differential investment patterns.

Other components of cash flows from investing activities include cash flows from investments in joint ventures and affiliates and long-term investments in securities.[8] The cash flow consequences of acquisitions and divestitures must also be reported in this category. Footnote disclosures (when available) should be used to segregate operating assets and liabilities obtained (relinquished) in acquisitions (divestitures). This analysis, as discussed below, may be necessary to calculate CFO.

Financing Cash Flow

Components of financing cash flow include inflows from additional borrowing and equity financing, and outflows for repayment of debt, dividend payments, and equity repurchases. Debt financing for the period is the sum of the changes in short- and long-term debt accounts.

The calculation of equity financing cash flows requires analysis of the change in stockholders' equity, separating:

- Net income
- Dividends declared
- Shares issued or repurchased
- Changes in valuation accounts included in equity (each of these may require reallocation to appropriate operating or investing cash flow categories[9])

Once this is done, every change in the balance sheet has been included (net income is included by incorporating each of its components) except cash. The net cash flow must, by definition, be equal to the change in cash. This identity provides a check on computations.[10]

The last step is to summarize the cash flows from operations, financing, and investing activities. The result is a direct method statement of cash flows, as shown in Exhibit 3-1A.

---

[7]Thus, the deduction for depreciation expense is not taken because depreciation represents a cash flow; rather, because it is needed to calculate the cash capital expenditures.

[8]The nature of the relationship between parent and subsidiary or joint venture affiliate should be reviewed periodically to ensure proper classification; in some cases, affiliates may be more accurately considered part of operations. However, contractual arrangements may constrain the parent's control over or access to cash flows from affiliates. (See Chapter 13 for a detailed discussion of these issues.)

[9]For example, the change in the unrealized gains (losses) on investments account must be reflected as a component of investment cash flows (see Chapter 13).

[10]As an additional check, make sure that the income statement components used in the transactional analysis add up to net income.

The Indirect Method

Exhibit 3-1B presents the indirect method statement of cash flows for the WSF Company. The reporting of investing and financing activities is identical to the direct method. *The reporting of cash flow from operations, however, is quite different.* Under the indirect method, the starting point is the period's net income. Two types of adjustment are then made to net income to arrive at the CFO:

1. All "non-cash" expense (revenue) components of the income statement are added (subtracted).
2. Changes in operating accounts are added/subtracted as follows:

   • Increases (decreases) in the balances of operating asset accounts are subtracted (added).
   • Increases (decreases) in the balances of operating liability accounts are added (subtracted).

The second type of adjustment represents the same balance sheet changes that were used to arrive at cash from operations under the direct method. As these adjustments are provided by the reconciliation in the indirect cash flow method, it is possible to use them to derive a direct method cash flow statement from an indirect one.

In Box 3-1, we demonstrate this process using duPont's indirect method Statement of Cash Flows reproduced in Exhibit 3-5. As the discussion in the box indicates, careful analysis of footnote information is required to make the necessary adjustments.

Two important requirements of SFAS 95 must, however, be explained before proceeding to Box 3-1:

1. *Changes in operating accounts shown on duPont's Statement of Cash Flows do not equal the balance sheet changes.* For example, in the 1994 cash flow statement, accounts receivable *decreases by $30;* on the balance sheet (Appendix A), it *increases by $319.* What accounts for this and similar discrepancies in other operating assets and liabilities?
2. DuPont's Statement of Cash Flows contains the *effect of exchange rate changes on cash* (in addition to the three cash flow categories: operating, investing, and financing). The 1994 amount is $94 million. What does it represent?

We address both issues below.

Reported Versus Operating Changes in Assets and Liabilities

The discrepancies between the changes in accounts reported on the balance sheet and those reported in the cash flow statement are due to two factors:

• Acquisitions and divestitures
• Foreign subsidiaries

BOX 3-1
DuPont—1994
Derivation of CFO Using Direct Method ($ in millions)

**EXHIBIT 3-5. E. I. DUPONT DE NEMOURS AND COMPANY AND
CONSOLIDATED SUBSIDIARIES**
Consolidated Statement of Cash Flows ($ in millions)

	1994	1993	1992
Cash and cash equivalents at beginning of year	$ 1,109	$ 1,640	$ 468
Cash provided by operations			
Net income (loss)	2,727	555	(3,927)
Adjustments to reconcile net income to cash provided by operations			
Extraordinary charge from early extinguishment of debt (Note 8)	—	11	69
Transition effect of accounting changes (Notes 1, 7, and 25)	—	—	4,833
Depreciation, depletion, and amortization	2,976	2,833	2,655
Dry hole costs and impairment of unproved properties	152	201	185
Other noncash charges and credits—net	(140)	843	(174)
Decrease in operating assets			
Accounts and notes receivable	30	103	104
Inventories and other operating assets	19	664	219
Increase (decrease) in operating liabilities			
Accounts payable and other operating liabilities	(432)	686	907
Accrued interest and income taxes (Notes 4 and 7)	332	(516)	(483)
Cash provided by operations	5,664	5,380	4,388
Investment activities (Note 24)			
Purchases of property, plant, and equipment	(3,050)	(3,621)	(4,448)
Investments in affiliates	(90)	(70)	(127)
Payments for businesses acquired	(5)	(409)	—
Proceeds from sales of assets	432	1,160	179
Investments in short-term financial instruments—net	(379)	(85)	(70)
Miscellaneous—net	(41)	(53)	(87)
Cash used for investment activities	(3,133)	(3,078)	(4,553)
Financing activities			
Dividends paid to stockholders	(1,247)	(1,201)	(1,182)
Net increase (decrease) in short-term borrowings	(517)	(2,024)	2,310
Long-term and other borrowings			
Receipts	824	1,806	2,976
Payments	(2,032)	(1,392)	(2,711)
Common stock issued in connection with compensation plans	94	67	86
Cash provided by (used for) financing activities	(2,878)	(2,744)	1,479
Effect of exchange rate changes on cash	94	(89)	(142)
Cash and cash equivalents at year-end	$ 856	$ 1,109	$ 1,640
Increase (decrease) in cash and cash equivalents	$ (253)	$ (531)	$ 1,172

75

		1994
Cash collections from customers		
Sales (not including excise taxes)	$ 34,042	
Change in accounts and notes receivable	30	**34,072**
Cash payments for inputs		
COGS	(21,977)	
Change in inventories and other operating assets	19	
Change in payables and operating liabilities	172	**(21,786)**
(see discussion)		
Cash payments for SG&A		
Selling, general and administrative	(2,888)	
Change in payables and operating liabilities	149	**(2,739)**
(see discussion)		
Cash for research and development		**(1,047)**
Exploration expenses including dry hole and impairment	(357)	
Less adjustment for noncash expense	152	**(205)**
Taxes other than income		
Excise taxes received	5,291	
Taxes other than income	(6,215)	
Change in taxes other than income (see discussion)	42	**(882)**
Miscellaneous		
Other income	926	
Change in payables and liabilities (see discussion)	(204)	
Other noncash charges and credits	(140)	**582**
Restructuring	142	
Change in payables and liabilities (see discussion)	(591)	**(449)**
Interest and debt expense		**(559)**
Income taxes		
Tax expense	(1,655)	
Change in accrued interest and income taxes	332	**(1,323)**
Cash from operations		**$ 5,664**

Discussion

The category "changes in accounts payable and other operating liabilities" appearing in duPont's (indirect) cash flow statement in Exhibit 3-5 is an aggregation of many categories. Details can be found in Notes 16 and 18 reproduced below. The sum of the changes in these accounts is 290 + (748) = (458). DuPont's cash flow statement shows a change of (432).

In order to obtain the direct cash flow statement, a number of assumptions and simplifications were made. First, as the difference between (458) and (432) (due to acquisitions and/or the effect of exchange rate changes) is not significant, (26), it can be safely ignored* without affecting the thrust of the analysis. Then, where possible, each of the individual categories in Notes 16 and 18 was identified with its "associated activity" (see last column).

Note 16: Accounts Payable

	1994	1993	Change	Associated Activity
Trade	$1,847	$1,675	$172	Inputs
Payables to banks	321	264	57	
Compensation awards	222	94	128	SG&A
Other	344	411	(67)	
	$2,734	$2,444	$290	

Note 18: Other Accrued Liabilities

	1994	1993	Change	Associated Activity
Payroll and other employee benefits	$ 725	$ 694	$ 31	SG&A
Taxes other than on income	422	380	42	Taxes other than income
Postretirement benefits other than pensions	333	343	(10)	SG&A
Restructuring charges	219	810	(591)	Restructuring
Miscellaneous	1,431	1,651	(220)	
	$3,130	$3,878	$(748)	

The identified items from Notes 16 and 18 are aggregated and listed below. These were used to modify their respective associated activity from the income statement to calculate the cash disbursement for that activity.

Changes in Payables and Operating Liabilities

Inputs	$ 172
SG&A	149
Taxes other than income	42
Restructuring	(591)
	$(228)

This leaves a remaining balance of (432) − (228) = (204) in the miscellaneous activity, comprised of:

Payables to banks	$ 57
Other	(67)
Miscellaneous	(220)
	(230)
Acquisition or exchange rate adjustment*	26
	$(204)

*Alternative approaches may be to assume that the 26 is associated with inputs or with inputs and SG&A and aggregate cash disbursement for inputs and expenses as one item.

Acquisitions and Divestitures

Changes in reported balances of operating asset and liability accounts may include the effects of both operating activities and acquisitions or divestitures. Thus, for example, the inventory account may be increased as a result of:

1. Purchase of inventory from a supplier (an operating activity)
2. Acquisition of (merger with) another firm that has inventory as a component of its balance sheet (an investing activity)

SFAS 95 requires that CFO include only operating transactions and events. Thus, for firms that acquire operating assets and liabilities, the changes reported in the statement of cash flows as adjustments to income to arrive at CFO will not match the increase or decrease reported on the balance sheet.

The difference between the changes reported in the two statements provides useful information to the analyst. If the difference for any balance sheet account represents the amount of that component acquired through a merger, *the analyst can reconstruct the assets and liabilities obtained by the firm through an acquisition.*[11] This information is generally not provided anywhere else.

It should be noted that although the reporting requirements accomplish the necessary segregation in the period of the acquisition (or divestiture), cash flows for subsequent periods may be distorted. For example, cash paid for the accounts receivable of an acquired firm is reported as an investment cash (out)flow. However, the subsequent cash collection of that receivable will be a component of operating cash flows. The result is overstated cash flows from operations as the cost of acquiring the accounts receivables was never reflected in cash outflows for operations.[12] *Acquisitions, divestitures, and continuing corporate reorganizations can therefore distort trends in both cash flows from operations and investing cash flows.* These issues are examined in greater detail in Chapter 14.

Translation of Foreign Subsidiaries

The second difference between the changes reported on the cash flow statement and those reported on the balance sheet relates to foreign operations. The assets and liabilities of foreign subsidiaries must be translated into the reporting currency (i.e., U.S. dollars) upon preparation of consolidated financial statements. This process generates a U.S. dollar balance for each asset and liability account that includes both operating changes (representing real cash flow effects) and exchange rate effects that have no current cash flow consequences.

For example, assume a firm has a foreign subsidiary that has an opening and closing accounts receivables balance of 10,000 lira. Assume further that at the beginning of the year 1 lira is worth $1.00, but at the end of the year a lira is worth $1.10. Upon consolidation, the parent's balance sheet will include

---

[11]This can be done if we assume that the confounding effect of exchange rate changes (discussed next) is not significant. Thus, ignoring that issue for the moment, one would estimate that duPont's accounts receivable increased by $349 million ($319 + $30) due to an acquisition.

[12]Similarly, cash received for accounts receivable of a divested business is reflected as an investment cash inflow, whereas the cash outflow required to generate the receivable (purchase of inventory, selling costs) was previously reported as a component of CFO.

Opening accounts receivable from foreign subsidiary (10,000 lira × opening exchange rate of 1)	$10,000
Closing accounts receivable from foreign subsidiary (10,000 lira × closing exchange rate of 1.1)	$11,000
Change	$ 1,000

This increase of $1,000 appears as part of the balance of accounts receivable on the balance sheet. However, it will not appear as a component of cash collections for the period because it is not a change resulting from operations. Thus, CFO does not include the effects of the translation process.

Effect of Exchange Rate Changes on Cash

An explanation of the item *effect of exchange rate changes on cash* follows directly from our previous discussion. Suppose the foreign subsidiary in our previous example had a cash balance of 4,000 lira at the beginning and end of the year. Upon consolidation, the parent's reported cash balance includes $4,000 at the beginning of the year and $4,400 (4,000 lira × 1.10) at the end of the year. This change of $400 needs to be reported as it does not appear as an operating, investing, or financing activity.

Translation gains and losses resulting from exchange rate changes are excluded from cash flows from operating, investing, and financing activities. The sum of these excluded gains and losses is reported as the effect of exchange rate changes on cash (further discussion of these issues occurs in Chapter 15).

EXAMPLE: DUPONT

DuPont's Statement of Cash Flows is reproduced in Exhibit 3-5. We examine each component of duPont's cash flow statement, in turn, to demonstrate the use and analysis of cash flow statements.

Cash from Operations. DuPont reports cash flows using the *indirect method.* As a result, the company provides a reconciliation of the difference between net income and CFO. The reconciling adjustments fall into three categories:

1. Noncash expenses
2. Nonoperating cash flows
3. Changes in operating assets and liabilities

Noncash expenses consist mostly of the amortization of past investment outflows. Although the matching principle requires amortization when computing net income, it is not a current period cash flow.

For 1992, the transition effects of adopting new accounting standards for income tax and other postemployment benefits must be removed. The adoption of these standards had no cash flow impact.[13]

---

[13]See Chapters 9 and 12.

Nonoperating cash flows relate to investment and financing activities. For example, gains and losses from the sales of investments result from investment activities (discussed below) and must be excluded from the CFO. Similarly, the 1992 and 1993 extraordinary losses relate to the early extinguishment of debt, a financing activity, and must also be excluded from the computation of the cash flows from operations.

Finally, cash from operations reports changes in balance sheet accounts that are operating in nature. Such accounts include inventories, accounts receivable and payable (excluding amounts relating to investing and financing activities), and accruals for such operating items as interest,[14] income taxes, and employee benefits.

The reconciliation only uses the changes due to operating activities and excludes two other sources of changes in operating assets and liabilities: acquisitions and the impact of changes in exchange rates. We will see shortly how these are treated in the cash flow statement.

Investing Cash Flow. DuPont's major investment activity from 1992 to 1994 has been the purchase of property, plant, and equipment (PP&E). There are additional outflows for acquisitions, investments in affiliates, and net investment in short-term financial instruments. DuPont has received cash inflows from the sale of assets.

Gains or losses from the sale of long-term assets are excluded from CFO. Although duPont's cash flow statement does not explicitly report such gains or losses, Note 2 (Appendix A) reveals that gains are included in other income. Thus, we assume that they have been removed from CFO (probably in the "other noncash charges and credits—net" entry).

Note 2 also reports duPont's equity in the earnings of affiliates. Note 14 states that, in 1994, affiliates paid $326 million in dividends to duPont, roughly the same as duPont's equity in the earnings of those affiliates. The difference[15] is another adjustment to CFO (again, probably included in the "other—net" item). Many companies report the deduction for "undistributed earnings" or "equity earnings in excess of dividends received" as a separate reconciling item in the CFO section of their cash flow statement.

The separate disclosure of cash outflows for acquisitions is an important feature of the cash flow statement. These amounts reflect the assets purchased less liabilities assumed in acquisitions accounted for using the purchase method (see Chapter 14 for a full discussion). *The cash outflows for the acquisitions of operating assets and liabilities of the acquired firm are excluded from CFO but included in CFI.*

The change in duPont's investment in short-term financing instruments requires some discussion. These investments are not considered "cash equivalents" because they do not meet the SFAS 95 definition (risk-free with maturities of less than three months). Nonetheless, from a practical point of view, they may be little different. If their risk is low and liquidity high, they should be treated analytically as cash equivalents as they represent additional short-term liquidity. Note that changes in the level of these investments are reported net, one of the exceptions to the "gross" reporting requirements of SFAS 95. Under that standard, changes in balance sheet assets and liabilities that turn over frequently (another example is credit card receivables) may be reported

---

[14]In a subsequent section of this chapter, we make the argument that cash flows for interest represent financing rather than operating activities.

[15]Generally, the cash dividends received from investees are more appropriately analyzed as components of investment cash flows.

net. Investments that are long-term, less liquid, and riskier (e.g., stocks or long-term bonds) should be treated differently (such investments are discussed in Chapter 13).

Financing Cash Flow. This category contains cash flows between the firm and suppliers of its debt and equity capital. For duPont, debt origination and repayment are the principal items. Note that whereas changes in long-term debt are gross, the change in short-term debt is shown net (another exception to the gross reporting requirement). Dividends paid to shareholders and cash received from the sale of common stock are also included in CFF.

Effect of Exchange Rate Changes on Cash. DuPont has foreign subsidiaries and cash balances denominated in foreign currencies. Changes in exchange rates create translation gains and losses that are not cash flows, but must be reported for the cash flow statement to balance. The $94 million reported by duPont captures, in a single number, the effect of exchange rate changes on the firm's foreign cash holdings.

Change in Cash and Cash Equivalents. The net reconciling number is the period's change in the balance of cash and equivalents, equal to the sum of the three major cash flow components (CFO, CFI, and CFF) and any exchange rate effects. This number is necessarily equal to the difference between cash at the beginning of the year and the amount at the end of the year. However, although this number is easy to measure, it has no analytic value. Firms can influence the net change by accelerating or delaying payments, or by making use of short-term financing facilities.

ANALYSIS OF CASH FLOW INFORMATION

The cash flow statement is intended to help predict the firm's ability to sustain (and increase) cash from current operations. In doing so, the statement provides more objective information about:

- A firm's ability to generate cash flows from operations
- Trends in cash flow components and cash consequences of investing and financing decisions
- Management decisions regarding such critical areas as financial policy (leverage), dividend policy, and investment for growth

Neither the statement of cash flows nor the income statement alone contain sufficient information for decision making. (See Box 2-2 for some empirical evidence in this respect.) Income statement and balance sheet data must be combined with cash flows for insights into the firm's ability to realize assets based on reported revenues and settle liabilities resulting from accrued expenses and thereby assist the analyst in the development of other valuation-relevant measures.

Free Cash Flows and Valuation

An important but elusive concept often used in cash flow analysis is *free cash flow* (FCF). It is intended to measure the cash available to the firm for discretionary uses after making all required cash outlays. The concept is widely used by analysts and in the finance literature as the basis for many valuation models (see Chapter 19). The basic elements required to calculate FCF are available from the cash flow statement. In practice, however, the definition of FCF varies widely, depending on how one defines required and discretionary uses.

The basic definition used by many analysts is cash from operations less the amount of capital expenditures required to maintain the firm's *present* productive capacity.[16] Discretionary uses include growth-oriented capital expenditures and acquisitions, debt reduction, and stockholder payments (dividends and stock repurchase). The larger the firm's FCF, the healthier it is because it has more cash available for growth, debt payment, and dividends.

The argument for this definition is similar to Hicks' argument regarding the computation of net income discussed in the previous chapter. If historical cost depreciation provided a good measure of the use of productive capacity, then FCF would equal CFO less depreciation expense. However (as discussed in Chapter 8), historical cost depreciation is arbitrary and measures the cost to replace operating capacity only by coincidence.

The obvious alternative to depreciation is the amount of capital expenditures made to maintain current capacity, excluding the expansion portion of capital expenditures. In practice, however, it is difficult to separate capital expenditures into expansion and replacement components. Lacking better information, all capital expenditures are subtracted from CFO to obtain FCF.

Subtracting all capital expenditures from CFO to arrive at FCF brings the definition of FCF closer to the one used in finance valuation models. In these models, required outflows are defined as operating cash flows less capital expenditures to replace current operating capacity *as well as capital expenditures necessary to finance the firm's growth opportunities.* Growth opportunities are defined as those in which the firm can make "above normal" returns. It is difficult to determine *a priori* the amount of capital expenditures required to maintain growth and the discretionary portion of these expenditures; pragmatically, FCF is generally measured as CFO less capital expenditures.

Valuation models do, however, differ as to whether FCF is measured by *FCF available to the firm [i.e., all providers of capital (debt and equity)]* or *FCF available to equity shareholders.* In the former case, required payments *do not* include outlays for interest and debt. In the latter case, they do. Thus, for FCF to the firm, one cannot use reported CFO because it includes outlays for interest expense. We return to this point later in this chapter. In Chapter 19, we elaborate on the differing definitions of FCF and their implications for valuation models.

Relationship of Income and Cash Flows

When periodic financial statements are prepared, estimates of the revenues earned and expenses incurred during the reporting interval are required. As discussed in the previous chapter, these estimates require management judgment and are subject to modification as more information about the operating cycle becomes available. Accrual accounting can therefore be affected by management's choice of accounting policies and estimates. Furthermore, accrual accounting *by itself* fails to provide adequate information about the liquidity of the firm and long-term solvency. Some of these problems can be alleviated by the use of the cash flow statement in conjunction with the income statement.

---

[16]IAS 7 on cash flow statements recommends this disclosure.

Cash flow is relatively (but not completely) free of the drawbacks of the accrual concept. It is less likely to be affected by variations in accounting principles and estimates, making it more useful than reported income in assessing liquidity and solvency.

As a result, the level and trend of cash flow and reported income vary, as illustrated in Figure 3-1. Three different types of company are presented: Kmart, Union Camp, and Intel. Reported income and CFO were taken directly from the firms' financial statements. Two measures of free cash flow are used:

FCF1 equals CFO minus (net) capital expenditures.
FCF2 equals CFO minus CFI and thus includes expenditures (receipts) for acquisitions (divestitures) and other investments.

Note that CFO (generally) exceeds income for all three companies because CFO is not reduced by the cost of productive capacity.[17] Depreciation is usually the largest component of the adjustment from income to CFO. When the cost of productive capacity is included, as in FCF1, the relationship is company-specific and varies from year to year.

Intel is a "growth" company; its income and CFO show steady growth from 1991 to 1994. FCF1 is below income in each period, reflecting capital expenditures for expansion as well as for replacement. FCF1 is positive in each year, a healthy sign given rapid growth. FCF2, on the other hand, is near or below zero each year. FCF patterns have to be monitored carefully for growth companies to ensure that they are not growing too fast, which can cause liquidity problems.

Kmart was experiencing operating difficulties during this time period as reflected in its income and cash flow patterns. CFO exceeded income in 1994; in 1993 and 1995, CFO was lower. In 1994, Kmart reported the highest CFO, but the lowest profitability! Finally, unlike Intel, its FCF2 exceeded CFO in 1995.

The explanation for Kmart's pattern of CFO and income is its (current) operating assets. Increases in receivables and inventories reduced CFO below reported income in some years. Revenues were recognized without receipt of cash, increasing receivables; cash outflows for (increased) inventories were not expensed.

Although Intel also reported higher receivables and inventory, the nature of the growth was not the same. *Intel's operating assets grew in proportion to the firm's sales.* As Intel grew, more working capital was required to maintain that growth. *In Kmart's case, the lack of sales growth, coupled with increases in working capital growth, reduced CFO, reflecting slow receivable collections and inventory buildup.* In 1994, on the other hand, Kmart cut back and decreased its operating assets, increasing CFO.

The FCF patterns for Kmart also differ considerably from those for Intel. Note the increase in FCF1 reported by Kmart in 1994 and FCF2 in 1994 and 1995. The increases in 1994 were partially due to the increases in CFO discussed earlier. Additionally, in 1994, Kmart cut capital expenditures. The sharp increase in FCF2 in 1995 is a result of Kmart's sale of some investments (in its noncore operations) to raise needed cash.

Union Camp is an example of a cyclical company. In 1992 and 1993, it was in the trough of the cycle. In 1991, it had just entered the trough and, in 1994, it was coming out of it. The differences between income and cash flows are largely due to timing

---

[17]This point is elaborated on further in the section entitled, "Cash Flow Classification Issues."

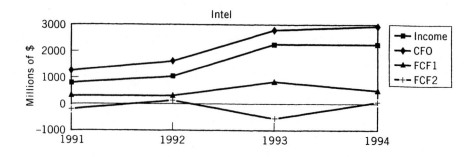

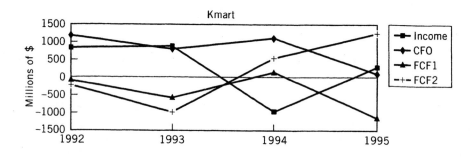

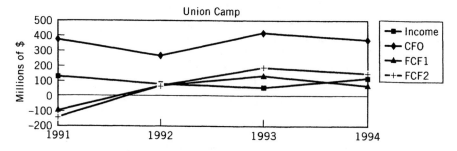

Legend: Income and CFO as per firm's financial statements.
FCF1 = CFO - (net) Capital Expenditures
FCF2 = CFO - CFI

FIGURE 3-1 Comparison of patterns of income, CFO, and free cash flows.

differences. The company cut production and capital expenditures during the downturn. However, depreciation on existing capacity had to be recognized. The result was high (relative to income) CFO, FCF1, and FCF2 in those years. Capital expenditures may not have been enough to replace existing capacity as all three cash flow measures were above income. In 1991 and 1994, however, the company increased capital expenditures, reducing FCF below income.

The above discussion indicates that cash flow statements should be used together with information from the income statement, the balance sheet, and footnotes to assess the cash-generating ability of a firm. This assessment should consider the firm's liquidity, the viability of income as a predictor of future cash flows, and the effect of timing and recognition differences. We elaborate on these points in the next sections.

4

FOUNDATIONS OF RATIO AND FINANCIAL ANALYSIS

INTRODUCTION

Financial ratios are used to compare the risk and return of different firms in order to help equity investors and creditors make intelligent investment and credit decisions. Such decisions range from an evaluation of changes in performance over time for a particular investment to a comparison among all firms within a single industry at a specific point in time.

The informational needs and appropriate analytical techniques used for these investment and credit decisions depend on the decision maker's time horizon. Short-term bank and trade creditors are primarily interested in the immediate liquidity of the firm. Longer-term creditors (e.g., bondholders) are interested in long-term solvency. Creditors seek to minimize risk and ensure that resources are available for the payment of interest and principal obligations.

Equity investors are primarily interested in the long-term earning power of the firm. As the equity investor bears the residual risk (which can be defined as the return from operations after all claims from suppliers and creditors have been satisfied), it requires a return commensurate to that risk. The residual risk is highly volatile and difficult to quantify, as is the equity investor's time horizon. Thus, analysis by the equity investor needs to be the most comprehensive, and it subsumes the analysis carried out by other users.

Purpose and Use of Ratio Analysis

A primary advantage of ratios is that they can be used to compare the risk and return relationships of firms of different sizes. *Ratios can provide a profile of a firm, its economic characteristics and competitive strategies, and its unique operating, financial, and investment characteristics.*

This process of standardization may, however, be deceptive as it ignores differences between industries, the effect of varying capital structures, and differences in accounting and reporting methods (especially when comparisons are international in scope). Given these differences, changes (trends) in a ratio and variability over time may be more informative than the level of the ratio at any point in time.

Four broad ratio categories measure the different aspects of risk and return relationships:

1. Activity analysis. Evaluates revenue and output generated by the firm's assets.
2. Liquidity analysis. Measures the adequacy of a firm's cash resources to meet its near-term cash obligations.
3. Long-term debt and solvency analysis. Examines the firm's capital structure in terms of the mix of its financing sources and the ability of the firm to satisfy its longer-term debt and investment obligations.
4. Profitability analysis. Measures the income of the firm relative to its revenues and invested capital.

These categories are interrelated rather than independent. For example, profitability affects liquidity and solvency, and the efficiency with which assets are used (as measured by activity analysis) impacts profitability. Thus, financial analysis relies on an integrated use of many ratios, rather than a selected few.

Ratio Analysis: Cautionary Notes

Ratio analysis is essential to comprehensive financial analysis. However, ratios are based on implicit assumptions that do not always apply. Ratio computations and comparisons are further confounded by the lack or inappropriate use of benchmarks, the timing of transactions, negative numbers, and differences in reporting methods. This section presents some important caveats that must be considered when interpreting ratios.[1]

---

[1]For explanatory purposes, this discussion uses specific ratios as examples; these ratios are defined later in the chapter.

Economic Assumptions

Ratio analysis is designed to facilitate comparisons by eliminating size differences across firms and over time. Implicit in this process is the *proportionality assumption* that the economic relationship between numerator and denominator does not depend on size. This assumption ignores the existence of fixed costs. When there are fixed costs, changes in total costs (and thus profits) are not proportional to changes in sales.

Moreover, the implicit assumption of a linear relationship between numerator and denominator may be incorrect even in the absence of a fixed component. For example, the inventory turnover ratio, COGS/inventory, implies a constant relationship between the volume of sales and inventory levels. Management science theory, however, indicates that the optimum relationship is nonlinear and inventory levels may be proportional to the square root of demand.[2] Thus, a doubling in demand should increase inventory by only 40% (approximately) with a consequent 40% increase in the turnover ratio. *The inventory turnover ratio is clearly not size-independent.*

Benchmarks

Ratio analysis often lacks appropriate benchmarks to indicate optimal levels. The evaluation of a ratio often depends on the question posed by the analyst. For example, from the point of view of a short-term lender, a high liquidity ratio may be a positive indicator. However, from the perspective of an equity investor, it may indicate poor cash or working capital management.

Using an industry average as the benchmark[3] may be useful for comparisons within an industry, but not for comparisons between companies in different industries. Even for intraindustry analysis, the benchmark may have limited usefulness if the whole industry or major firms in that industry are doing poorly.

Timing and Window Dressing

Data used to compute ratios are available only at specific points in time when financial statements are issued. For annual reports, the fiscal year-end may correspond to the low point of a firm's operating cycle, when reported levels of assets and liabilities may not reflect the levels typical of normal operations. As a result, especially in the case of seasonal businesses, ratios may not reflect normal operating relationships. For example, inventories and accounts payable may be understated. Reference to interim statements is one way of alleviating this problem. However, most foreign countries either do not require interim statements or require them less frequently.[4] Moreover, foreign filings are generally less timely than U.S. reports.

The timing issue leads to another problem. Transactions at year-end can lead to manipulation of the ratios to show the firm in a more favorable light, often called *window dressing*. For example, a firm with a current ratio (current assets/current liabilities) of 1.5 ($300/$200) can increase it to 2.0 ($200/$100) by simply using cash of $100 to reduce accounts payable immediately prior to the period's end.

---

[2] See Chapter 6 for a more detailed discussion of this issue.

[3] See the last section of the chapter, where we discuss databases that provide industry averages.

[4] Foreign firms using Form 20-F filings to sell securities in the United States are not required to provide interim statements if there is no home-country filing requirement.

Generally, any ratio where a transaction affects the numerator and denominator can be manipulated as follows. If the ratio is greater than 1, it can be increased by a transaction that subtracts the same amount from both the numerator and denominator. If it is less than 1, it can be increased by a transaction that adds the same amount to both the numerator and denominator.[5]

Negative Numbers

Two examples illustrate the care that must be taken in ratio analysis when negative numbers occur.

■ **Example 1: Return on Equity** $= \dfrac{\text{Income}}{\text{Equity}}$

	Income	Equity	ROE
Company A	$ 10,000	$ 100,000	10%
Company B	(10,000)	(100,000)	10%	■

Ratio analysis without reference to the underlying data can lead to wrong conclusions as it appears that both companies earn identical returns on their (equity) investment. Because much financial and ratio analysis today is computer-generated, the existence of negative numbers will be overlooked unless the program is well written.

■ **Example 2: Dividend Payout Ratio** $= \dfrac{\text{Dividend}}{\text{Income}}$

	Dividend	Income	Payout Ratio
Company A	$10,000	$ 50,000	20%
Company B	10,000	30,000	33%
Company C	10,000	(50,000)	(20%)	■

Ranking these firms by payout ratio (highest to lowest) would list them as B, A, and C. However, in reality, Company C has the highest payout ratio. That ratio is intended to measure the extent to which income is paid to shareholders rather than retained in the business. For the same income, a higher dividend increases the proportion paid out (higher payout ratio). As income approaches zero, the payout ratio approaches infinity. The payment of dividends despite negative income indicates a high payout ratio.

Accounting Methods

The choice of accounting methods and estimates can greatly affect reported financial statement amounts. In addition, as described in Chapter 3, even "pure" numbers such as cash flows from operations may be affected by accounting choices. Thus, ratios are

---

[5]To decrease the ratio, for ratios greater (less) than 1, the same amount is added to (subtracted from) the numerator and denominator.

not comparable between firms (with differing accounting methods) or for the same firm over time (when it changes accounting methods). To interpret such ratios, it may be necessary to convert from one accounting method to another. A strong understanding of accounting rules and a judicious eye for information contained in the notes to financial statements are musts for this type of analysis. Subsequent chapters will detail the impact of specific accounting methods on affected ratios.

The balance of this chapter describes specific ratios, primarily in narrative form. We illustrate the calculation and interpretation of these ratios in Exhibits 4-4, 4-6, 4-7, 4-8, and 4-12 through 4-14, using the financial statements of duPont, a leading firm in the chemical industry. DuPont's financial statements are presented in Appendix A at the end of the book. Case 4-1 asks you to compare the financial data and ratios of duPont with those of two competitors, Dow Chemical and ICI.

The calculations in these exhibits are intended for illustrative purposes; in most cases, they are based on data taken directly from financial statements without any adjustments. The required adjustments will become clearer as we progress through the book. Ratios should not be viewed as an end unto themselves, but rather as a starting point for further analysis. Ratios highlight where further investigation and adjustment may be needed. In that sense, even ratios calculated with unadjusted data can serve a useful purpose.

COMMON-SIZE STATEMENTS

A pervasive problem when comparing a firm's performance over time is that the firm's size is always changing. Firms of different sizes are also difficult to compare. Common-size statements are used to standardize financial statement components by expressing them as a percentage of a relevant base. For example, balance sheet components can be shown as a percentage of total assets; revenues and expenses can be computed as a percentage of total sales, and in the direct method cash flow statement, the components of cash flow from operations can be related to cash collections.

Common-size statements should not, however, be viewed solely as a scaling factor for standardization. They provide the analyst with useful information as a first step *in developing insights into the economic characteristics of different industries and of different firms in the same industry.* For example, significant changes in net income over time may be traced to variations in cost of goods sold (COGS) as a percentage of sales. Changes in this ratio may indicate the efficacy of the firm's efforts to streamline its operations and/or a change in pricing strategies. Additionally, differences over time in a single firm or between firms due to operating, financing, and investing decisions made by management and external economic factors are often highlighted by common-size statements.

Exhibit 4-1 compares the 1994 balance sheets and income statements of duPont, Dow Chemical, and ICI, including both the actual data and common-size statements. Exhibit 4-2 presents common-size balance sheets and income statements for the chemical industry and selected other industries. The scaling factors are total assets for the balance sheets and sales for the income statements.

Cross-Sectional Comparisons. Comparison of the three companies based on actual reported data is fraught with problems because of the disparity in size. Both duPont and Dow are considerably larger than ICI; comparisons of assets, working capital, and income cannot provide much insight unless the numbers are scaled.

EXHIBIT 4-1
Comparative Balance Sheets and Income Statements, 1994 Data

A. Comparative Balance Sheets

	As Reported			Common-Size (%)		
	DuPont ($ millions)	ICI (£ millions)	Dow ($ millions)	DuPont	ICI	Dow
Cash and marketable securities	$ 1,109	1,759	$ 1,134	3	20	4
Accounts receivable	5,213	1,629	4,458	14	18	17
Inventories	3,969	1,233	2,712	11	14	10
Prepaid expenses	259	112	—	1	1	0
Deferred taxes	558	—	389	2	0	1
Current assets	$ 11,108	4,733	$ 8,693	30%	53%	33%
Net property, plant, and equipment	21,120	3,861	8,726	57	43	33
Investment in affiliates	1,662	171	931	5	2	4
Other assets	3,002	239	8,195	8	3	31
Total assets	$ 36,892	9,004	$ 26,545	100%	100%	100%
Short-term debt	1,292	369	1,275	4	4	5
Accounts and notes payable	2,734	1,077	2,562	7	12	10
Income taxes payable	409	233	720	1	3	3
Other current liabilities	3,130	929	2,061	8	10	8
Current liabilities	$ 7,565	2,608	$ 6,618	21%	29%	25%
Long-term debt	6,376	1,529	5,303	17	17	20
Other liabilities	8,438	772	3,240	23	9	12
Deferred income taxes	1,494	21	644	4	0	2
Total liabilities	$ 23,873	4,930	$ 15,805	65%	55%	60%
Minority interests	197	338	2,506	1	4	9
Preferred stock	237	—	22	1	0	0
Common stock and APIC	5,179	1,293	1,144	14	14	4
Retained earnings	7,406	2,443	7,068	20	27	27
Total equity	$ 13,019	4,074	$ 10,740	35%	45%	40%
Total liabilities and equity	$ 36,892	9,004	$ 26,545	100%	100%	100%

Note: Common-size columns may not add due to rounding.

Common-size balance sheets and income statements provide such insight. Looking at the common-size balance sheets, we immediately see that:

- ICI is the strongest financially, as total debt (short- and long-term) of 21% of assets exceeds cash and marketable securities of 20%. Dow and duPont have total debt (short- and long-term) of 25% and 21% of assets respectively. As their cash and marketable securities are considerably lower than for ICI, their net debt burden is much higher. ICI also has the highest ratio of equity to total assets.

90

EXHIBIT 4-1 (*continued*)

B. Comparative Income Statements

	As Reported			Common-Size (%)		
	duPont ($ millions)	ICI (£ millions)	Dow ($ millions)	duPont	ICI	Dow
Sales	$ 39,333	9,189	$ 20,015	100	100	100
Cost of goods sold*	(24,953)	(6,502)	(13,219)	(63)	(71)	(66)
Selling, general, and administrative expenses	(2,888)	(2,005)	(3,061)	(7)	(22)	(15)
Research and development expenses	(1,047)	(184)	(1,261)	(3)	(2)	(6)
Interest expense	(559)	(186)	(537)	(1)	(2)	(3)
Restructuring and write-downs	142	(137)	—	0	(1)	—
Other operating expenses	(6,572)	(39)	(229)	(17)	(0)	(1)
Income from operations	$ 3,456	136	$ 1,708	9%	1%	9%
Other income	926	272	344	2	3	2
Income before taxes	4,382	408	2,052	11%	4%	10%
Provision for taxes	(1,655)	(164)	(779)	(4)	(2)	(4)
Income before minority interests, extraordinary items, and accounting changes	$ 2,727	244	$ 1,273	7%	3%	6%
Less minority interests, extraordinary items, and accounting changes	—	(56)	(335)	—	(1)	(2)
Net income	$ 2,727	188	$ 938	7%	2%	5%

*Includes depreciation.
Note: Common-size columns may not add due to rounding.

- DuPont has the largest relative property investment, at 57% of total assets, followed by ICI (43%) and Dow (33%).

- DuPont has a disproportionate amount of "other liabilities." We will find (in Chapter 12) that this liability reflects its unfunded postretirement benefit obligation.

Turning to the income statement, we find that:

- DuPont reports the highest net income as a percentage of sales. Dow reports much lower net income ($938 million versus $2,727 million for duPont), but the difference is much smaller as a percentage of sales (5% compared to 7%).[6] ICI reports the lowest net income relative to sales.

- DuPont has the lowest ratio of cost of goods sold to sales and the lowest relative selling expense. ICI has the highest ratios.

- Dow reports the highest R&D expense as a percentage of sales.

[6]This difference is affected by the inclusion of excise taxes in the sales figures reported by duPont. That firm's income as a percentage of sales increases to 8% if excise taxes are excluded.

EXHIBIT 4-2
Industry Comparisons, 1994: Common-size Balance Sheets and Income Statements

	Retailers		Manufacturers					
	Groceries	Depart-ment Stores	Rubber and Plastic Footwear	Pulp and Paper	Drugs and Medi-cines	Industrial Chemicals	Iron and Steel	Petroleum Refining
A. Comparative Balance Sheets (%)								
Cash and equivalents	11	6	6	7	14	7	6	7
Receivables	5	12	29	22	23	27	26	27
Inventories	32	49	23	18	24	22	25	22
Other	2	2	1	1	2	2	1	2
Current assets	50%	68%	59%	49%	63%	58%	57%	58%
Fixed assets (net)	37	24	33	42	27	32	34	32
Intangibles (net)	3	2	2	2	5	4	1	1
Other	10	7	5	8	6	7	8	9
Total assets	100%	100%	100%	100%	100%	100%	100%	100%
Notes payable	5	6	10	8	5	8	9	6
Current portion of long-term debt	5	3	4	3	3	3	4	3
Trade payables	20	16	15	15	14	17	14	20
Inc. taxes payable	1	1	2	1	1	1	2	1
Other	10	8	8	6	9	9	8	8
Current liabilities	41%	35%	39%	33%	32%	37%	36%	39%
Long-term debt	24	19	17	19	14	15	18	17
Deferred taxes	0	0	1	2	1	1	2	2
Other	3	3	4	3	3	4	5	2
Total liabilities	69%	57%	60%	57%	50%	56%	61%	60%
Equity	31%	43%	40%	43%	51%	44%	39%	41%
Total liabilities + equity	100%	100%	100%	100%	100%	100%	100%	100%
B. Comparative Income Statements (%)								
Sales	100	100	100	100	100	100	100	100
Cost of sales	−77	−67	−72	−75	−57	−68	−79	−78
Gross profit	23%	33%	28%	25%	43%	32%	21%	22%
Operating expenses	−22	−32	−23	−20	−35	−26	−17	−19
Operating profit	1%	2%	5%	5%	8%	6%	4%	3%
Other expenses	0	0	−2	−1	−1	−1	−2	−1
Profit before tax	1%	2%	4%	4%	7%	5%	3%	2%

Source: Reprinted with permission, copyright Robert Morris Associates 1994. Data adapted from the ALL SIZES column appearing in 1994 *Annual Statement Studies.* RMA cautions that the studies be regarded only as a general guideline and not as an absolute industry norm. This is due to limited samples within categories, the categorization of companies by their primary Standard Industrial Classification (SIC) number only, and different methods of operations by companies within the same industry. For these reasons, RMA recommends that the figures be used only as general guidelines in addition to other methods of financial analysis.

Differences in operating characteristics may explain some of these differences. Different accounting methods may also play some part. Common-size analysis has provided a starting point for analysis, however.

Industry Comparisons. Some of the differences among the three firms may reflect differences in the industry segments in which they operate. Industry comparisons in Exhibit 4-2 show that balance sheet compositions differ widely. For example:

- The two retailer categories (groceries and department stores) show (as would be expected) the lowest levels of receivables and highest inventory balances. Customers generally pay for purchases with cash (or with credit cards), keeping receivables low. Inventories are relatively high as customers demand a variety of goods.
- Pulp and paper manufacturers report the highest fixed assets, reflecting large required investments in plants and natural resources.
- The drugs and chemicals sectors report the highest intangibles, probably due to patents and acquisition intangibles.

Common-size income statements also delineate some critical income statement differences. Groceries show low gross margins and drugs the highest, reflecting the economic characteristics and cost structures of these industries. Groceries have the lowest operating profit margin, typical of a low-margin, high-turnover business. Drugs and medicines have the highest operating margins, reflecting their high-research, patent-protected position.

Comparisons over Time. Common-size statements can also be used to compare the performance of a single company over time. Exhibit 4-3A shows actual and common-size income statements for duPont over the period 1990 to 1994. Sales declined slightly from $40,047 million to $39,333 million, whereas profits increased 18% from $2,310 million to $2,727 million. The common-size statements indicate considerable stability in the components of operating expense, perhaps surprising for a company in a cyclical industry. Other income, restructuring charges, and write-downs were highly variable. Both interest expense and the provision for income taxes declined. Significant charges for restructuring (1991 to 1993) and the adoption of two new accounting methods in 1992 explain most of the variations in duPont's performance during the 1991 to 1993 period.

Exhibit 4-3A also illustrates the use of common-size statements for trend analysis. A base year is selected, 1990 in this case, and data for all subsequent years (1991 to 1994 for duPont) are shown as percentages of base year data. This statement reveals an 81% increase in other income and declines of 28% in interest expense and 10% for the provision for income taxes. The analyst must review the financial statements to determine the sources of other income, evaluate the cause of the decline in reported interest expense, and assess the reason for the lower income tax rate.

Changes in balance sheet and cash flow statement components can also be analyzed over time. Exhibit 4-3B applies common-size analysis to duPont's direct method statement of cash flows, derived in Chapter 3; cash collections is the appropriate scaling factor. The insights obtained from the analysis of common-size statements facilitate detailed analysis of the firm and comparative analysis of firms—issues discussed in the following sections.

EXHIBIT 4-3. E.I. DUPONT DENEMOURS
Common-Size Income Statements and Statement of Cash Flows, 1990 to 1994

	A. Common-Size Income Statements				
	1990	1991	1992	1993	1994
As Reported ($ in millions)					
Sales	$ 40,047	$ 38,695	$ 37,799	$ 37,098	$ 39,333
Cost of goods sold	(22,945)	(22,528)	(22,046)	(21,624)	(21,977)
Gross profit	17,102	16,167	15,753	15,474	17,356
Other operating expenses	(12,687)	(12,988)	(13,377)	(12,830)	(13,483)
Restructuring and write-downs	0	(828)	(475)	(1,835)	142
Income from operations	4,415	2,351	1,901	809	4,015
Other income	512	828	553	743	926
Income before interest and taxes	4,927	3,179	2,454	1,552	4,941
Interest expense	(773)	(752)	(643)	(594)	(559)
Income before taxes	4,154	2,427	1,811	958	4,382
Provision for taxes	(1,844)	(1,415)	(836)	(392)	(1,655)
Income before extraordinary items and accounting changes	2,310	1,012	975	566	2,727
Extraordinary items and accounting changes	—	—	(4,902)	(11)	—
Net income	$ 2,310	$ 1,012	$ (3,927)	$ 555	$ 2,727
As % of Total Sales					
Sales	100%	100%	100%	100%	100%
Cost of goods sold	−57	−58	−58	−58	−56
Gross profit	43	42	42	42	44
Other operating expenses	−32	−34	−35	−35	−34
Restructuring and write-downs	0	−2	−1	−5	0
Income from operations	11	6	5	2	10
Other income	1	2	1	2	2
Income before interest and taxes	12	8	6	4	13
Interest expense	−2	−2	−2	−2	−1
Income before taxes	10	6	5	3	11
Provision for taxes	−5	−4	−2	−1	−4
Income before extraordinary items and accounting changes	6	3	3	2	7
Extraordinary items and accounting changes	0	0	−13	0	0
Net income	6%	3%	−10%	1%	7%
As % of 1990 Level					
Sales	100%	97%	94%	93%	98%
Cost of goods sold	100	98	96	94	96
Gross profit	100	95	92	90	101
Other operating expenses	100	102	105	101	106
Restructuring and write-downs*	—	100	57	222	−17
Income from operations	100	53	43	18	91
Other income	100	162	108	145	181
Income before interest and taxes	100	65	50	31	100
Interest expense	100	97	83	77	72
Income before taxes	100	58	44	23	105

EXHIBIT 4-3 (*continued*)

A. Common-Size Income Statements

	1990	1991	1992	1993	1994
Provision for taxes	100	77	45	21	90
Income before extraordinary items and accounting changes	100	44	42	25	118
Extraordinary items and accounting changes					
Net income	100%	44%	−170%	24%	118%

*1991 used as base year as none in 1990.

B. Common-Size Statement of Cash Flows

Years ended December 31	1990	1991	1992	1993	1994
As % of Cash Collections					
Cash collections	100.0%	100.0%	100.0%	100.0%	100.0%
Cash inputs	−63.5	−64.0	−65.0	−65.0	−63.9
Cash expenses	−19.0	−19.0	−13.0	−17.0	−14.3
Cash taxes paid	−5.0	−5.5	−9.6	−3.0	−3.9
Cash interest paid	−3.0	−3.0	−2.8	−2.0	−1.6
Misc. cash flow	2.5	1.0	0.0	2.0	0.4
Cash flow from operations	12.0%	9.5%	9.6%	15.0%	16.6%
As % of 1990 Level					
Cash collections	100.0%	98.0%	93.0%	92.0%	95.0%
Cash inputs	100.0	98.0	96.0	93.0	96.0
Cash expenses	100.0	98.0	59.0	78.0	83.0
Cash taxes paid	100.0	116.0	205.0	58.0	72.0
Cash interest paid	100.0	102.0	90.0	84.0	75.0
Misc. cash flow	100.0	45.0	15.0	82.0	52.0
Cash flow from operations	100.0	80.0	76.0	118.0	108.0

Note: Common-size columns may not add due to rounding.

DISCUSSION OF RATIOS BY CATEGORY

The ratios presented here and their mode of calculation are neither exhaustive nor uniquely "correct." The definition of many ratios is not standardized[7] and may vary from analyst to analyst, textbook to textbook, and annual report to annual report.[8] Not all such variations are logical or useful; we believe that the ratios presented in this book meet both these criteria.

[7]In this chapter, when one of the components of the ratio comes from the balance sheet and the other from the income or cash flow statement, the balance sheet number is an average of the beginning and ending balances. An exception is the cash flow from operations to debt ratio. In practice, some analysts use beginning or ending balances for such "mixed" ratios.

[8]For example, see Gibson (1982, 1987), discussed in the section in this chapter entitled "Patterns of Ratio Disclosure, Definitions, and Use."

The analyst's primary focus should be the relationships indicated by the ratios, not the details of their calculation. As we proceed through this book, we will suggest many adjustments to and modifications of these basic ratios.

Activity Analysis

A firm's operating activities require investments in both short-term (inventory and accounts receivable) and long-term (property, plant, and equipment) assets. Activity ratios describe the relationship between the firm's level of operations (usually defined as sales) and the assets needed to sustain operating activities.

The higher the ratio, the more efficient the firm's operations, as relatively fewer assets are required to maintain a given level of operations (sales). Trends in these ratios over time and in comparison to other firms in the same industry can indicate potential trouble spots or opportunities. Furthermore, although these ratios do not measure profitability or liquidity directly, they are important factors affecting those performance indicators.

Activity ratios can also be used to forecast a firm's capital requirements (both operating and long-term). Increases in sales will require investments in additional assets. Activity ratios enable the analyst to forecast these requirements and to assess the firm's ability to acquire the assets needed to sustain the forecasted growth.

Short-Term (Operating) Activity Ratios

The *inventory turnover ratio*, defined as

$$\text{Inventory Turnover} = \frac{\text{Cost of Goods Sold}}{\text{Average Inventory}}$$

measures the efficiency of the firm's inventory management. A higher ratio indicates that inventory does not remain in warehouses or on the shelves but rather "turns over" rapidly from the time of acquisition to sale. This ratio is affected by the choice of accounting method; an explanation and an adjusted ratio are discussed in Chapter 6.

The inverse of this ratio can be used to calculate the average number of days inventory is held until it is sold:[9]

$$\frac{\text{Average No. Days}}{\text{Inventory in Stock}} = \frac{365}{\text{Inventory Turnover}}$$

The *receivables turnover ratio* and the *average number of days of receivables outstanding* can be calculated similarly as

$$\text{Receivables Turnover} = \frac{\text{Sales}}{\text{Average Trade Receivables}}$$

---

[9]For manufacturing firms, the computation is less straightforward. See the discussion in Box 4-1.

and

$$\frac{\text{Average No. Days}}{\text{Receivables Outstanding}} = \frac{365}{\text{Receivables Turnover}}$$

The receivables turnover ratios:

1. Measure the effectiveness of the firm's credit policies.
2. Indicate the level of investment in receivables needed to maintain the firm's sales level.

Receivables turnover should be computed using only trade receivables in the numerator in order to evaluate operating performance. Receivables generated from financing (unless customer financing is provided as a normal component of sales activities) and investment activities (e.g., receivables from the sale of an investment) should be excluded as they do not represent normal recurring operating transactions. Adjustments may also be necessary if the firm has sold receivables during the period.[10]

The *accounts payable turnover ratio* and *number of days payables are outstanding* can be computed in a similar fashion as

$$\text{Payables Turnover} = \frac{\text{Sales}}{\text{Average Accounts Payable}}$$

and

$$\frac{\text{Average No. Days}}{\text{Payables Outstanding}} = \frac{365}{\text{Payables Turnover}}$$

Although accounts payable are liabilities rather than assets, their trend is significant as they represent an important source of financing for operating activities. The time spread between when suppliers must be paid and when payment is received from customers is critical for wholesale and retail firms with their large inventory balances. The relationship among accounts payable, accounts receivable, and inventories will be seen shortly when we examine the operating and cash cycles.

The *working capital turnover ratio*, defined as

$$\text{Working Capital Turnover} = \frac{\text{Sales}}{\text{Average Working Capital}}$$

is a summary ratio that reflects the amount of working (operating) capital needed to maintain a given level of sales. Only operating items should be used to compute this measure. Short-term debt, marketable securities, and excess cash should be excluded as they are not required for operating activities.

In Chapter 1, we discussed the going concern assumption, a basic tenet of accrual accounting. The deferral of inventory cost until the item is sold and recognition of revenues prior to cash collection assume that the inventories will be sold and the receivables collected.

[10]See Chapter 11 for a discussion of this issue.

Similarly, the use of working capital as a proxy for cash flow (and liquidity—see the next section) is contingent on this assumption. The level and trends of turnover ratios provide information as to the validity of this assumption. Declining turnover ratios, indicating longer shelf time for inventory and/or slower collection of receivables, could be indicators of reduced demand for a firm's products or of sales to customers whose ability to pay is less certain. This might signal one or more of the following:

1. The firm's income may be overstated because reserves are required for obsolete inventory or uncollectable receivables.
2. Future production cutbacks may be required.
3. Potential liquidity problems may exist.

When activity ratios decline, the statement of cash flows helps assess whether income is overstated relative to cash collections. As will be discussed shortly, profitability and liquidity ratios can also improve our understanding of the cause(s) of lower turnover ratios.

Long-Term (Investment) Activity Ratios

The *fixed asset turnover ratio* measures the efficiency of (long-term) capital investment. The ratio, defined as

$$\text{Fixed Assets Turnover} = \frac{\text{Sales}}{\text{Average Fixed Assets}}$$

reflects the level of sales generated by investments in productive capacity.

The level and trend of this ratio are affected by characteristics of its components. First, sales growth is continuous, albeit at varying rates. Increases in capacity to meet that sales growth, however, are discrete, depending on the addition of new factories, warehouses, stores, and so forth. Compounding this issue is the fact that management often has discretion over the timing, form, and financial reporting of the acquisition of incremental capacity.

The combination of some of these factors, as Figure 4-1 shows, results in an erratic turnover ratio. The life cycle of a company or product includes a number of stages: startup, growth, maturity (steady state), and decline. Startup companies' initial turnover may be low, as their level of operations is below their productive capacity. As sales grow, however, turnover will improve continually until the limits of the firm's initial capacity are reached. Subsequent increases in capital investment decrease the turnover ratio until the firm's sales growth catches up to the increased capacity. This process continues until maturity when sales and capacity level off, only to reverse when the firm enters its decline stage.

Additional problems can result from the timing of a firm's asset purchases. Two firms with similar operating efficiencies, having the same productive capacity and the same level of sales, may show differing ratios depending on when their assets were acquired. The firm with older assets has the higher turnover ratio, as accumulated depreciation has reduced the carrying value of its assets. Over time, for any firm, the accumulation of depreciation expense improves the turnover ratio (faster for firms that use accelerated depreciation methods or short depreciable lives) without a corresponding improvement in actual efficiency. The use of gross (before depreciation)

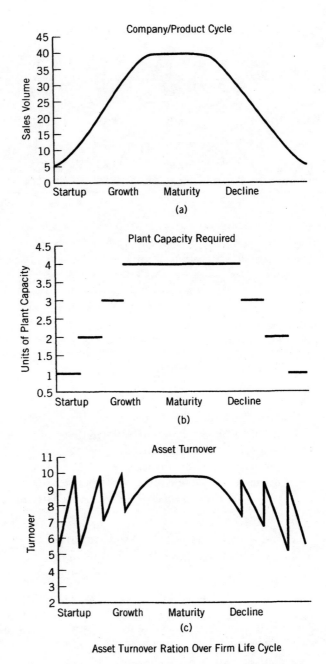

FIGURE 4-1 Asset turnover and capacity requirements.

rather than net fixed assets alleviates this shortcoming. However, this is rarely done in practice.

An offsetting and complicating factor is that newer assets generally operate more efficiently due to improved technology. However, due to inflation newer assets may be more expensive and thus decrease the turnover ratio. Using current or replacement cost rather than historical cost to compute the turnover ratio is one solution to this

EXHIBIT 4-4. E.I. DUPONT DENEMOURS AND COMPANY AND CONSOLIDATED SUBSIDIARIES
Activity Analysis

Years Ended December 31,	1990		1991		1992		1993		1994		Average	
Inventory turnover[a]	**4.68**		**4.83**		**4.95**		**5.21**		**5.64**		**5.06**	
No. of days[b]		78		76		74		70		65		72
Accounts receivable turnover[c]	**8.39**		**8.13**		**8.80**		**8.99**		**9.52**		**8.77**	
No. of days[d]		44		45		41		41		38		42
Fixed assets turnover[e]	**2.00**		**1.86**		**1.78**		**1.71**		**1.85**		**1.84**	
Total assets turnover[f]	**1.10**		**1.04**		**1.01**		**0.98**		**1.06**		**1.04**	

1994 Calculations:

[a]**Inventory Turnover = COGS/Avg. inventory = {21,977/[(3,969 + 3,818)/2]} = 5.64**

[b]Avg. No. Days Inventory Stock = 365/Inventory Turnover = 365/5.64 = 65

[c]**Accounts Receivable Turnover = Net Sales/Avg. AR(Trade) = {39,333/[(4,244 + 4,020)/2]} = 9.52**

[d]Avg. No. Days Receivables Outstanding = 365/AR Turnover = 365/9.52 = 38

[e]**Fixed Assets Turnover = Sales/Avg. Fixed Assets = {39,333/[(21,120 + 21,423)/2]} = 1.85**

[f]**Total Assets Turnover = Sales/Avg. Total Assets = {39,333/[(36,892 + 37,053)/2]} = 1.06**

Comments: DuPont does not provide a breakdown of the raw materials, work-in-process, and finished goods inventory balances. It is, therefore, not possible to compute turnover ratios for the components. The gross inventory turnover ratio has improved significantly from 4.68 (78 days) in 1990 to 5.64 (65 days) in 1994. The receivables turnover ratio shows similar improvement over the 1990 to 1994 period. These ratios reflect better operating performance.

problem. Finally, it should be noted that methods of acquisition (lease versus purchase) and subsequent financial reporting choices (capitalization versus operating lease reporting) also affect turnover ratios for otherwise similar firms. See Chapter 11 for a discussion of these issues.

Total asset turnover is an overall activity measure relating sales to total assets:

$$\text{Total Asset Turnover} = \frac{\text{Sales}}{\text{Average Total Assets}}$$

This relationship provides a measure of overall investment efficiency by aggregating the joint impact of both short- and long-term assets. This comprehensive measure is a key component of the disaggregation of return on assets, presented in a later section of this chapter. The computation and analysis of turnover measures are illustrated, using duPont as an example, in Exhibit 4-4.

Liquidity Analysis

Short-term lenders and creditors (such as suppliers) must assess the ability of a firm to meet its current obligations. That ability depends on the cash resources available as of the balance sheet date and the cash to be generated through the operating cycle of the firm.

Figure 4-2 is a schematic representation of the operating cycle of a firm. The firm purchases or manufactures inventory, requiring an outlay of cash and/or the creation of trade payables debt. The sale of inventory generates receivables that, when collected, are used to satisfy the payables, and the cycle is begun again. The ability to repeat

Operating and Cash Cycles

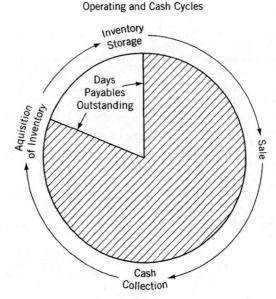

Shaded Area Circumference = Cash Cycle

FIGURE 4-2 Operating and cash cycles.

this cycle on a continuous basis depends on the firm's short-term liquidity and cash-generating ability.

Length of Cash Cycle

One indicator of short-term liquidity uses the activity ratios as a liquidity measure. The *operating cycle* of a merchandising firm is the sum of the number of days it takes to sell inventory and the number of days until the resultant receivables are converted to cash. The circumference of the circle in Figure 4-2 represents the length of this cycle. If a firm operates without credit, it also represents the total number of days cash is tied up in operating assets.

To the extent a firm uses credit, the length of the cash (operating) cycle is reduced. Subtracting the number of days of payables outstanding from the operating cycle results in the firm's *cash cycle*, the number of days a company's cash is tied up by its current operating cycle (the circumference of the shaded portion of the circle in Figure 4-2). The cash cycle[11] captures the interrelationship of sales, collections, and trade credit in a manner that the individual numbers may not. The shorter the cycle, the more efficient the firm's operations and cash management.

For a manufacturing firm, further refinements and approximations may be necessary to calculate the length of the operating and cash cycle. They are discussed in Box 4-1.

---

[11]The inverse of the working capital turnover ratio (times 365) is sometimes used as a crude approximation of the cash cycle. [See Richards and Laughlin (1980) for an extended discussion.]

BOX 4-1
Estimating the Operating and Cash Cycle for a Manufacturing Firm

A merchandising firm holds only one type of inventory: finished goods inventory. Consequently, the inventory turnover ratio measures only one time stage: the time from inventory purchase until its sale. For a manufacturing firm, on the other hand, inventory is held through three stages:

1. As raw material, from purchase to beginning of production
2. As work in process, over the length of the production cycle
3. As finished goods, from completion of production until sale

Only the last stage (as finished goods) is comparable to a merchandising firm. The inventory turnover ratio, COGS/average finished goods inventory, computes the length of time from completion until sale.

The length of time inventory is in the production cycle (stage 2) can be calculated as

$$365 \times \frac{\text{Average Work-in-Process Inventory}}{\text{Cost of Goods Manufactured}}$$

The length of time it takes for raw material to enter production is

$$365 \times \frac{\text{Average Raw Material Inventory}}{\text{Raw Materials Used}}$$

The breakdown among finished goods, work in process, and raw materials inventory is often available in the notes to financial statements. Cost of goods manufactured can be calculated from financial statements as cost of goods sold + ending (finished goods) inventory − beginning (finished goods) inventory. However, the amount of material used in production is rarely available making the calculation of the length of stage 1 infeasible. Some approximations are possible. The first involves calculating the combined length of stage 1 and 2 as

$$365 \times \frac{\text{Average (Work in Process and Raw Material) Inventory}}{\text{Cost of Goods Manufactured}}$$

The accuracy of this approximation depends on the proportion of the various inventories and the degree to which the individual ratios differ. Another (less accurate but perhaps simpler) approximation ignores this whole discussion and uses the composite turnover ratio, thereby mirroring the merchandising firm:

$$365 \times \frac{\text{Average (Total) Inventory}}{\text{Cost of Goods Sold}}$$

Exhibit 4-5 presents the operating and cash cycles for Kmart, a major discount retailer, over the 10-year period 1985 to 1994. Inventory turnover declined gradually over this period; receivables turnover declined sharply. Suppliers appear to have tightened credit terms in 1990, perhaps reflecting Kmart's poor operating performance. As a result, both the operating cycle and cash cycle lengthened considerably over the period. This analysis illustrates the importance of examining the relationship among cash cycle components.

EXHIBIT 4-5. KMART CORPORATION
Analysis of Operating and Cash Cycle

	1985	1986	1987	1988	1989	1990	1991	1992	1993	1994
				A. Turnover Ratios						
Inventory	3.7	3.5	3.6	3.5	3.5	3.5	3.5	3.6	3.5	3.2
Receivables	134.5	82.7	63.2	69.0	62.0	48.2	45.0	43.1	37.3	28.7
Payables	9.0	8.4	8.7	8.4	8.6	9.9	10.3	10.6	10.5	8.4
				B. Average No. of Days						
Inventory in stock	98	103	102	105	103	106	106	102	104	114
Receivables outstanding	3	4	6	5	6	8	8	8	10	13
Operating cycle	100	107	108	111	109	113	114	110	114	127
Less payables outstanding	41	43	42	43	42	37	35	35	35	43
Cash cycle	60	64	66	67	67	76	78	76	79	83

Comments: The decline in inventory and receivables turnover occurs steadily over the 10-year period shown. However, supplier concern is evident in the decline in number of days payables were outstanding beginning in 1989. These factors contributed to the significant deterioration in both the operating and cash cycles.

Working Capital Ratios and Defensive Intervals

The concept of working capital relies on the classification of assets and liabilities into "current" and "noncurrent" categories. *The traditional distinction between current assets and liabilities is based on a maturity of less than one year or (if longer) the operating cycle of the company.*

The typical balance sheet has five categories of current assets:

1. Cash and cash equivalents
2. Marketable securities
3. Accounts receivable
4. Inventories
5. Prepaid expenses

and three categories of current liabilities:

1. Short-term debt
2. Accounts payable
3. Accrued liabilities

By definition, each current asset and liability has a maturity (the expected date of conversion to cash for an asset; the expected date of liquidation for cash for a liability) of less than one year. However, in practice the line between current and noncurrent has blurred in recent years. Marketable securities and debt are particularly susceptible to arbitrary classification. For this reason, working capital ratios should be used with caution.

103

Short-term liquidity analysis compares the firm's cash resources with its cash obligations. Cash resources can be measured by either:

1. The sum of the firm's current cash balance and its potential sources of cash, or
2. Its (net) cash flows from operations

Cash obligations can be measured by either:

1. Current obligations requiring cash, or
2. Cash outflows arising from operations

The following table summarizes the ratios commonly used to measure the relationship between resources and obligations:

	Numerator Cash Resources	Denominator Cash Obligations
Level	Current assets	Current liabilities
Flow	Cash flow from operations	Cash outflows for operations

Conceptually, the ratios differ in whether *levels* (amounts shown on the balance sheet) or *flows* (cash inflows and outflows) are used to gauge the relationship.

Three ratios compare levels of cash resources with current liabilities as the measure of cash obligations. The *current ratio* defines cash resources as all current assets:

$$\textbf{Current Ratio} = \frac{\textbf{Current Assets}}{\textbf{Current Liabilities}}$$

A more conservative measure of liquidity is the *quick ratio:*

$$\textbf{Quick Ratio} = \frac{\textbf{Cash + Marketable Securities + Accounts Receivable}}{\textbf{Current Liabilities}}$$

which excludes inventory from cash resources, recognizing that the conversion of inventory to cash is less certain both in terms of timing and amount.[12] The included assets are "quick assets" because they can be quickly converted to cash.

Finally, the *cash ratio*, defined as

$$\textbf{Cash Ratio} = \frac{\textbf{Cash + Marketable Securities}}{\textbf{Current Liabilities}}$$

is the most conservative of these measures of cash resources as only actual cash and securities easily convertible to cash are used to measure cash resources.

The use of either the current or quick ratio implicitly assumes that the current assets will be converted to cash. In reality, however, firms do not actually liquidate their current assets to pay their current liabilities. Minimum levels of inventories and

---

[12]Inventory balances of actively traded commodities such as oil, metals, or wheat can be considered very liquid and should be included in the quick ratio.

receivables are always needed to maintain operations. If all current assets are liquidated, the firm has effectively ceased operations. As suggested earlier by Figure 4-2, the process of generating inventories, collecting receivables, and paying suppliers is ongoing. These ratios therefore measure the "margin of safety" provided by the cash resources relative to obligations rather than expected cash flows.

Liquidity analysis, moreover, is not independent of activity analysis. Poor receivable or inventory turnover limits the usefulness of the current and quick ratios. Obsolete inventory or uncollectible receivables are unlikely to be sources of cash. Thus, levels and changes in short-term liquidity ratios over time should be examined in conjunction with turnover ratios.

The *cash flow from operations ratio*:

$$\text{Cash Flow from Operations Ratio} = \frac{\text{Cash Flow from Operations}}{\text{Current Liabilities}}$$

measures liquidity by comparing actual cash flows (instead of current and potential cash resources) with current liabilities. This ratio avoids the issues of actual convertibility to cash, turnover, and the need for minimum levels of working capital (cash) to maintain operations.

An important limitation of liquidity ratios is the absence of an economic or "real-world" interpretation of those measures. Unlike the cash cycle liquidity measure, which reflects the number of days cash is tied up in the firm's operating cycle, there is no intuitive meaning to a current ratio of 1.5. For some companies that ratio would be high, for others dangerously low.

The *defensive interval*, in contrast, does provide an intuitive "feel" for a firm's liquidity, albeit a most conservative one. It compares the currently available "quick" sources of cash (cash, marketable securities, and accounts receivable) with the estimated outflows needed to operate the firm: projected expenditures. There are different definitions of both cash resources and projected expenditures.[13] We present here only the basic form:

$$\text{Defensive Interval} = 365 \times \frac{\text{Cash + Marketable Securities + Accounts Receivable}}{\text{Projected Expenditures}}$$

The calculation of the defensive interval for duPont (Exhibit 4-6) uses current year income statement data to estimate projected expenditures. The defensive interval represents a "worst case" scenario indicating the number of days a firm could maintain the current level of operations with its present cash resources but without considering any additional revenues.

Long-Term Debt and Solvency Analysis

The analysis of a firm's capital structure is essential to evaluate its long-term risk and return prospects. Leveraged firms accrue excess returns to their shareholders as long

---

[13]See Sorter and Benston (1960). The most conservative variation, the "no credit" interval, measures the number of days the firm could survive if it loses all access to trade credit. In this version, accounts payable are subtracted from the numerator.

DISCUSSION OF RATIOS BY CATEGORY

EXHIBIT 4-6. E. I. DUPONT DENEMOURS AND COMPANY AND CONSOLIDATED SUBSIDIARIES
Liquidity Analysis

Years Ended December 31,	1990	1991	1992	1993	1994	Average
Average no. of days inventory in stock[a]	78	76	74	70	65	72
+ Days of receivables outstanding[a]	44	45	41	41	38	42
Length of operating cycle	**122**	**121**	**115**	**111**	**103**	**114**
− Payables outstanding[b]	32	32	31	31	29	31
Length of cash cycle	**90**	**89**	**84**	**80**	**74**	**83**
Current ratio[c]	**1.22**	**1.45**	**1.20**	**1.15**	**1.47**	**1.30**
Quick ratio[d]	0.68	0.80	0.68	0.64	0.84	0.73
Cash ratio[e]	**0.06**	**0.06**	**0.16**	**0.13**	**0.15**	**0.11**
Cash from operations ratio[f]	0.51	0.73	0.43	0.57	0.75	0.60
Defensive interval no. of days[g]	**75**	**67**	**77**	**70**	**71**	**72**

1994 Calculations:

[a] Average no. of days inventory stock and receivables outstanding computed in Exhibit 4-4.

[b] Purchases = COGS + Change in Inventory = [21,977 + (3,969 − 3,818)] = 22,128

Average No. Days Payables Outstanding = 365*[Avg. AP(Trade)/Purchases] = {365*[((1,847 + 1,675)/2)/22,128]} = 29

[c] **Current Ratio = Current Assets/Current Liabilities = 11,108/7,565 = 1.47**

[d] Quick Ratio = (Cash + Marketable Securities + AR)/Current Liabilities = (856 + 253 + 5,213)/7,565 = 0.84

[e] **Cash Ratio = (Cash + Marketable Securities)/Current Liabilities = (856 + 253)/7,565 = 0.15**

[f] CFO = Operating Cash Flow (computed in the consolidated statement of cash flows)

Cash from Operations Ratio = CFO/Current Liabilities = 5,664/7,565 = 0.75

[g] **Projected Expenditures = Cost of Goods Sold + Other Operating Expenses except Depreciation Expense =**
21,977 + 2,888 + 357 + 1,047 + 6,215 = 32,484

Defensive Interval No. Days = 365*[(Cash + Marketable Securities + AR)/Projected Expenditures] =
365*(856 + 253 + 5,213)/32,484 = 71

Comments: Both the operating and cash cycle have improved over the last 5 years. Similarly, improved operating performance is seen in all the liquidity ratios. The defensive interval suggests that the firm has 71 days of expenditures on hand, compared to 75 days in 1990 and 72 days on average. This decline may be the result of improved operations and resource management.

as the rate of return on the investments financed by debt is greater than the cost of debt. The benefits of financial leverage bring additional risks, however, in the form of fixed costs that adversely affect profitability (see the next section) if demand or profit margins decline. Moreover, the priority of interest and debt claims can have a severe negative impact on a firm when adversity strikes. The inability to meet these obligations can lead to default and possible bankruptcy.

Debt Covenants

To protect themselves, creditors often impose restrictions on the borrowing company's ability to incur additional debt and make dividend payments. These *debt covenants* are often based on working capital, cumulative profitability, and net worth. It is, therefore, important to monitor the firm to ensure that ratios comply with levels specified in the debt agreements. Violations of debt covenants are frequently an "event of default" under loan agreements, making the debt due immediately. When covenants are violated, therefore, borrowers must either repay the debt (not usually possible) or obtain waivers from lenders. Such waivers often require additional collateral, restrictions on firm operations, or higher interest rates.[14]

Capitalization Table and Debt Ratios

Long-term debt and solvency analysis evaluate the level of risk borne by a firm, changes over time, and risk relative to comparable investments. A higher proportion of debt relative to equity increases the riskiness of the firm. Exhibit 4-7 presents capitalization tables for duPont. Two important factors should be noted:

1. The relative debt levels themselves, and

2. The trend over time in the proportion of debt to equity

Debt ratios are expressed either as

$$\textbf{Debt to Total Capital} = \frac{\textbf{Total Debt (Current + Long-Term)}}{\textbf{Total Capital (Debt + Equity)}}$$

or

$$\textbf{Debt to Equity} = \frac{\textbf{Total Debt}}{\textbf{Total Equity}}$$

The definition of short-term debt used in practice may include operating debt (accounts payable and accrued liabilities). The short-term debt shown in Exhibit 4-7 excludes operating debt because it is a function of the firm's operations and its essential business and contractual relationship to its suppliers rather than external lenders. However, many lenders define debt as equal to total liabilities.

As with other ratios, industry and economy-wide factors affect both the level of debt and the nature of the debt (maturities and variable or fixed rate). Capital-intensive industries tend to incur high levels of debt to finance their property, plant, and equipment. Such debt should be long-term to match the long time horizon of the assets acquired.

An important measurement issue is whether to use book or market values to compute debt ratios. Valuation models in the finance literature that use leverage ratios as inputs are generally based on the market value of debt and equity. Market values of both debt and equity are available or can readily be estimated, and their use can make the ratio a more useful analytical tool.

The use of market values, however, may produce contradictory results. The debt of a firm whose credit rating declines may have a market value well below face amount. A debt ratio based on market values may show an "acceptable" level of leverage. A ratio that would "control" for this phenomenon and can be used in conjunction with book- or market-based debt ratios is one that compares debt measured at book value to equity measured at market:

$$\frac{\textbf{Total Debt at Book Value}}{\textbf{Equity at Market}}$$

---

[14]The relationship between debt covenants and ratios is explored in greater detail in Chapter 10.

If the market value of equity is higher than its book value, the above ratio will be lower than the debt-to-equity ratio using book value.[15] This indicates that market perceptions of the firm's earning power would permit the firm to raise additional capital at an attractive price. If this ratio, however, exceeds the book value debt-to-equity measure, it signals that the market is willing to supply additional capital only at a discount to book value.

The measurement of debt and equity used to compute leverage ratios may require adjustments to reported data. Leases (whether capitalized or operating), other off-balance-sheet transactions such as contractual obligations not accorded accounting recognition, deferred taxes, financial instruments with debt and equity characteristics, and other innovative financing techniques must all be considered when making these calculations. These issues are discussed in later chapters. Exhibit 4-7 shows the computation and interpretation of long-term debt and solvency measurements for duPont.

Interest Coverage Ratios

Debt-to-equity ratios examine the firm's capital structure and, indirectly, its ability to meet current debt obligations. A more direct measure of the firm's ability to meet interest payments is

$$\text{Times Interest Earned} = \frac{\text{Earnings Before Interest and Taxes (EBIT)}}{\text{Interest Expense}}$$

This ratio, often referred to as the *interest coverage ratio*, measures the protection available to creditors as the extent to which earnings available for interest "cover" interest expense.[16] A more comprehensive measure, the *fixed charge coverage ratio*, includes all fixed charges:

$$\text{Fixed Charge Coverage} = \frac{\text{Earnings Before Fixed Charges and Taxes}}{\text{Fixed Charges}}$$

where fixed charges include contractually committed interest and principal payments on leases as well as funded debt.

This coverage ratio may also be computed using adjusted operating cash flows (cash from operations + fixed charges + tax payments) as the numerator:

$$\text{Times Interest Earned (Cash Basis)} = \frac{\text{Adjusted Operating Cash Flow}}{\text{Interest Expense}}$$

$$\text{Fixed Charge Coverage Ratio (Cash Basis)} = \frac{\text{Adjusted Operating Cash Flow}}{\text{Fixed Charges}}$$

Capital Expenditure and CFO-to-Debt Ratios

Internally generated cash flows are needed for investment as well as debt service. The coverage ratios discussed do not take this into consideration. Cash flow from opera-

---

[15]The analysis assumes that all debt has been included. See Chapter 11 for a discussion of off-balance sheet financing techniques.

[16]Because firms may capitalize some interest expense, using reported interest expense may overstate the coverage ratio. See Chapter 10 for a discussion of capitalized interest and adjustments to coverage ratios.

EXHIBIT 4-7. E. I. DUPONT DENEMOURS AND COMPANY AND CONSOLIDATED SUBSIDIARIES
Long-Term Debt and Solvency Analysis

Years Ended December 31,	1990	1991	1992	1993	1994	Average
Capitalization Table ($ in millions)						
Short-term debt	2,932	693	3,223	1,499	714	1,812
Current long-term debt	996	1,148	576	1,297	578	919
Long-term debt	5,663	6,456	7,193	6,531	6,376	6,444
Total debt	**9,591**	**8,297**	**10,992**	**9,327**	**7,668**	**9,175**
Trade payables[a]	3,437	3,174	3,372	3,145	3,565	3,339
Total debt (including trade)	**13,028**	**11,471**	**14,364**	**12,472**	**11,233**	**12,514**
Capital stock	4,981	5,058	5,193	5,304	5,416	5,190
Retained earnings	11,437	11,681	6,572	5,926	7,406	8,604
Total equity	**16,418**	**16,739**	**11,765**	**11,230**	**12,822**	**13,795**
Total capital	**26,009**	**25,036**	**22,757**	**20,557**	**20,490**	**22,970**
Total capital (including trade)	**29,446**	**28,210**	**26,129**	**23,702**	**24,055**	**26,308**
Debt						
To equity[b]	**0.58**	**0.50**	**0.93**	**0.83**	**0.60**	**0.67**
To capital[c]	0.37	0.33	0.48	0.45	0.37	0.40
Debt (including trade)						
To equity[d]	**0.79**	**0.69**	**1.22**	**1.11**	**0.88**	**0.91**
To capital[c]	0.44	0.41	0.55	0.53	0.47	0.48
Times interest earned[f]	**6.37**	**4.75**	**3.82**	**2.61**	**8.84**	**5.28**
Capital expenditure ratio[g]	0.95	2.26	0.88	1.58	2.16	1.56
CFO to debt[h]	**0.54**	**0.66**	**0.40**	**0.58**	**0.74**	**0.58**

1994 Calculations:

[a]Trade Payables = Accounts Payable + "Nonincome Taxes" + Income Taxes = 2,734 + 422 + 409 = 3,565

[b]**Debt to Equity = Total Debt/Total Equity = 7,668/12,822 = 0.60**

[c]Debt to Capital = Total Debt/Total Capital = 7,668/20,490 = 0.37

[d]**Debt (including trade) to Equity = Total Debt (including trade)/Total Equity = 11,233/12,822 = 0.88**

[e]Debt (including trade) to Capital = Total Debt (including trade)/Total Capital (including trade) =
    11,233/24,055 = 0.47

[f]**Times Interest Earned = EBIT/Interest Expense = 4,941/559 = 8.84**

[g]CFO/Capital Expenditures
  Capital Expenditure Ratio = 5,664/2,618 = 2.16

[h]**CFO to Debt = CFO/Total Debt = 5,664/7,668 = 0.74**

Comments: Leverage ratios show substantial improvement since the lows of 1992. However, lower reported equity in 1992 is due to significant charges taken for accounting changes. Restructuring charges reduced earnings in 1993.

tions, as noted in Chapter 3, ignores the cost of additions to operating capacity. Net income, with its provision for depreciation, amortizes the original cost of existing fixed assets. However, given their relatively long service life, the replacement costs of these assets (even with minimal inflation) may be significantly higher, and historical cost depreciation cannot adequately provide for their replacement.[17] Neither net income

[17]See Chapter 8 for a discussion of these issues.

nor cash from operations, of course, makes any provision for the capital required for growth.

A firm's long-term solvency is a function of:

1. Its ability to finance the replacement and expansion of its investment in productive capacity, as well as
2. Its generation of cash for debt repayment

The *capital expenditure ratio*

$$\text{Capital Expenditure Ratio} = \frac{\text{Cash from Operations (CFO)}}{\text{Capital Expenditures}}$$

measures the relationship between the firm's cash-generating ability and its investment expenditures. To the extent the ratio exceeds 1, it indicates the firm has cash left for debt repayment or dividends after payment of capital expenditures.

The *CFO-to-debt ratio*[18]

$$\text{CFO to Debt} = \frac{\text{CFO}}{\text{Total Debt}}$$

measures the coverage of principal repayment requirements by the current CFO. A low CFO-to-debt ratio could signal a long-term solvency problem as the firm does not generate enough cash internally to repay its debt.

Profitability Analysis

Equity investors are concerned with the firm's ability to generate, sustain, and increase profits. Profitability can be measured in several differing but interrelated dimensions. First, there is the relationship of a firm's profits to sales, that is, the residual return to the firm per sales dollar. Another measure, return on investment (ROI), relates profits to the investment required to generate them. We briefly define these ratios and then elaborate on their use in financial statement analysis.

Return on Sales

One measure of profitability is the relationship between the firm's costs and its sales. The ability to control costs in relation to revenues enhances earnings power. A common-size income statement shows the ratio of each cost component to sales. In addition, six summary ratios measure the relationship between different measures of profitability and sales:

1. The *gross (profit) margin* captures the relationship between sales and manufacturing or merchandising costs:

$$\text{Gross Margin} = \frac{\text{Gross Profit}}{\text{Sales}}$$

---

[18]The definition of debt may depend on the objective of the analysis. It should include all short- and long-term debt and may include trade debt.

2. The *operating margin*, calculated as

$$\text{Operating Margin} = \frac{\text{Operating Income}}{\text{Sales}}$$

provides information about a firm's profitability from the operations of its "core" business, excluding the effects of:
- Investments (income from affiliates or asset sales)
- Financing (interest expense)
- Tax position

3. A profit margin measure that is independent of both the firm's financing and tax position is the

$$\text{Margin Before Interest and Tax} = \frac{\text{EBIT}}{\text{Sales}}$$

4. The pretax margin is calculated after financing costs (interest) but prior to income taxes:

$$\text{Pretax Margin} = \frac{\text{Earnings Before Tax (EBT)}}{\text{Sales}}$$

5. Finally, the overall profit margin is net of all expenses:

$$\text{Profit Margin} = \frac{\text{Net Income}}{\text{Sales}}$$

The five ratios listed above can be computed directly from a firm's financial statements.

6. Another useful profitability measure is the contribution margin ratio, defined as

$$\text{Contribution Margin} = \frac{\text{Contribution}}{\text{Sales}}$$

where contribution = sales − variable costs.

The contribution margin ratio, however, cannot be computed directly from a firm's financial statements as the breakdown between fixed and variable costs is rarely provided. Appendix 4-A, however, discusses how to estimate this breakdown.

Return on Investment

Return on investment (ROI) measures the relationship between profits and the investment required to generate them. Diverse measures of that investment result in different forms of ROI.

Return on Assets. The return on assets (ROA) compares income with total assets (equivalently, total liabilities and equity capital). It can be interpreted in two ways.

111

First, it measures management's ability and efficiency in using the firm's assets to generate (operating) profits. Second, it reports the total return accruing to all providers of capital (debt and equity), independent of the source of capital.

The return is measured by net income prior to the cost of financing and is computed by adding back (after-tax) interest expense to net income:[19]

$$ROA = \frac{\text{Net Income} + \text{After-Tax Interest Cost}}{\text{Average Total Assets}}$$

ROA can also be computed on a pretax basis using EBIT as the return measure. This results in a ROI measure that is unaffected by differences in a firm's tax position as well as financial policy:

$$ROA = \frac{\text{EBIT}}{\text{Average total assets}}$$

In practice, however, the ROA measure is sometimes computed using either net income or EBT as the numerator. Such postinterest ROI ratios make leveraged firms appear less profitable by charging earnings for payments (interest) to some capital providers (lenders) but not others (stockholders). Preinterest ROI ratios, in contrast, facilitate the comparison of firms with different degrees of leverage. Therefore, ROI ratios that use total assets in the denominator should *always* include total earnings (before interest) in the numerator. As interest is tax-deductible, posttax profit measures should add back net-of-tax interest payments.

Return on Total Capital. One particularly useful ROI measure is the *return on total capital* (ROTC). This ratio uses the sum of *external* debt and equity instead of total assets as the base against which the firm's return is measured. ROTC measures profitability relative to all (nontrade) capital providers.

Return can be measured either (pretax) by EBIT or (after tax) by net income plus after-tax interest:[20]

$$ROTC = \frac{\text{EBIT}}{\text{Average (Total Debt} + \text{Stockholders' Equity)}}$$

or

$$ROTC = \frac{\text{Net Income} + \text{After-Tax Interest Expense}}{\text{Average (Total Debt} + \text{Stockholders' Equity)}}$$

Return on Equity. The return on total stockholders' equity (ROE) excludes debt in the denominator and uses either pretax income (*after* interest costs) or net income:

$$ROE = \frac{\text{Pretax Income}}{\text{Average Stockholders' Equity}}$$

[19]The after-tax interest cost is calculated by multiplying the interest cost by $(1 - t)$, where t is the firm's marginal tax rate.

[20]As in the case of ROA, preinterest measures of profitability should be used to compute ROTC, as total capital includes debt obligations.

Relationship of ROA and ROE to Providers of Investment Base

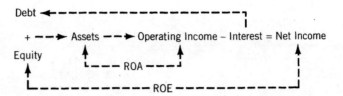

FIGURE 4-3 Relationship of ROA and ROE to providers of investment base.

or

$$ROE = \frac{\text{Net Income}}{\text{Average Stockholder's Equity}}$$

For companies with preferred equity, another ROI measure focuses on the returns accruing to the residual owners of the firm—common shareholders:

$$\text{Return on Common Equity (ROCE)} = \frac{\text{Net Income} - \text{Preferred Dividends}}{\text{Average Common Equity}}$$

The relationship between ROA and ROE reflects the firm's capital structure. As shown in Figure 4-3, creditors and shareholders provide the capital needed by the firm to acquire the assets used in the business. In return, they receive their share of the firm's profits.

ROA and ROTC measure returns to all providers of capital. ROCE measures returns to the firm's common shareholders and is calculated after deducting the returns paid to the creditors (interest) and other providers of equity capital (preferred shareholders).

Profitability and Cash Flows

Profitability ratios traditionally use accrual-based income measures, as shown for duPont in Exhibit 4-8. Cash flow analogues for these ratios should also be calculated. Examples include cash gross margin (cash collections less cash paid for inputs) and ROI measures using CFO in the numerator (either before or after interest, depending on the denominator). A direct method cash flow statement is required for ratios such as cash gross margin and operating margin. There is empirical evidence (see the discussion of Gombola and Ketz, 1983 that follows) that such cash-flow-based ratios have different properties from traditional profitability measures.

Operating and Financial Leverage

Profitability ratios imply that profits are proportional to sales, which may belie the true relationship among sales, costs, and profits. Generally, a doubling of sales would be expected to double income only if all expenses were variable. Conceptually, expenses can be classified into variable (V) and fixed (F) components. Variable expenses

113

EXHIBIT 4-8. E. I. DUPONT DENEMOURS AND COMPANY AND CONSOLIDATED SUBSIDIARIES
Profitability Analysis

Years Ended Dedember 31,	1990	1991	1992	1993	1994	Average
Gross margin (%)[a]	42.70	41.78	42.18	42.33	44.13	42.62
Operating margin (%)[a]	**11.02**	**8.22**	**6.29**	**7.13**	**9.85**	**8.50**
Preinterest and tax margin (%)[a]	12.30	9.23	6.49	4.18	12.56	8.95
Pretax margin (%)[a]	**10.37**	**7.28**	**4.79**	**2.58**	**11.14**	**7.23**
Profit margin (%)[a]	**5.77**	**3.63**	**(10.39)**	**1.50**	**6.93**	**1.49**
ROA (preinterest)						
After tax (%)[b]	**7.52**	**4.79**	**(9.55)**	**2.39**	**8.32**	**2.69**
Pretax (%)[c]	13.53	9.62	6.55	4.09	13.36	9.43
ROE						
After tax (%)[d]	**14.34**	**8.46**	**(27.55)**	**4.83**	**22.68**	**4.55**
Pretax (%)[e]	25.79	17.00	12.71	8.33	36.44	20.05
ROTC (preinterest)						
After tax (%)[f]	**11.00**	**6.96**	**(14.99)**	**4.18**	**14.98**	**4.43**
Pretax (%)[g]	19.79	13.99	10.27	7.17	24.07	15.06

1994 Calculations:

[a]Return on sales and margins from Exhibit 4-3.

[b]**After Tax (%) = {[Net Income + (Interest Expense*(1 − Effective Tax Rate))]/Avg. Assets}*100 =**
  {2,727 + [559*(1 − 0.378)/(36,892 + 37,053)/2)]}*100 = 8.32%

[c]Pretax (%) = (EBIT/Avg. Assets)*100 = {4,941/[(36,892 + 37,053)/2)]}*100 = 13.36

[d]**After Tax (%) = (Net Income/Avg. Equity)*100 = (2,727/[12,822 + 11,230]/2)*100 = 22.68%**

[e]Pretax (%) = (EBT/Avg. Equity)*100 = {4,382/[(12,822 + 11,230)/2]}*100 = 36.44%

[f]**After Tax (%) = {[Net Income + (Interest Expense*(1 − Effective Tax Rate))]/Avg. Total Capital [Debt + Equity]}*100**
  = {[2,727 + (559*(1 − 0.378))]/(20,490 + 20,557)/2}*100 = 14.98%

[g]Pretax (%) = [EBIT/Avg. Total Capital (Debt + Equity)]*100 = {4,941/[(20,490 + 20,557)/2]}*100 = 24.07%

Comments: See the section on "common-size statements" for a discussion of trends in margins. Trends in ROA/ROE are discussed later with reference to Exhibits 4-12 and 4-14.

tend to be operating in nature, whereas fixed costs are the result of operating, investing, and financing decisions.[21]

The mix of variable and fixed operating cost components in a firm's cost structure often reflects the industry in which the firm operates. Fixed investing and financing costs depend on the asset intensity of the firm's operations and (somewhat related) on the amount of debt financing used by the firm.

Leverage, which is the proportion of fixed costs in the firm's overall cost structure, can be subdivided into fixed operating costs that reflect *operating leverage* (the proportion of fixed operating costs to variable costs), and fixed financing costs or *financial leverage*.

Leverage trades risk for return. Increases in fixed costs are risky because they must still be paid as demand declines, depressing the firm's income. At high levels of demand, fixed costs are spread over a larger base, enhancing profitability. These concepts are illustrated in Exhibit 4-9.

[21]Financial markets sometimes create investing and financing transactions with variable payment streams such as lease payments tied to revenues (e.g., retailers) and adjustable rate loans. These payments may have both variable and fixed components.

EXHIBIT 4-9
Illustration of Operating, Financial, and Total Leverage Effects

General Assumptions	Company V	Company F
Fixed costs	$ 0	$ 40
Variable costs/sales	80%	40%
Assets	$200	$200

A. Assume 0% Financing, Debt $0, Equity $200

	No Leverage Company V			Operating Leverage Company F		
Scenario	A	B	C	A	B	C
Sales	$50	$100	$150	$50	$100	$150
Variable cost	40	80	120	20	40	60
Contribution	$10	$ 20	$ 30	$30	$ 60	$ 90
Fixed cost	0	0	0	40	40	40
Operating income	$10	$ 20	$ 30	($10)	$ 20	$ 50
Return						
On sales	20%	20%	20%	(20%)	20%	33%
On assets	5%	10%	15%	(5%)	10%	25%
On equity	5%	10%	15%	(5%)	10%	25%

B. Assume 50% Financing, Debt 100, Equity 100, Interest rate = 5%

	Financial Leverage Company V			Total Leverage Company F		
Scenario	A	B	C	A	B	C
Operating income	$10	$ 20	$ 30	($10)	$ 20	$ 50
Interest	5	5	5	5	5	5
Net income	$ 5	$ 15	$ 25	($15)	$ 15	$ 45
Return						
On assets	5%	10%	15%	(5%)	10%	25%
On equity	5%	15%	25%	(15%)	15%	45%

Operating Leverage

Part A of Exhibit 4-9 illustrates operating leverage. With sales of $100 (scenario B), Company V and Company F have the identical return on sales of 20% and ROA (= ROE) of 10%. The return on sales is constant for Company V, since its operating costs are completely variable. Changes in net income are directly proportional to changes in demand—a 50% increase in sales to $150 results in a 50% increase in income to $30. Company F's profitability, on the other hand, varies by more than changes in demand. A 50% change in demand changes net income by 150%. Because of fixed costs, the return on sales does not remain constant with volume.

The *contribution margin ratio* is a useful measure of the effects of operating leverage on the firm's profitability:

$$\text{Contribution Margin Ratio} = \frac{\text{Contribution}}{\text{Sales}} = 1 - \frac{\text{Variable Costs}}{\text{Sales}}$$

This ratio indicates the incremental profit resulting from a given dollar change in sales. For Company V this ratio is 20% (1 − 80%), and for Company F it is 60% (1 − 40%). Thus, a change of $50 in sales results in a change in operating income of

Company V: 20% × $50 = $10

Company F: 60% × $50 = $30

The *operating leverage effect (OLE)* is defined as

$$\text{OLE} = \frac{\text{Contribution Margin Ratio}}{\text{Return on Sales}} = \frac{\text{Contribution}}{\text{Operating Income}}$$

and is the ratio of the contribution margin to operating income. The OLE can t used to estimate the percentage change in income (and ROA) resulting from a giv percentage change in sales volume:

% Change in Income = OLE × % Change in Sales

When OLE is greater than 1, operating leverage exists. However, this measu operating leverage is not constant across all levels of activity.[22] *The OLE is a re measure and varies with the level of sales.*

For Company V, the OLE is equal to 1, at all sales levels, because its co: completely variable. Thus, for Company V, a given percentage change in sales in equivalent percentage changes in income and ROA.

For Company F, however, the OLE varies: It is equal to 3 (60%/20%) for s B. A 50% change in sales (to scenario A or scenario C) will result in a t' percentage change (3 × 50% = 150%) in income and ROA. Using scenario base starting point, however, results in an OLE measure of 1.8 (60%/33% drop in sales from scenario C to scenario B ($150 to $100) results in a 6(33%) drop in income ($50 to $20) and ROA.[23]

Financial Leverage

The effects of financial leverage can also be measured. From the poin common shareholders, financial leverage is, like operating leverage, a ris trade-off. The firm takes on the risk of fixed financing costs, anticipatin returns will accrue to the common shareholders at higher levels of dem

In part B of Exhibit 4-9, we assume that each company is 50% fin: and interest costs = $5 (5% interest rate). For Company V (which ha leverage), changes in net income are now proportionally higher than

[22]Similarly, the financial leverage measure discussed shortly is also a function of the c

[23]In all cases, the ROE is identical to ROA, as we have assumed no financing i

mand; changes of 50% in volume are accompanied by changes of 67% in profit and ROE. (Note that ROA, because it is computed before interest expense, is unaffected by the existence of financial leverage.)

The *financial leverage effect* (FLE) relates operating income to net income:

$$FLE = \frac{Operating\ Income}{Net\ Income}$$

The FLE for Company V is (at scenario B) $20/$15 = 1.33. Thus, a 50% change in sales (and operating income) results in a 67% (1.333 × 50%) shift in income (from $15 to $25) and ROE (from 15% to 25%).

For Company F, the changes in income relative to changes in demand are even higher. Here, the effects of *both* operating and financial leverage work together, giving a *total leverage effect* (TLE) equal to the product of the individual leverage effects:

$$TLE = OLE \times FLE = \frac{Contribution}{Net\ Income}$$

$$TLE = 3 \times 1.333 = 4.00$$

A 50% decline in Company F's sales (from $100 to $50) results in a 200% (4 × 50%) decline in income (from $15 to $−15). This suggests that firms with high operating leverage take on high financial leverage only at their peril. Traditionally, high debt ratios have been considered acceptable only for firms with low operating leverage with stable operations (such as public utilities), where the risk of combining operating and financial leverage was low. In recent years, however, financial leverage has be applied to companies with high operating leverage as well (airlines, for example resulting in financial distress or even bankruptcy during periods of economic adversit

CHAPTER 5

ANALYZING THE FIRM'S ENVIRONMENT

OVERVIEW

In Chapters 5 and 6 we review the information needed to build an accurate pro-forma model of the firm. This information has two aspects:

- In order to project sales for the firm, you have to analyze the firm's operating environment and the firm's place within this environment. This is the topic of the current chapter.
- To convert the marketing view of the firm's prospects (expressed as sales projections) into full financial projections, you need to project the *efficiency* with which the firm will generate the projected sales. The analysis of the firm's efficiency is described in the following chapter. This analysis will show you how to model individual balance sheet and income statement items.

Combining the sales projections derived in this chapter with the projected operating efficiency, you will have the information that is necessary to build a complete pro-forma model of the firm.

The process of valuing a firm begins with a thorough analysis of its environment: You cannot predict the firm's sales, costs, or capital investments unless you understand the conditions under which the firm produces and sells its products. Accordingly, the study of the firm's environment typically is a "top-down" process: From your understanding of the broadest environment you can deduce the prospects of the firm's immediate environment. *The objective of the analysis of the firm's environment is to estimate the firm's sales in future years* by:

- *Projecting the sales of the industry as a whole.* This depends on the analyst's projections of macroeconomic conditions and the industry's characteristics.

• *Projecting the market share of the firm within the industry.* This depends on the analyst's evaluation of the industry's main players and their strengths and weaknesses.

A typical analysis of the firm's environment has three steps:

Step 1 Begin by considering the firm's macroeconomic environment—prospects for future employment, inflation, income, regulations, and taxes. This macroanalysis is often extended beyond national boundaries to take into account foreign competition, to project raw material prices when these are imported from other countries, or to project the foreign macroenvironment when the firm's products are exported.

Step 2 Once you understand the macroenvironment, analyze the prospects of the industry to which the firm belongs. In projecting industrywide sales, you should take into account how the industry is affected by the projected macroconditions. For example, a projected decline in economic activity—a recession—calls for a shift in consumer demand from luxury goods and high-quality brands to low-cost substitutes. Alternatively, in a period of high inflation you should reasonably expect the industry's sales to grow faster—in nominal terms—than if you expect low inflation.

Step 3 Once you understand both the macroenvironment and the overall industry prospects, you can consider the future of the firm you value. Suppose, for example, that you project poor economic conditions and a shift in consumer demand to low-cost brands. If the firm that you are analyzing is the industry's price leader, it will probably *increase* its market share as customers gravitate to this firm from high-quality, high-price competitors. Macroeconomic conditions do not necessarily affect all the firms of an industry equally!

Although, in principle, a full analysis of a firm includes all the stages just described, often the labor is divided: Some analysts specialize in macroanalysis—analyzing and predicting macroeconomic conditions—and some specialize in microanalysis—following specific industries and firms. In many investment banks these analyses are performed by different departments of the bank. Since our focus is on valuation issues, we take a user perspective in describing how macroeconomic analysis is done. Accordingly, in this chapter we describe how to read a macroanalysis rather than how to do one. We focus more on the microinterpretations of macroanalysis and, obviously, on microanalyses of industries and firms.

The chapter is organized according to the deductive process of projecting the sales prospects of a firm. We begin by describing how macroeconomic activity is analyzed, proceed with a discussion of industry's sales projection, and conclude with a discussion of the projection of the sales of individual firms. Clearly, the economic and marketing models and tools that are covered in a few semester-long courses cannot be fully described in one chapter. However, since we have a specific application in mind—using economic and marketing models to value projects, firms, and securities—in this chapter we give a bird's-eye view of these models, focusing on their application to the prediction of sales.

5.1 THE ANALYSIS OF MACROECONOMIC ACTIVITY

Economic activity varies over time. This suggests that it is worthwhile to measure and to try to predict changes in economic activity. Although the preceding sentence seems trivially true, this statement is not innocuous: We must consider how we *want* and *can* measure economic activity.

Measuring the Level of Economic Activity

The two most widely used aggregates of the level of macroeconomic activity are the **gross national product (GNP)** and the **gross domestic product (GDP):**

• The *gross national product* is the value of all goods and services produced by using the resources *owned* by a nation. The GNP calculation doesn't distinguish between resources located in the country and resources owned by the citizens of the country that are physically located abroad. On the other hand, the GNP doesn't include the value of products produced locally by resources owned by foreigners.

• The *gross domestic product* measures the value of the products produced domestically, independent of who owns the resources used in the production.

In Figure 5.1 we plot the U.S. GNP and the GDP for 1970 through 1992 (in dollars of constant value—1987 dollars). Clearly, we see that the GNP and the GDP are highly correlated and, indeed, are virtually identical. Nonetheless, as their

FIGURE 5.1 The U.S. gross national product (GNP) versus the gross domestic product (GDP), 1971–1992, in constant (1987) dollars.

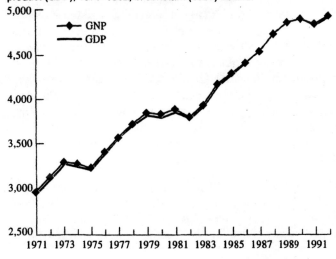

121

definitions suggest, the GNP is more related to the nation's *income* than the GDP. Thus, the GNP may be more useful than the GDP in predicting sales of consumption goods (such as books, air transportation, and cars), whereas the GDP, being more related to the nation's *production*, may be more useful in predicting the sales of intermediate products (such as personal computers, machinery, and raw materials). Today, the standard measurement of national economic activity is based on the GDP, which means that the GDP series are more readily available for international comparison and analysis. Thus, from now on we will primarily refer to the GDP while keeping in mind the high correlation between the two measures of activity.

Because no one person or entity knows the quantities and prices of *all* goods and services produced in any given period, the GDP is easier to define than to measure. In practice, the level of economic activity is only *estimated* so that we use *estimates* of activity to measure and predict the level of economic activity. In the United States the GDP is estimated by the Bureau of Economic Analysis, an agency of the U.S. Commerce Department. It is estimated on a quarterly basis, and the first estimate of a given quarter is published in the third week after the end of the quarter. Revised estimates are released in the following 2 months as more accurate information is collected and processed. This means that, as with all accounting figures, we know what really occurred—that is, the accurate national product of a given quarter—only after it actually happened.[1]

Despite the fact that the measurement of the level of economic activity can be done accurately only after the fact (and even then with a lag), for the purpose of decision making we would like to know roughly where the economy is now and where it is headed in a timely fashion. Toward that end, various government and private agencies report *indicators* of the level of economic activity. There are three types of economic indicators: **leading indicators, coincidental indicators,** and **lagging indicators.**

• *Leading economic indicators* are indicators that tend to rise and fall *ahead* of similar changes in the level of economic activity. Therefore, leading economic indicators are useful in predicting *future* trends in economic activity.

• *Coincidental economic indicators* tend to move *with* the level of economic activity. Therefore, the coincidental indicators are useful in assessing the *current state of the economy* even before the actual GDP figures are estimated.

• *Lagging indicators* lag the movement of economic activity. They are useful in assessing, after the fact, the relations between various economic statistics and the actual level of economic activity. (Such analysis can help us to formulate better models and indicators of economic activity.)

Ostensibly, for valuations (which are based on discounting *future* cash flows) the leading economic indicators are the most relevant indicators. There are quite a few intuitive statistics of macroeconomic activity that can be indicators of future trends of the economy. Each of these indicators, however, will have its own

---

[1]Even then, the figures are often corrected in subsequent months.

idiosyncratic behavior. A better way to estimate trends in the economy is to aggregate a few of these indicators; the Bureau of Economic Analysis of the Department of Commerce does this monthly: The Bureau publishes a monthly index that averages 11 series of leading indicators. The 11 components of the **index of leading economic indicators** are listed in Exhibit 5.1.

Exhibit 5.1

Components of the Index of Leading Economic Indicators

Average workweek of production workers in manufacturing

Initial claims for state unemployment insurance (inverted before inclusion in the index)[2]

New orders for consumer goods (adjusted for inflation)

Vendor performance—companies receiving slower deliveries from suppliers

Contracts and orders for plant and equipment (adjusted for inflation)

New private housing building permits issued

Change in manufacturers' unfilled orders (durable goods industries)

Change in sensitive materials prices

Stock prices (S&P 500 index)

Money supply (M2, adjusted for inflation)

Index of consumer expectations

The index of leading economic indicators leads the level of activity in the economy by about one-half year. By itself, this is bad news: It suggests that the index of leading economic indicators is useful in forecasting economic activity only in the short run—in the next 6 months. To compound the problem, monthly changes in the index of leading economic indicators, which are used to measure *changes* in the trend of economic activity, are typically less important than three or four consecutive changes in the same direction. Thus, only after observing several consecutive changes in the index can we conclude that a change in the *direction* of the economy is actually taking place. This further reduces the usefulness of the leading indicators in assessing future economic conditions.

Figure 5.2 shows quarterly percentage changes in the real GDP (annualized) and the percentage changes in the previous quarter's leading economic indicators (LEI). As you can see, there is a fair degree of correlation. Regressing the changes one on the other gives an $R^2 = 31\%$, which is respectable for regressions of this type; however, it is clear that the LEI do not, by themselves, fully predict changes in economic activity, even in the short run.

The inability to use empirical relations to predict long-run macroeconomic activity is a reflection of a theoretical gap in understanding and predicting long-run trends of economic activity. Although history shows that macroeconomic activity is cyclical, economists can only partially explain the phenomenon. For example, economists argue that the fact that it takes time to build factories (or

---

[2]An *increase* in this leading indicator component indicates a *decrease* in unemployment.

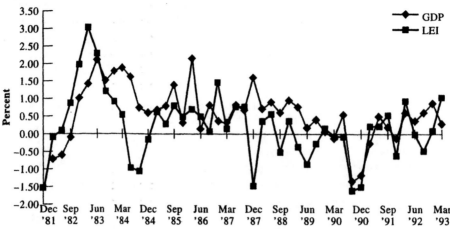

FIGURE 5.2   Real GDP changes versus changes in leading economic indicators.

more generally, to adjust the level of production) creates fluctuations in economic activity. Rigidities in employment contracts—the fact that it is difficult to adjust wages upward or downward in relation to economic conditions—and other long-term relations may exacerbate these fluctuations.

From the perspective of someone who tries to value a firm based on projected macroeconomic conditions, the fact that we do not fully understand why economic activity is cyclical means that it is difficult to predict business cycles and their duration from theoretically founded relations. Instead, we rely on statistical relations between leading indicators and the level of economic activity (which can only be measured after the fact!) to predict *short-run* fluctuations in macroeconomic activity. For example, history shows that a few consecutive increases in the index of leading economic indicators indicates an upturn in economic activity over the next half a year or thereabouts. In the long run, however, we typically assume that economic activity will be average—neither a recession nor a boom. This is the first time we encounter the problem of "blurriness": As we look further into the future, our vision becomes more and more hazy; we have a relatively clear view of the future only in the short run. You will face the same problem when projecting industry's characteristics and the firm's performance. Unfortunately, most of the value of firms and their securities is in their distant future, about which we have only a faint knowledge (at best . . .).

The predictions of various economists for the future economic trends are often surveyed and published. This is very useful information. Evidence suggests that the average prediction is a much better indicator of future economic conditions than any individual prediction. In essence, by averaging a few predictions, we get rid of the idiosyncrasies of each of the forecaster's opinions and obtain a more accurate prediction. Thus, when valuing a firm and its securities, we should preferably use consensus predictions, published monthly, for example, by Blue Chip Economic Indicators—a private firm.

The consensus predictions typically state projected economic growth over the next 2 years, as well as two other important statistics—projected unemployment and projected inflation rates. You can use all three projections in estimating projected industry and firm sales. Projected growth in the GDP and projected changes in unemployment can be used to project growth in unit sales—**real sales growth rates.** Projected inflation rates can be used to project changes in unit price, which when multiplied by the projected real growth rate will give the projected sales growth in *dollar* terms—**nominal sales growth rate.** In the following section we describe some ways of estimating these growth rates.

5.2 THE EFFECT OF MACROECONOMIC CONDITIONS ON INDUSTRIES

In the previous section we described how economists attempt to project future macroeconomic conditions. You deduce from these projections the likely effect of future macroconditions on the prospects of the industry that you analyze. To reemphasize, macroeconomic projections are typically of any accuracy only in the short run, which means that for long-run sales projections we have little choice but to assume average macroeconomic conditions.

We distinguish between two possible effects of macroeconomic conditions on industries: (1) the effect on the *level* of the industry's sales and (2) the effect on the *composition* of the sales. We start our discussion with an analysis of the dependence of the level of the industry's sales on macroconditions.

The Level of the Industry's Sales and Macroeconomic Conditions

The industry's sales and profits typically reflect macroeconomic conditions. Obviously, the *extent* to which an industry's performance reflects macroeconomic conditions depends on the industry. Some industries, such as food, health care, and other consumer staples, are less affected by changes in economic conditions. Sales of other industries, such as airlines or luxury consumption goods, critically depend on macroconditions: They rise when the economic conditions improve and decline when economic conditions deteriorate.

Figure 5.3 presents an example of an industry where sales are highly correlated with macroeconomic conditions: It depicts domestic car sales, in millions of cars per year, and annual changes in the GDP (adjusted for inflation). Evidently, when the economy flourishes, that is, when national income grows at a fast rate, sales of domestic cars increase, whereas when the economy is in a slump, that is, when national income hardly grows or even declines, car sales decline.

The high correlation of automobile sales and changes in the GDP is useful since you can use *published* projections of GDP growth rates to predict future car sales. If you think that macroconditions are a key determinant of the activity of an industry, you will be able to project the industry's (short-run!) sales based on projected macrogrowth rates. To do so, you:

• Estimate the relation between the sales of the industry and growth rates by using historical values

125

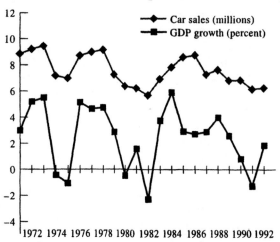

FIGURE 5.3   U.S. auto sales and changes in the GDP, 1971–1992.

• Forecast industry sales by applying the estimated relation to the forecasted growth rate

To illustrate, we can use the GDP and car sales to project next year's expected car sales based on GDP growth projections. We begin by regressing annual automobile sales on real annual changes in the GDP. Here is the regression output from a spreadsheet, which gives respectable results:[3]

Regression Output

Constant	6.75831076
Std Err of Y Est	0.77496101
R Squared	0.58287254
No. of Observations	22
Degrees of Freedom	20
X Coefficient(s) 0.375086374	
Std Err of Coef. 0.070951875	

Two parameters are estimated in this regression—an intercept and a slope co-efficient. The intercept corresponds to the number of cars that are estimated to be sold when the nation's income doesn't change—for a 0 percent growth rate in the GDP, 6.76 million cars are sold on average. The slope coefficient suggests that for each 1 percent inflation-adjusted increase in the GDP 375,000 more cars will be sold. Figure 5.4 depicts the actual and fitted annual car sales.

---

[3]When estimating economic relations such as those illustrated in this chapter a "respectable" R^2 is anything in the range of 30 to 60 percent. Anything more than 60 percent is extraordinary. (One of our colleagues has a rule of thumb for regressions in finance: Any R^2 greater than 80 percent is bogus!—there simply aren't any economic relations that can be estimated with this degree of linearity.)

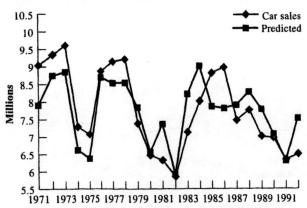

FIGURE 5.4 Auto sales—actual versus predicted.

Data Mining—Being Ex-Post Smart

How did we know that auto sales correlate well with *changes in the GDP*? The answer is that we didn't! Instead, we looked at the data in another way before determining that the same relation was meaningful both economically and statistically. Figure 5.5 shows the data as we first looked at them—the raw data depicted in the graph of annual automobile sales and the *level of the GDP* (in billions of 1987 dollars).

As you can see, the first attempt to correlate auto sales with a measure of economic activity did not go so well: The regression data on car sales versus the GDP doesn't work nearly as well as the previous model:

Regression Output

Constant	10.9560329
Std Err of Y Est	1.07732705
R Squared	0.19387164
No. of Observations	22
Degrees of Freedom	20
X Coefficient(s) −0.82009396	
Std Err of Coef. 0.373932812	

Having failed in this attempt, we reexamined the data and ended up with *changes in the GDP,* as opposed to the *level* of the GDP, as a measure of the economic activity that can explain the volume of car sales. Academic economists snidely refer to such a procedure as *data mining,* but it is done all the time.[4] Instead of sneering at data mining, we prefer to use it judiciously—by using economic reasoning to figure some potential determinants of an industry's activity and selecting

[4]We like to call it "playing with the data," which makes it sound as if you are having fun trying to figure out how things work.

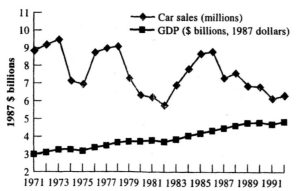

FIGURE 5.5   Auto sales and the GDP, 1971–1992—an exercise in data mining?

the statistical representation of the relation which fit the data best. Hopefully, the best-fitting relation will agree with economic intuition as well. In that case not only will you play with the data, but you may learn something from it too!

Adjusting for Inflation

When estimating the relation between the industry's sales and economic activity, you should use inflation-adjusted figures. Analyses based on current-dollar values—dollars of differing purchasing power—may lead to misleading or spurious results. The problem may arise whenever inflation affects both the dependent variable (such as dollar sales of an industry) and the explanatory variables (such as the GDP). The use of inflation-adjusted figures avoids spurious correlations and allows you to estimate the economically meaningful relations that determine economic activity.

When using inflation-adjusted figures in the analysis of possible relations between the industry's sales and macroeconomic activity, you have to make sure of the end results of your predictions. Specifically, after adjusting all historical figures to *current-year* dollars and relating one variable to another (e.g., using regression techniques), you end up predicting the industry's sales in terms of *current* dollars—dollars of the current year's purchasing power. To arrive at *current-dollar* sales for future years, you should adjust for the expected inflation rates. To illustrate the technique, let's go back to our regression example. In this example car sales figures don't need to be adjusted for inflation as they are in terms of the number of cars, but the GDP figures that we use are in *constant dollars*—dollars of 1987. Regressing the number of cars sold annually on the annual changes in the GDP, we estimated the following relation:

$$\text{Annual car sales} = 6.76\text{MM} + 0.375 \cdot \text{GDP growth (\%)} \qquad R^2 = 58.3\%$$

Suppose the consensus economic predictions are of a 2 percent growth rate for 1993. This means that, based on these projections and the estimated regression relation, we expect that 6.76MM + 0.375 · 2 = 7.51 million cars will be sold in 1993. To translate the expectation for sales of 7.5 million car sales to expected *dollar* sales, we use the average car price. For example, suppose the average car price for 1992 was $11,000. This implies that expected sales of 7.5 million cars is equivalent to a *1992-dollar* sales figure of $82.5 billion. However, we probably don't expect the average car price in 1993 to be the same as the average car price in 1992. Suppose inflation is projected to be 4 percent in 1993. We then may project an average 1993 car price of $11,000 · (1 + 4%) = $11,440 and *1993-dollar* sales of $86.6 billion next year. Obviously, you may think that 1993 car prices will change by more (or less) than the projected inflation rate. In this case you may project the domestic auto industry's sales in 1993 based also on your expected rate of car price changes.

Short-Run Effects of Macroconditions on Industries

Industry dependence on macroconditions is different in different stages of the business cycle. Figure 5.6 presents a typical business cycle and a corresponding cycle in stock prices. The figure depicts the fact that stock prices lead the economic activity. This is because stock values reflect the firm's *future* profitability so that an anticipated change in economic activity, which implies a corresponding change in profits, leads to a *current* change in stock prices. Historically, stock prices have led the economy by about one-half year and have been a most consistent leading economic indicator.

Three points of reference in the economic cycle are marked on the graph: Point 1 denotes the time at which the economy slows down or even enters a recession; point 2 denotes the time at which the economy begins recovering from a slow-down; and point 3 denotes the peak of economic activity. When the economy slows

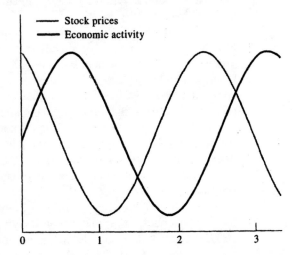

FIGURE 5.6 The three points of reference in the economic cycle: point 1—at the time that the economy slows down, or enters a recession; point 2—at the time that the economy begins to recover; and point 3—at the time of the peak of economic activity.

down, point 1 in the figure, most industries suffer in sales, and consequently profits decline. Some industries, however, do relatively well. These are typically consumer staples industries whose demand is fairly independent of macroeconomic conditions. For these industries the relatively small decline in revenues may be more than offset by lower labor and material costs that are typical of such recessionary periods. (It also turns out that cosmetic goods sell well when the economy turns south. Apparently, people like to look especially good when they are looking for employment.) When the economy begins to pick up momentum, point 2 in the figure, most industries' profit outlook improves and capital investment projects, which have been postponed in the down years, are reinstituted. As a result, capital goods tend to sell well in this period (and, accordingly, profits of manufacturers of capital goods are among the first to recoup when the economy gains momentum). For similar reasons, housing construction picks up so that housing supply product sales also pick up. When the economy is growing at full steam, point 3, all industries do well. The products that sell especially well are luxury goods that are the latest to join the party of increased sales following a downturn in the economy. When you consider macroconditions an estimating an industry's sales, these regularities may help to fine-tune industry's sales projections.

The Composition of the Industry's Sales and Macroeconomic Conditions

In the top-down approach to forecasting the firm's sales you proceed from the projection of the industry's sales to the projection of the firm's sales effectively by forecasting the firm's future market share. We discuss how market shares and the industry's sales are related and projected in the following sections. Prior to the discussion of market shares, however, we need to emphasize that market shares may also depend on macroeconomic conditions, even in industries where total industry demand is relatively independent of economic conditions (such as food and health care).

Firms choose differing marketing strategies, such as product characteristics, pricing, and placement. The different positioning of firms in the same industry implies that, depending on macroeconomic conditions, consumers switch from one brand to another to match the characteristics of their consumption to the desired consumption basket. In particular, when economic conditions are poor, consumers tend to switch from high-quality and high-cost brands to lower-quality and to lower-cost brands. For example, one of the phenomena of the early 1990s' recession was the flourishing of discount outlets, where lower-price substitutes for goods typically bought in department stores can be found, whereas department stores lost sales, some to the point of being forced into bankruptcy. Obviously, a reverse trend is typical of good economic times.

To illustrate this point, we plot in Figure 5.7 the ratio of the annual sales of K-Mart (discount stores) to those of Macy's and the GNP in the years 1988 through 1992. We see in the figure that when economic conditions worsen, as indicated by a decline in the GNP, the market share of K-Mart increases, whereas when eco-

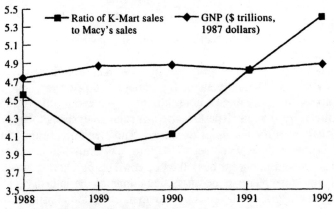

FIGURE 5.7   K-Mart/Macy's sales and the GNP.

nomic conditions improve, the market share of Macy's increases.[5] Although there are many other determinants of market shares, Figure 5.7 illustrates the fact that the positioning of the firm in the marketplace is a key determinant of the variation of its market share as macroeconomic conditions change.

The discussion and the example make it clear that in your projection of the industry's sales you should consider not only the effect of macroeconomic conditions on the *level* of sales but also on its *composition*. In particular, when the economy is expected to get into or remain in a slump, you should expect that producers of low-cost products will increase their market shares while producers of high-cost products will see their market shares decline. You should expect the reverse to happen when the economy flourishes.

5.3 PROJECTING LONG-RUN INDUSTRY SALES

The analysis of the dependence of industries on macroeconomic conditions is useful in forming expectations about the very short-run prospects of industries. This is mostly because macroeconomic conditions can be predicted, at least with any accuracy, only in the short run—at most 1 or 2 years forward. Lacking ability to predict reliably distant economic conditions, you should *assume that macroeconomic conditions will be average in the long run*—neither a slump nor high prosperity. The projection of long-run industry sales, therefore, depends only slightly on macroeconomic conditions. Rather, these projections depend mostly on the industry's fundamentals, which means that we need to understand these fundamentals in order to be able to predict the industry's sales. Since each industry has a different story, we cannot give a recipe "The Best Way to Predict the

[5]What happened in 1991? Why did the GNP improve but K-Mart's sales relative to Macy's improved even more? Macy's filed for Chapter 11. If you are going to get in the prediction business, you will need to have an explanation for everything!

Industry's Sales.'' Instead, we present some general principles and tools that are useful in many projections.

Many predictions of an industry's sales begin by looking for historical patterns, that is, relating the annual industry sales, for example, to prior year sales, to the size of the economy (e.g., number of households), to the age profile of the population, and to the average wage. The first trick in such analyses is to try *to offset the effects of inflation on the variables examined*: The prediction of the industry's sales is more accurately done when separated into real terms—in terms of either the number of units sold in a year or dollars of constant purchasing power—and to an inflation adjustment. This is because predictions of the industry's sales are often driven by an analysis of the consumer demand, and the consumer demand, in the long run, is independent of the price level. The simplest way to see why this must be true is to consider what will happen to the consumer demand for goods and to the industry's sales if existing dollars were to be exchanged for ''new dollars,'' for example, at a rate of five new dollars for each one old dollar. Suddenly, all prices will increase fivefold—a 400 percent change in the price level. Since income and wealth will also suddenly increase fivefold, demand for goods *denominated in real units* will remain the same. The reported sales of all industries and firms, however, will suddenly ''jump'' by 400 percent, commensurate with the change in the price level. Clearly, this ''change'' in sales, which has no fundamental economic reason, is something we don't want to include in an analysis of patterns of sales. Moreover, when inflation affects both the dependent variable and the explanatory variable of a statistical analysis (such as regression analysis), failure to convert all numbers to dollars of equal purchasing power may cause the effects of inflation to mask fundamental economic-driven relations that truly explain sales. Thus, your best bet is to analyze the consumer demand for goods *only after adjusting for the effects of inflation*.

The adjustment of sales for the effect of inflation can be done to dollars of any purchasing power, to dollars of any year. However, since you probably will have the best intuition (and data) for dollars of *current* purchasing power—current dollars—it makes sense to convert all historical sales figures to equivalent sales in terms of *today's* dollars. The conversion of prior years' sales to current-dollar sales is done by using a price index, say, the **consumer price index (CPI)** and the following relation:

$$\text{Sales}_{\text{current dollars}} = \text{Sales}_{\text{original year's dollars}} \cdot \frac{\text{current CPI}}{\text{original year's CPI}}$$

Although the adjustment may seem small and of little importance for low levels of inflation, you have to keep in mind the type of sales analyses that we have in mind—analyses oriented to the prediction of *long-run* industry and firm's sales. This means that we are likely to analyze *long* histories of sales, to analyze *long-term* relations, and to project *long-term* sales prospects. For such long-term relations and predictions, *even under low levels of annual inflation*, the *accumulated* effect of inflation may be significant as even small annual inflation adjustments compound to substantial effects on sales. To illustrate the adjustment method and the magnitude of the effect of inflation, we use the sales figures of J. M. Smucker Inc., the largest U.S. producer of jams and jellies, that are analyzed in detail in Chapter 7. Exhibit 5.2 shows the conversion of Smucker's prior years' sales to constant dollar sales. We begin with the sales figures reported in Smucker's income statements, which are sales in dollars of changing purchasing power, and convert them to sales in terms of 1992 dollars by multiplying by the CPI ratios.

Exhibit 5.2

Adjusting Smucker's Sales for Inflation

Fiscal year (ending April 30)	Sales ($M)	Average CPI in year	Constant dollar sales (1992 $)
1986	262.80	108.57	333.07
1987	288.26	110.62	358.57
1988	314.25	115.18	375.41
1989	366.86	120.25	419.79
1990	422.36	126.12	460.80
1991	454.98	132.97	470.82
1992	483.47	137.60	483.47

Note: Smucker's financial year ends April 30. The CPI in each row of the table is the *average monthly CPI for the year ending April 30.*

The average annual inflation rate in the period was about 4 percent. Yet the accumulated effect on 1986 sales is 27 percent. More importantly, the annual growth rate of Smucker's sales, which judging by Smucker's income statements is 10.8 percent, is only 6.5 percent when the effect of inflation is neutralized. This is an important number to estimate and project, as it may critically affect the *projected* long-term growth rate of Smucker's sales. Obviously, if you use the 6.5 percent average annual growth rate to base the projected growth rate of Smucker, this can only serve as the base for projecting *real* growth rates. To obtain *current-dollar* sales projections, you should inflate the constant-dollar projected sales by the projected inflation rate.

A second trick in projecting industry sales is to "think at the margin": Rather than predict the *level* of the industry's sales, it is often simpler to think in terms of *changes* in the level of sales—or in the growth rate of sales. By doing so, you implicitly recognize an inherent inability to understand fully why the industry's sales levels are what they are. Consequently, you think about and try to predict possible *changes* in the industry's sales levels. In practical terms, this means that the focus of the analysis is on predicting *growth rates* of sales rather than on levels of sales: growth driven by technological changes, by changes in consumer tastes or income, and by changes in competition (within the industry and from substitute products). (Remember that growth can be negative!)

A conceptual tool that is often used in analyzing and predicting the industry's sales is the **product life-cycle model.** This model describes common stages in the life cycle of a consumer product. Figure 5.8 is a graphical presentation of the

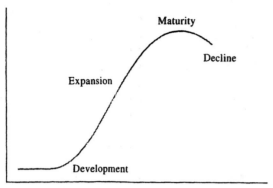

FIGURE 5.8   The product life cycle.

model: On the horizontal axis we plot time delineating the different stages in the life cycle of a product; on the vertical level we plot annual unit sales. The model describes four stages that are typical of consumer products.

- In the first stage the product is being developed and early versions of it are introduced. Consumers are not yet familiar with the product, so sales levels are typically low. The same is true of competition: Since at this stage only a few producers possess the necessary knowledge for production and distribution of the product, there is hardly any competition to consider.
- As the product and its potential gain recognition, the consumer demand increases and the industry enters a stage of rapid expansion. The initial producers of the product, capitalizing on their initial success and presence in an expanding market, generate large profits.
- The high profits of the initial producers attract additional firms to enter the market, which increases competition and reduces profits. Sales continue to expand, although at a much smaller pace, as the industry is now a mature one.
- As consumers become satiated with the product, some industries experience declining sales. Other industries continue to operate at existing levels without further expansion.

A case in point is any generation of personal computers (PCs) that you want to consider. Take, for instance, the 486 generation of IBM-compatible PCs. Soon after Intel's 486 processor became available, PC producers began manufacturing 486-based PCs. Initially, few producers had the necessary know-how, the 486 chip was expensive relative to the 386 chips, and few software vendors had programs that used the full capabilities of the new chip. Hence, few 486-based PCs were sold (relative to the total sales of PCs) and their prices and profit margins were higher than those of other PCs. As the 486 chip became the standard, its cost declined, more software became available, and clone chips were introduced, sales volume picked up substantially while prices and profit margins declined. Finally, Pentium-based machines began replacing the 486-based machines as the industry standard, which reduced the sales volume, prices, and margins of the 486-based PCs.

The example of the 486-based PCs illustrates both the usefulness of the product life-cycle model and its shortcoming. The product life-cycle model is a useful *starting point* for the analysis of the industry's sales. Knowing which stage of its life cycle the industry's product is in, we can reasonably accurately predict what will happen in future stages. The problem in implementing the model, however, is that *most industries are not single product industries.* Rather, most industries produce a multitude of products, the nature of which may change over time but not necessarily change the nature of the industry as a whole. The PC industry is a case in point. The product life-cycle theory may well describe the sales of any *generation* of PCs—the 8086, 286, 386, 486, or Pentium-based machines: Introduction, when few and expensive PCs use the newly introduced processor; rapid growth, when all PC producers introduce models that use the new processor; and maturity and eventual decline, when the processor is replaced by the next generation. Yet the PC industry as a whole merely changes the platform on which it builds the machines: While the machines become faster and more powerful, the nature of the business—designing, producing, marketing, and servicing the latest-generation PC at the lowest possible cost—remains essentially the same over many product generations.

Another example of a product life cycle is illustrated in Figure 5.9. This graph

FIGURE 5.9 The life cycles for dynamic random access memory (DRAM) chips of different sizes—the 1-megabit (mb) chip is on the declining portion of its life cycle; the 4-mb chip is at maturity; the 16-mb chip is in its expansion phase; and the 64-mb chip is still in its developmental stage. (*Source: The Economist,* August 26, 1995.)

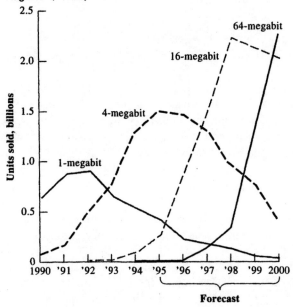

shows life cycles for dynamic random access memory (DRAM) chips of different sizes.

A similar example to that of the PC industry is the music business where the medium has changed from 45-rpm long-play records, to 33-rpm vinyl records, to audio cassettes, to CDs. Yet the business of producing and selling music has remained essentially the same, with the necessary technical adaptation. In some industries, such as the fashion industry, product cycles may be even faster than the prior two examples. Should we conclude that the fashion industry's sales will decline when the current mode will no longer be in vogue? Thus, when using the product life-cycle model, do so with care.

Despite its limitation, the product life-cycle model corresponds to an economically sound and empirically documented phenomena: When an industry generates high profits, it attracts new entrants; these new entrants cause prices and profit margins to decline. An opposite phenomenon occurs in industries where profit margins are too low: In such industries companies are being bought by competitors or get out of business via bankruptcies. (Recent examples of such consolidations driven by excess capacity and too low profits include the air transportation business, department stores, and the banking industry.) The consolidation of such industries reduces competition and restores profitability to normal levels. The two phenomena are, in fact, two facets of the same thing—**regression toward the mean.** In the context of predicting the industry's sales and profit margins regression toward the mean implies that, in the long run, the industry's profits tend to revert to normal levels—levels that are commensurate with the industry's risks. You should take into account this phenomenon in projecting long-term market shares and profit margins.

5.4 COMPETITION ANALYSIS AND THE PROJECTION OF THE FIRM'S SALES

Once you understand the prospects of the industry, it is fairly easy to translate these projections to projections about the prospects of the firm you value. This is because market shares of firms are typically slow to change. Therefore, knowing the current market share of the firm and the industry's projected sales allows you to obtain an initial estimate of the firm's sales potential:

Projected firm sales = projected industry sales · projected market share

Obviously, the current market share is only the starting point for the analysis: You should estimate *changes* in the market share that reflect your perception of the strong and weak points of the firm you value.

It will be presumptuous on our part to try to summarize a whole set of market-share theories and models in one section. Yet some things are worth stressing. First, as in the case of predicting the industry's sales, it is often simpler to think in terms of *changes* rather than in terms of *absolute values*. In the context of predicting the firm's sales, marginal thinking means that, based on the marketing strategy of the firm, you analyze and project *changes* in market shares. Changes in market shares are driven by recent and expected:

- Changes in consumer tastes
- Entry or exit of firms from the industry
- Relative strengths and weaknesses of firms in the industry
- Shifts in demand that are driven by economic conditions at large
- Marketing strategies of the firms in the industry

Marketing models of market shares can be grouped into those models that stress consumer attitudes toward products and those that stress sellers' efforts and characteristics. In the first type of models the emphasis is on modeling consumer choice and in the second the emphasis is on modeling marketing efforts and their effects. Consider, for example, a market-response model similar to the model presented in Kotler (1984).[6] In this model M_i denotes the marketing efforts of firm i and *market shares are assumed to be proportional to the firm's marketing efforts.* A little algebraic manipulation shows that the proportionality assumption implies that the market share of firm i, denoted by λ_i, equals

$$\lambda_i = \frac{M_i}{\sum_{j=1}^{N} M_j}$$

where N is the number of firms in the industry and ΣM_i denotes the sum of the marketing efforts of the firms in the industry. A variant of this model allows for marketing efforts that are of differing efficiency. Let κ_i denote the relative efficiency of the marketing efforts of firm i. Then the preceding market-share equation should be only slightly modified:

$$\lambda_i = \frac{\kappa_i \cdot M_i}{\sum_{j=1}^{N} \kappa_j \cdot M_j}$$

For the purpose of predicting *future* market shares, an important implication of this model (and of several variants of it) is that *the percentage change in a firm's market share is proportional to the percentage change in its marketing efforts*:

$$\frac{\Delta \lambda_i}{\lambda_i} \propto \frac{\Delta M_i}{M_i}$$

($\propto$ means "proportional to.") This observation has two important implications for the prediction of the firm's sales:

[6]P. Kotler, *Marketing Managements: Analysis, Planning, and Control*, 5th ed., Prentice-Hall, Englewood Cliffs, N.J., 1984.

- Recent changes in marketing efforts of firms imply similar imminent changes in market shares.
- To project future changes in market shares, we should project the marketing strategies of the firms in the industry, of both current players and the potential entrant.

The focus on changes in market shares reflects marginal analysis—the analysis that focuses on marginal effects rather than on predicting levels. It also is a practical way to reflect our prior analysis of the firm's environment, both economywide and industry specific, in the projection of the firm's sales: There is an intuitive and simple relation among projected changes in market shares, projected growth of the industry, and projected changes in the sales of individual firms:

$$(1 + \text{growth of firm sales}) = (1 + \text{growth of industry sales})$$
$$\cdot (1 + \text{fractional change of market share})$$

For example, suppose you project that sales of the XYZ industry will grow at the fast rate of 20 percent next year. As a result of the fast growth rate of the industry, new firms (for which the factories are currently being built) will start producing next year. You estimate that this added competition and production capacity will reduce the market share of the firm you value from 8 percent to 7 percent. These two estimates jointly imply that you project that the sales of the firm next year will grow at the rate of 5 percent over this year's sales:

$$1 + \text{growth} = (1 + 20\%) \left[1 + \left(\frac{7\% - 8\%}{8\%} \right) \right] = 1 + 5\%$$

The starting point for many projections of the firm's sales is often an analysis of prior years' sales growth. Like the analysis of industry sales, it is desirable to separate growth into *unit* sales growth and changes in unit *price*. There are two reasons for this separation. First, prices and quantities often move in different directions. Accordingly, marketing strategies are designed to optimally exploit this trade-off.[7] This means that in order to predict the future sales of firms in a way that reflects the expected marketing strategies of the firm and its competitors, one must consider separately the two components of dollar sales. The second reason for the separation is that typically production costs are tied to *unit* sales, not to *dollar* sales. Therefore, to predict firm profitability better, we need to be able to measure volume in the same units that we use to estimate costs.

The need to estimate unit sales and price changes separately is problematic to outsiders who are evaluating firms, such as stock analysts and M&A specialists, who often are not privy to information about the firm's unit sales and unit prices. When such analysts look at prior years' sales and try to decompose them into unit

---

[7]Recall the four Ps of marketing strategy: *product, price, promotion,* and *place.*

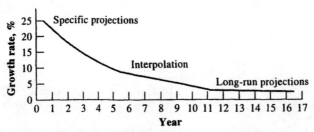

FIGURE 5.10   The three stages in growth projections.

sales growth and price changes, they must *estimate* the appropriate decomposition. One way to do this is to deflate reported sales, which are in terms of current dollars, by a price index. The preferred price index to use is the industry's price index. If no industry-specific index exists, a general price index, such as the CPI, will do. The example of adjusting Smucker's sales given in Section 5.3 is a case in point.

In predicting the firm's sales growth, we often use a **three-stage growth model.** In this model we make three types of growth projections for the short, medium, and long run. In the short run, given that we typically have a good understanding of the industry and the firm's relative position in the industry, we make specific projections on an annual basis. In the long run, given the tendency of industries' and firms' profits to regress toward the mean, we project that the firm's sales will grow at the long-run growth rate of the economy. In the intermediate run we interpolate between the latest specific projection we made for the short-run and the long-run growth prospects. Figure 5.10 describes a typical three-stage growth model. We see three distinct periods here:

• In the first 6 years we estimate specific growth rates that decline from 25 percent in the first year to 10 percent in the sixth year.

• After the first 12 years we estimate that the firm (and the industry) will enter a steady-state growth of 3 percent per annum.

• Between years 6 and 12 we interpolate the growth rates down from 10 percent to 3 percent at equal steps.

The three-stage model entails making specific growth projections in the first years, making long-run growth projections, *and specifying the periods to which these rates are applicable*; or in other words, specifying the transition years—from the short-run identifiable firm-specific prospects to the intermediate regression-toward-the-mean period to the long-run period.

SUMMARY

In this chapter we reviewed several models and techniques that are used to predict the industry's and the firm's sales. The overall approach of predicting the firm's sales is top-down:

- Begin with an analysis and prediction of macroeconomic conditions.
- Proceed with an analysis and prediction of the industry's prospects in the context of the expected macroconditions.
- Culminate with an analysis and prediction of firm-specific sales that reflect the projected industry's sales and composition.

The three levels of analysis are typically carried out by separate groups of people: The macroanalysis is typically the domain of macroeconomists, whereas analysts and corporate specialists focus on the industry-level and firm-specific parts of the process.

The macrolevel analysis is the most problematic part: We know that macroeconomic activity is cyclical, yet there is little theory to explain this cyclicality. Consequently, macroeconomists rely on empirical regularities and leading indicators of economic activity to predict trends in macroeconomic activity *in the short run*. In fact, since valuations require the prediction of the firm's performance over several years, specific macroeconomic predictions are useful only in the *very* short run—typically 1 to 2 years ahead. For longer prediction horizons we simply assume that macroeconomic activity will be average—neither a boom nor a bust.

In converting the short-run macropredictions into industry-specific predictions, we want to take into account the effects of these conditions on both the *level* of the industry's sales and its *composition*: Industries respond differently to changing macroconditions, and the within-industry composition of sales depends on macroconditions.

In the analysis of sales (as well as many other valuation-related issues) we prefer *to think at the margin*. In the context of analyzing and predicting industry and the firm's sales this means that we prefer to think of *changes* in sales—the *growth rates* of sales—instead of analyzing and predicting the *level* of sales. The underlying reasoning is that we cannot fully understand how industry sales are determined and we have a better chance to understand *changes* in consumer preferences, budgets, costs, and competition as determinants of *changes* in sales.

Another element in the analysis of growth rates of sales is the separation of growth into *real growth*—growth in unit sales—and *inflation effects*—the effect of changing the purchasing power of money on unit prices. Economic activity— consumer demand and producer supplies—primarily reflects *real* not *nominal* factors. Hence, to be able to analyze the industry's sales and its determinants meaningfully, we should think in real terms. We do so by translating prior years' figures into equivalent figures in terms of dollars of current purchasing power. For example, to translate sales of prior years to current-dollar equivalent sales, we can use the CPI and the following relation:

$$\text{Sales}_{\text{current dollars}} = \text{Sales}_{\text{original year's dollars}} \cdot \frac{\text{current CPI}}{\text{original year's CPI}}$$

To convert predictions of the *industry's* sales growth to consistent predictions of the *individual firm's* sales, we need to think of the firm's current and future

140

market shares. We can project the firm's sales by directly projecting market shares and multiplying the projected market shares by the projected industry's sales or, once more, think at the margin: Relate the industry's sales growth to the firm's sales growth via projected *changes* in market shares:

$$(1 + \text{growth of firm sales}) = (1 + \text{growth of industry sales})$$
$$\cdot (1 + \text{fractional change of market share})$$

Market shares of mature industries are slow to change, especially in industries where brand loyalty is commonplace (such as food stuff and health products). This suggests that in mature industries the sales growth of individual firms are not expected to differ materially from the industry's expected growth rate. On the other hand, when market-share changes are expected, you can use marketing models of market shares to try to predict market-share changes. A common thread in several such models is the prediction that changes in market shares are proportional to changes in marketing efforts of the firms in the industry. This result can help to predict changes in market shares in particular short-run changes in shares that can be traced to recent changes in marketing efforts.

A common paradigm in which the firm's sales are projected is the *three-stage model.* In this model we make three types of growth:

• In the short run, given that we typically have a good understanding of the industry and the firm's relative position in the industry, we make specific projections on an annual basis.

• In the long run, given the tendency of the profits of industries and firms to regress toward the mean, we project that the firm's sales will grow at the long-run growth rate of the economy.

• In the intermediate run, we interpolate between the latest specific projection we made for the short-run and the long-run growth prospects.

The three-stage model entails making specific growth projections in the first years, making long-run growth projections, *and specifying the periods to which these rates are applicable*; or in other words, specifying the transition years—from the short-run identifiable firm-specific prospects to the intermediate regression-toward-the-means period to the long-run period.

EXERCISES

5.1 Consider the relation between annual car sales and the annual GDP growth estimated in the Section 5.2.

   a If you expect the relation to continue to hold and that GDP growth rates for 1997, 1998, and 1999 will be 2, 3, and 2 percent, respectively, how many cars do you expect the industry to sell in each of these years?

   b Suppose in 1996 the average car sold for $15,000 and inflation is expected to be 3 percent per year in each of the following 3 years. What are the expected dollar sales of the industry? What are the expected sales in dollars of constant value—say, of 1996?

c Suppose the market share of *foreign* car manufacturers is expected to increase in 1997 to 50 percent from the 40 percent share it was in 1996. What do you expect the *domestic* producers to sell in 1997?

5.2 Assume that the widget industry has only four manufacturers—A, B, C, and D—whose market shares in 1997 are 35, 30, 25, and 10 percent, respectively. Further, assume that marketing expenses are the only determinants of market shares.

a Suppose in 1998 manufacturer A plans to increase its marketing expenses by 20 percent and, following this change, B, C, and D will also increase their marketing expenses but only by 10 percent. What are the expected market shares of A, B, C, and D in 1996?

b Suppose the total industry's sales in 1997 ("the market") were $600 million and marketing expenses in 1997 were 5 percent of sales. Suppose now, instead of increasing its marketing expenses by 20 percent, A plans to reduce its unit prices by 2 percent in 1998. The other producers in the industry are not expected to lower their unit prices in response. What effect do you expect this change to have on the market shares of A, B, C, and D? (*Hint:* Think of the price reduction as another form of marketing expense, say, a coupon.)

5.3 Suppose you expect the sales of the ABC Co. to grow at the rates of 12, 9, and 7 percent in 1997, 1998, and 1999, respectively. You also expect that ABC's industry will be in a steady state with a constant long-term growth rate of 2 percent from the year 2001 and onward. If ABC's sales in 1996 were $240 million, what can you reasonably expect ABC's sales to be in the years 1997 through 2005?

"J.M. Smucker - Projecting Financial Performance"
Simon Z. Benninga and Oded H. Sarig

7.1 A SHORT DESCRIPTION OF SMUCKER

The J. M. Smucker Company, based in Orrville, Ohio, is the leading producer of jams, preserves, and jellies in the United States. The company was founded in 1897, and to this day the firm is actively managed by the Smucker family, which owns about 30 percent of the shares. Brand names of the company include Smucker's, Knudsen Family, Dickenson's, and Simply Fruit.

Smucker's hallmarks are its commitment to product quality and its conservative financial policies. The company has a negligible amount of debt in its capital structure.

Although over 90 percent of the company's 1992 sales were domestic, Smucker has made an increasing commitment to expanding its international sales. The company's main marketing efforts outside the United States are concentrated in the United Kingdom, Australia, and Canada.

7.2 SALES PROJECTION

Smucker sells food products both in the United States and abroad—Australia, Canada, and the United Kingdom. Since Smucker is an established brand name in the United States while it is still in the process of penetrating the international arena, we project Smucker's domestic and international sales separately. Although at the date of this analysis, the end of 1992, the company is expanding its international operations, these still constitute less than 10 percent of its total sales.

Smucker's products, jellies and jams, enjoy a relatively stable market. This is a mature industry where relatively few innovative products emerge. The stable demand is coupled with an established technology to produce jellies and jams. These two factors suggest that the prices of Smucker's products rise roughly at the rate of inflation. A food-industry analyst following Smucker would check this prediction by examining the actual prices of Smucker's products over time and by comparing them to the rate of inflation. Since this is just an illustrative example, we take this prediction as correct without further verifying its validity.

Under the assumption that the price of Smucker's goods appreciates at the rate of inflation we can estimate the *constant-dollar* sales of Smucker by adjusting the reported annual sales to changes in the consumer price index (CPI). This is not quite as accurate as knowing the actual tonnage of jellies and jams that are shipped each year, but it is a close enough estimate. In Exhibit 7.1 we show the conversion of the Sales of Smucker as reported in its financial statements for the years 1986 through 1992 to Sales figures expressed in 1992 dollars.

Exhibit 7.1

J. M. SMUCKER CO.
Adjusting Sales for Inflation

Fiscal year ending April 30	Sales ($M)	Average CPI	Constant-dollar sales
1986	262.80	108.57	333.07
1987	288.26	110.62	358.57
1988	314.25	115.18	375.41
1989	366.86	120.25	419.79
1990	422.36	126.12	460.80
1991	454.98	132.97	470.82
1992	483.47	137.60	483.47

Note: Smucker's fiscal year ends April 30. The consumer price index (CPI) in each row of the table is the average monthly CPI for the year ending April 30.

The adjustment of Sales for the inflation of a single year makes only a small difference. The cumulative effect of adjusting for inflation over many years, however, can be substantial. To illustrate this, in Figure 7.1 we plot the annual Sales figures as they were originally reported in the financial statements of 1986 through 1992, in *current dollars,* and adjusted for the different purchasing power of dollars in these years, in terms of *constant dollars* (specifically, 1992 dollars).[1]

[1]Since Smucker's fiscal year ends April 30, references to years refer to the fiscal year ending on April 30. Thus, for example, "1992" refers to Smucker's fiscal year ending April 30, 1992.

FIGURE 7.1   Smucker's Sales in current and constant dollars.

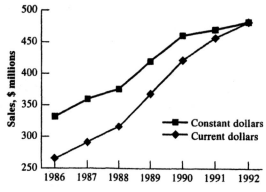

We can calculate compound growth rates of Sales for the 1986 through 1992 period by taking the

$$\text{Compound growth rate} = \left[\frac{1992 \text{ Sales}}{1986 \text{ Sales}} \right]^{1/6} - 1$$

There is a substantial difference between the inflation-unadjusted (i.e., nominal) annual Sales growth of 10.69 percent and the inflation-adjusted (i.e., real) growth of 6.41 percent. Although Sales growth driven by changes in the price level should be accounted for in valuations, it is not a growth that is due to the firm's efforts, and therefore should be considered separately from sales growth driven by further market penetration, market expansion, and the like. If inflation rates of the past are expected to prevail in the future, it will make no difference whether we analyze current-dollar or constant-dollar Sales figures. Typically, this is not the case, and thus it makes better economic sense to consider separately the growth in real Sales and the increase in Sales due to the adjustment of prices for changes in the purchasing power of money.

Smucker's products are consumer staples, that is, basic goods, of which the consumption varies only slightly with economic conditions. We don't expect, for example, people to say, "Since this year I earn less money than I usually do, I'll eat less" or, perhaps more importantly for predicting Smucker's sales, "I'll make my kids eat less this year." Thus, in the long run we expect Smucker's U.S. sales to grow with the growth of the U.S. population. This means that as a first pass at predicting Smucker's sales we should see how past sales in the United States are related to the size of the U.S. population. In Figure 7.2 we present Smucker's sales, restated to 1992 dollars, against the number of U.S. households.

As is evident from Figure 7.2, Smucker's sales are highly correlated with the size of the U.S. population. Calculating the ratio of sales to the number of households, we see that the average household consumed $4.47 of Smucker's products

FIGURE 7.2   Smucker's Sales versus the number of U.S. households, 1986–1992.

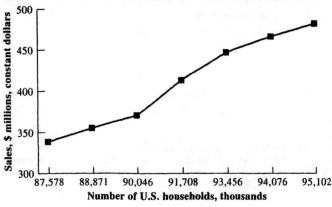

145

per annum. Regressing the percentage change in real sales on the percentage change in the number of households for the last 6 years gives

% change in real Sales

$$= -0.0087 + 5.1284 \cdot \text{\% change in households}, \qquad R^2 = 0.5865$$

As might be expected, the y-intercept of -0.0087 is not statistically significantly different from zero, and the coefficient of the percent change in households is highly significant. Thus, extrapolating the trend from data for the last 6 years leads us to conclude that a 1 percent increase in the number of U.S. households will lead to an approximate 5 percent change in Smucker's real sales. We will use this 5 percent figure to estimate *short-term growth prospects for domestic Smucker's sales.* Estimating the growth in the number of U.S. households at 1.4 percent (its average growth over the preceding 5 years) gives 7 percent as the short-term real growth of Smucker's sales.[2]

What about the longer run? It is unreasonable to expect that in the long run Smucker's sales will continue to grow 5 times faster than the number of households. At this rate Smucker would soon capture the whole U.S. jam and jelly market! In the long run it is more reasonable to expect that the increase in Smucker's sales will roughly parallel the increase in U.S. household formation. Thus, we expect that *Smucker's long-run real sales growth will be 1.4 percent.*

In estimating the long-run growth rate of Smucker's sales on the basis of the growth in the population, we implicitly make two assumptions:

- Future per-capita consumption of jams and jellies will remain the same as it was in the past few years.
- Smucker's share of the jam and jelly market will remain the same as it was in the past few years.

These are assumptions that we should examine carefully. Specifically, to go beyond the basic projection of annual sales growth of 1.4 percent per year, we need to consider trends in food consumption and in the strengths and weaknesses of Smucker relative to its competitors as determinants of Smucker's market share. Probably the most noteworthy recent trend in food consumption is toward low-fat, low-sugar "healthier" foods and ingredients. On the one hand, this suggests a decline in the overall consumption of jams and jellies. On the other hand, Smucker's high-quality product probably makes Smucker more likely to benefit from this trend than low-cost competitors in the industry. The recent increase in Smucker's market share and the management discussion of this point in its 1992 financial statements suggest this is a change that is already taking place. Moreover, the emergence of the U.S. economy from a recession may further benefit Smucker as

[2]Students often feel that the R^2 of 58.65 percent of the regression is low; we, on the other hand, think this is a very reasonable number: It says that about 60 percent of Smucker's sales growth variability is attributable to household formation. The rest, presumably, has to do with factors that depend on the company and its competitors—advertising, product mix, and so on.

the high-quality, high-price producer of jellies and jams at the expense of the lower-quality, lower-cost producers. This is because as personal income growth returns to normal (i.e., nonrecession) levels, families that switched to low-cost substitutes will resume buying Smucker's more costly but higher-quality products. For this reason we expect Smucker's short-term Sales growth to be higher than its basic, longer-term Sales growth.

The upshot of these considerations is that we may expect Smucker's U.S. sales to grow at 7 percent in 1993 and 1994 and to revert to a long-term growth rate of 1.4 percent per year from, say, 1996. Interpolating the growth rates of 7 percent in 1994 and 1.4 percent in 1996, we arrive at a projected intermediate growth rate of 4 percent for 1995.

Smucker is attempting to penetrate international markets. Its international sales increased by more than 20 percent in 1990 but increased barely 3 percent in 1992. For illustration purposes we project that Smucker will be able to attain faster growth rates internationally than it has in 1992 but not as high a growth as that achieved in 1991. Specifically, we project a 10 percent annual growth in Smucker's international sales in the years 1993 through 1995. From 1997 onward we expect Smucker's international Sales to grow no faster than its domestic sales, that is, at the annual rate of 1.4 percent. In 1996 we interpolate the growth rate to 6 percent.[3]

Using the projected growth rates and levels of domestic and international sales in 1992, we can project Smucker's Sales in the fiscal years 1993 through 1997. Exhibit 7.2 provides the detailed calculation of the projected Sales.

[3]Obviously, a more realistic analysis of Smucker requires a more detailed analysis of its sales' prospects. Since our intention in this chapter is to illustrate the techniques with a *reasonable* number, we consider past values and gross trends in establishing the projected sales growth rates.

Exhibit 7.2

J. M. SMUCKER CO.
Projected Real Growth, 1993–1997

	Year					
	1992 (base)	1993	1994	1995	1996	1997
U.S. real growth rate		7%	7%	4%	1.4%	1.4%
U.S. Sales (in $ millions)	$442.88	$473.88	$507.05	$528.35	$535.75	$543.25
International real growth rate		10%	10%	10%	6%	1.4%
International Sales	$ 40.59	$ 44.65	$ 49.11	$ 54.03	$ 57.27	$ 58.07
Constant-dollar Sales	483.47	518.53	556.17	582.37	593.01	601.32
Projected real Sales growth		7.25%	7.26%	4.71%	1.83%	1.40%

The projected Sales in Exhibit 7.2 are in terms of *1992 dollars*. These projections will be enough if you plan to project *real* cash flows and discount them at a *real* discount rate. If, on the other hand, you prefer to do *nominal* projections, as we do here, *the constant-dollar projections should be converted to current-dollar projections by using the projected inflation rate.* Macroeconomists project that U.S. inflation will be moderate in 1993—roughly 3 percent. For future years it is not clear whether the picture is equally rosy on U.S. inflation prospects: The economies of many developed countries are likely to recover from the long-lasting downturn and with it inflation is more likely to increase. Thus, we use a rate of 4 percent inflation for the years 1994 and onward. By using these projected inflation rates, we can convert the constant-dollar Sales projections to current-dollar Sales projections. Exhibit 7.3 demonstrates how this is done.

Exhibit 7.3

J. M. SMUCKER CO.
Projected Nominal Sales, 1993–1997

	Year					
	1992	1993	1994	1995	1996	1997
Constant-dollar Sales	$483.47	$518.53	$556.17	$582.37	$593.01	$601.32
Annual inflation rate		3%	4%	4%	4%	4%
Cumulative adjustment factor	1.00	1.0300	1.0712	1.1140	1.1586	1.2050
Current-dollar (nominal) Sales	$483.47	$534.09	$595.77	$648.79	$687.07	$724.56
Projected nominal Sales growth		10.47%	11.55%	8.90%	5.90%	5.46%

Note: Sales in $ millions.

7.3 RATIO ANALYSIS

Given the projected Sales of Smucker in the next 5 years, we can turn to the estimation of Smucker's financial performance. Toward that end, we analyze the *past* performance of Smucker relative to past sales. The discussion in this section refers to the financial statements of Smucker in the years 1986 through 1992, which are given in Exhibit 7.4.

It is important to note that Smucker has gone through a rather rapid expansion during the period analyzed. Some of this expansion was achieved by acquiring firms with related business. A full ratio analysis should explicitly examine whether Smucker's ratios before and after the acquisitions remain the same. If the ratios prior to the acquisitions differ from the postacquisition ratios, only the postacquisition ratios should be used to predict the performance of Smucker in future years. Since ours is only an illustrative example, we don't perform a full analysis of this issue but, rather, consider it only when relevant.

Exhibit 7.4

J. M. SMUCKER CO.
Financial Statements, 1986–1992

	Year ending April 30*						
	1986	1987	1988	1989	1990	1991	1992
Assets (in $ thousands)							
Cash and Cash Equivalents	$ 18,095	$ 25,227	$ 27,111	$ 36,652	$ 18,402	$ 24,513	$ 36,268
Trade Receivables, Net	21,096	26,192	24,799	29,640	35,591	42,328	41,565
Finished Goods	12,923	13,122	17,885	19,856	22,775	27,791	34,604
Raw Materials, Containers, and Supplies	25,683	29,824	29,115	27,324	38,720	38,740	43,173
Other Current Assets	2,125	2,096	2,937	4,657	4,459	7,664	5,961
Land and Land Improvements	4,569	4,802	5,190	7,095	9,475	10,473	11,985
Buildings and Fixtures	24,853	25,658	32,157	34,960	41,818	45,233	47,191
Machinery and Equipment	34,817	39,324	47,670	58,039	67,908	78,893	88,781
Construction in Progress	1,221	5,129	3,019	2,390	2,967	2,123	2,922
Accumulated Depreciation	(22,805)	(28,597)	(34,053)	(40,570)	(46,750)	(53,813)	(62,556)
Intangible Assets	8,533	8,145	11,594	14,011	23,459	22,460	20,961
Amounts Due from ESOP†	5,092	5,012	4,922	8,807	8,815	9,876	11,103
Other Assets	1,064	1,950	2,601	4,403	6,016	6,024	6,913
Total Assets	$137,266	$157,884	$174,947	$207,264	$233,655	$262,305	$288,871

*Smucker's fiscal year ends April 30. Thus, "1986" refers to figures for the fiscal year ending April 30, 1986, and so on.
† "Amounts Due from ESOP" refers to loans that Smucker makes to its employees to finance their purchase of equity as part of an employee stock ownership plan (ESOP).

Th : ESOP purchases shares in Smucker, financing these purchases with loans it receives from the company itself (loans that subsequently appear on the Balance Sheet of Smucker as an asset). From the point of view of a financial analysis these loans are more properly subtracted from Smucker's Equity. In our projections (the pro-forma model at the end of this chapter), we will ignore these loans; we do this by subtracting the ESOP loans from the Assets and the Equity accounts.

149

Exhibit 7.4 continued

J. M. SMUCKER CO.
Financial Statements, 1986–1992

				Year ending April 30			
	1986	1987	1988	1989	1990	1991	1992
			Liabilities (in $ thousands)				
Accounts Payable	$ 19,145	$ 23,341	$ 23,517	$ 18,368	$ 21,992	$ 24,819	$ 28,363
Salaries, Wages, and Additional Compensation	4,418	4,808	5,239	5,922	6,741	7,405	7,934
Accrued Marketing and Merchandising	0	0	0	9,524	6,680	7,121	6,444
Income Taxes Payable	1,934	3,638	4,581	1,357	2,624	3,795	2,249
Dividends Payable	1,100	1,323	1,620	1,913	2,511	2,806	3,101
Current Portion of Long-Term Debt	1,666	2,503	667	0	0	0	0
Other Current Liabilities	0	0	0	4,772	5,194	4,083	5,469
Long-Term Debt	4,503	4,150	3,081	4,954	4,277	4,267	3,827
Deferred Federal Income Taxes	0	4,067	4,254	5,641	6,150	6,374	6,692
Other Liabilities	4,940	1,496	1,744	1,470	1,546	1,536	1,474
Class A Common	3,670	3,675	3,681	3,678	3,692	3,692	3,692
Class B Common	0	0	0	0	0	0	3,692
Additional Capital	3,385	4,408	5,746	7,733	10,158	10,544	7,034
Retained Income	93,340	105,946	122,797	143,383	165,436	186,919	209,586
Less: Deferred Compensation	(835)	(1,471)	(1,980)	(1,017)	(2,818)	(1,728)	(947)
Currency Translation Adjustment	0	0	0	(434)	(528)	672	261
Total Liabilities and Shareholder Equity	$137,266	$157,884	$174,947	$207,264	$233,655	$262,305	$288,871

Exhibit 7.4 continued

J. M. SMUCKER CO.
Financial Statements, 1986–1992

					Year ending April 30		
	1986	1987	1988	1989	1990	1991	1992
			Annual Income Statement (in $ thousands)				
Net Sales	$262,802	$288,263	$314,245	$366,855	$422,357	$454,976	$483,472
Cost of Goods Sold (COGS)	(175,735)	(192,169)	(206,144)	(240,227)	(281,450)	(295,681)	(314,133)
Gross Profit	87,067	96,094	108,101	126,628	140,907	159,295	169,339
Selling, General, and Administrative Expenses (SG&A)	(58,063)	(62,032)	(70,529)	(83,907)	(91,908)	(107,750)	(114,888)
Operating Income	29,004	34,062	37,572	42,721	48,999	51,545	54,451
Interest Income	1,729	993	1,360	2,048	1,969	1,280	1,510
Other Income, Net	574	273	85	234	62	544	568
Total	$ 31,307	$ 35,328	$ 39,017	$ 45,003	$ 51,030	$ 53,369	$ 56,529
Interest Expense	$ (1,238)	$ (598)	$ (425)	$ (421)	$ (1,086)	$ (788)	$ (446)
Income before Income Taxes	30,069	34,730	38,592	44,582	49,944	52,581	56,083
Federal Currently Payable	11,328	14,520	14,332	14,265	16,057	18,402	18,236
Federal Deferred Taxes	1,087	608	(918)	708	690	(692)	434
State and Local	1,794	1,923	2,308	2,054	3,020	3,127	3,295
Net Income	15,860	17,679	22,870	27,555	30,177	31,744	34,118
Dividend					(8,112)	(10,267)	(11,451)
Change in Retained Earnings	$ 15,860	$ 17,679	$ 22,870	$ 27,555	$ 22,065	$ 21,477	$ 22,667

151

Security Analysis: How to Analyze Accounting and Market Data to Value Securities

Robert W. Holthausen and Mark E. Zmijewski

Chapter 6

Analyzing Financial Statement Relations

1. **Reasons for Analyzing Financial Statement Relations (Ratio Analysis).**

   There are a variety of reasons that financial statements are analyzed.

   A.   Financial analysts use financial statement relations to evaluate internal strategic planning or to identify inefficient managements, to assess whether a firm is operating in a manner similar to other firms which are its direct competitors and also to assess whether there have been any changes in the firm's operations over time. Though financial statement relations need not directly indicate that a firm operations have improved or worsened, they help identify areas where additional investigation is appropriate. Financial statement relations are used as an aid in economic decisions.

   B.   Financial ratios are used in a variety of decision contexts as one input to be considered. Ratios are used in bank credit analysis, in rating decisions made by bond rating agencies, in valuation exercises by equity analysts, and by auditors in setting the scope of their engagements.

   C.   Financial statement relations play an important role in contracts to restrict and monitor managers' actions, or to compensate managers for performance. Financial statement relations are used in compensation contracts, which provide the incentives for managers to perform, and in bond indenture agreements which limit the actions that the firm can take.

   D.   In a valuation setting, there are three primary uses of analyzing financial statements:

      (1)   Used to gain a general understanding of the firm and the industry, and to determine the firm's position within the industry. Financial relations can provide insights into the key drivers of the business.

      (2)   Used in the forecasting of financial statements which leads to forecasts of future free cash flows. Forecasts are typically generated by first identifying one or more key factors and then driving the forecasts of the financial statements from those key factors. Examination of the firm's history of interrelations between various financial statement items aids in forecasting the firm's statements.

      In addition, a variety of financial statement relations provide information about the likely validity (or at least internal consistency) of our forecasts.

Security Analysis: How to Analyze Accounting and Market Data to Value Securities
   Robert W. Holthausen and Mark E. Zmijewski
   \C0693A.W51

Do not reproduce without permission.
July 29, 1998 - 2:45 pm

153

(3) Another area where financial statement relations are important in a valuation context is the identification of "comparable firms." Necessary for using price-multiple valuation techniques and estimating the firm's cost of capital.

2. Choosing Comparable Firms for Price Multiple Work (Chapter 9).

A. Note, to implement the P/E, or other price multiple methods, it is important to identify firms that are comparable along the dimensions that affect the magnitude of the price multiple. For the P/E valuation approach, the following list indicates factors important to consider when identifying comparable firms.

(1) Differences in growth Rates.
(2) Differences in the time profile of earnings (growth rates not constant over time).
(3) Differences in risk (financial and business).
(4) Differences in reinvestment requirements.
(5) Differences in return on investments.
(6) Differences in the "Quality" or sustainability of earnings.
(7) Different accounting techniques.
(8) Under performing/idle assets.

B. Other price multiples may require you to consider different factors when identifying comparable firms.

C. The key is that when choosing the set of comparable companies to estimate the multiple, one must attempt to construct a set of firms where the factors that drive cross-sectional variation in multiples is similar between the firm being valued and the comparable firms. Thus, it would be important that growth, risk, reinvestment etc., be the same for the firm being valued and the set of comparable companies.

3. Equity Cost of Capital Estimates Based on Industry Comparables (Chapter 10).

Individual firms betas are much less precise than portfolio betas (consider the plot previously shown in Chapter 3 where the standard error of beta for one security is on average 0.22 and the standard error for a portfolio of 15 securities is on average 0.07). This translates into 95% confidence intervals that are approximately equivalent to the point estimate +/- 0.44 or +/- 0.14 (this assumes that one has estimated beta with 60 observations). For example, using these standard errors, a point estimate for beta of 1.00 has either a 95% confidence interval of 0.56 to 1.44 or 0.86 to 1.14.

Industry portfolio betas are potentially more accurate assessments of an individual firm's beta because of the greater precision in estimation. Thus, even if a firm has data available publicly you may still want to use a portfolio of firms for estimation purposes. If the firm you are valuing does not have data publicly available, you will have to use comparable firms to estimate your firm's beta.

How do you implement this approach?

Security Analysis: How to Analyze Accounting and Market Data to Value Securities
Robert W. Holthausen and Mark E. Zmijewski
\C0693A.W51

Do not reproduce without permission.
July 29, 1998 - 2:45 pm

154

Consider whether the firm being valued is similar to other firms in the industry or does it operate itself very differently?

Use comparable firms, not just SIC codes to define an industry. Emphasis here is on the operating risks of the firm, not the financing risks because we can control for differences in capital structure.

Determinants of the unlevered beta would include variables like the lines of business of an enterprise as well as the operating leverage of a firm (the ratio of fixed to variable costs ignoring financing). Firm size does not matter in the context of using the CAPM unless you believe it affects beta. Leverage is a determinant of the equity beta but not the unlevered beta and we believe we know how to control for variation in capital structure.

Differences in capital structure can be controlled via levering and unlevering betas or cost of capital estimates directly (see the levering and unlevering formulas).

4. Steps in the Analysis of Financial Statements

A. Competitive Analysis

(1) Identify the key profit drivers, the key business risks for the firm.

(2) Analyze the firm and its industry to determine the competitive nature of the industry and whether profitability can be sustained.

B. Analysis of Accounting

(1) Evaluate the extent to which the accounting captures the economic transactions of the firms. How do required accounting treatments mask what is happening? How do choices made by management when there is accounting discretion affect the reliability of the financial statements?

(2) Is it necessary to recast the financial statements in anyway to more accurately depict the firm?

C. Financial Analysis

The goal of this analysis is to evaluate current performance and strategy and to assess whether the current performance and strategy are sustainable. Moreover, the analysis may allow insights into how the strategy will have to evolve.

D. Prospective Analysis

Forecasting the firm's future by forecasting the firm's entire set of financial statements and performing the valuation.

Security Analysis: How to Analyze Accounting and Market Data to Value Securities
Robert W. Holthausen and Mark E. Zmijewski
\C0693A.W51

Do not reproduce without permission.
July 29, 1998 - 2:45 pm

155

5. Competitive Analysis

Competitive analysis is an analysis of the underlying economics of the industry in which the firm operates. It is typically a qualitative analysis which allows the analyst to identify the key drivers of success and the key risks. This in turn allows assessment of the sustainability of the firm's performance.

A firm's value depends on whether it can earn a return on its capital in excess of the cost of capital. The cost of capital is determined by the capital markets, but the amount earned by a firm depends on its business strategy, its efficiency and the degree of competition with other firms.

There are two components of this analysis -- industry analysis and competitive analysis of the firm

A.   Industry Analysis

Industry's vary widely in their profitability across industries at a point in time and over time for an industry.

The industrial organization literature suggests that profitability in an industry is determined by the degree of actual and potential competition within an industry, which is driven by:

(1)   Rivalry among firms

    (a)   Industry growth-if industry is growing rapidly, existing firms need not grab market share from each other to grow

    (b)   Industry concentration-if there is only one dominant firm (IBM in the 1970's), they set the rules of competition. If there are only two or three equal-sized players, they can implicitly cooperate.

    (c)   Differentiation-if firms can differentiate their products, they can avoid head on price competition. However, if customers view the products as commodities, customers will be willing to switch on the basis of price.

    (d)   Switching costs-if switching costs are low, only price will matter

    (e)   Scale/Learning economies-if there is a steep learning curve or other scale economies, size is important and there will be aggressive competition for market share

    (f)   Fixed/variable costs-scale economies can be driven by cost factors.

    (g)   Excess capacity-if capacity exceeds demand there is a strong incentive to cut price to fill capacity

    (h)   Exit barriers-problems of excess capacity are exacerbated if there are significant barriers for exit (assets are specialized or regulations make exit costly).

(2)   Threat of new entrants

    (a)   Scale economies-large scale economies make entry harder. Either a large investment is needed right away or firms have to enter with a less than optimal capacity. Could arise from R&D, advertising or physical plant

Security Analysis: How to Analyze Accounting and Market Data to Value Securities
Robert W. Holthausen and Mark E. Zmijewski
\C0693A.W51

and equipment.

(b)   First mover advantage-if first entrants set industry standards or enter into exclusive arrangements with suppliers for materials, or acquire scarce government licenses to operate in regulated industries threat of entry is lower. First mover advantages can also occur when switching costs are large (consider computer operating system software).

(c)   Distribution access-limited capacity in existing distribution channels and high cost of developing new ones limit entry. For example, new entry into the domestic auto industry is difficult because of costs of developing a dealer network.

(d)   Relationships-New consumer good manufacturers may find it difficult to obtain supermarket shelf space.

(e)   Legal barriers-copyrights, patents, licensing regulations

(3)   Threat of substitute products

    (a)   Relative price and performance
    (b)   Buyers' willingness to switch

Together these drive industry profits.

How much of the industry profits are retained in the industry depends on the relative bargaining power of industry's buyers and suppliers.

(4)   Bargaining power of buyers

Determined primarily by price sensitivity and the relative bargaining power.

    (a)   Switching costs-if switching costs are low, buyers are more price sensitive

    (b)   Differentiation-if products are undifferentiated, buyers are more price sensitive

    (c)   Importance of product for cost and quality-if product is small part of cost and quality, buyer will not engage in many search costs

    (d)   Number of buyers-more buyers reduces the buyers relative bargaining power

    (e)   Volume per buyer-if volume of a buyer is higher than others, bargaining power increases

(5)   Bargaining power of suppliers-similarly

    (a)   Switching costs
    (b)   Differentiation
    (c)   Importance of product for cost and quality
    (d)   Number of suppliers
    (e)   Volume per supplier

Security Analysis: How to Analyze Accounting and Market Data to Value Securities
Robert W. Holthausen and Mark E. Zmijewski
\C0693A.W51

B.   Competitive Analysis of the Firm

There are two generic ways to characterize a firm's business strategy-cost leadership or differentiation.

(1)   Cost Leadership - may be the only way to achieve superior performance if the product is a commodity-like product. Cost leadership is typically attained through

      (a)   economics of scale and scope
      (b)   efficient production
      (c)   simpler product designs
      (d)   lower input costs
      (e)   low-cost distribution
      (f)   little R&D or advertising
      (g)   tight cost controls

(2)   Differentiation-firm seeks to be unique in the industry along some dimension valued by customers. As such first needs to identify one or more attributes of a product or service that customers value. Second, must find a unique way to supply the chosen attribute. Differentiation attained through

      (a)   superior product quality
      (b)   superior product variety
      (c)   superior customer service
      (d)   more flexible delivery
      (e)   investment in brand image, marketing capabilities
      (f)   investment in R&D
      (g)   focus on creativity and innovation

C.   Achieving and Sustaining Competitive Advantage

Choice of a competitive strategy does not lead to a competitive advantage. The firm has to have the appropriate capabilities and has to be able to implement the strategy and sustain the chosen strategy. This involves creation of the firms core competencies (the economic assets the firm possesses) required for the strategy and appropriate structuring of the firm's value chain (the process that converts inputs into outputs).

The more unique the firm's core competencies and value chain and the more difficult they are to imitate, the more sustainable the firm's competitive advantage. Asking the following types of questions may be useful.

(1)   What are the key success factors and risks associated with the firm's chosen competitive strategy?
(2)   Does the firm currently have the resources and capabilities to deal with the key success factors and risks?
(3)   Has the firm made commitments to bridge the gap between its current capabilities

Security Analysis: How to Analyze Accounting and Market Data to Value Securities
Robert W. Holthausen and Mark E. Zmijewski
\C0693A.W51

Do not reproduce without permission.
July 29, 1998 - 2:45 pm

158

and the capabilities required for the strategy.

(4) Has the firm structured its activities (R&D, design, manufacturing, market and distribution and support activities) consistent with the strategy

(5) Is the competitive advantage sustainable? Are there barriers that make imitation difficult?

(6) Are there any foreseeable changes in the firm's industry structure that might disrupt the firm's competitive advantage such as new technologies, changes in regulations, changes in customer requirements? Can the firm address the potential changes?

6. Analysis of Accounting

A. Identify Key Accounting Policies

To the extent that there are key factors and key risks of a firm which have been identified through strategic analysis, accounting analysis should see how the financial statements measure and portray the key factors and risks.

As such, the analysts should attempt to see how the accounting measures capture these constructs and the key estimates embedded in these policies. For example, if a firm has concentrated on quality initiatives, how have warranty estimates been estimated? How do banks estimate credit risk, etc.

B. Assess Accounting Flexibility

Not all firms have equal flexibility in choosing accounting policies because of accounting rules. For example, a companies whose R&D initiatives are important has to expense all R&D under U.S. GAAP. Advertising is also required to be expensed. In other cases, say establishing loan loss reserves, there is tremendous discretion.

When managers have little discretion, accounting estimates are unlikely to be informative. When managers do have discretion, accounting numbers have the potential to be informative if the manager chooses to communicate through the disclosures. (Of course, managers can also use the discretion to obfuscate the truth).

C. Evaluate Accounting Strategy

(1) How do the firm's policies compare to industry norms. If dissimilar, is it because the firm's competitive advantage is unique (lower warranty costs because of higher quality or is the firm understating warranty liabilities?)

(2) Does management have strong incentives to distort earnings (bonuses tied to accounting numbers, close to default on accounting based bond covenants, current union negotiations or proxy contests, tax considerations, etc.)

(3) Has the firm recently changed any policies or estimates? What is the justification? What is the impact of the changes?

Security Analysis: How to Analyze Accounting and Market Data to Value Securities
Robert W. Holthausen and Mark E. Zmijewski
\C0693A.W51

      (4)   Has the company's/manager's policies been realistic in the past? Reputation effects.

      (5)   Does the firms appear to structure certain transactions to achieve certain accounting treatments? Why? (lease terms, structure of takeover transactions, etc.)

D.   Evaluate Disclosure Strategy

      (1)   Does the firm provide adequate disclosure to assess firm's strategy and its economic consequences. Does management letter indicate the firm's competitive position in the industry? Are future plans discussed? Or does the letter merely discuss historical numbers?

      (2)   Are key accounting policies explained and is any logic provided, especially if policies deviate from industry norms?

      (3)   Does the firm explain its current performance? Do they link performance to business and industry conditions? If changes in margins or expenses occurred do they provide any insights as to why?

      (4)   Even if accounting rules do not allow management to communicate certain factors (such as successful R&D and advertising expenditures), management can discuss these issues and indicate how these areas are managed.

      (5)   What is quality of segment and geographic disclosure for firms in multiple segments and geographic areas?

      (6)   How forthcoming is management with respect to communicating bad news. Does it explain why the poor performance occurred and how it is dealing with the poor performance? Is the strategy reasonable?

One force which of course limits the extent to which the firm wants to make adequate disclosure is the extent to which competitors will be able to use those disclosures to their advantage.

E.   Identify Red Flags

      (1)   Unexplained changes in accounting, especially when performance is poor
      (2)   Unexplained changes that boost profits
      (3)   Unusual increases in accounts receivable relative to sales
      (4)   Unusual increases in inventories relative to sales
      (5)   An increasing gap between reported income and cash flow from operations
      (6)   An increasing gap between reported income and taxable income
      (7)   A tendency to use financing mechanisms like R&D limited partnerships and sale of receivables without recourse
      (8)   Unexpected large asset writeoffs
      (9)   Large fourth-quarter adjustments
     (10)   Qualified audit opinions or changes in auditors
     (11)   Related party transactions

Security Analysis: How to Analyze Accounting and Market Data to Value Securities
Robert W. Holthausen and Mark E. Zmijewski
\C0693A.W51

F.   Undo Accounting Distortions

If you think accounting numbers suggest numbers are misleading or not as informative as they could be, restate the numbers to reduce the distortions.

Things to consider include off balance sheet financing, guarantees, legal judgments, intangibles, minority interests, equity interests in other companies, differences from industry norms, etc.

Some analysts use a process that attempts to "purify" the accounting numbers. Adjustments for off balance sheet financing, under or over funded pensions, post retirement health benefits, non-capitalized operating leases, guarantees, and legal judgements can all be important when comparing firms. The treatment of intangible assets is also important. Some analysts include intangibles in assets and the amortization of intangibles as an expense, however, other analysts write-off intangibles, mostly goodwill, against retained earnings, resulting in no amortization on the income statement. The difference between these two approaches can be significant. Recall that firms are allowed to write-off goodwill directly against retained earnings in the United Kingdom.

Some other issues are master limited partnerships (oil royalty trusts) -- some of the firm's assets may have been spun off to master limited partnerships over which the firm still has some control. Or another is the capitalization of operating leases.

The basis of consolidation (purchase vs. pooling) can be an important consideration. Were assets written up and was goodwill created? Different treatments lead to very different financial statements. Income recognition (e.g., full cost vs. successful efforts in the oil and gas exploration industries) can be an important consideration. Other income recognition have revolved around land sale companies like Thousand Trails and Patten Corporation concerning the timing difference between income recognition and collection of cash. Depreciation methods and estimated useful lives vary across firms leading to differential costs and differential asset values; inventory pricing (e.g., LIFO vs FIFO) also leads to differences in cost of goods sold as well as differences in asset values.

Rating agencies, like Moody's and Standard & Poor's, expend significant resources to "purify" the accounting numbers before they begin their analysis.

7.   An Important Caveat -- Understanding Financial Statements

The analysis of financial statements, regardless of the reason, hinges on the utilization of the financial statements of the firm. As such, gaining expertise in financial statement analysis requires a thorough understanding of the economics of the transactions in which entities engage and in how the accounting system records those transactions. Thus, the more one understands about accounting principles, the better equipped one is to engage in meaningful financial analysis. These notes do not provide the detailed knowledge of accounting principles required, however, there are many excellent introductory, intermediate, and advanced accounting texts available for this purpose.

Security Analysis: How to Analyze Accounting and Market Data to Value Securities
   Robert W. Holthausen and Mark E. Zmijewski
\C0693A.W51

Do not reproduce without permission.
July 29, 1998 - 2:45 pm

161

Generally accepted accounting standards are continually evolving, in the United States and throughout the world. Accounting standards and the transactions firms enter into are in a constant state of change. Knowledge of changes in standards is important for conducting financial statement analysis. For example, some firms engage in a variety of mechanisms to obtain financing that does not appear on the balance sheet. Standard setting bodies, such as the Financial Accounting Standards Board, change accounting principles over time in response to these changes. However, as soon as one type of off-balance sheet financing vehicle is brought on to the balance sheet by the standards setting board, another type of transaction which is not disclosed on the balance sheet will be created.

Understanding appropriate accounting principles becomes more complicated as one performs valuations of companies in different countries, as accounting principles vary from country to country. Thus, apparent differences between two companies from different countries may be driven entirely by differences in accounting principles between the two countries. For example, the audited financial statements in many countries are tied very closely to the income tax regulations, whereas in the United States there are very few ties between income tax accounting and accounting for the preparation of financial statements.[1] Close ties to income tax regulations provides an additional incentive to reduce reported income in the financial statements in these countries.

In the United Kingdom, goodwill can be written off directly against retained earnings without affecting net income. In the United States, goodwill amortization passes directly through the income statement. Also in the United Kingdom, fixed assets can be written up annually to their replacement cost. The adjustment in value goes directly to shareholders equity. In the United States, no asset write-ups are allowed. In Germany, companies can at their own discretion, increase expenses in a given year for anticipated costs associated with maintenance and upkeep that will be incurred in the following year. This discretion allows managers to manipulate income, at least in the short run. No such discretion is allowed in the United States. Finally, in many countries, firms are not required to record liabilities such as pension liabilities or post-retirement health benefits on the basis of actuarial methods, whereas in the United States, the recording of such actuarial measured liabilities is required.

8.   Types of Financial Statement Relations (Ratios).

In these notes we do not discuss the calculation of specific financial statement relations (ratios). Other textbooks discuss those issues thoroughly (see most introductory accounting textbooks and financial statement analysis textbooks, such as *Financial Statement Analysis: Theory, Application and Interpretation* by Leopold A. Bernstein (Richard D. Irwin, Homewood, IL). We do, however, discuss the major types of financial statement relations, how they are calculated, and some important considerations when calculating them.

A.   Rates of Return.

Rates of return measure the profitability of the firm. It is important to have a consistent numerator and denominator in the rate of return measure your are analyzing. The denominator dictates

---

[1]One well known exception in the United States is inventory accounting; a firm that uses the Last-in First-out inventory method for income tax calculations must also use this method for financial reporting purposes.

Security Analysis: How to Analyze Accounting and Market Data to Value Securities
Robert W. Holthausen and Mark E. Zmijewski
\C0693A.W51

the measurement of the numerator. The denominator dictates the claim holders of interest (for example, equity holders, or all claim holders), and the numerator should be the earnings (or flow) that is available to those claim holders. For the rate of return on assets (or investment), the income number should represent flows to all claim holders, so it should be measured before interest flows but after tax. For the rate of return on equity, the relevant income number should represent flows available to common equity holders.

How do you define equity? Preferred stock should not be considered part of common equity. Deferred taxes are sometimes as equity, depending on the analyst. The decision to treat as equity or debt is usually driven by the horizon over which the deferred taxes are likely to reverse. There are no general guidelines regarding the treatment of intangibles when using book values. Some analysts writeoff intangibles against shareholders equity in calculating return measures.

Profit margin analysis analyzes the extent to which the company's sales cover its cost of goods sold (sales less cost of goods sold divided by sales) or the extent to which sales dollars are converted into net income (some income number divided by sales). Most often analysts measure profit margin on sales as net income after taxes divided by sales. If you are comparing the profitability across firms, however, measuring profit margin on sales as income after taxes plus interest less interest tax shields (i.e., adjust net income to put it on a 100% equity financed basis) divided by sales is potentially useful. The second calculation is more useful if there is wide variation in financial leverage across the firms you are analyzing.

Cash flow rate of return ratios have become more popular since the standardization of cash flow statements in 1987. Many analysts examine cash flows from operations as the numerator in these rate of return measures. One note of caution regarding cash flows from operations is that it does not contain any provision for the replacement of assets, whereas income numbers at least include a depreciation charge. One measure of cash return on assets is defined as cash flow from operations before interest but after taxes divided by total assets; another is free cash flow of the unlevered firm divided by total assets. The limitation of using free cash flow of the unlevered firm in the numerator, however, is that capital expenditures are "lumpy," and it may not be reflective of the future cash flow requirements. Some type of averaging of capital expenditures can be used to addressed this issue. Cash return on common stockholders' equity is defined as cash flow from operations less preferred dividends divided by common equity. Again, you can also calculate this ratio as free cash flows of the common equity divided by the common equity. (The same capital expenditure comments apply here.)

B.   Financial Risk Analysis.

Financial Leverage.

Financial leverage is the proportion of non-common equity capital used to finance the firm's investments. Usually, financial leverage refers to the amount of debt financing used by the firm. It is usually measured relative to assets or equity; measures may be based on book values or market values depending on the use. Many analysts eliminate intangibles in book value measures

What is debt? Debt is sometimes difficult to define. For example, firms often use many off-balance sheet financing instruments. There are issues concerning the treatment of deferred taxes, the

Security Analysis: How to Analyze Accounting and Market Data to Value Securities
  Robert W. Holthausen and Mark E. Zmijewski
  \C0693A.W51

Do not reproduce without permission.
July 29, 1998 - 2:45 pm

163

value of the debt in convertible debt issues, and the treatment of preferred stock. Although preferred stock is not debt, preferred stockholders have a higher priority of claims than commons stockholders, so preferred stock must be analyzed as well. The issue of what constitutes debt has become more complicated over time as companies have entered into more non-traditional transactions. Conducting financial analysis hinges on understanding the economics underlying a transaction as well as how the transaction is disclosed by the accountant.

For example, unconditional purchase obligations are future obligations to transfer funds for fixed or minimum quantities. SFAS #47 requires firms to disclose the requirements of these unconditional requirements for the next five years, but does not require that the firm book a liability. However, understanding the nature of these obligations is important for understanding commitments of future cash flows that the firm has made. Various project financing arrangements is another area that deserves special consideration. For example, research and development arrangements typically entail one company advancing funds to a company engaged in research and development (R&D Company) in exchange for a claim on the value of any products or technologies produced. These arrangements have become popular because depending on how the contract is structured, firms may avoid the expensing of research and development. The FASB issued SFAS #68 in order to at least set guidelines concerning the appropriate disclosure of these transactions.

Financial Instruments is another "hot" topic in accounting at this time. The number of new financial products introduced since the mid-1980s has been incredible (Arthur Andersen reports that more than 600 new financial products were introduced between 1986 and 1989). Financial instruments include contracts like exchangeable debentures, interest rate swaps, recourse obligations on receivables sold, options, financial guarantees, interest rate caps and floors, futures contracts, forward contracts, etc. The FASB is currently in the process of developing accounting standards for financial instruments and some have already appeared. Many financial instruments have debt and equity like features associated with them and it is important to understand the economics of these transactions as well as how the accountant records and discloses them. Disclosures of financial instruments are not consistent across firms and do not provide all necessary information for appropriately evaluating their potential risk reduction or risk increasing properties. Many of these are off-balance sheet and some are not adequately described in footnotes.

Coverage Ratios.

The coverage of fixed costs (cash outflows) is another measure of financial risk analysis. Coverage ratios assess the funds that are generated from operations to cover fixed costs (interest, rental commitments, principal repayments, etc.) Typical ratios are often based on earnings numbers before interest and taxes. More recently, individuals have been interested in coverage ratios defined using cash flows before interest and taxes. For example cash interest coverage might be defined as cash flows from operations before interest and taxes divided by fixed cash payments such as cash interest, or cash interest plus cash rental payments, or cash interest plus cash rental payments plus principal repayments.

Liquidity.

Liquidity ratios assess the amount and type of resources that are currently available to meet current liabilities. It is important to assess lines of credit and other pre-approved short-term financing in

Security Analysis: How to Analyze Accounting and Market Data to Value Securities
Robert W. Holthausen and Mark E. Zmijewski
\C0693A.W51

Do not reproduce without permission.
July 29, 1998 - 2:45 pm

164

order to assess the liquidity of a firm.

C.   Operating Risk Analysis.

Analyzing operating leverage requires an assessment of how a firm's expenses respond to changes in short-term demand, what percent of the firm's expenses (cash outflows) are variable, and the identification of the firm's fixed expenses (cash outflows)? Consider two companies like Toy's R Us and COMSAT. Toys grows primarily through building new stores. Thus, "fixed costs" go up directly with sales as do variable costs. COMSAT launches satellites for communications. Once the satellite is launched, COMSAT can experience tremendous variation in revenue with virtually no changes in costs.

Efficiency answer the question, "How well do you ...?"

(1)   Collect accounts receivable (receivables turnover and aging analysis).
(2)   Manage accounts payable (payables turnover).
(3)   Manage inventory (inventory turnover).
(4)   Utilize fixed assets (asset turnover measures).
(5)   Income/Sales and related measures (see common sized financial statements).
(6)   Expense/Sales ratios (see common sized financial statements).

In the case of banks we might be very concerned about how well interest rate risk and credit risk are managed. Analysis of interest rate risk requires an understanding of the maturity structure of the assets and liabilities of the bank as well as any hedging activities of the bank.

D.   Common sized financial statements.

Common sized financial statements express all income statement and balance sheet items by a size measure. The deflator is typically sales for the income statement and total assets for the balance sheet, although it is also useful to use sales (or some key factor used to forecast sales) as the deflator for the balance sheet when identifying relations used for forecasting. This analysis shows ratios in a financial statement format which is sometimes useful when attempting to comprehend a firm's big picture, and when comparing the same firm through time or different firms at some point in time.

E.   Market ratios.

There are numerous market ratios that are used to compare and value the common equity (or total assets) of firms. Many market relations can be calculated on both a per share and total firm basis. We discuss these ratios when we discuss price multiple valuation methods in chapter 9.

F.   Other measures.

It is sometimes useful to compute ratios based on other information as well (e.g., square footage, number of stores, number of warehouses, barrels of beer or oil or salad dressing, etc.)

G.   Per share items.

Per share items provide very little information in their own right. Controlling for the number of

Security Analysis: How to Analyze Accounting and Market Data to Value Securities
Robert W. Holthausen and Mark E. Zmijewski
\C0693A.W51

Do not reproduce without permission.
July 29, 1998 - 2:45 pm

165

shares, however, is important in many types of analyses and decision processes. Per share numbers can sometimes be deceiving because the firm can buy back shares with excess cash and reduce the number of shares outstanding. Per share items play a key role in calculating some market relations.

9.   Other Financial Statement Relations.

Growth.

What are the important factors that affect the level of operations of the firm? Some factors are sales, the number of stores, availability of certain raw materials, capital expenditure decisions, etc. Past growth rates of sales may not be very good predictors of future growth rates. Growth in sales is usually analyzed carefully to assess the source of the company's growth. Knowing the growth rate in sales alone is not sufficient; in particular, the proportion of growth that comes from increases in volume, increases in unit pricing, acquisitions, and foreign currency translation are all important components of an analysis of sales.

Analysis of the determinants of growth is important for estimating future growth. If growth is coming from unit growth, then you must assess the cost of producing that growth; for example, in a retail business, does growth come from increased utilization of stores or does it come from building more stores? In a manufacturing facility, has growth come from idle plant capacity or from building new production facilities. If it came from idle plant capacity, how much more growth can occur before plant expansion is required. Some analysts suggest analyzing the ratios of cash from sales to sales as an indicator of the "quality of sales." This is most easily done if the statement of cash flows is prepared using the direct method, though you can approximate the same calculation if the statement of cash flows is prepared using the indirect method.[2]

For most companies the cash from sales to sales ratio will approximate one. However, for some companies, that would not be the case. Take for example, Thousand Trails which sold access to campsites in parks they constructed across the United States. They booked the complete revenue from the sale at the time the contract was signed but the actual funds were received in installments over 24 to 84 months (average of 61 months). In their growth period, their ratio of cash from sales to sales was considerably lower than one. Thousand Trails ultimately experienced significant collection problems on its installment sales.

What is the source of the firm's *growth opportunities*? Is the firm well positioned for growth? What are the prospects for international growth, and in what regions, Eastern Europe, Western Europe, Pacific Rim, etc. What are the strategic trends in the industry affecting future growth opportunities? Can the firm grow with existing customers, and who are the new customers? What are the competitive forces in the industry that affect growth (highly competitive with easy entry and exit or not competitive with difficult entry). What are the technological changes in the industry that are affecting growth opportunities?

---

[2]Refer to chapter 5 for a discussion of the direct and indirect cash flow statements.

Security Analysis: How to Analyze Accounting and Market Data to Value Securities
Robert W. Holthausen and Mark E. Zmijewski
\C0693A.W51

The Relation between Earnings and Cash Flows.

How different are cash flows from operations and operating income? What are the causes of the differences betweens earnings and cash flows. If earnings far exceed cash flows, when are the cash flows going to rebound?

Reinvestment.

What proportion of the firm's cash flow from operations is the firm reinvesting into old projects, in new projects? How important is new financing for reinvestment or has reinvestment come from internally generated funds. Is the extent of investment sufficient to sustain the current operating level of the organization? Is the plant and equipment up-to-date and pristine or is it antiquated and nearing the end of its useful life? Is the extent of investment sufficient to sustain a reasonable level of growth?

10.   Measurement Issues.

We use ratios to analyze a firm to scale for size differences. The calculation of financial statement relations is an explicit attempt to control for size. Consider the two firms, A and B, firm A has net income equal to $100 and firm B $1,000; which firm is more profitable? To answer this question you must first adjust the net incomes for the size of the two firms. Merely looking at the two net incomes indicate which firm made more money, but would give no indication of which firm was more profitable given their investment in the business. One method of adjusting for size is to divide both net incomes by the number of common shares outstanding (earnings per share). This method does not control for total investment. Another size adjustment is to divide both net incomes by sales or common equity. Relations such as net income/sales attempt to provide information about a firm's efficiency (the proportion of sales are converted to the bottom line).

If you think about it for a minute, you can see that ratios essentially assume direct proportionality, that is they implicitly assume that the correct adjustment for size of firm is one of direction proportionality. Suppose that within an industry, firms which are efficient will realize a net income which is directly proportional to sales (that is, $NI = B*Sales$). Then net income/sales is the correct way to adjust for size. If the median firm in the industry is efficient, the median net/income to sales ratio will equal B. Firms with ratios below B are less efficient than the industry in general and firms with ratios above B are more efficient. On the other hand, if direct proportionality is not the appropriate adjustment, then ratios are an inappropriate means of inferring efficiency. For example, typical EOQ (economic order quantity) inventory models assume that inventory should increase with the square root of sales. Based on these models, the inventory turnover ratio, calculated as cost of good sold/inventory, is a misspecified adjustment for size (assuming the EOQ model is correct)

Some basic rules to follow when you are calculating financial statement relations are

1.   Flow divided by a flow - divide the most recent flow by the most recent flow. Types of relations that fall under this rule are profit margin (but not rate of return on assets or rate of return on equity), coverage of fixed cost (earnings before interest and taxes to interest), and expense ratios (cost of goods sold to sales).

Security Analysis: How to Analyze Accounting and Market Data to Value Securities
Robert W. Holthausen and Mark E. Zmijewski
\C0693A.W51

Do not reproduce without permission.
July 29, 1998 - 2:45 pm

167

2.   Stock divided by a stock - use the ending balances. Types of relations that fall under this rule are liquidity relations (current assets to current liabilities) and financial leverage relations (total debt to equity).

3.   Flow divided by a stock or a stock divided by a flow - use the most recent flow and the average stock. Types of relations that fall under this rule are rate of return on assets and rate of return on equity, some efficiency relations (days sales in accounts receivable, days sales in inventory, fixed asset turnover).

4.   Using quarterly data. If quarterly data are available, you must adjust the data for the effects of seasonality. For example, for flows, you can aggregate data on a rolling four quarter basis so that the annual last observation contains the most recent four quarters available to control for the effects of seasonality; for stocks, you can use a weighted average of the stock.

Inflation adjustments.

What is the appropriate adjustment factor, if any? Use an economy wide inflation factor, or measure price index of the asset as narrowly as possible. The evidence on GPLA statements is that they don't tell us much. Most people don't inflation adjust their numbers before performing ratio analysis in countries in which inflation is not too great.

Inflation adjustments can be important when you use a measure of units in the calculation; for example, it would be useful to inflation adjust sales when attempting to interpret a relation such as the dollars of sales per square foot of retail floor space, especially over time. Sales per square foot for TOY'S R US in U.S. stores increased from $175 (thousands) to $206 between 1986 and 1990 which suggests real growth in the operating efficiency of the stores. However, when those numbers are inflation adjusted, the sales per square foot was almost constant. As such, real growth in TOY'S R US's domestic sales was accomplished through increases in square footage, primarily through increases in the number of stores. In comparison, TOY'S R US's international stores did experience increases in sales per square foot in real terms.

Seasonality.

Some firms have highly seasonal businesses. For example, approximately 49% of Toys' R Us sales occur during the fourth quarter, which ends at the end of January. The company's cash position is highest in January and is lowest in October. Inventories hit their highest level in October and their lowest level in January. Examination of the annual reports for Toy's R Us would mislead an analyst regarding Toy's R Us' average inventory level, cash position, and short term debt requirements. Further, seasonality adjustments must be made when analyzing quarterly data. Two methods of adjusting quarterly data are to construct an annual income statement and cash flow statement by combining the previous four quarters, and a balance sheet that represents the weighted average of the previous four balance sheets, and to examine this quarter relative to the quarter one year ago.

Security Analysis: How to Analyze Accounting and Market Data to Value Securities
Robert W. Holthausen and Mark E. Zmijewski
\C0693A.W51

Potentially Misleading Relations.

In certain circumstances, financial statement relation can be misleading and incorrect. For example, changes in a firm's fiscal year end overtime (less than full year's results reported), or examining firms with different fiscal year-ends can be misleading. Typically this is not a very big issue unless there were great differences in economic activity through time. Also, firms in the same industry tend to cluster to a specific fiscal year end because of industry factors. For example, most retail stores in the United States pick January 31 as their fiscal year as opposed to December 31 because of the seasonal sales in December. Changes in accounting principles not adjusted retroactively can cause a problem.

The outlier or influential observation can result in misleading financial statement relations. Sometimes an outlier is a data error and sometimes it is just an observation that is very different from all the others. ow do you treat an outlier? First identify if it is a data error. Secondly identify if there is an economic rationale for why it should be excluded from your analysis (e.g., the firm is not really in the line of business that you presumed). If you want to mitigate the effect of the outlier, truncate (or delete) the observation, windsorize the data -- set extreme observation at the limit you consider believable, or use a statistic that is not influenced by outliers such as medians.

Relations that have negative denominators are usually misleading; in general, you cannot use observations with negative denominators. A reasonable solution is to substitute a denominator that cannot have a negative value, if possible. It is sometime possible to invert a ratio to avoid a negative denominator. For example, it is reasonable to invert a price to earnings ratio. An earnings/price ratio can never have a negative denominator. Databases are particularly bad at ignoring the effects of negative denominators. You should be careful in your analysis if you use databases that calculate ratios for you.

Acquisitions and divestitures can cause problems when calculating financial statement relations because year-to-year changes are not reflective of the true underlying economic conditions of the firm. When using data bases like COMPUSTAT, prior year numbers are not adjusted for acquisitions and divestitures, even if the company adjusts its prior financial statements in reports subsequent to the acquisition or divestiture. Thus, significant changes in ratios may be observed at the time of acquisitions or divestitures. One way to deal with this problem is to create historical financial statements for the firm based on the separate financial statements of the merged firms.

Relative Comparisons -- Choosing a Benchmark.

One of the major problems in conducting financial analysis is interpreting financial ratios. Consider two firms. Is a current ratio of 4 better than a current ratio of 2? There are no universally applicable standards or ideals for any given ratio. Thus, you need to define some benchmark for comparison. While a larger current ratio might seem to indicate a firm which is more liquid, it is possible that the firm with the greater current ratio has built up its inventory to inefficient levels and financed the inventory build up with long-term debt.

One solution to this problem is to judge the firm relative to it competitors. A benchmark commonly used is an industry norm or a peer (comparable) group of firms. Why do we use industry norms? Because we know that capital requirements, technologies, types of products, etc., will affect the magnitudes of financial statement relations; hence, if looking for a benchmark for a firm, comparison to firms in similar businesses is probably relevant.

Security Analysis: How to Analyze Accounting and Market Data to Value Securities
Robert W. Holthausen and Mark E. Zmijewski
\C0693A.W51

While using an industry benchmark is a potential solution to this problem, knowing that a firm deviates from the industry norm is not necessarily evidence that the firm is operating suboptimally. Toys "R" Us is an example of a firm that is an industry leader and may be able to operate with different current ratios, financial leverage, etc., than other firms in the industry. Closer analysis is required.

Assume you observe the following days to collect accounts receivable for firms A and B.

	Firm A	Firm B
1981	80	150
1982	70	130
1983	90	110
1984	90	150
1985	80	110
1986	80	140
1987	90	150
1988	70	120
1989	80	130
1990	60	100

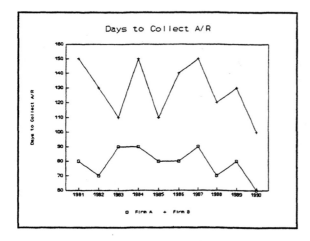

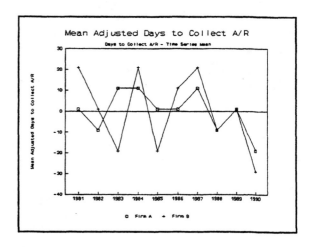

Security Analysis: How to Analyze Accounting and Market Data to Value Securities
Robert W. Holthausen and Mark E. Zmijewski
\C0693A.W51

Which firm is more efficient in its account collections? Is the more efficient firm the one pursuing the best policy (that is, are common shareholders' claims affected more positively by one policy over another)? How can you find out? The same type of problem arises here as in the cross-sectional comparisons. One needs to ask questions like, if the firm's are in the same line of business over this period, why are their days sales in receivables so different. Perhaps A is too tight fisted with its credit policy and is thus losing significant sales to firm B which is willing to extend credit to more marginal firms. The question is which is the more profit maximizing policy. Are the changes over time a rational response to variation in the cost of money? Find out about industry practice. Estimate the effect of more strict or lax collection policies on differences in sales and assess the how the cost of carrying the greater receivables compares to the increased profits.

If we observe that a firm's ratio and an industry norm for that ratio are different, that does not imply that the two are statistically different from one another. The bad news is that judging statistical significance is somewhat hampered by the tremendous skewness in the data. One way to get a feel for how different a firm is from the "norm" is to look at the distribution. But this is only useful if we have a reasonably sized peer group.

We could discuss statistical techniques for dealing with the skewness in the data, but I don't think that would resolve the interpretation issues. One major problem is that if I observe that two firms have different ratios (e.g., leverage), does that mean that one firm has not optimized. The notion behind a "norm" basically implies that the "norm" is in some sense optimal and that deviations from the norm represent suboptimum behavior. If you think about it for a few minutes, you can begin to see problems in assuming that deviations from a norm represent suboptimum behavior. For example, what is the optimal capital structure for a firm? What is the optimal dividend policy for a firm?

11.   The Distributions of Financial Statement Relations.

Inter-firm distribution.

In Exhibit 6.1 we present the 1985 and 1989 distributions of eight financial ratios for the population of Compustat firms. The relevant questions to address when analyzing this exhibit are: Do financial ratios vary across firms? Do financial ratios vary over time across firms? Is inter-firm cross-sectional variation the same over time? The eight ratios are current assets to current liabilities (CRx), total debt to total assets (DAT%), income before interest and taxes to interest (ICBTx), inventory turnover (INVXx), income before extraordinary items and discontinued operations to sales (NPM%), receivables turnover (RECXx), return on assets (ROA%), and return on common equity (ROE%).

Inter-industry distribution.

In Exhibit 6.2 we present the 1985 and 1989 weighted average of eight financial ratios for the 29 four digit SIC codes. The relevant question to answer when analyzing this exhibit are: Do financial ratios vary across industries? Do financial ratios vary over time across industries? Is inter-industry cross-sectional variation the same over time?

Security Analysis: How to Analyze Accounting and Market Data to Value Securities
  Robert W. Holthausen and Mark E. Zmijewski
  \C0693A.W51

The eight ratios are current assets to current liabilities (CRx), total debt to total assets (DAT%), income before interest and taxes to interest (ICBTx), inventory turnover (INVXx), income before extraordinary items and discontinued opeations to sales (NPM%), receivables turnover (RECXx), return on assets (ROA%), and return on common equity (ROE%). Not shown in Exhibit 6.2 is the variation of these ratios within industries. An analysis of intra-industry variation indicates that financial ratios vary within industries and financial ratios vary over time within industries. The implication is that it is important to use comparable firms (not a random sample) when evaluating financial statement relations.

Security Analysis: How to Analyze Accounting and Market Data to Value Securities
Robert W. Holthausen and Mark E. Zmijewski
\C0693A.W51

Do not reproduce without permission.
July 29, 1998 - 2:45 pm

172

Exhibit 6.1

Distribution of Financial Ratios Across Compustat Population

Statistic	CRx	DAT%	ICBTx	INVXx	NPM%	RECXx	ROA%	ROE%
Panel A: 1985 Distribution								
Mean	4.1	31.6	19.7	14.7	-42.5	15.4	-9.8	-25.9
Standard Deviation	20.9	106.9	476.5	59.6	376.7	90.3	205.3	1078.4
Kurtosis	882	3,753	1,588	449	325	1,721	4,418	2,208
(std error)	0.07	0.07	0.07	0.08	0.07	0.08	0.07	0.07
Skewness	26.5	56.8	38.1	18.1	-16.3	36.5	-63.8	-43.3
(std error)	0.04	0.03	0.04	0.04	0.03	0.04	0.03	0.03
01st Percentile	0.1	0.0	-173.9	0.2	-935.8	0.2	-181.2	-531.7
05th Percentile	0.5	0.0	-24.7	1.1	-139.3	1.8	-57.5	-103.3
10th Percentile	0.8	0.4	-8.0	1.6	-42.0	2.8	-27.5	-41.9
25th Percentile	1.2	8.9	0.1	2.6	-2.8	4.4	-3.3	-2.8
50th Percentile	1.9	23.9	2.4	4.4	3.1	6.2	2.8	9.8
75th Percentile	3.1	40.9	6.2	9.5	7.4	8.9	6.6	16.8
90th Percentile	5.5	60.7	19.7	26.6	13.5	17.1	11.0	31.2
95th Percentile	8.6	75.3	46.3	50.8	19.9	41.5	14.5	62.4
99th Percentile	41.0	140.7	265.4	162.3	76.4	175.6	27.1	367.1
Panel B: 1989 Distribution								
Mean	3.4	44.3	13.5	20.7	-32.7	14.2	-10.9	6.0
Standard Deviation	16.0	554.6	508.9	292.5	418.1	51.4	174.2	943.7
Kurtosis	898	4,800	4,941	3,908	1,230	362	2,094	1,604
(std error)	0.07	0.06	0.07	0.07	0.06	0.07	0.06	0.06
Skewness	27.2	66.4	67.9	60.7	15.2	15.5	-42.1	19.4
(std error)	0.03	0.03	0.03	0.04	0.03	0.03	0.03	0.03
01st Percentile	0.1	0.0	-161.3	0.2	-1025.2	0.0	-197.3	-659.2
05th Percentile	0.4	0.0	-22.9	1.1	-119.0	0.3	-53.2	-132.5
10th Percentile	0.7	0.2	-6.7	1.7	-40.3	1.6	-27.1	-55.8
25th Percentile	1.1	9.2	-0.1	2.8	-5.1	4.0	-4.9	-6.9
50th Percentile	1.7	26.7	1.8	4.7	2.5	6.0	2.0	8.6
75th Percentile	2.8	45.0	5.2	10.7	7.3	8.8	6.4	16.9
90th Percentile	5.0	68.2	17.2	30.0	13.8	18.1	11.2	32.5
95th Percentile	7.5	81.4	40.1	58.1	21.6	44.7	15.3	82.5
99th Percentile	23.0	152.5	287.6	182.4	84.8	190.0	29.0	542.0
Panel C: % Change in Ratio [(1989-1985)/1985*100%]								
Mean	-17%	40%	-32%	40%	-23%	-8%	11%	-123%
25th Percentile	-10%	3%	-300%	8%	82%	-9%	48%	146%
50th Percentile	-7%	12%	-23%	7%	-19%	-3%	-27%	-12%
75th Percentile	-7%	10%	-16%	12%	-1%	-0%	-3%	1%

Security Analysis: How to Analyze Accounting and Market Data to Value Securities
Robert W. Holthausen and Mark E. Zmijewski
\C0693A.W51

Exhibit 6.2

Distribution of Financial Ratios Industries

INDUSTRY AGGREGATE	SIC	CRx	DAT%	ICBTx	INVXx	NPM%	RECXx	ROA%	ROE%
Panel A: 1985 Weighted Average									
ALL INDUSTRIAL		1.3	34.7	3.0	5.5	4.5	4.3	4.5	14.4
S & P 500		1.1	27.6	2.0	5.2	5.1	3.0	2.8	13.9
DRILLING OIL AND GAS WELLS	1381	1.8	41.6	-0.2	9.1	-14.0	4.2	-5.0	-12.0
APPAREL & OTHER FINISHED PDS	2300	1.8	37.2	3.5	4.0	5.3	9.7	8.5	34.5
MEN,YTH,BOYS FRNSH,WRK CLTHG	2320	2.5	43.6	3.0	2.9	3.7	8.0	5.5	15.5
CONVRT PAPR,PAPRBRD,EX BOXES	2670	1.9	23.0	8.1	3.6	7.7	6.2	9.6	20.6
NEWSPAPER:PUBG, PUBG & PRINT	2711	1.2	33.8	4.1	20.4	8.9	7.2	6.4	16.8
PLASTICS,RESINS,ELASTOMERS	2821	1.4	42.5	2.7	5.8	6.1	6.7	5.7	-20.9
PHARMACEUTICALS	2834	1.8	20.3	10.2	2.5	13.2	5.6	12.6	26.5
MISC CHEMICAL PRODUCTS	2890	2.0	17.7	8.9	4.8	5.9	5.9	6.8	13.8
PETROLEUM REFINING	2911	1.1	21.8	4.6	10.1	5.1	8.9	5.2	13.3
PLASTICS PRODUCTS, NEC	3089	1.9	34.2	3.9	4.2	4.2	6.4	5.4	14.5
CUTLERY,HAND TOOLS,GEN HRDWR	3420	2.2	34.7	4.9	2.8	6.9	4.7	8.5	32.7
SPECIAL INDUSTRY MACHY, NEC	3559	2.2	24.5	8.3	2.9	6.4	4.5	7.0	14.1
AIR COND,HEATING,REFRIG EQ	3585	1.2	51.3	2.0	4.7	4.5	2.1	3.4	17.1
ELECTRIC LIGHTING,WIRING EQ	3640	2.0	25.2	4.9	3.1	5.7	6.1	5.5	11.5
TELE & TELEGRAPH APPARATUS	3661	1.7	18.4	4.7	2.8	4.8	3.6	4.7	12.8
AIRCRAFT PARTS, AUX EQ, NEC	3728	2.2	56.5	1.7	3.3	3.0	7.3	3.1	17.5
RAILROADS,LINE-HAUL OPERATNG	4011	0.9	28.1	2.6	16.6	5.7	7.8	3.1	9.4
TRUCKING, EXCEPT LOCAL	4213	1.1	29.1	2.1	130.8	0.9	9.5	1.6	4.6
TELEVISION BROADCAST STATION	4833	1.7	37.5	5.1	46.4	17.9	6.0	9.6	28.9
WATER SUPPLY	4941	0.7	42.9	2.3	24.3	10.0	5.9	2.9	10.5
DRUGS AND PROPRIETARY-WHSL	5122	1.5	22.6	1.9	9.3	0.6	12.4	1.9	6.6
GROCERY STORES	5411	1.2	51.5	1.8	10.5	0.9	92.5	3.0	27.5
WOMEN'S CLOTHING STORES	5621	2.3	18.3	7.4	5.1	4.6	13.9	8.7	16.5
FAMILY CLOTHING STORES	5651	1.9	30.3	4.7	3.9	4.0	11.6	7.9	20.4
EATING PLACES	5812	1.0	51.2	2.0	22.2	2.9	18.9	3.0	15.2
CATALOG, MAIL-ORDER HOUSES	5961	2.4	42.3	2.7	4.9	2.6	5.9	3.5	10.3
HOTELS,MOTELS,TOURIST COURTS	7011	1.0	51.7	2.0	40.3	8.2	7.5	3.7	11.4
HELP SUPPLY SERVICES	7363	1.9	28.1	5.7	297.4	2.8	6.3	8.6	23.9
ENGINEERING SERVICES	8711	1.8	25.9	3.2	10.8	2.8	4.6	4.1	9.0
Panel B: 1989 Weighted Average									
ALL INDUSTRIAL	1	1.5	23.9	4.2	5.9	3.7	8.6	4.4	11.0
S & P 500	6	1.2	22.6	2.3	5.2	4.5	9.2	2.8	11.8
DRILLING OIL AND GAS WELLS	1381	0.7	45.1	-0.7	8.2	-25.8	4.9	-7.4	-20.9
APPAREL & OTHER FINISHED PDS	2300	2.4	21.6	6.8	2.6	3.9	6.4	7.0	13.1
MEN,YTH,BOYS FRNSH,WRK CLTHG	2320	2.9	20.0	6.8	4.0	4.7	8.5	8.3	14.6
CONVRT PAPR,PAPRBRD,EX BOXES	2670	2.1	15.4	9.8	3.2	7.1	6.1	9.1	15.8
NEWSPAPER:PUBG, PUBG & PRINT	2711	1.3	26.9	10.2	16.0	8.9	8.1	8.9	19.4
PLASTICS,RESINS,ELASTOMERS	2821	1.3	31.8	0.2	4.6	-2.9	6.0	-2.6	-7.9
PHARMACEUTICALS	2834	2.1	16.9	9.9	2.4	10.8	5.7	9.6	17.5
MISC CHEMICAL PRODUCTS	2890	2.2	17.8	9.6	4.3	6.8	5.8	7.3	13.6
PETROLEUM REFINING	2911	1.1	22.5	5.0	9.9	3.8	10.1	4.4	11.9
PLASTICS PRODUCTS, NEC	3089	2.5	8.8	11.1	4.9	5.1	8.5	6.7	10.1
CUTLERY,HAND TOOLS,GEN HRDWR	3420	2.2	26.4	6.2	2.8	7.0	5.0	8.1	17.0
SPECIAL INDUSTRY MACHY, NEC	3559	2.3	31.8	1.3	2.2	-0.0	5.0	0.0	-0.1
AIR COND,HEATING,REFRIG EQ	3585	1.2	26.5	3.8	5.9	4.0	5.8	4.6	13.2
ELECTRIC LIGHTING,WIRING EQ	3640	2.2	25.4	5.6	2.9	5.4	6.9	5.8	12.3
TELE & TELEGRAPH APPARATUS	3661	2.0	22.7	1.8	2.2	2.0	3.8	2.0	5.7
AIRCRAFT PARTS, AUX EQ, NEC	3728	2.4	22.0	7.9	3.3	6.1	6.9	7.9	16.8
RAILROADS,LINE-HAUL OPERATNG	4011	1.2	24.6	3.3	11.9	5.1	6.9	3.1	8.2
TRUCKING, EXCEPT LOCAL	4213	1.4	15.4	9.0	130.8	3.8	9.5	6.5	13.3
TELEVISION BROADCAST STATION	4833	1.7	45.7	4.1	46.4	6.7	6.0	5.8	34.2
WATER SUPPLY	4941	1.1	41.7	2.9	28.7	11.6	7.0	3.8	13.1
DRUGS AND PROPRIETARY-WHSL	5122	1.6	18.9	2.3	10.1	0.3	11.4	0.8	2.2
GROCERY STORES	5411	1.3	23.3	5.0	10.8	1.4	120.3	5.9	15.2
WOMEN'S CLOTHING STORES	5621	2.0	27.9	7.8	4.8	5.4	26.8	10.1	21.9
FAMILY CLOTHING STORES	5651	1.8	20.8	8.3	3.8	3.1	65.7	7.0	15.7
EATING PLACES	5812	1.0	29.3	4.5	22.2	5.5	18.9	6.1	14.7
CATALOG, MAIL-ORDER HOUSES	5961	2.7	42.2	2.6	4.9	2.4	5.9	3.8	12.9
HOTELS,MOTELS,TOURIST COURTS	7011	1.0	50.8	1.7	36.1	3.3	9.9	1.9	6.0
HELP SUPPLY SERVICES	7363	2.1	25.2	4.9	47.7	2.1	7.0	6.5	14.6
ENGINEERING SERVICES	8711	1.6	13.9	11.0	10.7	5.5	4.4	8.3	17.8
Panel C: Rank Correlation between 1985 and 1989 Weighted Average									
Rank Correlation		0.825	0.426	0.370	0.964	0.563	0.900	0.527	0.645

Security Analysis: How to Analyze Accounting and Market Data to Value Securities
Robert W. Holthausen and Mark E. Zmijewski
\C0693A.W51

12. Internal Strategic Planning and Identifying (In)Efficient Managements.

An important use of financial ratios is to analyze a firm relative to its comparable firms, and assess where the firm is better and worse than its comparable firms.

(1) Before you begin this analysis, you must first identify the comparable firms.

(2) Where is the firm inefficient or different? Where can the firm improve?

(3) Are present operating and financing strategies working?

(4) What is the firm's growth potential?

(5) How would new operating and financing initiatives affect the firm.

(6) How risky is the firm?

(7) How stable is the firm?

13. Financial Statement Relations as an Aid in Economic Decisions.

Ratios are used in the following decisions.

(1) Decisions by banks to issue credit and monitor existing loans.
(2) Decisions by rating agencies in setting bond ratings.
(3) Decisions by auditors in setting scope for their engagements.
(4) Allocating resources within a firm.

For example, Standard & Poor's (a bond rating agency) considers subjective assessments of the risk of the firm's position within an industry and the industry the firm operates within, in conjunction with financial information. Firms which are considered to be less risky on grounds are allowed to have more risky financial characteristics (as measured by ratios) in determining a rating. Consider the following guidelines published by S&P for "total debt as a percentage of capitalization" in the food and beverage industry as a function of their subjective assessment of the firm's competitive position within the industry.

FOOD AND BEVERAGE INDUSTRY
Competitive Position vs. Peer Group

Rating Category	Excellent	Above Average	Industry Average	Median
BBB	60%	55%	50%	35%
A	50%	45%	40%	30%
AA	40%	35%	30%	25%
AAA	30%	25%	N.A.	15%

Security Analysis: How to Analyze Accounting and Market Data to Value Securities
  Robert W. Holthausen and Mark E. Zmijewski
  \C0693A.W51

Do not reproduce without permission.
July 29, 1998 - 3:13 pm

175

Analysts also develop statistical models to predict economic events. See chapter 7, "Using Financial Statement Relations to Predict Economic Events," for a discussion of prediction models of this type.

14. Using Financial Statement Relations for Forecasting Financial Statements and Cash Flows.

Financial analysts use ratios as an aid to generate forecasts (e.g, required cash balance, inventory, capital expenditures, relation between various expenses and sales, etc.). We discuss this topic in more detail in chapter 8. As will be discussed, we favor the forecasting of the firm's financial statements, not just the firm's cash flows. Typically, the financial statement forecasts are driven by one or a few key factors. Once you forecast those key factors, then you forecast the remainder of the financial statements by forecasting various relations among financial statement items. The time series of a company's various financial statement relations is useful in that it provides information about the stability of a particular relation over time. Obviously changes in economic factors or in the company's operating policies can affect the stability of various relations.

Analysts use other ratios as an aid to judge the reasonableness of forecasts. One of the benefits of forecasting financial statements is that a variety of ratios can be examined to assess if various historical relations have been inadvertently altered in the forecasts. For example, it is often difficult to make forecasts of capital expenditures. Various asset turnover ratios, such as sales/total assets often make it clear that historical relations have been altered in the forecasts.

15. The Role of Financial Statement Relations in Contracts.

Financial statement relations play an important role in the control and monitoring of management actions. Ratios are used in contracts to place limits on the actions that managers of firms can take. For example, it is common to write restrictive covenants to lending agreements that restrict the firm's ability to issue new debt, pay dividends, merge with other companies, and sell off assets as a function of various leverage tests (such as debt to net tangible assets) and liquidity constraints (current ratios).

These contracts become binding for some firm's and often prohibit the firm's ability to take actions which might make the stockholders better off at the expense of the bondholders. In addition, not meeting certain minimum ratios can accelerate the due date of the loan to the present (a so-called event of default). Events of default typically give the bondholders the right to have a greater influence on how the company will be run, or force it into bankruptcy proceedings; for example, the following paragraph appears in Fort Howard's 12/31/90 10-K.

Among other restrictions, the Bank Credit Agreement and subordinated securities: (1) restrict payments of dividends, repayments of subordinated debt, purchases of the Company's stock, additional borrowing and acquisition of property, plant and equipment; (2) require that the ratios of current assets to current liabilities, senior debt to net worth plus subordinated debt and earnings before non-cash charges, interest and taxes to cash interest be maintained at prescribed levels, (3) restrict the ability of the Company to make fundamental changes and to enter into new lines of business, the pledging of the

Security Analysis: How to Analyze Accounting and Market Data to Value Securities
  Robert W. Holthausen and Mark E. Zmijewski
  \C0693A.W51

Do not reproduce without permission.
July 29, 1998 - 3:13 pm

176

Company's assets and guarantees of the indebtedness of others; and (4) limit dispositions of assets, the ability of the Company to enter lease and sale-leaseback transactions and investments which might be made by the Company. The Company believes such limitations should not impair its plans for expansion, continued modernization of the facilities, or other operating activities.

Of course, Fort Howard is highly levered. Some companies don't have any constraints, such as General Motors and John Harland. Readers of the financial press will remember that RJR didn't have any restrictions prior to its LBO. Many other companies have some type of constraint. In a recent study by Press and Weintrop, of a random sample of firms, 49% had debt constraints, 45% had working capital constraints and 61% had dividend constraints. For example, under its debt covenants, Computer Factory had to have a total liabilities to tangible net worth ratio less than 1.5, had to maintain a current ratio of at least 2.00, could pay no dividends and had to maintain net worth of at least $8.6 million.

We also see ratios used in employment contracts. For example, top management's bonus compensation is often set at some specified percentage of earnings in excess of some proportion of invested capital. For example;

$$\text{Bonus} = Y\% \ [\text{Net Income} - X\% \ \text{Capitalization}].$$

Depending on the definition of capitalization, this essentially sets a lower bound on ROE or ROA in setting the bonus. A recent contract used by Bank-America was to pay out a maximum bonus pool to eligible employees of 0.75% [Consolidated Net Income - Taxes]. But there were no awards if:

$$\text{ROE} < 15\%, \ \text{ROA} < \text{average ROA of the 15 largest banks.}$$

Security Analysis: How to Analyze Accounting and Market Data to Value Securities
Robert W. Holthausen and Mark E. Zmijewski
\C0693A.W51

Chapter 6

Problems for Review

1. A rather infamous compensation contract between Archie McCardell and International Harvester (I-H) allowed Archie to have a $1.8 million loan forgiven in McCardell's second year as CEO. The loan had been used to buy 60,000 shares of I-H stock. The contract called for averaging I-H's return on assets, return on shareholder's equity and return on sales. I-H's average was to be compared with the average of the same 3 ratios on six identified competitors (Caterpillar Tractor, Deere & Co., Ford Motor, General Motors, Massey-Ferguson and Paccar (made Kenworth trucks)). The entire loan could be forgiven in any year that I-H's average topped the average of the 18 ratios of the competitors. The contract called for a competitor's ratios to be dropped from the analysis if it lost money (but it did not provide for marginal performances or unusual circumstances). The contract was designed by Booz Allen.

    In the year in which McCardell's loan was forgiven, Massey-Ferguson was on the edge of bankruptcy proceedings but barely profitable and Ford's earnings fell 25%. About one-quarter of I-H's income came from foreign currency translation gains and a one-time credit for a change in the U.K. tax law. The contract did stipulate that the compensation committee should check to see if McCardell took steps to increase profits through short term manipulations. The compensation board could have reduced the loan by only 20% per year had they wished.

    The announcement that McCardell's loan would be forgiven for the results achieved in the fiscal year ending October 31, 1979 was made in August of 1980. More than a few employees and shareholders were disgruntled since Harvester had reported a $417.5 million loss for the first 9 months of the 10/31/80 fiscal year end. Harvester lost more money in 1980 than it made in 1979. The shareholders of the corporation filed a suit against McCardell (chairman and CEO), the then president and chief operating officer, and the board of directors of Harvester.

    Required:

    Discuss the aspects of McCardell's compensation contract that are well conceived and the aspects that are poorly conceived.

Security Analysis: How to Analyze Accounting and Market Data to Value Securities
Robert W. Holthausen and Mark E. Zmijewski
\C0693A.W51

2. Examples of Some Financial Statement Relation Calculations.

Below we present financial statement and other data for six publicly traded firms. Included with the list of companies below, we provide the rate of return on equity (ROE) and the rate of return on assets (ROA) that is reported by a well known database for these firms.

Firm Name	Ticker	SIC	Industry Description	Stock Exchange	Database ROE	ROA
NEW AMERICAN SHOE CO	NSO	3021	RUBBER AND PLASTICS FOOTWEAR	New York	31.0%	-75.0%
ANACOMP INC	AAC	3861	PHOTOGRAPHIC EQUIP & SUPPLY	New York	39.3%	4.5%
EAGLE-PICHER INDS	EPI	3714	MOTOR VEHICLE PART,ACCESSORY	New York	-23.0%	9.5%
LINDBERG CORP	LIND	3390	MISC PRIMARY METAL PRODUCTS	NASDAQ	13.0%	6.7%
PERSONAL COMPUTER PRODUCTS	PCPI	3577	COMPUTER PERIPHERAL EQ, NEC	NASDAQ	-35.0%	-9.9%
ASTROSYSTEMS INC	ASTR	3823	INDUSTRIAL MEASUREMENT INSTR	NASDAQ	1.1%	0.8%

STATEMENT OF FINANCIAL POSITION	TICKER--> NSO Jun88	AAC Sep88	EPI Nov90	LIND Dec90	PCPI Jun90	ASTR Jun88
ASSETS						
Cash & Equivalents	0.179	23.715	16.092	0.314	1.090	28.262
Receivables - Total (Net)	5.157	140.383	121.691	9.560	3.587	7.604
Inventories - Total	5.610	105.173	75.602	1.550	2.041	7.190
Current Assets - Other	0.483	90.772	15.061	1.502	1.180	36.867
Current Assets - Total	11.429	360.043	228.446	12.926	7.898	44.807
Plant, Property & Equip (Gross)	14.009	200.117	357.627	81.001	1.268	1.943
Accumulated Depreciation	6.995	41.076	210.894	49.850	0.904	0.920
Plant, Property & Equip (Net)	7.014	159.041	146.733	31.151	0.364	1.023
Investments and Advances - Other	0.000	21.664	10.315	1.978	0.376	0.648
Intangibles	0.000	391.777	14.589	0.000	0.000	0.000
Assets - Other	0.219	30.851	13.612	1.821	0.762	0.000
TOTAL ASSETS	18.662	963.376	413.695	47.876	9.400	46.478
LIABILITIES						
Accounts Payable	3.561	41.205	43.363	2.049	1.662	0.725
Notes Payable	3.565	0.000	19.700	0.000	0.000	0.000
Accrued Expenses	2.866	88.286	31.765	4.207	0.588	1.087
Taxes Payable	0.000	29.799	5.733	0.000	0.000	0.000
Debt (Long-Term) Due In One Year	0.737	78.300	102.419	0.290	4.409	0.000
Other Current Liabilities	0.000	0.000	40.000	0.000	0.068	0.000
Total Current Liabilities	10.729	237.590	242.980	6.546	6.727	1.812
Long Term Debt	53.034	541.878	3.618	5.440	0.014	0.000
Deferred Taxes	0.000	0.000	0.000	8.702	0.000	9.778
Liabilities - Other	0.000	73.041	338.579	2.461	0.000	0.000
TOTAL LIABILITIES	63.763	852.509	585.177	23.149	6.741	11.590
SHAREHOLDERS' EQUITY						
Preferred Stock	0.000	24.000	0.000	0.000	4.107	0.000
Common Stock	0.340	0.363	13.906	14.183	0.021	0.568
Capital Surplus	25.259	139.318	37.644	1.576	4.611	10.801
Retained Earnings (Net Other)	(70.700)	(50.360)	(219.697)	14.644	(6.080)	23.519
Less: Treasury Stock	0.000	2.454	3.335	5.676	0.000	0.000
TOTAL SHAREHOLDERS' EQUITY	(45.101)	110.867	(171.482)	24.727	2.659	34.888
TOTAL LIABILITIES & EQUITY	18.662	963.376	413.695	47.876	9.400	46.478

Security Analysis: How to Analyze Accounting and Market Data to Value Securities
Robert W. Holthausen and Mark E. Zmijewski
\C0693A.W51

INCOME STATEMENT	TICKER-->	NSO Jun88	AAC Sep88	EPI Nov90	LIND Dec90	PCPI Jun90	ASTR Jun88
Sales (Net)		21.473	450.503	699.347	76.141	13.375	13.965
Cost of Goods Sold		29.626	277.597	561.400	52.196	8.060	12.517
Gross Profit		(8.153)	172.906	137.947	23.945	5.315	1.448
Selling, General, & Admin Expenses		5.265	79.203	66.016	14.641	5.153	2.824
Operating Income Before Depreciation		(13.418)	93.703	71.931	9.304	0.162	(1.376)
Depreciation, Depletion, & Amortiz		1.908	21.072	24.227	3.763	0.142	0.285
Operating Income After Depreciation		(15.326)	72.631	47.704	5.541	0.020	(1.661)
Interest Expense		0.221	23.471	12.579	0.635	0.384	0.000
Non-Operating Income/Expense		0.000	3.702	(1.292)	(0.101)	(0.508)	2.289
Special Items		(2.497)	0.000	10.227	0.496	0.000	(0.384)
Pretax Income		(18.044)	52.862	44.060	5.301	(0.872)	0.244
Income Taxes - Total		0.000	23.747	4.700	2.096	0.058	(0.135)
Minority Interest		0.000	0.000		0.000	0.000	0.000
Income Before Extraordinary Items & Discontinued Operations (EI&DO)		(18.044)	29.115	39.360	3.205	(0.930)	0.379
Extraordinary Items		4.043	14.470	0.000	0.000	0.000	0.000
Discontinued Operations		0.000	0.000	0.000	0.000	0.000	0.000
Net Income (Loss)		(14.001)	43.585	39.360	3.205	(0.930)	0.379
Income Before EI&DO		(18.044)	29.115	39.360	3.205	(0.930)	0.379
Preferred Dividends		0.000	2.165	0.000	0.000	0.234	0.000
Available for Common Before EI&DO		(18.044)	26.950	39.360	3.205	(1.164)	0.379
Common Stk Equivalents - Savings		0.000	0.000	0.000	0.000	0.000	0.000
Adjusted Available for Common		(18.044)	26.950	39.360	3.205	(1.164)	0.379

STATEMENT OF RETAINED EARNINGS	Jun88	Sep88	Nov90	Dec90	Jun90	Jun88
Retained Earnings - Beginning Balance	(56.699)	(91.289)	(260.590)	12.918	(5.150)	23.140
Net Income	(14.001)	43.585	39.360	3.205	(0.930)	0.379
Cash Dividends	0.000	2.062	0.000	1.321	0.000	0.000
Retained Earnings After Dividends	(70.700)	(49.766)	(221.230)	14.802	(6.080)	23.519
Change - Foreign Curr Translation Adj	0.000	(0.541)	1.533	0.000	0.000	0.000
Adj to Long-Term Marketable Securities	0.000	0.000	0.000	0.000	0.000	0.000
Other CMP Adj (Stock Splits/Retirement)	0.000	0.000	0.000	(0.158)	0.000	0.000
Non-CMP (COMPUSTAT) Adjustments - PLUG CALCULATION	0.000	(0.053)	(0.000)	(0.000)	0.000	(0.000)
Retained Earnings - Ending Balance	(70.700)	(50.360)	(219.697)	14.644	(6.080)	23.519
Retroactive Adjustments (Acct'g Chgs)		0.000	0.000	0.000	0.000	0.000
Retained Earnings - After Adjustments	(70.700)	(50.360)	(219.697)	14.644	(6.080)	23.519

A. How did the database calculate ROE? Recalculate ROE and ROA using the best approach possible. (Note, there is only one year of a balance sheet so it is not possible to calculate the average balance sheet over two years.)

B. Recalculate ROE for LIND and ASTR assuming deferred taxes are not a liability.

C. Recalculate ROE and ROA for AAC and EPI assuming that all intangibles are written off against retained earnings and intangibles have been amortized over 10 years.

Security Analysis: How to Analyze Accounting and Market Data to Value Securities
Robert W. Holthausen and Mark E. Zmijewski
\C0693A.W51

Do not reproduce without permission.
July 29, 1998 - 3:13 pm

180

3.   An Analysis of TOYS "R" US (TOY).

Below we present some information on TOY and other firms. Use this information to assess where TOY is efficient, inefficient, or different, where TOY can improve, if TOY's present operating and financing strategies are working, what its growth potential is over, say, the next decade, what TOY's financing strategy is, how risky it is, and how stable it is. Also, use this information to identify which of these firms are potentially comparable to TOY, and what other type of firms may be comparable to TOY. We present data for TOY, CWLD (Child World), GMN (Greenman which operates Circus World, Playland and Playworld stores), LIO (Lionel which operates Lionel Playworld, Kiddie City and TOY Warehouse), GPS which is the GAP and GOSHA which is OSHKOSH B'GOSH (kids clothes manufacturer).

2 TICKER REF#	VARIABLE DESCRIPTION	1984	1985	1986	1987	1988	1989
3							
4 TOY	-100 Sales $ (Nominal) / Store - US TOY	8.258	7.897	8.063	8.486	9.115	9.379
5 TOY	-99 Sales $ (Nominal) / Store - Intern'l	3.000	4.167	5.476	6.176	7.667	7.853
6 TOY	-98 Sales $ (Nominal) / Store - Kids	2.273	2.391	2.674	3.243	3.125	3.394
7 TOY	-97 Sales $ (GPLA) / Store - US TOY	5.311	4.894	4.941	4.981	5.123	5.037
8 TOY	-96 Sales $ (GPLA) / Store - Intern'l	1.929	2.582	3.356	3.625	4.309	4.218
9 TOY	-95 Sales $ (GPLA) / Store - Kids	1.462	1.482	1.639	1.904	1.757	1.823
10 TOY	-94 Operating Profit $ (Nominal) / Store - US TOY	1.005	0.927	1.022	1.086	1.154	1.208
11 TOY	-93 Operating Profit $ (Nominal) / Store - Intern'l	-0.500	-0.167	0.143	0.088	0.375	0.574
12 TOY	-92 Operating Profit $ (Nominal) / Store - Kids	-0.273	-0.087	0.070	0.081	0.107	0.139
13 TOY	-91 Operating Profit $ (GPLA) / Store - US TOY	0.646	0.575	0.626	0.638	0.648	0.649
14 TOY	-90 Operating Profit $ (GPLA) / Store - Intern'l	-0.322	-0.103	0.088	0.052	0.211	0.308
15 TOY	-89 Operating Profit $ (GPLA) / Store - Kids	-0.175	-0.054	0.043	0.048	0.060	0.074
16 TOY	-88 Sales $ (Nominal) / Sq ft - US TOY	183.543	174.955	178.120	187.042	200.553	206.081
17 TOY	-87 Sales $ (Nominal) / Sq ft - Intern'l	65.217	90.580	119.048	134.271	166.667	170.716
18 TOY	-86 Sales $ (Nominal) / Sq ft - Kids	108.225	113.872	127.353	154.440	148.810	161.627
19 TOY	-85 Sales $ (GPLA) / Sq ft - US TOY	118.038	108.427	109.155	109.782	112.729	110.689
20 TOY	-84 Sales $ (GPLA) / Sq ft - Intern'l	41.942	56.136	72.954	78.809	93.682	91.694
21 TOY	-83 Sales $ (GPLA) / Sq ft - Kids	69.600	70.571	78.044	90.646	83.645	86.812
22 TOY	-82 Operating Profit $ (Nominal) / Sq ft - US TOY	22.339	20.538	22.581	23.944	25.384	26.542
23 TOY	-81 Operating Profit $ (Nominal) / Sq ft - Intern'l	-10.870	-3.623	3.106	1.918	8.152	12.468
24 TOY	-80 Operating Profit $ (Nominal) / Sq ft - Kids	-12.987	-4.141	3.322	3.861	5.102	6.604
25 TOY	-79 Operating Profit $ (GPLA) / Sq ft - US TOY	14.367	12.728	13.838	14.053	14.268	14.256
26 TOY	-78 Operating Profit $ (GPLA) / Sq ft - Intern'l	-6.990	-2.245	1.903	1.126	4.582	6.697
27 TOY	-77 Operating Profit $ (GPLA) / Sq ft - Kids	-8.352	-2.566	2.036	2.266	2.868	3.547
28 TOY	-76 Operating Margin (OPNI/SALE) US TOYs	0.122	0.117	0.127	0.128	0.127	0.129
29 TOY	-75 Operating Margin (OPNI/SALE) Intern'l	-0.167	-0.040	0.026	0.014	0.049	0.073
30 TOY	-74 Operating Margin (OPNI/SALE) KIDS	-0.120	-0.036	0.026	0.025	0.034	0.041
31 AG5651	457 LIFE OF GROSS PLANT	13.8084	13.4251	12.5532	12.8137	11.8141	11.9287
32 AG5945	457 LIFE OF GROSS PLANT	21.7372	17.3867	17.2913	17.6150	17.9396	19.2089
33 CWLD	457 LIFE OF GROSS PLANT	NA	8.0048	8.3414	8.4617	8.4635	7.3044
34 GMN	457 LIFE OF GROSS PLANT	12.8747	13.8432	9.5074	8.3870	8.8524	9.9798
35 GOSHA	457 LIFE OF GROSS PLANT	12.6456	11.9325	13.0559	14.9276	17.2813	15.3635
36 GPS	457 LIFE OF GROSS PLANT	9.0337	8.4472	8.3006	9.3996	9.1085	9.2830
37 LIO	457 LIFE OF GROSS PLANT	11.4442	12.1125	12.9636	12.9185	11.7377	15.0972
38 TOY	457 LIFE OF GROSS PLANT	28.1926	27.9992	29.4343	29.4989	29.3132	29.8348
39 AG5651	459 AGE OF REMAINING PLANT	9.8383	9.8494	9.0024	9.0109	8.2385	8.2101
40 AG5945	459 AGE OF REMAINING PLANT	17.6348	14.6667	14.4150	14.5133	14.6146	15.6602
41 CWLD	459 AGE OF REMAINING PLANT	NA	6.9575	6.5903	6.0619	5.4792	4.7580
42 GMN	459 AGE OF REMAINING PLANT	7.6525	9.5747	6.1992	5.1500	4.6962	4.5937
43 GOSHA	459 AGE OF REMAINING PLANT	8.6654	7.8794	8.3841	10.3767	12.7152	10.8237
44 GPS	459 AGE OF REMAINING PLANT	5.8871	5.4909	5.4010	6.2986	6.0894	6.2801
45 LIO	459 AGE OF REMAINING PLANT	6.1276	5.8132	7.7625	8.3606	7.4189	9.1173
46 TOY	459 AGE OF REMAINING PLANT	24.4904	24.4383	25.6971	25.7232	25.6023	25.8657
47 AG5651	460 CURRENT ASSETS / CURRENT LIABILITIES	1.8444	1.7570	1.7920	1.8738	1.9306	1.8143
48 AG5945	460 CURRENT ASSETS / CURRENT LIABILITIES	1.7623	1.5696	1.4640	1.4222	1.4590	1.3586
49 CWLD	460 CURRENT ASSETS / CURRENT LIABILITIES	NA	1.4705	1.3703	1.3582	1.4882	1.5480
50 GMN	460 CURRENT ASSETS / CURRENT LIABILITIES	1.5969	2.0121	1.9063	2.0830	2.2927	2.1945
51 GOSHA	460 CURRENT ASSETS / CURRENT LIABILITIES	3.2648	3.8425	3.4089	3.9355	2.7698	4.2632
52 GPS	460 CURRENT ASSETS / CURRENT LIABILITIES	2.1714	1.8880	1.9268	2.0109	1.6992	1.6892
53 LIO	460 CURRENT ASSETS / CURRENT LIABILITIES	3.3328	2.2889	2.4253	2.7877	2.4795	2.4298
54 TOY	460 CURRENT ASSETS / CURRENT LIABILITIES	1.5315	1.4555	1.3115	1.3404	1.2899	1.2167
55 AG5651	463 DAYS SALES IN ACCOUNTS RECEIVABLES	9.5692	5.4789	5.3506	10.2187	29.1089	30.6315
56 AG5945	463 DAYS SALES IN ACCOUNTS RECEIVABLES	NA	5.6415	5.1482	5.6280	5.4985	4.4423
57 CWLD	463 DAYS SALES IN ACCOUNTS RECEIVABLES	NA	NA	1.0794	0.8172	0.7443	0.9934
58 GMN	463 DAYS SALES IN ACCOUNTS RECEIVABLES	27.7696	22.2167	21.3313	24.6963	19.7996	16.7237
59 GOSHA	463 DAYS SALES IN ACCOUNTS RECEIVABLES	NA	30.8692	29.8231	31.3511	29.8508	24.7340
60 GPS	463 DAYS SALES IN ACCOUNTS RECEIVABLES	4.1707	3.5823	2.5684	2.7798	2.1281	1.3268
61 LIO	463 DAYS SALES IN ACCOUNTS RECEIVABLES	18.8590	15.7254	3.0330	2.2883	2.9457	3.0598
62 TOY	463 DAYS SALES IN ACCOUNTS RECEIVABLES	4.3703	4.4977	4.6730	5.7184	5.8575	4.5538
63 AG5651	466 DAYS TO SELL INVENTORY	91.1566	95.0719	91.0462	91.1647	131.1814	96.5950
64 AG5945	466 DAYS TO SELL INVENTORY	NA	99.1922	113.7269	118.5315	122.9820	129.7294
65 CWLD	466 DAYS TO SELL INVENTORY	NA	NA	131.2316	130.9954	143.4852	142.8845
66 GMN	466 DAYS TO SELL INVENTORY	82.4306	105.6304	122.3599	131.5689	123.5770	117.7032
67 GOSHA	466 DAYS TO SELL INVENTORY	NA	98.0560	114.3270	119.8870	123.0064	143.3895
68 GPS	466 DAYS TO SELL INVENTORY	88.4575	96.6270	99.2621	93.7758	85.8296	77.9662
69 LIO	466 DAYS TO SELL INVENTORY	111.2270	140.1711	115.7383	127.0514	141.6624	154.5954
70 TOY	466 DAYS TO SELL INVENTORY	104.6473	110.4002	101.6886	108.6311	110.8646	117.5569
71 AG5651	467 ACID-TEST	0.2798	0.2412	0.2677	0.3949	0.7317	0.6283

Security Analysis: How to Analyze Accounting and Market Data to Value Securities
Robert W. Holthausen and Mark E. Zmijewski
\C0693A.W51

2 TICKER REF# VARIABLE DESCRIPTION	1984	1985	1986	1987	1988	1989
72 AG5945 467 ACID-TEST	0.6895	0.4125	0.3361	0.2351	0.2075	0.1152
73 CWLD 467 ACID-TEST	NA	0.2118	0.2706	0.3314	0.0705	0.1458
74 GMN 467 ACID-TEST	0.6061	0.7239	0.5004	0.4866	0.4622	0.4108
75 GOSHA 467 ACID-TEST	1.0707	1.3748	1.1364	1.4422	0.5987	0.9703
76 GPS 467 ACID-TEST	0.3404	0.3075	0.5965	0.3185	0.3441	0.2379
77 LIO 467 ACID-TEST	1.5252	0.9029	1.0405	0.9390	0.5531	0.3839
78 TOY 467 ACID-TEST	0.5724	0.4077	0.2443	0.1636	0.2174	0.0855
79 AG5651 471 TOTAL LIABILITIES / TOTAL ASSETS	0.5339	0.5575	0.5677	0.5694	0.5560	0.5733
80 AG5945 471 TOTAL LIABILITIES / TOTAL ASSETS	0.5481	0.5018	0.5224	0.5999	0.5853	0.5562
81 CWLD 471 TOTAL LIABILITIES / TOTAL ASSETS	NA	0.4644	0.5217	0.5477	0.4917	0.4736
82 GMN 471 TOTAL LIABILITIES / TOTAL ASSETS	0.5582	0.5377	0.5466	0.5730	0.5176	0.5302
83 GOSHA 471 TOTAL LIABILITIES / TOTAL ASSETS	0.3597	0.3279	0.3246	0.2635	0.3011	0.2120
84 GPS 471 TOTAL LIABILITIES / TOTAL ASSETS	0.3985	0.4419	0.4175	0.3715	0.4255	0.4168
85 LIO 471 TOTAL LIABILITIES / TOTAL ASSETS	1.0246	0.4037	0.5439	0.6116	0.6292	0.6318
86 TOY 471 TOTAL LIABILITIES / TOTAL ASSETS	0.4728	0.4148	0.4084	0.4399	0.4428	0.4454
87 AG5651 472 TOTAL DEBT / TOTAL ASSETS	0.5091	0.5272	0.5356	0.5075	0.5080	0.5465
88 AG5945 472 TOTAL DEBT / TOTAL ASSETS	0.5327	0.4770	0.4959	0.5725	0.5548	0.5245
89 CWLD 472 TOTAL DEBT / TOTAL ASSETS	NA	0.4619	0.5172	0.5417	0.4851	0.4651
90 GMN 472 TOTAL DEBT / TOTAL ASSETS	0.5538	0.5343	0.5404	0.5500	0.4910	0.5115
91 GOSHA 472 TOTAL DEBT / TOTAL ASSETS	0.3587	0.3259	0.3193	0.2579	0.2960	0.2078
92 GPS 472 TOTAL DEBT / TOTAL ASSETS	0.3985	0.4419	0.4175	0.3715	0.4255	0.4168
93 LIO 472 TOTAL DEBT / TOTAL ASSETS	0.9985	0.4037	0.5439	0.6021	0.6137	0.6159
94 TOY 472 TOTAL DEBT / TOTAL ASSETS	0.4579	0.3935	0.3819	0.4136	0.4119	0.4140
95 AG5651 477 OIADP / INTEREST	6.8080	7.7650	8.3193	5.0535	8.1357	6.5801
96 AG5945 477 OIADP / INTEREST	21.9107	5.5043	6.9211	5.2506	4.5179	4.2465
97 CWLD 477 OIADP / INTEREST	NA	3.6352	5.8445	4.4298	4.1544	1.7188
98 GMN 477 OIADP / INTEREST	27.6102	6.7039	-0.0524	-0.7656	1.6988	1.8132
99 GOSHA 477 OIADP / INTEREST	22.6475	23.2097	44.0429	64.3374	19.5823	21.1605
100 GPS 477 OIADP / INTEREST	6.2174	20.6435	84.6756	33.3114	39.8220	63.8620
101 LIO 477 OIADP / INTEREST	8.7782	10.2143	3.2424	1.6262	1.2967	0.7945
102 TOY 477 OIADP / INTEREST	29.5269	19.6512	20.2846	16.0220	13.4450	10.3415
103 AG5651 483 RETURN ON COMMON EQUITY	0.1826	0.1729	0.1516	0.2030	0.0560	0.1131
104 AG5945 483 RETURN ON COMMON EQUITY	NA	0.1994	0.1377	0.1504	0.1831	0.1997
105 CWLD 483 RETURN ON COMMON EQUITY	NA	NA	0.0621	0.0759	0.0623	0.0277
106 GMN 483 RETURN ON COMMON EQUITY	0.2755	0.1647	-0.0602	-0.0541	0.0345	0.0442
107 GOSHA 483 RETURN ON COMMON EQUITY	NA	0.3360	0.3688	0.3234	0.2079	0.3330
108 GPS 483 RETURN ON COMMON EQUITY	0.0989	0.1995	0.3746	0.2871	0.2703	0.3178
109 LIO 483 RETURN ON COMMON EQUITY	NA	1.2833	0.1214	0.0731	0.0476	0.0040
110 TOY 483 RETURN ON COMMON EQUITY	0.2145	0.1848	0.1881	0.2003	0.2095	0.2052
111 AG5651 484 RETURN ON TOTAL ASSETS	0.1003	0.0888	0.0753	0.1026	0.0371	0.0645
112 AG5945 484 RETURN ON TOTAL ASSETS	NA	0.1134	0.0787	0.0805	0.0942	0.1056
113 CWLD 484 RETURN ON TOTAL ASSETS	NA	NA	0.0376	0.0430	0.0415	0.0297
114 GMN 484 RETURN ON TOTAL ASSETS	0.1268	0.0881	-0.0084	-0.0054	0.0381	0.0469
115 GOSHA 484 RETURN ON TOTAL ASSETS	NA	0.2309	0.2543	0.2327	0.1564	0.2607
116 GPS 484 RETURN ON TOTAL ASSETS	0.0717	0.1224	0.2169	0.1798	0.1666	0.1872
117 LIO 484 RETURN ON TOTAL ASSETS	0.1223	0.2506	0.0762	0.0477	0.0440	0.0249
118 TOY 484 RETURN ON TOTAL ASSETS	0.1200	0.1083	0.1162	0.1222	0.1260	0.1258
119 AG5651 488 INCOME / SALES	0.0328	0.0305	0.0252	0.0343	0.0149	0.0260
120 AG5945 488 INCOME / SALES	0.0606	0.0472	0.0377	0.0360	0.0402	0.0473
121 CWLD 488 INCOME / SALES	NA	0.0183	0.0174	0.0191	0.0156	0.0070
122 GMN 488 INCOME / SALES	0.0409	0.0328	-0.0139	-0.0118	0.0068	0.0081
123 GOSHA 488 INCOME / SALES	0.0935	0.0866	0.1041	0.1056	0.0742	0.1193
124 GPS 488 INCOME / SALES	0.0229	0.0428	0.0803	0.0655	0.0593	0.0615
125 LIO 488 INCOME / SALES	0.0584	0.1609	0.0307	0.0169	0.0098	0.0008
126 TOY 488 INCOME / SALES	0.0655	0.0606	0.0623	0.0650	0.0670	0.0671
127 AG5651 490 SALES / AVG TOTAL ASSETS	2.6269	2.5515	2.6306	2.5527	1.6428	1.9000
128 AG5945 490 SALES / AVG TOTAL ASSETS	NA	2.0325	1.7783	1.7952	1.8161	1.7687
129 CWLD 490 SALES / AVG TOTAL ASSETS	NA	NA	1.7991	1.8412	1.9172	2.0427
130 GMN 490 SALES / AVG TOTAL ASSETS	2.9893	2.2886	1.9890	2.0194	2.3141	2.5874
131 GOSHA 490 SALES / AVG TOTAL ASSETS	NA	2.5516	2.3874	2.1699	2.0052	2.0843
132 GPS 490 SALES / AVG TOTAL ASSETS	2.6279	2.6894	2.6685	2.6614	2.7357	2.9918
133 LIO 490 SALES / AVG TOTAL ASSETS	1.7825	1.5473	2.0295	1.8050	1.8466	1.8387
134 TOY 490 SALES / AVG TOTAL ASSETS	1.7737	1.7003	1.7788	1.7671	1.7460	1.7009
135 AG5651 491 COST OF GOODS SOLD / SALES	0.7063	0.7095	0.7210	0.7350	0.6782	0.6805
136 AG5945 491 COST OF GOODS SOLD / SALES	0.6770	0.6561	0.6586	0.6653	0.6646	0.6673
137 CWLD 491 COST OF GOODS SOLD / SALES	NA	0.6929	0.6980	0.7113	0.6966	0.6962
138 GMN 491 COST OF GOODS SOLD / SALES	0.7419	0.6927	0.6808	0.6598	0.6426	0.6437
139 GOSHA 491 COST OF GOODS SOLD / SALES	0.6859	0.6861	0.6516	0.6709	0.7301	0.6499
140 GPS 491 COST OF GOODS SOLD / SALES	0.6816	0.6118	0.5640	0.6161	0.6501	0.6355
141 LIO 491 COST OF GOODS SOLD / SALES	0.6807	0.7037	0.6776	0.7106	0.7155	0.7299
142 TOY 491 COST OF GOODS SOLD / SALES	0.6693	0.6695	0.6823	0.6877	0.6916	0.6913
143 AG5651 492 SELLING. GEN & ADMIN / SALES	0.2104	0.2114	0.2025	0.2018	0.2237	0.2181
144 AG5945 492 SELLING. GEN & ADMIN / SALES	0.2058	0.2458	0.2427	0.2392	0.2346	0.2309
145 CWLD 492 SELLING. GEN & ADMIN / SALES	NA	0.2336	0.2358	0.2353	0.2407	0.2593
146 GMN 492 SELLING. GEN & ADMIN / SALES	0.1664	0.2372	0.2980	0.3249	0.3055	0.3052
147 GOSHA 492 SELLING. GEN & ADMIN / SALES	0.1151	0.1291	0.1284	0.1322	0.1350	0.1379
148 GPS 492 SELLING. GEN & ADMIN / SALES	0.2480	0.2515	0.2467	0.2394	0.2161	0.2295
149 LIO 492 SELLING. GEN & ADMIN / SALES	0.2216	0.2629	0.2798	0.2452	0.2417	0.2401
150 TOY 492 SELLING. GEN & ADMIN / SALES	0.2023	0.2067	0.1875	0.1862	0.1841	0.1810
151 AG5651 493 DEPREC & AMORTIZATIONS / SALES	0.0163	0.0174	0.0175	0.0175	0.0225	0.0230
152 AG5945 493 DEPREC & AMORTIZATIONS / SALES	0.0125	0.0155	0.0169	0.0173	0.0171	0.0166
153 CWLD 493 DEPREC & AMORTIZATIONS / SALES	NA	0.0198	0.0181	0.0170	0.0176	0.0186
154 GMN 493 DEPREC & AMORTIZATIONS / SALES	0.0069	0.0144	0.0220	0.0278	0.0242	0.0206
155 GOSHA 493 DEPREC & AMORTIZATIONS / SALES	0.0129	0.0142	0.0127	0.0123	0.0135	0.0135
156 GPS 493 DEPREC & AMORTIZATIONS / SALES	0.0246	0.0264	0.0256	0.0234	0.0251	0.0239
157 LIO 493 DEPREC & AMORTIZATIONS / SALES	0.0216	0.0125	0.0150	0.0170	0.0179	0.0145
158 TOY 493 DEPREC & AMORTIZATIONS / SALES	0.0108	0.0132	0.0136	0.0139	0.0136	0.0138
159 AG5651 494 INTEREST EXPENSE / SALES	0.0099	0.0079	0.0071	0.0090	0.0093	0.0119
160 AG5945 494 INTEREST EXPENSE / SALES	0.0048	0.0150	0.0118	0.0149	0.0185	0.0201
161 CWLD 494 INTEREST EXPENSE / SALES	NA	0.0148	0.0082	0.0082	0.0109	0.0151
162 GMN 494 INTEREST EXPENSE / SALES	0.0031	0.0083	0.0150	0.0163	0.0163	0.0168
163 GOSHA 494 INTEREST EXPENSE / SALES	0.0082	0.0074	0.0047	0.0029	0.0062	0.0094
164 GPS 494 INTEREST EXPENSE / SALES	0.0074	0.0053	0.0019	0.0036	0.0027	0.0017
165 LIO 494 INTEREST EXPENSE / SALES	0.0087	0.0020	0.0085	0.0167	0.0192	0.0195
166 TOY 494 INTEREST EXPENSE / SALES	0.0040	0.0056	0.0057	0.0070	0.0082	0.0110

Security Analysis: How to Analyze Accounting and Market Data to Value Securities
Robert W. Holthausen and Mark E. Zmijewski
\C0693A.W51

2 TICKER REF#		VARIABLE DESCRIPTION	1984	1985	1986	1987	1988	1989
3		....						
167 AG5651	495	INCOME TAXES / SALES	0.0273	0.0268	0.0272	0.0245	0.0289	0.0288
168 AG5945	495	INCOME TAXES / SALES	0.0491	0.0333	0.0355	0.0267	0.0257	0.0301
169 CWLD	495	INCOME TAXES / SALES	NA	0.0223	0.0240	0.0147	0.0124	0.0070
170 GMN	495	INCOME TAXES / SALES	0.0408	0.0146	-0.0077	-0.0126	0.0046	0.0055
171 GOSHA	495	INCOME TAXES / SALES	0.0883	0.0793	0.1010	0.0810	0.0462	0.0755
172 GPS	495	INCOME TAXES / SALES	0.0155	0.0517	0.0815	0.0519	0.0412	0.0410
173 LIO	495	INCOME TAXES / SALES	0.0316	0.0074	0.0072	0.0086	0.0036	0.0004
174 TOY	495	INCOME TAXES / SALES	0.0557	0.0506	0.0540	0.0453	0.0402	0.0402
175 AG5651	584	SALES (Index)	1.00	1.28	1.69	1.97	1.36	1.43
176 AG5945	584	SALES (Index)	1.00	1.66	2.02	2.50	3.02	3.30
177 CWLD	584	SALES (Index)		1.00	1.23	1.46	1.57	1.62
178 GMN	584	SALES (Index)	1.00	1.26	1.41	1.40	1.54	1.71
179 GOSHA	584	SALES (Index)	1.00	1.18	1.44	1.65	1.84	2.29
180 GPS	584	SALES (Index)	1.00	1.21	1.59	1.99	2.34	2.97
181 LIO	584	SALES (Index)	1.00	0.69	0.80	0.96	1.15	1.21
182 TOY	584	SALES (Index)	1.00	1.16	1.44	1.84	2.35	2.81
183 AG5651	585	EPS - Primary - Excluding EI&DO (Index)	1.00	1.17	1.18	1.70	1.63	1.92
184 AG5945	585	EPS - Primary - Excluding EI&DO (Index)	1.00	0.95	1.13	NA	1.81	2.39
185 CWLD	585	EPS - Primary - Excluding EI&DO (Index)		1.00	1.04	1.10	1.21	0.56
186 GMN	585	EPS - Primary - Excluding EI&DO (Index)	1.00	0.86	NA	NA	0.20	0.26
187 GOSHA	585	EPS - Primary - Excluding EI&DO (Index)	1.00	1.10	1.61	1.87	1.47	2.94
188 GPS	585	EPS - Primary - Excluding EI&DO (Index)	1.00	2.79	5.32	5.38	5.66	7.64
189 LIO	585	EPS - Primary - Excluding EI&DO (Index)	1.00	0.17	0.44	0.19	0.20	0.02
190 TOY	585	EPS - Primary - Excluding EI&DO (Index)	1.00	1.07	1.35	1.80	2.35	2.84
191 AG5651	644	Operating Income After Depreciation (Index)	1.00	1.18	1.48	1.34	1.53	1.67
192 AG5945	644	Operating Income After Depreciation (Index)	1.00	1.31	1.57	1.87	2.41	2.68
193 CWLD	644	Operating Income After Depreciation (Index)		1.00	1.10	0.99	1.32	0.78
194 GMN	644	Operating Income After Depreciation (Index)	1.00	0.83	-0.01	-0.21	0.50	0.61
195 GOSHA	644	Operating Income After Depreciation (Index)	1.00	1.08	1.61	1.63	1.20	2.45
196 GPS	644	Operating Income After Depreciation (Index)	1.00	2.92	5.68	5.26	5.56	7.21
197 LIO	644	Operating Income After Depreciation (Index)	1.00	0.19	0.29	0.34	0.38	0.25
198 TOY	644	Operating Income After Depreciation (Index)	1.00	1.09	1.42	1.76	2.21	2.73
199 AG5651	651	INCOME BEFORE EI&DO (Index)	1.00	1.24	1.32	1.93	1.85	1.98
200 AG5945	651	INCOME BEFORE EI&DO (Index)	1.00	1.10	1.37	1.56	2.16	2.77
201 CWLD	651	INCOME BEFORE EI&DO (Index)		1.00	1.17	1.23	1.34	0.62
202 GMN	651	INCOME BEFORE EI&DO (Index)	1.00	1.01	-0.48	-0.55	0.26	0.34
203 GOSHA	651	INCOME BEFORE EI&DO (Index)	1.00	1.09	1.61	1.86	1.46	2.93
204 GPS	651	INCOME BEFORE EI&DO (Index)	1.00	2.82	5.57	5.69	6.07	7.98
205 LIO	651	INCOME BEFORE EI&DO (Index)	1.00	0.18	0.82	0.36	0.38	0.03
206 TOY	651	INCOME BEFORE EI&DO (Index)	1.00	1.07	1.37	1.83	2.41	2.88
207 AG5651	5840	SALES	5552.800	7132.500	9365.700	10954.600	7531.100	7918.900
208 AG5945	5840	SALES	2342.400	3883.000	4720.100	5859.300	7080.900	7727.100
209 CWLD	5840	SALES	NA	513.148	628.834	749.127	807.067	830.269
210 GMN	5840	SALES	172.879	218.009	244.238	242.701	266.706	295.955
211 GOSHA	5840	SALES	137.423	162.109	198.197	226.298	252.994	315.076
212 GPS	5840	SALES	534.127	647.333	848.009	1062.021	1252.097	1586.596
213 LIO	5840	SALES	354.703	246.076	282.667	340.839	408.920	428.848
214 TOY	5840	SALES	1701.699	1976.133	2444.902	3136.568	4000.192	4787.828

Security Analysis: How to Analyze Accounting and Market Data to Value Securities
Robert W. Holthausen and Mark E. Zmijewski
\C0693A.W51

Do not reproduce without permission.
July 29, 1998 - 3:13 pm

183

Forecasting Financial Statements (and Free Cash Flows)

1. Introduction.

The purpose of our discussion is to understand the mechanics of forecasting financial statements as well as to develop skills in judging the reasonableness of forecasts. Our purpose is not to train expert statistical forecasters. Take courses in time-series and regression (econometrics) to become a statistical expert.

2. Developing Financial Statement (and Free Cash Flow) Forecasts.

There are three key issues in beginning to develop forecasts.

1. What is the forecast horizon? The forecast horizon is a choice variable for the analyst. As discussed in Chapter 1, we typically forecast the cash flows year-by-year for a finite horizon and then use either a cash flow perpetuity model, a price-multiple model, or a liquidation or breakup scenario to determine the terminal value. The explicit year-by-year forecast should be extended until the firm reaches "steady-state." By that, we mean that it is expected that the firm will enter a period of no-growth or relatively modest growth. The growth rate assumption is usually tied to expected inflation.

    Steady state is usually defined as the point where the firm now earns a rate of return on its invested capital which is expected to persist in perpetuity. In most cases, it is expected that the firm's projected return on capital would be equal to its cost of capital, otherwise we are projecting that the firm will be earning rents in perpetuity. Evidence clearly indicates that firms which earn above their industry ROE, typically revert back to their industry ROE over time. Thus, if firm is earnings rents on its activities, you will want to forecast out to the point where the rents have disappeared. Steady-state also encompasses the assumption that the firm will reinvest a constant proportion of its cash flows into the business in each year to sustain the assumed constant growth. In addition, steady state typically involves also reaching some steady state with regard to capital structure.

2. Ascertain what financial forecasts are required. Ultimately, the aim in valuation is to forecast the free cash flows of the firm and potentially, the free cash flows of the equity. Calculation of the free cash flows of the firm typically starts from either cash flow from operations or earnings before interest and taxes; thus, the forecasts must include projections of: revenues, expense amounts for cost of goods sold, selling, general & administrative, depreciation, etc., capital expenditures, required changes in working capital, research and development, advertising, financing requirements (or excess marketable securities), income taxes, interest expense. As such, we typically forecast the entire income statement and balance sheet.

Security Analysis: How to Analyze Accounting and Market Data to Value Securities
   Robert W. Holthausen and Mark E. Zmijewski
   \CH8.W51

Do not reproduce without permission.
July 29, 1998 - 3:28 pm

185

3. What is the appropriate aggregation level? What levels of data aggregation are available? Should you forecast the consolidated firm only, or should you forecast smaller business units such as subsidiaries, divisions, geographic regions, cost centers, profit centers, lines of business, or product lines? Forecasting at the consolidated firm level can be inherently difficult. Suppose we have two divisions which have different growth rates and different operating margins. First of all, even if the two divisions have constant (but different) growth rates, there is no constant growth rate which can be applied to the firm. Moreover, with different operating margins in the two divisions, the operating margin for the firm will vary through time according to the operating margins of the two divisions and their relative sizes. In this case, forecasting at the divisional level would be preferred.

    There are several reasons for forecasting multinational companies by geographic regions (e.g., by the various currencies the company does business in). More on this when we discuss multinational valuation.

Here is a list of procedures to use when forecasting.

1. Identify the key factors that drive the firm's operations. Sales (in units or dollars) is usually a key factor. Sales (and earnings) generally appear to be a random walk or random walk with drift, thus most recent sales is a good starting point (average sales for the last three years is not typically a good starting point). Are there others? If we assume that the firm can sell all of the products it produces, than plant capacity may be the critical factor for forecasting sales. Forecasting the capacity of the firm's total production facilities requires forecasts of plant openings and plant closings. Inflation is another potentially important factor to forecast. Since we want to develop forecasts of nominal cash flows, the growth in sales and net income will depend on real growth in those line items as well as the effects of inflation on those items.

    Number of store openings for a retail establishment is important. Sometimes the expected supply of a scarce commodity used in the production process is a key factor. Identifying the key factors is based on understanding the industries in which the firm competes and the economics which underlie those industries. What is the strategy of the firm? How does it anticipate that it will grow?

2. Forecast the key factors. Statements or plans of management may help guide the forecast. Understanding the industry and firm is key in developing forecasts of the key factors. Again, what is the firm's strategy? Various mechanical models may be of some aid, though typically we forecast with relatively little time series data, hence more sophisticated statistical models may not be reliable.

3. Identify the accounts that have a relatively constant relation with the key factors (e.g., cost of goods sold is typically X% of sales and accounts receivable are Y% of sales). Make adjustments to the historical relations for projected changes in the firm's operations. For example, if an industry becomes more competitive, we would expect operating margins to shrink.

4. Devise a suitable means for forecasting accounts which do not have a predictable relation with the key factors. For example, other current assets may be a constant dollar number. Capital expenditures may be tied to store openings or plant capacity additions, or replacement of existing plant.

Security Analysis: How to Analyze Accounting and Market Data to Value Securities
Robert W. Holthausen and Mark E. Zmijewski
\CH8.W51

Do not reproduce without permission.
July 29, 1998 - 3:28 pm

186

5.   Some factors are not typically forecasted like long-term changes in foreign currency exchange rates.

6.   Forecast corporate income tax rates which are affected by changes in the firm's profitability as well as changes in income tax laws; for example, a firm could have net operating loss carryforwards which affect the amount of income taxes expected to be paid in the next few years. Usually try to understand what gives rise to deferred taxes and model those. Forecast depreciation off of capital expenditures and estimates of average useful lives for equipment in conjunction with current depreciation guidelines for tax purposes.

7.   In a first pass of the forecast, set the dividends of the firm equal to the free cash flows to the equity holders. Thus, dividends may be positive or negative (where negative dividends indicates that the firm must do financing). If you know specifics about the firm's required paydowns of debt, you can also incorporate those in a first pass as well.

    On another pass, you can make adjustments to the dividends and capital structure required to achieve desired results. If the change in cash will be positive for several years and then turn negative, you may want to retain the cash but not paying out dividends to avoid additional financing (usually a debt issue) later. Continuing negative changes in cash may require financing plans. If you hold up paying out cash flows because of financing that will be required in the near term, those cash flows cannot be treated as free cash flows. Those cash flows should be put into a short term investments account and treated as a required investment, on which interest can be earned. If your model puts *excess* cash flows into a short-term investments accounts, for valuation purposes you should treat those as free cash flows and not treat the short term investment accounts as one that either earns interest or has some residual value. Note that if you truly model a firm to hold short term investments, even if you invest in Treasury Bills, that changes the risk of the firm.

    As it turns out, the importance of forecasting the financial structure depends on what method is used to value the firm. Proforma forecasts of the capital structure of the firm are necessary when discounting the free cash flows of the equity at the equity cost of capital or when discounting the free cash flows of the unlevered firm at the unlevered cost of capital and then adding the net present value of the interest tax shield. When discounting the free cash flows of the unlevered firm at the weighted average cost of capital, proformas which explicitly forecast the target capital structure are not required, however they are useful to understand whether the assumed capital structure is feasible.

7.   Check that financial statements articulate (e.g., ending retained earnings is equal to beginning retained earnings + net income - dividends; ending accounts receivable is equal to beginning accounts receivable + sales - cash collections; ending inventory is equal to beginning inventory + purchases -cost of goods sold; change in cash flows ties to the statement of cash flows, etc.).

8.   Forecasts of income statements and balance sheets provide a forecast of statement of cash flows. Free cash flows can be developed from there.

9.   Check the reasonableness of your forecasts by comparing them to some mechanical model if you believe there is some model which reasonably captures the process. Sometimes you can check the reasonableness of your forecasts by using your forecasting process on earlier years

Security Analysis: How to Analyze Accounting and Market Data to Value Securities
  Robert W. Holthausen and Mark E. Zmijewski
 \CH8.W51

for which data are available, that is back test your model. However, if you used those earlier years to develop your model, do not take much comfort in your back testing procedure. You should have forecasts which are very close.

10. **WHEN YOU THINK YOU ARE DONE, STEP BACK FROM THE NUMBERS--DO THEY MAKE SENSE?**

Suppose that your projections indicate an increase in sales over the next five years. What factors are responsible for this projected sales increase? Is the sales increase achievable with the projected level of marketing expenses? Is the projected level of production consistent with planned staffing and capital expenditure? Are inventory and other working capital forecasts consistent with the sales increase? Does the increase reflect only the effects of inflation? Does the increase reflect a constant market share in an expanding market? If so, why is the market expanding? Does that assumption agree with industry projections? If it is an expanding market, why will we be able to maintain a constant market share (i.e., why don't new entrants compete away some of our market share in the expanding market?). Does the increase reflect a rising market share in a stagnant market? Why will our market share increase? Are some firms leaving the industry? Why?

It is important to check the reasonableness of your forecasts by identifying financial statement relations (or market relations) that can be used to examine the consistency (reasonableness) of the forecasts. For example, you should examine the return on total assets, return on equity, asset turnover ratios (inventory turnover, receivables turnover, sales turnover, etc.), Gross, operating and profit margins, reinvestment requirements, any other appropriate relations that will give an indication of the reasonableness of your forecasts.

The checks of reasonableness of the forecasts are critical. When forecasting for even a short period of time, it is relatively easy to have inadvertent changes in various financial relations take place. For example, you could inadvertently alter return on assets or the investment in assets required to produce increases in sales, which would have a material impact on the reasonableness of your forecasts over time.

Other considerations. How timely must the forecast be? How often is a forecast required? What are the cost/benefits of accuracy/errors? How is accuracy measured? What is the cost of developing the model? What are the time constraints for developing the model?

3. **A Simple Example - The Future Looking Company (FLC).**

Prepare FLC's financial statement and free cash flow forecasts (balance sheet, income statement, statement of retained earnings, cash flow statement, and free cash flow statement beginning with cash flow from operations) for the years ended December 31, 2002 through December 31, 2004, making the following assumptions.

(1)   The manufacturing operations, which produce all products sold by FLC, have been operating at their long-run optimal capacity since the firm began its operations in late, 1999. Plants will continue to run at capacity for the future.

(2)   Capital expenditures are expected to be $11,000 (measured in 2001 dollars). These expenditures are for maintenance only.

Security Analysis: How to Analyze Accounting and Market Data to Value Securities
  Robert W. Holthausen and Mark E. Zmijewski
\CH8.W51

(3)   Sales orders are expected to equal capacity for the next few years, and sales prices are expected to keep pace with inflation, as are the cost of goods sold and selling and administrative expenses (you expect inflation to be 5% per year).

(4)   FLC does not plan to issue any long-term debt or common equity during the next few years. The firm uses short-term debt to finance short-term cash shortages, and the average amount of short-term debt is approximately 40% of accounts receivable, rounded to the nearest $1,000. The interest rate on all debt is 10%.

(5)   FLC intends to pay all free cash flows of the common equity in dividends each year.

(6)   Assume that all flows occur on the last day of the year; therefore, no depreciation is charged for capital expenditures during the year, and no interest is paid on debt issued during the year.

(7)   FLC's income tax forms and financial statements are identical, the tax rate is 30% on taxable income.

(8)   The firm expects no changes its basic operations (e.g., expense ratios, operating profitability, etc.)

Below are FLC's actual financial statements.

	Actual Dec-00	Actual Dec-01
17 The Future Looking Company (FLC)		
18 Income Statement		
19		
20 Revenue	150,000	157,500
21 Cost of Goods Sold	75,000	78,750
22 Total Depreciation & Amortization	10,000	11,050
23 Sell, Gen & Admin	45,000	47,250
24		
25 Net Operating Income	20,000	20,450
26 Interest on Short-term Investments	0	0
27 Interest on Debt	4,900	5,000
28		
29 Pre-tax Income	15,100	15,450
30 Income Taxes	4,530	4,635
31		
32 Net Income	10,570	10,815
33		
34		
35 The Future Looking Company (FLC)	Actual Dec-00	Actual Dec-01
36 Statement of Retained Earnings		
37		
38 Beginning Retained Earnings	0	9,575
39 Net Income	10,570	10,815
40 Dividends	995	9,655
41		
42 Ending Retained Earnings	9,575	10,735
43		
44		
45 .		

Security Analysis: How to Analyze Accounting and Market Data to Value Securities
  Robert W. Holthausen and Mark E. Zmijewski
  \CH8.W51

```
47 The Future Looking Company (FLC)          Actual    Actual
48 BALANCE SHEET                             Dec-00    Dec-01
49 ---------------------------------------------------------------
50 ASSETS:
52 Total Cash & Cash Equivalents              3,000     3,150
53 Accounts Receivable                       12,500    13,125
54 Inventory                                 10,417    10,938
55                                          -----------------
56 Total Current Assets                      25,917    27,213
57                                          -----------------
58 Property, Plant, & Equipment - Cost      110,500   121,500
59 Accumulated Depreciation                  10,000    21,050
60                                          -----------------
61 Net PPEQ                                 100,500   100,450
62                                          -----------------
63 Total Assets                             126,417   127,663
64                                          =================
65 EQUITIES:
66 Accounts Payable                           7,842     7,927
67 Short-term Debt                            5,000     5,000
68                                          -----------------
69 Total Current Liabilities                 12,842    12,927
70 Long-term Debt                            45,000    45,000
71                                          -----------------
72 Total Liabilities                         57,842    57,927
73                                          -----------------
74 Paid-in Capital                           59,000    59,000
75 Retained Earnings                          9,575    10,735
76                                          -----------------
77 Shareholders' Equity                      68,575    69,735
78                                          -----------------
79 Total Equities                           126,417   127,663
80                                          =================
```

Security Analysis: How to Analyze Accounting and Market Data to Value Securities
Robert W. Holthausen and Mark E. Zmijewski
\CH8.W51

Do not reproduce without permission.
July 29, 1998 - 3:28 pm

190

81			
82	The Future Looking Company (FLC)	Actual	Actual
83	CASH FLOW STATEMENT	Dec-00	Dec-01
84	------------------------------------		
85	Net Income	10,570	10,815
86	Total Depreciation & Amortization	10,000	11,050
87	Change in Accounts Receivable	(12,500)	(625)
88	Change in Inventory	(3,417)	(521)
89	Change in Accounts Payable	7,842	85
90		------------	
91	Net Cash Provided by Operations	12,495	20,805
92	Capital Expenditures	(10,500)	(11,000)
93	Cash Flows from Financing		
94	Equity Changes	0	0
95	Short-term Debt Changes	1,000	0
96	Long-term Debt Changes	0	0
97	Dividends	(995)	(9,655)
98		------------	
99	Net Change in Cash & Equivalents	2,000	150
100			
101	Cash Interest Paid	4,900	5,000
102			
103	Cash Income Taxes Paid	4,530	4,635
104			

Security Analysis: How to Analyze Accounting and Market Data to Value Securities
Robert W. Holthausen and Mark E. Zmijewski
\CH8.W51

Here are the forecasts for the years 2002 to 2004:

```
16
17 The Future Looking Company (FLC)              Actual   Actual   Actual   F'cast   F'cast   F'cast
18 Income Statement                              Dec-99   Dec-00   Dec-01   Dec-02   Dec-03   Dec-04
19 --------------------------------------------------------------------------------------------------
20 Revenue (5 % inflation per year)                       150,000  157,500  165,375  173,644  182,326
21 Cost of Goods Sold (50% of sales)                       75,000   78,750   82,688   86,822   91,163
22 Depr. & Amort (10 year life on prior year ending balance)10,000  11,050   12,150   13,305   14,518
23 Sell, Gen & Admin (30% revenue)                         45,000   47,250   49,613   52,093   54,698
24                                                        ---------------------------------------------
25 Net Operating Income (Summed)                           20,000   20,450   20,925   21,424   21,947
26 Interest on Short-term Investments (none)                    0        0        0        0        0
27 Interest on Debt (10% interest on prior ending balance) 4,900    5,000    5,000    5,100    5,100
28                                                        ---------------------------------------------
29 Pre-tax Income (Summed)                                 15,100   15,450   15,925   16,324   16,847
30 Income Taxes   (30% assumed tax rate)                    4,530    4,635    4,778    4,897    5,054
31                                                        ---------------------------------------------
32 Net Income (Summed)                                     10,570   10,815   11,148   11,427   11,793
33                                                        =============================================
34
35 The Future Looking Company (FLC)              Actual   Actual   Actual   F'cast   F'cast   F'cast
36 Statement of Retained Earnings                Dec-99   Dec-00   Dec-01   Dec-02   Dec-03   Dec-04
37 --------------------------------------------------------------------------------------------------
38 Beginning Retained Earnings                                  0    9,575   10,735   10,100    9,935
39    Net Income (Per income statement)                   10,570   10,815   11,148   11,427   11,793
40    Dividends (Assumption #5 - FCF to equity)              995    9,655   11,783   11,592   12,514
41                                                        ---------------------------------------------
42 Ending Retained Earnings (Summed)                  0     9,575   10,735   10,100    9,935    9,214
43                                                        =============================================
44
45 The Future Looking Company (FLC)              Actual   Actual   Actual   F'cast   F'cast   F'cast
46 BALANCE SHEET                                 Dec-99   Dec-00   Dec-01   Dec-02   Dec-03   Dec-04
47 --------------------------------------------------------------------------------------------------
48 ASSETS:
49 Cash Balance (Required) (2% of revenues)      1,000    3,000    3,150    3,308    3,473    3,647
50 Short-term Investments (Not used)                 0        0        0        0        0        0
51                                                        ---------------------------------------------
52 Total Cash & Cash Equivalents (Summed)        1,000    3,000    3,150    3,308    3,473    3,647
53 Accounts Receivable (30 days sales)               0   12,500   13,125   13,781   14,470   15,194
54 Inventory (50 days cost of goods sold)        7,000   10,417   10,938   11,484   12,059   12,662
55                                                        ---------------------------------------------
56 Total Current Assets                          8,000   25,917   27,213   28,573   30,002   31,502
57                                                        ---------------------------------------------
58 Property, Plant, & Equipment - Cost (See CAPEX)100,000 110,500 121,500  133,050  145,178  157,911
59 Accumulated Depreciation (Beg. + Depr Exp)            10,000   21,050   33,200   46,505   61,023
60                                                        ---------------------------------------------
61 Net PPEQ (Summed)                           100,000  100,500  100,450   99,850   98,673   96,889
62                                                        ---------------------------------------------
63 Total Assets (Summed)                       108,000  126,417  127,663  128,423  128,674  128,390
64                                                        =============================================
65 EQUITIES:
66 Accounts Payable (10% of purchases)               0    7,842    7,927    8,323    8,740    9,177
67 Short-term Debt (40% of accounts receivable)  4,000    5,000    5,000    6,000    6,000    6,000
68                                                        ---------------------------------------------
69 Total Current Liabilities (Summed)            4,000   12,842   12,927   14,323   14,740   15,177
70 Long-term Debt (constant)                    45,000   45,000   45,000   45,000   45,000   45,000
71                                                        ---------------------------------------------
72 Total Liabilities (Summed)                   49,000   57,842   57,927   59,323   59,740   60,177
73                                                        ---------------------------------------------
74 Paid-in Capital (Constant)                   59,000   59,000   59,000   59,000   59,000   59,000
75 Retained Earnings (Retained Earnings Statement)  0     9,575   10,735   10,100    9,935    9,214
76                                                        ---------------------------------------------
77 Shareholders' Equity (Summed)                59,000   68,575   69,735   69,100   68,935   68,214
78                                                        ---------------------------------------------
79 Total Equities (Summed)                     108,000  126,417  127,663  128,423  128,674  128,390
80                                                        =============================================
81
```

Security Analysis: How to Analyze Accounting and Market Data to Value Securities
Robert W. Holthausen and Mark E. Zmijewski
\CH8.W51

		Actual	Actual	Actual	F'cast	F'cast	F'cast
82	The Future Looking Company (FLC)	Dec-99	Dec-00	Dec-01	Dec-02	Dec-03	Dec-04
83	CASH FLOW STATEMENT						
84	-----						
85	Net Income	0	10,570	10,815	11,148	11,427	11,793
86	Total Depreciation & Amortization	0	10,000	11,050	12,150	13,305	14,518
87	Change in Accounts Receivable	0	(12,500)	(625)	(656)	(689)	(724)
88	Change in Inventory	(7,000)	(3,417)	(521)	(547)	(574)	(603)
89	Change in Accounts Payable	0	7,842	85	396	416	437
90							
91	Net Cash Provided by Operations	(7,000)	12,495	20,805	22,491	23,885	25,421
92	Capital Expenditures (Grows at Inflation)	(100,000)	(10,500)	(11,000)	(11,550)	(12,128)	(12,734)
93	Cash Flows from Financing						
94	Equity Changes	59,000	0	0	0	0	0
95	Short-term Debt Changes	4,000	1,000	0	1,000	0	0
96	Long-term Debt Changes	45,000	0	0	0	0	0
97	Dividends (from FCF statement)	0	(995)	(9,655)	(11,783)	(11,592)	(12,514)
98							
99	Net Change in Cash & Equivalents	1,000	2,000	150	158	165	174
100							
101	Cash Interest Paid		4,900	5,000	5,000	5,100	5,100
102							
103	Cash Income Taxes Paid		4,530	4,635	4,778	4,897	5,054
104							
105							

106 CALCULATION of the Free Cash Flows of the Unlevered Firm and the Common Equity.

		Actual	Actual	F'cast	F'cast	F'cast
108	The Future Looking Company (FLC)	Dec-00	Dec-01	Dec-02	Dec-03	Dec-04
109	Statement of Free Cash Flows					
110	-----					
111	Marginal Tax Rate	30.00%	30.00%	30.00%	30.00%	30.00%
112						
113						
114	Operating Activities - Net Cash Flow	12,495	20,805	22,491	23,885	25,421
115	Less - Change in Required Cash Balance	(2,000)	(150)	(158)	(165)	(174)
116						
117	Adjusted Operating Cash Flow	10,495	20,655	22,333	23,719	25,248
118						
119	Plus - Interest Expense = Cash Interest Paid	4,900	5,000	5,000	5,100	5,100
120	Less - Income Tax Shelter from Debt Financing	(1,470)	(1,500)	(1,500)	(1,530)	(1,530)
121						
122	Effects of Interest and the Interest Tax Shield	3,430	3,500	3,500	3,570	3,570
123						
124	Cash Flow From Operations of the Unlevered Firm	13,925	24,155	25,833	27,289	28,818
125						
126	Less - Purchases of Property, Plant and Equipment	(10,500)	(11,000)	(11,550)	(12,128)	(12,734)
127						
128	Net Capital Expenditure Cash Flows	(10,500)	(11,000)	(11,550)	(12,128)	(12,734)
129						
130	Free Cash Flow of the Unlevered Firm	3,425	13,155	14,283	15,162	16,084
131						
132	Less - Total Effects of Financial Leverage	(3,430)	(3,500)	(3,500)	(3,570)	(3,570)
133	Plus - Change in Short-Term Debt Financing	1,000	0	1,000	0	0
134	Plus - Change in Long-Term Debt Financing	0	0	0	0	0
135						
136	Cash Flows to (from) Non-Equity Security Holders	(2,430)	(3,500)	(2,500)	(3,570)	(3,570)
137						
138	Free Cash Flow of the Common Equity	995	9,655	11,783	11,592	12,514
139						
140	Items to Reconcile to the Statement of Cash Flows:					
141	Changes in Common Equity	0	0	0	0	0
142	Cash Dividends - Common	(995)	(9,655)	(11,783)	(11,592)	(12,514)
143						
144	Change in Excess Cash	0	0	0	0	0
145	Plus - Change in Required Cash Balance	2,000	150	158	165	174
146						
147	Change in Cash Balance - FCF Statement	2,000	150	158	165	174
148						
149	Change in Cash Balance - B/S	2,000	150	158	165	174
150						

Security Analysis: How to Analyze Accounting and Market Data to Value Securities
Robert W. Holthausen and Mark E. Zmijewski
\CH8.W51

4. Overview of Business Forecasting Methods.

Informal and Formal Methods (interocular -- plot the data and guess).

May be based on plotting a series by itself over time and extrapolating to the future. Alternatively, it may be based on understanding the relations between several different series. Extrapolation of the series is based on an understanding of the firm, its industry, the markets it operates within, and key factors likely to affect the firm and the industry in the future. Quantitative. Explanatory -- using one series to explain another (GNP to explain earnings). Time series statistical models -- a series related to itself over time.

Identify the patterns in the data.

Is the series stationary? Are the parameters of the distribution (e.g., mean and variance) constant overtime? (Depending on the type of model, stationarity also refers to covariance structure of series with itself over time or covariance with another series.) Often we don't have enough data to test these notions formally. Nevertheless, we should examine the data to ask whether the forecasting methods we are considering are sensible.

Do mergers, accounting changes, regulatory changes, changes in the competitive environment and technological change affect stationarity (i.e., how the series will evolve over time or how the series relates to another series)? The answer is undoubtedly YES in many, but not all situations. Is there a trend? Is there seasonality (especially quarterly or monthly data)? Not likely with annual data. Is there a cycle? That is are there peaks and valleys apparent in the data that can be exploited to predict the future. Can the pattern in the series be related to patterns in other series? Other contemporaneous series may be useful to understand the determinants of the variable being forecast (e.g., McDonald's sales may be related to the disposable incomes of consumers and the price of gas. McDonald's costs may be affected by minimum wage laws and price of beef. If so, we may want to use predictions of the determinants of McDonald's sales and costs to predict. Lagged series sometimes make excellent predictor variables. For example, last period's sales may be useful for predicting this periods sales. Or the sales of autos today may be related to last periods disposable income.

Do the forecasts possess the desired characteristics? Accuracy -- how measured (variety of ways we discuss below in Section 7). Unbiased -- forecast neither <u>systematically</u> overestimates or underestimates the series being forecast. For example, some claim that analysts are in general optimistic when predicting. White noise errors -- mean zero, no autocorrelation -- that is no patterns, that is no time series dependence. If patterns in the forecast errors exist, then there is still information in the series that has not been exploited by the time-series model. Again, we may not have enough data to perform precise statistical tests of this characteristics, but these are the properties we are looking for.

5. Mechanical Forecasting Methods.

A very popular forecasting method is regression analysis. In regression analysis, variation in dependent variable is explained by variation(s) in the independent variable(s). Multiple regression analysis tells us about "conditional" relations. For example, regression analysis could tell us the expected variable costs conditional on the number of labor hours worked. This is an very popular statistical method; 65% of firms surveyed use this method. Regression analysis, however, is not always applied properly.

Consider an index model (a regression model) used for forecasting earnings.

Security Analysis: How to Analyze Accounting and Market Data to Value Securities
Robert W. Holthausen and Mark E. Zmijewski
\CH8.W51

Do not reproduce without permission.
July 29, 1998 - 3:28 pm

194

Define: $\Delta Earnings_{j,t}$ = change in earnings from t-1 to t for firm j.

$\Delta Index_{m,t}$ = change in some market (economy)-wide or industry-wide index (maybe GNP or earnings of all U.S. Corporations) from t-1 to t.

An index model for earnings is then,

$$\Delta Earnings_{j,t} = a_j + b_j \Delta Index_{m,t} + e_{j,t}$$

where $e_{j,t}$ =   mean zero, constant variance, serially independent disturbance term (serial independence implies zero autocorrelation).

This index model assumes that two independent components make up a firm's earnings, a component due to market wide influences (how the economy is doing) and a component which is firm specific. This is not based on economic theory -- it's just an empirical regularity. If slope coefficient, $b_j > 0$ then firm's earnings are related positively to the economy. A $b_j < 0$ implies a countercyclical company. We sometimes see index models estimated in the levels as opposed to the changes.

The index is usually a economy wide measure of activity such as GNP, total corporate profits, etc. Can include other indices as well (e.g., some measure of industry activity). Note if we want to forecast using an index model, we must forecast the index once we have the model parameters. That is we can estimate the intercept and slope coefficient for a firm from past data, but to actually forecast then we need a forecast of the index for the period being forecast. WARNING: Regression analysis always assumes no autocorrelation in the residuals. If there is autocorrelation, R^2, F and t statistics are biased upward.

Consider an example of the above warning. Examine Caterpillar Tractor's annual earnings for 1947-1968 and two indexes I will label as index 1 and index 2. When I ran the model in levels, that is

$$Earnings_{j,t} = a_j + b_j \, Index_{m,t} + e_{j,t}$$

Index 1 had an R^2 of 83% and the slope coefficient had a t-statistic of 10.02. Index 2 had an R^2 of 84% and the slope coefficient had a t-statistic of 10.30. Based on the regression in the levels, you would say that the two indices were equally good at explaining Caterpillar's earnings. If you were to run these two models in the differences, you would have found index 1 had an R^2 of 18% and the slope coefficient had a t-statistic of 2.04; index 2 had an R^2 of 4% and the slope coefficient had a t-statistic of 0.89. Neither model is nearly as good as we originally thought and clearly index 2 doesn't tell us anything about Caterpillar's annual earnings.

Had we looked at the first order autocorrelation coefficient of the residuals from the levels models, you would have observed an autocorrelation coefficient of 0.57 on index 1 and 0.50 on model 2. Both are highly significant and indicate that the R^2's, t-statistics and F-statistics will be seriously biased upwards. The model in the differences bears that out. There is no significant autocorrelation in the residuals when the models are estimated in the differences.

What were the indices? INDEX 1 -- Annual Per Capital Income from 1947-1968; INDEX 2 -- Quarterly GNP from 1947 to 1952. How can you estimate the autocorrelation of the residuals in any model you might run. Estimate a regression with the residual at t as the dependent variable and the residual at t-m as the independent variable for the mth order autocorrelation coefficient (thus, t on t-1 gives you the 1st order autocorrelation coefficient). The slope coefficient is the degree of autocorrelation. If the regression is

Security Analysis: How to Analyze Accounting and Market Data to Value Securities
  Robert W. Holthausen and Mark E. Zmijewski
\CH8.W51

significant or the t-statistic on the slope coefficient is significant, you have autocorrelation. NOTE, we could have run an index model on sales or some other series. Also we could have included many other variables besides some measure of economy wide activity. Many times an index model will be estimated with both an economy-wide index and an industry index. Suppose you were running an index model for McDonald's sales. What might be relevant factors to include in the regression model?

Security Analysis: How to Analyze Accounting and Market Data to Value Securities
Robert W. Holthausen and Mark E. Zmijewski
\CH8.W51

Do not reproduce without permission.
July 29, 1998 - 3:28 pm

196

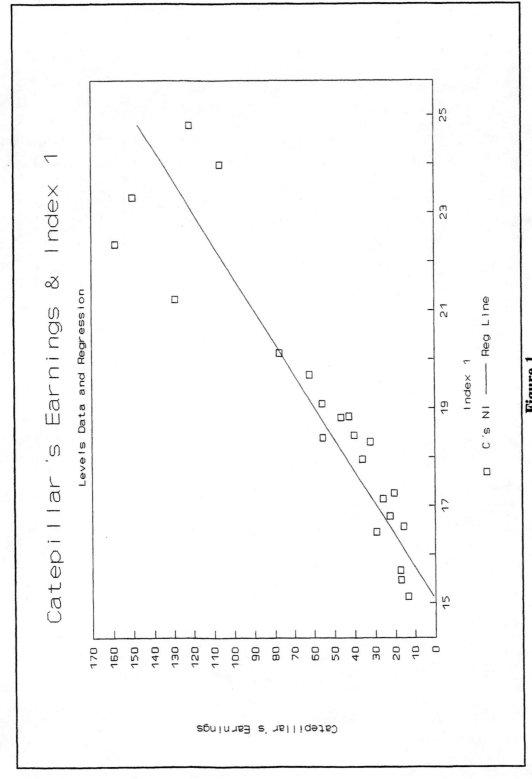

Figure 1

R-squared = 83%, Slope Coefficient t-statistic = 10.0, Autocorrelation Coefficient = .573

197

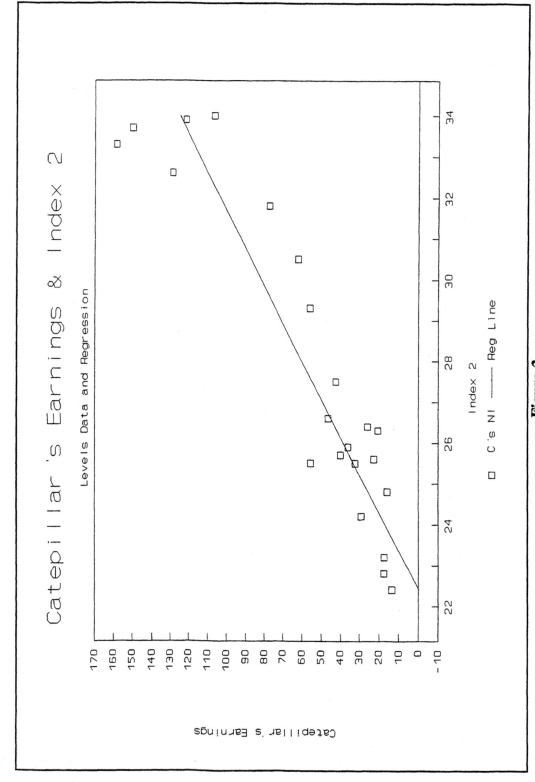

Catepillar's Earnings & Index 2

Levels Data and Regression

Figure 2

R-squared = 84%, Slope Coefficient t-statistic = 10.3, Autocorrelation Coefficient = .495

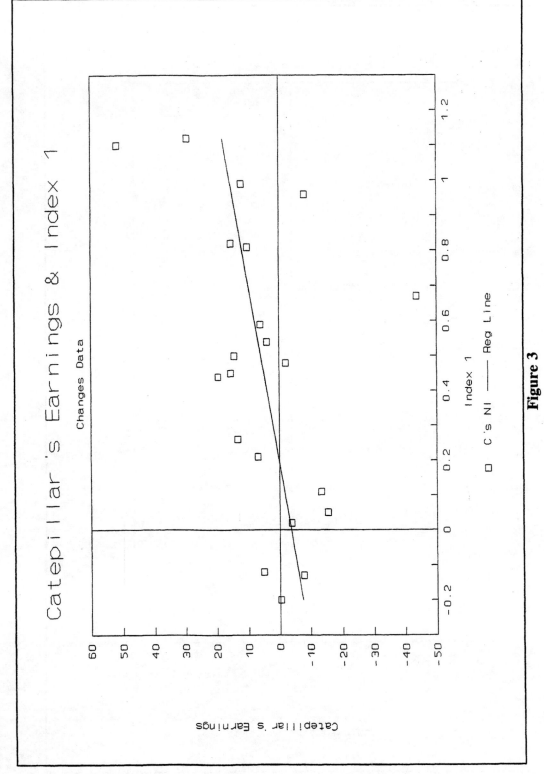

Figure 3

R-squared = 18%, Slope Coefficient t-statistic = 2.00, Autocorrelation Coefficient = .180

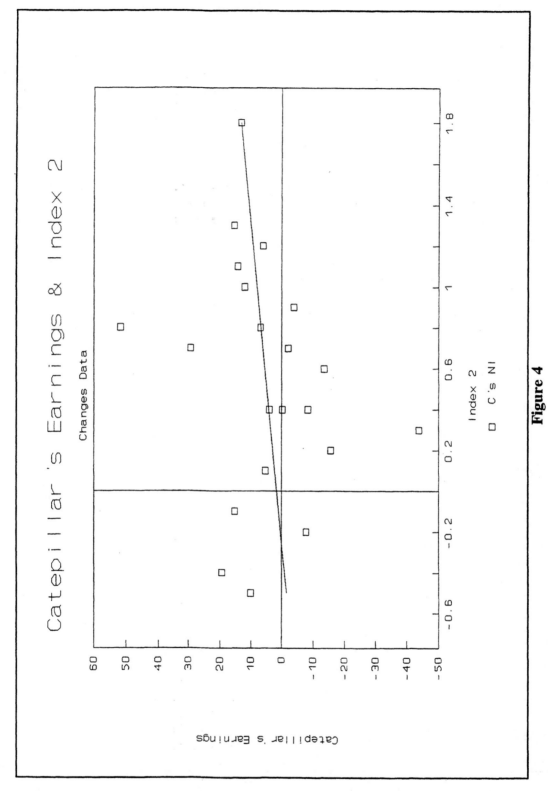

Figure 4

R-squared = 4%, Slope Coefficient t-statistic = 0.9, Autocorrelation Coefficient = .566

We discuss other quantitative methods below.

Structural models.

Description - Simultaneous systems of regression equations. Econometric Models are useful when the dependent variable is not exogenous. For example, if we want to estimate the impact of advertising on sales, we need a second equation which takes account of the fact that sales levels affect advertising levels. Primarily used in Economic forecasting by macro economists.

Trend extrapolation.

Description - Entails the simple extrapolation of past trends in the data. For example, if sales appear to have grown by 10% each year, we would predict growth of 10% in subsequent years. Popular extrapolation methods are linear and exponential extrapolations. Usage for business forecasting -- 50% of firms use this method.

Smoothing.

Description - Forecasts are obtained by smoothing, averaging, past actual values in a linear or exponential manner. Types of models: moving average, exponential, linear, and linear-exponential. Usage for business forecasting - 40% of firms use this method.

Example -- forecast of the variable Z at time period t, $E(Z_t)$ is

$$E(Z_t) = 1/5\ (Z_{t-1} + Z_{t-2} + Z_{t-3} + Z_{t-4} + Z_{t-5})$$

A more general formulation of smoothing is

$$E(Z_t) = (1-B)Z_{t-1} + (1-B)B\ Z_{t-2} + (1-B)B^2\ Z_{t-3} + (1-B)B^3\ Z_{t-4}....$$

where $\quad 0 > B < 1$.

Hence small B implies rapid decline in weights (most recent observation gets the most weight) while large B implies slow decline. But B is ad hoc, that is, the weights are chosen arbitrarily.

Filters.

Description--Forecasts are expressed as a linear combination of past actual values. Parameters or model can "adapt to changes in data."

Autoregressive/Moving Averages (ARMA/Box Jenkins).

Description--Forecasts are expressed as a linear combination of past actual values and/or past errors. These models are developed by examining the autocorrelation functions of stationary series. The autocorrelation function is just a description of what the autocorrelations of the series are at various lags. From these functions we make guesses about the generating mechanism driving the series. Box-Jenkins models subsume trend extrapolation, smoothing and filters and are based on statistical theory. Popular technique of academics. Usage for business forecasting - 20% of the firms use this method.

Security Analysis: How to Analyze Accounting and Market Data to Value Securities
Robert W. Holthausen and Mark E. Zmijewski
\CH8.W51

Examples would be autoregressive models of various orders

$$AR(1) \quad E(\text{Earnings}_t) = \phi_1 \text{ Earnings}_{t-1} + \gamma + u_t$$

$$AR(2) \quad E(\text{Earnings}_t) = \phi_1 \text{ Earnings}_{t-1} + \phi_2 \text{ Earnings}_{t-2} + \gamma + u_t$$

These models can be estimated using regression techniques. The AR(1) turns out to be a fairly useful model for forecasting annual earnings. But be wary of autocorrelated residuals. Don't assume the model is an appropriate one without checking. If we were using quarterly data, we might have a seasonal model that we could estimate or identify with Box Jenkins techniques. The first order autoregressive process in the seasonal differences is

$$E(Q_t) = Q_{t-4} + \phi_1(Q_{t-1} - Q_{t-5}) + \gamma$$

where: Q_t = earnings for quarter t

Note this model can easily be estimated via regression by regressing

$$(Q_t - Q_{t-4}) = a + b(Q_{t-1} - Q_{t-5})$$

In this regression a, the intercept, is the estimate of γ, and b, the slope, is the estimate of ϕ_1. This model is quite useful for forecasting quarterly earnings. Another representation of the quarterly earnings process which is quite simple (but probably not as good as the first order autoregressive process in the seasonal differences is the seasonal random walk:

$$E(Q_t) = Q_{t-4} + \gamma$$

where γ is referred to as the drift term and is estimated by the average change in seasonally differenced earnings over the last few years.

Steps performed in Box-Jenkins work:

(1)   Look at the data and determine if its a stationary series.
(2)   Identify the type of time-series process through various procedures.
(3)   Estimate the parameters of the process.
(4)   Perform various diagnostic checks to see if its a good model.
(5)   Forecast with the estimated parameters.

The advantage of Box-Jenkins models is that the techniques allow you to identify the type of time series process from the data and then estimate the parameters of the process. One disadvantage is that the technique (like all others) assumes the process is stationary. If the time series process experiences structural shifts, then Box-Jenkins techniques are inappropriate (BUT SO ARE ALL OTHER MECHANICAL TECHNIQUES WHICH REQUIRE ESTIMATION).

There are also some other methods. Decision trees -- subjective probabilities are assigned to each event and the approach of Bayesian Statistics is used. Sales force estimates -- a bottom-up approach aggregating salesmen's forecasts. Usage for business forecasting; 20% of the firms use this method. Juries of executive opinion -- marketing, production and finance executives jointly prepare forecasts; 70% of firms use this method.

Security Analysis: How to Analyze Accounting and Market Data to Value Securities
Robert W. Holthausen and Mark E. Zmijewski
\CH8.W51

Do not reproduce without permission.
July 29, 1998 - 3:28 pm

202

Anticipatory surveys market research -- learning about intentions of potential customers or planes of businesses; 40% of the firms use this method.

Three Simple (Deterministic, Extrapolation) Time-Series Models.

Simple linear trend model.

$$Y_t = b_0 + b_1 t$$

where:

t	=	time period (1967, 1968, ..., 1985).
Y_t	=	the dollar value of Y at time t.

Y grows at a constant dollar basis, b_1.

Exponential growth curve.

$$Y_{t+1} = A * e^{n+1}$$

$$\ln(Y_t) = c_0 + c_1 t$$

where:

c_0	=	$\ln(A)$.
c_1	=	r.

Y grows at a constant percent, c_1.

Autoregressive model.

$$Y_t = d_0 + d_1 * Y_{t-1}.$$

6.   **Evaluating Forecasts.**

Dispersion.

Intimately intertwined with the nature of the decision context and the user's loss function. Forecast error measures are Mean Absolute Error (MABE) and Mean Square Error (MSE). Mean Absolute Error is calculated as the mean of the absolute values of the forecast errors. Mean square error is calculated as the mean of the squared values of the forecast errors. MSE metrics weight larger errors more heavily than a MABE metric. Implies loss function increases with the square of the size of the error. These two measures respectively assume a linear and a quadratic loss function.

Bias.

Forecasts are unbiased if the expected value of the forecast error is zero. Common metric is the average error (AVE), which allows forecast errors of differing signs to cancel out. A deflator is often used to adjust for cross-sectional differences. Deflator typically forced to have a non-negative sign. Alternative: omit observations with negative denominators. The deflator can play a role in the ranking

Security Analysis: How to Analyze Accounting and Market Data to Value Securities
   Robert W. Holthausen and Mark E. Zmijewski
\CH8.W51

and it certainly relates to the loss function. Potential deflators are: absolute value of actual, absolute value of forecast, standard error of forecast error, standard error of actuals, standard error of forecasts, and stock price.[1] The choice of the deflator should be made on the basis of the loss function. Outliers may be a problem, and the standard solutions are employed (e.g., trimming).

Other Issues.

Forecasts may rank differently on the three dimensions: MABE, MSE and AVE. The "best" method is the one that best captures the loss function, but academics in their research typically have trouble determining an appropriate loss function since uses of forecasts may vary. The loss function may be asymmetric (e.g., bank loan example). Forecast horizon - do different model predict different forecast horizons better?

7. How Well Do We Forecast?

Financial Analysts.

Financial analysts' forecasts may be optimistic, however, none of the results indicate a bias that is statistically different from zero. All analysts do not revise their forecasts at the same time. In fact, it appears that more than 75% of the analysts do not revise their forecasts in a given month. Potential explanations, little information typically arrives during a month that would require a revision unless a detailed analysis is conducted - however, detailed analyses are not conducted on a monthly basis. Value Line conducts detailed forecasts every 13 weeks, otherwise, it only revises upon major events. Analysts revise forecasts with a shorter time horizon more often. Analysts generally revise long term forecasts in the same direction as the revision of short term forecasts. Analysts' forecasts are more accurate than are mechanical models. Analysts typically have a shorter time horizon for their forecasts (e.g., Value Line has a 40 day horizon while the mechanical models have a 90 day horizon). Analysts have access to a broader information set. For Value Line, mean absolute percentage errors in forecasts are approximately 22%, 26% and 29% for forecasts which are one quarter, two quarters and three quarters ahead. Similar numbers for Box-Jenkins time series model would be 26%, 32% and 33%.

Management Forecasts.

These forecasts are voluntary and only a small set of firms provide forecasts. The same firm does not always provide forecasts. Characteristics of firms with voluntary forecasts are that the firms have less variable earnings, they are larger firms, and the forecast typically conveys good news, but not always. Management forecasts are more accurate than analysts. Holding forecast horizon constant, management's median absolute forecast error is about 40% of the median security analysts forecast error on the same company. Can management manipulate income? You bet, but the real question is how often do they do it and under what circumstances.! Incentives for manipulation -- compensation plans, bond contracts, etc. The magnitude of the absolute forecast error is generally an increasing function of forecast horizon.

---

[1]Deflating by actual or forecast can result in the problem of negative denominators.

Security Analysis: How to Analyze Accounting and Market Data to Value Securities
Robert W. Holthausen and Mark E. Zmijewski
\CH8.W51

Consensus Forecasts.

How do you aggregate forecasts across analysts? Do you use the mean, median, weighted average based on other criterion? difficult to control for the timing of the forecasts. Ideally, you would like to use forecasts that are contemporaneous. However, in the databases that are available today, old and new forecasts are mixed. Evidence indicates that the latest forecast is often the most accurate forecast - even better than the consensus. This indicates a potential weighting by the age of the forecast. Analysts on the All-American Team are slightly more accurate than analysts as a whole who follow the same firm (both over the prior and next year after being name to the team).

Security Analysis: How to Analyze Accounting and Market Data to Value Securities
Robert W. Holthausen and Mark E. Zmijewski
\CH8.W51

Do not reproduce without permission.
July 29, 1998 - 3:28 pm

205

Chapter 8

Problems for Review

1.   **Basic Forecasting, Inc. (BFI).**

It is December 31, 2001; your consulting firm has been hired by the board of directors of BFI to prepare forecasts of BFI's financial statements and free cash flows for the next four years based on the assessments of BFI's management (note you need not forecast all four years but you should at least forecast two years). Your firm has also been hired to present and evaluate these forecasts sometime in early 2002 and the intention is that you will perform a valuation as of December 31, 2001. You have been given this assignment. [Note-this is a hard and time consuming problem].

Your interviews with BFI's management revealed the following information.

(1)   The manufacturing operations, which produce all products sold by BFI, have been operating at their long-run optimal capacity since the firm began its operations in late 1999.

(2)   BFI paid $10,000 for all of the land it owns (all purchased on December 31, 1999). Plant and equipment is depreciated for financial reporting purposes using straight-line depreciation.

(3)   The capital expansion program, which BFI began in 2001, is expected to increase BFI's 2001 capacity by 30% for the fiscal year beginning January 1, 2003, after the firm makes additional capital expenditures of $30,000 in 2002; capital expenditures in subsequent years are expected to be $3,000, measured in 2001 dollars, which are expected to increase with inflation.

(4)   Sales orders are expected to equal capacity in 2002, 90% of capacity in 2003, and 100% of capacity afterward. Sales prices are expected to keep pace with inflation, as are the cost of goods sold and selling and administrative expenses (you expect inflation to be 5% per year).

(5)   Management expects to decrease the cost of good sold and selling and administrative expenses (as a percent of net sales) by 2% in each of the next two years.

(6)   BFI expects to increase its efficiency in managing working capital by decreasing the average collection period for accounts receivable and the average number of days it holds inventory by 5 days in each of the next three years.

(7)   BFI uses short-term debt to finance short-term cash shortages, and the average amount of short-term debt is approximately 50% of accounts receivable, rounded to the nearest $1,000.

Security Analysis: How to Analyze Accounting and Market Data to Value Securities
   Robert W. Holthausen and Mark E. Zmijewski
   \CH8.W51

(8)   BFI plans to issue long-term debt (at the current 10% interest rate) if it has insufficient cash to fund its capital investments, and to repay long-term debt if it has any excess cash (after consideration of short-term debt financing decision discussed above). Long-term debt is issued and repaid in $100 increments.

(9)   BFI intends to pay dividends equal to the free cash flows to the common equity.

(10)   Interest on long-term debt issued December 31, 2001 (pertinent to the construction of the new capacity) will be capitalized until the plant is placed in operation (January 1, 2003).

(11)   Assume that all flows occur on the last day of the year; therefore, no depreciation is charged for capital expenditures during the year, and no interest is paid on debt issued during the year.

(12)   BFI's tax rate is 40% of taxable income. Only interest expense is tax deductible in the year it accrues; that is, interest capitalized for financial reporting purposes is also capitalized for income tax purposes. Property, plant, and equipment is depreciated over 25 years for income tax purposes using the straight line method.

(13)   The firm invests its excess cash in short-term investments that earn 7% per year.

(14)   Use historical relations among financial statement accounts to forecast the remaining accounts. This involves detective work on your part.

A.   Prepare BFI's financial statement and free cash flow forecasts (balance sheet, income statement, statement of retained earnings, cash flow statement, and free cash flow statement beginning with cash flow from operations) for the years ended December 31, 2002 through December 31, 2005 (again you need only do two years).

B.   Evaluate the forecasts.

HINTS

This is a very difficult problem. Spend some time figuring out how deferred taxes could look as they do. In addition, be very careful of the treatment of net operating losses. Remember that you must keep track of the value of interest tax shields in order to do a valuation. Thus, for your forecasts, you must determine the extent to which those future interest tax shields are actually useful. It is possible that an interest tax shield will have benefit in a given year, be reversed in a subsequent year and be reinstated in a later year. Good luck. Set aside a lot of time for this one.

Security Analysis: How to Analyze Accounting and Market Data to Value Securities
Robert W. Holthausen and Mark E. Zmijewski
\CH8.W51

```
 2
 3 Basic Forecasting, Inc. (BFI)
 4 Income Statement                               Dec-00   Dec-01
 5 .............................................................
 6 Revenue                                        110,000  116,871
 7 Cost of Goods Sold                              54,450   56,098
 8 Total Depreciation & Amortization                1,333    1,500
 9 Sell, Gen & Admin                               54,450   56,098
10                                                -----------------
11 Net Operating Income                             (233)    3,175
12 Interest on Short-term Investments                  0        0
13 Interest on Debt                                 2,400    4,180
14                                                -----------------
15 Pre-tax Income                                 (2,633)  (1,005)
16 Income Tax Expense                                  0        0
17                                                -----------------
18 Net Income                                     (2,633)  (1,005)
19                                                =================
20
21 Basic Forecasting, Inc. (BFI)
22 Statement of Retained Earnings                 Dec-00   Dec-01
23 .............................................................
24 Beginning Retained Earnings                         0   (2,717)
25 Net Income                                     (2,633)  (1,005)
26    Dividends                                       84       72
27                                                -----------------
28 Ending Retained Earnings                       (2,717)  (3,794)
29                                                =================
30
```

Security Analysis: How to Analyze Accounting and Market Data to Value Securities
Robert W. Holthausen and Mark E. Zmijewski
\CH8.W51

```
31 Basic Forecasting, Inc. (BFI)
32 BALANCE SHEET                                   Dec-00    Dec-01
33 ................................................................
34 ASSETS:
35 Cash Balance (Required for Operations)           5,761     5,564
36 Short-term Investments                               0         0
37                                                 ---------  ---------
38 Total Cash & Cash Equivalents                    5,761     5,564
39 Accounts Receivable                             18,044    19,478
40 Inventory                                       13,839    14,024
41                                                 ---------  ---------
42 Total Current Assets                            37,645    39,067
43                                                 ---------  ---------
44 Property, Plant, & Equipment - Cost             55,000    85,000
45 Accumulated Depreciation                         1,333     2,833
46                                                 ---------  ---------
47 Net PPEQ                                        53,667    82,167
48                                                 ---------  ---------
49 Total Assets                                    91,312   121,234
50
51 EQUITIES:
52 Accounts Payable                                 5,429     5,628
53 Income Taxes Payable                                 0         0
54 Short-term Debt                                  9,000    10,000
55                                                 ---------  ---------
56 Total Current Liabilities                       14,429    15,628
57 Long-term Debt                                  34,600    64,400
58 Deferred Income Taxes                               0         0
59                                                 ---------  ---------
60 Total Liabilities                               49,029    80,028
61                                                 ---------  ---------
62 Paid-in Capital                                 45,000    45,000
63 Retained Earnings                              (2,717)   (3,794)
64                                                 ---------  ---------
65 Shareholders' Equity                            42,283    41,206
66                                                 ---------  ---------
67 Total Equities                                  91,312   121,234
68
```

Security Analysis: How to Analyze Accounting and Market Data to Value Securities
Robert W. Holthausen and Mark E. Zmijewski
\CH8.W51

```
69
70 Basic Forecasting, Inc. (BFI)
71 CASH FLOW STATEMENT                              Dec-00    Dec-01
72 ·······································································
73 Net Income                                      (2,633)   (1,005)
74   Total Depreciation & Amortization              1,333     1,500
75   Change in Deferred Income Taxes                    0         0
76   Change in Accounts Receivable                (18,044)   (1,434)
77   Change in Inventory                              161      (185)
78   Change in Accounts Payable                     5,429       199
79   Change in Income Taxes Payable                     0         0
80                                                  ·················
81 Net Cash Provided by Operations               (13,755)     (925)
82 Capital Expenditures                           (5,000)  (30,000)
83 Cash Flows from Financing
84   Equity Changes                                     0         0
85   Short-term Debt Changes                        4,000     1,000
86   Long-term Debt Changes                        14,600    29,800
87   Dividends                                        (84)      (72)
88                                                  ·················
89 Net Change in Cash & Equivalents                 (239)     (197)
90                                                  =================
91 Cash Interest Paid                               2,400     4,180
92                                                  =================
93 Cash Income Taxes Paid                               0         0
94                                                  =================
```

Security Analysis: How to Analyze Accounting and Market Data to Value Securities
Robert W. Holthausen and Mark E. Zmijewski
\CH8.W51

14

ANALYSIS OF BUSINESS COMBINATIONS

INTRODUCTION

Corporate reorganizations have become an increasingly important aspect of the inte
national financial landscape in recent years. Acquisitions and divestitures of portio
of operating segments or entire lines of business are used to modify existing levels
horizontal and vertical integration, diversify, increase market share, improve operati
efficiency, and increase the market value of the firm.

211

Financial restructuring, on the other hand, alters the capital structure of a firm, increasing its debt burden. Capital structure may also be changed through reorganizations in bankruptcy, quasireorganizations, recapitalizations, and initial public offerings or secondary issues of stock in subsidiaries.

In the case of mergers or acquisitions, the use of a new accounting basis or continuation of the historical carrying amounts affects the preparation of subsequent financial statements for the combined operations of the two entities. The most significant issue for financial analysts is the comparability of reported results before and after acquisitions, given different reporting methods. Since sales, income, and return measures of the combined entity following the combination differ from those of the acquirer alone, the question is whether and how to restate reported results to facilitate comparisons of pre- and postmerger operations.

When a subsidiary acquired using the purchase method provides separate financial statements, another issue arises. Should the new basis be "pushed down" into those separate statements? This issue is important because these transactions often generate substantial goodwill and the implications for equity and liability valuation can be quite complex.

Many economic and financial reporting considerations affect the accounting method chosen to report acquisitions; it is important to understand management incentives for these choices. Much has been written in recent years regarding the comparative merits of the different methods of accounting for business combinations, their differential ability to obscure the "true" operating results, and their impact on international competition because of international tax and reporting differences. Although this chapter shows how each of these methods may have these effects, its objectives are to enable the financial analyst to interpret postacquisition financial statements prepared using either method and to provide some insights into management decisions.

The chapter begins with an explanation and simplified illustration of the purchase and pooling methods of accounting for mergers and acquisitions, followed by a comparison of their impact on financial statements and ratios. The SmithKline Beecham merger shows how differences in acquisition accounting methods hamper the comparison of firms in different countries. Next, we provide a discussion of the issue of acquisition goodwill followed by a review of empirical research into market reaction and management incentives to engage in acquisition activities.

The following sections examine push-down accounting and the significant accounting and analysis issues raised by spinoffs.

The chapter contains two cases that extend the analysis to two actual business combinations. The first case, based on the purchase method acquisition of Great Northern Nekoosa by Georgia Pacific, requires restatement to the pooling method, with very different financial statement effects. The second case reverses direction, asking for the restatement of the ConAgra–Golden Valley merger, which was reported using the pooling method, as a purchase. These restatements facilitate a comparison of financial statements and ratios resulting from the use of these two methods.

ACCOUNTING FOR ACQUISITIONS

Financial reporting rules for acquisitions in the United States depend on whether the transaction results in a change in control. Transactions in which one entity acquires the ownership interest of the stockholders of another entity trigger changes in control, requiring a new accounting basis for the acquired assets and liabilities. The *purchase method* of accounting treats such acquisitions as a purchase of the assets and assumption of the liabilities of the acquired or target firm, by the buyer.

The purchase method requires the allocation of the purchase price to all identifiable tangible and intangible assets and liabilities, regardless of whether they were recognized in the financial statements of the acquired company. *As a result, the assets and liabilities of the acquired company are received into the financial statements of the acquirer at their fair market values at the acquisition date.* The resulting postmerger balance sheets are not comparable to the preacquisition balance sheet of the acquirer.

The income and cash flow statements include the operating results of the acquired company effective with the date of acquisition. Operating results prior to the merger are not restated, although pro forma *data on a combined basis may be disclosed.* Like the balance sheet, pre- and postmerger income and cash flow statements are not comparable.

Some business combinations are assumed to merge the ownership interests of two firms rather than transfer control from the stockholders of one entity to those of the surviving firm. When such transactions meet certain restrictive conditions, they are reported using the *pooling of interests method* (merger accounting). The nature of the pooling of interests method is clearly defined in para. 12 of APB 16 (1970):

> The pooling of interests method accounts for a business combination as the uniting of the ownership interests of two or more companies by exchange of equity securities. No acquisition is recognized because the combination is accomplished without disbursing resources of the constituents. Ownership interests continue and the former bases of accounting are retained.

Pooling differs from the purchase method in the following respects:

1. The two parties are treated identically; there is no acquirer or acquired firm.
2. The financial statements are consolidated without adjustment; fair market values are not recognized for either company.
3. Operating results for the combined firm are restated for periods prior to the merger date.

Conditions Necessary for Use of the Pooling of Interests Method

APB 16 sets the conditions under which the pooling method can be used to account for an acquisition. The major requirements follow:

1. Each of the combining companies is independent; pooling is precluded when either has been a subsidiary or division of another company within two years prior to the merger. Significant intercompany stockholdings also preclude pooling.
2. Only voting common shares can be issued; the use of multiple classes of common or other securities (e.g., nonvoting preferred) violates the risk sharing that underlies the pooling concept.
3. Stock reacquisitions (other than normal purchases, such as for use in employee benefit plans) are prohibited, as are special distributions or other changes in

capital structure prior to the merger. These provisions are also intended to preserve the "uniting of equity interests." In the SmithKline Beecham example, discussed later in the chapter, special distributions to stockholders prior to the merger precluded pooling in the United States.

4. Absence of planned transactions that have the effect of benefiting some shareholders. For example, the combined company could not agree to tender for shares to guarantee some stockholders a fixed price for their shares.

5. The combined company must not intend to dispose of a significant portion of the existing businesses of the combining companies, other than duplicate facilities or excess capacity.

The pooling of interests method of accounting can be used only if *all* these conditions are met. The purchase method is required if any one of the conditions is violated. Thus, strictly speaking, the methods are not alternatives for any given transaction.

In practice, however, transaction terms are usually designed to achieve specific reporting objectives. Companies planning an acquisition prepare *pro forma* financial statements to estimate the impact of a proposed transaction and evaluate different terms and their different accounting consequences.[1] Even in the case of unfriendly acquisitions, for example, American Telephone's acquisition of NCR in 1991, pooling treatment can be obtained by restructuring the terms after the surrender.

ILLUSTRATION OF THE PURCHASE AND POOLING METHODS

The application of the purchase and pooling methods of accounting is illustrated by the Acquire Corporation's acquisition of the Target Company for $490 million on June 30, 1996. Scenario A assumes that Acquire raises the funds by selling new common stock. This assumption isolates the accounting effects of the two methods so that their impact on the financial statements and ratios of the combined firm can be seen. In practice, purchase transactions are rarely financed by equity alone. Scenario B assumes that the acquisition of Acquire by Target is financed by a mix of cash, debt, and equity.

Exhibit 14-1 presents the preacquisition balance sheets of both companies and the fair market values of Target's assets and liabilities on the acquisition date. Prior to the acquisition, Target has common equity of $250 million ($500 million assets less $250 million liabilities). The adjustments of Target's assets and liabilities to fair market value are typical of those found in real companies.

The Purchase Method

Application of the purchase method requires that all assets and liabilities of the target entity be revalued to fair market value. In addition, previously unrecognized contingencies and off-balance-sheet items must also be recognized. Examples include lawsuits and environmental contingencies as well as employee benefit plans.

---

[1]See, for example, Michael S. Devine, "Using Pro Forma Allocations to Evaluate Business Purchases," *Financial Executive*, June 1981, pp 15–18.

214

EXHIBIT 14-1. ACQUIRE AND TARGET
Comparative Balance Sheets at June 30, 1996 ($ in millions)

	Historical Cost				Fair Value	
	Acquire		Target		Target	
Cash	$100		$ 75		$ 75	
Inventories	200		100		150	
Receivables	200		75		75	
Current assets		$ 500		$250		$300
Property		500		250		350
Goodwill*		0		0		70
Total assets		$1,000		$500		$720
Payables	150		50		50	
Accrued liabilities	100		50		50	
Current liabilities		$ 250		$100		$100
Long-term debt		250		150		130
Common stock	400		225			
Retained earnings	100		25			
Common equity		500		250		490†
Total equities		$1,000		$500		$720

*See text discussion of the purchase method for allocation rules.

†Acquire has agreed to pay $490 million for Target's net assets; the $490 million presented for common equity reflects that purchase price.

Inventories carried at the lower of cost or market value are frequently reported at amounts below fair value, especially when the last-in, first-out (LIFO) inventory method is employed. Property is another common area of adjustment; in an inflationary world, fair value usually exceeds historical cost. The use of accelerated depreciation methods by the acquired firm may also result in understated asset values.

The adjustment to long-term debt depends on the current level of interest rates, as compared with the interest rate imbedded in the company's long-term debt. In the case of Target, we assume that the interest rate on the company's long-term debt is below current rates. The fair market value of this debt is the present value, at the current interest rate, of the cash flows (both principal and interest) required by the company's debt or $130 million in this case, which is below the face amount ($150 million) of the debt. When the current interest rate is below the historic rate, then the present value exceeds the face amount.[2]

[2]Note that SFAS 107, Disclosures About Fair Value of Financial Instruments, requires footnote disclosures of the fair value of debt and other financial assets and liabilities.

Having determined the fair values of assets and liabilities, we compare the net amount with the purchase price:

Assets at fair market value	$650 million
Liabilities at fair market value	(230)
Net assets at fair market value	$420 million

The purchase price of $490 million is $70 million higher than the fair value of net assets. Once all tangible assets and liabilities are restated at fair market value, any excess, residual purchase price must be allocated to intangible assets. Identifiable intangibles include:

- Patents
- Customer lists
- Licenses
- Brand names

Any excess purchase price that cannot be attributed to identifiable intangibles must be accounted for as a general intangible, usually called goodwill.[3] In Target's case, we cannot attribute any of the purchase price to identifiable intangibles and the $70 million excess purchase price must be treated as goodwill.

Alternatively, the fair value of the net assets acquired may exceed the purchase price of the entire company.[4] In this case, the purchase method requires that the fair value of property be reduced to the extent necessary to equate the net fair value of assets to the purchase price. In such cases, the new carrying amount of property may be less than its fair market value.

Exhibit 14-2A (column 5) shows the postmerger consolidated balance sheet under the purchase method. Note that Target's common equity has not been carried forward; it has been eliminated as a result of the merger. The combined common equity equals the sum of Acquire's preacquisition and newly issued equity, the latter stated at market value.

The combined balance sheet carries forward the assets and liabilities of Acquire without any change; adjustments are made only to the assets and liabilities of Target. If Target had purchased Acquire, the results would be quite different. Acquire's assets and liabilities would be restated, and Target's would remain unchanged.

The application of the purchase method of accounting to the balance sheet can be summarized as follows:

1. The purchase price is allocated to the assets and liabilities of the acquired firm; all assets and liabilities are restated to their fair market value.

---

[3]Goodwill is the excess purchase price over the fair market value of all identifiable assets net of all identifiable liabilities. It is one of the most controversial subjects in the accounting literature, as discussed in a later section of this chapter. Both the FASB and U.K. Accounting Standards Board have undertaken projects on accounting for goodwill.

[4]This may be due to unrecognized obligations or a low rate of return on assets.

216

EXHIBIT 14-2A
Comparison of Purchase and Pooling Methods: Scenario A (All Stock)

Consolidated Balance Sheets at June 30, 1996 ($ in millions)

| | (1) Historical Cost | | (3) Pooling Consolidated | (4) Purchase Method | (5) |
	Acquire	Target		Adjustments	Consolidated
Cash	$ 100	$ 75	$ 175	$ 0	$ 175
Inventories	200	100	300	50	350
Receivables	200	75	275	0	275
Current assets	$ 500	$250	$ 750	$ 50	$ 800
Property	500	250	750	100	850
Goodwill*	0	0	0	70	70
Total assets	$1,000	$500	$1,500	$220	$1,720
Payables	150	50	200	0	200
Accrued liabilities	100	50	150	0	150
Current liabilities	$ 250	$100	$ 350	0	$ 350
Long-term debt	250	150	400	(20)	380
Common stock	400 / 225		625	265 / 890	
Retained earning	100 / 25		125	(25) / 100	
Common equities	500	250	750	240†	990
Total equity	$1,000	$500	$1,500	$220	$1,720
Current ratio	2.00X	2.50X	2.14X		2.29X
Debt-to-equity ratio	50.00%	60.00%	53.33%		38.38%

*See text discussion of the purchase method for allocation rules.
†The net adjustment of $240 million reflects the purchase and retirement of all Target's equity ($225 million common stock + $25 million retained earnings) and the issuance of Acquire common stock with a market value of $490 million: $490 million − $250 million = $240 million.

2. The restated net fair value is compared with the purchase price; any excess purchase price over net fair value is attributed to identifiable intangible assets when possible, otherwise to goodwill.

3. If the restated net fair value exceeds the purchase price, then the write-up of property is reduced until equality is achieved.

4. The common equity of the acquired firm is eliminated.

The Pooling of Interests Method

The pooling method is illustrated using the same purchase method transaction. How-ever, to meet the pooling method's requirement for an exchange of common stock, we restructure the transaction. We now assume that Acquire exchanges its shares directly for those of Target. The postmerger balance sheet is also shown in Exhibit 14-2A (column 3) and is simply the summation of Target and Acquire's balance sheets.

Notice that the pooling method is similar to consolidation of a previously unconsolidated subsidiary, as discussed in Chapter 13. All assets and liabilities of the two firms are combined (and intercompany accounts eliminated), without any adjustment for fair values. When the pooling method is used, fair market values are irrelevant to recording the combination. *The actual market price and premium paid for the acquired firm are suppressed from both the balance sheet and income statement.*

Unlike the purchase method, the pooling method is symmetrical. The accounting result is identical whether Target is being acquired or is the firm making the acquisition. Note that the common equity of the two firms is simply combined. Neither company's share price has any bearing on the accounting result.[5]

EFFECTS OF ACCOUNTING METHODS

Comparison of Balance Sheets

Scenario A: Acquisition Funded by Sales of Common Stock. Exhibit 14-2A shows that the two methods produce very different postmerger balance sheets. Yet the economic reality resulting from the transaction is identical (if we ignore, for the moment, income tax effects), regardless of the accounting method used.

The differences between the balance sheets under the purchase method (column 5) and the pooling method (column 3) result from recognition of the market value of the transaction and the fair values of Target's assets and liabilities. As a result, a number of financial ratios are changed; we show two examples within the exhibit.

The current ratio is higher under the purchase method because of the adjustment of the acquired firm's current assets to their higher fair market value. The debt-to-equity ratio is lower under the purchase method because the newly issued equity of Acquire is reported at market value rather than at the preacquisition equity of Target.

These ratio effects are dependent on the use of equity as the acquisition medium. We now evaluate the differences between the purchase and pooling method using a more realistic purchase transaction involving the use of a mixture of cash, debt, and equity.

Scenario B: Acquisition Funded by Cash, Debt, and Equity. Exhibit 14-2B depicts the balance sheets under the two methods when the purchase is funded with the following mixture of cash, debt, and equity:

---

[5]Share prices have no effect on the accounting result once the terms of the deal have been set. They do, however, affect the basic terms of the transaction and the exchange ratio and may affect, as will be discussed, the choice of accounting method.

EXHIBIT 14-2B
Comparison of Purchase and Pooling Methods: Scenario B (Cash + Debt + Stock)

Consolidated Balance Sheets at June 30, 1996 ($ in millions)

	(1)		(2)	(3)	(4)		(5)
	Historical Cost			Pooling	Purchase Method		
	Acquire		Target	Consolidated	Adjustments		Consolidated
Cash	$ 100		$ 75	$ 175	$(100)		$ 75
Inventories	200		100	300	50		350
Receivables	200		75	275	—		275
Current assets	$ 500		$250	$ 750	$ (50)		$ 700
Property	500		250	750	100		850
Goodwill*	0		0	0	70		70
Total assets	$1,000		$500	$1,500	$ 120		$1,620
Payables	150		50	200	0		200
Accrued liabilities	100		50	150	0		150
Current liabilities	$ 250		$100	$ 350	0		$ 350
Long-term debt†	250		150	400	170		570
Common stock‡	400	225		625	(25)	600	
Retained earning	100	25		125	(25)	100	
Common equity	500		250	750	(50)		700
Total equities	$1,000		$500	$1,500	$ 120		$1,620
Current ratio	2.00X		2.50X	2.14X			2.00X
Debt-to-equity ratio	50.00%		60.00%	53.33%			81.43%

*See text discussion of the purchase method for allocation rules.
†The net adjustment of $170 million reflects the issuance of $190 million of debt less the write-down of Target's debt by $20 million to its fair value.
‡The net adjustment of $(50) million is the issuance of $200 million of Acquire common stock less the elimination of Target's equity ($225 million of common stock and $25 million of retained earnings).

Cash	$100 million
Debt (issued at the current interest rate[6])	190
Equity	200
Total purchase price	$490 million

As in Exhibit 14-2A, the balance sheet differences reflect the recognition of the market value of the transaction and the fair values of Target's assets and liabilities. The use of cash depresses the current ratio, but that decline is partially offset by the recognition of the fair value of Target's current assets. The net impact is a function

[6]Note that the actual cost of borrowing depends on market and firm-specific factors including, but not limited to, postacquisition leverage, market perceptions of the acquisition, and the debt maturity.

of the proportion of cash and other current assets used relative to the adjustment for fair value of the target's current assets.

The use of debt generates a substantial increase in leverage as depicted by the higher reported debt-to-equity ratio. The lower equity and total assets also affect return measures after the acquisition.

The pooling method balance sheet, *which* (consistent with APB16) *still assumes an all-stock transaction,* is unchanged from Exhibit 14-2A.

Comparison of Income Statements

The acquisition method also affects the income statement. The funding mix is another factor; we will discuss the impact of both purchase method scenarios. Exhibit 14-3

EXHIBIT 14-3. ACQUIRE AND TARGET
Income Statements, 1995 to 1997 ($ in millions)

	Years Ended December 31			
	1995	1996	1996*	1997
Target				
Sales	$ 600	$ 660	$ 340	$ 726
Cost of goods sold	(300)	(330)	(170)	(363)
Gross margin	$ 300	$ 330	$ 170	$ 363
Selling expense	(115)	(125)	(65)	(135)
Depreciation expense	(25)	(28)	(14)	(32)
Interest expense	(10)	(10)	(5)	(10)
Pretax income	$ 150	$ 167	$ 86	$ 186
Income tax expense	(50)	(56)	(29)	(62)
Net income	$ 100	$ 111	$ 57	$ 124
Gross margin as a % of sales	50.00%	50.00%	50.00%	50.00%
Interest coverage ratio	16.00	17.70	18.20	19.60
Acquire				
Sales	$1,000	$1,000	$ 500	$1,000
Cost of goods sold	(600)	(600)	(300)	(600)
Gross margin	$ 400	$ 400	$ 200	$ 400
Selling expense	(130)	(130)	(65)	(130)
Depreciation expense	(50)	(50)	(25)	(50)
Interest expense	(20)	(20)	(10)	(20)
Pretax income	$ 200	$ 200	$ 100	$ 200
Income tax expense	(68)	(68)	(34)	(68)
Net income	$ 132	$ 132	$ 66	$ 132
Gross margin as a % of sales	40.00%	40.00%	40.00%	40.00%
Interest coverage ratio	11.00	11.00	11.00	11.00

*Six months ended December 31.

EXHIBIT 14-4
Purchase Method Consolidated Income Statements: Scenario B, 1996 and 1997
($ in millions)

I. Year Ended December 31, 1996

	Acquire	Target	Adjustments	Consolidated
Sales	$1,000	$ 340	$—	$1,340
Cost of goods sold	(600)	(170)	(30)	(800)
Gross margin	$ 400	$ 170	$(30)	$ 540
Selling expense*	(130)	(65)	(1)	(196)
Depreciation expense	(50)	(14)	(5)	(69)
Interest expense	(20)	(5)	(10)	(35)
Pretax income	$ 200	$ 86	$(46)	$ 240
Income tax expense	(68)	(29)	15	(82)
Net income	$ 132	$ 57	$(31)	$ 158
Gross margin (% of sales)	40.00%	50.00%	NA	40.30%
Interest coverage ratio	11.00	18.20	NA	7.86

II. Year Ended December 31, 1997

	Acquire	Target	Adjustments	Consolidated
Sales	$1,000	$ 726	$—	$1,726
Cost of goods sold	(600)	(363)	(20)	(983)
Gross margin	$ 400	$ 363	$(20)	$ 743
Selling expense*	(130)	(135)	(2)	(267)
Depreciation expense	(50)	(32)	(10)	(92)
Interest expense	(20)	(10)	(22)	(52)
Pretax income	$ 200	$ 186	$(54)	$ 332
Income tax expense	(68)	(62)	17	(113)
Net income	$ 132	$ 124	$(37)	$ 219
Gross margin (% of sales)	40.00%	50.00%	NA	43.05%
Interest coverage ratio	11.00	19.60	NA	7.38

*Includes goodwill amortization.

contains condensed income statements for Target and Acquire for 1995, 1996, and 1997 as well as for the second half of 1996. Exhibit 14-4 contains combined income statements for Scenario B. We have assumed that Acquire is in a steady state, reporting a constant gross margin (40%) and interest coverage ratio (11X). Target reports annual sales growth of 10%, constant gross margin of 50%, and interest coverage that increases from 16X in 1995 to 19.6X in 1997.

Under the purchase method, Acquire's income statement includes Target's operations only after the effective date of the merger. Thus, the 1996 combined income statement (see panel I of Exhibit 14-4) includes the operations of Acquire for the entire year, but the operations of Target only for the six months following the merger on June 30, 1996. The restatement of Target's assets and liabilities to their fair market values affects certain categories of expense as well. These include:

- Cost of goods sold (COGS), which may increase as inventory that has been written up in value is sold.
- Higher depreciation expense, due to recognition of the higher fair values of Target's property.
- Amortization of goodwill recognized in the allocation of the purchase price.
- Higher interest expense due to amortization, over the remaining life of the debt, of the debt discount created by revaluing long-term debt. As Exhibit 14-4 shows, when debt is used to fund the acquisition, the additional cost of borrowing is another adjustment.[7]

When inventory is accounted for by using either first-in, first-out (FIFO) or average cost, written-up inventory values flow into the cost of goods sold fairly quickly, depressing gross margins. Although reported income is reduced, some of the acquisition cost is recovered quickly as the higher costs reduce taxable income in a taxable purchase transaction. When last-in, first-out (LIFO) inventory accounting is used, the higher costs remain in inventory indefinitely unless a LIFO invasion (reduction of inventory quantities) takes place.

For the acquisition of Target, we assume use of the average cost method, and that $30 million of the inventory write-up flows through COGS prior to the end of 1996. The remainder ($20 million) flows through COGS in 1997.

Additional depreciation expense is a consequence of the higher depreciable base of property assets. The same depreciation methods and lives applied to that higher cost increase depreciation expense and lower reported income, but also generate income tax savings in taxable purchases.

If we assume use of the straight-line method, it appears that Target's fixed assets have an average life of 10 years (property/depreciation expense). Applying this factor to the property write-up of $100 million increases depreciation expense by $10 million per year, or $5 million (one-half) for the six months ended December 31, 1996.[8]

Amortization of goodwill is deductible for tax purposes in the United States only in some cases. Unless goodwill is tax-deductible, companies prefer to allocate the cost of an acquisition to depreciable property, even though this results in faster amortization in the financial statements. Under APB 17 (1970), goodwill may be amortized over any period from 10 to 40 years.

For Target, we assume a write-off over 35 years; this is within the normal range in the United States. This assumption results in a goodwill amortization expense of $2 million for 1997 and $1 million (one-half) for the last six months of 1996.

---

[7]The derivation of income statements for 1996 and 1997 under Scenario A is not shown in the interest of brevity. The only difference is that, under Scenario A, there is no additional interest expense as the acquisition is financed entirely by issuing shares.

[8]Note that this assumes all Target's property is written up by the same percentage. If the write-up is disproportionately high in a class of property with an average life significantly different from the company average, this assumption does not hold.

The treatment of debt discount follows the method used when a bond is issued at a discount (see Chapter 10). The effective interest rate is higher as it reflects the stated (coupon) interest rate as well as amortization of the discount. This principle, when applied to discounted debt, increases interest expense. Otherwise, the reported debt liability would be insufficient at maturity, resulting in a loss. We assume an increase in interest expense of $1 million for the second half of 1996 and $3 million for 1997. The purchase method debt of $190 million under Scenario B generates additional interest expense of $9 million during the second half of 1996 and a further $19 million in 1997.

The purchase method income statement for the year ended December 31, 1996 includes Acquire's operations for the full year, Target's operations for the six months following the merger, and the effects of the purchase method adjustments (net of applicable tax savings). Panel II of Exhibit 14-4 shows the income statement for 1997 for the combined firm, also under Scenario B.

We see the full impact of purchase accounting from Acquire's income statements for the three years ended December 31, 1997, shown in Exhibit 14-5 for both scenarios. 1995 sales and expenses are those of Acquire only; 1996 and 1997 data include Target for the period following the merger on June 30, 1996 (for Scenario B, their derivation is shown in Exhibit 14-4).

First, note the distortion of the sales trend. From 1995 to 1997, Acquire reports a sales increase of 72.6%, none of which is due to its own internal growth. Most of the growth is due to the inclusion of Target's sales starting with the second half of 1996; part is due to the sales growth of Target following its acquisition.

The second problem is the distortion of profitability ratios. Acquire alone (see Exhibit 14-3) has a constant gross margin (sales less COGS) of 40% of sales; Target has a constant gross margin of 50% of sales. The combined gross margin percentage (Exhibit 14-5) shows a rising trend, reflecting Target's growing importance.

The reported interest coverage ratio, however, declines for Scenario B. The additional debt reduces the coverage ratio to 7.38X in 1997 from the 11X reported for 1995. The decline is a function of the proportion of debt used to finance the purchase, the assumption of Target's debt, and the relative cost of debt. For Scenario A (panel A of Exhibit 14-5), the assumption that the acquisition is financed by selling equity results in higher interest coverage and net income due to lower interest expense.

Without the underlying data (from Exhibits 14-3 and 14-4), it is impossible to determine whether the rising profitability of Acquire is due to improvement in its own operations, the higher profitability of Target, efficiencies from the merger, or the impact of purchase method adjustments. In some cases, we can keep track of an acquired company through the use of segment data (see Chapter 13). However, as the frequency of acquisition rises, the ability to discern the impact of any single acquisition diminishes. When there are many small acquisitions or acquisitions within existing segments, their effect cannot be isolated.

For comparison purposes, we now examine the income statements for the years 1995 through 1997 that result from accounting for the merger as a pooling of interests. These income statements, presented in Exhibit 14-6, are obtained by simply adding together (without any adjustment) the income statements of Acquire and Target for the respective years.

Exhibits 14-5 and 14-6 show considerable differences. When the pooling method is used, the operating results of Target are included for all three years, including the

EXHIBIT 14-5. ACQUIRE CORP.
Purchase Method Consolidated Income Statements, 1995 to 1997,
Years Ended December 31 ($ in millions)

Scenario A: All Equity

	1995	1996	1997
Sales	$1,000	$1,340	$1,726
Cost of goods sold	(600)	(800)	(983)
Gross margin	$ 400	$ 540	$ 743
Selling expense*	(130)	(196)	(267)
Depreciation expense	(50)	(69)	(92)
Interest expense	(20)	(26)	(33)
Pretax income	$ 200	$ 249	$ 351
Income tax expense	(68)	(85)	(119)
Net income	$ 132	$ 164	$ 232
Gross margin (% of sales)	40.00%	40.30%	43.05%
Interest coverage ratio	11.00	10.58	11.64

Scenario B: Cash, Debt, and Equity

	1995	1996	1997
Sales	$1,000	$1,340	$1,726
Cost of goods sold	(600)	(800)	(983)
Gross margin	$ 400	$ 540	$ 743
Selling expense*	(130)	(196)	(267)
Depreciation expense	(50)	(69)	(92)
Interest expense	(20)	(35)	(52)
Pretax income	$ 200	$ 240	$ 332
Income tax expense	(68)	(82)	(113)
Net income	$ 132	$ 158	$ 219
Gross margin (% of sales)	40.00%	40.30%	43.05%
Interest coverage ratio	11.00	7.86	7.38

*Includes goodwill amortization.

periods prior to the merger. The restatement of prior period results is one of the salient features of the pooling of interests method of accounting, and it facilitates comparability.

Because the operating results of all three years include both Acquire and Target, the purchase method's "illusion of growth" is absent. Sales growth over the period 1995 to 1997 is 7.9%, reflecting only the internal sales growth of Target. All categories of expense are comparable as well. The gross margin percentage shows small year-to-year increases, reflecting the growing importance of Target's higher margin operations. The interest coverage ratio reflects the addition of Acquire's higher cost debt.

EXHIBIT 14-6. ACQUIRE CORP.
Pooling Method Income Statements, 1995 to 1997,
Years Ended December 31 ($ in millions)

	1995	1996	1997
Sales	$1,600	$1,660	$1,726
Cost of goods sold	(900)	(930)	(963)
Gross margin	$ 700	$ 730	$ 763
Selling expense	(245)	(255)	(265)
Depreciation expense	(75)	(78)	(82)
Interest expense	(30)	(30)	(30)
Pretax income	$ 350	$ 367	$ 386
Income tax expense	(118)	(124)	(130)
Net income	$ 232	$ 243	$ 256
Gross margin (% of sales)	43.75%	43.98%	44.21%
Interest coverage ratio	12.67	13.23	13.87

However, the pooling of interests method can also mislead. The first problem is that it creates a fictitious history. Results for 1995 have been restated as if the two companies were combined in that year. In reality, they were separate enterprises, with different managements. The pooling method permits the management of Acquire to take credit for the operating results of Target for the period prior to its acquisition.

The pooling method allows companies whose shares sell at high price/earnings ratios to improve earnings per share via acquisition. When a company uses its highly valued shares (i.e., high price/earnings multiple) to acquire a company whose shares sell at a low multiple of earnings under the pooling method, then earnings per share increase. This technique is sometimes known as "bootstrapping," as the acquired company can raise earnings per share through financial engineering rather than operating improvement. This effect is illustrated in Case 14-2, using the ConAgra acquisition of Golden Valley. In theory, this technique should fail as the market assigns a lower price/earnings ratio to the postmerger firm to reflect the inclusion of "lower-quality" earnings.[9] In practice, the technique can be effective for many years.

In the extreme case, an acquisition can be made after the close of the fiscal year to meet sales and earnings objectives. Because of the restatement feature of the pooling method, a company can include in its reported results the operations of firms acquired after the end of the year but before release of the annual report.[10]

Another serious problem with the pooling method of accounting *is the suppression of the true cost of the acquisition.* Since the pooling method carries forward historical

[9]The efficient markets hypothesis suggests that the market price of the acquirer should adjust instantaneously.

[10]National Student Marketing, a "high-flyer" in the late 1960s and early 1970s until its collapse, was reported to have made acquisitions *after the end of each fiscal year* to bring reported earnings up to the forecasted level.

costs, *no recognition is given to the true value of the assets acquired or any securities used to pay for the acquired company* (see Exhibit 14-2A, column 3).

There are several consequences of this failure to recognize the fair values acquired and paid for. One is that the acquiring company may sell acquired assets whose carrying cost is well below fair or market value. As a result, reported income includes fictitious gains. Although the acquirer presumably paid the full value of the assets acquired, the price paid was not recognized by the pooling method. Similarly, depreciation and amortization reflect the historical cost of assets acquired rather than their market value. As a result, income is overstated.[11]

Cash Flow Statement Effects

When the pooling method is used, the merger itself (an exchange of shares) is not reported in the cash flow statement as no cash flows have taken place. The postacquisition cash flow statement is the sum of the individual cash flow statements. As in the case of the income statement, previously issued cash flow statements are restated on a combined basis.

Under purchase method accounting, however, cash flows associated with the acquisition are reported on the cash flow statement, but in abbreviated form. The net assets acquired are reported as cash used for investment and the applicable financing sources as cash from financing. To illustrate this recognition in a simplified setting, assume that Acquire prepares a cash flow statement for the acquisition date of June 30, 1996, reflecting only the acquisition (during that short time period, no operations take place). The balance sheet changes and cash flow statement for Scenario B are presented in Exhibit 14-7.

The purchase method balance sheet (panel I) reflects the acquisition of the assets and liabilities (at their fair values) of Target. However, the cash flow statement (panel II) shows only cash outflows for investing of $415 million, equal to the purchase price of $490 million less $75 million of preacquisition cash on Target's balance sheet. None of the individual assets and liabilities acquired (shown in italics in panel I) are reported in the cash flow statement. Financing cash flow includes Acquire's issuance of $190 million of debt and $200 million of equity, for a total of $390 million generated from lenders and owners. The decrease in cash of $25 million is the net amount of cash used by Acquire to complete the acquisition. If we assume that the transaction was financed entirely with equity (Scenario A), the cash flow statement would report cash for investment of $415 million and cash from equity financing equal to $490 million with a net increase in cash of $75 million.

SFAS 95 (see Chapter 3) specifically requires that reported cash flows exclude the effect of acquisitions (other than actual cash flows). The failure to report the

---

[11]Abraham J. Briloff has written extensively over the years on the problems associated with the use of the pooling method. For example, see Briloff, "Distortions Arising from Pooling-of-Interests Accounting," *Financial Analysts Journal,* March–April 1968, pp 71–80. Despite the venerable age of this article, it remains a superb illustration of the suppression of the fair value of the acquisition in the pooling method, permitting the reporting of "gains" on acquired assets.

EXHIBIT 14-7
Impact of the Acquisition of Target on Statement of Cash Flows of Acquire,
Scenario B: Cash + Debt + Stock

I. Acquire Corp. Pre- and Postacquisition Balance Sheets

$ in millions	Preacquisition*		Postacquisition†		Change
Cash		$ 100		$ 75	($ 25)
Inventories		*200*		*350*	*150*
Receivables		*200*		*275*	*75*
Current assets		$ 500		$ 700	$200
Property		*500*		*850*	*350*
Goodwill		*0*		*70*	*70*
Total assets		$1,000		$1,620	$620
Payables		*150*		*200*	*50*
Accrued liabilities		*100*		*150*	*50*
Current liabilities		250		350	100
Long-term debt		*250*		*570*	*320*
Common stock	400		600		200
Retained earnings	100		100		0
Common equity		500		700	200
Total equities		$1,000		$1,620	$620

II. Effect of Acquisition on Acquire's Statement of Cash Flows

($ in millions)

Cash from operations		
Net income	$0	
Changes in operating accounts	0	$ 0
Cash for investment		(415) Net assets of Target (net of cash)
Cash from financing		
Debt financing	$190	
Equity financing	200	390
Net change in cash		($ 25)

*Exhibit 14-2B, column 1.
†Exhibit 14-2B, column 5.
Changes not shown explicitly in cash flow statement shown in italics; note that new debt is reported although assumed debt of Target is ignored.

individual asset and liability changes for purchase method acquisitions has two consequences:

1. Consecutive balance sheets and the cash flow statement can be used to deduce the assets and liabilities acquired.
2. Operating cash flow (CFO) can be distorted.

We consider each of these consequences in turn.

Deducing Assets and Liabilities Acquired

Because SFAS 95 requires the exclusion of acquisition balance sheet changes from the cash flow statement, balance sheet changes for any period have three components:

1. Operating changes for the period
2. Effect of acquisitions
3. Effect of foreign currency changes

For companies with no foreign operations, only the first two components exist. In that case, we can deduct the operating change component from the total change and deduce the acquisition effects.

Exhibit 14-7 illustrates this process in a simplified way. Panel I shows the balance sheet of Acquire just before and just after its acquisition of Target. We have assumed that the period is so short that there are no operations. In this case, therefore, the balance sheet changes are due entirely to the acquisition. If we did not have the consolidating balance sheet (Exhibit 14-2B) for Scenario B, we could deduce it.

For example, inventories rose by $150 million. As the operating change was zero, the acquired inventories of Acquire must have been $150 million (at fair value). This same analysis can be applied to receivables, property, goodwill, and payables.

The analysis of debt is more complicated. The total change is $320 million, of which $190 is new debt issued to finance the acquisition. The assumed debt of Target must be $130 million (reflecting the $20 million write-down to fair value).

The debt example illustrates the general procedure used to deduce acquisition assets and liabilities: Subtract the operating change shown in the cash flow statement from the actual balance sheet change for the period. The difference should be the effect of acquisitions or divestitures.

Use of this procedure is illustrated in Case 14-1 (Georgia Pacific) and Problem 8. Its accuracy, however, depends on an absence of foreign currency effects; these are discussed in Chapter 15.

Distortion of Cash from Operations

Although the acquisition increases operating assets and liabilities, that increase is not included in cash from operations (CFO). The cash flow change in operating accounts does not equal the actual balance sheet change. Because the additional inventories and receivables are acquired as part of an acquisition, the cash paid for their acquisition is included in cash for investment.

However, CFO reported in the year of the acquisition (and in subsequent years) may still be distorted. The degree of distortion depends on whether the levels of operating assets and liabilities immediately after the acquisition are maintained over time.

The potential distortion can be illustrated by considering the inventory acquired. Although the cash paid for the acquisition of the inventory does not flow through cash from operations, the cash received when the inventory is sold does. Thus, CFO is inflated as the proceeds of sale are included, whereas the cost of acquiring the inventory is not.

This distortion is minimal if inventory is continually replaced, as the cash outflows for new inventory offset cash inflows from sales. However, if there is a reduction in the acquired firm's net operating assets, CFO may be distorted, and careful analysis is required to understand the impact. An example appears in Case 14-1, the analysis of Georgia Pacific's acquisition of Great Northern Nekoosa.

Impact on Ratios

Financial statement ratios under the two methods differ, reflecting recognition of the purchase price and the fair values of the assets and liabilities of Target by Acquire under the purchase method; the pooling method suppresses both the purchase price and fair values.

Exhibits 14-2A and 14-2B show that the purchase method reports higher asset values and higher common equity (for the all-equity Scenario A) than the pooling of interests method when the purchase price exceeds the stated net worth of the acquired company. As a result, the base for activity and return ratios is higher. In addition, adjustments required by the purchase method usually reduce reported earnings. (Acquire's 1997 earnings are $256 million under the pooling method, but only $232 million under the purchase method for Scenario A.) The result is that profitability ratios are generally lower when the purchase method is used. Interest coverage ratios are reduced in this case by the increase in interest expense and further lowered when the acquisition is financed with debt.

The purchase method makes financial ratios difficult to interpret in other ways. Acquire's assets and liabilities are carried forward at historical cost, whereas Target's are restated to fair market values,[12] generating a mixture of historical costs and market values in the combined accounts. As a result, activity ratios are difficult to compare with those of other companies.

In addition, postacquisition ratios are not comparable with preacquisition ratios, because:

- Target may have had a different turnover ratio than Acquire (both the level and trend may differ), reflecting the nature of its business; the postmerger ratio is a blend of the ratios of the two companies.
- Turnover ratios are reduced solely because of the fair value adjustments required by the purchase method.

Comparison of a company that has made a purchase method acquisition with one that has made a pooling acquisition (or none at all) is also affected by these same problems.

A purchase method acquisition creates a discontinuity throughout the financial statements of the acquiring company. Comparison with preacquisition data for the same company and comparison with other companies are hampered by the inclusion of the acquired entity at the acquisition date (balance sheet effects), and by the subsequent purchase method adjustments (balance sheet and income statement effects).

---

[12]Property, however, is restated to an amount less than fair value when the purchase price is below the fair value of net assets.

229

Because the pooling method restates preacquisition financial statements, it produces comparable financial statements. However, this comparability is fictitious; the combined companies were not operated as one or by the same management prior to the combination. The restated levels and trends in ratios may not represent expected performance over time under different management.

The reader is cautioned that ratio effects described in this section are company- and transaction-specific. Depending on the purchase price relative to book value, the fair values of assets and liabilities acquired, the means of financing, and the earnings of the target firm, the effect on ratios of use of the purchase method or pooling method will vary in practice. Use of trend data for such companies can easily lead to misleading conclusions. *We can, however, make the general statement that the choice of method does affect the ratios of the combined enterprise, often significantly.*

COMPLICATING FACTORS IN PURCHASE METHOD ACQUISITIONS

The Target–Acquire scenarios are both simplistic. In actual transactions, there are two complicating factors that sometimes appear:

- Contingent payments
- In-process research and development

We discuss each issue briefly.

Contingent Payments

Some acquisition agreements provide that the acquisition price is dependent on future earnings of the acquired entity or other future events. APB 16 states that the additional purchase price is recognized by the acquirer as soon as those conditions are met.

The purchase price increase must be allocated to the assets and liabilities acquired. If some assets (e.g., property) were not fully written up to fair value, then a further write-up would occur. The usual case, however, is that the contingent compensation increases goodwill.

For example, Russ Berrie, a gift and toy marketer, reported that

> in October 1993, the Company acquired substantially all of the assets of Cap Toys, Inc., a toy company based in Ohio, and $13,606,000 of goodwill was recorded. Under the purchase agreement, additional payments may be required based on the attainment of certain operating profit levels of Cap Toys, Inc. During the years ended December 31, 1995 and 1994, $1,047,000 and $2,563,000, respectively, was charged to goodwill related to these additional payments.[13]

As Russ Berrie amortizes acquisition goodwill over 15 years, the additional goodwill increases amortization expense, offsetting some of the increased profitability of the

---

[13]Russ Berrie, *1995 Annual Report*, Note 1.

acquired firm. Such disclosures are also helpful indications of the performance of acquisitions in following years.

In-Process Research and Development

The acquisition price of computer, biotechnology, and other firms with high technological content recognizes that such firms have significant assets in the form of research and development in progress. APB 16 requires that such "in-process research and development" be expensed immediately when the purchase method of accounting is used. For example, when IBM acquired Lotus in 1995, $1,840 million (more than half) of the purchase price was expensed.

There are two important effects of such expensing:

1. Reported income of the acquirer is reduced in the period of the acquisition. As this effect is nonoperating, it should be considered a nonrecurring expense for analysis purposes.

2. The immediate write-off reduces the amount of goodwill that would otherwise be recognized, reducing future goodwill amortization. In effect, there is an immediate write-off of goodwill. This may create an incentive for firms to allocate as much of the purchase price as possible to in-process research and development.[14]

INCOME TAX EFFECTS OF BUSINESS COMBINATIONS

The income tax aspects of accounting for business combinations have always been complex. Changes in U.S. tax laws in recent years have only increased that complexity. A thorough discussion of this subject is well beyond the scope of this book. However, a few general comments may be helpful.

Most pooling of interests acquisitions are nontaxable events under the Internal Revenue Code (the Code) of the United States. Nontaxability has two consequences:

1. Shareholders of the acquired company do not recognize gain or loss as a result of the merger. They transfer the cost basis of their shares in the acquired company to the shares of the acquirer that they receive in exchange.

2. The cost basis of the assets and liabilities of the acquired company is not affected by the merger. There is no income tax recognition of the fair value of assets and liabilities and no change in tax benefits or deductibility as these assets are used or liabilities paid.

A purchase method acquisition, in contrast, is usually a taxable event under the Code. In a taxable exchange, selling shareholders must recognize gain or loss on the sale of their shares, even if they receive securities of the acquiring company. In addition,

---

[14]See the discussion in Elizabeth McDonald, "More Firms Write Off Acquisition Costs," *Wall Street Journal,* Dec. 2, 1996, p. A2.

the tax basis of assets and liabilities of the acquired firm is changed from original cost to fair value, reflecting the price paid for the company.

In most cases, the accounting treatment and the income tax treatment are identical. In these circumstances, the postmerger accounting and tax basis of assets and liabilities are the same. However, the accounting and tax rules do differ in some respects, and there are times when the tax treatment of an acquisition is different from the accounting treatment. In such cases, care must be taken to discern the impact of the difference on future earnings and cash flows. Careful reading of the income tax footnote (see Chapter 9) may reveal different tax and accounting bases for some assets and liabilities. Differential merger treatment is usually the cause of such differences.

When a merger is tax-free, but accounted for as a purchase, the tax basis of the assets is below the accounting basis (if we assume that the purchase price exceeds historical equity). As a result, the additional depreciation and other expenses resulting from purchase method adjustments are not tax-deductible. This increases the firm's effective tax rate.

Another effect is that recognized gains on the sale of assets are higher for tax purposes than for accounting purposes, reducing after-tax cash proceeds and adversely affecting the after-tax gain or loss from the sale.

CHOOSING THE ACQUISITION METHOD

The analyses of Acquire–Target and SmithKline Beecham may suggest that the purchase and pooling methods of acquisition accounting are optional alternatives. Strictly speaking, that is not the case; the conditions mandating the use of the purchase or pooling method in the United States are delineated in APB 16. However, it is naive to believe that acquirers ignore the accounting consequences of planned acquisitions.

APB 16 (1970)[27] was intended to eliminate abuses of the pooling method during the acquisition binge of the 1960s and the optional nature of acquisition accounting by defining the conditions under which each method would be applicable. For example,

[27]On August 21, 1996, the FASB added a project to its agenda that will reconsider APB Opinions 16 and 17.

233

to be eligible for pooling treatment, 12 separate criteria related to the structure of the transaction, its tax effect, and the mode of payment must be satisfied. Thus, the accounting method depends on the characteristics of the transaction.

From the corporate viewpoint, the pooling method is usually preferred under the following conditions:

1. Purchase price greatly exceeds stated equity or book value of target.
2. Target does not have significant depreciable assets that can be written up substantially for tax purposes, creating higher tax deductions.
3. Acquiring company does not wish to increase its leverage or has limited borrowing power.
4. Target has securities or other assets with market values above historic cost. Under pooling, the cost is unchanged; after the acquisition these assets can be sold, increasing reported income.

Under the purchase method, the first two conditions would generate a large amount of goodwill and subsequent amortization reducing reported earnings without a cash (tax reduction) benefit. The SmithKline-Beecham merger is a good example of the adverse impact of purchase accounting on acquisitions meeting the first two conditions.

The third condition needs some elaboration. Purchase method acquisitions can substantially increase the acquiring company's debt load (see Exhibit 14-2B) as compared with the result under a stock transaction. Case 14C-1 illustrates this issue using Georgia Pacific's acquisition of GNN. Apparently, GP felt that the large cash flow of GNN, combined with asset sales, would make the debt load manageable.

In general, acquisitions of service companies and others with low asset intensity (few assets to write up) and targets with high returns on equity (implying purchase prices well above stated equity) lend themselves to pooling.

On the other hand, purchase accounting can be advantageous under different conditions:

1. Target is "asset rich" allowing write-ups, consequent tax reduction, and quick recovery of the investment. Allocation of the purchase price to inventory is a good example.
2. Purchase price is below stated book value facilitating a write down of assets, reducing depreciation and increasing reported earnings.
3. Purchase accounting includes the Target's "off-balance-sheet" obligations (e.g., underfunded postretirement plans) in the allocation of the purchase price, reducing future charges to earnings.
4. Shareholders of the acquirer do not wish to dilute their voting control or equity interest by issuing additional shares. They may prefer to use cash or securities with little or no voting power to effect the acquisition.

Thus, the accounting method is a consequence of the acquisition terms and the specific circumstances of the acquirer, target company, and shareholders. Although not truly optional, it is subject to management control, and the terms of the merger can be fashioned to achieve the desired accounting alternative. Anecdotal evidence suggests that the accounting treatment can significantly affect the negotiated terms[28] and that certain mergers would not have been consummated if pooling could not be used.

Both the choice of accounting method and different market reactions to mergers accounted for as pooling or purchases must, therefore, be understood in the context of the overall motivation for mergers. These issues can be illustrated by examining the income maximization hypothesis often used to explain the accounting choice.

Income Maximization as Motivation for the Pooling/Purchase Choice

Many researchers have explored income maximization and price (P) to book value (BV) ratio as motivations for the pooling/purchase choice. Under this hypothesis, when the price paid exceeds the target's book value ($P > BV$), pooling is preferred as subsequent reported income, return on equity (ROE), and return on assets (ROA) will be higher. On the other hand, when $P < BV$, purchase accounting is preferred.

Robinson and Shane (1990) summarize the results of a number of studies of this hypothesis. They find that when $P > BV$ there is a strong preference for the pooling method (84% overall). For $P < BV$, although the purchase method does not dominate, there is clearly less of a preference for the pooling method. Thus the results are generally consistent with the overall hypothesis, albeit in an asymmetric fashion.

Davis (1990) also documents that the price to book value differential is considerably larger for poolings. This differential is related to the bid premium (the price paid for the target relative to the premerger price of the target) Robinson and Shane found to be larger for poolings.

Thus, consistent with the income maximization hypothesis, the evidence indicates that pooling is the preferred method of accounting for mergers where:

1. $P > BV$ and

2. Relatively higher prices are paid for targets.

Market Reaction and the Pooling/Purchase Choice

For mergers in general, Morck et al. (1990) report that

> average returns to bidding shareholders are at best slightly positive and significantly negative in some studies.[29]

Hong et al. (1978) compared the abnormal returns of acquiring firms using the pooling method with those using the purchase method to evaluate the impact of the choice of accounting method. They also tested whether the market reacts positively to the higher income reported when the pooling method is used.

Little or no market reaction was observed for pooling firms, either in the period

---

[28]The AT&T–NCR merger is an example. Moreover, the FASB Discussion Memorandum, An Analysis of Issues Relating to Accounting for Business Combinations and Purchased Intangibles (August 19, 1976), reports that two-thirds of its respondents concurred with the statement that many of the mergers that used the pooling of interests would not have been consummated had they been required to use the purchase method. Only 14% disagreed with the statement.

[29]Randall Morck, Andrei Shleifer, and Robert W. Vishny, "Do Managerial Objectives Drive Bad Acquisitions?," *Journal of Finance*, March 1990, pp. 31–48. These results contrast with those of target shareholders, who generally fare well as a result of the merger.

leading up to the merger or around the first post-merger earnings announcement. However, for a smaller sample of purchase method firms, they found significant positive reaction in the 12-month period preceding the effective date of the merger.

Davis (1990), using weekly data and an expanded sample of firms, found similar results. Unlike pooling firms, purchase method acquirers show abnormal positive returns over a 26-week period prior to the merger announcement.

Hong et al. and Davis studied two separate time periods (1954 to 1964 and 1971 to 1982, respectively), but both found positive returns to bidder firms using the purchase method. Bradley et al. (1988),[30] noted that although target firms almost always earn abnormal positive returns, acquiring firms realized a significant positive reaction only during the unregulated period 1963–1968 and in fact suffered a significant loss during the sub-period 1981–1984.[31]

Interpreting the Research Results

It is difficult to draw conclusions from this research for two reasons. First, as cash or debt (taxable) transactions cannot be accounted for by use of the pooling method, comparable purchase method transactions are confined to nontaxable acquisitions using shares of the acquirer. In many cases, however, factors that preclude the use of pooling are characteristic of higher bid premia. When cash is used, the bid premium tends to be higher.[32] Moreover, when the transaction is taxable to the target shareholders, a higher bid premium may be required to compensate them for the tax consequences.

Thus, these studies are limited to those transactions where the bid premia are *a priori* smaller. This self-selection bias may explain smaller price to book value differentials associated with purchase accounting and limit the generalizability of these results.

Similarly, the positive market reaction to the purchase acquisitions may be associated with the bargain purchase implied by the low bid premia. On the other hand, relatively higher payments for the pooling transactions may indicate overpayment (or at least no bargain) and hence the muted market reaction. Thus, the market reaction may be related to the level of payment rather than the choice of accounting method.

This explanation assumes that the market reacts to mergers that had been anticipated because of leaks in the weeks leading up to the merger announcement.[33] An alternative explanation offered by Hong et al. was that the firms that instigated purchase transactions were better performing firms and that

> firms who choose the purchase method can "afford" to report the lower earnings caused by the use of this method.[34]

We return to this point later.

---

[30]Bradley et al. (1988) did not differentiate between purchase and pooling transactions.

[31]J. Bradley, A. Desai, and E. H. Kim, "Synergistic Gains from Corporate Acquisitions and Their Division Between the Stockholders of Target and Acquiring Firms," *Journal of Financial Economics,* May 1988, pp. 3–40.

[32]See Robinson and Shane (1990), p. 81.

[33]As most of the reaction was in the 11-week period leading up to the merger announcement this is a plausible explanation.

[34]Hai Hong, Robert S. Kaplan, and Gershon Mandelker, "Pooling vs. Purchase: The Effects of Accounting for Mergers on Stock Prices," *The Accounting Review,* Jan. 1978, pp. 31-47.

The second issue in interpreting research results is related to the question of *cause and effect*. First, we explore reasons why firms are interested in income maximization. One possibility is that managers with compensation plans based on earnings, ROA, or ROE are motivated to choose pooling over purchase to enhance their compensation.

This line of reasoning is consistent with theories of merger activity that argue that managers initiate mergers for their own self-interest and consequently may overpay for the target. They enter into mergers to "buy" growth or to diversify their own risk even if this growth or diversification is not (necessarily) in the best interests of their shareholders.[35]

This underlying motivation may explain (1) the merger, (2) the accounting choice, and (3) the degree of overpayment. If the accounting choice is deemed desirable, then it may be that the accounting choice itself was one of the terms of the negotiation. The acquirer may have paid more for the target to obtain a deal structure permitting it to use the pooling method.

Thus, the choice of accounting method cannot be viewed separately from the acquisition itself. In many ways it is endogenous to the overall terms of the merger. This is true not only for the effects implied by the income maximization theory and the differential market reactions discussed above. Similar patterns can be shown in the context of other merger characteristics. These are discussed in the next section.

Other Factors Influencing Mergers, Bid Premia, and the Pooling/Purchase Choice

Exhibit 14-14 lists a number of factors that can impact the pooling/purchase choice either directly or indirectly (through its influence on the bid premium). In addition, (some of) these factors have been found in other studies to be associated with positive market reaction to mergers. The discussion of these categories should serve to illustrate the complexities involved in analyzing the relationship of accounting choice and economic characteristics of mergers.

The three categories are characteristics of:

1. The transaction
2. The acquiring firm
3. The target firm

Characteristics of the Transaction

(1) Cash Transaction and (2) Tax Status. These were discussed earlier. Under APB 16, pooling is permissible only if the merger is a noncash transaction. Moreover, pooling transactions tend to be nontaxable acquisitions. Generally, higher bid premia are associated with mergers that involve cash payments and are taxable to the target's shareholders. These factors result in higher bid premia for purchase rather than pooling transactions and also preclude the use of pooling.

(3) Percentage Acquired. The larger the percentage of the target acquired, the larger the bid premium. Under APB 16, unless the acquisition exceeds 90% of the shares of the target, it must be accounted for as a purchase. Thus a higher bid premia is implied for a pooling rather than purchase transaction.

---

[35]See Morck et al. (1990) pp. 31–36. Roll (1986) goes so far as to suggest that managers suffer from hubris and are convinced that they can do a better job with the target than its current management.

EXHIBIT 14-14
Merger Characteristics, Bid Premia, and Choice of Accounting Method

	+ Indicates Preference for Pooling	+ Indicates Larger Bid Premia
Characteristics of Transaction		
1. Cash payment	−	+
2. Tax status	−	+
3. Small percentage acquired	−	−
Characteristics of Acquirer		
4. $P > BV$ and management compensation contract	+	
5. $P > BV$ and bond covenant, debt constraint	−	
6. $P > BV$ and bond covenant, dividend constraint	+	
7. "Good" managers Owner versus manager control	−	−
Characteristics of Target		
8. Low leverage High liquidity		+
9. Relative size of target to acquirer	−	−
10. "Poor" managers Low market to book ratio Low Q ratio		−
11. Low price-earnings multiple	+	

Characteristics of Acquirer

The first three aspects of the acquirer are tied to the nature of the price to book value differential.

(4) Compensation Plans. When $P > BV$, compensation plans can induce managers to increase their compensation by choosing the pooling method (Dunne, 1990).

(5) and (6) Effects of Bond Covenants. The firm's debt covenants may affect preference for the purchase or pooling method. When $P > BV$, the purchase method reports higher assets and equity. This improves the current and debt-to-equity ratios. Thus, firms with binding debt covenants in terms of liquidity and leverage ratios prefer the purchase method.[36] Davis, for example, found that purchase method firms had significantly higher leverage ratios than pooling firms.[37]

---

[36]However, Leftwich (1981) argues that firms with high leverage ratios prefer pooling as it reports higher income. His argument, it seems to us, ignores the increased equity reported at the time of the purchase and focuses on the income stream realized over time.

[37]Davis did not discuss whether the firms had bond covenants based on leverage ratios. Thus, we cannot speculate whether the positive market reaction associated with the choice of the purchase method was in any way related to wealth transfers from bondholders to equityholders.

On the other hand, if restrictions on dividends are related to levels of retained earnings, then the pooling method may be preferred. Although it reports lower total equity, the pooling method reports higher retained earnings, as the retained earnings of the acquirer and target are combined. Under purchase accounting, only the acquirer's retained earnings are carried forward. Because debt covenants usually contain liquidity, leverage, and dividend restrictions, both the terms of the merger and accounting method preference depend on the most limiting of these covenants.

(7) Type of Management. Empirical evidence (e.g., Servaes, 1991) indicates that better managers make better acquisitions. One of the signs of better managers is superior market performance of their firms. Thus, the evidence with respect to acquisitions using the purchase method may indicate a combination of:

1. Firms with better managers (making better acquisitions) explaining the abnormal positive reaction prior to the merger;
2. Since better managers make better acquisitions, they do not tend to overpay, explaining lower bid premia;
3. Better managers do not need or use artificial income increasing methods. This argument was advanced earlier by Hong et al. (1978).

Consistent with these propositions, Dunne (1990) found that owner-controlled firms were more prone to choose the purchase method. They are more likely to take actions that are beneficial to the welfare of the firm, as opposed to manager-controlled firms that may attempt to maximize their own welfare at the expense of the firm.

Characteristics of Target

(8) High Liquidity/Low Leverage. Firms with excess cash are often acquisition targets and would likely receive higher bid premia as the acquiring firm wants to capture the liquid assets. Firms with excess liquidity may have been strong performers in the past in industries whose growth potential has declined.

(9) Relative Size of Target. Robinson and Shane note that the larger the size of the target relative to the acquirer, the less likely the acquirer would be willing to give the target's shareholders common shares with full voting rights. The acquirer's shareholders would be fearful of losing control of the firm. Under APB 16, lack of voting rights precludes use of the pooling method. Robinson and Shane cite empirical evidence that bid premia tend to be lower when the target is relatively large. Again, we have a situation when lower bid premia are consistent with the accounting choice of purchase, independent of any income/asset manipulation motivation.

(10) Type of Management. Firms run by poor managers are often viewed as prime takeover targets. The new managers feel they can do a better job of running the firm. The relationship of the firm's price to its book value is often viewed as an indicator of poor management, as the firm is not valued favorably by the market.

Tobin's Q ratio, the ratio of a firm's market value to the replacement value of its assets, is another indicator of poor managerial performance. Low Q ratios (below 1, for example) indicate that a dollar invested internally in the firm will generate a return whose present value is less than $1.

There are alternative explanations (to poor management) for low market price to book value ratios and low Q's. Such firms may be in industries with few growth opportunities as it is too expensive to grow by investing internally. The efficient way to expand is to acquire another company in the same industry. It may be cheaper to buy a firm with existing assets than to replace the assets directly. In any event, target firms with low market to book value and/or low Q ratios can typically be bought with low bid premia.

(11) Low P/E Ratios. A low P/E ratio may be another manifestation of the poor performance noted earlier. However, we discuss it separately as it is often given another dimension relating to the bootstrapping phenomenon noted earlier. It is hypothesized that a firm with a high P/E ratio can increase its own market price by acquiring companies with low P/E ratios. The newly acquired earnings will be valued by the market at the acquirer's higher P/E ratio. For this to work, the market has to be naive. When companies using this technique make many insignificant mergers (with little disclosure), however, it may be hard for analysts to see through the technique.[38]

Summary

The discussion indicates that the relationship between choice of accounting method and the underlying motivation for mergers is quite complex. One should, therefore, not draw immediate conclusions as to managers' motivations and/or potential market reaction. The effects and implications of the accounting method cannot be understood without a thorough examination of the merger's economic characteristics.

9

ANALYSIS OF INCOME TAXES

INTRODUCTION

Income taxes are a troublesome issue in financial reporting. The difference in the objectives of financial and tax reporting is an important reason for this difficulty. The objective of financial reporting is to provide users with information needed to evaluate a firm's financial position, performance, and cash flows. At the same time, the accrual basis of financial reporting allows management to select revenue and expense recognition methods that permit it to smooth or otherwise manage (maximize or minimize) reported net income. As discussed throughout the text, management incentives to manage reported income result from management compensation, bond covenants, political considerations, and the (presumed) effect on financial markets.

Tax reporting, in contrast, is the product of political and social objectives. The current period taxable income is measured using the modified cash basis; revenue and expense recognition methods used in tax reporting often differ from those used for financial reporting as the firm has strong incentives to select methods allowing it to minimize taxable income and, therefore, taxes paid, maximizing cash from operations.[1]

Thus, differences between taxes payable for the period and the tax expense recognized in the financial statements result from:

- The difference between accrual and modified cash bases of accounting
- Differences in reporting methods and estimates

These differences create deferred tax liabilities (credits) and deferred tax assets (debits or prepaid taxes) that are difficult to interpret. There is disagreement as to whether

[1]In countries such as Japan, Germany, and Switzerland, statutory financial reporting is required to conform to tax reporting. In these countries, the problems discussed in this chapter do not occur for statutory (usually, parent company only) statements. However, consolidated financial statements, for example, those prepared under IASC GAAP, do not conform with tax reporting and deferred tax issues must be dealt with. See the discussion of financial reporting practices outside the United States later in this chapter.

they are true assets or liabilities and their usefulness as indicators of future cash flows. When these deferrals become very large, their interpretation can have a significant effect on the financial analysis of a firm or group of firms.

Note: Terminology related to income tax accounting can be confusing as two terms that may seem similar to the reader can have very different meanings. A glossary of terms used in this chapter is therefore provided in Box 9-1. Each term in the glossary is shown in italics when first used in the chapter.

BOX 9-1
Glossary: Income Tax

Based on Tax Return

Taxable income	Income subject to tax.
Taxes payable (current tax expense)	Tax return liability resulting from current period taxable income. SFAS 109 calls this "current tax expense or benefit."
Income tax paid	Actual cash flow for income taxes, including payments (refunds) for others years.
Tax loss carryforward	Tax return loss that can be used to reduce taxable income in future years.

Based on Financial Reporting

Pretax income	Income before income tax expense.
Income tax expense	Expense resulting from current period pretax income; includes taxes payable and deferred income tax expense.
Deferred income tax expense	Accrual of income tax expense expected to be paid (or recovered) in future years; difference between taxes payable and income tax expense. Under SFAS 109, this results from changes in deferred tax assets and liabilities.
Deferred tax asset	Balance sheet amounts expected to be recovered from future operations.
Deferred tax liability	Balance sheet amounts expected to result in future cash outflows.
Valuation allowance	Reserve against deferred tax assets based on likelihood that those assets will be realized.
Timing difference	The result of tax return treatment (timing or amount) of transaction that differs from financial reporting treatment.
Temporary difference	Differences between tax reporting and financial reporting that will affect taxable income when those differences reverse. Similar to but slightly broader than timing differences (see footnote 6).

Note: SFAS 109 contains a more technical glossary of terms used in that standard.

ACCOUNTING FOR INCOME TAXES: BASIC ISSUES

The central accounting issue is whether the tax effects of transactions for which GAAP-based and tax-based accounting rules differ should be recognized in the period(s) in which they affect *taxable income* or in the period(s) in which they are recognized in the financial statements. These alternatives produce different measures of operating and financial performance, affecting the evaluation of a firm's operating performance and earning power. Cash flows for taxes are not affected by financial reporting choices except when conformity between tax and financial reporting is required.

Exhibit 9-1 uses a simplified example to illustrate the issues faced when tax accounting differs from accounting for financial statements. In this example, depreciation is the only item of expense.

EXHIBIT 9-1
Alternative Approaches to Tax Expense and Taxes Payable

Assumptions

- A firm purchases a machine costing $6,000 with a three-year estimated service life and no salvage value.
- For financial reporting purposes, the firm uses straight-line depreciation with a three-year life.
- For income tax reporting, the machine is depreciated straight-line over two years.
- The machine is used to manufacture a product that will generate annual revenue of $5,000 for three years.
- The tax rate is 40% in all three years.

A. Income Tax Reporting: Straight-Line Depreciation over Two Years

	Year 1	Year 2	Year 3	Total
Revenue	$5,000	$5,000	$5,000	$15,000
Depreciation	3,000	3,000	0	6,000
Taxable income	$2,000	$2,000	$5,000	$ 9,000
Taxes payable @ 40%	800	800	2,000	3,600
Net income	$1,200	$1,200	$3,000	$ 5,400

B. Financial Statement Reporting: Straight-Line Depreciation over Three Years

B1. Method Rejected by APB and FASB

- No recognition of deferred taxes
- Tax expense defined as taxes payable

	Year 1	Year 2	Year 3	Total
Revenue	$5,000	$5,000	$5,000	$15,000
Depreciation	2,000	2,000	2,000	6,000
Pretax income	$3,000	$3,000	$3,000	$ 9,000
Tax expense = payable	800	800	2,000	3,600
Net income	$2,200	$2,200	$1,000	$ 5,400

EXHIBIT 9-1 (*continued*)

B2. Required Presentation Under GAAP (SFAS 109)

- Recognition of deferred taxes
- Tax expense differs from taxes payable

	Year1	Year 2	Year 3	Total
Revenue	$5,000	$5,000	$5,000	$15,000
Depreciation	2,000	2,000	2,000	6,000
Pretax income	$3,000	$3,000	$3,000	$ 9,000
Tax expense @ 40%	1,200	1,200	1,200	3,600
Net income	$1,800	$1,800	$1,800	$ 5,400
Taxes payable (from part A)	800	800	2,000	3,600
Deferred tax expense	400	400	(800)	0
Deferred tax credit (on balance sheet)	400	800	0	0

Journal Entries

Years 1 and 2

Tax expense	$1,200	
Deferred tax liability		$ 400
Taxes payable		800

Year 3

Tax expense	$1,200	
Deferred tax liability	800	
Taxes payable		$2,000

Part A depicts the income tax reporting choice. The company depreciates a $6,000 asset over two years, giving rise to *taxes payable* of $800, $800, and $2,000 over the three-year period.

For financial reporting (part B), the firm depreciates the asset over three years. *Pretax income* exceeds taxable income in the first two years; taxable income is higher in year 3.[2] What *tax expense* should the company report in its financial statements?

One approach (not permitted under U.S. GAAP) would make tax expense equal to taxes payable. Part B1 shows tax expense equal to taxes payable for each year. As a result, the relationship between tax expense and pretax income is inconsistent over time and with the prevailing tax rate. Pretax income is the same for all three years, but tax expense differs as the tax deferred in earlier years is paid in year 3. For example, although the statutory tax rate is 40%, the tax rate reported in part B1 is 26.7% for the first two years and 66.7% for year 3.

Part B2 illustrates the U.S. GAAP treatment. At the end of year 1, it is recognized that the tax on the deferred $1,000 *timing difference* will be paid in year 3. Consequently, a *deferred tax liability* of $400 is created equal to the $1,000 timing difference multiplied

---

[2]Of the $3,000 pretax income reported in years 1 and 2, $1,000 (the excess tax depreciation) is not subject to taxes in those years. The $2,000 (2 × $1,000) deferred in the first two years becomes subject to taxation in the third as taxable income ($5,000) exceeds pretax income ($3,000) by $2,000.

by the 40% tax rate. This liability is recognized in year 1 and becomes a portion of that year's tax expense. Thus, total income tax expense equals $1,200: taxes payable ($800) plus *deferred income tax expense* ($400). The matching principle is satisfied as the relationship between revenues and expenses (40% tax rate) is maintained. From the balance sheet perspective, a liability is recorded equal to the amount of tax that will be paid in year 3 when the difference in accounting methods reverses. In year 2, a similar deferred tax is recognized. At the end of year 2, the cumulative timing difference is $2,000 and the aggregate deferred tax liability is $800.

No tax depreciation remains to be recorded in year 3, but book depreciation expense equals $2,000. At the end of year 3, there is no remaining timing difference as the machine is fully depreciated for both tax and financing reporting purposes. Thus, year 3 income tax expense equals taxes payable ($2,000) *less* the reversal of the deferred tax liability of $800 accumulated over the first two years for a net amount of $1,200.

Deferred Tax Assets and Liabilities

Deferred tax liabilities are required when future taxable income is expected to exceed pretax income, as illustrated in Exhibit 9-1. Pretax income exceeds taxable income in years 1 and 2, but year 3 taxable income is expected to exceed pretax income by $2,000. Differences between financial accounting and tax accounting can also give rise to *deferred tax assets* when future pretax income is expected to be less than taxable income.

Exhibit 9-2 extends our example of Exhibit 9-1 by introducing warranty expense, a timing difference that gives rise to a deferred tax asset in years 1 and 2. As warranty

EXHIBIT 9-2
Basic Example: Accounting for Income Taxes

Assumptions

Identical to Exhibit 9-1

- A firm purchases a machine costing $6,000 with a three-year estimated service life and no salvage value.
- For financial reporting purposes, the firm uses straight-line depreciation with a three-year life.
- For income tax reporting, the machine is depreciated straight-line over two years.
- The machine is used to manufacture a product that will generate annual revenue of $5,000 for three years.
- The tax rate is 40% in all three years.

Additional for Exhibit 9-2

- Warranty expenses are estimated at 10% of revenues each year; all repairs are provided in year 3.

A. Deferred Tax Assets and Liabilities

In years 1 and 2, the difference in depreciation lives generates a temporary difference of $1,000 (pretax income *exceeds* taxable income), resulting in a deferred tax liability of $400 ($1,000 × 0.40) each year. At the end of the second year, the cumulative temporary difference is $2,000, and the cumulative deferred tax liability is $800.

No tax depreciation remains to be recorded in year 3, but a book depreciation of $2,000 is recognized. Pretax income is *less than* taxable income, resulting in a temporary difference in

245

EXHIBIT 9-2 (*continued*)

the opposite direction and the elimination of the deferred tax liability accumulated during the first two years.

Warranty expense of $500 is recognized each year. Since no expenditures are incurred in years 1 and 2, no expense can be recognized on the tax return for those years. The temporary difference (pretax income is *less than* taxable income) results in a deferred tax asset of $200 for each year. In year 3, an expense of $500 is recognized in the financial statements, but tax-deductible expenditures of $1,500 are made for repairs; pretax income *exceeds* taxable income by $1,000, and the cumulative deferred tax assets are eliminated.

Journal Entries

Years 1 and 2

Tax expense	$1,000	
Deferred tax asset	200	
Deferred tax liability		$ 400
Taxes payable		800

Year 3

Tax expense	$1,000	
Deferred tax liability	800	
Deferred tax asset		$ 400
Taxes payable		1,400

Each year, the deferred tax assets and liabilities have been shown separately to highlight their different sources and expected cash consequences. Note that over the entire three-year period, tax expense and taxes payable are identical. By the end of the third year, all temporary differences have reversed so that all deferred tax assets and liabilities have been offset.

B. Financial Statements

Year	Gross Revenues	Total Expense	Pretax Income	Tax Expense*	Net Income
1	$ 5,000	$2,500†	$2,500	$1,000	$1,500
2	5,000	2,500†	2,500	1,000	1,500
3	5,000	2,500†	2,500	1,000	1,500
	$15,000	$7,500	$7,500	$3,000	$4,500

*Tax expense is 40% (tax rate) × pretax income.

†Depreciation expense is $2,000 ($6,000/3); warranty expense is $500 ($5,000 × 10%).

C. Tax Return

Year	Gross Revenues	Total Expense	Taxable Income	Taxes Payable*	Posttax Income
1	$ 5,000	$3,000†	$2,000	$ 800	$1,200
2	5,000	3,000†	2,000	800	1,200
3	5,000	1,500‡	3,500	1,400	2,100
	$15,000	$7,500	$7,500	$3,000	$4,500

*Taxes payable are 40% (tax rate) × taxable income.

†Annual depreciation expense is $6,000/2 = $3,000; no expenditures are incurred for warranties during the first two years.

‡There is no depreciation expense, as equipment is fully depreciated at the end of year 2; repair expenditures of $1,500 are incurred.

payments are tax-deductible when paid rather than when accrued, the amount charged to warranty expense for financial statement purposes is generally larger than that allowed for tax purposes.

As shown in Exhibit 9-2A, the firm recognizes a warranty expense of $500 in each of years 1 and 2, but receives no tax deduction. As pretax income exceeds taxable income (for this expense only), a deferred tax asset must be created.

Thus, the tax computations for each year must reflect both the deferred tax liability resulting from depreciation and the deferred tax asset resulting from warranty expense. The journal entries in part A, financial statements in part B, and tax return data in part C incorporate both. In practice, firms have many deferred tax assets and liabilities, resulting from different timing differences.

Income tax expense is based on pretax income, which reflects the use of machinery (financial statement depreciation) and estimated warranty expense for products sold. Taxes payable are measured as the tax rate times taxable income and reflect the effects of tax depreciation and allowable warranty deductions on the tax return. Over the three-year period, total revenues are $15,000, total depreciation expense is $6,000, and total warranty expense is $1,500 for both financial and tax reporting. The timing of expense recognition differs, but the total amount is the same.[3]

Deferred Tax Liabilities

The calculation of the deferred tax liability is identical to that shown in Exhibit 9-1.

Deferred Tax Assets

Warranty expenses of $500 are accrued each year. Since no expenditures are incurred in years 1 and 2, no deductions can be taken on the tax return for those years. The higher taxable income results in a prepayment of taxes; tax expense in the financial statements reflects lower pretax income. The difference of $500 in each of the first two years generates a deferred tax asset of $200 ($500 × 0.40) each year and increases tax expense by that amount each year. At the end of year 2, there is a deferred tax asset of $400.

In year 3, tax-deductible expenditures of $1,500 are incurred for repairs, reducing taxable income and tax payments. These expenditures exceed year 3 expense ($500) by $1,000, equal to the total additional expense recognized in years 1 and 2. The temporary difference reverses, deferred income tax expense is reduced by $400 ($1,000 × 0.40), and the deferred tax asset generated during the first two years is eliminated.[4]

Do the deferred tax liabilities at the end of years 1 and 2 actually represent a liability for tax payments due in year 3? Similarly, does the deferred tax asset qualify as an asset? In this simple case, they do, as the forecast reversals occur as expected. In the real world, the answer is not so clear; these are important issues from an analytical perspective and we will return to them shortly.

---

[3]Warranty expense and actual repair costs are assumed to be identical for illustration only; it is difficult to predict the frequency and level of repair costs perfectly. Bad debt expenses and litigation losses are other examples of timing differences where predictions are uncertain.

[4]In the examples of Exhibit 9-1 and 9-2, income tax expense could also have been computed by applying the income tax rate of 40% directly to pretax income in each year. However, in more complex situations, discussed in the next section, this approach would produce a different result.

SFAS 109: THE LIABILITY METHOD

Accounting for taxes in the United States is based on SFAS 109 (1992), whose two objectives are to recognize:

1. Taxes payable or refundable for the current year
2. The deferred tax liabilities and assets (adjusted for recoverability) measured as the future tax consequences of events that have been recognized in financial statements or tax returns

Statement 109 replaced APB 11 and shifted the emphasis from the deferral method to the liability method.[5] The deferral method has an income statement focus; balance sheet deferred tax assets and liabilities result from the calculation of deferred tax expense. The focus of the liability method is the balance sheet, as deferred tax assets and liabilities are calculated directly; deferred tax expense used to determine reported income is a consequence of the balance sheet calculations. As the deferral method is now used only in a few countries, we defer further discussion of that method to the section entitled, "Financial Reporting Outside the United States" and Appendix 9-A.

SFAS 109 recognizes the deferred tax consequences of temporary differences.[6] *The standard mandates the recognition of deferred tax liabilities for all temporary differences expected to generate net taxable amounts in future years.*

The FASB argues that deferred tax consequences of temporary differences that will result in net taxable amounts in future years meet the SFAC 6 definition of liabilities.[7] The board contended that deferred taxes are legal obligations imposed by tax laws and temporary differences will affect taxable income in future years as they reverse.

The expected reversal of the temporary difference is confirmed by the firm's decision to report the machine (in Exhibit 9-1) on its balance sheet; use of the machine in operations suggests continued depreciation on the financial statements and therefore a reversal of that difference. These considerations are the basis of the FASB view that the only question is when, not whether, the use of the machine will generate taxable income in future periods.

The financial statement effects of the liability method can best be highlighted by examining its treatment of tax rate changes.

---

[5]SFAS 96 (1987) was an interim step in this process. As that standard, which used the liability method, was superseded by SFAS 109, we do not discuss it here.

[6]This concept is broader than the timing difference concept used in APB 11, as it also considers other events that result in differences between the tax bases of assets and liabilities and their carrying amounts in financial statements. Such differences arise when (1) the tax basis of an asset is reduced by tax credits, (2) investment tax credits are accounted for under the deferred method, (3) the tax basis of a foreign subsidiary's assets is increased as a result of indexing, and (4) carrying amounts and tax bases of assets differ in purchase method acquisitions.

[7]The temporary difference in Exhibit 9-1 derives from the firm's use of different depreciation lives for financial reporting than for tax return reporting, creating a difference between the carrying amount of the asset and its tax basis. Use of the asset in operations will result in taxable income in year 3, when no depreciation can be recorded on the tax return. The board acknowledged that other events may offset the net taxable amounts that would be generated when temporary differences reverse, but because those events have not yet occurred, and they are not assumed in the financial statements, their tax consequences should not be recognized. See para. 75 to 79, SFAS 109, for more discussion of this issue.

Effect of Tax Rate and Tax Law Changes

Exhibit 9-3 depicts the impact of a change in tax rates using the example in Exhibit 9-2. The corporate tax rate is assumed to decrease from 40% to 35% at the beginning of year 2.

In panel A, we assume that the upcoming tax decrease *was enacted before* the year 1 financial statements were prepared. In panel B, however, we assume that the year 2 tax decrease *was enacted after* year 1 financial statements were prepared.

EXHIBIT 9-3
Impact of Tax Rate Change: The Liability Method

Assumptions

Identical to Exhibit 9-2

- A firm purchases a machine costing $6,000 with a three-year estimated service life and no salvage value.
- For financial reporting purposes, the firm uses straight-line depreciation with a three-year life.
- For income tax reporting, the machine is depreciated straight-line over two years.
- The machine is used to manufacture a product that will generate annual revenue of $5,000 for three years.
- Warranty expenses are estimated at 10% of revenues each year; all repairs are provided in year 3.

A. Year 2 Tax Rate Change Enacted in Year 1

Year 1: Tax Rate = 40%

Year 2 Tax Rate Will Be 35%

Selected T-Accounts

			Deferred Tax Asset		Deferred Tax Liability	
Income tax expense	975					
Deferred tax asset	175		$175			$350
Deferred tax liability		350	$175			$350
Taxes payable		800				

Year 2: Tax Rate = 35%

			Deferred Tax Asset		Deferred Tax Liability	
			$175			$350
Income tax expense	875		175			
Deferred tax asset	175					$350
Deferred tax liability		350				
Taxes payable		700	$350			$700

Year 3: Tax Rate = 35%

			Deferred Tax Asset		Deferred Tax Liability	
			$350			$700
Income tax expense	875				700	
Deferred tax liability	700					
Deferred tax asset		350		350		
Taxes payable		1,225	$ 0			$ 0

EXHIBIT 9-3 (*continued*)

Calculations

Temporary Differences

	Depreciation (Liability)	Warranty (Asset)	Taxes Payable	Income Tax Expense
Year 1	35% × $1,000	35% × $(500)	40% × $2,000	$350 − $175 + 800
Year 2	35% × 1,000	35% × (500)	35% × 2,000	$350 − $175 + 700
Year 3	35% × (2,000)	35% × 1,000	35% × 3,500	−$700 + $350 + $1,225

B. Year 2 Tax Rate Change Enacted in Year 2

Year 1: Tax Rate = 40%

Selected T-Accounts

			Deferred Tax Asset		Deferred Tax Liability	
Income tax expense	1,000					
Deferred tax asset	200					
Deferred tax liability		400	$200			$400
Taxes payable		800	$200			$400

Year 2: Tax Rate Reduced to 35%

(i) *Adjustment of Prior-Year Deferrals*

			Deferred Tax Asset		Deferred Tax Liability	
Deferred tax liability	50		$200			$400
Deferred tax asset		25		25	50	
Income tax expense		25	$175			$350

(ii) *Current Year Operations*

			Deferred Tax Asset		Deferred Tax Liability	
Income tax expense	875					
Deferred tax asset	175		$175			$350
Deferred tax liability		350	175			350
Taxes payable		700	$350			$700

Year 3: Tax Rate = 35%

			Deferred Tax Asset		Deferred Tax Liability	
			$350			$700
Income tax expense	875				700	
Deferred tax liability	700			350		
Deferred tax asset		350				
Taxes payable		1,225	$ 0			$ 0

Calculations

Temporary Differences

	Depreciation (Liability)	Warranty (Asset)	Taxes Payable	Income Tax Expense
Year 1	40% × $1,000	40% × $(500)	40% × $2,000	$400 − $200 + $800
Year 2	(5%) × 1,000	(5%) × (500)		−$50 + $25
	35% × 1,000	35% × (500)	35% × 2,000	$350 − $175 + $700
Year 3	35% × (2,000)	35% × 1,000	35% × 3,500	−$700 + $350 + $1,225

Panel A: Future Tax Rate Change Enacted in Current Year. The balance sheet orientation of SFAS 109 requires adjustments to deferred tax assets and liabilities to reflect the impact of a change in tax rates or tax laws. Thus, in panel A for year 1, although taxes payable are based on the current tax rate of 40%, the calculation for deferred tax assets and liabilities is based on the tax rate expected to be in effect when the differences reverse, 35%.

Calculation of Year 1 Income Tax Expense

Taxes payable = $2,000 taxable income × 40%	= $ 800
Deferred tax asset = $500 temporary difference × 35%	= (175)
Deferred tax liability = $1,000 temporary difference × 35%	= 350
Total income tax expense	= $ 975

Note that year 1 tax expense as a percentage of pretax income (the effective tax rate) is 39%: a weighted average of the current tax rate of 40% and the 35% rate that will be in effect when the timing differences that gave rise to the deferred taxes reverse. There is no attempt to match income tax expense directly with pretax income, and one cannot calculate tax expense directly by multiplying pretax income by the current tax rate.

For years 2 and 3, the calculations are similar to those in Exhibit 9-2 except that the new tax rate of 35% (rather than 40%) is used for all calculations.

Panel B: Future Tax Rate Change Enacted Subsequently. In panel B, we assume that the tax rate decrease for year 2 is enacted after year 1 statements have been prepared. Calculations for year 1 tax expense, taxes payable, and deferred taxes therefore use the year 1 tax rate of 40% and are identical to those in Exhibit 9-2. A deferred tax asset of $200 and a deferred tax liability of $400 are created.

In year 2, when the rate decrease is effective, two steps are necessary to calculate the current year's tax expense:

1. The deferred tax asset and liability balances at the end of year 1 must be restated at the new (lower) tax rate of 35% (assumed to be in effect when the deferred taxes will be paid). This calculation is shown in Exhibit 9-3B. Year 2 tax expense is reduced (income is increased) since the lower rate reduces the expected tax payment when the depreciation difference reverses, partially offset by a lower expected tax benefit when the warranty expense difference reverses. The adjustment results in a deferred tax asset of $175 and liability of $350.[8]

2. The taxes payable and deferred taxes arising from current year operations are calculated using the new rate of 35%.

---

[8]These balances are now identical to those shown in panel A of the exhibit when the tax law change was known prior to the issuance of the year 1 financial statements. The only difference between the two panels is the timing of the restatement at the lower rate.

Tax expense for year 2 is calculated as follows:

Adjustment of Year 1 Balances to New Rate

Deferred tax asset of $200 restated to $175	$ 25
Deferred tax liability of $400 restated to $350	(50)

Year 2 Taxes Payable and Temporary Differences

Taxes payable = $2,000 taxable income × 35%	700
Deferred tax asset = $500 temporary difference × 35%	(175)
Deferred tax liability = $1,000 temporary difference × 35%	350
Income tax expense	$ 850

Note that, as in panel A, the income tax expense of $850 is affected by changes in the deferred tax liability and asset accounts and there is no attempt to directly match the relationship of tax expense to pretax income.[9]

Under SFAS 109, the liability method requires that changes in tax rates (or other tax regulations) that affect the estimated future tax liability are recognized in reported income in the year the change is enacted.

Treatment of Operating Losses

Operating losses are due to an excess of tax deductions over taxable revenues. Tax losses can be carried back and applied to prior years to obtain refunds of taxes paid; the impact of the carryback on income tax expense is recognized in the loss period because it can be measured and is recoverable.

Tax losses may also be carried forward to future periods if insufficient taxes were paid during the carryback period or the firm would lose valuable tax credits if losses were carried back to that period. Because the realization of *tax loss carryforwards* depends on future taxable income, the expected benefits are recognized as deferred tax assets. Under SFAS 109, such assets are recognized in full but a *valuation allowance* may be required if recoverability is unlikely.

Deferred Tax Assets and the Valuation Allowance

SFAS 109 is permissive regarding the recognition of deferred tax assets. The standard permits recognition of a deferred tax asset whenever a deductible temporary difference results in an operating loss or tax credit carryforward. However, management (and its auditors) must defend recognition of all deferred tax assets. A valuation allowance reducing the deferred tax asset is required if an analysis of the sources of future taxable

---

[9]Under the deferral method, however, the change in tax rates is ignored until the year when the reversal occurs and current year tax expense is simply the current tax rate times pretax income (see Appendix 9-A).

income suggests that it is more likely than not that some portion or all of the deferred tax asset will not be realized.[10]

Tax-planning strategies can be used to reduce required valuation allowances, but they must be disclosed. SFAS 109 provides examples of positive and negative evidence that must be weighed to determine the need for a valuation allowance and to measure the amount of the allowance.[11] *Changes in the valuation allowance are included in income from continuing operations except when they are generated by unrecognized changes in the carrying amount of assets or liabilities.*[12]

Financial Statement Presentation and Disclosure Requirements

The disclosure requirements of SFAS 109 incorporated U.S. Securities and Exchange Commission disclosure requirements that had been in effect for many years.

Large multinational companies operate in dozens of tax jurisdictions and their financial reports must summarize their tax position for all consolidated entities. Such firms often generate deferred tax assets and liabilities in different tax jurisdictions. *Statement 109 permits offsets of deferred tax effects only within each tax-paying component and tax jurisdiction of the firm.*

Deferred tax assets and liabilities must be separated into current and noncurrent components based on the classification of the assets and liabilities generating the deferral. However, deferred tax assets due to carryforwards are classified by reference to expected reversal dates. SFAS 109 specifically requires:

1. Separate disclosure of all deferred tax assets and liabilities, any valuation allowance, and the net change in that allowance for each reporting period.

2. Disclosure of any unrecognized deferred tax liability for the undistributed earnings of domestic or foreign subsidiaries and joint ventures. These disclosures should facilitate the comparison of the operating results of firms that have different policies with respect to deferred tax recognition or the remission of income from such affiliates.

3. Disclosure of the current year tax effect of each type of temporary difference.

4. Disclosure of the components of income tax expense.

5. Reconciliation of reported income tax expense with the amount based on the statutory income tax rate (the reconciliation can use either amounts or percentages of pretax income).

6. Disclosure of tax loss carryforwards and credits.

---

[10]Sources of future taxable income include existing taxable temporary differences, future taxable income net of reversing temporary differences, taxable income recognized during qualifying carryback periods, and applicable tax-planning strategies.

[11]Existing contracts or backlogs expected to be profitable, appreciated assets, earnings over the past few years, and the nature (nonrecurring) of the loss would suggest that a valuation allowance is not needed. Examples of negative evidence include cumulative losses in recent years and the past inability to use loss or tax credit carryforwards.

[12]The most common example is the deferred tax assets that arise when the market value of "available-for-sale" securities is less than cost; the unrealized loss is included in equity, under SFAS 115, net of the related deferred income tax asset. See Chapter 13 for further discussion.

These requirements determine the income tax disclosures in duPont's Note 7 (see Appendix A). These disclosures are the raw material for the analysis provided later in this chapter.

Effective Date and Transition Method

SFAS 109 was effective for fiscal years beginning after December 15, 1992. The standard allowed significant flexibility with respect to adoption methods and effective dates. Firms adopting SFAS 109 could do so either retroactively or prospectively.[13]

DuPont adopted the new standard effective January 1, 1992 (see Note 7). Adoption increased deferred tax liabilities by $1,045 million, mainly due to required adjustments (discussed later in this chapter) to purchase method acquisitions.

DEFERRED TAXES: ANALYTICAL ISSUES

Estimates of the firm's future cash flows and earning power, and the analysis of financial leverage must consider changes in deferred tax assets and liabilities, deferred tax expense, and any changes in the valuation allowance. *The key analytic issue is whether the deferred tax assets and liabilities will reverse in the future. If they will not, then it is highly debatable whether to classify deferred taxes as assets or liabilities; it may be more appropriate to consider them as decreases or increases to equity.*

To resolve that issue, we need to understand the factors that determine the level of and trends in reported deferred taxes, to decide whether they are assets (or liabilities) and to evaluate their expected cash consequences.

Factors Influencing the Level and Trend of Deferred Taxes

In general, temporary differences originated by individual transactions will reverse and offset future taxable income and tax payments. However, *these reversals may be offset by other transactions, for example, newly originating temporary differences.* The cash consequences of deferred tax debits and credits depend on the following factors:

- Future tax rates and tax laws
- Changes in accounting methods
- The firm's growth rate
- Firm-specific and general price level changes
- Nonrecurring items and equity adjustments

We discuss these factors next.

Effects of Changes in Tax Laws and Accounting Methods

Management incentives for choosing revenue and expense recognition methods on the tax return and financial statements differ, as mentioned previously. Choices (and subsequent changes) of tax and/or accounting methods determine taxes payable, income tax expense, and both the amounts and rate of change of reported deferred tax balances.

---

[13]For firms that had adopted SFAS 96, the effect of adopting SFAS 109 was often immaterial.

Under the liability method, as seen in Exhibit 9-3, when a new tax law is enacted, its effects must be recognized immediately. Thus, lower tax rates will reduce deferred tax liabilities and assets, increase equity (if we assume net deferred tax liabilities), and affect income tax expense for the year. The larger the net deferred tax liability, the greater the impact of the tax cut, as previous-year deferrals are adjusted to the lower rate. For analytic purposes, one need not wait for the actual tax change to be enacted; estimates can be made when legislation is proposed.

Changes in GAAP can also significantly impact deferred taxes. For example, in 1992 duPont adopted SFAS 106, Accounting for Postretirement Benefits Other Than Pensions. The standard (see Chapter 12) required accrual accounting for postretirement costs (mainly medical benefits for current employees after retirement) rather than cash basis accounting. As cash basis accounting was used for income tax purposes, there was no temporary difference associated with these benefits prior to the adoption of SFAS 106.

Upon adoption, duPont recognized a postretirement benefit liability of $5.9 billion and deferred tax asset of $2.1 billion. Is this $2.1 billion an asset? Can it be used to reduce future taxes? That depends on the $5.9 billion liability associated with it. As postretirement benefits are paid, future taxes payable will be reduced, but the amounts are uncertain. If, for example, duPont reduces future medical benefits and payments are below the estimated liability, then the deferred tax asset of $2.1 billion will not fully materialize. Thus, *realization of a deferred tax asset or liability depends on the realization of the temporary difference that created it.*

Effect of the Growth Rate of the Firm

For most firms, the deferred tax liability grows over time; temporary differences do not reverse on balance.[14] For growing firms, increased or higher-cost investments in fixed assets result in ever-increasing deferred tax liabilities due to the use of accelerated depreciation methods for tax reporting.

Exhibit 9-4 extends the Exhibit 9-1 example by focusing on the deferred tax consequences of depreciation differences. Assume that the firm acquires one machine each year and it continues to use the depreciation lives in Exhibit 9-1. The depreciation differences will produce a deferred tax expense of $400 in each year during the first two years of each machine's operation, with a reversal of $800 in its third year to eliminate the deferred tax liability generated over the first two years.

The $400 deferred tax liability at the end of the first year represents the effect of the temporary difference from the single machine in use. In year 2, machine 1 adds an additional deferred tax liability of $400. The acquisition of a second machine in year 2 adds another difference of $400; there is now an accumulated deferred tax liability of $1,200 at the end of year 2.

---

[14]A similar analysis can be made for deferred tax assets. We focus on deferred tax liabilities because they are generally larger. Deferred tax assets (more precisely, prepaid taxes) stem from both recurring transactions (such as warranty expenses, management compensation, employee benefits, and bad debt reserves), and from more irregular events (such as restructuring costs, impairments, environmental remediation obligations, and provisions for litigation losses) that are accrued on the financial statements prior to their deduction on the tax return.

Management often has substantial discretion over the amount and timing of the origination of these debit balances as it controls the recognition of these expenses. However, the amount and timing of their reversal may not be as discretionary or predictable as the temporary differences (such as depreciation differences) that generate deferred tax liabilities.

EXHIBIT 9-4
Impact of Growth on Deferred Tax Liability

Assumptions

A firm purchases one machine during each year of operation. All other assumptions are identical to those used in Exhibit 9-1. Most important, temporary differences are originated and reversed as in Exhibit 9-1 and at the same tax rate, which is assumed to remain constant over time.

Deferred Tax Liability

Year 1	$ 400	Machine 1 (origination)
Year 2	400	Beginning balance
	400	Machine 1 (origination)
	400	Machine 2 (origination)
Year 3	$1,200	Beginning balance
	(800)	Machine 1 (reversal)
	400	Machine 2 (origination)
	400	Machine 3 (origination)
Year 4	$1,200	Beginning balance
	(800)	Machine 2 (reversal)
	400	Machine 3 (origination)
	400	Machine 4 (origination)
Year 5	$1,200	Beginning balance

Note: The balance stabilizes at $1,200 in this example at the end of year 3, with the originations exactly offset by the reversals. This result assumes constant levels of asset acquisitions, price levels, tax rates, and regulations. Increases in either price levels or acquisitions would result in rising balances of deferred tax liabilities.

In year 3, the firm acquires and uses the third machine that generates its first year temporary difference, and the asset acquired in year 2 originates its second year difference. However, the machine acquired in year 1 now generates a reversal of temporary difference; whereas depreciated in the financial statements, no depreciation remains to be recorded for the asset on the tax return. The originating temporary differences from the second and third machine offset the reversal due to the first machine; there is no change in the net deferred tax liability.

Note that the deferred tax consequences of one asset have reversed, generating taxable income that is offset by other originating differences. The deferred tax liability remains $1,200 and *stabilizes at that level* if asset acquisitions, depreciation methods, and tax rates and tax laws remain unchanged. Increased asset purchases above present levels (either in physical quantity or due to higher prices) will result in a growing deferred tax liability as originations exceed reversals. Thus, as a result of growth, either in real or nominal terms, the net deferred tax liability will increase over time; *in effect, it will never be paid.*

If the firm reduces its acquisition of fixed assets and reversals exceed originations, the related deferred tax liability will decline. The cash consequences of this scenario, however, are uncertain. If the decrease in asset acquisitions results from declining product demand, then lower asset acquisitions may be accompanied by poor profitability. Without taxable income, the deferred taxes will never be paid. Alternatively, the·

firm may originate other temporary differences that offset depreciation reversals; in the aggregate, deferred tax liabilities may not decline.

The cash consequences of reversing temporary differences, therefore, depend on both future profitability and other activities of the firm that affect future taxable income.

Effects of Nonrecurring Items and Equity Adjustments

The following may also affect income tax expense, taxes paid, and deferred tax assets and liabilities:

- Nonrecurring items
- Extraordinary items
- Accounting changes
- Equity adjustments

Nonrecurring items (such as restructuring charges) may have future as well as current period tax consequences, and complicate the analysis of the firm's tax position. DuPont, for example, had restructuring changes in 1992 and 1993, partly reversed in 1994, as detailed in Note 6. These charges generated significant deferred tax assets, as discussed later in this chapter.

Extraordinary items, such as duPont's loss from the early retirement of debt (Note 8), are reported after tax; the tax effect is shown separately in duPont's tax footnote. Transition effects of accounting changes often generate deferred tax effects, especially when the new method is not a permitted method of tax reporting. The large deferred tax asset resulting from duPont's adoption of SFAS 106 (postretirement benefits other than pensions) is a typical example.

Finally, equity adjustments that bypass the income statement may have current and deferred tax consequences. Common examples include:

- Unrealized gains or losses on marketable securities (see Chapter 13)
- Currency translation adjustments (see Chapter 15)

The cash and deferred tax effects of continuing operations may be obscured by the items discussed above. Although firms generally disclose their associated tax effect, discerning their cash and deferred tax impact may require careful reading of the tax footnote supplemented by discussions with management.

Liability or Equity?

How should analysts treat deferred tax liabilities in the analysis of a firm's solvency?

As indicated above, changes in a firm's operations or tax laws may result in deferred taxes that are never paid (or recovered). Moreover, a firm's growth may continually generate deferred tax liabilities. Even if temporary differences do reverse, future losses may forestall tax payments. These factors suggest that, in many cases, deferred taxes are unlikely to be paid.

Even if deferred taxes are eventually paid, the present value of those payments is considerably lower than the stated amounts. Thus, the deferred tax liability should be discounted at an appropriate interest rate.[15]

These arguments suggest that the components of the deferred tax liability should be analyzed to evaluate the likelihood of reversal or continued growth. Only those components that are likely to reverse should be considered a liability.[16] In addition, the liability should be discounted to its present value based on an estimate of the year(s) of reversal. If the temporary differences giving rise to deferred tax liabilities are not expected to reverse, those amounts should not be considered liabilities.

SFAS 109 requires disclosure of the components of the deferred tax liability at each year-end. These components should be examined over time to see which tend to reverse and which do not. For example, the effect of using accelerated depreciation methods for tax reporting tends not to reverse.[17] If reversal occurs gradually, as capital expenditures decline, the liability should be discounted to present value. Similar analysis can be applied to other major differences, keeping in mind any changes in the tax law.

To the extent that deferred taxes are not a liability, then they are stockholders' equity. Had they not been recorded, prior-period tax expense would have been lower and net income higher. Thus, equity should be increased. This adjustment reduces the debt-to-equity ratio, in some cases considerably.[18]

In some cases, however, deferred taxes are neither liability nor equity. For example, if tax depreciation is a better measure of economic depreciation (see Chapter 8) than financial statement depreciation, adding the deferred tax liability to equity overstates the value of the firm. However, if the deferred tax liability is unlikely to result in a cash outflow, it is not a liability either. Ultimately, the financial analyst must decide on the appropriate treatment of deferred taxes on a case-by-case basis.

In practice, the analytic treatment of deferred tax liabilities varies. Some creditors, notably banks, do not consider them to be liabilities (but neither do they include them as part of equity). In calculating solvency and other ratios, most analysts ignore deferred taxes altogether.

Standard and Poor's, a major U.S. rating agency, includes noncurrent deferred taxes in permanent capital for its computation of pretax return on permanent capital. However, it does not consider deferred tax liabilities as debt.[19]

---

[15]Discounting of deferred taxes is not allowed under U.S. GAAP and is rare elsewhere. It is currently allowed in the Netherlands; however, few firms discount. The most recent proposal from the U.K. Accounting Standards Board calls for discounting under certain conditions.

[16]The United Kingdom allows partial allocation and deferred taxes are recognized only when reversal is expected within the foreseeable future (see Exhibit 9-7 and related discussion).

[17]However, the recognition of fixed asset impairment (see the discussion in Chapter 8) may instantaneously offset many years of accelerated depreciation. Such write-downs do not affect tax reporting until the affected assets are sold. As a result, previously established deferred tax liabilities relating to these assets reverse. If the carrying value of the impaired assets is reduced below their tax basis, deferred tax assets must be established. But this reversal has no effect on taxable income or, therefore, taxes payable. This is another case where the reversal of temporary differences may not generate income tax cash outflows. For an example, see the discussion of Glatfelter's impairment provision in Chapter 8. Problem 7 in Chapter 9 considers the income tax consequences of that write-down.

[18]Some creditors treat deferred tax liabilities as debt. In this case, there is a double effect; debt is decreased and equity increased by the same amount, with an even greater decrease in the debt-to-equity ratio.

[19]See Standard and Poor's "Formulas for Key Ratios," *Corporate Finance Criteria* (New York: McGraw-Hill, 1994), p. 75.

Box 9-2 discusses evidence provided by market research regarding the relevance of deferred taxes to securities valuation. The evidence indicates that the market does consider firm growth rates, the probability of reversal, and present value factors in assessing whether to treat deferred taxes as liability or equity.

Analysis of Deferred Tax Assets

Deferred tax assets may be indicators of future cash flow, reported income, or both. Therefore, as with liabilities, one should examine the source of those assets and evaluate the likelihood and timing of reversal. Any valuation allowance should also be reviewed. To the extent that deferred tax assets have been offset by a valuation allowance, realization of those assets will increase reported income (and stockholders' equity) as well as generate cash flow. If no valuation allowance has been provided, then realization will have no effect on reported income or equity, although cash flow will still benefit.

Conversely, when deferred tax assets are no longer realizable, if no valuation allowance had been provided, then the establishment of such an allowance reduces reported income and equity.

Given management discretion, the valuation allowance has become another factor used to evaluate the quality of earnings. Some firms are conservative, offsetting most or all deferred tax assets with valuation allowances. Other firms are more optimistic and assume that no valuation allowance is necessary.

BOX 9-2
Market Valuation of Deferred Taxes

Surprisingly, there have not been many empirical studies that examined whether the market as a whole treats deferred tax liabilities as debt. Earlier discussion noted that the extent to which deferred tax liabilities should be treated as debt is a function of the probability that the deferrals will be reversed and the debt (if considered) should be discounted to its present value.

Givoly and Hayn (1992) examined these issues in the context of the Tax Reform Act (TRA) of 1986. The TRA cut the statutory tax rate for U.S. corporations from 46 to 34%. This affected a firm's current tax position as well as the amount that would have to be repaid if and when future reversals of temporary differences occurred.

The TRA was debated for over two years in Congress. Givoly and Hayn examined the effects on stock prices of events that indicated an improved chance of the measure passing as well as events that indicated a decreased chance of the measure passing. After controlling for the effects on current tax payments,* they argued that if the market treated the deferred tax as a liability:

1. The larger the deferred taxes, the more positive the impact of the TRA on the firm's market price.

2. No matter how large the firm's deferred tax account is, if temporary differences will not be reversed or future tax losses will result in nonpayment of the tax at reversal, the effects of the TRA should be minimal. Thus, they argued that the larger the growth rate in the deferred tax account and the greater the probability of tax losses,† the less likely there would be a positive impact on stock prices.

If the market ignored the deferred tax liability, there would be no impact of any of these factors. Overall, their results confirmed that the market incorporated the deferred tax liability into valuation.

When chances of the TRA being adopted increased (decreased), then:

1. The larger the deferred tax account, the more positive (negative) the market reaction.

2. A large growth rate and increased probability of losses decreased (increased) the abnormal return.

A by-product of their study was the indication that the market incorporated a discount factor in valuing the deferred tax liability. The deferred tax accounts of high-risk‡ firms tended to affect market valuation less than low-risk firms. This result is consistent with a higher discount rate being applied to the higher-risk firms.

The Givoly and Hayn study focused on the deferred tax account in the balance sheet. It found that deferred tax accounting is incorporated in balance sheet valuation. Focusing on earnings, an earlier study by Beaver and Dukes (1972) also found that the market "favors" the deferral process. They found market reaction tended to be more closely associated with income that incorporated deferrals than with income that ignored deferrals and calculated taxes on the basis of current tax expense.§ Rayburn (1986), however, found that the association between deferred tax accruals and security returns was dependent on the expectations model assumed.

---

*Givoly and Hayn also controlled for other factors such as the present stock and age of machinery and equipment.

†The probability of losses was estimated using the frequency of losses that occurred in the previous five years.

‡High risk was determined on the basis of the firm's market beta.

§The authors found this result surprising as they expected the number closer to cash flows (earnings without deferral) to be more closely associated with security prices. In a subsequent paper (Beaver and Dukes, 1973), the authors offered a different explanation. They demonstrated (see the discussion in Chapter 8) that the market generally imputes a more accelerated form of depreciation than straight-line depreciation. As deferred taxes increase expense shown for firms using straight-line depreciation, they argued that the observed results with respect to deferred taxes may be a function of deferred taxes masking as a form of accelerated depreciation.

The important point is that changes in the valuation allowance often affect reported earnings and can be used to manage them.

DuPont's reported valuation allowance declined by $88 million in 1994, from $445 million at December 31, 1993 to $357 million at December 31, 1994. A change in the tax status of some affiliates reduced the allowance by $105 million. That reduction was partly offset by an unexplained $17 million net increase. The $88 million net change in the valuation allowance ($0.13 per share) increased reported income.

Effective Tax Rates

Valuation models that forecast future income or cash flows use the firm's effective tax rate as one input. Moreover, trends in effective tax rates over time for a firm and the relative effective tax rates for comparable firms within an industry can help assess operating performance and the income available for stockholders. Several alternative measures can be used to assess the firm's effective tax rate.

The *reported* effective tax rate is measured as:

$$\frac{\textbf{Income Tax Expense}}{\textbf{Pretax Income}}$$

EXHIBIT 9-5. DUPONT
Effective Tax Rates

	1992	1993	1994	1992 to 1994
Taxes payable	$ 896	$1,100	$1,407	$3,403
Deferred tax expense	(221)	(737)	306	(652)
Other	161	29	(58)	132
Income tax expense	$ 836	$ 392	$1,655	$2,883
Income tax paid	$1,213	$ 896	$1,344	$3,453
Pretax income	$1,811	$ 958	$4,382	$7,151
Statutory tax rate	34%	35%	35%	34.7%
Income tax expense/pretax income	46.2%	40.9%	37.8%	40.3%
Taxes payable/pretax income	49.5%	114.8%	32.1%	47.6%
Income tax paid/pretax income	67.0%	93.5%	30.7%	48.3%

Both reported tax expense and pretax income, however, are affected by management choices of revenue and expense recognition methods. Although it is useful to retain pretax income, a key indicator of financial performance, as the denominator, other numerators generate tax rates that provide additional information.[20]

The first alternative tax rate uses taxes payable (current tax expense) for the period, based on revenue and expense recognition methods used on the tax return:

$$\frac{\text{Taxes Payable}}{\text{Pretax Income}}$$

This ratio may also be used with cash taxes paid instead of taxes payable. The resulting ratio focuses more on cash flows:

$$\frac{\text{Income Tax Paid}}{\text{Pretax Income}}$$

The amount of cash taxes paid can be easily obtained as SFAS 95, Statement of Cash Flows, requires separate disclosure of this amount. Due to interim tax payments and refunds, cash taxes paid may be quite different from taxes payable.

Exhibit 9-5 calculates these differing measures of an effective tax rate for duPont.

The first calculation is the reported effective tax rate (income tax expense/pretax income). DuPont's effective tax rate decreased from 46.2% in 1992 to 37.8% in 1994; the three-year average rate is 40.3%. All these rates exceed the U.S. statutory rate for the period.[21]

---

[20]Some empirical evidence (see Zimmermann, 1983) indicates that effective tax rates calculated using income tax paid and/or current tax expense tend to be higher for large firms. This is cited as evidence of the political cost hypothesis as large firms, being more politically sensitive, are required to make (relatively) larger wealth transfers than smaller firms. As the research results are largely due to the oil and gas industry, it is difficult to tell whether the political costs result from size or industry classification. Wang (1991) notes that smaller firms are more likely to have net operating losses than larger firms, at which time their effective tax rate is zero. Ignoring these losses may bias the research results.

[21]The average statutory rate for a multiyear period should be a weighted average, with pretax income providing the weights.

Two questions are suggested by these data:

1. Why is duPont's effective tax rate above the statutory rate?

2. What is duPont's effective tax rate likely to be in the future?

We seek answers to these questions shortly.

The second effective tax rate (taxes payable/pretax income) calculated in Exhibit 9-5 is highly variable over the 1992 to 1994 period, ranging from a high of 114.8% in 1993 to a low of 32.1% in 1994. The average rate is 47.6% over the three-year period, well above *both* the first effective rate and the statutory rate. Again, we will try to understand the factors in this high rate and the likelihood that they will persist in the future.

The third measure of effective tax rate, which compares income tax paid with pretax income, is also variable over the three-year period. The average rate of 48.3% is close to the average rate for taxes payable. This congruence should be expected as the timing of taxes paid is affected by technical payment requirements and by errors in management's forecast of tax liability in each jurisdiction. Over time, these factors should cancel out.

We return to the analysis of duPont's income tax position shortly. To provide additional background for that analysis, we must first discuss the effect of temporary versus permanent differences on effective tax rates and other specialized issues that highlight differences between tax and financial reporting.

ACCOUNTING FOR TAXES: SPECIALIZED ISSUES

Temporary Versus Permanent Differences

The different objectives of financial and tax reporting generate temporary differences between pretax financial income and taxable income. Some differences, however, are permanent because they result from revenues and expenses that are reportable on either tax returns or in financial statements but not both. In the United States, for example, interest income on tax-exempt bonds, premiums paid on officers' life insurance, and amortization of goodwill (in some cases) are included in financial statements but are never reported on the tax return. Similarly, certain dividends are not fully taxed, and tax or statutory depletion may exceed cost-based depletion reported in the financial statements.

Tax credits are another type of permanent difference. The alternative fuels credit reported by duPont is one example. Such credits directly reduce taxes payable and are different from tax deductions that reduce taxable income.

No deferred tax consequences are recognized for *permanent differences*; however, they result in a difference between the effective tax rate and the statutory tax rate that should be considered in the analysis of effective tax rates.

Indefinite Reversals

The amount and timing of the reversal of some temporary differences are subject to management influence or control. Some differences may never reverse at all. The accounting for these differences is especially troublesome. The uncertainty as to the amount and timing of their cash consequences affects the estimation of cash flows and firm valuation.

The undistributed earnings of unconsolidated subsidiaries and joint ventures are the most common example of this problem. The U.S. tax code requires 80% ownership to consolidate for tax purposes, ruling out joint ventures and many subsidiaries that are consolidated for accounting purposes. In addition, foreign subsidiaries are not consolidated in the U.S. tax return.[22]

As a result, the income of these affiliates is taxable on the parent's (U.S.) tax return only when dividends are received or the affiliate is sold, not when earnings are recognized. There is a difference between (tax return) taxable income and (financial reporting) pretax income. If the affiliate earnings are permanently reinvested, then affiliate earnings may never be taxable on the parent company tax return.

APB 23 permitted firms to omit deferred tax provisions on the reinvested earnings of affiliates that met the "indefinite reversal" criteria of that standard.[23] APB 24 provided different reporting rules for equity method investments (other than controlled subsidiaries and joint ventures) as the assumption of permanent reinvestment of undistributed earnings could be justified only when the parent controls the investee. The deferred tax effects of undistributed earnings were computed based on whether they were expected to be received as dividends or capital gains.[24]

SFAS 109 superseded APB 23[25] by requiring the recognition of deferred tax liabilities for temporary differences due to the undistributed earnings of essentially permanent domestic subsidiaries and joint ventures for fiscal years beginning on or after December 15, 1992.[26] However, SFAS 109 maintained the APB 23 exemption from the provision of deferred tax liabilities in the following cases:

- Undistributed earnings of a foreign subsidiary or joint venture that are considered to be permanently reinvested.
- Undistributed earnings of a domestic subsidiary or joint venture for fiscal years prior to December 15, 1992.

In its income tax note (Note 7), duPont reports that the firm has not recorded deferred taxes on undistributed earnings of foreign affiliates in the amount of $4,333 million (59% of the reported retained earnings of $7,406 million) at December 31, 1994. If the indefinite reversal assumption had not been applicable, the firm would have reported an additional unspecified deferred tax liability.

---

[22]In some cases, even wholly owned U.S. subsidiaries may not be consolidated for tax purposes. Insurance subsidiaries, which are governed by special tax regulations, are one example.

[23]Criteria for "indefinite reversal" included a history of reinvestment (lack of dividend payments) and operational budgets (showing the intent to reinvest earnings).

[24]Since dividends from qualifying investments are eligible for an 80% dividends received exclusion in the US, the effective tax rate is much lower than the rate applicable to income received as capital gains.

[25]SFAS 109 also amended APB 23 as follows: Deferred taxes must be provided on bad debt reserves of U.S. thrift lenders originating after 1987, on deposits in statutory reserve funds of U.S. steamship enterprises, and on post-1992 policyholders' surplus of stock life insurance companies; these issues are beyond the scope of this book.

[26]But if the parent has the statutory ability to realize those earnings tax free, no deferred tax provision is required (para. 33, SFAS 109).

Accounting for Acquisitions

SFAS 109 requires separate recognition of the deferred tax effects of any differences between the financial statement carrying amounts and tax bases of assets and liabilities recognized in purchase method acquisitions (see Chapter 14). APB 16 required firms to record acquired assets and liabilities *net* of related deferred taxes. As a result, many firms that had made purchase method acquisitions had to record additional deferred tax liabilities when adopting SFAS 109. DuPont reports that this requirement was the principal reason why the adoption of the new standard increased deferred tax liabilities by more than $1 billion (see duPont's Note 7).

In some cases, a valuation allowance must be recorded for deferred tax assets due to the acquired firm's temporary differences or its operating loss or tax credit carryforwards. The tax benefits of subsequent reversals of the valuation allowance must be used, first, to reduce all related goodwill, second, to eliminate all other related noncurrent intangible assets, and third, to reduce reported income tax expense.

ANALYSIS OF INCOME TAX DISCLOSURES: DUPONT

Accounting for income taxes is complex; a large company may have many permanent and temporary differences between financial statement income and taxable income. A large multinational pays taxes in a number of jurisdictions, further complicating the process. From an analyst's perspective, unraveling these layers can seem daunting indeed.

Some analysts respond to this complexity by ignoring the issues. They analyze corporate performance on a pretax basis and simply accept that variations in the reported tax rate occur. We agree that analysis on a pretax basis is sound, but also believe that a firm's income tax accounting is too important to ignore.

The goals of income tax analysis are to:

1. Understand why the firm's effective tax rate differs (or does not differ) from the statutory rate in its home country.
2. Forecast changes in the effective tax rate, improving forecasts of earnings.
3. Review the historical differences between income tax expense and income taxes paid.
4. Forecast the future relationship between income tax expense and income tax payments.
5. Examine deferred tax liabilities and assets, including any valuation allowance, for

   • Possible effects on future earnings and cash flows.
   • Their relevance to firm valuation.
   • Their relevance in assessing a firm's capital structure.

We pursue these goals, using duPont as an example, and illustrate the insights regarding a firm that can be derived from its income tax disclosures.

Analysis of the Effective Tax Rate

The first step is an examination of the firm's tax rate, the trend in that rate, and the rate relative to similar companies. Variations are generally the consequence of:

1. Different statutory tax rates in different jurisdictions; analysis can offer important clues as to the sources of income.

2. Tax holidays that some countries offer; earnings from such operations usually cannot be remitted without payment of tax. Be alert to possible changes in the operations in such countries or the need to remit the accumulated earnings.

3. Permanent differences between financial and taxable income: tax-exempt income, tax credits, and nondeductible expenses.

4. The effect of tax rate and other tax law changes that, under SFAS 109, are included in income tax expense (a separate disclosure of this effect is required).

5. Deferred taxes provided on the reinvested earnings of foreign affiliates and unconsolidated domestic affiliates.

As noted earlier, duPont's effective tax rate averaged 40.3% over the 1992 to 1994 period. DuPont's tax footnote provides the required reconciliation between its statutory rate and effective rate for each year.[27] Because of the significance of some of these differences and variation in pretax income over the period, the rate-based disclosures are difficult to analyze. For that reason, Exhibit 9-6 converts them to dollar-based disclosures.

Starting with the three-year totals, we see that a higher tax rate on non-U.S. earnings is the largest single factor in duPont's high effective tax rate, adding $1.3 billion or 18 percentage points for the three-year period. DuPont's petroleum operations accounted for 43% of revenues and 26% of operating profit in 1994. Three-quarters of those operations are outside the United States, mostly in Europe.[28] Under U.S. tax law, oil royalties are tax-deductible expenses, whereas foreign income tax payments are tax credits. For that reason, foreign countries generally structure royalties as "income taxes" and U.S. companies with foreign petroleum operations report high effective tax rates. Thus, duPont's high effective tax rate is largely a function of its non-U.S. petroleum operations. Forecasting future effective tax rates, therefore, requires explicit forecasts of the earnings of these operations.

Partly offsetting this effect is lower tax rates paid by duPont operations in (unspecified) U.S. possessions. This factor reduced the composite three-year tax rate by two percentage points, adding an average of nearly $50 million to net income. No further data are provided regarding these operations. Another continuing benefit is the alternative fuels credit, whose dollar amount grew each year. Discussion with management should result in a better understanding of the source and likelihood of continuation of these benefits.

Several factors in duPont's effective tax rate are nonrecurring in nature. One is the benefit ($274 million) from 1993 changes in the U.K. Petroleum Revenue Tax law. Another is the 1994 benefit ($105 million) from "tax status changes" affecting the valuation allowance.

---

[27]The reconciliation can be done in either percentages (relative to the statutory tax rate) or monetary amounts (relative to "statutory" income tax expense equal to pretax income multiplied by the statutory rate).

[28]Based on duPont's reported segment data, discussed in detail in Chapter 13.

EXHIBIT 9-6.   DUPONT
Reconciliation of Effective and Statutory Tax Rates

	1992	1993	1994	1992 to 1994	
				Total	Rate
Pretax income	$1,811	$958	$4,382	$7,151	
Statutory rate	34%	35%	35%		
Variations from Statutory Rate					
Non-U.S. income	20.5	51.9	9.9		
U.S. possessions	(2.4)	(5.6)	(1.1)		
Alternative fuels	(2.0)	(6.9)	(2.1)		
Tax rate changes	—	(28.6)			
Tax status change	—		(2.4)		
Other—net	(3.9)	(4.9)	(1.5)		
Net effect	12.2	5.9	2.8		
Effective tax rate	46.2	40.9	37.8		
Tax in Millions of Dollars = Rate × Pretax Income					
At statutory rate	$ 616	$335	$1,534	$2,485	34.8%
Effect of					
Non-U.S. income	$ 371	$497	$ 434	$1,302	18.2%
U.S. possessions	(43)	(54)	(48)	(145)	−2.0
Alternative fuels	(36)	(66)	(92)	(194)	−2.7
Tax rate changes	—	(274)	—	(274)	−3.8
Tax status change	—	—	(105)	(105)	−1.5
Other—net	(71)	(47)	(66)	(183)	−2.6
Net effect	$ 221	$ 57	$ 123	$ 400	5.6%
Income tax expense	$ 837	$392	$1,656	$2,885	40.3%

Source: Adapted from duPont Note 7, *1994 Annual Report.*

Now that we understand the reasons for duPont's high effective tax rate in the past, we turn to the future. A forecast of future income tax expense should start with estimated pretax income and apply the statutory rate of 35%. The analyst should then adjust for the effects of the:

- Higher tax rate on petroleum income
- Lower tax rate on U.S. possession operations
- Alternative fuels credit
- "Other" effects

These adjustments may require input from duPont management or trade publications. Some firms provide periodic forecasts of their tax rate because of the difficulty of making such forecasts externally.

Analysis of Deferred Income Tax Expense

We now examine the effects of temporary differences on income tax expense. Companies are required to provide details of these differences, although formats vary. DuPont's disclosure is typical, showing a breakdown in dollars for each year.

Temporary differences are generally the result of the use of different accounting policies or estimates for tax purposes than for financial reporting differences. Some of these differences are systematic; others are transaction-specific. Frequent examples include:

1. *Depreciation.* Different methods and/or lives results in different measures of depreciation expense.

2. *Impairment.* Financial reporting write-downs do not generate tax deductions until assets are sold.

3. *Restructuring costs.* Usually tax-deductible when paid rather than when accrued.

4. *Inventories.* Companies using last-in, first-out (LIFO) accounting for tax purposes in the United States must also use LIFO for reporting purposes, but when other methods are used, differences may occur.

5. *Postemployment benefits.* The accruals required by SFAS 87 (pensions), SFAS 106 (other retiree benefits), and SFAS 112 (other postemployment benefits) are discussed in Chapter 12. Tax treatment of these costs is generally cash-based, generating deferred tax effects.

6. *Deferred compensation.* Tax-deductible only when payments are made.

On a cumulative basis, duPont generated negative deferred tax expense (taxes payable > income tax expense) over the 1992 to 1994 period, although deferred tax expense was positive in 1994.[29] Depreciation was the only factor generating positive deferred tax expense over this period. Although duPont used accelerated depreciation methods for most property (see the discussion in Chapter 8), its tax depreciation is higher still. This effect may be due to petroleum property (depreciated using the straight line method) or to the use of shorter lives for tax accounting. As duPont switched to the straight-line method for all property effective January 1, 1995, deferred tax expense from this source should increase.

Note, however, that in 1993 depreciation generated negative deferred tax expense. As reported in Note 6, duPont wrote down fixed assets in that year, reversing a portion of the excess tax depreciation from prior years.

The 1993 restructuring charges had other deferred tax effects. Although the disclosure is not clear, the "other accrued expenses" line in the deferred income tax disclosure probably reflects charges that did not generate tax deductions in that year. *When a large restructuring charge is taken, the tax effects generally occur as expenditures are made, with significant effects on deferred tax expense both in the year of the charge and the year(s) of payment.*

The two nonrecurring adjustments for tax rate and tax status changes (both discussed above) affected deferred tax expense. Neither adjustment had any effect on cash flow.

---

[29]See Note 7 to duPont financial statements and data in Exhibit 9-5.

Because duPont's deferred tax expense was negative over the 1992 to 1994 period, taxes payable (and income tax paid) exceeded income tax expense. Absent write-offs or other "restructuring" charges and given the 1995 change in depreciation method, it appears unlikely that deferred tax expense will be negative in the future.

Using Deferred Taxes to Estimate Taxable Income

Deferred tax expense reflects the difference between taxable income reported to tax authorities and pretax income reported to shareholders. This relationship can be used to estimate components of taxable income. The difference between taxable income and pretax income equals

$$\frac{\textbf{Deferred Tax Expense}}{\textbf{Statutory Tax Rate}}$$

For example, duPont's 1994 depreciation expense (financial reporting) was $2,976 million. Deferred tax expense related to depreciation was $144 million in 1994 (Note 7). Using that amount and the statutory tax rate of 35%, we estimate that the additional depreciation expense under tax reporting was $411 million ($144 million divided by 0.35) and tax basis depreciation was $3,387 million ($2,976 + $411).

These calculations should be viewed as estimates. They are most reliable when they relate to a single tax jurisdiction as the appropriate tax rate and the difference between tax and financial reporting rules are clear. Although this method can, in theory, be used to calculate taxable income for the entire firm, such calculations for large multinationals are less reliable.

Similar calculations can be made for the cumulative financial reporting-tax differences using deferred tax asset and liability data. The calculation for duPont's fixed assets is shown in the next section of this chapter.

Deferred tax disclosures can also be used, in some cases, to estimate the taxes paid associated with components of income and expense. Problem 11B applies this approach to the gain on an asset sale by Honda.

Analysis of Deferred Tax Assets and Liabilities

Our final step is an examination of the balance sheet consequences of duPont's income tax accounting. As required by SFAS 109, Note 7 contains a table of significant deferred tax assets and liabilities, as well as the valuation allowance, at each balance sheet date.

The most significant deferred tax asset relates to accrued employee benefits. As previously discussed, the adoption of SFAS 106 (postretirement benefits) generated a large deferred tax asset.

The second largest asset results from "other accrued expenses," presumably accruals that have not yet generated tax deductions. Possible sources include deferred compensation, accruals for the fungicide recall (see Note 3) and restructuring charges. Note 18 lists duPont's "other accrued liabilities."

Tax loss and tax credit carryforwards are a third significant source of deferred tax assets. Although duPont does not say so, it is likely that this source has generated the valuation allowance.

DuPont's largest single source of deferred tax liabilities, as for most firms, is depreciation. This difference usually reflects the use of accelerated methods and shorter lives for tax return depreciation calculations.

If we assume a 35% tax rate for all depreciation-related deferred tax assets, the reporting difference can be estimated as $8.4 billion ($2.94/0.35) or 30% of accumulated depreciation of $27.7 billion. Given duPont's use of accelerated methods for nonpetroleum property, this large difference is surprising. Although much of this difference may relate to petroleum property, some may reflect the use of shorter lives for tax reporting.

Although the remaining deferred tax liabilities are small, several deserve comment. While duPont uses the LIFO inventory method for "substantially all" inventories, there is a $310 million deferred liability from this source. This liability may reflect obsolescence write-downs that cannot be recognized for tax purposes under LIFO or different varieties of LIFO used for financial and tax reporting.[30]

Although duPont has several significant affiliates accounted for by the equity method (see Note 14 and Chapter 13), there is only a small deferred tax liability from this source. Note 14 indicates that virtually all of duPont's share of earnings is paid out as dividends, which are taxed currently.

DuPont reported a valuation allowance of $357 million at December 31, 1994 ($445 million at December 31, 1993). Although there is no discussion in the financial statements, the tax loss/tax credit carryforwards are the most likely reason for that allowance.

If we put together all these pieces, duPont's net balance sheet liability for income tax is:

Deferred tax assets	$ 4,592
Less: Valuation allowance	(357)
Less: Deferred tax liability	(5,152)
Net liability	$ (917)

Where does this liability appear on duPont's balance sheet? The answer is—in several places. Fortunately, SFAS 109 requires the disclosure of all deferred tax components on the balance sheet. In the case of duPont, these are ($ in millions):

Assets		Liabilities	
Deferred income taxes	$558	Income taxes	$ 63
Other assets	82	Deferred income taxes	1,494
Totals	$640		$1,557
Net liability			$ 917

Is this $917 million a real liability? Or, to rephrase the question, what are the likely future cash flow effects of duPont's deferred tax assets and liabilities?

Given its large size, the deferred tax liability associated with accumulated depreciation is the logical starting point. On the one hand, capital expenditures have been declining (41% since 1990), although the Management Discussion and Analysis forecasts an increase for 1995. In addition, the switch to straight line depreciation for nonpetroleum property will tend to increase the deferred tax liability from this source. Thus, unless there are further decreases in capital spending, it seems unlikely that the deferred tax liability from depreciation will decline over the next few years. The trend

[30]Appendix 6-A contains a discussion of the different varieties of LIFO.

in capital spending must, however, be monitored. Based on data available in the annual report, no other deferred tax liability seems likely to reverse.

On the other hand, duPont's largest deferred tax asset, related to accrued employee benefits, may start to reverse at some point. As retiree benefit payments increase, they may exceed the accrual for additional benefits earned. Trends in these amounts can be monitored using the analytic techniques in Chapter 12.

In total, therefore, it appears unlikely that duPont's deferred tax accruals will generate any significant cash outflow over the next few years. In addition, given the unlikelihood of near-term reversal, the net liability should be discounted for the time value of money. The combination of these factors suggests that a liability should not be recognized for valuation purposes.

Other Issues in Income Tax Analysis

The following issues, although not relevant to an analysis of duPont, occur frequently enough to warrant brief mention:

- Watch for companies that report substantial income for financial reporting purposes but little or no taxes payable (implying little or no taxable income). Such differences often reflect aggressive revenue and expense recognition methods used for financial reporting, and low quality of earnings. In such cases, caution is indicated as the methods used for financial reporting purposes may be based on optimistic assumptions.

- Look for current or pending reversals of past temporary differences. For example a decline in capital spending may result in a greater proportion of depreciatio coming from old assets that have already been heavily depreciated for tax pu poses. Thus, financial reporting depreciation may exceed tax depreciation, gene ating a tax liability.

- Remember that deferred tax assets and liabilities may point to near-term cɛ consequences. Restructuring provisions often generate little cash or tax eff in the year they occur, but substantial effects in following years.

- Tax law changes may also result in the reversal of past temporary differen In the United States, tax law changes in recent years have curtailed the us the completed contract and installment methods for tax purposes, generɛ substantial tax liabilities for affected companies.

1.   **Overview**

In this chapter we discuss estimating the cost of capital. We begin by discussing the estimation of the equity cost of capital. Estimates of the equity cost of capital can then be used to determine either the weighted average cost of capital or the unlevered cost of capital once assumptions are made about how the capital structure will be managed and the cost of debt capital is estimated. Whether you are ultimately interested in the weighted average cost of capital or the unlevered cost of capital depends on the valuation technique that you are using (the adjusted present value method or the adjusted cost of capital method -- see Chapters 1, 2, and 4).

The exact procedure that one uses to estimate the cost of capital depends on whether the firm being valued is publicly traded or not.

A.   If the firm you are valuing is publicly traded (or if you are just trying to estimate the cost of capital for a publicly traded firm for purposes of investment project evaluation), you can use market data available for the firm itself. If the firm you are valuing is private, any cost of capital estimate will necessarily entail choosing some comparable publicly traded firms to obtain estimates of the cost of capital.

In some cases when the firm is publicly traded, you may still want to use comparable firms to estimate the cost of capital because of the potential reduction in measurement error associated with estimating the cost of equity capital for a portfolio.

B.   If you have decided to just use data on the firm you are valuing (which presumes it is publicly traded), you always begin by estimating the equity cost of capital and debt cost of capital, regardless of whether you are using the adjusted present value method or adjusted cost of capital method for valuing the firm.

Once you have estimated the equity and debt costs of capital for your firm, you may then develop estimates of either the unlevered cost of capital or the weighted average cost of capital. Estimating the unlevered cost of capital will entail using the levering and unlevering formulas discussed in Chapters 2 and 3.

C.   If you are using comparable firms whose capital structure is different from the firm you are valuing, you must first estimate the unlevered cost of capital for each of your comparable firms using the unlevering formulas discussed in Chapters 2 and 3. The unlevering of each comparable firm's equity cost of capital is based on that firm's capital structure. Once unlevered cost of capital estimates are derived for each firm, aggregate those estimates into a single estimate.

Security Analysis: How to Analyze Accounting and Market Data to Value Securities
   Robert W. Holthausen and Mark E. Zmijewski
   \CH10.W51

Do not reproduce without permission.
July 30, 1998

271

If you only need an estimate of the unlevered cost of capital because you are using the adjusted present value method you are now done. If however, you want an estimate of the weighted average cost of capital, you must lever up the unlevered cost of capital estimate from the comparable firms using the appropriate formulas from Chapters 2 and 3. The levering is based on the capital structure of the firm you are valuing.

(1)   This can be done by first estimating the equity cost of capital and then plugging into the traditional weighted average cost of capital formula. Estimate the equity cost of capital by levering up the unlevered cost of capital using the appropriate formulas from Chapters 2 and 3.

(2)   Alternatively, the weighted average cost of capital can be estimated by using one of the weighted average cost of capital formulas written in terms of the unlevered cost of capital and debt cost of capital (see Chapters 2 and 3, but note these formula only work if you have a firm with only debt and equity in its capital structure).

This chapter, in conjunction with the cost of capital issues discussed in Chapters 2 and 3, should provide you with a reasonably detailed guideline for estimating the cost of capital in a variety of situations.

2.   **An Aside on Levering and Unlevering Formulas**

Chapters 2 and 3 provide information on levering and unlevering cost of capital estimates and betas given a capital structure of debt and equity under certain assumptions about valuation of interest tax shields. The derivations presented in Chapter 2 provide sufficient information to derive the same formulas under more complicated capital structures (for example, the inclusion of preferred stock).

Preferred stock is equity but pays a periodic fixed dividend. Preferred stock generally has no maturity date and preferred shareholders cannot force the firm into bankruptcy proceedings or accelerate a principal payment like a debtholder. Preferred shareholders can generally keep the firm from paying common dividends if the preferred dividend payments are in arrears.

In the U.S. preferred dividends are taxable to individuals but 70% of preferred dividends paid to a corporation are tax exempt. The remaining 30% are taxed at ordinary corporate income tax rates. Therefore, the effective tax on preferred dividends is roughly 10%. We generally observe that preferred shares are held by corporations because of the tax advantages and are generally issued at lower effective yields then debt of similar risk. The disadvantage of preferred stock is that the preferred dividends are not tax deductible for the issuing corporation. Issuing corporations are usually firms who cannot effectively use the tax advantage of debt or are regulated utilities who get to charge their customers for the tax disadvantage of preferred.

Floating rate preferred shares are like regular preferred but the rate of dividend payment is reset periodicly to either a given spread off of a particular short-term government instrument or by dutch auction. Trust preferreds, which are relatively new allow firms to deduct the preferred

Security Analysis: How to Analyze Accounting and Market Data to Value Securities
Robert W. Holthausen and Mark E. Zmijewski
\CH10.W51

Do not reproduce without permission.
July 30, 1998

272

dividend payments as interest expense and still maintains the preferred dividend exclusion for the corporation which holds them.

If a firm had issued preferred stock, the economic balance sheet would now include preferred stock on the equities side at the cost of capital of preferred stock. The derivations that follow assume that interest tax shields are either valued at the cost of debt or the cost of capital of the unlevered firm.

Here are some variable definitions for variables we use below.

V_t	=	market value of the levered firm at time $t = E_t + D_t + R_t$
k_U	=	cost of capital for the unlevered firm assumed constant
k_{Et}	=	cost of equity capital for the equity at time t
k_{Dt}	=	cost of debt capital at time t
k_{Rt}	=	cost of preferred capital at time t
E_t	=	market value of the equity at time t
D_t	=	market value of the debt at time t
R_t	=	market value of the preferred stock at time t
$DVTS_t$	=	present value of all interest tax shields at time t.
$DVTS_{t,kd}$	=	present value of the interest tax shield at time t discounted at discount rate k_D at time t.
$DVTS_{t,ku}$	=	present value of the interest tax shield at time t discounted at discount rate k_u at time t.
T	=	the appropriate tax rate for calculating the value of the interest tax shield.

The general, Case I, Case II, Case III and Case IV formulas are repeated below given the inclusion of preferred stock in the economic balance sheet. We do not rederive the formulas but suggest you do that on your own given the derivations in Chapter 2. If you understand the derivations in Chapter 2, deriving these formulas is very similar. For those of you interested, the left hand side of the first equation in every case's derivation is identical. The right hand side of each first equation now includes an additional term $R_t * k_{Rt}$. In addition, in the step where you substitute an expression for V_{ut} remember now that $V_{ut} = D_t + E_t + R_t - DVTS_t$ (where you substitute an appropriate expression for $DVTS_t$ given the particular case you are deriving). The advantage for understanding the derivation of these equations is that you will then be able to handle even more complicated capital structures should you face them in your valuation work.

The formulas below lever and unlever the cost of capital. Remember from the Chapter 3 notes that levering and unlevering formulas for betas (given the CAPM) are identical except for the substitution of the appropriate asset's beta for its cost of capital in the formulas.

A.   The equity cost of capital for a firm.

The General Formulation

The equity cost of capital for the firm in terms of the unlevered cost of capital, debt cost of capital and capital structures is given by the following general formula.

Security Analysis: How to Analyze Accounting and Market Data to Value Securities
Robert W. Holthausen and Mark E. Zmijewski
\CH10.W51

$$k_{Et} = k_U + (k_U-k_{Dt})*(D_t-DVTS_{t,kd})/E_t + (k_U-k_{Rt})*R_t/E_t$$

Remember that $DVTS_{t,kd}$ is the value of the interest tax shields which are discounted at k_d, this period. As in Chapter 2, there are certain special cases of the general formulation.

Case I - No tax deduction for interest.

The equity cost of capital for the firm in terms of an the unlevered cost of capital and debt cost of capital is equal to

$$k_{Et} = k_U + (k_U-k_{Dt})*D_t/E_t + (k_U-k_{Rt})*R_t/E_t \; .$$

Assume that $k_U = 0.2$, $k_{Dt} = 0.15$, $k_{Rt} = 0.12$, $E_t = 5$, $D_t = 6$ and $R_t = 4$. Convince yourself that $k_{Et} = 0.3240$.

Case II - Interest tax shelters do not depend on the value of the levered firm.

In this case, the interest tax shelters are known and do not depend on the value of the firm; therefore, they are discounted at the debt cost of capital. The equity cost of capital is:

$$k_{Et} = k_U + (k_U-k_{Dt})*(D_t-DVTS_{t,kd})/E_t + (k_U-k_{Rt})*R_t/E_t$$

Assume that $k_U = 0.2$, $k_{Dt} = 0.15$, $k_{Rt} = 0.12$, $E_t = 5$, $D_t = 6$, $R_t = 4$, and $DVTS_{t,kd} = 1$. Convince yourself that $k_{Et} = 0.3140$.

Under certain circumstances, it is possible to make simplifying perpetuity assumptions regarding the present value of the interest tax shields. One simplifying assumption is that the firm is going to have a fixed dollar amount of debt and that the firm is expected to generate the same free cash flow in perpetuity. Given this assumption, the value of the interest tax shields ($DVTS_{t,kd}$) is equal to T*D. Substituting T*D into the above formula yields

$$k_{Et} = k_U + (k_U-k_{Dt})*(1-T)*D_t/E_t + (k_U-k_{Rt})*R_t/E_t$$

Assume that $k_U = 0.2$, $k_{Dt} = 0.15$, $k_{Rt} = 0.12$, $E_t = 5$, $D_t = 6$, $R_t = 4$ and $T = 0.40$. Convince yourself that $k_{Et} = 0.30$.

Alternatively, assume that the firm's debt is going to grow at some rate, g, and that the firm is expected to grow at approximately the same rate as the debt. Given this assumption, the value of the interest tax shields ($DVTS_{t,kd}$) is equal to $(k_D*T*D)/(k_D-g)$. Substituting this result into the above formula yields

$$k_{Et} = k_U + (k_U-k_{Dt})*[1-(Tk_D/(k_D-g))]*D_t/E_t + (k_U-k_{Rt})*R_t/E_t$$

Assume that $k_U = 0.2$, $k_{Dt} = 0.15$, $k_{Rt} = 0.12$, $E_t = 5$, $D_t = 6$, $R_t = 4$, $T = 0.40$ and the growth rate in debt, g, equals 5% per year. Convince yourself that $k_{Et} = 0.288$.

Case III - Constant debt/value capital structure strategy.

Here it can be shown that the value of next period's interest tax shield is equal to $D_t Tk_D/(1 + k_D)$; further, the cost of equity capital and cost of debt capital does not change through time. The equity cost of capital for this case is

$$k_E = k_U + (k_U-k_D)*[1-(Tk_D/(1+k_D))]*D_t/E_t + (k_U-k_{Rt})*R_t/E_t$$

Assume that $k_U = 0.2$, $k_{Dt} = 0.15$, $k_{Rt} = 0.12$, $E_t = 5$, $D_t = 6$, $R_t = 4$ and $T = 0.40$. Convince yourself that $k_{Et} = 0.3209$.

Case IV - Interest Tax Shields Discounted at k_U

The equity cost of capital for the firm in terms of an the unlevered cost of capital and debt cost of capital is equal to

$$k_{Et} = k_U + (k_U-k_{Dt})*D_t/E_t + (k_U-k_{Rt})*R_t/E_t .$$

Assume that $k_U = 0.2$, $k_{Dt} = 0.15$, $k_{Rt} = 0.12$, $E_t = 5$, $D_t = 6$ and $R_t = 4$. Convince yourself that $k_{Et} = 0.3240$.

Note, while these notes are not developing the formulas for the weighted average cost of capital in terms of k_U and k_D (you can just use the standard textbook formula as presented in section 14 of this chapter). You should convince yourself that the formula for the WACC in terms of k_U and k_D for Case IV, is the same with preferred stock as is shown in Chapter 2, when preferred was not considered. That is,

$$WACC_t = k_U - [k_{Dt}*T*(D_t/V_t)]$$

B.   The unlevered cost of capital.

It is most often the case that the cost of capital for the unlevered firm is not observable, although the cost of equity capital and the cost of debt capital are observable, or at least straight-forward to estimate. In these situations you can use the equity cost of capital formulae we present above to calculate the unlevered cost of capital.

The General Formulation

The most general formula for determining the unlevered cost of capital from the equity and debt costs of capital and knowledge of the capital structure is given by:

$$k_U = k_{Et}*E_t/(E_t+D_t-DVTS_{t,kd}+R_t) + k_{Dt}*(D_t-DVTS_{t,kd})/(E_t+D_t-DVTS_{t,kd}+R_t)$$

$$+ k_{Rt}*R_t/(E_t+D_t-DVTS_{t,kd}+R_t),$$

Security Analysis: How to Analyze Accounting and Market Data to Value Securities
Robert W. Holthausen and Mark E. Zmijewski
\CH10.W51

Do not reproduce without permission.
July 30, 1998

275

As in prior discussions of this material. There are several special cases of the general formulation.

Case I - No tax deduction for interest.

In this case, issuing debt does not increase the value of the firm (i.e., interest is not tax deductible). The unlevered cost of capital is equal to

$$k_U \ = \ k_{Et}*E_t/(E_t+D_t+R_t) \ + \ k_{Dt}*D_t/(E_t+D_t+R_t) \ + \ k_{Rt}*R_t/(E_t+D_t+R_t),$$

Case II - Interest tax shelters do not depend on the value of the levered firm.

In this case, the interest tax shelters are known and do not depend on the value of the firm; therefore, they are discounted at the debt cost of capital. The unlevered cost of capital is

$$k_U \ = \ k_{Et}*E_t/(E_t+D_t-DVTS_{t,kd}+R_t) \ + \ k_{Dt}*(D_t-DVTS_{t,kd})/(E_t+D_t-DVTS_{t,kd}+R_t)$$

$$+ \ k_{Rt}*R_t/(E_t+D_t-DVTS_{t,kd}+R_t),$$

Under certain assumptions outlined above, we can assume that $DVTS_{t,kd} = T*D$. In that case, we can substitute $T*D$ for $DVTS_{t,kd}$ in the above formulas.

$$k_U \ = \ k_{Et}*E_t/(E_t+(1-T)D_t+R_t) \ + \ k_{Dt}*(1-T)D_t/(E_t+(1-T)D_t+R_t)$$

$$+ \ k_{Rt}*R_t/(E_t+(1-T)D_t+R_t),$$

which can be rewritten as,

$$k_U \ = \ [k_{Et}+k_{Dt}*(1-T)D_t/E_t+k_{Rt}*R_t/E_t]/(1+(1-T)D_t/E_t+R_t/E_t).$$

An alternative simplification is to assume that the firm is going to grow at some rate, g, then

$$k_U \ = \quad k_{Et}*E_t/(E_t+D_t*(1-Tk_D/(k_D-g))+R_t)$$

$$+ \ k_{Dt}*D_t*(1-Tk_D/(k_D-g))/(E_t+D_t*(1-Tk_D/(k_D-g))+R_t)$$

$$+ \ k_{Rt}*R_t/(E_t+D_t*(1-Tk_D/(k_D-g))+R_t)$$

which can be rewritten as,

$$k_U \ = \quad [k_{Et}+k_{Dt}*D_t/E_t*(1-Tk_D/(k_D-g))+k_{Rt}*R_t/E_t]/(1+D_t/E_t*(1-Tk_D/(k_D-g))+R_t/E_t)$$

Security Analysis: How to Analyze Accounting and Market Data to Value Securities
Robert W. Holthausen and Mark E. Zmijewski
\CH10.W51

Do not reproduce without permission.
July 30, 1998

276

Case III - Constant debt/value capital structure strategy.

The unlevered cost of capital for this case is

$$k_U = k_E * E_t / (E_t + D_t * (1 - Tk_D / (1 + k_D)) + R_t)$$

$$+ k_D * D_t * (1 - Tk_D / (1 + k_D)) / (E_t + D_t * (1 - Tk_D / (1 + k_D)) + R_t)$$

$$+ k_R * R_t / (E_t + D_t * (1 - Tk_D / (1 + k_D)) + R_t)$$

which can be rewritten as,

$$k_U = [k_E + k_D * D_t / E_t * (1 - Tk_D / (1 + k_D)) + k_R * R_t / E_t] / (1 + D_t / E_t * (1 - Tk_D / (1 + k_D)) + R_t / E_t)$$

You should convince yourself for each of the above cases that you can use the information given in the problems where you estimated the equity cost of capital (except the unlevered cost of capital and including the estimate of the equity cost of capital), to determine that $k_U = 0.20$ in each of the above cases. [Remember, you must use the appropriate k_E in every case since it changes with each case.]

Case IV - Interest Tax Shields Discounted at k_U

In this case, issuing debt increases the value of the firm (i.e., interest is tax deductible), but it does not create an asset with a different risk from the underlying assets. The unlevered cost of capital is equal to

$$k_U = k_{Et} * E_t / (E_t + D_t + R_t) + k_{Dt} * D_t / (E_t + D_t + R_t) + k_{Rt} * R_t / (E_t + D_t + R_t),$$

3. **The Sharpe-Lintner CAPM model -- Expected Return and Risk.**

   A. Sharpe-Lintner Capital Asset Pricing Model -- Statement.

$$E(\tilde{R}_i) = R_f + \beta_i [E(\tilde{R}_m) - R_f]$$

where:

$E(\tilde{R}_i)$	$\equiv$	expected rate of return on asset i.
R_f	$\equiv$	rate of return on a risk free asset.
$E(\tilde{R}_m)$	$\equiv$	expected rate of return on the market portfolio.
β_i	$\equiv$	Beta of security i defined as covariance$(\tilde{R}_i, \tilde{R}_m)$/variance$(\tilde{R}_m)$.

Security Analysis: How to Analyze Accounting and Market Data to Value Securities
Robert W. Holthausen and Mark E. Zmijewski
\CH10.W51

B. Things to Note.

(1) The model is defined in terms of expectations, thus investors are compensated in an "expected" sense. Actual return realizations will typically deviate from expectations.

(2) The model prices securities relative to the market risk premium.

(a) The market risk premium is the return expected to be earned on the market above the risk free rate, that is

$$E(\tilde{R}_m) - R_f.$$

(3) In order to use the CAPM to estimate the cost of equity capital, we need estimates of:

(a) the security's beta,
(b) the market risk premium, and
(c) the risk free rate of interest.

We discuss each of these in turn

4. **Estimation Issues -- BETA.**

A. Regression Techniques -- Build Your Own Beta.

Estimate a simple regression where the return of the relevant asset is the dependent variable (left-hand side variable) and the contemporaneous return on the market is the independent variable (right-hand side variable). This is often called the market model.

$$R_{it} = \alpha_i + \beta_i R_{mt} + \epsilon_{it} \qquad t=1\ldots\ldots T.$$

The estimated slope coefficient $\hat{\beta}$ is the slope of the fitted regression line and the estimated α_i is the intercept of the regression line on the Y axis.

Assuming the data meet the assumptions of ordinary least squares regression (primarily normality, stationarity and serial independence of the error terms), the estimate of beta from a regression, β_i is an unbiased estimate of the true beta. That is,

$$E(\hat{\beta}) = \beta_i$$

The Standard error of the estimate describes the sampling variability of the estimate and thus measures the confidence you have in the estimate.

For example, the 95% confidence level for an estimated beta (with 120 or more observations) is equal to the beta estimate +/- 1.96 X standard error of the estimate.

Security Analysis: How to Analyze Accounting and Market Data to Value Securities
Robert W. Holthausen and Mark E. Zmijewski
\CH10.W51

Do not reproduce without permission.
July 30, 1998

278

B.   If you do not have a series of returns available to you, you will have to create the return series. The return on asset i from t-1 to t is given by:

$$R_{i,t} = (P_{i,t} - P_{i,t-1} + D_{i,t}) / P_{i,t-1}$$

where $P_{i,t}$ is the price of asset i at time t, and $D_{i,t}$ is any cash distribution made between t-1 and t. If there are changes in the number of shares outstanding due to stock splits or stock dividends, adjustments must be made. Assume a stock had a 2-for-1 stock split between t-1 and t after the dividend, $D_{i,t}$ had been paid. In that case, $P_{i,t}$ would have to be multiplied by 2 to properly calculate the return to shareholders between t-1 and t.

C.   Issues in estimating beta.

   (1)   Choice of index.

      (a)   Use a series with dividends, not without dividends (be careful, the actual S&P500 index excludes dividends. Of course, there are indices of the S&P500 available, which include the effect of dividends.

      (b)   Weighting scheme (e.g., equal or value weighted).

            Theory tells us value weighted -- its important to use the same index for measuring beta and for measuring the market risk premium -- most U.S. practitioners use the S&P500 because of its availability and it is value-weighted. We prefer use of a value-weighted index.

      (c)   Securities included (e.g., S&P500, all NYSE Common Stocks, NYSE + AMEX + OTC Common Stocks, Indices containing stocks, bonds, etc.).

            Theory tells us its the value weighted index of all risky assets -- practitioners tend to rely on an index of just common stocks and most use only the S&P500 because of its availability and long history relative to alternative indices.

      (d)   Betas will vary as a function of the index chosen because beta is simply a scaled measure of covariance and that measure will vary depending on the index.

   (2)   How much data?

      (a)   What is the interval of return measurement?

            Daily, weekly or monthly data:

            more statistical issues with daily data such as autocorrelation of returns, non-trading and non-synchronous trading between a firm and the index.

Security Analysis: How to Analyze Accounting and Market Data to Value Securities
Robert W. Holthausen and Mark E. Zmijewski
\CH10.W51

We suggest monthly data if sufficient observations are available. Otherwise use weekly data. Recent research suggests some advantage to measuring returns over longer intervals.

(b)   Has there been an operating/financing change?

You must assess the tradeoff between more observations vs. recent observations; or precision vs. stationarity

Use observations from a period subsequent to a large change in operating and financing policies.

For example, when Marathon Oil and U.S. Steel merged, neither firm's prior beta would be a good estimate of the combined entity's beta, nor would the pre LBO beta for RJR be a good estimate of the post LBO beta

(c)   Little improvement in precision of the estimates is likely with more than 500 daily observations (roughly 2 years), 100 weekly observations (roughly 2 years) or 60 monthly observations (5 years). These are useful guidelines for usage. Use fewer numbers of observations if there have been structural changes.

(3)   Typical U.S. Betas

Utilities	0.40
Retail Grocery Stores	0.70
Department Stores	0.90
Motor Vehicles	1.00
Steel Firms	1.10
Air Transportation	1.30
Petroleum Refining	1.30
Electronic Components	1.50
Electronic Computing	1.60
Drilling Oil and Gas Wells	1.90

(4)   Stability of beta estimates.

(a)   Evidence indicates that betas of common stocks vary over time due to changes in firm's operating and financing policies, due to changes in competition, regulation etc.

Security Analysis: How to Analyze Accounting and Market Data to Value Securities
    Robert W. Holthausen and Mark E. Zmijewski
    \CH10.W51

Do not reproduce without permission.
July 30, 1998

280

(b)   Mean reversion in beta estimates.

Beta estimates represent true beta + noise -- empirical evidence indicates that betas which are greater than one, <u>on average</u> have positive noise terms, and betas which are less than one, <u>on average</u> have negative noise terms. Thus, betas estimated in two consecutive periods tend to revert back to the mean of one. So called bayesian estimates of beta, will take into consideration the typical degree of mean reversion.

Portfolio Number	Period 1 1988-1992	Period 2 1993-1997	Portfolio Number	Period 1 1993-1997	Period 2 1988-1992
1	0.381	0.522	1	0.393	0.558
2	0.561	0.634	2	0.566	0.709
3	0.774	0.780	3	0.727	0.825
4	0.850	0.872	4	0.833	0.921
5	1.093	0.940	5	1.149	0.974
6	1.251	1.061	6	1.177	1.139
7	1.621	1.480	7	1.510	1.318

(c)   Beta estimates of portfolios vs. securities.

Portfolio betas tend to be more stable than individual security estimates, thus some advocate estimating the beta of a firm by using a portfolio of firms in the same industry (more on this later).

D.   Some Commercial Services - "STORE BOUGHT BETAS."

(1)   Some advocate using store bought betas, but a critical factor here is knowing what index the beta was estimated against -- many people who do valuations, inadvertently use a commercial estimate based on an index other than the S&P500 and then use the S&P500 to measure the market risk premium.

(2)   Commercial services use a common time period for estimation (e.g. 60 months of monthly data) and typically make no adjustments for recent changes in operating and financing characteristics -- the valuation expert has much more information on recent changes within the firm than is used by these commercial services which may be estimating betas on 2000 to 5000 companies.

(3)   Merrill Lynch Beta Estimates.

$$\hat{\beta}^{ML} = 0.35 + 0.65 \times \hat{\beta}^{OLS}$$

where

$$\hat{\beta}^{ML} \equiv \text{Merrill Lynch beta estimate}$$

Security Analysis: How to Analyze Accounting and Market Data to Value Securities
Robert W. Holthausen and Mark E. Zmijewski
\CH10.W51

$$\hat{\beta}_{OLS} \equiv \text{Regression estimate of beta}$$

As such, a $\hat{\beta}^{OLS}$ of 2.0 implies a $\hat{\beta}^{ML}$ of 1.65. Likewise, a $\hat{\beta}^{OLS}$ of 0.4 implies a $\hat{\beta}^{ML}$ of 0.61. (Note Bloomberg uses a very similar adjustment. Their adjustment at the time of this writing is:

$$\hat{\beta}^{Bloomberg} = 0.33 + 0.67 \times \hat{\beta}^{OLS}$$

(4) Bayesian techniques.

    (a) Adjustment to the mean beta of the market (i.e., most bayesian techniques will shade the beta estimate toward 1, just like the Merrill Lynch estimate).

    (b) Adjustment to an industry beta (either totally or partially) is an alternative. In other words, adjust to the average beta in the industry as opposed to adjusting to the average beta in the market.

(5) Some estimation techniques rely on financial data (e.g., BARRA).

(6) Many other beta estimates available as well, Value Line, Bloomberg, ALCAR, Ibbotson, etc.

(7) Here are some alternative estimates from Commercial Services

	American Express	Anheuser Busch	Apple Computer
BARRA-Historical	1.04	0.48	1.94
BARRA-Predicted	1.21	0.83	1.78
Merrill Lynch	1.11	0.48	1.99
Value Line	1.30	0.80	1.70
Wilshire-5 year	1.24	0.55	1.72
Wilshire-future	1.50	0.83	1.77

E.   Equity Cost of Capital Estimates Based on Industry Comparables.

Individual firms betas are much less precise than portfolio betas (consider the plot previously shown in Chapter 3 where the standard error of beta for one security is on average 0.22 and the standard error for a portfolio of 15 securities is on average 0.07). This translates into 95% confidence intervals that are approximately equivalent to the point estimate +/- 0.44 or +/- 0.14 (this assumes that one has estimated beta with 60 observations). For example, using these standard errors, a point estimate for beta of 1.00 has either a 95% confidence interval of 0.56 to 1.44 or 0.86 to 1.14.

Security Analysis: How to Analyze Accounting and Market Data to Value Securities
  Robert W. Holthausen and Mark E. Zmijewski
  \CH10.W51

Industry portfolio betas are potentially more accurate assessments of an individual firm's beta because of the greater precision in estimation. Thus, even if a firm has data available publicly you may still want to use a portfolio of firms for estimation purposes. If the firm you are valuing does not have data publicly available, you will have to use comparable firms to estimate your firm's beta.

How do you implement this approach?

(1)   Consider whether the firm being valued is similar to other firms in the industry or does it operate itself very differently? Is it subject to the same demand and supply shocks.

Use comparable firms, not just SIC codes to define an industry. Emphasis here is on the operating risks of the firm, not the financing risks because we can control for differences in capital structure. Is the firm in financial distress?

(2)   Examine whether the operating leverage for the two firms is similar. Operating leverage for a project is basically the ratios of the present value of the fixed costs of a project divided by the net present value of the project. A project with no fixed costs has no operating leverage. Basically trying to determine if the ratio of fixed costs to total costs for two firms is the same. This can be estimated via regression or if there is little data available, one can use two representative years to estimate.

(3)   Differences in capital structure can be controlled via levering and unlevering betas or cost of capital estimates directly (see the levering and unlevering formulas).

(4)   Estimate equity betas of industry comparables yourself or use a commercial service to obtain the estimates, but the same rationale for using your own estimates exists as before.

(5)   Once equity betas are estimated (or purchased from a commercial service) for each comparable firm, calculate each comparable firms unlevered beta (or unlevered cost of capital). The unlevering is based on each firm's capital structure and your assessment of how each firm intends to manage its capital structure.

(6)   The unlevered beta (or cost of capital) is then a mean (equal weighted, value-weighted or standard error weighted) or median of the comparable firms.

(7)   Equity betas (or the equity cost of capital) can then be derived (if required) from the unlevered beta (or unlevered cost of capital) in conjunction with the levering formulas. Application of these formulas depends on the capital structure decision of the firm being valued.

Security Analysis: How to Analyze Accounting and Market Data to Value Securities
   Robert W. Holthausen and Mark E. Zmijewski
   \CH10.W51

F. Adjusting Beta Estimates for Changes in Operating Assets

An issue which sometimes arises is that you want to adjust an estimated beta for changes in operations which take place subsequent to the time period you have used for estimation. Alternatively, suppose you have a firm which is in two lines of business and you can estimate betas for each line of business separately. The issue then is what is the firm's overall beta. In either case, adjustments can be made as long as you remember the following.

$$\beta_{\text{unlevered firm}} \quad = \quad \Sigma x_i \, \beta_i$$

where

$\beta_{\text{unlevered firm}}$ $\quad\equiv\quad$ the beta of the unlevered firm (or equivalently the firm's projects or assets).

β_i $\quad\equiv\quad$ the beta of project i of the firm.

x_i $\quad\equiv\quad$ the proportion of the market value of the unlevered firm in project i.

Understanding this relation is important because it allows us to see how betas change through various events such as acquisitions or divestitures; for example, if a firm worth $200 million dollars with an asset beta of 2.0 acquires another firm worth $100 million whose asset beta is 1.0. The asset beta of the combined firm will be 1.67 = 2/3*2.0 + 1/3*1.0.

Consider another example. Suppose a firm worth $200 million with an asset beta of 1.0 sells off $50 million dollars of marketable securities (excess cash) and distributes the cash to the shareholders. What happens to the asset beta of the firm, assuming the marketable securities had an average beta of 0.40? The asset beta of the firm should be X where 1.0 = 150/200*X + 50/200*0.40. Hence, X = 1.20.

These techniques allow you to adjust the unlevered beta. One could then estimate an equity beta by relevering the adjusted unlevered beta.

5. **Estimation Issues -- Market Risk Premium.**

A. What is $[E(R_m) - R_f]$?

Estimates of the expected market risk premium are typically determined by estimating the historical average spread between the return on the market and a proxy for risk free rates.

Security Analysis: How to Analyze Accounting and Market Data to Value Securities
  Robert W. Holthausen and Mark E. Zmijewski
  \CH10.W51

B.   Some useful data for getting started.

TOTAL ANNUAL RETURNS   1926-1997

Return Series	Geometric Mean	Arithmetic Mean	Standard Deviation
S&P500	11.0%	13.0%	20.3%
Small Stocks (Bottom Quintile of NYSE)	12.7%	17.7%	33.9%
Long Term Corp Bonds (High Grade Bond Index)	5.7%	6.1%	8.7%
Long Term Govt Bonds	5.2%	5.6%	9.2%
Inter Term Govt Bonds	5.3%	5.4%	5.7%
U.S. Treasury Bills (Rolling one-month T-Bills)	3.8%	3.8%	3.2%
Inflation	3.1%	3.2%	4.5%

C.   Things to Note.

(1)   Real returns — Historically, what has been the real gain in the purchasing power of an investment in U.S. Treasury Bills? Approximately, 0.6%

(2)   Maturity Premiums — Historically, what is the extra return associated with investing in long-term government bonds as opposed to very short term treasury bills? Approximately, 1.8%. Note however, there is no significant maturity premium offered historically between intermediate and long-term government bonds (0.2%). In fact, other evidence indicates that the maturity premium observed here is available on one-year bonds and there is no incremental maturity premium available beyond maturities of one-year.

(3)   Default Premium — Historically, what is the extra return associated with investing in long term high grade corporate bonds as opposed to long term government bonds? Approximately 0.5%.

Security Analysis: How to Analyze Accounting and Market Data to Value Securities
Robert W. Holthausen and Mark E. Zmijewski
\CH10.W51

Do not reproduce without permission.
July 30, 1998

(4)   Market Risk Premium   Historically, what is the extra return associated with investing in the S&P500 as opposed to U.S. Treasury Bills? Approximately 9.2%. But could also define the market risk premium relative to long-term government bonds.

(5)   Where is the difference between the geometric and arithmetic means the greatest? When the standard deviation of the series is the greatest.

D.   Estimating Inflation

(1)   Suppose you wanted an estimate of expected inflation for the next month. Assume that a one month T-Bill was yielding 3.6% on an annualized basis.

Some would suggest a reasonable estimate is to use the relation between inflation, real and nominal rates to estimate inflation, in particular,

Expected inflation = [(1 + Nominal rate)/(1 + Real rate)] -1.

The historical real return on U.S. Treasury Bills over the 1926-1997 period has been approximately 0.6%. A one month annualized T-Bill rate of 3.6% suggests expected inflation of (1.036/1.006) - 1.0 = 3.0% for the next month (on an annualized basis).

The exact real rate to subtract from the nominal rate is not known for certain as there is variation in real rates over time. During the 1970's, real rates on U.S. Treasury Bills were actually negative. During the 1980's real rates on U.S. Treasury Bills were extremely high.

Others have suggested using the most recent 12 month real return on Treasury Bills as opposed to the historical real return on U.S. Treasury Bills. This approach entails estimating the real return on U.S. Treasury Bills over the last 12 months and subtracting that number from the current yield. For the year ended 12/31/97, the real return on U.S. Treasury Bills was 3.5% (very high in historical terms).

(2)   Estimates of average inflation over a longer time period can be obtained in a similar fashion. The historical real return on long term U.S. Government Bonds has been approximately 2.4%. Assume 20 year government bonds were yielding approximately 6.0%, hence one estimate of the average (time weighted) expected inflation for the next 20 years (using the same formula as above is (1.06/1.024) - 1.0 = 3.5%. Again, the exact real rate to use is uncertain.

Security Analysis: How to Analyze Accounting and Market Data to Value Securities
Robert W. Holthausen and Mark E. Zmijewski
\CH10.W51

286

E.   Issues in Estimating the Market Risk Premium.

(1)   Which estimate do we use -- Arithmetic vs. Geometric Mean.

(a)   CAPM is a one-period model but it is used in a multi-period world.

(b)   Arithmetic mean return is simply the equally weighted average of the returns (monthly, yearly, etc.) over the period used for estimation.

$$\bar{R}_A = \frac{1}{T} \sum_{t=1}^{T} R_t$$

(c)   Geometric mean return is the average (monthly, yearly, etc.) compounded rate of return over the period used for estimation.

$$\bar{R}_G = \left[\prod_{t=1}^{T} (1 + R_t) \right]^{1/T} - 1$$

where $\Pi \equiv$ multiplication operator.

(d)   Choice of geometric vs. arithmetic is more critical as the volatility of the series increases. Note that the geometric mean return is always less than the arithmetic mean unless the variable is a constant.

This is an important issue as the market risk premium judged on the S&P500 would vary by 2.0% depending on whether the geometric or arithmetic mean were used to estimate it.

(e)   The arithmetic mean is the conceptually correct estimate of the mean if you believe that returns are independent through time. The geometric mean measures the historical buy and hold return an investor would have earned if they had held a particular asset, and may provide an appropriate expectation, if returns are dependent through time and if similar patterns in returns are observed. In fact, average annual returns on the S&P500 or NYSE in excess of the risk free rate are virtually uncorrelated through time (correlation of 0.01), providing strong support for use of the arithmetic mean.

The practicing profession is somewhat divided on this issue with most academics arguing for the arithmetic mean. Many practitioners use the arithmetic mean return, but there is not unanimity. Most of the major IBANKS have now switched to the arithmetic mean return.

Security Analysis: How to Analyze Accounting and Market Data to Value Securities
Robert W. Holthausen and Mark E. Zmijewski
\CH10.W51

(2) Choice of a market proxy -- Same issues as before.

    (a) Which securities should be included? S&P500, NYSE, NYSE & AMEX, indices which include bonds, real estate etc.

    (b) Weighting? Equal vs. value weighted.

    (c) What does the CAPM say about the choice theoretically?

    (d) Current practice is to use broadly based stock index, most typically the S&P500 because of availability.

    (e) Maintain consistency with index used for beta estimation.

    (f) Looming issue given globalization of the capital markets.

        Choice may depend on how freely funds can move from one country to another. For example, suppose funds invested in the U.S.S.R. cannot be removed. For funds internally reinvested in the U.S.S.R., then the opportunity cost of funds is determined solely by opportunity costs measured there. For example, the Moscow McDonald's will not be able to easily move profits outside of Russia.

        If funds can be freely moved between countries, then opportunity costs may be more appropriately defined through some type of global index.

    (g) Data on market returns in various countries is improving, but at this time there is not nearly as much data (both types of securities and length of return series) on other countries as on the U.S. securities markets. The Morgan Stanley Capital International series is one such data base which provides returns by country.

(3) Time Period for Estimation.

    (a) Data quirks -- it is useful to thoroughly understand the details underlying data to be used. For example, from 1940 to 1953 U.S. Treasury Bill rates were set by the government and not by a free market. Thus, T-Bill rates may not have been able to vary with expected inflation during that period. Thus, using interest rates on U.S. Treasury Bills subsequent to 1953 may be more appropriate for some purposes.

    (b) Short vs. long horizons -- If you believe the distribution of the market risk premium is stationary, then you would want to use the longest time series available. However, some advocate that the market risk premium should be based on a shorter horizon, say the last 20 years, because they are not convinced the market risk premium is stationary (ALCAR). Using the last 20 years of data can provide a very different estimate of the market risk premium than using the period since 1926. If one based the market risk premium on the arithmetic mean for the prior 20 years, market risk premium estimates (calculated relative to the returns on U.S. T-Bills) would have ranged between 1.9% and 16.6% using the data from 1926-1997. If one were to use the most recent 20 years, the arithmetic market risk premium (relative to T-Bills) would be 10.0% compared to 9.2% using the 1926-1997 period.

We suggest assuming that the market risk premium is stationary through time and that you use the maximum amount of data available to estimate the market risk premium. Using the arithmetic mean yields a market risk premium estimate of 9.2% (relative to U.S. Treasury Bills). The last 70 years of history has included wars, peacetime, expansion, recession, major oil shocks, major changes in world governments, bull markets, bear markets, market crashes, etc. Since these are all hard to predict, a history which includes all of these events is relevant. Using data for the past 200 years in this country yields similar estimates of the market risk premium (though the data is not nearly as good going back far in time).

This of course becomes difficult to implement in countries with short market histories.

(4)   Variation through time.

    (a)   Does the market risk premium vary through time? Yes, but it is only predictable for at most four years. Models based on market dividend yields seem to have reasonable predictive power (adjusted R^2's of 50%). At this time, it is rare in practice to estimate varying market risk premiums when applying the CAPM. For company valuation, there is little to be gained in attempting to consider time series variation in market risk premiums. There may be merit in attempting to estimate differential risk premiums through time if you are valuing very short lived assets (e.g., not companies).

    (b)   Evidence suggests that the expected return on the stock market varies inversely with expected inflation, but the adjusted R^2's of these regressions are approximately 3%. Thus periods of high expected inflation lead to relatively high Treasury Bill rates, low expected returns on common stocks and thus, relatively low market risk premiums. In practice, most still assume a constant risk premium which does not vary with expected inflation, especially in valuations of long term assets.

    (c)   Evidence indicates a very weak relation between expected return on the market and anticipated market volatility, however the latter is very difficult to measure and hence this is currently not a fruitful path.

Security Analysis: How to Analyze Accounting and Market Data to Value Securities
Robert W. Holthausen and Mark E. Zmijewski
\CH10.W51

Do not reproduce without permission.
July 30, 1998

289

F. Choice of a proxy for the risk free rate in estimating the market risk premium.

(a) Market risk premiums are also often measured relative to long-term government bonds. If one pursues this alternative, one has to decide whether to just calculate the income returns on government bonds or whether to include the total return.

You will see some estimates of the market risk premium using the long-term government bond yield as the risk free rate and using the historical arithmetic mean difference between the market index (like the S&P500) and the total return on long-term government bonds. The historical risk premium measured this way is 7.4%. Another alternative is the procedure recommended by Ibbotson Associates. They calculate the risk premium from the historical mean arithmetic difference between the S&P500 and the income returns of Long-Term Government Bonds, yielding a 7.8% market risk premium.

(b) Some do not advocate using long-term government bonds because there is inflation risk associated with those instruments, hence they are not risk-free (there is potential inflation risk with one-month U.S. Treasury Bills, but the risk is rather small, especially since the series is being rolled over monthly). The market risk premium is often measured relative to U.S. Treasury Bills, because they are the most risk free asset available. The historical difference in returns between the S&P500 and U.S. Treasury Bills has been 9.2%.

(c) If one were to calculate the market risk premium between the S&P500 and the total return on intermediate term bonds based on the historical arithmetic mean difference, the resulting risk premium is 7.6%. The premium based off the S&P500 and intermediate term government bond income returns is 8.2%.

G. Some market risk premium estimation choices by those in the practice of valuation.

(1) Stern Stewart and Company (according to the Quest for Value, by G. Bennett Stewart, III uses a 6% market risk premium when using 20 year U.S. Treasury Bonds as the risk free instrument.

(2) McKinsey Company, according to Tom Copeland, Tim Koller and Jack Murrin in Valuation: Measuring and Managing the Value of Companies recommends using a market risk premium of 5% to 6%. This is based on the belief that the geometric mean return is a better estimate of the market risk premium than the arithmetic mean return. Moreover, they believe a long time period should be used to estimate the risk premium and appear to use data back to 1926 available from Ibbotson Associates in drawing their conclusions.

Security Analysis: How to Analyze Accounting and Market Data to Value Securities
Robert W. Holthausen and Mark E. Zmijewski
\CH10.W51

(3)   Ibbotson recommends the mean arithmetic difference between the S&P500 and the income returns on either the long-term or intermediate term government bonds, depending on the duration of the cash flows you are valuing (7.8% and 8.2% respectively).

6.   Estimation Issues -- Risk Free Rate

A.   Choice of a proxy for the risk free rate.

How you define the market risk premium affects how you define the risk free rate.

(1)   U.S. Treasury Bills are proxies for the risk free return over a very short period. Are U.S. Treasury Bills risk-free? Default free maybe, but certainly not totally risk free. There is risk of unexpected shifts in real rates of return and inflation, but that risk is minor in a strategy of rolling over one-month Treasury Bills.

(2)   When valuing a firm or a project with a relatively long horizon, it is probably better to use a longer term proxy for the risk free return, to capture the market's long term assessment of the risk free rate. In this case, we can use intermediate or long-term government bonds.

(3)   If we estimate the market risk premium as 9.2% (the mean arithmetic difference between the S&P500 and U.S. Treasury Bills), one has to subtract the maturity premium from the yield on the intermediate term or long term government bond (whatever you are using) because these instruments contain a maturity premium relative to U.S. Treasury Bills, and that must be subtracted from their yields to estimate the long-term risk free rate of return. This premium reflects the extra risk associated with being invested in a fixed nominal payoff security for a longer period which is not an issue with common stock.

The maturity premium on long-term government bonds over Treasury Bills has been approximately 1.4% (based on income returns, not total returns). Therefore, if the yield on a long-term government bond today were 6.2%, the appropriate estimate of the risk free rate for use in the CAPM would be 6.2% - 1.4% = 4.8%.

If you were using an intermediate government bond (three to ten years), the maturity premium (based on income returns) has been 1.0%, thus we would subtract 1.0% from the yield on an intermediate term government bond to determine the risk free rate of return for that period.

(4)   What is our forecast horizon? If using a single discount rate, choose an instrument whose <u>duration</u> is similar to the cash flows being forecast. **If you are valuing a company and are discounting flows over many future years, you are probably best served by choosing an intermediate or long term government bond.**

Security Analysis: How to Analyze Accounting and Market Data to Value Securities
Robert W. Holthausen and Mark E. Zmijewski
\CH10.W51

(5)   If using varying discount rates for cash flows received in different years, one might use a continuum of risk free rates where each is obtained from a government bond with the appropriate duration. This approach is seldom used.

(6)   Using different rates may be appropriate when the yield curve is steeply sloped or where the risk of the firm is changing.

B.   Date of Yield Estimation

The estimated yield for the risk free rate should be based on the date your valuation is effective. For example, if you are estimating the value of a company as of **today**, the relevant yield is what is the current yield on the appropriate term government security. If you have decided to use a 20 year U.S. Government Bond as your proxy for the risk free rate, you would determine the current yield on a 20 year government bond to estimate R_f **today**.

7.   **Putting It All Together -- Some Common Estimation Techniques.**

A.   Define the market risk premium relative to long-term (7.8%) or intermediate-term government bonds (8.2%), based on income returns only. Estimate the risk free rate using the current yield on the U.S. Government instrument of the appropriate duration (long-term or intermediate-term).

(1)   Assume 10 year U.S. Government bonds yield about 6.0%. Therefore, the CAPM estimate would be: $Ke = 6.0\% + Beta * 8.2\%$.

(2)   Assume 25 year U.S. Government bonds yield about 6.5%. Therefore, the CAPM estimate would be: $Ke = 6.5\% + Beta * 7.8\%$

B.   Define the market risk premium relative to U.S. Treasury Bills (9.2%). Estimate the risk free rate using the current yield on a Government instrument of the appropriate duration (long-term or intermediate term) and subtract the average maturity premium for the long-term (1.4%) or intermediate term (1.0%) based on income returns to obtain the estimate of the risk free rate of return.

(1)   Assume 10 year U.S. Government bonds yield about 6.0%. Therefore, after subtracting the 1.0% average maturity premium for intermediate bonds over treasury bills, the CAPM estimate would be: $Ke = 6.0\%-1.0\% + Beta * 9.2\%$.

(2)   Assume 25 year U.S. Government bonds yield about 6.5%. Therefore, after subtracting the 1.4% average maturity premium for long-term bonds over treasury bills, the CAPM estimate would be: $Ke = 6.5\%-1.4\% + Beta * 9.2\%$.

Security Analysis: How to Analyze Accounting and Market Data to Value Securities
Robert W. Holthausen and Mark E. Zmijewski
\CH10.W51

Suppose you obtained the following estimates of the betas of the following stocks:

Stock	Beta
AT&T	0.81
DEC	1.21
MCI	1.52
Compaq	1.73
Genentech	1.95

Assume yields on 25 year U.S. Government Bonds are approximately 6.4% and that we have decided to estimate the market risk premium as the historical difference between the S&P 500 and U.S. Treasury Bills (9.2%). Subtracting the 1.4% maturity premium on U.S. long-term bonds vs. U.S. treasury bills bonds yields a risk free rate of 5.00%. Assume that the market risk premium is expected to remain at its long term historical arithmetic average relative to U.S. Treasury Bills (9.2%). A long term estimate of the cost of equity capital for these firms would be

Stock	Equity Beta	Cost of Equity Capital $R_f + Beta (R_m - R_f)$
AT&T	0.81	12.45%
DEC	1.21	16.13%
MCI	1.52	18.98%
Compaq	1.73	20.92%
Genentech	1.95	22.94%

Remember these are estimates of the cost of equity capital for these firms which in part reflects their capital structure. Choosing a lower market risk premium would obviously lower the estimates of the cost of equity capital. These are not estimates of the weighted average cost of capital or unlevered cost of capital for these firms.

If we were to go through this same exercise defining the market risk premium relative to long-term government bonds (7.8%), the estimates we would obtain would be:

Stock	Equity Beta	Cost of Equity Capital $R_f + Beta (R_m - R_f)$
AT&T	0.81	12.71%
DEC	1.21	15.83%
MCI	1.52	18.25%
Compaq	1.73	19.89%
Genentech	1.95	21.61%

Security Analysis: How to Analyze Accounting and Market Data to Value Securities
  Robert W. Holthausen and Mark E. Zmijewski
  \CH10.W51

8.   Privately Held Firms and the Equity Cost of Capital.

A.   First ascertain the purpose of the valuation of the private company. If the company is being taken public through an IPO, it is not relevant to assess the cost of capital presuming that the company is private. Instead, it should be viewed as a public company. Here, techniques like the CAPM are appropriate. On the other hand, if you are valuing a private company for a purchaser who is going to keep it as a private company and who is going to be poorly diversified because of the purchase, then the valuation should consider that it is a private company. This would determine the value of the company to the purchaser, not the value of the company if it were held in a well diversified portfolio. Note, if the cost of capital is much higher under this scenario for a private company, it isn't clear that this individual would be able to purchase the business because others may be willing to bid more for it.

The CAPM (like all modern asset pricing theories such as the APT which we will shortly discuss) relies on diversification as a key element in the pricing of securities and assumes that the firms shares are perfectly marketable. How does one then estimate the cost of equity capital for the owner of a private company who has a majority of his/her wealth tied up in the assets of an enterprise, or for a private company where the shares are not liquid. To the extent the CAPM relies on diversification and assumes perfectly marketable assets, one can argue that pricing the security based on using the CAPM may sometimes not be appropriate. Evidence in a variety of academic articles indicates that less liquid stocks have higher costs of capital than that predicted by the CAPM.

If one wanted to stay within the spirit of the CAPM, one could estimate the cost of equity capital using the variance of the stock rather than its beta. Remember that the equation of the capital market line

$$E(\widetilde{R}_p) = R_f + \frac{E(\widetilde{R}_m) - R_f}{\sigma(\widetilde{R}_m)} \sigma(\widetilde{R}_p)$$

indicates what the expected return on a portfolio should be given its variance. Since private companies don't have publicly traded stocks, one would have to estimate the variance by observing publicly traded firms that are in the same industry.

B.   Data on Discounts for Lack of Marketability

Shannon P. Pratt in his book <u>Valuing a Business: The Analysis and Appraisal of Closely Held Companies</u> (Chapter 10, "Data on Discounts for Lack of Marketability", discusses the topic of discounting the value of the firm due to the lack of marketability of the shares for firms which are private.

Security Analysis: How to Analyze Accounting and Market Data to Value Securities
    Robert W. Holthausen and Mark E. Zmijewski
\CH10.W51

Do not reproduce without permission.
July 30, 1998

294

(1)   Studies on Restricted Stock

One source of data on the lack of marketability is data on letter stock transactions. Letter stock is identical to the shares of a public company in all respects, except that there are restrictions on trading that security in the open market for a certain period. The duration of the restrictions vary across issues.

A 1971 SEC institutional investor study documented the size of discounts for restricted stocks by size of company and exchange on which the public shares traded. Discounts were greatest for OTC companies, next largest for AMEX securities and smallest for NYSE companies. Average discounts across all of these markets was 25.8%. Discounts on the NYSE companies were between 10% and 30% over half of the time. Discounts on the ASE companies were between 20% and 40% over half of the time. Discounts on the OTC companies were between 10% and 40% over half of the time.

In another study on restricted securities, Milton Gelman found that median discounts were 33% on restricted stock. Robert Moroney found median discounts of 33% in a 146 transactions where registered investment companies bought large blocks of restricted securities.

(2)   Studies on IPOs shortly after a private sale of stock

One disadvantage of the restricted stock studies is that they may understate the discount, since the restrictions on marketability are just temporary. Two studies, one using data from 1980 to 1981 and one using data from 1985-1986 examined cases where a company went public within five months of selling some common stock in a private sale. In the 1980 to 1981 study, the mean (median) discount from the IPO price was 60% (66%). In the study using study from 1985-1986, the mean (median) discount from the IPO price was 43% (43%). In all cases, the fair market value was approved by the Board of Directors (but are these truly arms-length transactions?) Moreover, did they go public because prospects changed?

(3)   Tax Court Decisions on Lack of Marketability

Data on discounts for lack of marketability from court decisions in the U.S. clearly accept the notion that there are discounts for lack of marketability (though remember, the outcome of court decisions need not reflect appropriate economic treatment). It is not uncommon to observe discounts ranging from 35% to 50% in these cases.

(4)   Use of this Data

The way in which these discounts for lack of marketability are applied in practice is that a valuation is done first assuming the company is publicly traded. Thus, the CAPM is routinely used for determining the cost of capital. Then, the value obtained from the CAPM estimate, is reduced for the lack of marketability by applying the information on discounts resulting from these studies.

Security Analysis: How to Analyze Accounting and Market Data to Value Securities
Robert W. Holthausen and Mark E. Zmijewski
\CH10.W51

It should be noted that many different things are done in practice. In some cases, the value of the firm is calculated based on an estimate of the cost of capital from a model like the CAPM, and then a premium is added to the value of the firm for the fact that an individual has complete control over the firm. These premiums for control are often in the 10% to 20% range.

C.   Other Considerations with Private Companies

One final issue should be mentioned in passing (though this does not really belong here). In valuing private companies, some attention to the tax status of the private company should be considered. Suppose for example, a Corporation has Subchapter S status, which means that it is not taxed on income at the corporate level, but is taxed at the individual level. Therefore, suppose as an investor in the corporation (assuming you own all of the corporation), that you are debating making the firm an all equity firm vis-a-vis one with debt and equity. For simplicity, assume you will hold all of the claims. Under this scenario, there is no tax on either debt or equity at the corporate level and there is tax at the personal level on both. Moreover, you cannot postpone the tax on equity because the profits of the corporation are taxed at the personal level. In this situation, it should be clear that there is no tax advantage of debt.

9.   The Equity Cost of Capital, Firm Size and Other Anomalies.

A.   Early Tests of Sharpe-Lintner.

Early tests of the CAPM did not support the model perfectly, but there was clearly a very strong association between beta and expected return, but as discussed in Chapter 3, researchers have provided strong evidence that small firms outperform large firms on a risk-adjusted basis. Interestingly, a large portion (and maybe all) of the size effect occurs in the month of January. The other months do not indicate nearly as severe departures from the CAPM. In fact, some researchers have concluded that there is no size effect other than in the month of January.

One interpretation of this evidence is that the CAPM is not measuring expected returns properly. The other, is that the market was not efficient with respect to pricing small stocks.

At present, we have no acceptable theory which explains the mispricing in the CAPM with respect to size. Most researchers do not think that size per se matters. Rather, to the extent they believe the size effect, they believe that size proxies for some element of risk which is priced, but not included in the CAPM. A variety of explanations for the size effect have been considered, including: bid-ask spreads, taxes, transactions costs and others. To date we have no satisfactory explanation for the phenomenon.

B.   Other correlated variables.

You will no doubt read about other anomalies (besides size) in the popular press.

Security Analysis: How to Analyze Accounting and Market Data to Value Securities
Robert W. Holthausen and Mark E. Zmijewski
\CH10.W51

Examples include the following.

(a)   P/E ratios.
(b)   Market/Book ratios.
(c)   Dividend Yield.
(d)   Price.

However, these variables are each correlated with size, so in large part we are simply "rediscovering" the size effect. The debate about which variable subsumes the other rages.

A recent paper by Eugene Fama and Kenneth French entitled " A Cross-Section of Expected Stock Returns" received considerable attention in the non-academic press in 1991. In their paper, they claim that size and book-to-market equity ratios combine to capture all of the cross-sectional variation in average stock returns associated with market beta, size, leverage, book-to-market equity and earnings-price ratios. Like the empirical work on size, their results have implications for estimating the cost of capital. However, that has not been well fleshed out at this time. As the authors themselves state in discussing estimating the cost of capital with their model, "We predict, however, that sampling error will be a serious problem in the parameter estimates for individual securities."

C.   Using Firm Size to Estimate the Cost of Capital.

One reason for us to be interested in the size effect, is that it represents another means for determining a firm's equity cost of capital. Given the clear relation between size and returns, an alternative technique for determining a firm's cost of capital is to add the typical risk premium (above a risk free rate) for the size decile of which the firm is currently a member, to the current risk free rate. That is

Equity cost of capital $= R_f +$ Appropriate size decile risk premium

This is admittedly ad hoc and requires some approximate knowledge of how large the firm is. Would probably have to use a price multiple technique to approximate the market value in the absence of any other indication. Of course, if the firm grows through time sufficiently quickly to change deciles, this technique suggests that the required rate of return would decline through time.

As an example, the arithmetic mean return on firms in the ninth decile of the NYSE has been 18.2% (through 12/31/97) Geometric mean returns have been 12.5% for ninth decile firms. U.S. Treasury Bills over this period have earned 3.8% (arithmetic mean). Therefore, the 9th decile risk premium (relative to U.S. Treasury Bills) has been 14.4% (arithmetic mean). If long term government bonds were yielding 6.85%, this would suggest that the equity cost of capital for firms in the 9th decile of firm size (defining the market risk premium relative to U.S. Treasury Bills) is 19.85% = (6.85%-1.4%) + 14.4% (using the arithmetic mean risk premium).

Security Analysis: How to Analyze Accounting and Market Data to Value Securities
Robert W. Holthausen and Mark E. Zmijewski
\CH10.W51

Do not reproduce without permission.
July 30, 1998

297

Another alternative would be to estimate the cost of capital from the standard CAPM and add or subtract the historical deviation from CAPM pricing for firm of that size.

$$E(\tilde{R}_i) = R_f + \beta_i [E(\tilde{R}_m) - R_f] + \text{adjustment for historical size mispricing.}$$

To see how this might work examine the arithmetic mean returns for deciles firm size in the Ibbotson Data (data from January, 1926 through December 31, 1997--data primarily gives estimates of expected returns and firm size by decile of the NYSE, only since 1982 does the data reflect returns earned on the American Stock Exchange and OTC companies).

Decile	Arithmetic Mean	Size Premium to S&P 500	Size Premium to CAPM	Common Stock Market Cap (Largest Firm)
1-Largest	11.98%	-1.02%	-0.30%	222,298,251,000
2	13.69%	0.69%	0.42%	8,647,751,000
3	14.29%	1.29%	0.65%	4,013,856,000
4	15.00%	2.00%	1.04%	2,346,253,000
5	15.75%	2.75%	1.56%	1,358,517,000
6	15.82%	2.82%	1.45%	945,146,000
7	16.39%	3.39%	1.60%	656,601,000
8	17.46%	4.46%	2.36%	431,840,000
9	18.21%	5.21%	2.56%	261,261,000
10-Small	21.83%	8.83%	5.36%	130,402,000
Mid-Cap	14.76%	1.76%	0.92%	4,013,856,000
Low-Cap	16.33%	3.33%	1.68%	945,146,000
Micro	19.17%	6.17%	3.30%	261,261,000

Using this data one could calculate the CAPM return and then add the size premium to the S&P 500 as the adjustment. Of course, one needs to have a gross idea of what the value of your firm's equity is (probably use a price multiple to approximate).

For example, if you had a 9th decile firm whose Beta was 1.2, what would you do? If LT Government bonds were yielding 6.85% this would suggest an equity cost of capital (defining the market risk premium relative to U.S. Treasury Bills) of 19.05% = (6.85% - 1.4%) + 1.2 (9.2%) + 2.56%.

Security Analysis: How to Analyze Accounting and Market Data to Value Securities
Robert W. Holthausen and Mark E. Zmijewski
\CH10.W51

Could also calculate cost of capital adjustments using Mid-Cap (stocks in portfolios 3-5), Low-Cap (portfolios 6-8) and Micro-Cap (portfolios 9 and 10) with no adjustment from the CAPM for portfolios 1 & 2 (the procedure recommended by Ibbotson to the extent one wants to implement a firm size adjustment). For a 9th decile firm this would imply (using the example from the paragraph above) an equity cost of capital of 19.79% = (6.85% - 1.4%) + 1.2 (9.2%) + 3.30%.

Note that we have still been using arithmetic means to do all this instead of geometric means, which assumes that returns are reasonably independent through time. Note that returns are reasonably independent overall for the NYSE or S&P500 (correlation of 0.01) which is why we support using the arithmetic mean. It should be noted however that correlations for portfolios 8, 9 and 10 start to increase (0.1, 0.1 and 0.18 respectively). While these correlations are statistically significant, understand the implication. A time series correlation of 0.1 (0.2) would imply that 1% (4%) of future variation in the portfolio's return could be explained by past behavior, indicating that use of the arithmetic mean return is probably still warranted for even these portfolios.

At this time, it is not clear that the firm-size adjustment to the CAPM is a reasonable adjustment to make to the CAPM. The original paper documenting this phenomenon was published by Rolf Banz in 1981. The interpretation of this evidence by academics was that it could have been due to a risk factor that the CAPM didn't incorporate correctly, or it could have been due to a market inefficiency. Since 1980, the size premium of the mid-cap portfolio has been 0.1%, the size premium of the low-cap portfolio has been 0.0% and the size premium for the micro-cap portfolio has been -1.2%. Thus, there has been no evidence of a size effect since the original Banz paper was circulated. This is consistent with two interpretations, either the size premium represented a prior capital market inefficiency that has been corrected, or it represented an element of risk that was formerly priced, but is no longer priced (perhaps, because capital markets have become more efficient and the liquidity of small-cap stocks has improved sufficiently to eliminate some prior risk factor). Under either interpretation, addition of the size adjustment to the CAPM would be unwarranted. Another potential interpretation is that the premium still exists, but by chance, is has not been observed over the past 14 years.

10.   **Arbitrage Pricing Theory.**

A.   The APT is an equilibrium pricing model that has become a strong competitor for the Sharpe-Lintner CAPM. As such, it is another contending model to estimate the cost of equity capital.

B.   The Model.

Assumes that expected rates of return are influenced by more than one factor; for example, suppose that there are four factors labeled one to four.

Security Analysis: How to Analyze Accounting and Market Data to Value Securities
    Robert W. Holthausen and Mark E. Zmijewski
    \CH10.W51

The APT states:

$$E(R_j) = R_f + \beta_{j1} [E(RF_1) - R_f] + \ .... \ + \beta_{j4} [E(RF_4) - R_f]$$

where

$E(R_j)$	$\equiv$	expected return on security j.
R_f	$\equiv$	risk free rate of return.
β_{jk}	$\equiv$	the sensitivity of asset j to factor k (i.e., the covariance of asset j's returns with changes in factor k).
$E(RF_k)$	$\equiv$	expected return on a portfolio with an average sensitivity to factor k

BUT, the APT identifies neither the number of factors nor the economic nature of those factors.

C. Pre-specification of factors.

Recently, users of the APT have just posited a set of economic factors that they believe influence expected returns and they then use those returns in multi-index models. The economic factors or "forces" typically include:

(1) Industrial production.

(2) Inflation.

(3) The spread between long and short term bonds.

(4) The spread between high and low grade bonds.

Pre-specification of the factors has become the technique of choice for APT researchers attempting to reach the practicing (and paying) audience. Inspiration for the factors (such as inflation, and general economic conditions) that might or should influence returns are obtained more from intuition and experience with data than from rigorous economic analysis.

To implement the APT using prespecification of factors one has to identify the risk premium associated with each factor and then to determine the sensitivity of a stock to each factor. This is analogous to estimating the beta of a stock and the market risk premium when using the CAPM.

(a) To calculate the risk premium associated with each factor, construct a portfolio of stocks which are perfectly correlated with the underlying

Security Analysis: How to Analyze Accounting and Market Data to Value Securities
Robert W. Holthausen and Mark E. Zmijewski
\CH10.W51

Do not reproduce without permission.
July 30, 1998

300

factor of interest, so called "mimicking portfolios" which are uncorrelated with the other factors. Then the historical return on these portfolios in excess of the risk free rate of interest is the risk premium for that factor.

(b) Next, estimate the sensitivity of a stock to each of the factors. This can be accomplished by either estimating the sensitivity to the factor perse or to the mimicking portfolio. This is done in a manner similar to estimating the beta of a firm with respect to the market, except we now identify the sensitivity to all the identified factors.

(c) Finally, the expected return is calculated simply by plugging into the APT formula, the current risk free rate of interest, a stock's sensitivity to each of the factors and the risk premium associated with each factor.

D. Is The APT Usable?

APT is the first serious competitor to the S-L CAPM

We are now beginning to see the APT used in practice. It has started to appear in testimony relating to rate of return regulation.

APT also appears in a new release of ALCAR to determine the cost of capital. Now the user of ALCAR can choose between an APT cost of capital or a CAPM cost of capital.

11. Another Alternative Cost of Equity Estimate -- Constant Dividend Growth Model.

A. If we assume that a firm's dividend will grow by a constant proportion each year, then it is true that the price per share of the firm is equal to

$$P_0 = DIV_1 / (k_E - g)$$

where

P_0 $\equiv$ the price per share of the firm's stock today.

DIV_1 $\equiv$ the expected dividend per share for the next year.

k_E $\equiv$ the cost of equity capital.

g $\equiv$ the expected annual growth rate in dividends.

B. Rearranging this equation suggests that the cost of equity capital is

$$k_E = g + (DIV_1 / P_0)$$

where DIV_1 / P_0 is often referred to as the firm's dividend yield.

Security Analysis: How to Analyze Accounting and Market Data to Value Securities
Robert W. Holthausen and Mark E. Zmijewski
\CH10.W51

C.   This formulation is a simplification in that it assumes that the firm's dividends will grow by the same amount per year, FOREVER. As such, this alternative only provides reasonable estimates for firms which are very stable relatively low growth companies.

One would never estimate the cost of equity capital for a firm that had experienced recent high growth in dividends using this formulation. More often this is used for firms which are relatively low growing high dividend yielding securities (e.g., many utilities).

As such, we don't generally recommend the use of this constant dividend growth model as a means of estimating the cost of equity capital. Despite our lack of faith in this model, on occasion you will see it used to derive estimates of the cost of equity capital in valuation work.

D.   Consider the following example (stolen from Brealey and Myers).

At the beginning of 1986 Sears Roebuck was selling for $45 per share and the dividend payments expected in 1986 were $1.76. Thus, Sears Roebuck's dividend yield was $1.76/$45.00 which equals 3.9%.

The question then becomes what is Sears growth rate in dividends expected to be.

One way to estimate the growth rate is to use the historic growth rate in dividends if you thought that was a good indicator of the future.

An alternative way to estimate the growth rate is to determine what proportion of earnings Sears reinvests in the company (the so-called plowback ratio) and multiply it by Sear Roebuck's return on equity.

Plowback ratio = 1 - dividend payout ratio = $1 - DIV_1/EPS_1$, where EPS_1 is the expected earnings per share for this year.

For Sears the plowback ratio = 1 - ($1.76/$3.90) = 1 - 45% = 55%, because EPS was expected to be $3.90 in 1986.

The return on equity is given by the following, ROE = EPS_1 / Book Equity per share. For Sears the Book Equity per share at the beginning of 1986 is approximately $30.00, so ROE = $3.90/ $30.00 = 13%.

Therefore the growth rate g = plowback ratio X ROE = 55% X 13% =   7.2%

As such, the cost of equity capital for Sears is approximately 3.9% + 7.2% = 11.1%.

12.   Summary -- Cost of Equity Capital

At this time, there are several alternatives for estimating the cost of equity capital. For purposes of this course, we rely primarily on the CAPM. However, a variety of other means exist for

Security Analysis: How to Analyze Accounting and Market Data to Value Securities
Robert W. Holthausen and Mark E. Zmijewski
\CH10.W51
Do not reproduce without permission.
July 30, 1998

estimating the cost of equity capital. The primary alternatives to the CAPM that are used in valuation work at this time are estimates derived from Arbitrage Pricing Theory (ALCAR) and estimates based on firm size.

13. **The Cost of Straight-Debt Capital**

    A.   The cost of debt (the borrowing rate) is related to the probability of default of a given issue. Default is associated with the riskiness of the firm's cash flows and the leverage ratio the firm maintains. Debt ratings by rating agencies such as Moody's, Standard and Poor's and Fitch's, provide assessments of the default risk associated with debt issues.

        (1)   Firms with higher debt ratings have lower probabilities of default and can issue debt at lower cost.

        (2)   So called junk bonds (high grade equity) carry low ratings and are issued at relatively high interest rates. Junks bonds default more often than high grade bonds.

        (3)   As firms approach bankruptcy, their debt begins to behave more like common stock.

    B.   Estimates of the cost of debt can be readily obtained in a variety of ways if the firm has publicly traded debt.

        (1)   If the firm has publicly traded debt, you can determine the yield on that debt and often will be able to determine the rating of that debt if it is rated by one of the rating agencies. Sources for yields include many daily financial newspapers. More extensive data on yields are available from sources like "Bloomberg's", Moody's Bond Record and Standard and Poor's Bond Guide.

        (2)   On occasion a firm will have publicly rated debt, but you will not be able to find a yield on the debt. In that case use the average yield on companies with similar ratings. That information can be obtained from sources like Moody's Bond Record and Standard and Poor's Bond Guide.

    C.   Estimates of the cost of debt can still be obtained for firms which don't have publicly traded debt by examining the cost of debt capital associated with recent debt issues by firms which have similar likelihoods of default.

        (1)   Debt ratings by Moody's, Standard and Poor's and others are one way to choose firms of equivalent default risk to the firm of interest. In order to implement this, you need a model to estimate the rating of a company given its financial statements.

            (a)   A model of this type was presented in Chapter 7.

Security Analysis: How to Analyze Accounting and Market Data to Value Securities
Robert W. Holthausen and Mark E. Zmijewski
\CH10.W51

(b)   The ALCAR cost of capital module includes such a model.

(c)   Stern Stewart & Co. has a model called the Stern Stewart & Co. Bond Rating System which is part of their PC software system called FINANSEER™, which is a valuation package. The Stern Stewart bond rating model is discussed in detail (including definitions of the variables, their associated coefficients and the cutoff-scores for predicting various ratings in The Quest for Value by G. Bennett Stewart, III (pp. 396-408).

(d)   Statistics published by various agencies (for example Credit Stats by Standard and Poor's) would allow you to classify a company's debt using a firm's financial ratios.

(2)   If the firm has recently issued debt, whether public or not, the yield on that debt can serve as a mechanism for estimating the current cost of debt, assuming that there have been no major shifts in the leverage and operations of the firm as well as no major shifts in economy wide interest rates.

D.   The yields on debt calculated in all financial publications (of which we are aware) are always promised yields. Promised yields are the yield associated with debt **assuming all of the payments required under a debt instrument are made on a timely basis.** Bonds can be readily valued by discounting promised payments by the yield-to-maturity (which is not the expected yield or expected return on the debt). However, the expected yield on a debt instrument (or expected return), which is really the appropriate cost of debt capital, allows for some probability of default. Using promised yields as the cost of debt capital essentially assumes that the debt is free of default risk. Unfortunately expected yields on debt are not observable. It should be obvious that the difference between promised yields and expected yields increases with default risk.

If one could estimate the default probability associated with a bonds payments, you could simply substitute the expected payments for the promised payments and solve for the yield which equates the current price with the expected payments. Conceivably, one could obtain data on default by ratings and make differential adjustments as a function of rating class.

Most people engaged in valuation work do not typically calculate expected yields directly, either because they don't know the expected default rate associated with a particular issue, what the value of the bond would be if it were in default and potentially what the current price of the bond is. As such, more heuristic approaches are used. For example, McKinsey & Company (according to Valuation: Measuring and Managing the Value of Companies by Tom Copeland, Tim Koller and Jack Murrin) uses the actual promised yield to maturity for any bond rated BBB or higher, and uses the promised yield to maturity on BBB bonds for all bonds rated below BBB. This has obvious pitfalls in that it implies there is no increase in expected returns for debt as it becomes more risky below BBB. Nevertheless, it demonstrates the point of distinguishing promised and expected yields.

Security Analysis: How to Analyze Accounting and Market Data to Value Securities
  Robert W. Holthausen and Mark E. Zmijewski
\CH10.W51

I have however, recently seen a study which estimates the following adjustments to observed yields to obtain expected returns (view these as crude estimates).

Rating	Adjustment to Yield
AAA (Aaa)	0.01%
AA (Aa)	0.03%
A (A)	0.08%
BBB (Baa)	0.17%
BB (Ba)	0.50%
B (B)	1.34%
CCC (Caa)	2.36%
CC (Ca)	3.77%
C (C)	5.57%

To use these take the promised yield and subtract the adjustment to yield to calculate the expected return.

E.   Other debt which has "caps", "collar", conversion features, etc. contain components that have option like characteristics. We often deal with these issues by analyzing the straight-debt and option like characteristics separately. Thus, the value of the straight-debt and option components are valued separately and the appropriate cost of capital for each separate component are applied to each. Courses in options and in financial instruments address the issue of valuing these more complicated debt instruments.

14.   Measurement Issues in Estimating WACC.

A.   Introduction

As discussed previously, the weighted average cost of capital is the method used for calculating the adjusted discount rate. The adjusted cost of capital method or weighted average cost of capital is not easy to implement in all situations. The adjusted cost of capital method is most easily implemented when it is assumed that the firm manages the capital structure to have a constant debt to value ratio.

The weighted average cost of capital (including preferred) is defined as:

$$WACC_t = . \ k_{Et} \ (E_t/V_t) \ + \ k_{Dt} \ (1\text{-}T) \ (D_t/V_t) \ + \ k_{Rt} \ (R_t/V_t)$$

where $WACC_t$ =   the weighted average cost of capital at time t (adjusted discount rate)

k_{Et} =   cost of equity capital at time t

k_{Dt} =   cost of debt capital at time t

Security Analysis: How to Analyze Accounting and Market Data to Value Securities
Robert W. Holthausen and Mark E. Zmijewski
\CH10.W51

$$k_{R_t} \quad = \quad \text{cost of preferred capital at time t}$$

$$R_t \quad = \quad \text{market value of the preferred at time t}$$

$$E_t \quad = \quad \text{market value of the equity at time t}$$

$$D_t \quad = \quad \text{market value of the debt at time t}$$

$$V_t \quad = \quad \text{market value of the firm at time } t = E_t + D_t + R_t$$

$$T \quad = \quad \text{the appropriate tax rate for calculating the value of the}$$
interest tax shield of the debt.

The weighted average cost of capital is the average cost of capital for the firm as a whole given a capital structure.

Note that the weighted average cost of capital is just a weighted average of the cost of equity, debt and other forms of capital. The cost of debt capital is multiplied by (1-T) in order to reduce the effective cost of debt capital because of the tax deductibility of interest.

NOTE: k_E, k_D and k_R change as leverage changes.

As leverage goes up, the cost of equity capital, cost of debt capital and cost of preferred capital increase.

Avoid the common error of applying one estimate of k_E, k_D and k_R applied at all possible leverage ratios.

If you are using a constant weighted average cost of capital over time, then the weighted average cost of capital presumes that the firm will always keep the proportion of the market values of the debt, preferred, and equity equal. Thus, if the value of the equity unexpectedly increases or decreases, management is assumed to make appropriate adjustments in the capital structure to keep the debt/equity proportions constant.

B.   When is the Weighted Average Cost of Capital useful?

The weighted average cost of capital is the discount rate appropriate for valuing "scale expansions" or projects that have the "average" risk of the existing operating assets (unlevered firm), assuming the firm's debt/equity ratio is unchanged.

The weighted average cost of capital is appropriate for valuing the entire firm (i.e., when discounting the cash flows to the firm) assuming the assumptions required for the weighted average cost of capital are met.

Security Analysis: How to Analyze Accounting and Market Data to Value Securities
  Robert W. Holthausen and Mark E. Zmijewski
\CH10.W51

The weighted average cost of capital is not an appropriate discount rate for all of the firm's projects. For example it is not appropriate for:

-- projects which are either riskier or safer than the firm's <u>existing operating assets</u> (unlevered firm)

-- projects which will induce changes in the capital structure of the firm.

For projects, the use of project specific hurdle rates is appropriate.

C. Major Issues in Estimating WACC

-- What are the appropriate definitions of the weights of each type of capital ?

-- What is T?

-- Where can we obtain estimates of the cost of debt, preferred and equity capital?

-- What is the effect of changes in leverage on k_E, k_D and k_R?

Remember -- The Cost of Capital is a forward looking estimate.
(Thus it is based on future information not historical information).

D. Calculation of the Weights for Each Type of Capital.

(1) Weights should be based on Market values (if available).

If there is private debt in the capital structure or debt for which no price is currently available, attempt to value the debt by discounting the promised payments at current promised yields of debt of the same rating. If coupon rates are close to promised yields, the book value of debt is a reasonable proxy for the market value.

(2) Use target weights, not current weights, if current weights do not reflect the target capital structure for the firm. You must assume however that the firm will quickly adjust to its target capital structure if a valuation based on the weighted average cost of capital is to have merit.

(3) If the weights are targeted to vary significantly through time, then WACC varies through time, and we might want to rely on a adjusted present value calculation. Consider LBO's for example.

(4) If the coupon rate is different from the cost of debt, then the value of debt is going to change through time as the debt approaches maturity. If the coupon and cost of debt are not equal, the WACC method and APV method will give slightly

Security Analysis: How to Analyze Accounting and Market Data to Value Securities
Robert W. Holthausen and Mark E. Zmijewski
\CH10.W51

Do not reproduce without permission.
July 30, 1998

307

different answers with APV yielding the correct answer. The WACC method can't quite get the value of the interest tax shields correct when coupons and cost of debt are different.

    (5)   Weights are based on debt excluding short term liabilities that are included in working capital.

    (6)   Off balance sheet financing and leases are included in the capital structure.

E.   Calculation of the appropriate tax rate.

Use the expected future marginal tax rate of the corporation. If the corporation is unable to use the tax shields from interest expense because of heavy losses, T can be equal to 0.

F.   Estimation of the cost capital for each type of financing?

    (1)   How do we estimate the cost of equity capital?

Use a model like the CAPM or APT as previously discussed.

    (2)   How do we estimate the cost of debt capital for straight debt?

Use current long term debt rates on similar debt (i.e., debt with a similar rating or riskiness). We have previously discussed the use of a model to rate debt and determine from that the cost of debt capital. That approach is similar to one adopted by ALCAR.

    (3)   How do we estimate the cost of preferred for straight preferred?

The cost of capital for non-callable, non-convertible preferred that is perpetual is simply the preferred dividend yield. For a fixed life preferred, the cost of capital calculation is the same as calculating the yield on a bond. Preferred dividends are not deductible by the issuing corporation.

Utilities often issue preferred stock because they do get compensated for tax payments in the setting of rates, thus tax deductibility is not a major concern, as long at the regulatory authority allows the capital structure. Preferred dividends received by a corporation are taxed at the 30% rate, not the 34% corporate tax rate (soon to be 35%).

G.   More complicated capital structures.

How do you deal with more complicated capital structures?

For example, suppose a firm has convertible debt outstanding, industrial revenue bonds (a form of subsidized debt), income bonds, etc.

Security Analysis: How to Analyze Accounting and Market Data to Value Securities
Robert W. Holthausen and Mark E. Zmijewski
\CH10.W51

Do not reproduce without permission.
July 30, 1998

308

In this case the WACC is a blended rate of all of the forms of financing.

The more you know about valuing various types of fixed income securities that have provisions like "caps", "collars", etc., the more able you will be able to deal with estimation issues.

Many of the instruments which make up a firm's capital structure include option like features. The pricing of options is not considered in this course, but studying options and fixed income securities is certainly relevant for performing valuations.

H.   A Very Simple Exercise in Determining the Weighted Average Cost of Capital

Assume the following facts. Sutton's Department Stores is in the retailing business and is considering making a capital expenditure whereby it expands its entire business. Sutton's is a private company and therefore does not know its beta. However, you have determined that the capital structure of Sutton's is very similar to the capital structure in the industry.

Sutton's, as well as the retailing industry in general has obtained approximately one-third of its capital in long term debt and two-thirds have come from equity. The average equity beta in the retailing industry is 0.90.

Sutton's recently borrowed money on a five year note at 9%, though two years ago they were charged 14% on a 5 year note.

Assume U.S. Government obligations are currently yielding:

Instrument	Yield
1 month bill	3.6%
5 year notes	6.5%
20 year notes	7.2%

Sutton's tax rate is currently 33%.

Required: Estimate Sutton's weighted average cost of capital and be prepared to defend your estimate. Assume that the project Sutton's is considering has a life of approximately 5 years.

(1)   First, we require an estimate of Beta. Fortunately, one is given (0.90). This estimate can be used directly because the stated assumption is that Sutton's capital structure is similar to the capital structure generally used in the industry. If Sutton's capital structure were different, we would have to use the unlevering formulas for the industry beta (or the industry equity cost of capital) and then relever back up for Sutton's capital structure.

Security Analysis: How to Analyze Accounting and Market Data to Value Securities
  Robert W. Holthausen and Mark E. Zmijewski
  \CH10.W51

(2)   Second, we need to use the CAPM to come up with a cost of capital for the equity. In this example, we'll use the market risk premium relative to intermediate term government bonds (using the arithmetic mean and income returns only) which is 8.2%. The appropriate risk free rate here is to take the yield on five year government notes of 6.5%. Therefore, R_f = 6.5%. We find that Sutton's cost of equity capital is

$$k_e = R_f + \text{Beta} (R_m - R_f)$$

Therefore, k_e = 6.5% + 0.90 (8.2%) = 13.9%

(3)   Third, we require an estimate of WACC.

$$WACC_t = k_{Et} (E_t/V_t) + k_{Dt} (1-T) (D_t/V_t)$$

Therefore, $WACC_t$ = 13.9% (2/3) + 9% (1 - 0.33) (1/3)

= 9.27% + 2.01% = 11.28%

15.   Comprehensive Example -- Toys 'R Us

In this comprehensive example, we go through the logic of computing the cost of capital for Toys 'R Us using data available as of 11/1/90.

A.   Estimating the equity cost of capital.

(1)   Estimate TOYS Beta

Since TOYS is a publicly traded company, we have the choice of using the beta of TOYS or we can use a portfolio of comparable firms. In addition, we have the option of using our own estimate of beta or commercial service estimates (for example, Value Line estimates TOYS beta at 1.30). We opt for our own estimates since that gives us control over the time period for estimation as well as determination of the index used.

Beta Estimates were estimated by regressing monthly returns for various Toy companies on the S&P500 index from September 1985 to June 1990.

	TOYS	Child World	Greenman	Lionel	Toy Industry Aggregate	TOY+Child+ Lionel+Green
Beta	1.25	1.38	1.25	1.52	1.27	1.35
Std. error	0.12	0.28	0.29	0.37	0.12	0.19
R-Squared	0.65	0.30	0.25	0.23	0.68	0.48

In this case, unlike more typical cases, there is nothing gained from using a portfolio

Security Analysis: How to Analyze Accounting and Market Data to Value Securities
Robert W. Holthausen and Mark E. Zmijewski
\CH10.W51

Do not reproduce without permission.
July 30, 1998

310

approach to estimate the equity beta for TOYS. The standard error of the beta estimate for TOYS is no larger than the standard error for the Toy Industry aggregate or an equally weighted portfolio composed of TOYS, Child World, Greenman Brothers and Lionel. Thus, we do not gain any precision in our estimate of TOYS beta by using an industry approach. As such, there is no levering and unlevering of industry comparables required. In addition, we looked at beta estimates based on the last three years of operations (when international operations started to increase and we found no evidence of any risk shifts occurring because of the emerging importance of international operations).

We conclude that a reasonable estimate of TOYS beta is 1.25.

(2)   Estimating the Equity Cost of Capital.

As of 11/1/90, 20 year U.S. Government Bonds were yielding 8.5%. Assuming a market risk premium of 8.6% (which was the estimate commonly used in 1990 relative to U.S. Treasury Bills) and a maturity premium on long-term government bonds to Treasury Bills of 1.7% (which was the estimate commonly used in 1990), the equity cost of capital (using the CAPM) would be

$$k_E = (8.5\% - 1.7\%) + 1.25*8.6\% = 17.55\%.$$

Using a market risk premium of 6.6% (geometric mean) would yield an estimate of k_E of

$$k_E = (8.5\% - 1.7\%) + 1.25*6.6\% = 15.05\%.$$

Thus, a reasonable range of estimates for TOYS equity cost of capital is 15% to 18%. I prefer the estimate based on the arithmetic risk premium. **Remember the market risk premium and maturity premium in this example are based on data through 1990 only.**

B.   Estimating the Current Weighted Average Cost of Capital.

Instead of calculating the current weighted average cost of capital, we could have measured the cost of capital using an assumed weighting for the various components of the cost of capital. In this case, we illustrate a weighted average cost of capital computation in the context of estimating TOYS current capital structure. The implicit assumption here is that the current capital structure is in fact the target capital structure. Here are some facts from the 1/28/90 10-K as well as some other sources.

(1)   The contingencies footnote in TOYS annual report (see Chapter 5B for a copy) indicates that TOYS has commitments for operating leases of $86,696, $87,121, $87,591, $87,219 and $87,048 for the next 5 years and total

Security Analysis: How to Analyze Accounting and Market Data to Value Securities
Robert W. Holthausen and Mark E. Zmijewski
\CH10.W51

commitments at this time for all years beyond year 5 of $1,569,371 (all figures in thousands).

(2)   Capitalized leases on the balance sheet are $14.4 million.

(3)   Short Term Notes at year end are $205.5 million. However, scrutiny of the short term debt balances during the year suggests that the average short debt balance is 2.75 times higher than the year-end balance because of the seasonality of TOYS' business. TOYS' borrowing rate on their short term debt is 9%.

(4)   TOYS has an industrial revenue bond outstanding in the amount of $61.7 million, which carries an interest rate of 6.9%.

(5)   TOYS has $1.4 million in mortgage notes outstanding with a coupon rate of 9.5%.

(6)   TOYS has $96.9 million of debentures outstanding, with a coupon rate of 8.25%. The debt is currently selling at $80 per $100 and it is currently yielding 9.85%. TOYS debt is rated AA by Standard and Poor's.

(7)   There are 296,961,000 shares outstanding and the current price is $22 per share.

(8)   The number of options outstanding is currently insignificant.

(9)   TOYS marginal tax rate is 37.5%. TOYS is currently profitable and is expected to remain profitable for the foreseeable future.

Given these facts we estimate the weighted average cost of capital.

To estimate the effect of the operating leases, we calculate the present value of the lease payments using the current yield on long term debt of 9.85%. In order to estimate the present value we have to make an assumption about the $1,569,371 commitments beyond year 5. We assume that commitment is based on the same amount of commitment as year 5 ($87,048), which implies that the commitment beyond year 5 continues for 18 years beyond year 5. The present value of the operating lease payments at 9.85% is therefore $782.1 million.

The assumed rate of interest on capitalized leases is the same as the long term debt.

Short term notes are assumed to have an average outstanding balance of 2.75 times the amount outstanding at year end. As such we assume the average outstanding balance of short term debt is 2.75 X $205.5 million which is equal to $565 million.

Security Analysis: How to Analyze Accounting and Market Data to Value Securities
Robert W. Holthausen and Mark E. Zmijewski
\CH10.W51

Do not reproduce without permission.
July 30, 1998

312

Part of long term debt borrowing is Industrial Revenue Bonds. The rate of interest on industrial revenue bonds is less than the rate of interest on the corporations regular bonds because the interest received by the holders of those bonds is tax free. Therefore, these bonds are priced more like a tax-free municipal bond. The default risk associated with the bonds is based on TOYS default risk.

The mortgage notes are trivial in amount and we expend virtually no effort on estimating their value or interest rate. Since the companies AA debentures yield 9.85%, a slightly lower interest rate for mortgage notes of 9.5% seems reasonable.

TOYS bonds are selling at a discount (0.80 or $800 per $1000 bond) as of 11/1/90. As such we multiply the amount of debt outstanding. To estimate their value in the capital structure we take their face value of 96.9 million and multiply by 0.80 to determine their market value which is approximately $77.5 million.

The current value of the common equity is $22 X 296,961,000 = $6,533.1 million.

Based on these values the calculation of the weighted average cost of capital for TOYS as of 11/1/90 appears below.

	Dollar Amount (Millions)	"Target" Weight (%)	Before Tax Cost (%)	After Tax Cost (%)	WACC Contribution (%)
Operating Leases	782.1	9.73	9.85	6.16	0.60
Capitalized Leases	14.4	0.18	9.85	6.16	0.01
Short Term Notes	565.0	7.03	9.00	5.63	0.40
Long Term Financing:					
Industrial Revenue	61.7	0.77	6.90	4.31	0.03
Mortgage Notes	1.4	0.02	9.50	5.94	0.00
Debentures	77.5	0.96	9.85	6.16	0.06
Common Equity	6.533.1	81.31	17.55	17.55	14.26
Total	8.035.2	100.00			15.35

Therefore, under this set of assumptions, the weighted average cost of capital is 15.35%. Had we run through the same set of calculations having ignored the operating leases, we would have obtained an estimate of the weighted average cost of capital of 16.6%.

C.   Estimate TOYS Unlevered Cost of Capital.

Examination of TOYS capital structure since 1983, indicates that debt (including the capitalization of operating leases) has been a relatively constant proportion of total firm value and has been fluctuating between approximately 15% and 20% of firm value. As such we assume that TOYS intention is to run its capital structure with a constant debt to value ratio of 20% (assuming the capitalization of operating leases). As discussed in part B above, TOYS marginal tax rate is 37.5%. Moreover, TOYS blended cost of debt (weighted average of all its debt) is 9.41%.

Security Analysis: How to Analyze Accounting and Market Data to Value Securities
Robert W. Holthausen and Mark E. Zmijewski
\CH10.W51

Do not reproduce without permission.
July 30, 1998

313

Because TOYS has maintained a relatively constant debt/value ratio we presume that the appropriate valuation of the interest tax shields uses Case III. As such, our estimate of the unlevered cost of capital for TOYS using D/V of 20%, tax rate of 37.5%, cost of debt of 9.4%, cost of equity of 17.55% is

$$k_U = (k_E + k_D*((1-Tk_D/(1+k_D))*D_t/E_t))/(1+(1-Tk_D/(1+k_D))*D_t/E_t).$$

$$= [.1755+.094*((1-.375*.094/(1.094))*(.2/.8))]/[1+(1-.375*.094/(1.094))*(.2/.8)]$$

$$k_U = 15.96\%$$

Note that this calculation assumes that the market is also implicitly capitalizing the operating leases in determining how risky TOYS equity is.

D.   What are the Effects of Capitalizing Operating Leases on Free Cash Flows?

A complex issue which we have not raised previously is the role of operating leases. A comprehensive treatment of this subject is contained in the supplement to Chapter 10.

One of the lessons from this treatment is that the value of the firm is in part determined by how you treat a particular item.

Note that if you capitalize operating leases and value the firm using the weighted average cost of capital method, the value will include the value of the capitalized operating lease obligation. If you want to value the equity, you must take your estimate of firm value and subtract the value of all non-equity claims (which would now include the value of the capitalized operating leases).

If you do not capitalize operating leases and value the firm using the weighted average cost of capital, the value of the firm will not include the value of the capitalized operating lease obligation, because the cash flows of the unlevered firm have been reduced by the rental expense in each future period.

Similar situations can occur with other types of transactions. For example, post-medical retirement benefits.

Security Analysis: How to Analyze Accounting and Market Data to Value Securities
Robert W. Holthausen and Mark E. Zmijewski
\CH10.W51

Security Analysis: How to Analyze Accounting and Market Data to Value Securities

Robert W. Holthausen and Mark E. Zmijewski

Supplement to Chapter 10

Capitalizing Operating Leases

---

1.   Introduction.

The issue of whether to capitalize operating leases is a potentially important issue for companies with significant amounts of operating leases. If operating leases are insignificant then recasting the financial statements by capitalizing them is not an important issue. However, if leases are important, the issue can be important. In this supplement we provide information about the potential importance of capitalizing leases and consider an example of how to capitalize operating leases.

2.   Valuation of a Company with an Operating Lease

Consider the case of a company that has a perpetual lease on land. The land is worth $1000, the cost of debt for the firm is 10% and their lease payment is $100 per year. They are able to earn revenues from usage of the land of $1000 per year (without any costs other than the rent). Consider the income statement and free cash flow statement for this company under the situation where it treats the lease as an operating lease and in the situation where it is treated as a capital lease. We assume that the tax rate is 40%.

In the case of an operating lease the income statement will show revenues of $1000 and rent expense of $100 per year. In the case of a capitalized lease, the income statement will show revenues of $1000 and interest expense of $100 per year. The balance sheet under the operating lease will show no asset and no liability. Under the capitalization of the lease, the balance sheet will show an asset and a liability of $1000 (the capitalized value of the lease payments at 10% in perpetuity). For purposes of this example, assume that the lease transaction had occurred in a prior year.

Security Analysis: How to Analyze Accounting and Market Data to Value Securities
  Robert W. Holthausen and Mark E. Zmijewski
  \CH5BSUPP.W51

	Operating Lease	Capitalized Lease
Income Statement:		
Revenues	1000	1000
Rent Expense	100	
Interest Expense	____	100
Pretax Income	900	900
Income Taxes	<360>	<360>
Net Income	540	540

Note for this simple firm, the cash flows from operations are also $540.

Statement of Free Cash Flows:

	Operating Lease	Capitalized Lease
Cash Flow from Operations	540	540
After Tax Interest	0	60
	540	600
Less Capital Expenditures	0	0
Free Cash Flows-Unlevered	540	600
After Tax Interest	0	< 60>
Change in Debt	0	0
Free Cash Flows-Equity	540	540

Note, for this simple firm, that the free cash flows of the equity are identical regardless of how the lease is treated. However, the free cash flows of the unlevered firm are higher by the amount of the after-tax interest expense in the case where we have capitalized the lease.[1] Why? Because we have treated the rental payment as a financing rather than as an operating activity.

---

[1]As we shall show in a more complicated example, the free cash flows of the unlevered firm when we capitalize the leases are equal to the free cash flows of the unlevered firm (given no capitalization of leases) plus the after-tax interest expense, plus the difference between the lease payment and the interest expense (the reduction in the lease liability), minus any capital expenditures stemming from new leases (i.e., any new capitalized value of leased assets). In this simple example with a perpetual lease, there is no difference between the lease payment and the interest expense and there is no new capitalized value of leased assets. Therefore, the free cash flows of the unlevered firm are only higher by the after-tax interest expense.

Security Analysis: How to Analyze Accounting and Market Data to Value Securities
Robert W. Holthausen and Mark E. Zmijewski
\CH5BSUPP.W51

Now consider a valuation of this firm. Assuming that the market is reasonably efficient, it will understand that the firm has a fixed obligation regardless of whether we treat this as an operating lease or as a capitalized lease. Thus, the market will assign the same cost of equity capital to the firm in either case. In this case, we assume that the cost of equity capital is 0.20.

Thus, in either case the value of the equity (this is a perpetuity, no growth case) is equal to

$$E = 540/0.2 = 2700.$$

Now lets consider how we would value the firm in the case where we treat the lease as operating for valuation purposes. In this case, the firm is treated as having no debt. Therefore, the unlevered cost of capital, K_u, is equal to 0.2 as well. Moreover, the value of the firm is equal to,

$$V = 540/0.2 = 2700.$$

Thus, the value of the firm is identical to the value of the equity (this is not a surprise since the firm is treated as having no debt).

Now consider the firm when we treat the lease as being capitalized for valuation purposes. In this case the value of the firm is not the same, because now the value of the firm includes the value of the equity and the value of the capitalized lease obligation ($2700 + $1000 = $3700).

Suppose we had valued the firm using the weighted average cost of capital. In this case,

$$WACC = K_e \, E/V + K_d \, (1\text{-}T) \, D/V = 0.2 \, (2700/3700) + 0.1 \, (1\text{-}0.4) \, (1000/2700)$$

$$= 0.16216$$

If we value the firm using WACC, then the value of the firm is equal to

$$V = 600/0.16216 = \$3700.$$

But remember, this value includes the value of the capitalized lease obligation. Therefore, the value of the equity is equal to the value of the firm less the value of the capitalized lease obligation which is equal to $3700 - $1000 = $2700, which is the same value we obtained earlier.

Now consider an APV valuation. We first need to calculate the unlevered cost of capital, K_u. In this case, the debt (the capitalized lease obligation) is permanent and the firm is not expected to grow so we will use K_d to value the interest tax shields (Case II). Therefore,

$$K_u = K_e \, (E/(E+D(1\text{-}T))) + K_d \, (D(1\text{-}T)/(E+D(1\text{-}T)))$$

$$K_u = 0.2 \, (2700/(2700+1000(1\text{-}0.4))) + 0.10 \, (1000(1\text{-}0.4)/(2700+1000(1\text{-}0.4))) = 0.18182$$

Security Analysis: How to Analyze Accounting and Market Data to Value Securities
Robert W. Holthausen and Mark E. Zmijewski
\CH5BSUPP.W51

Notice that when the leases are capitalized, the unlevered cost of capital is **not** the same as in the case where leases are treated as operating. Why? Because when leases are treated as an operating activity, we have additional operating leverage (a fixed cost) which we do not have in the case where leases are capitalized. When leases are capitalized, we substitute financial leverage for operating leverage and when we calculate the unlevered cost of capital we get the financial leverage affects out of the cost of capital.

Continuing the valuation, we now discount the free cash flows of the unlevered firm at the unlevered cost of capital and add in the value of the interest tax shields. In this case, the value of the interest tax shields is equal to $1000*0.10*0.4/0.10 = 400$. Therefore,

$$V = 600/0.18182 + 400 = 3300 + 400 = 3700.$$

Thus, the value of the firm is again \$3700 which again includes the value of the capitalized lease obligation and the value of the equity is still \$2700.

Summary:

What have we learned from this simple example?

1. We have learned that the value of the equity is not affected by the treatment of a lease as either operating or capitalized. The value of the firm is affected however, because in the case of the operating lease the value of the firm does not include the lease obligation whereas in the case of capitalization, the value of the firm treats the capitalized lease obligation as debt.

2. The free cash flows of the equity are the same whether we treat leases as capitalized or not. However, the free cash flows of the unlevered firm when treating leases as capitalized are equal to the free cash flows of the unlevered firm assuming leases are not capitalized, plus after tax interest expense, plus the difference between the lease payment and the interest expense (the reduction in the lease liability), minus any capital expenditures stemming from new leases (i.e., any new capitalized value of leased assets).

3. The cost of equity capital is the same regardless of whether we treat the lease as operating or capitalized, but the unlevered cost of capital is different. In the case where the lease is treated as capitalized, the unlevered cost of capital will be lower than in the case where the lease is treated as an operating activity. When the lease is treated as an operating activity, the lease payment increases operating leverage, whereas when the lease is treated as capitalized, the lease payment increases financial leverage, but the unlevering removes the effect of the financial leverage.

One tempting conclusion to draw from this example is that given the value of the equity is the same in either case, it makes no difference whether we treat the lease as operating or capitalized since the value of the equity is the same. All one would have to remember is that if the leases are treated as capitalized, then we need to subtract the capitalized value of the leases from the value of the firm in calculating the value of the equity.

Security Analysis: How to Analyze Accounting and Market Data to Value Securities
    Robert W. Holthausen and Mark E. Zmijewski
\CH5BSUPP.W51

The above conclusion is appropriate *if you can directly observe* the cost of equity capital *for your firm* without resorting to the use of comparable companies. What do we mean by directly? For purposes of discussion, assume we are using the CAPM. In this case, we simply estimate the beta of the company being valued and use the CAPM to determine the equity cost of capital.

Suppose however, we have to resort to comparable companies. Now the situation is quite a bit messier, because as we have seen, the unlevered cost of capital is affected by how the leases are treated. So what does this imply.

1)   If the comparable companies rely on leases to the exact same extent as the firm you are valuing, then again it will not matter how you treat the leases (this is tantamount to saying that if all my comparable companies have the same capital structure as the firm I am valuing then I know that firm's equity cost of capital without worrying about unlevering and levering the cost of capital estimates simply by knowing the equity cost of capital for my comparable companies).

2)   If there are differences in the lease structures across firms, however, the only way to do the levering and unlevering appropriately, is to treat the operating leases as capitalized leases for both the comparable companies and the firm you are valuing. If this is not done, then otherwise identical firms will have different unlevered costs of capital simply due to whether the lease was treated as capitalized or operating. To avoid this situation, treat all operating leases as capitalized.

Obviously, if the industry in which you are dealing has a trivial amount of operating leases, you would not go through the steps required to capitalize all the firms' leases.

3. An Illustration of Capitalizing Operating Leases

In the example which follows, we take a firm with leases, and show the difference in the income statement, balance sheet, statement of cash flows and statement of free cash flows under two scenarios. The first presentation treats the leases as operating leases and the second presentation treats the leases as capital leases. The tax rate in the problem is 40%. The first presentation is easy and we will not comment on that in any detail. Note that we have a firm which has no debt, rental payments are $1000 in 1990 and capital expenditures are $20,000 in 1990.

At the end of the first presentation, we provide a typical lease footnote for operating leases (lines 363-377). The typical footnote disclosure would only provide information about the minimum cash payments. It would not include information on the present values of those cash payments (as on lines 378-406) since these are operating leases which are not capitalized. The interest rate used to capitalize the leases in the example is 13%. In capitalizing the leases, we use the following method. Consider the 1989 data. The amount payable after 1994 is 5,000 and the amount payable in 1994 is 1,000. We therefore assume lease payments are 1000 a year for each of the five years beginning after 1994 (1995-1999). Total capitalized values of operating leases are 6,000 at the end of 1989 and 7,000 at the end of 1990.

Security Analysis: How to Analyze Accounting and Market Data to Value Securities
    Robert W. Holthausen and Mark E. Zmijewski
    \CH5BSUPP.W51

We also provide information about the 1989 and 1990 journal entries used to capitalize the leases (lines 495-540). Note that the capitalized leases are depreciated using a nine year life. Note also that the amount charged to interest expense is 13% times the liability recognized for the present value of lease obligations (13% * 6000) for 1990. Depreciation on the capitalized leases in 1990 is $667 = 6000/9$, given our assumption about straight-line depreciation and a nine-year life for the assets.

Note also that a deferred tax asset and liability are created (lines 520-540) because for tax purposes, the deductible expense is the rent expense whereas the financial statements portray the expenses as interest and depreciation which will not equal the rental expense generally. A deferred tax asset arises from the liability associated with capitalizing the leases and a deferred tax liability arises associated with the leasehold asset. Since these values are not the same once the asset begins to be depreciated, a net deferred tax asset or liability arises.

We provide the income statement, balance sheet, statement of cash flows and statement of free cash flows under the assumption that operating leases are capitalized. We also provide an additional column to make it easy to compare those statements when the leases are treated as an operating activity.

At this point you should be able to work through the example on your own. Note that:

Free cash flows of unlevered firm (with operating leases)	5000
Plus: after tax interest (780-312)	468
Plus: Rent Expense	1000
Less: Interest Expense	<780>
Less: New Equipment Acquired Under Operating Leases	<1220>
Free cash flows of unlevered firm (with capitalized leases)	4468

Security Analysis: How to Analyze Accounting and Market Data to Value Securities
Robert W. Holthausen and Mark E. Zmijewski
\CH5BSUPP.W51

Do not reproduce without permission.
July 30, 1998 - 11:16 am

320

		1990
97		
98	THE BASIC CASH FLOW COMPANY (BCF) – Income Statement	
	NET SALES	100,000
101		
102	Selling, general, & admin exp	(60,000)
103	Depreciation	(4,000)
104	Rent Expense	(1,000)
105		
106	Total Expenses	(65,000)
107		
108	INCOME FROM OPERATIONS	35,000
109	Interest Expense	0
110		
111	INCOME BEFORE INCOME TAXES	35,000
112	Income Tax Expense	(14,000)
113		
114	NET INCOME	21,000
115	Beginning Retained Earnings	0
116	Dividends	0
117		
118	Ending Retained Earnings	21,000
119		========

Robert W. Holthausen & Mark E. Zmijewski

	THE BASIC CASH FLOW COMPANY (BCF) – Balance Sheet	1989	1990	CHANGE
120				
121	THE BASIC CASH FLOW COMPANY (BCF) – Balance Sheet	1989	1990	CHANGE
122				
123	ASSETS			
124	Cash and short–term investments	0	10,000	10,000
125	Accounts receivable	0	0	0
126	Inventories	0	0	0
127				
128	Total current assets	0	10,000	10,000
129				
130	PROPERTY, PLANT, AND EQUIPMENT	10,000	30,000	20,000
131	Less accumulated depreciation	0	(4,000)	(4,000)
132				
133	Net Property, plant, and equipment	10,000	26,000	16,000
134				
135	Other	0	0	0
136				
137	TOTAL	10,000	36,000	26,000
138		========	========	========
139				
140	LIABILITIES AND SHAREHOLDERS' EQUITY			
141	Accounts payable — trade	0	0	0
142	Short–term Notes to Banks	0	0	0
143	Interest Payable	0	0	0
144	Income Taxes Payable	0	0	0
145				
146	Total current liabilities	0	0	0
147				
148	Long–term Debt–A (net of discount)	0	0	0
149	Long–term Debt–B (net of premium)	0	0	0
150	Long–term Debt–C	0	0	0
151	Long–term Debt–D	0	0	0
152	Deferred Income Taxes	0	0	0
153				
154	Long–term liabilities	0	0	0
155				
156	Total liabilities	0	0	0
157				
158	Common Stock at Par	10,000	15,000	5,000
159	Additional paid–in capital	0	0	0
160	Foreign currency translation adj	0	0	0
161	Retained earnings	0	21,000	21,000
162				
163				
164		10,000	36,000	26,000
165	Treasury Stock, at cost	0	0	0
166				
167	Total shareholders, equity	10,000	36,000	26,000
168				
169	TOTAL	10,000	36,000	26,000
170		========	========	========
171				

172
17?

	ACCOUNT	REF #	DEBIT	CREDIT

٠...

176	CFO – Income	1	21,000	
177	Retained Earnings			21,000
178				
179	Retained Earnings	2	0	
180	CF – Financing – Dividends			0
181				
182	Accounts receivable	3	0	
183	CFO			0
184				
185	CFO – Deferred Income Taxes	4	0	
186	Deferred Income Taxes			0
187				
188	CFO	5	0	
189	Accounts payable — trade			0
190				
191	CFO	6	0	
192	Interest Payable			0
193				
194	CFO	7	0	
195	Income Taxes Payable			0
196				
197	CF – Financing	8	0	
198	Short–term Notes to Banks			0
199				
200	CFO – Adjustment	9	0	
201	Long–term Debt–A (net of discount)			0
202				
	Long–term Debt–B (net of premium)	10	0	
	CFO – Adjustment			0
20ɔ				
206	CFO	11	0	
207	Long–term Debt–C			0
208				
209	CF – Financing	12	0	
210	Long–term Debt–D			0
211				
212	CF – Financing	13	5,000	
213	Common Stock at Par			5,000
214				
215	CFO	14	4,000	
216	Depreciation			4,000
217				
218	Net Property, plant, and equipment	15	20,000	
219	CF – Investing			20,000
220				
221	Treasury Stock	16	0	
222	CF – Financing			0
223				

323

Robert W. Holthausen & Mark E. Zmijewski

#	THE BASIC CASH FLOW COMPANY (BCF) – Cash Flow Statement	1990	REF #
224			
225	THE BASIC CASH FLOW COMPANY (BCF) – Cash Flow Statement	1990	REF #
226	———————————————————————————— ———— ———— ————	————	————
227	Net Income	21,000	1
228			
229	Adjustments:		
230	Depreciation	4,000	14
231	Deferred income taxes	0	4
232	Change in Accounts receivable	0	3
233	Change in A/P	0	5
234	Change in Interest Payable	0	6
235	Change in Income Taxes Payable	0	7
236	Amortization of Debt–A Discount	0	9
237	Amortization of Debt–B Premium	0	10
238	Accrual of Debt–C Interest	0	11
239		————	
240	Cash Flow from Operations	25,000	
241		————	
242	Investing Activities		
243	Purchases of PPEQ –net	(20,000)	15
244	PPEQ Sold		
245	Other – net		
246		————	
247		(20,000)	
248		————	
249	Financing Activities:		
250	Change in Short–term Notes to Banks	0	8
251	Issue of Long–Term Debt	0	12
252	Change in Common Stock	5,000	13
253	Dividends paid	0	2
254	Purchase of Treasury Stock	0	16
255		————	
256		5,000	
257		————	
258	Change in cash balance	10,000	0
259		========	
260			
261	Additional Schedules		
262			
263	Total Interest Expensed & Capitalized	0	
264	Chg Int/P	0	
265	Discount Debt–A	0	
266	Premium Debt–B	0	
267	Interest Accrued LTD	0	
268		————	
269	Amount Paid	0 Check	0
270		========	========
271			
272	Income Tax Expense	14,000	
273	Change in Income Taxes Payable	0	
274	Deferred income taxes	0	
275		————	
276	Amount Paid	14,000 Check	14,000
277		========	========

Robert W. Holthausen & Mark E. Zmijewski

278		
279	FREE CASH FLOW MEASUREMENT	1990
	—————————————————————	————
	Assumed Marginal Tax Rate	40.0%
282		========
283	Cash Flow from Operations	25,000
284	Less – Capitalized Interest (Assets)	0
285	Less – Interest Accrued to Long–Term Debt	0
286	Less (Plus) – Inc (Dec) in Required Cash Balance	
287		————
288	Adjusted Operating Cash Flow	25,000
289		————
290	Plus – Total Effects of Financial Leverage	
291	Plus – Interest Expense	0
292	Plus – Capitalized Interest (Assets)	0
293	Plus – Amortization of Premium	0
294	Less – Change in Interest Payable	0
295	Less – Amortization of Discount (Deferred Charges)	0
296		————
297	Plus – Total Cash Interest Paid	0
298	Less – Income Tax Shelter from Debt Financing	0
299		————
300	Plus – Total Effects of Financial Leverage	0
301		————
302	Operating Cash Flow of the Unlevered Firm	25,000
303		————
304	Less – Net Capital Expenditure Cash Flows	
305	Less – Purchases of Property, Plant, and Equipment	(20,000)
306	Plus – Capitalized Interest (Assets)	0
307		————
308	Less – Net Capital Expenditure Cash Flows	(20,000)
	FREE CASH FLOWS OF THE UNLEVERED FIRM	5,000
311		————
312	Less – Total Effects of Financial Leverage	0
313		————
314	Less (Plus) – Other CFs to (from) Non–equity Claims	
315	Plus – Change in Short–Term Debt Financing	0
316	Plus – Change in Long–Term Debt Financing	0
317	Plus – Interest Accrued to Long–Term Debt	0
318		————
319	Less (Plus) – Other CFs to (from) Non–equity Claims	0
320		————
321	FREE CASH FLOWS TO COMMON EQUITY	5,000
322	Changes in Common Equity	5,000
323	Cash Dividends – Common	0
324		————
325	Change in Excess Cash	10,000
326	Plus (Less) – Inc (Dec) in Required Cash Balance	0
327		————
328	Change in Cash Balance – FCF Statement	10,000
329		========
330	Change in Cash Balance – B/S	10,000
331		========

Robert W. Holthausen & Mark E. Zmijewski

		1990
332		
333	EBIT Calculation of Free Cash Flows	
334	────────────────────────────────	
335	Net Income (Loss)	21,000
336	Interest Expense	0
337	Income Taxes – Total	14,000
338		────────
339	EBIT	35,000
340		
341	Required Changes in Working Capital:	
342	Required Change in Cash Balance	0
343		
344		
345	Change in Accounts receivable	0
346	Change in A/P	0
347	Change in Income Taxes Payable	0
348		
349	Depreciation	4,000
350	Deferred income taxes	0
351		────────
352	Subtotal	39,000
353	Less – Cash Tax Payments without any Interest Tax Shield	(14,000)
354	Less – Net Capital Expenditures	(20,000)
355		────────
356	FREE CASH FLOWS OF THE UNLEVERED FIRM	5,000
357		========
358		0
359		
360		

326

Robert W. Holthausen & Mark E. Zmijewski

361
362

Minimum Cash Payments for Equipment Under Operating Leases

					Lease Value Check	
365		Minimum Cash Payment at the End of:				
366			1989	1990	13.0000%	13.0000%
367						
368		1990	1,000		1989	1990
369		1991	1,300	1,200		
370		1992	1,312	1,400	(6,000)	(7,000)
371		1993	1,200	1,502	1,000	1,200
372		1994	1,000	1,400	1,300	1,400
373		1995		1,200	1,312	1,502
374	Amount Payable After 1994		5,000		1,200	1,400
375	Amount Payable After 1995			6,000	1,000	1,200
376			————	————	1,000	1,200
377	Total Minimum Cash Payments		10,812	12,702	1,000	1,200
378	Amount Representing Interest		(4,812)	(5,702)	1,000	1,200
379			————	————	1,000	1,200
380	Present Value of Operating Lease Payments		6,000	7,000	1,000	1,200
381			========	===========		
382						
383						
384	Interest Rate on Leases		13%	13%		
385	Average Payments/Year, 1995–1999 (1996–2000)		1000	1,200		
386	Years in Amount Payable after 1994 (1995)		5.00	5.00		
387						
388	Present Value of Payments Calculations, as of:		1989	1990		
389						
390		1990	885			
391		1991	1,018	1,062		
		1992	909	1,096		
		1993	736	1,041		
		1994	543	859		
395		1995		651		
396	Present Value of Post 1994 Payments, as of 1989		1909			
397	Present Value of Post 1995 Payments, as of 1990			2291		
398	Total Present Value of Payments		6,000	7,000		
399						
400						
401						
402	Present Value of Post 1994 Payments, as of 1994		3,517			
403	Present Value of Post 1995 Payments, as of 1995			4,221		
404						
405						
406	NOTE: Leased assets all have a nine year life.					

327

Robert W. Holthausen & Mark E. Zmijewski

493				
494				
495	Journal Entries to Capitalize Operating Leases	Lease Interest Rate	13%	
496				
497	1989 Entries			
498				
499	Equipment Under Operating Lease	6000		
500	Present Value of the Lease Obligation		6000	
501				
502	1990 Entries			
503				
504	Interest Expense	780		
505	Present Value of Lease Obligation	220		
506	Rent Expense		1,000	
507				
508	Amortization Expense	667		
509	Accumulated Amortization		667	
510				
511	Equipment Under Operating Lease	1,220		NOTE: New leases.
512	Present Value of the Lease Obligation		1,220	
513				
514	Adjusting Tax Entry			
515	Deferred Income Taxes	179		
516	Tax Expense		179	
517				
518				
519				

520	Deferred Income Tax Calculation for Capitalizing Leases	Income Tax Rate	40%
521			

		Leasehold Asset	Leasehold Obligation
522		Leasehold	Leasehold
523		Asset	Obligation
524			
525	Book Basis	6,553	7,000
526	Tax Basis	0	0
527		————	————
528	Difference Between Tax & Book	6,553	7,000
529	Tax Rate	40.00%	40.00%
530		————	————
531	Deferred Tax Asset or Liability	2,621	2,800
532		========	===========
533			
534	Deferred Tax Asset From Leases	2,800	
535	Deferred Tax Liability from Leases	(2,621)	
536		————	
537	Net Deferred Tax Asset from Leases	179	
538			
539			
540	NOTE: Leased assets all have a nine year life. Assume straight–line depreciation.		

407

⌐∩ℑ This sheet presents the financial statements and
free cash flow calculations for Basic Cash Flow Company
restated for the capitalization of leases.

411
412
413

	1990	W/O Cap 1990	Difference
THE BASIC CASH FLOW COMPANY (BCF) – Income Statement			
NET SALES	100,000	100,000	0
Selling, general, & admin exp	(60,000)	(60,000)	0
Depreciation	(4,000)	(4,000)	0
Rent Expense	0	(1,000)	1,000
Leasehold Amortization Expense	(667)		(667)
Total Expenses	(64,667)	(65,000)	333
INCOME FROM OPERATIONS	35,333	35,000	333
Interest Expense	(780)	0	(780)
INCOME BEFORE INCOME TAXES	34,553	35,000	(447)
Income Tax Expense	(13,821)	(14,000)	179
NET INCOME	20,732	21,000	(268)
Beginning Retained Earnings	0	0	0
Dividends	0	0	0
Ending Retained Earnings	20,732	21,000	(268)

Robert W. Holthausen & Mark E. Zmijewski

		1989	w/ Cap 1990	Change	W/O Cap 1990	Difference
438						
439						
440	THE BASIC CASH FLOW COMPANY (BCF) – Balance Sheet					
441	————————————————					
442	ASSETS					
443	Cash and short–term investments	0	10,000	10,000	10,000	0
444	Accounts receivable	0	0	0	0	0
445	Inventories	0	0	0	0	0
446						
447	Total current assets	0	10,000	10,000	10,000	0
448						
449	PROPERTY, PLANT, AND EQUIPMENT	10,000	30,000	20,000	30,000	0
450	Less accumulated depreciation	0	(4,000)	(4,000)	(4,000)	0
451	Operating Lease Equipment Capitalized	6,000	7,220	1,220		7,220
452	Less accumulated amortization	0	(667)	(667)		(667)
453						
454	Net Property, plant, and equipment	16,000	32,553	16,553	26,000	6,553
455						
456	Other	0	0	0	0	0
457						
458	TOTAL	16,000	42,553	26,553	36,000	6,553
459		===========	========	========	========	========
460						
461	LIABILITIES AND SHAREHOLDERS' EQUITY					
462	Accounts payable — trade	0	0	0	0	0
463	Short–term Notes to Banks	0	0	0	0	0
464	Interest Payable	0	0	0	0	0
465	Income Taxes Payable	0	0	0	0	0
466						
467	Total current liabilities	0	0	0	0	0
468						
469	Present Value of the Lease Obligation	6,000	7,000	1,000		7,000
470	Long–term Debt–A (net of discount)	0	0	0	0	0
471	Long–term Debt–B (net of premium)	0	0	0	0	0
472	Long–term Debt–C	0	0	0	0	0
473	Long–term Debt–D	0	0	0	0	0
474	Deferred Income Taxes	0	(179)	(179)	0	(179)
475						
476	Long–term liabilities	6,000	6,821	821	0	6,821
477						
478	Total liabilities	6,000	6,821	821	0	6,821
479						
480	Common Stock at Par	10,000	15,000	5,000	15,000	0
481	Additional paid–in capital	0	0	0	0	0
482	Foreign currency translation adj	0	0	0	0	0
483	Retained earnings	0	20,732	20,732	21,000	(268)
484	Treasury Stock, at cost	0	0	0	0	0
485						
486	Total shareholders, equity	10,000	35,732	25,732	36,000	(268)
487						
488	TOTAL	16,000	42,553	26,553	36,000	6,553
489		===========	========	========	========	========
490						
491	Check: A = L + SE	0	0			
492						

541
5̄4̄2̄

ACCOUNT	REF #	DEBIT	CREDIT
545			
546 CFO – Income	1	20,732	
547 Retained Earnings			20,732
548			
549 Retained Earnings	2	0	
550 CF – Financing – Dividends			0
551			
552 Accounts receivable	3	0	
553 CFO			0
554			
555 CFO – Deferred Income Taxes	4	(179)	
556 Deferred Income Taxes			(179)
557			
558 CFO	5	0	
559 Accounts payable — trade			0
560			
561 CFO	6	0	
562 Interest Payable			0
563			
564 CFO	7	0	
565 Income Taxes Payable			0
566			
567 CF – Financing	8	0	
568 Short–term Notes to Banks			0
569			
570 CFO – Adjustment	9	0	
571 Long–term Debt–A (net of discount)			0
Long–term Debt–B (net of premium)	10	0	
574 CFO – Adjustment			0
575			
576 CFO	11	0	
577 Long–term Debt–C			0
578			
579 CF – Financing	12	0	
580 Long–term Debt–D			0
581			
582 CF – Financing	13	5,000	
583 Common Stock at Par			5,000
584			
585 CF – Financing	14	1,000	
586 Leasehold Obligation – Net of Repayments			1,000
587			
588 CFO	15	4,000	
589 Depreciation			4,000
590			
591 CFO	16	667	
592 Amortization			667
593			
594 Net Property, plant, and equipment	17	20,000	
595 CF – Investing			20,000
596			
597 Operating Lease Equipment Capitalized	18	1,220	
598 CF – Investing			1,220
599			
600 Treasury Stock	19	0	
601 CF – Financing			0

Robert W. Holthausen & Mark E. Zmijewski

603				
604				
605		W/ Cap	W/O Cap	
606	THE BASIC CASH FLOW COMPANY (BCF) – Cash Flow Statement	1990	1990	Difference
607				
608	Net Income			
609		20,732	21,000	(268)
610	Adjustments:			
611	Depreciation	4,000	4,000	0
612	Amortization	667	0	667
613	Deferred income taxes	(179)	0	(179)
614	Change in Accounts receivable	0	0	0
615	Change in A/P	0	0	0
616	Change in Interest Payable	0	0	0
617	Change in Income Taxes Payable	0	0	0
618	Amortization of Debt–A Discount	0	0	0
619	Amortization of Debt–B Premium	0	0	0
620	Accrual of Debt–C Interest	0		0
621				
622	Cash Flow from Operations	25,220	25,000	220
623				
624	Investing Activities			
625	Purchases of PPEQ –net	(20,000)	(20,000)	0
626	Operating Lease Equipment Capitalized	(1,220)		(1,220)
627	Other – net	0	0	0
628				
629		(21,220)	(20,000)	(1,220)
630				
631	Financing Activities:			
632	Change in Short–term Notes to Banks	0	0	0
633	Issue of Long–Term Debt	0	0	0
634	Change in Operating Lease Equipment Capitalized	1,000		1,000
635	Change in Common Stock	5,000	5,000	0
636	Dividends paid	0	0	0
637	Purchase of Treasury Stock	0	0	0
638				
639		6,000	5,000	1,000
640				
641	Change in cash balance	10,000	10,000	0
642				
643				
644	Ending Cash Balance	10,000	10,000	0
645	Beginning Cash Balance	0	0	0
646				
647	Change in Cash Balance	10,000	10,000	0
648				
649				
650	Additional Schedules			
651				
652	Total Interest Expensed	780	0	780
653	Interest Capitalized	0		0
654	Chg Int/P	0	0	447
655	Discount Debt–A	0	0	(179)
656	Premium Debt–B	0	0	0
657	Interest Accrued LTD	0	0	268
658				
659	Amount Paid	780	0	1,316
660				
661				
662	Income Tax Expense	13,821	14,000	(179)
663	Change in Income Taxes Payable	0	0	0
664	Deferred income taxes	179	0	179
665				
666	Amount Paid	14,000	14,000	0
667				

Robert W. Holthausen & Mark E. Zmijewski

668

		W/ Cap 1990	W/O Cap 1990	Difference
671	FREE CASH FLOW MEASUREMENT			
672	———————————————————	———	———	———
673	Assumed Marginal Tax Rate	40.0%	40.0%	0.0%
674		========	========	========
675	Cash Flow from Operations	25,220	25,000	(220)
676	Less – Capitalized Interest (Assets)	0	0	0
677	Less – Interest Accrued to Long–Term Debt	0	0	0
678	Less (Plus) – Inc (Dec) in Required Cash Balance	0	0	0
679		———	———	———
680	Adjusted Operating Cash Flow	25,220	25,000	(220)
681		———	———	———
682	Plus – Total Effects of Financial Leverage			
683	Plus – Interest Expense	780	0	(780)
684	Plus – Capitalized Interest (Assets)	0	0	0
685	Plus – Amortization of Premium	0	0	0
686	Less – Change in Interest Payable	0	0	0
687	Less – Amortization of Discount (Deferred Charges)	0	0	0
688		———	———	———
689	Plus – Total Cash Interest Paid	780	0	(780)
690	Less – Income Tax Shelter from Debt Financing	(312)	0	312
691		———	———	———
692	Plus – Total Effects of Financial Leverage	468	0	(468)
693		———	———	———
694	Operating Cash Flow of the Unlevered Firm	25,688	25,000	(688)
695		———	———	———
696	Less – Net Capital Expenditure Cash Flows			
697	Less – Purchases of Property, Plant, and Equipment	(20,000)	(20,000)	0
698	Less – Equipment Acquired Under Capital Lease	(1,220)	0	1,220
	Plus – Capitalized Interest (Assets)	0		0
		———	———	———
701	Less – Net Capital Expenditure Cash Flows	(21,220)	(20,000)	1,220
702		———	———	———
703	FREE CASH FLOWS OF THE UNLEVERED FIRM	4,468	5,000	532
704		———	———	———
705	Less – Total Effects of Financial Leverage	(468)	0	468
706		———	———	———
707	Less (Plus) – Other CFs to (from) Non–equity Claims			
708	Plus – Change in Short–Term Debt Financing	0	0	0
709	Plus – Change in Long–Term Debt Financing	0	0	0
710	Plus – Interest Accrued to Long–Term Debt	0	0	0
711	Plus – Increase in Obligations for Capital Leases	1,000		(1,000)
712		———	———	———
713	Less (Plus) – Other CFs to (from) Non–equity Claims	1,000	0	(1,000)
714		———	———	———
715	FREE CASH FLOWS TO COMMON EQUITY	5,000	5,000	(0)
716	Changes in Common Equity	5,000	5,000	0
717	Cash Dividends – Common	0	0	0
718		———	———	———
719	Change in Excess Cash	10,000	10,000	(0)
720	Plus (Less) – Inc (Dec) in Required Cash Balance	0	0	0
721		———	———	———
722	Change in Cash Balance – FCF Statement	10,000	10,000	(0)
723		========	========	========
724	Change in Cash Balance – B/S	10,000		
725		========		

333

	W/ Cap 1990	W/O Cap 1990	Difference
726			
727 EBIT Calculation of Free Cash Flows			
728 ————————————————			
729 Net Income (Loss)	20,732	21,000	(268)
730 Interest Expense	780	0	780
731 Income Taxes – Total	13,821	14,000	(179)
732			
733 EBIT	35,333	35,000	333
734 Required Changes in Working Capital:			
735 Required Change in Cash Balance	0	0	0
736 Change in Accounts receivable	0	0	0
737 Change in A/P	0	0	0
738 Change in Income Taxes Payable	0	0	0
739 Depreciation	4,000	4,000	0
740 Amortization	667		667
741 Deferred income taxes	(179)	0	(179)
742			
743 Subtotal	39,821	39,000	821
744 Less – Cash Tax Payments without any Interest Tax Shield	(14,133)	(14,000)	491
745 Less – Net Capital Expenditures	(20,000)	(20,000)	0
746 Less – Equipment Acquired Under Capital Lease	(1,220)		1,220
747			
748 FREE CASH FLOWS OF THE UNLEVERED FIRM	4,468	5,000	2,532
749	========	========	========
750 Check – CFO vs. EBIT Method			
751 FCFU – CFO Method	4,468	5,000	(532)
752 FCFU – EBIT Method	4,468	5,000	(532)
753			
754 Difference	(0)	0	(0)
755	========	========	========
756 Check – FCFU Base Case vs. FCFU Restated			
757 FCFU – Base Case	5,000		
758 Plus: After–tax Lease Interest Expense	468		
759 Plus: Lease Payment minus Interest Expense	220		
760 Less: Acquisition of Equipment Under Capital Lease	(1,220)		
761			
762 FCFU – Simple Restatement	4,468		
763 FCFU – Complete Restatement	4,468		
764			
765 Difference	(0)		
766	========		
767 Check – FCFCE Base Case vs. FCFCE Restated			
768 FCFCE – Base Case	5,000		
769 FCFCE – Restated	5,000		
770			
771 Difference	(0)		
772	========		

334

Robert W. Holthausen & Mark E. Zmijewski

7

Forecasting
Performance

Once you've analyzed the company's historical performance, you can move on to forecasting its future performance. The key to projecting performance is to develop a point of view on how the company can or will perform on the key value drivers: growth and return on invested capital. Since growth and ROIC are not constant over time, a third dimension, time itself, must also be considered. While we cannot provide specific forecasting rules, here are some basic steps to consider when developing forecasts.

1. Evaluate the company's strategic position, considering both the industry characteristics as well as the company's competitive advantages or disadvantages. This will help you assess the company's growth potential and its ability to earn returns above its cost of capital.

2. Develop performance scenarios for the company and its industry that describe qualitatively how the company's performance will evolve and the critical events that are likely to impact that performance.

3. Forecast individual income-statement and balance-sheet line items based on the scenarios. These line items will then be aggregated to forecast free cash flow, ROIC, and the other key value drivers.

4. Check the overall forecast for reasonableness, particularly the key value drivers.

EVALUATE STRATEGIC POSITION

In order to earn returns on capital in excess of the opportunity cost of capital, companies must develop and exploit a competitive advantage. Without a competitive advantage, competition would force all the companies in the industry to earn only their cost of capital (or even less). Therefore, to develop a point of view about a company's ability to earn an attractive ROIC over time, we must identify the company's potential for generating competitive advantages, given the nature of the industry in which it competes and its own assets and capabilities.

Competitive advantages that translate into a positive ROIC versus WACC spread can be categorized into three types:

1. Providing superior value to the customer through a combination of price and product attributes that cannot be replicated by competitors. These attributes can be tangible (the fastest computer) or intangible (a strong relationship between salesperson and buyer).
2. Achieving lower costs than competitors.
3. Utilizing capital more productively than competitors.

A competitive advantage must ultimately be expressed in terms of one or more of these characteristics. Describing competitive advantages this way also helps to begin to shape the financial forecast.

Three techniques for identifying competitive advantages include customer segmentation analysis, competitive business system analysis, and industry structure analysis.

Customer Segmentation Analysis

The purpose of customer segmentation analysis is to help estimate potential market share by explicitly identifying why customers will choose one company's products over others. It also tells us how difficult it will be for a competitor to differentiate itself and helps to identify how profitable each type of customer is likely to be, based on their needs and cost to serve.

Customer segmentation analysis segments customers from two

perspectives: the customer and the producer. From the customer perspective, product attributes have different importance to different groups of customers. For example, after-sale service may be more important to a small manufacturing customer than a large customer with its own in-house maintenance staff. In addition, different competitors may include different attributes in their product offering and, therefore, deliver different benefits to customer groups.

A customer segment is a group of customers to whom similar product attributes provide similar benefits. Segmenting customers forces the analyst to understand why customers prefer one product over another, often despite the fact that the products appear very similar. This then helps to identify why competitive market share may differ across customer groups and to find opportunities for differentiation to segments. For example, in the overnight package delivery business, detailed billing information on each package is important to some customers, while others are content with summary data. Some customers want to be able to know instantaneously where a package is at any point in time, while other customers can wait for the information. So, while all customers receive the same overnight delivery, other less apparent attributes may also be important.

From the producer perspective, different customers have different costs to serve. For example, in the salt industry, distance to the customer has a major impact on the costs to serve because of salt's low value-to-weight characteristics. Accordingly, some customers may be simply too far away to serve if competitors are much closer. On the other hand, customers close by may be important to lock up because their proximity creates a major competitive advantage.

By segmenting customers according to both the customer and producer attributes, and then comparing a company's ability to satisfy those customers relative to competitors, you can begin to identify current or potential competitive advantages.

Competitive Business System Analysis

The business system is the way a company provides product attributes to the customer, as illustrated in Exhibit 7.1. The business system extends from product design to after-sales service. Analysis of the business system provides insight into how a company can

337

Exhibit 7.1 **BUSINESS SYSTEM ANALYSIS**

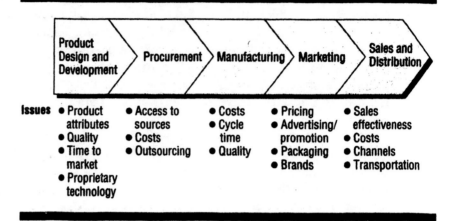

achieve a competitive advantage through lower costs, better capital utilization, or superior customer value. To do this, the analyst needs to lay out the business systems of the major competitors and identify:

- What product attributes does each competitor provide with its business system?

- What costs and capital are associated with providing these attributes? Ideally, this should be done for each component of the business system. In addition, linkages between the components should be considered.

- What are the reasons for differences in performance between competitors?

For example, a competitor may have a manufacturing cost advantage because its labor force is not unionized. In order to overcome this labor cost advantage, other competitors must achieve greater labor productivity or cost savings elsewhere in the business system, or provide a superior product to their customers.

Recently, a variation on this business system analysis has been introduced. It focuses on core processes rather than the functional orientation of the traditional business system. For example, a core process for a fast food chain might be site development (including

The existence of substitute products can place significant limits on an industry. For example, railroads and trucks compete for the movement of freight. Rail movement is relatively cheap for large, long hauls but is not as flexible and inexpensive as truck movement for small, short hauls. However, for some shipments between the very long and very short, a shipper could use either rail or truck transportation and could try to create bidding competitions between them.

Entry and exit barriers determine the likelihood of new competitors entering the industry and old competitors leaving the industry. Entry barriers arise when there are skills or assets that only a few competitors can obtain. Access to capital is rarely an entry barrier because it is easy to obtain. Access to a new technology and patents, on the other hand, where only a handful of scientists can use the technology, can shut out new competitors. Exit barriers exist when competitors are better off staying in the industry, even though they are not earning their cost of capital. Exit barriers often arise in capital intensive industries where companies may be earning more than their marginal costs so they do not wish to exit, but the returns on capital are very low. Furthermore, managements may continue to invest capital in low return industries for long periods of time, because they do not wish to dismantle their organization or they are hoping someone else will leave first.

The bargaining power of suppliers determines what share of the total pool of customer revenues can be retained by the industry. If a company can increase its bargaining power, its share of the revenue will increase. Walmart, the discount retailer, has exploited its purchasing power and information technology about customer wants very successfully to obtain from its vendors lower prices and better service than its competitors. Attempts to extract value from suppliers do not always work. For example, many department stores have attempted to cut out the manufacturers altogether by developing their own house brands for which they design the products and contract out the manufacturing. Unfortunately, many of these retailers have found that their costs for design and manufacturing are not low enough to make up for the lower prices they generally have to charge.

The bargaining power of customers also affects the industry's share of revenues. For example, in carpet manufacturing, the major competitors have found ways to skip the wholesalers—who traditionally distributed their products to retailers—and deal directly site selection and construction), which might cut across many traditional functional areas, including marketing, real estate, construction, and finance. The advantage of this perspective is that it highlights the competitive advantages that can be gained from better cross-functional management.

Industry Structure Analysis

The third framework for assessing competitive advantages is industry structure analysis. Industry structure analysis looks outside the industry at the forces that will shape the industry's profitability. Michael Porter of Harvard is best known for having formalized industry structure models.[1] An approach to industry structure analysis is shown in Exhibit 7.2. In this model, four key external forces drive an industry's profit potential: substitute products, supplier bargaining power, customer bargaining power, and entry/exit barriers.

Exhibit 7.2 **INDUSTRY STRUCTURE MODEL**

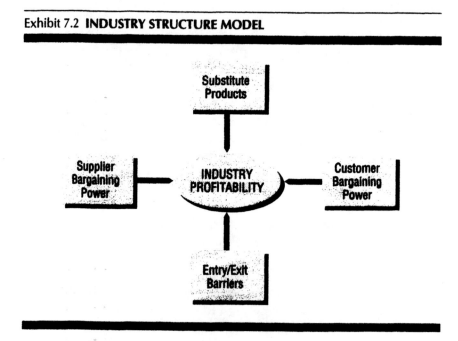

---

[1] Michael E. Porter, *Competitive Strategy: Techniques for Analyzing Industries and Competitors* (New York: Free Press, 1980).

340

Exhibit 7.3 **STRUCTURE-CONDUCT-PERFORMANCE MODEL**

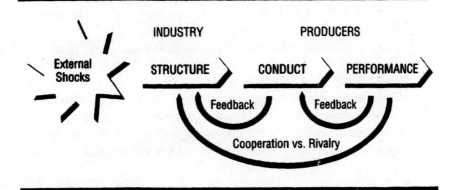

with the retail stores. They have thus been able to extract a significant share of the total revenue pool away from the wholesalers.

The Structure-Conduct-Performance model adds a dynamic element to industry structure analysis as illustrated in Exhibit 7.3. The S-C-P model adds external shocks to the system to analyze how external shocks will affect the structure, how competitors are likely to respond, and how the performance of the industry and competitors will be affected.

These three types of analyses (customer segmentation, business system, and industry structure) should provide insights into whether the industry as a whole is likely to earn returns exceeding the cost of capital and how the company being valued is positioned within the industry.

DEVELOP PERFORMANCE SCENARIOS

Once you have developed a point of view about the company's ability to achieve and sustain a competitive advantage, the next step is to develop performance scenarios. By using scenarios we acknowledge that forecasting financial performance is at best an educated guess. The best we can do is narrow down the range of likely future performance. Consider a high tech company that is developing a proprietary new product. If the company successfully develops the product, its competitive advantage will be a product that delivers superior value to customers. Accordingly, its growth and returns on capital are likely to be huge. If it fails to develop the product, it will likely go out of business. A scenario that projects moderate growth and returns is highly unlikely, even though it could be considered "most likely" from a statistical perspective. While this situation may be extreme, we strongly believe it is better to develop a number of scenarios for a company, and to understand the company's value under each scenario, than to build a single "most likely" forecast and value.

Once the scenarios are developed and valued, an overall value of the company can be estimated as a weighted average of the values of the independent scenarios, assigning probabilities to each scenario. The following table shows how we valued a steel company:

Scenario ($ millions)	Entity value	Debt	Equity value	Probability	Weighted value
Business as usual	$2,662	$2,520	$142	15%	
Industry behavior improves slightly	3,694	2,520	1,174	65%	$1,228
Sustained improvement in industry behavior	4,736	2,520	2,216	20%	

Developing scenarios does not mean mechanically changing the sales growth rate by 10 percent. Instead, it means developing a comprehensive set of assumptions about how the future may evolve and how that is likely to affect industry profitability and the company's financial performance. For example, the industry may be characterized by rapid growth and few substitutes. One scenario may assume these conditions will continue for a certain time period after which the introduction of substitutes will slow growth (for example, the way personal computers have caused the demand for mainframes to decline). Here are two simple sample scenarios:

- *The company introduces a major new product line and sales take off.* The scenario should factor in how the competition would respond in terms of competing products and pricing. It should also deal with how the company would handle the strain of the higher sales level in areas like manufacturing and distribution.

- *A substitute product enters the market.* How would the company respond? Would it just lose sales, or would it retaliate? What organizational changes would be made to compete in the new environment?

In addition to the competitive advantage assessment just described, consider these shocks that could affect industry and company performance:

- The potential for new products or technological breakthroughs that would affect demand for the company's products.
- Potential changes in government policy or regulation, such as environmental laws or international trade barriers.
- Changes in consumer tastes or lifestyles, or other factors that may affect demand for the industry's products.
- The availability of key raw materials.
- Changes in the overall health of the domestic and world economy.

FORECAST INDIVIDUAL LINE ITEMS

Before forecasting individual line items you must decide on the structure of the forecast. The structure of the forecast is the order in which the variables are forecasted and the way in which they relate to each other. The best forecast structure begins with an integrated income statement and balance sheet forecast. The free cash flow and other value drivers can then be derived from them.

It is possible to forecast free cash flow directly rather than going through the income statement and balance sheet; however, we do not recommend it. If you forecast free cash flow first, you must still construct the balance sheet to properly evaluate the relationships between the cash flow or income statement items and the balance sheet accounts. If you do not construct the balance sheet, it is easy to lose sight of how all the pieces fit together. A recent experience provides an example. A team doing a valuation tried to simplify the forecasting process by ignoring the balance sheet. The company's history showed that it usually generated about two dollars in sales for each dollar of net fixed assets. By the end of the team's forecast, the company was generating five dollars in sales for each dollar of net fixed assets. The team had not intended this result and did not even know it was happening, because it had not constructed a balance sheet and supporting ratios. The balance sheet also helps to identify the financing implications of the forecast. It shows how much capital must be raised or how much excess cash will be available.

The most common approach to forecasting the income statement and balance sheet for nonfinancial companies is a demand-driven forecast. A demand-driven forecast starts with sales. Most other variables (expenses, working capital) are driven off the sales forecast. Use the ROIC tree to organize the forecast and as a consistency check.

Forecasts of individual line items should draw upon a careful analysis of industry structure and a company's internal capabilities. Analyzing the historical level of valuation variables is a useful starting point. Once these levels have been calculated, several questions will help you gain insight into the future level of each valuation variable.

- What characteristics of the industry have had the greatest impact on value drivers in the past?
- What company-specific capabilities have had the greatest impact on historical value drivers?
- Are industry characteristics and company capabilities expected to maintain historical patterns in the future? If not, what is expected to change?
- What must change in the industry or the company to cause a significant shift in the historical level of the company's value drivers?

While we will not talk about individual line items, two topics merit special mention: inflation and the length of the forecast.

Inflation

We recommend that financial forecasts and discount rates be estimated in nominal rather than real currency units as discussed in Chapter 5. *For consistency, both the free cash flow forecast and the discount rate must be based on the same expected general inflation rate.*

Individual line items, however, could have specific inflation rates that are higher or lower than the general rate, but they should still drive off the general rate. To provide a specific example, the revenue forecast should reflect the growth in units sold and the expected increase in unit prices. The increase in unit prices, in turn, should reflect the general expected level of inflation in the economy, plus or minus an inflation rate differential for that specific product. Suppose that general inflation is expected to be 4.0 percent and that unit prices for the company's products were expected to increase at 1 percent faster than general inflation. Overall, the company's prices would be expected to increase at 5.0 percent per year. Assuming a 3 percent annual increase in units sold would lead to a forecast of 8.2 percent annual revenue growth ($1.05 \times 1.03 - 1.00$).

We can derive the expected general inflation rate that is consistent with the discount rate from the term structure of interest rates. The term structure is based on yields to maturity of U.S. government bonds. Nominal interest rates reflect lenders' expectations of future inflation. Lenders expect to be compensated for expected losses due to inflation as well as default and market risk. Exhibit 7.4 shows the term structure of interest rates at three points in time. Inflationary expectations are clearly reflected in each. In 1981, short-term interest rates were high, reflecting the market's belief at that time that future inflation would be lower than near-term inflation. In 1988, inflationary expectations were lower than in 1981, and the market believed long-term inflation would be higher than short-term inflation. In 1992, inflationary expectations were even lower.

The term structure of interest rates provides a market-based estimate of expected inflation over time. This should be the best estimate for valuation purposes, for these reasons:

- Most economists', or econometric, forecasts of inflation rarely extend beyond one or two years, far too short a period for valuation.

- Market-based estimates provide a broader consensus view (with investors' money at stake) than individual forecasts.

- Empirical analysis suggests that market-based estimates are the least biased.[2]

[2] See E. Fama and M. Gibbons, "A Comparison of Inflation Forecasts," *Journal of Monetary Economics* (May 1984): 327–348; or G. Hardouvelis, "The Predictive Power of the Term Structure during Recent Monetary Regimes," *Journal of Finance* (June 1988): 339–356.

Exhibit 7.4 **TERM STRUCTURE OF INTEREST RATES AT THREE POINTS IN TIME**

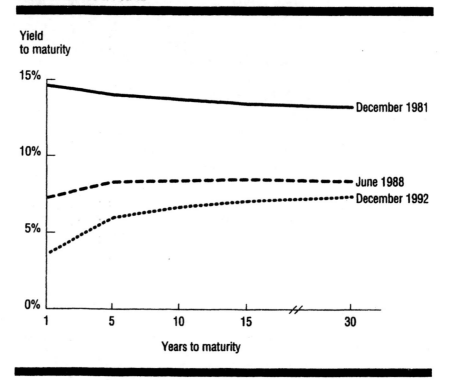

The expected inflation rate over a given period can be derived from the term structure of interest rates as follows:

1. Determine the nominal risk-free rate of interest for the time period over which you want to estimate inflation (use the same interval that will be used to calculate the weighted average cost of capital, usually ten or more years).

2. Estimate the real rate of interest. This is a controversial issue and different sources provide different estimates. Ibbotson Associates estimate the real rate as the difference between the annualized rate of return on U.S. Treasury bills and the Consumer Price Index (for all urban consumers, not seasonally adjusted). For the interval 1926 to 1991, their real rate is 0.5 percent per year. However, this rate fluctuates wildly. Looking at individual decades, real rates have ranged from −5.4 percent in the 1940s to 4.1 percent in the 1980s. Given

346

this volatility and the sense that investors are less likely to be surprised by inflation going forward as they were in the 1940s and 1970s, we recommend using a real rate estimate of 2–3 percent, which is in the range of the long-term growth in GDP.

3. Calculate the expected inflation rate from the nominal and real rates using the following formula:

$$\text{Expected inflation} = \frac{(1 + \text{Nominal rate})}{(1 + \text{Real rate})} - 1$$

Suppose the 10 year rate on government bonds is 7.0 percent and the real rate of interest is expected to be 3.0 percent. Then, the expected general inflation rate over the next ten years would be 3.9 percent. Note that the expected inflation rate is not the same for all time periods. For example, if the one year rate on government securities is 5.0 percent and if we expect the short term real rate to be 3.0 percent then the expected inflation for the next year would be 1.9 percent. If the expected inflation for the next year is 1.9 percent and the ten-year expected inflation is 3.9 percent then the rate over the last nine years must be higher than 3.9 percent so that the 10-year average will be 3.9 percent. In fact, you could estimate the expected inflation rate for each year of the forecast using the term structure of interest rates and use it for your forecast.

Length of Forecast

For practical purposes, most forecasts should be divided into two periods: an explicit forecast period (say, ten years) and the remaining life of the company (Year 11 on). A detailed forecast is done for the first period. Cash flow from the second, more distant, period is valued using a continuing-value formula as described in detail in Chapter 9.

The explicit forecast period should be long enough so that the company reaches a steady state by the end of the period. The steady state can be described as follows:

- The company earns a constant rate of return on all new capital invested during the continuing-value period.
- The company earns a constant rate of return on its base level of invested capital.

- The company invests a constant proportion of its earnings back into the business each year.

The most common approach is to make the forecast period as long as you expect the company to have sustainable rates of return on new investment above the company's cost of capital. Microeconomic analysis suggests that over time, competition will drive the returns in many industries to the level of the cost of capital. Once the company's returns have converged on its cost of capital, it is relatively simple to estimate the company's continuing value. Therefore, forecasting until convergence simplifies the continuing-value problem. If this is your approach, the forecast periods should be for as long as returns above the weighted average cost of capital are sustainable.

When in doubt, make a longer rather than shorter forecast. We would rarely use a forecast period of less than seven years. The forecast period should never be determined by the company's own internal planning period. Just because the company forecasts out only three years does not justify using three years for the valuation. A rough forecast beyond three years is certainly better than no forecast.

If a company is in a cyclical industry, it is important that your forecast capture a complete cycle. Failure to do so may result in wildly unrealistic continuing-value assumptions, because the up or down phase of the cycle may be projected to last forever. It is best to put long-run forecasts (averaging out cyclical effects) into your continuing-value assumptions.

CHECK OVERALL FORECAST FOR REASONABLENESS

The final step in the forecasting process is to construct the free cash flow and value drivers from the income statements and balance sheets and to evaluate the forecast. The forecast should be evaluated the same way the company's historical performance was analyzed. To understand how the key value drivers are expected to behave, ask:

- Is the company's performance on the key value drivers consistent with the company's economics and the industry competitive dynamics?

- Is revenue growth consistent with industry growth? If the company's revenue is growing faster than the industry's, which competitors are losing share? Will they retaliate? Does the company have the resources to manage that rate of growth?

- Is the return on capital consistent with the industry's competitive structure? If entry barriers are coming down, shouldn't expected returns decline? If customers are becoming more powerful, will margins decline? Conversely, if the company's position in the industry is becoming much stronger, should you expect increasing returns? How will returns and growth look relative to the competition?

- How will technology changes affect returns? Will they affect risk?

- Can the company manage all the investment it is undertaking?

Finally, you must understand the financing implications of the forecast. Will the company have to raise large amounts of capital? If so, can it obtain the financing? Should it be debt or equity? If the company is generating excess cash, what options does it have for investing the cash or returning it to shareholders?

PRESTON CORPORATION

In Chapter 6, we presented a historical analysis of Preston Corporation. In this section, we will develop a forecast of Preston's financial performance. Recall from Chapter 6 that Preston's return on capital has been consistently lower than its WACC and also lower than its major competitors.

EVALUATE STRATEGIC POSITION

Preston's strategic position is fundamentally unattractive. While average returns on invested capital in the industry will probably improve somewhat, these returns are unlikely to exceed the industry's cost of capital by much. Furthermore, Preston does not appear to have any significant competitive advantage that will help it to beat the rest of the industry.

We developed the following insights after conducting analyses of customer segmentation, competitive business systems, and industry structure.

- The customers that Preston has targeted are a broad range of small-to-medium shippers with fairly similar needs. They are mainly concerned with price and on-time delivery. Most customers currently believe that almost all truckers provide comparable on-time delivery and therefore focus mostly on price. Preston has done nothing to carve out a niche for itself by providing a differentiating service to any group of customers.

- A business system analysis provided similarly discouraging information.

  - Preston and many of its competitors have unionized labor. The non-unionized truckers have significant cost advantages.

  - Other than labor costs, all competitors have access to the same equipment and technology.

  - The larger competitors appear to enjoy significant economies of scale in their ability to efficiently consolidate their shipments from many customers and to ensure that their trucks are always full.

  - Several smaller competitors have carved out niches that they dominate through superior service and knowledge of the customers shipping needs.

  - Unfortunately, Preston does not have the scale economies of the larger players nor has it taken control of any customer segment.

- An industry structure analysis demonstrated that the primary factors affecting the industry are entry/exit barriers. Substitutes, supplier bargaining, and customer bargaining power are not critical factors in the industry. On the negative side, entry barriers are low. Just about anyone can buy a truck and set up a trucking business. On the positive side, exit barriers are also low and many competitors were leaving the market as they realized they could not compete profitably.

In summary, while the overall outlook for the industry is improving (as evidenced by firming prices), the fundamental outlook is unattractive, except perhaps for the largest carriers who may be able achieve cost advantages through larger scale and for the niche players who dominate certain market segments. Preston appears to be attempting to achieve the size necessary in selected markets to realize the scale economies of the largest players in those markets. It is not clear whether Preston will succeed. Overlying all this, however, is the uncertainty about competitive behavior. Since competition is primarily on price, future price wars are always possible.

DEVELOP PERFORMANCE SCENARIOS

We developed three performance scenarios for Preston.

1. *Moderate Performance.* Under this scenario, the industry avoids major price wars so overall industry returns on capital improve to approximately the cost of capital. Preston's performance also improves as management moves to emphasize several geographic regions where it is better positioned to achieve some scale economies, and as management completes several initiatives to improve productivity. However, Preston never really achieves the scale or segment dominance to earn outstanding returns.

2. *Downside.* Under this scenario, the industry price wars continue, keeping industry returns below the cost of capital. Preston's performance continues to be weak.

3. *Upside.* Like the first scenario, the industry avoids price wars and industry returns approach the cost of capital. In this scenario, however, Preston finds several geographic niches and is able to gradually achieve returns somewhat above the industry.

FORECAST INDIVIDUAL LINE ITEMS

We present the line item forecast for the moderate performance scenario. The detailed projections are laid out in Exhibits 7.5 and 7.6. We forecasted Preston's performance for ten years because we believe that was a sufficient period for the industry to shake out and for Preston's long-term performance level to be established.

The Preston forecast is a demand-driven forecast. Most items are driven by the sales forecast. Our approach to forecasting each item is certainly not the only appropriate technique. It would be impossible to enumerate all the possibilities. Therefore, we have chosen to present one method to indicate the types of issues that should be addressed.

Revenues

Revenue growth is determined by the growth in the quantity of carrier services provided (tonnage) and prices (rates). Tonnage is largely determined by the level of industrial production and by the ability of the company to capture increased market share as the industry continues to undergo consolidation. Through the first half of 1988, Preston's tonnage was 18.7 percent higher than it was during the same period of 1987. After taking into account

Exhibit 7.5 PRESTON CORPORATION, MODERATE CASE, FORECAST OPERATING ASSUMPTIONS

	1988	1989	1990	1991	1992	1993	1994	1995	1996	1997	Perp
Operations											
Revenue growth	20.8%	14.8%	12.6%	10.8%	9.3%	9.5%	9.4%	9.6%	9.7%	9.9%	9.4%
Operating expense/revenues	91.5%	90.7%	90.0%	89.5%	89.0%	89.0%	89.0%	89.0%	89.0%	89.0%	89.0%
Other expense/revenues	0.0%	0.0%	0.0%	0.0%	0.0%	0.0%	0.0%	0.0%	0.0%	0.0%	0.0%
EBDIT Margin	8.5%	9.3%	10.0%	10.5%	11.0%	11.0%	11.0%	11.0%	11.0%	11.0%	11.0%
Operating lease adjustments/revenues	-0.2%	-0.2%	-0.2%	-0.2%	-0.2%	-0.2%	-0.2%	-0.2%	-0.2%	-0.2%	-0.2%
Depreciation/revenues	4.6%	4.7%	4.8%	4.8%	4.9%	5.0%	5.0%	5.0%	5.1%	5.1%	5.1%
Operating margin	4.1%	4.9%	5.5%	5.9%	6.3%	6.3%	6.2%	6.2%	6.2%	6.2%	6.1%
Working capital/revenues											
Operating cash	1.9%	1.9%	1.9%	1.9%	1.9%	1.9%	1.9%	1.9%	1.9%	1.9%	1.9%
Accounts receivable	13.3%	13.3%	13.3%	13.3%	13.3%	13.3%	13.3%	13.3%	13.3%	13.3%	13.3%
Inventories	2.5%	2.5%	2.5%	2.5%	2.5%	2.5%	2.5%	2.5%	2.5%	2.5%	2.5%
Other current assets	0.9%	0.9%	0.9%	0.9%	0.9%	0.9%	0.9%	0.9%	0.9%	0.9%	0.9%
Accounts payable	3.9%	3.9%	3.9%	3.9%	3.9%	3.9%	3.9%	3.9%	3.9%	3.9%	3.9%
Other current liabilities	6.1%	6.1%	6.1%	6.1%	6.1%	6.1%	6.1%	6.1%	6.1%	6.1%	6.1%
Net working capital	8.6%	8.6%	8.6%	8.6%	8.6%	8.6%	8.6%	8.6%	8.6%	8.6%	8.6%
Property, Plant, and Equipment Input Values:											
CapX/revs (Input, Mode 1)	6.9%	9.8%	9.0%	8.3%	7.8%	7.4%	7.5%	7.5%	7.5%	7.5%	7.5%
NPPE/Revs (Input, Mode 2)	37.0%	36.5%	36.0%	35.5%	35.0%	34.5%	34.0%	33.5%	33.0%	32.5%	32.0%
Depr/Last year's GPPE	9.5%	9.5%	9.5%	9.5%	9.5%	9.5%	9.5%	9.5%	9.5%	9.5%	9.5%
Retirements/last year's GPPE	4.0%	4.0%	4.0%	4.0%	4.0%	4.0%	4.0%	4.0%	4.0%	4.0%	4.0%

Exhibit 7.6 PRESTON CORPORATION, MODERATE CASE, OTHER FORECAST ASSUMPTIONS, $ MILLIONS

	1988	1989	1990	1991	1992	1993	1994	1995	1996	1997	Perp
Taxes											
EBIT tax rate	39.0%	39.0%	39.0%	39.0%	39.0%	39.0%	39.0%	39.0%	39.0%	39.0%	39.0%
Marginal tax rate	39.0%	39.0%	39.0%	39.0%	39.0%	39.0%	39.0%	39.0%	39.0%	39.0%	39.0%
Incr def tax/tax on EBIT	10.0%	10.0%	10.0%	10.0%	10.0%	10.0%	10.0%	10.0%	10.0%	10.0%	10.0%
Financing											
Int rate on excess marketable securities	8.0%	8.0%	8.0%	8.0%	8.0%	8.0%	8.0%	8.0%	8.0%	8.0%	8.0%
Int rate on short-term debt	8.1%	8.1%	8.1%	8.1%	8.1%	8.1%	8.1%	8.1%	8.1%	8.1%	8.1%
Int rate on long-term debt	8.1%	8.1%	8.1%	8.1%	8.1%	8.1%	8.1%	8.1%	8.1%	8.1%	8.1%
Int rate on new long-term debt	10.8%	10.8%	10.8%	10.8%	10.8%	10.8%	10.8%	10.8%	10.8%	10.8%	10.8%
Dividend payout ratio	45.0%	45.0%	45.0%	45.0%	45.0%	45.0%	45.0%	45.0%	45.0%	45.0%	45.0%
Rate on operating leases	10.8%	10.8%	10.8%	10.8%	10.8%	10.8%	10.8%	10.8%	10.8%	10.8%	10.8%
Minority interest											
Min Int(IS)/income after-tax	0.0%	0.0%	0.0%	0.0%	0.0%	0.0%	0.0%	0.0%	0.0%	0.0%	0.0%
Minority Int payout ratio	0.0%	0.0%	0.0%	0.0%	0.0%	0.0%	0.0%	0.0%	0.0%	0.0%	0.0%
Minority interest (BS)	0.0	0.0	0.0	0.0	0.0	0.0	0.0	0.0	0.0	0.0	0.0

Exhibit 7.6 Continued

	1988	1989	1990	1991	1992	1993	1994	1995	1996	1997	Perp
Other ratios											
Nonoperating income growth	0.0%	0.0%	0.0%	0.0%	0.0%	0.0%	0.0%	0.0%	0.0%	0.0%	0.0%
Other assets/revenues	1.6%	1.6%	1.6%	1.6%	1.6%	1.6%	1.6%	1.6%	1.6%	1.6%	1.6%
Nonoperating assets growth rate	0.0%	0.0%	0.0%	0.0%	0.0%	0.0%	0.0%	0.0%	0.0%	0.0%	0.0%
Other liabs/revenues	0.0%	0.0%	0.0%	0.0%	0.0%	0.0%	0.0%	0.0%	0.0%	0.0%	0.0%
Cap operating leases/revenues	2.2%	2.2%	2.2%	2.2%	2.2%	2.2%	2.2%	2.2%	2.2%	2.2%	2.2%
Other values ($)											
Amortization of goodwill ($)	0.6	0.6	0.6	0.6	0.6	0.6	0.6	0.6	0.6	0.6	0.6
Special items ($)	0.0	0.0	0.0	0.0	0.0	0.0	0.0	0.0	0.0	0.0	0.0
Extraordinary items ($)	0.0	0.0	0.0	0.0	0.0	0.0	0.0	0.0	0.0	0.0	0.0
Effects of accounting change ($)	0.0	0.0	0.0	0.0	0.0	0.0	0.0	0.0	0.0	0.0	0.0
Short-term debt ($)	0.0	0.0	0.0	0.0	0.0	0.0	0.0	0.0	0.0	0.0	0.0
Long-term debt ($)	118.1	115.5	51.4	49.7	48.7	32.1	31.2	30.5	30.0	29.5	29.5
Preferred stock ($)	0.0	0.0	0.0	0.0	0.0	0.0	0.0	0.0	0.0	0.0	0.0
Preferred dividends ($)	0.0	0.0	0.0	0.0	0.0	0.0	0.0	0.0	0.0	0.0	0.0
Capitalized operating leases ($)	13.4	15.4	17.4	19.2	21.0	23.0	25.2	27.6	30.3	33.3	36.4

a seasonal drop in tonnage during the fourth quarter, we project total tonnage growth to be 16.2 percent in 1988.

The industry is currently facing a large upswing in demand, and as a result, many companies are operating at levels near their short-term capacity. For these reasons, we forecast a large increase in Preston's tonnage, slowing over the next several years to a permanent real growth level of 3 percent, which is our forecast of the long-term rate of real industrial production growth.

As discussed earlier, rates in the industry are firming. The industry enacted a 3.3 percent rate increase in October 1987 and additional 3.5 percent rate increases in April and late June 1988. This growth is in contrast to the recent rate stagnation faced by the industry due to increased competition since deregulation, and it is allowing the industry to move closer to achieving normal returns on its invested capital. However, rate increases are implemented slowly because approximately half of the industry's demand is locked in at defined rates in contracts. Thus, full rate increases cannot be achieved until these contracts expire.

We are therefore forecasting the recent and future rate increases to be gradually phased in, and thus we expect an increase of 4 percent during 1988 and a slow growth in rates over the next several years. We forecast the rate growth to eventually level off to the rate of expected inflation. Our revenue growth forecast is as follows (the total revenue growth is the product rather than the sum of the component growth rates):

	Tonnage growth	Rate growth	Revenue growth
1988	16.2%	4.0%	20.8%
1989	9.5	4.8	14.8
1990	7.0	5.2	12.6
1991	4.8	5.7	10.8
1992	3.0	6.1	9.3
1993	3.0	6.3	9.5
1994	3.0	6.2	9.4
1995	3.0	6.4	9.6
1996	3.0	6.5	9.7
1997	3.0	6.7	9.9

Operating Expenses

Preston's operating expenses as a percentage of revenues have fluctuated between 91.6 percent and 93.6 percent during the last five years. Over the past several years a few trends are apparent in specific components of this category. Claims and insurance costs as a percentage of revenues have risen by almost 40 percent since 1985. Much of this increase has been due to the occurrence of an unusually high number of severe accidents; therefore, we believe this trend will stop. Over the same period, salaries, wages, and fringes as a percentage of revenues, and purchased transportation as a percentage of revenues, have experienced small yet steady increases and declines, respectively.

We forecast operating expenses to decline as a percentage of revenues during the next several years. A primary reason for this forecast is our expectation of continued rising rates. We believe the recent rate increases enacted by Preston will more than offset the effects of the new three-year labor contract that took effect April 1, 1988, between the Teamsters and the trucking industry. (The contract calls for a 7 percent wage-cost increase in the first year, and a 2.5 percent to 3 percent increase in each of the following years.) In addition, because of its relatively slow growth, Preston's labor costs as a percentage of revenues will be less affected by the new contract than those of faster-growing firms. This is because newly and recently hired employees will receive the largest pay increases, and these employees are most prevalent at quickly growing firms. Overall, rates should rise more quickly than costs in the near future, and thus Preston's gross margin should also rise.

Depreciation Expense

Depreciation as a percentage of gross property, plant, and equipment has remained in the 9 to 10 percent range over the past six years. This should not change, so we have forecasted depreciation to equal 9.5 percent of the prior period's gross property, plant, and equipment.

Working Capital

For valuation purposes, operating working capital is defined as the sum of the operating cash, accounts receivable, inventories, and prepaid expenses less accounts payable and other current liabilities. We did not discern any clear trends in Preston's working capital as a percentage of revenues. Over the last three years, net operating working capital has remained in the range of 8.2 percent to 9.1 percent of revenues. None of the individual components has shown significant change, either. We will forecast Preston's working capital to remain about where it has been relative to revenues.

Consider the following when forecasting working capital:

- How does the company's inventory accounting method (LIFO versus FIFO) affect its reported inventories?
- Does the company's changing mix of business affect its need for working capital?

- Is the company planning any action to reduce its working capital (for example, just-in-time inventory system)?
- If a trend in working capital is discernible, will the improvement/deterioration continue or will it stabilize?

Year-end working capital can be fairly volatile simply because it is measured only on the last day of the year. Average measures are probably more stable, yet not generally available. Therefore, do not give too much weight to minor, random, year-to-year fluctuations. Focus instead on major trends.

Fixed Assets

Preston owns a variety of fixed assets, including trailers, tractors, trucks, freight terminals, retail outlets for the sale of salvaged freight, and tire-recapping facilities. Fixed assets are probably the trickiest part of the forecast. Most of the company's revenues, costs, and working capital are affected somewhat equally by inflation. Since fixed assets are not replaced each year, however, it is difficult to forecast the cost of replacing old assets that wear out.

For Preston, we have made some fairly simple assumptions. We assume it takes a stable amount of fixed assets to generate each dollar of sales. We expect that the relatively low levels of inflation experienced over the past several years will persist in the near future and will not materially alter this assumption. Therefore, we predict that over the forecast period, the ratio of revenue to property, plant, and equipment will gradually move closer to its historical average. Note that these assumptions would not work well with fast-growing companies or in an unstable inflationary environment.

Accumulated depreciation is the prior period's accumulated depreciation, plus the current period's depreciation expense, minus the book value of assets retired in the current period.

We will assume that fixed assets are used until they are fully depreciated and that they have no material scrap value. Therefore, the amount of assets retired from gross property, plant, and equipment will equal the amount of the reduction in accumulated depreciation. We have set the level of retirements at 4 percent of gross property, plant, and equipment, near recent historical levels.

Income Taxes

We estimated Preston's historical marginal income tax rate to be about 49 percent. This was a 46 percent federal rate, plus an effective 3 percent state and local rate. The 1986 Tax Reform Act reduced Preston's marginal federal rate to 40 percent in 1987 and to 34 percent beginning in 1988.

Adding a provision for state and local taxes (net of the federal tax benefit derived from them), we estimate Preston's marginal income tax rate will be 45 percent in 1987 and 39 percent beginning in 1988.

Preston's EBIT tax rate has historically been below its marginal rate, as shown in Exhibit 6.18. This was primarily due to investment tax credits that have been eliminated by the 1986 Tax Reform Act. Therefore, we have forecasted Preston's EBIT tax rate to equal its marginal income tax rate.

The total income tax provision on the income statement is the sum of two elements: Preston's EBIT multiplied by the EBIT tax rate, and the marginal tax rate multiplied by Preston's net interest income and nonoperating income less interest expense.

The increase in accumulated deferred income taxes as a percentage of the income tax provision has fluctuated widely. Deferred taxes can have a significant effect on the timing of free cash flow, because they represent the delay of a cash outflow—taxes. They arise because, in calculating its taxes, a company uses a depreciation schedule that is different from the schedule it uses to produce its financial statements. We are forecasting the increase in accumulated deferred taxes to be 10 percent of Preston's taxes on EBIT.

Financing

The amortization schedule for Preston's existing debt is provided in the annual report. New debt or marketable securities are created automatically in our forecast to balance the sources and uses of cash.

The interest rate on existing debt is forecast to equal the effective rate in 1987, 8.1 percent. The rate on new debt and operating leases is equal to Preston's current marginal borrowing rate of 11 percent. This rate is derived in Chapter 8, on estimating the cost of capital.

We also expect Preston to have a $0.53 per share dividend payout in 1988. For the remainder of the forecast period, we expect dividends to average approximately 45 percent of net income.

Other

Goodwill amortization should remain constant at $0.6 million per year since we are not forecasting any acquisitions. The amount of goodwill on the balance sheet will decline each year by the amount of the amortization.

We expect nonoperating income to be zero. It is impossible to generalize about the treatment of nonoperating items; just be careful and remember to take them into consideration in your valuation.

Other assets on the balance sheet are forecast to remain at the same percentage of revenues as they were in 1987. Since we possess no information regarding what this category contains, we are assuming that a certain level of these assets is necessary to generate each dollar of revenue.

CHECK OVERALL FORECAST FOR REASONABLENESS

Exhibits 7.7 to 7.14 show the resulting forecast of Preston's financial performance for the moderate performance scenario. The following table summarizes Preston's performance in this scenario.

	1983–87	Forecast 1988–1992	Forecast 1993–1997
Revenue growth	13.1*	13.6%	9.6%
EBIT growth	12.6	36.3	9.1
Pretax ROIC	9.4	12.3	14.7
After-tax ROIC	7.6	8.0	9.5
WACC	11.1	9.7	9.7

* Excludes acquisition

As anticipated, Preston's performance in this scenario is substantially improved over recent years, but its ROIC does not beat its WACC, even in the long run. Therefore, Preston's marginal ROIC is less than its WACC. As a result, the strong growth will not create any value. Overall, the results are consistent with the scenario we outlined.

As for the financing implications of this scenario, Preston's coverage ratio remains between 2 and 3 times EBIT. This is because Preston's relatively high growth rate coupled with moderate return on capital means that its investment rate averages near 100 percent. As a result, Preston must borrow to pay dividends and interest expense. This level of coverage probably does not provide enough cushion in this volatile environment. Preston should probably consider reducing its dividends to conserve financial flexibility if performance does not improve substantially.

Exhibit 7.7 **PRESTON CORPORATION, MODERATE CASE, FORECASTED INCOME STATEMENT**, $ MILLIONS

	1988	1989	1990	1991	1992	1993	1994	1995	1996	1997	Perp
Revenues	610.5	700.9	789.2	874.4	955.7	1,046.5	1,144.9	1,254.8	1,376.5	1,512.8	1,655.0
Operating expenses	(588.6)	(635.7)	(710.3)	(782.6)	(850.6)	(931.4)	(1,019.0)	(1,116.8)	(1,225.1)	(1,346.4)	(1,473.0)
Other expenses	0.0	0.0	0.0	0.0	0.0	0.0	0.0	0.0	0.0	0.0	0.0
Depreciation expense	(28.3)	(32.8)	(37.5)	(42.2)	(47.1)	(51.9)	(57.3)	(63.1)	(69.6)	(76.6)	(84.4)
Operating income	23.6	32.3	41.4	49.6	58.1	63.2	68.6	74.9	81.8	89.8	97.7
Amortization of goodwill	(0.6)	(0.6)	(0.6)	(0.6)	(0.6)	(0.6)	(0.6)	(0.6)	(0.6)	(0.6)	(0.6)
Nonoperating income	0.0	0.0	0.0	0.0	0.0	0.0	0.0	0.0	0.0	0.0	0.0
Interest income	0.3	0.0	(0.0)	0.0	0.0	(0.0)	(0.0)	0.0	0.0	(0.0)	(0.0)
Interest expense	(11.6)	(16.0)	(19.5)	(24.3)	(26.9)	(29.0)	(31.8)	(34.3)	(37.1)	(40.1)	(43.4)
Special items	0.0	0.0	0.0	0.0	0.0	0.0	0.0	0.0	0.0	0.0	0.0
Earnings before taxes	11.7	15.8	21.3	24.7	30.6	33.6	36.2	40.0	44.2	49.1	53.7
Income taxes	(4.8)	(6.4)	(8.6)	(9.9)	(12.1)	(13.3)	(14.4)	(15.8)	(17.5)	(19.4)	(21.2)
Minority interest	0.0	0.0	0.0	0.0	0.0	0.0	0.0	0.0	0.0	0.0	0.0
Income before extra items	6.9	9.4	12.8	14.8	18.4	20.2	21.9	24.2	26.7	29.7	32.5
Extraordinary items	0.0	0.0	0.0	0.0	0.0	0.0	0.0	0.0	0.0	0.0	0.0
Effect of accounting change	0.0	0.0	0.0	0.0	0.0	0.0	0.0	0.0	0.0	0.0	0.0
Net income	6.9	9.4	12.8	14.8	18.4	20.2	21.9	24.2	26.7	29.7	32.5

Exhibit 7.7 Continued

	1988	1989	1990	1991	1992	1993	1994	1995	1996	1997	Perp
Statement of retained earnings											
Beginning retained earnings	85.8	89.6	94.8	101.8	109.9	120.1	131.2	143.2	156.5	171.2	187.6
Net income	6.9	9.4	12.8	14.8	18.4	20.2	21.9	24.2	26.7	29.7	32.5
Common dividends	(3.1)	(4.2)	(5.7)	(6.7)	(8.3)	(9.1)	(9.8)	(10.9)	(12.0)	(13.4)	(14.6)
Preferred dividends	0.0	0.0	0.0	0.0	0.0	0.0	0.0	0.0	0.0	0.0	0.0
Adjustments to retained earnings	0.0	0.0	0.0	0.0	0.0	0.0	0.0	0.0	0.0	0.0	0.0
Ending retained earnings	89.6	94.8	101.8	109.9	120.1	131.2	143.2	156.5	171.2	187.6	205.4

Exhibit 7.8 PRESTON CORPORATION, MODERATE CASE, FORECASTED BALANCE SHEET, $ MILLIONS

	1988	1989	1990	1991	1992	1993	1994	1995	1996	1997	Perp
Operating cash	11.6	13.4	15.0	16.7	18.2	19.9	21.8	23.9	26.2	28.8	31.5
Excess marketable securities	0.0	0.0	0.0	0.0	0.0	0.0	0.0	0.0	0.0	0.0	0.0
Accounts receivable	81.2	93.3	105.0	116.3	127.2	139.2	152.3	167.0	183.2	201.3	220.2
Inventories	15.3	17.6	19.8	21.9	24.0	26.3	28.7	31.5	34.5	38.0	41.5
Other current assets	5.5	6.4	7.2	7.9	8.7	9.5	10.4	11.4	12.5	13.7	15.0
Total current assets	113.7	130.6	147.0	162.9	178.0	195.0	213.3	233.8	256.4	281.8	308.3
Gross property plant and equipment	345.7	394.6	444.6	495.4	546.7	603.3	664.7	732.4	806.5	888.3	975.1
Accum. depreciation	(119.8)	(138.8)	(160.5)	(184.9)	(212.2)	(242.2)	(275.4)	(312.0)	(352.3)	(396.6)	(445.5)
Net property plant and equipment	225.9	255.8	284.1	310.4	334.5	361.1	389.3	420.4	454.3	491.7	529.6
Goodwill	23.8	23.2	22.6	22.0	21.4	20.8	20.2	19.6	19.0	18.4	17.8
Other operating assets	9.8	11.2	12.6	14.0	15.3	16.7	18.3	20.1	22.0	24.2	26.5
Investments and advances	0.0	0.0	0.0	0.0	0.0	0.0	0.0	0.0	0.0	0.0	0.0
Total assets	373.2	420.8	466.4	509.3	549.3	593.6	641.1	693.8	751.7	816.1	882.2

Exhibit 7.8 Continued

	1988	1989	1990	1991	1992	1993	1994	1995	1996	1997	Perp
Short-term debt	0.0	0.0	0.0	0.0	0.0	0.0	0.0	0.0	0.0	0.0	0.0
Accounts payable	23.7	27.3	30.7	34.0	37.2	40.7	44.5	48.8	53.5	58.8	64.3
Other current liabilities	37.5	43.1	48.5	53.8	58.8	64.4	70.4	77.2	84.7	93.0	101.8
Total current liabilities	61.3	70.4	79.2	87.8	95.9	105.0	114.9	126.0	138.2	151.9	166.1
Long-term debt	118.1	115.5	51.4	49.7	48.7	32.1	31.2	30.5	30.0	29.5	29.5
New long-term debt	59.3	94.0	186.1	212.0	232.3	270.4	294.1	320.2	348.4	379.6	409.6
Deferred income taxes	21.3	22.6	24.3	26.3	28.7	31.2	34.0	37.0	40.4	44.0	48.0
Other non-interest liabilities	0.0	0.0	0.0	0.0	0.0	0.0	0.0	0.0	0.0	0.0	0.0
Minority interest	0.0	0.0	0.0	0.0	0.0	0.0	0.0	0.0	0.0	0.0	0.0
Preferred stock	0.0	0.0	0.0	0.0	0.0	0.0	0.0	0.0	0.0	0.0	0.0
Common stock and paid-in capital	23.6	23.6	23.6	23.6	23.6	23.6	23.6	23.6	23.6	23.6	23.6
Retained earnings	89.6	94.8	101.8	109.9	120.1	131.2	143.2	156.5	171.2	187.6	205.4
Treasury stock	0.0	0.0	0.0	0.0	0.0	0.0	0.0	0.0	0.0	0.0	0.0
Cumulative translation and other adjustments	0.0	0.0	0.0	0.0	0.0	0.0	0.0	0.0	0.0	0.0	0.0
Total common equity	113.2	118.4	125.4	133.5	143.7	154.8	166.8	180.1	194.8	211.2	229.0
Total liabilities and equity	373.2	420.8	466.4	509.3	549.3	593.6	641.1	693.8	751.7	816.1	882.2

363

Exhibit 7.9 **PRESTON CORPORATION, MODERATE CASE, FORECASTED NOPLAT,** $ MILLIONS

	1988	1989	1990	1991	1992	1993	1994	1995	1996	1997	Perp
NOPLAT											
Net Sales	610.5	700.9	789.2	874.4	955.7	1,046.5	1,144.9	1,254.8	1,376.5	1,512.8	1,655.0
Operating expenses	(558.6)	(635.7)	(710.3)	(782.6)	(850.6)	(931.4)	(1,019.0)	(1,116.8)	(1,225.1)	(1,346.4)	(1,473.0)
Other expenses	0.0	0.0	0.0	0.0	0.0	0.0	0.0	0.0	0.0	0.0	0.0
Depreciation expense	(28.3)	(32.8)	(37.5)	(42.2)	(47.1)	(51.9)	(57.3)	(63.1)	(69.6)	(76.6)	(84.4)
Adj for operating leases	1.5	1.7	1.9	2.1	2.3	2.5	2.7	3.0	3.3	3.6	3.9
EBIT	25.1	34.0	43.3	51.7	60.3	65.7	71.3	77.9	85.1	93.4	101.6
Taxes on EBIT	(9.8)	(13.3)	(16.9)	(20.1)	(23.5)	(25.6)	(27.8)	(30.4)	(33.2)	(36.4)	(39.6)
Change in deferred taxes	1.0	1.3	1.7	2.0	2.4	2.6	2.8	3.0	3.3	3.6	4.0
Deferred taxes accounting change	0.0	0.0	0.0	0.0	0.0	0.0	0.0	0.0	0.0	0.0	0.0
NOPLAT	16.3	22.1	28.1	33.5	39.2	42.6	46.3	50.5	55.2	60.6	65.9
Taxes on EBIT											
Provision for income taxes	4.8	6.4	8.6	9.9	12.1	13.3	14.4	15.8	17.5	19.4	21.2
Tax shield on interest expense	4.5	6.2	7.6	9.5	10.5	11.3	12.4	13.4	14.5	15.6	16.9
Tax shield on operating lease interest	0.6	0.6	0.7	0.8	0.9	1.0	1.1	1.2	1.3	1.4	1.5
Tax on interest income	(0.1)	0.0	0.0	0.0	0.0	0.0	0.0	0.0	0.0	0.0	0.0
Tax on nonoperating income	0.0	0.0	0.0	0.0	0.0	0.0	0.0	0.0	0.0	0.0	0.0
Taxes on EBIT	9.8	13.3	16.9	20.1	23.5	25.6	27.8	30.4	33.2	36.4	39.6

Exhibit 7.9 Continued

	1988	1989	1990	1991	1992	1993	1994	1995	1996	1997	Perp
Reconciliation to net income											
Net income	6.9	9.4	12.8	14.8	18.4	20.2	21.9	24.2	26.7	29.7	32.5
Add: increase in deferred taxes	1.0	1.3	1.7	2.0	2.4	2.6	2.8	3.0	3.3	3.6	4.0
Add: Goodwill amortization	0.6	0.6	0.6	0.6	0.6	0.6	0.6	0.6	0.6	0.6	0.6
Add: Extraordinary items	0.0	0.0	0.0	0.0	0.0	0.0	0.0	0.0	0.0	0.0	0.0
Add: Special items after tax	0.0	0.0	0.0	0.0	0.0	0.0	0.0	0.0	0.0	0.0	0.0
Add: Minority interest	0.0	0.0	0.0	0.0	0.0	0.0	0.0	0.0	0.0	0.0	0.0
Adjusted net income	8.5	11.3	15.1	17.5	21.4	23.4	25.2	27.8	30.6	34.0	37.1
Add: Interest expense after tax	7.1	9.7	11.9	14.8	16.4	17.7	19.4	20.9	22.6	24.4	26.5
Add: Interest expense on operating leases	0.9	1.0	1.1	1.3	1.4	1.5	1.7	1.8	2.0	2.2	2.4
Total income available to investors	16.4	22.1	28.1	33.5	39.2	42.6	46.3	50.5	55.2	60.6	65.9
Less: Interest income after tax	(0.2)	0.0	0.0	0.0	0.0	0.0	0.0	0.0	0.0	0.0	0.0
Less: Nonoperating income after tax	0.0	0.0	0.0	0.0	0.0	0.0	0.0	0.0	0.0	0.0	0.0
NOPLAT	16.3	22.1	28.1	33.5	39.2	42.6	46.3	50.5	55.2	60.6	65.9

Exhibit 7.10 **PRESTON CORPORATION, MODERATE CASE, FORECASTED INVESTED CAPITAL**, $ MILLIONS

	1988	1989	1990	1991	1992	1993	1994	1995	1996	1997	Perp
Operating current assets	113.7	130.6	147.0	162.9	178.0	195.0	213.3	233.8	256.4	281.8	308.3
Noninterest bearing liabilities	(61.3)	(70.4)	(79.2)	(87.8)	(95.9)	(105.0)	(114.9)	(126.0)	(138.2)	(151.9)	(166.1)
Operating working capital	52.5	60.2	67.8	75.1	82.1	89.9	98.4	107.8	118.3	130.0	142.2
Net property plant and equipment	225.9	255.8	284.1	310.4	334.5	361.1	389.3	420.4	454.3	491.7	529.6
Other assets net of other liabilities	9.8	11.2	12.6	14.0	15.3	16.7	18.3	20.1	22.0	24.2	26.5
Value of operating leases	13.4	15.4	17.4	19.2	21.0	23.0	25.2	27.6	30.3	33.3	36.4
Operating invested capital	301.5	342.7	381.9	418.8	452.9	490.7	531.1	575.9	624.8	679.1	734.7
Excess marketable securities	0.0	0.0	0.0	0.0	0.0	0.0	0.0	0.0	0.0	0.0	0.0
Goodwill	23.8	23.2	22.6	22.0	21.4	20.8	20.2	19.6	19.0	18.4	17.8
Nonoperating investments	0.0	0.0	0.0	0.0	0.0	0.0	0.0	0.0	0.0	0.0	0.0
Total investor funds	325.3	365.9	404.5	440.8	474.3	511.5	551.3	595.5	643.8	697.5	752.5
Equity	113.2	118.4	125.4	133.5	143.7	154.8	166.8	180.1	194.8	211.2	229.0
Deferred income taxes	21.3	22.6	24.3	26.3	28.7	31.2	34.0	37.0	40.4	44.0	48.0
Adjusted equity	134.5	141.0	149.7	159.9	172.3	188.0	200.8	217.1	235.2	255.2	277.0
Interest bearing debt	177.4	209.5	237.5	261.7	281.0	302.5	325.3	350.7	378.4	409.1	439.1
Value of operating leases	13.4	15.4	17.4	19.2	21.0	23.0	25.2	27.6	30.3	33.3	36.4
Total investor funds	325.3	365.9	404.5	440.8	474.3	511.5	551.3	595.5	643.8	697.5	752.5

Exhibit 7.11 PRESTON CORPORATION, MODERATE CASE, FORECASTED FREE CASH FLOW, $ MILLIONS

	1988	1989	1990	1991	1992	1993	1994	1995	1996	1997	Perp
EBIT	25.1	34.0	43.3	51.7	60.3	65.7	71.3	77.9	85.1	93.4	101.6
Taxes on EBIT	(9.8)	(13.3)	(16.9)	(20.1)	(23.5)	(25.6)	(27.8)	(30.4)	(33.2)	(36.4)	(39.6)
Change in deferred taxes	1.0	1.3	1.7	2.0	2.4	2.6	2.8	3.0	3.3	3.6	4.0
NOPLAT	16.3	22.1	28.1	33.5	39.2	42.6	46.3	50.5	55.2	60.6	65.9
Depreciation	28.3	32.8	37.5	42.2	47.1	51.9	57.3	63.1	69.6	76.6	84.4
Gross cash flow	44.5	54.9	65.6	75.8	86.2	94.6	103.6	113.7	124.8	137.2	150.3
Increase in working capital	9.8	7.8	7.6	7.3	7.0	7.8	8.5	9.4	10.5	11.7	12.2
Capital expenditures	60.0	62.8	65.8	68.5	71.1	78.5	85.5	94.2	103.5	114.0	122.3
Increase in other assets	1.5	1.4	1.4	1.4	1.3	1.5	1.6	1.8	1.9	2.2	2.3
Inv in operating leases	2.4	2.0	1.9	1.9	1.8	2.0	2.2	2.4	2.7	3.0	3.1
Gross investment	73.6	74.0	76.7	79.1	81.2	89.7	97.7	107.9	118.5	130.9	140.0
Free cash flow before goodwill	(29.1)	(19.1)	(11.1)	(3.3)	5.0	4.8	5.9	5.8	6.3	6.3	10.4
Investment in goodwill	0.0	0.0	0.0	0.0	0.0	0.0	0.0	0.0	0.0	0.0	0.0
Free cash flow	(29.1)	(19.1)	(11.1)	(3.3)	5.0	4.8	5.9	5.8	6.3	6.3	10.4
Nonoperating cash flow	0.0	0.0	0.0	0.0	0.0	0.0	0.0	0.0	0.0	0.0	0.0
Foreign currency translation effect	0.0	0.0	0.0	0.0	0.0	0.0	0.0	0.0	0.0	0.0	0.0
Cash flow available to investors	(29.1)	(19.1)	(11.1)	(3.3)	5.0	4.8	5.9	5.8	6.3	6.3	10.4

Exhibit 7.11 Continued

	1988	1989	1990	1991	1992	1993	1994	1995	1996	1997	Perp
Financing flow											
AT interest income	(0.2)	0.0	0.0	0.0	0.0	0.0	0.0	0.0	0.0	0.0	0.0
Incr/(Decr) excess marketable securities	(3.2)	0.0	0.0	0.0	0.0	0.0	0.0	0.0	0.0	0.0	0.0
AT interest expense	7.1	9.7	11.9	14.8	16.4	17.7	19.4	20.9	22.6	24.4	26.5
Interest on operating leases	0.9	1.0	1.1	1.3	1.4	1.5	1.7	1.8	2.0	2.2	2.4
Decr/(Incr) in debt	(34.3)	(32.0)	(28.0)	(24.2)	(19.3)	(21.5)	(22.8)	(25.4)	(27.7)	(30.7)	(30.0)
Decr/(Incr) in operating leases	(2.4)	(2.0)	(1.9)	(1.9)	(1.8)	(2.0)	(2.2)	(2.4)	(2.7)	(3.0)	(3.1)
Minority interest (IS and BS)	0.0	0.0	0.0	0.0	0.0	0.0	0.0	0.0	0.0	0.0	0.0
Common dividends	3.1	4.2	5.7	6.7	8.3	9.1	9.8	10.9	12.0	13.4	14.6
Share repurchases	0.0	0.0	0.0	0.0	0.0	0.0	0.0	0.0	0.0	0.0	0.0
Preferred dividends	0.0	0.0	0.0	0.0	0.0	0.0	0.0	0.0	0.0	0.0	0.0
Incr/(Decr) in treasury stock	0.0	0.0	0.0	0.0	0.0	0.0	0.0	0.0	0.0	0.0	0.0
Decr/(Incr) in preferred	0.0	0.0	0.0	0.0	0.0	0.0	0.0	0.0	0.0	0.0	0.0
Decr/(Incr) in common	0.0	0.0	0.0	0.0	0.0	0.0	0.0	0.0	0.0	0.0	0.0
Total financing flow	(29.1)	(19.1)	(11.1)	(3.3)	5.0	4.8	5.9	5.8	6.3	6.3	10.4

Exhibit 7.12 PRESTON CORPORATION, MODERATE CASE, KEY PERFORMANCE RATIOS

	1988	1989	1990	1991	1992	1993	1994	1995	1996	1997	Perp
Return on invested capital (Beg. of year)											
All operating exp/revenues	91.3%	90.5%	89.8%	89.3%	88.8%	88.8%	88.8%	88.8%	88.8%	88.8%	88.8%
Depreciation/revenues	4.6%	4.7%	4.8%	4.8%	4.9%	5.0%	5.0%	5.0%	5.1%	5.1%	5.1%
EBIT/revenues	4.1%	4.9%	5.5%	5.9%	6.3%	6.3%	6.2%	6.2%	6.2%	6.2%	6.1%
Net PPE/revenues	31.8%	32.2%	32.4%	32.5%	32.5%	32.0%	31.5%	31.0%	30.5%	30.0%	29.7%
Working capital/revenues	7.0%	7.5%	7.6%	7.8%	7.9%	7.8%	7.9%	7.8%	7.8%	7.8%	7.9%
Net other assets/revenues	3.2%	3.3%	3.4%	3.4%	3.5%	3.5%	3.5%	3.5%	3.5%	3.5%	3.5%
Revenues/invested capital	2.4	2.3	2.3	2.3	2.3	2.3	2.3	2.4	2.4	2.4	2.4
Pretax ROIC	9.8%	11.3%	12.6%	13.5%	14.4%	14.5%	14.5%	14.7%	14.8%	14.9%	15.0%
Cash tax rate	35.1%	35.1%	35.1%	35.1%	35.1%	35.1%	35.1%	35.1%	35.1%	35.1%	35.1%
After-tax ROIC	6.4%	7.3%	8.2%	8.8%	9.4%	9.4%	9.4%	9.5%	9.6%	9.7%	9.7%
After-tax ROIC (including goodwill)	5.8%	6.8%	7.7%	8.3%	8.9%	9.0%	9.1%	9.2%	9.3%	9.4%	9.5%
Return on invested capital (avg.)											
Net PPE/revenues	34.4%	34.4%	34.2%	34.0%	33.7%	33.2%	32.8%	32.3%	31.8%	31.3%	30.9%
Working capital/revenues	7.8%	8.0%	8.1%	8.2%	8.2%	8.2%	8.2%	8.2%	8.2%	8.2%	8.2%
Net other assets/revenues	3.6%	3.6%	3.6%	3.6%	3.6%	3.6%	3.6%	3.6%	3.6%	3.6%	3.6%
Revenues/invested capital	2.2	2.2	2.2	2.2	2.2	2.2	2.2	2.3	2.3	2.3	2.3
Pretax ROIC	9.0%	10.6%	12.0%	12.9%	13.8%	13.9%	14.0%	14.1%	14.2%	14.3%	14.4%
After-tax ROIC	5.8%	6.9%	7.8%	8.4%	9.0%	9.0%	9.1%	9.1%	9.2%	9.3%	9.3%
After-tax ROIC (including goodwill)	5.4%	6.4%	7.3%	7.9%	8.6%	8.6%	8.7%	8.8%	8.9%	9.0%	9.1%

369

Exhibit 7.12 Continued

	1988	1989	1990	1991	1992	1993	1994	1995	1996	1997	Perp
Growth rates											
Revenue growth rate	20.8%	14.8%	12.6%	10.8%	9.3%	9.5%	9.4%	9.6%	9.7%	9.9%	9.4%
EBIT growth rate	95.9%	35.6%	27.3%	19.3%	16.8%	8.8%	8.6%	9.1%	9.3%	9.7%	8.8%
NOPLAT growth rate	101.9%	35.6%	27.3%	19.3%	16.8%	8.8%	8.6%	9.1%	9.3%	9.7%	8.8%
Invested capital growth rate	17.7%	13.6%	11.4%	9.7%	8.2%	8.3%	8.2%	8.4%	8.5%	8.7%	8.2%
Investment rates											
Gross investment rate	165.3%	134.7%	117.0%	104.4%	94.2%	94.9%	94.3%	94.9%	95.0%	95.4%	93.1%
Net investment rate	278.7%	186.3%	139.6%	110.0%	87.2%	88.7%	87.3%	88.5%	88.7%	89.6%	84.3%
Financing											
Coverage (EBIT/interest)	2.2	2.1	2.2	2.1	2.2	2.3	2.2	2.3	2.3	2.3	2.3
Debt/total capital (book)	62.8%	65.5%	67.0%	67.8%	67.8%	67.8%	67.8%	67.7%	67.7%	67.7%	67.5%
Average ROE	6.2%	8.1%	10.5%	11.5%	13.3%	13.6%	13.6%	13.9%	14.3%	14.7%	14.8%

Exhibit 7.13 **PRESTON CORPORATION, MODERATE CASE, FORECASTED ECONOMIC PROFIT**, $ MILLIONS

	1988	1989	1990	1991	1992	1993	1994	1995	1996	1997	Perp
Return on invested capital	6.4%	7.3%	8.2%	8.8%	9.4%	9.4%	9.4%	9.4%	9.5%	9.6%	9.7%
WACC	9.7%	9.7%	9.7%	9.7%	9.7%	9.7%	9.7%	9.7%	9.7%	9.7%	9.7%
Spread	−3.3%	−2.4%	−1.5%	−0.9%	−0.3%	−0.3%	−0.3%	−0.3%	−0.2%	−0.1%	0.0%
Invested capital (beg of year)	256.2	301.5	342.7	381.9	418.8	452.9	490.7	531.1	575.9	624.8	679.1
Economic profit (before goodwill)	(8.6)	(7.2)	(5.1)	(3.5)	(1.5)	(1.3)	(1.3)	(1.0)	(0.6)	0.0	0.1
NOPLAT	16.3	22.1	28.1	33.5	39.2	42.6	46.3	50.5	55.2	60.6	65.9
Capital charge	(24.9)	(29.3)	(33.2)	(37.0)	(40.6)	(43.9)	(47.6)	(51.5)	(55.9)	(60.6)	(65.9)
Economic profit	(8.6)	(7.2)	(5.1)	(3.5)	(1.5)	(1.3)	(1.3)	(1.0)	(0.6)	0.0	0.1

Exhibit 7.14 PRESTON CORPORATION, MODERATE CASE, SUPPORTING CALCULATIONS, $ MILLIONS

	1988	1989	1990	1991	1992	1993	1994	1995	1996	1997	Perp
Change in working capital											
Incr in operating cash	1.5	1.7	1.7	1.6	1.5	1.7	1.9	2.1	2.3	2.6	2.7
Incr in accts receivable	17.8	12.0	11.8	11.3	10.8	12.1	13.1	14.6	16.2	18.1	18.9
Incr in inventories	3.4	2.3	2.2	2.1	2.0	2.3	2.5	2.8	3.1	3.4	3.6
Incr other current assets	0.5	0.8	0.8	0.8	0.7	0.8	0.9	1.0	1.1	1.2	1.3
(Incr) in accts payable	(4.8)	(3.5)	(3.4)	(3.3)	(3.2)	(3.5)	(3.8)	(4.3)	(4.7)	(5.3)	(5.5)
(Incr) other current liabilities	(8.7)	(5.6)	(5.4)	(5.2)	(5.0)	(5.6)	(6.0)	(6.8)	(7.5)	(8.4)	(8.7)
Net change in working capital	9.8	7.8	7.6	7.3	7.0	7.8	8.5	9.4	10.5	11.7	12.2
Capital expenditures											
Increase in net PPE	31.7	29.9	28.3	26.3	24.1	26.5	28.2	31.1	33.9	37.4	37.9
Depreciation	28.3	32.8	37.5	42.2	47.1	51.9	57.3	63.1	69.6	76.6	84.4
Capital expenditures (net of disposals)	60.0	62.8	65.8	68.5	71.1	78.5	85.5	94.2	103.5	114.0	122.3
Investment in goodwill											
Inc/(dec) bal sheet goodwill	(0.6)	(0.6)	(0.6)	(0.6)	(0.6)	(0.6)	(0.6)	(0.6)	(0.6)	(0.6)	(0.6)
Amortization of goodwill	0.6	0.6	0.6	0.6	0.6	0.6	0.6	0.6	0.6	0.6	0.6
Investment in goodwill	0.0	0.0	0.0	0.0	0.0	0.0	0.0	0.0	0.0	0.0	0.0
Nonoperating cash flow											
Extraordinary items	0.0	0.0	0.0	0.0	0.0	0.0	0.0	0.0	0.0	0.0	0.0
AT nonoperating income	0.0	0.0	0.0	0.0	0.0	0.0	0.0	0.0	0.0	0.0	0.0
Change in investments and advances	0.0	0.0	0.0	0.0	0.0	0.0	0.0	0.0	0.0	0.0	0.0
Nonoperating cash flow	0.0	0.0	0.0	0.0	0.0	0.0	0.0	0.0	0.0	0.0	0.0

11

LEASES AND OFF-BALANCE-SHEET DEBT

INTRODUCTION

Rapid changes in manufacturing and information technology and expanding international trade and capital markets have resulted in the growth of multinational corporations that must cope with increasingly mobile capital, labor, and product markets. These changes have been accompanied by volatile commodity and other factor price levels, fluctuating interest and foreign currency exchange rates, and a frenzy of domestic and international tax and regulatory changes. In addition, general inflation and industry-specific price changes have raised most asset prices and have increased the risks of operations and investments.

This economic climate has required increasing amounts of capital as firms acquire operating capacity (both for expansion and replacement purposes) at ever higher prices. Because of the volatility of prices and cash flows, the risks of owning operating assets have also increased. These trends have driven firms to seek methods of:

1. Acquiring the rights to assets through methods other than traditional direct purchases (financed by debt)
2. Controlling the risks of operations through derivative and hedging transactions

"Executory contracts" are the primary alternative form of transactions used by firms to acquire operating capacity, supplies of raw materials, and other inputs. Such contracts or arrangements are the subject of this chapter. Hedging transactions will be discussed in Chapter 16.

The trend toward these financing techniques and hedging transactions has been encouraged by drawbacks in the historical cost-based financial reporting system, in which recognition and measurement depend primarily on actual transactions. As contracts are considered legal promises, and neither cash nor goods may be exchanged at the inception of these contracts, accounting recognition is not required in many cases. The emphasis on accounting assets and liabilities rather than the recognition of economic resources and obligations further encourages firms to keep resources and *obligations* off the balance sheet.

Firms may engage in these transactions to avoid reporting high debt levels and leverage ratios and to reduce the probability of technical default under restrictive covenants in debt indentures. Off-balance-sheet transactions may also keep assets and potential gains out of the financial statements but under the control of management, which can orchestrate the timing of gain recognition to offset periods of poor operating performance.

Footnote disclosures constitute the best source of information about off-balance-sheet activities. Additional information may be available from disclosures in 10-K filings and from other company publications. In some cases, the economic meaning behind the disclosures requires explanation from management. Thus, a complete analysis of the firm must include a review of all financial statement disclosures to obtain data on off-balance-sheet activities. In many cases, straightforward adjustments can be used to reflect off-balance-sheet assets and liabilities on the balance sheet. Such adjustments result in a balance sheet that presents a more complete portrait of the firm's resources and obligations and financial ratios that are more comparable to those of competitors whose use of off-balance-sheet techniques is different.

The chapter begins with a discussion of leases, the most common form of executory contract entered into by firms. The methods used to analyze and adjust for leases serve as a model for the analysis of other off-balance-sheet activities that comprise the second part of the chapter.

LEASES

Accounting policy makers have grappled with leases for years to develop reporting requirements that emphasize the economic substance rather than the legal form of the leasing transaction. We begin our discussion of leases with a review of incentives for leases. A discussion of reporting requirements and the analysis of leases complete this section of the chapter.

Incentives for Leasing

Firms generally acquire rights to use property, plant, and equipment by outright purchase, partially or fully funded by internal resources or externally borrowed funds. In a purchase transaction, the buyer acquires (and the seller surrenders) ownership, which includes all the benefits and risks embodied in the asset. A firm may also acquire the use of property, including some or all of the benefits and risks of ownership, for specific periods of time and stipulated rental payments through contractual arrangements called leases.

Short-term, or *operating,* leases allow the lessee to use leased property for only a portion of its economic life. The lessee accounts for such leases as contracts reporting (as rental expense) only the required rental payments as they are made. Because the lessor retains substantially all the risks of ownership of leased property, the leased assets remain on its balance sheet and are depreciated over their estimated economic lives; rental payments are recognized as revenues over time according to the terms of the lease.

Alternatively, longer-term leases may effectively transfer all (or substantially all) the risks and rewards of the leased property to the lessee. Such leases are the economic equivalent of sales with financing arrangements designed to effect the purchase (by the lessee) and sale (by the lessor) of the leased property. *Such leases, referred to as finance or capital leases, are treated for accounting purposes as sales.* The asset and associated debt are carried on the books of the lessee, and the lessor records a gain on "sale" at the inception of the lease. The lessee depreciates the asset over its life, and treats lease payments as payments of principal and interest. The financial reporting differences between accounting for a lease as an operating or capital lease are far-reaching and affect the balance sheet, income statement, cash flow statement, and associated ratios.

One motivation for leasing rather than borrowing and buying an asset is to avoid recognition of the debt and asset on the lessee's financial statements. Lease capitalization eliminates this advantage. Whether a lease is reported as operating or capitalized depends, as we shall see, on the terms of the lease and their relationship to criteria specified by SFAS 13.

Notwithstanding these financial reporting requirements, leases may be structured to qualify as operating leases to achieve desired financial reporting effects and capital structure benefits. Operating leases allow lessees to avoid recognition of the asset and report higher profitability ratios and indicators of operating efficiency. Reported leverage is also lower because the related liability for contractual payments is not recognized.

Extensive use of operating leases needs careful evaluation and the analyst must adjust financial statements (to reflect unrecognized assets and liabilities) and the leverage, coverage, and profitability ratios for the effects of operating leases.

Box 11-1 reviews the finance literature on the competing incentives of the lease versus purchase decision. The impact of the financial reporting alternatives (operating vs. capitalization) on this decision is also discussed.

Lease Classification: Lessees

The preceding discussion suggests that lessees generally structure and report leases as operating leases. Their counterparts, lessors, however, prefer to structure leases as capital leases. This allows earlier recognition of revenue and income by reporting transactions that are in substance installment sales or financing arrangements as completed sales. The resulting higher profitability and turnover ratios are powerful incentives for lessors. Appendix 11-A is devoted to a discussion of lease accounting from the perspective of the lessor. The chapter itself retains the lessee perspective.

Lease classifications are not intended to be alternative reporting methods. However, management actively negotiates the provisions of lease agreements and the preferred accounting treatment is an important element of these contractual negotiations.

SFAS 13 attempted to promulgate "objective" and "reliable" criteria that facilitate the evaluation of the economic substance of lease agreements. One goal was to discourage off-balance-sheet financing by lessees and front-end loading of income by lessors. The criteria were designed to ensure that either the lessee or lessor recognize the leased assets on their books.

Capital Leases

A lease that, in economic substance, transfers to the lessee substantially all the risks and rewards inherent in the leased property is a financing or capital lease and should be capitalized. A lease meeting *any one* of the following SFAS 13 criteria at the inception of the lease must be classified as a capital lease by lessees:

1. The lease transfers ownership of the property to the lessee at the end of the lease term.
2. The lease contains a bargain purchase option.
3. The lease term is equal to 75% or more of the estimated economic life of the leased property (not applicable to land or when the lease term begins within the final 25% of the economic life of the asset).

375

BOX 11-1
Incentives for Leasing and Their Effect on the Capital Versus Operating
Lease Choice

Management may have a number of reasons to prefer leasing compared to outright asset purchases. The choice may be a function of strategic investment and capital structure objectives, the comparative costs* of leasing versus equity or debt financing, the availability of tax benefits, and perceived financial reporting advantages. Some of these reasons influence whether the lease will be treated as an operating or capital lease; others are unrelated to the accounting choice.

Tax Incentives

The tax benefits of owning assets can be exploited best by transferring them to the party in the higher marginal tax bracket. Firms with low effective tax rates more readily engage in leasing than firms in high tax brackets as the tax benefits can be passed on to the lessor. El-Gazzar et al. (1986) provide evidence consistent with this hypothesis; firms with lower effective tax rates had a higher proportion of lease debt to total assets than did firms with higher effective tax rates. Moreover, El-Gazzar et al. argue that tax effects also influence the choice of accounting method as the lessee attempts to influence the tax interpretation (by the IRS) of lease contracts. That is, it is more difficult to argue for capital lease treatment for tax purposes if the lease is treated as an operating lease for book purposes. Citing evidence by Mellman and Bernstein (1966) of substantial conformity (pre-SFAS 13)† between tax and book accounting for lessees, they note that

> apparently, a high-tax-rate lessee's claim of material equity on the tax return could be enhanced by showing ownership for reporting purposes.‡

Their sample of firms confirmed this finding as firms with high effective tax rates tended to capitalize their leases.

Nontax Incentives

Smith and Wakeman (1985) analyzed nontax incentives related to the lease versus purchase decision. Their list of eight nontax factors that make leasing more likely than purchase is presented here. Some of these factors are not directly related to the lessee's choice, but are motivated by the manufacturer or lessor and/or the type of asset involved. We have sorted these conditions by their potential impact on the operating versus capitalization accounting choice.

Nontax Incentives for Leasing Versus Purchase: Incentives Classified by Potential Impact on Operating Versus Capital Lease Choice

Favors Operating Lease as per SFAS 13

1. Period of use is short relative to the overall life of the asset.
2. Lessor has comparative advantage in reselling the asset.

Favors Structuring Lease as Operating Lease

3. Corporate bond covenants contain specific covenants relating to financial policies that the firm must follow.
4. Management compensation contracts contain provisions expressing compensation as a function of returns on invested capital.

376

Not Relevant to Operating Versus Capital Lease Decision

5. Lessee ownership is closely held so that risk reduction is important.

6. Lessor (manufacturer) has market power and can thus generate higher profits by leasing the asset (and controlling the terms of the lease) than selling it.

7. Asset is not specialized to the firm.

8. Asset's value is not sensitive to use or abuse (owner takes better care of asset than lessee).

Based on Smith and Wakeman (1985).

Short periods of use and the resale factor favor the use of operating leases, and under GAAP, these conditions would lead to lease agreements consistent with operating leases. The bond covenant and management compensation incentives also favor the *negotiated structuring of* the agreement as an operating lease.

Consistent with the foregoing, both Abdel-Khalik (1981) and Nakayama et al. (1981) note that the expected covenant violations resulting from SFAS 13 influenced firms to lobby against its adoption. Furthermore, Abdel-Khalik notes that firms renegotiated the terms of their leases during SFAS 13's transition period to make them eligible for treatment as operating leases. Imhoff and Thomas (1988) found that subsequent to SFAS 13, there was a general decline in leases as a form of financing. Further evidence with respect to the choice of accounting method is provided by El-Gazzar et al., who note that in the pre-SFAS 13 period, firms that had high debt-to-equity ratios and/or had incentive-based contracts based on income after interest expense were more likely to have leases classified as operating leases. Taken together, these results confirm that debt covenant and compensation factors affect both the choice of leasing as a form of financing as well as the choice of accounting treatment of the lease.

---

*Related to these costs are the risks related to residual values and obsolescence.

†Prior to SFAS 13, GAAP also required that certain leases be treated as capital leases. The effect of SFAS 13 was to tighten the requirements, making more leases qualify as capital leases.

‡Samir El-Gazzar, Steven Lilien, and Victor Pastena, "Accounting for Leases by Lessees," *Journal of Accounting and Economics,* 1986, pp. 217–237.

4. The present value[1] of the minimum lease payments[2] (MLPs) equals or exceeds 90% of the fair value of leased property to the lessor.

The ownership and bargain purchase criteria imply a transfer of all the risks and benefits of the leased property to the lessee; in economic substance, such leases are financing arrangements. Lease terms extending to at least 75% of the economic life of the leased asset are also considered to achieve such a transfer; there is an implicit assumption that most of the value of an asset accrues to the user within that period. Finally, a lease must be capitalized when the present value of the minimum lease payments is equal to or exceeds 90% of the fair value of the leased property at the inception of the lease. In effect, the lessee has contractually agreed to payments ensuring that the lessor will recover its investment along with a reasonable return.

---

[1]The discount rate used to compute the present values should be the lessee's incremental borrowing rate or the implicit interest rate of the lessor, whichever is lower. The use of the lower rate generates the higher of two present values, increasing the probability that this criterion will be met and the lease capitalized.

[2]MLPs include residual values when they are guaranteed by lessees since the guarantee results in a contractually fixed residual value and effectively transfers the risk of changes in residual values to the lessee.

The transaction is, therefore, an installment purchase for the lessee financed by the lessor, and capitalization reflects this economic interpretation of the leasing transaction.[3]

Operating Leases

Leases not meeting any of the four criteria listed above are not capitalized and no asset or obligation is reported in the financial statements since no purchase is deemed to have occurred. Such leases are classified as operating leases, and payments are reported as rental expense. SFAS 13 mandates the use of the straight-line method of recognizing periodic rental payments unless another, systematic basis provides a better representation of the use of leased property. As a result, for leases with rising rental payments, lease expense and cash flow will not be identical.

Financial Reporting by Lessees: Capital Versus Operating Leases

Financial reporting by lessees will be illustrated using a noncancellable lease beginning December 31, 19X0, with annual MLPs of $10,000 made at the end of each year for four years. Ten percent is assumed to be the appropriate discount rate.

Operating Lease. If the lease does not meet any criteria requiring capitalization:

- No entry is made at the inception of the lease.
- Over the life of the lease, only the annual rental expense of $10,000 will be charged to income and CFO.

Capital Lease. If the lease meets any one of the four criteria of a capital lease, then:

- At the inception of the lease, an asset (leasehold asset) and liability (leasehold liability) equal to the present value of the lease payments, $31,700, is recognized.
- Over the life of the lease:

1. The annual rental expense of $10,000 will be allocated between interest and principal payments on the $31,700 leasehold liability according to the following amortization schedule:

| Year | Opening Liability | Allocation of Payment of $10,000 | | Closing Liability† |
		Interest*	Principal	
X0				$31,700
X1	$31,700	$3,170	$6,830	24,870
X2	24,870	2,487	7,513	17,357
X3	17,357	1,735	8,265	9,092
X4	9,092	909	9,092	0

*10% of the opening liability.
†Equals the opening liability less the periodic amortization of the lease obligation. Also equals the present value of the remaining MLPs.

[3]Leases are classified at the inception of the lease; the classification is not changed when the lessee or lessor is acquired unless the provisions of the lease agreement are changed. See FASB Interpretation 21 (1978).

2. The cost of the leasehold asset of $31,700 is charged to operations (annual depreciation is $7,925) using the straight-line method over the term of the lease.[4]

Comparative Analysis of Capitalized and Operating Leases

Balance Sheet Effects. No assets or liabilities are recognized if the lease is treated as an operating lease. When leases are capitalized, there is a major impact on a firm's balance sheet at inception and throughout the life of the lease. At the inception of the lease, an asset and a liability equal to the present value of the lease payments are recognized.

Balance Sheet Effect of Lease Capitalization

	19X0	19X1	19X2	19X3	19X4
Assets					
Leased assets	$31,700	$31,700	$31,700	$31,700	$31,700
Accumulated depreciation	0	7,925	15,850	23,775	31,700
Leased assets, net	$31,700	$23,775	$15,850	$ 7,925	0
Liabilities					
Current portion of lease obligation	6,830	7,513	8,265	9,092	0
Long-term debt: lease obligation	24,870	17,357	9,092	0	0
	$31,700	$24,870	$17,357	$ 9,092	0

The gross and net (of accumulated depreciation) amounts are reported at each balance sheet date. The current and noncurrent components of the lease obligation are reported as liabilities under capitalization. The current component is the principal portion of the lease payment to be made in the following year. Note that, at the inception of the lease, the leased asset and liability are equal at $31,700. Since the asset and liability are amortized using different methods, this equality is not again observed until the end of the lease term when both asset and liability are equal to zero.

Effect on Financial Ratios. Lease capitalization increases asset balances, resulting in lower asset turnover and return on asset ratios, as compared with the operating lease method, which does not record leased assets.

The most important effect of lease capitalization, however, is its impact on leverage ratios. As lease obligations are not recognized for operating leases, leverage ratios are understated. Lease capitalization adds both current and noncurrent liabilities to debt, resulting in a corresponding decrease in working capital and increases in the debt-to-equity and other leverage ratios.

Income Statement Effects. The income statement effects of lease reporting are also significant and impact operating income as well as net income. The operating

---

[4]Generally, depreciation methods used for similar purchased property are applied to leased assets over their estimated economic lives when one of the transfer of ownership criteria (1 and 2) is met and over the lease term when one of the other capitalization criteria (3 and 4) is satisfied.

lease method charges the periodic rental payments to expense as accrued, whereas capitalization recognizes depreciation and interest expense over the lease term.

Income Effects of Lease Classification

| | Operating Lease | Capital Lease | | |
| | Operating = Total Expense | Operating Expense | Nonoperating Expense | |
Year	Rent	Depreciation	Interest	Total Expense
X1	$10,000	$ 7,925	$3,170	$11,095
X2	10,000	7,925	2,487	10,412
X3	10,000	7,925	1,735	9,660
X4	10,000	7,925	909	8,834
	$40,000	$31,700	$8,300	$40,000

Operating Income. Capitalization results in higher operating income (earnings before interest and taxes, or EBIT) since an annual straight-line depreciation expense of $7,925 is lower than the annual rental expense of $10,000 reported under the operating lease method. For an individual lease, this difference is never reversed and remains constant over the lease term given use of the straight-line depreciation method. Accelerated depreciation methods would generate smaller differences in early years, with an increasing difference as depreciation declines, increasing both the level and trend of EBIT.

Total Expense and Net Income. Under capitalization, lease expense includes interest expense and depreciation of the leased asset. Initially, total expense for a capital lease exceeds rental expense reported for an operating lease, but declines over the lease term as interest expense falls.[5] In later years, total lease expense will be less than rental expense reported for an operating lease.

Note that total expense (interest plus depreciation) for a capital lease must equal total rental expense for an operating lease over the life of the lease.[6] Consequently, although total net income over the lease term is not affected by capitalization, the timing of income recognition is changed; lower net income is reported in the early years, followed by higher income in later years. This relationship holds for individual leases, but the effect on a firm depends on any additional leases entered into in subsequent periods. The effect of inflation on asset prices (and lease rentals) means that the impact of old leases nearing expiration may be swamped by the impact of new leases. If a firm enters into new leases at the same or increasing rate over time, reported net income will remain lower under capitalization.

Effect on Financial Ratios. In general, firms with operating leases report higher profitability, interest coverage (as interest expense is lower), return on equity, and return on assets ratios. The higher ROE ratios are due to the higher profitability

[5]If the company uses accelerated depreciation, then the difference in earlier years will be greater but the subsequent decline will also be rapid.

[6]This equality does not hold when the residual value is not zero.

(numerator effect), whereas the higher ROA is due primarily to the lower assets (denominator effect).

Cash Flow Effects of Lease Classification. Lease classification provides another example where accounting methods affect the classification of cash flows.[7] Under the operating lease method, all cash flows are operating and there is an operating cash outflow of $10,000 per year. However, lease capitalization results in both operating and financing cash flows as the rental payments of $10,000 are allocated between interest expense (treated as CFO) and amortization of the lease obligation (reported as cash from financing).

Cash Flow Effect of Lease Classification

Year	Operating Lease Operations	Capital Lease Operations	Financing
X0			
X1	$10,000	$3,170	$6,830
X2	10,000	2,487	7,513
X3	10,000	1,735	8,265
X4	10,000	909	9,091

In 19X1, for example, CFO differs between the two methods by $6,830, the amortization of the lease obligation. Because interest expense declines over the lease term and an increasing proportion of the annual payment is allocated to the lease obligation, the difference in CFO increases over the lease term. Thus, lease capitalization systematically decreases the operating cash outflow while increasing the financing cash outflow.

Therefore, although the capital lease method adversely affects some financial statement ratios, it allows firms to report higher operating cash flows compared to those reported using the operating lease method.

Before proceeding, it is important to point out that *at the inception of the lease (year X0), no cash flows are reported.* This is true even though a capital lease implies the purchase of an asset (cash outflow for investment) financed by the issuance of new debt (cash inflow from financing). Disclosure of the event is reported as part of the "significant noncash financing and investing activities." Analysts attempting to estimate a firm's cash flow requirements for operating capacity should however include the present value of such leases as a cash requirement. Moreover, free cash flow calculations for valuation purposes should incorporate the present value of leases as a cash outflow for investment at the inception of the lease (see Chapter 19).

Analysis of Lease Disclosures

A noncancellable lease, whether reported as a capital or operating lease, in effect, constitutes debt and the right to use an asset. If the lease is reported as a capital lease,

---

[7]We discuss only the classification of cash flows. After-tax cash flows are not affected by lease classification as *generally* even firms that use the capital lease method for financial reporting purposes are required to use the operating lease method for tax purposes. Tax payments and actual cash flows are therefore identical. Under the capital lease method, the lease expense under financial reporting exceeds the lease expense reported for tax purposes, resulting in a deferred tax asset.

this information is on-balance-sheet. If it is reported as an operating lease, then the debt and asset are off-balance-sheet and the analyst must adjust accordingly.

This is especially true in industries such as airlines and retail department stores where some firms own operating assets (i.e., airplanes or stores), other firms lease them and report the leases as capital leases, and still other lessees account for them as operating leases. Given the same conditions, the firms using operating leases may report the "best" results as they will show minimal debt and their higher profits will appear to be generated by a relatively smaller investment in assets.

However, the disclosure requirements of firms with leases, capital or operating, are sufficiently detailed to provide the information required for adjustments.

Lease Disclosure Requirements

SFAS 13 requires the disclosure of gross amounts of capitalized lease assets as of each balance sheet date, by major classes or grouped by their nature or function; they may be combined with owned assets.

Lessees must also disclose future MLPs for each of the five succeeding fiscal years and the aggregate thereafter as well as the net present value of the capitalized leases. Separate disclosure of minimum sublease rentals receivable from noncancellable subleases is also required.

Lessees using operating leases must also disclose future MLPs for each of the five succeeding fiscal years and in the aggregate thereafter. The present value of the MLPs is not required but may occasionally be provided. The rental expense under operating leases (classified as to minimum, contingent, and sublease rentals) for each period for which an income statement is presented must be disclosed as of the balance sheet date.[8]

For both operating and capital leases, lessees must also disclose aggregate minimum rentals receivable under noncancellable subleases. Information regarding renewal terms, purchase options, contingent rentals, any escalation clauses, and restrictions on dividends, additional debt, and leasing is also required. Such disclosure is usually general in nature.

Financial Reporting by Lessees: An Example

Exhibit 11-1 contains the lease disclosure of AMR (the parent of American Airlines). From the balance sheet alone, it would seem that AMR is inclined to purchase rather than lease its airplanes. The carrying value of purchased equipment is over six times that of leased equipment.

The footnote paints an entirely different picture. AMR engages heavily in leasing, but the leases are mostly structured as operating leases. Capital lease obligations and operating leases are shown separately. Future MLPs for the next five years, and the aggregate thereafter, are disclosed for both capital and operating leases. For capital leases, interest has been deducted to report their present value of $2,403 million ($128 million is reported as current and $2,275 million as long-term debt).

Note that the (aggregate) operating lease payments of $20,011 million are more than five times the capital lease payments ($3,839 million). Moreover, the data suggest that the operating leases are of longer term than the capital leases.

Aggregate MLPs of the capital leases for the next five years are about 36% of total future MLPs or $1,399 million. Total MLPs for the remaining years are $2,440

---

[8]Unlike the case of capital leases, disclosure of the interest component of operating lease MLPs and their present value is not mandated by SFAS 13; it is occasionally provided.

EXHIBIT 11-1. AMR
Excerpts from Balance Sheet and Lease Footnotes

		December 31, 1994
Assets		
Equipment and property (net of accumulated depreciation of 5,465)		$12,020
Equipment and property under capital leases (net of accumulated amortization of 1,166)		1,878
Total assets		19,486
Liabilities		
Long-term debt		
Current maturity	590	
Noncurrent	5,603	6,193
Capital lease obligations		
Current	128	
Noncurrent	2,275	2,403
Total long-term debt and capital lease obligations		8,596
Shareholders equity		$ 3,380

Leases

AMR's subsidiaries lease various types of equipment and property, including aircraft, passenger terminals, equipment, and various other facilities. The future minimum lease payments required under capital leases, together with the present value of net minimum lease payments, and future minimum lease payments required under operating leases that have initial or remaining noncancelable lease terms in excess of one year as of December 31, 1994, were ($ in millions):

Year Ending December 31	Capital Leases	Operating Leases
1995	$ 273	$ 946
1996	300	924
1997	280	920
1998	276	931
1999	270	912
2000 and subsequent	2,440	15,378
	$3,839	$20,011
Less amount representing interest	1,436	
Present value of minimum lease payments	$2,403	

At December 31, 1994, the Company had 216 jet aircraft and 123 turboprop aircraft under operating leases and 82 jet aircraft and 63 turboprop under capital leases.

Source: AMR, *1994 Annual Report.*

million or 64% of the total MLPs of $3,839 million over the lease terms. The capitalized MLPs generally decline slowly over time, and a substantial proportion of the payments occurs after the initial five years, suggesting long-term leases. The average lease term of the capitalized leases can be estimated by computing the number of payments included in the "later years" amount of $2,440 million; that is, ($2,440 million/$270 million) if we assume that annual payments remain at the 1999 level. This suggests a lease term of approximately 14 (initial five plus the estimated nine) years.

For operating leases, the proportion of payments after the first five years is ($15,378/$20,011) 77% of total payments. This suggests a longer term than for the capital leases. Dividing the remaining payments of $15,378 by the 1999 payment of $912 yields 17, suggesting a lease term of 22 years (5 plus 17) or 50% longer than for the capital leases.

The note indicates that 216 jet aircraft and 123 turboprops are under operating leases. *Neither these assets nor the debt associated with them appear on the balance sheet.*

Investors and analysts can use the lease disclosures to adjust the balance sheet appropriately. The present value of the operating leases can be estimated by discounting the future cash flows. This estimate requires assumptions about the pattern of MLPs after the first five years and the discount rate. This estimation procedure is "robust," with the calculated present value relatively invariant to the assumptions.

Assumed Pattern of MLPs. Footnote disclosures reflect the payments to be made over each of the next five years and the total payments thereafter. The present value computation requires an estimate of the number of payments implicit in the latter lump sum. Either the rate of decline suggested by the cash outflows for the next five years or a constant amount over the remaining term may be used to derive the present value of the operating lease payments.

Discount Rate. The discount rate should reflect the risk class of the leased assets as well as the company being analyzed. The interest rate implicit in the reported capital leases is a good approximation of that rate.[9]

Box 11-2 uses AMR to illustrate the estimation method(s). The procedure yields a rate of between 6 and 7% depending on the assumptions made; we use 6.5%. The two assumptions regarding pattern of cash flows over the lease term generate present value estimates of $10.5 and $10.2 billion, a difference of only 3%.

Impact of Operating Lease Adjustments

Liabilities. The impact of the adjustment is highly significant. AMR's reported long-term debt and capital leases total $8.6 billion. Adding approximately $10.5 billion for off-balance-sheet operating leases more than doubles debt to approximately $19 billion. *AMR has more debt off the balance sheet than on the balance sheet.* With equity of $3.4 billion, an already high debt-to-equity ratio of 2.5 increases to 5.6.

AMR: Effects of Operating Lease Adjustment ($ in billions)

	As Reported	+ Operating Leases	= Adjusted
Debt	$ 8.6	$10.5	$19.1
Equity	3.4		3.4
Debt/equity	2.5X		5.6X
Assets	$19.5	$10.5	$30.0

[9]Because the implicit rate is an average rate based on terms at inception, it may be significantly different from either the reported or marginal long-term borrowing rate the company faces in the capital markets and it may not reflect the market value of equivalent debt. The analyst may want to use an estimated (from the debt footnote or based on current market conditions) long-term borrowing rate.

BOX 11-2
Estimation of the Present Value of Operating Leases

A. The Implicit Discount Rate of a Firm's Capital Leases

Two approaches may be employed to estimate the average discount rate used to capitalize a firm's capital leases. The first uses only the next period's MLP; the second incorporates all future MLPs in the estimation procedure.

1. Using Next Period's MLP

The 1995 MLP for AMR's capital leases is $273 million. That payment includes interest and principal. The principal portion is shown in AMR's current liabilities section as $128 million. The difference between the two, $145 million, represents the interest component of the MLP. As the present value of AMR's capital leases equals $2,403, the interest rate on the capitalized leases can be estimated as ($145/$2,403) 6.03%.

This calculation assumes that the principal payment of $128 million will be made at the end of the year. If it is made early in the year, then the interest expense is based on the principal outstanding after payment of the current portion. If the current portion is a significant portion of the overall liability, then the results can be biased. An alternative estimate of the implicit interest rate may be derived using the average liability balance; that is, $145/[0.5 \times ($2,403 + $2,275)] = 6.2\%$.

2. Using All Future MLPs

The interest rate can also be estimated by solving for the implicit interest rate (internal rate of return) that equates the MLPs and their present value. This calculation requires an assumption about the pattern of MLPs after the first five years. As discussed further in the next section (with reference to operating leases), the simplest assumption is that the payment level ($270 million) in the fifth year (1999) continues to the future, implying the following payment stream:

Year	Payments
1995	$ 273
1995	300
1997	280
1998	276
1999	270
2000–2008	270
2009 (residual)	10
	$3,839

The internal rate of return that equates this stream to the present value of $2,403 is 7.0%.

Alternatively, one can assume a declining rate of payments with a decline rate based on the payment pattern of the first five years. In AMR's case, payments increase initially and then decline slowly as the payment levels of 1998 and 1999 are approximately 98% of the previous year. Using this pattern and assuming payments of

$$(0.98 \times \$270) = \$264 \text{ in the year } 2000$$
$$(0.98 \times \$264) = \$256 \text{ in the year } 2001$$

and so on result in an internal rate of return of 6.9%, very close to the 7.0% based on the constant rate assumption. Generally, the differences are not significantly different, and unless the rate of decline is very steep, the constant rate assumption simplifies the computation.

The first procedure yields an estimate of 6.0 to 6.2%; the second yields estimates of 6.9 to 7.0%. Based on these estimates, we use 6.5% for our analysis of AMR's operating leases.

B. Assumed Pattern of MLPs

The MLPs for the first five years (1995 to 1999) are given. From the year 2000 and on, two assumptions are possible:

1. Constant rate, or
2. Declining rate

Under the constant rate assumption, it is assumed that MLPs from the year 2000 and on equal the 1999 payment of $912. Alternatively, and more realistically, one would expect the payments to decline over time. The rate of decline implicit in the MLPs reported individually for the first five years may be used to estimate the payment pattern after the initial five years. Based on that payment pattern,* we use a decline rate of 1.8%. The assumed patterns and the resultant present values are presented below.

Assumed Pattern of MLPs for Operating Leases

Initial five-year given payments

Year	MLPs
1995	$946
1996	924
1997	920
1998	931
1999	$912

	Assumed Payment Rate	
Year	Constant Amount	Declining Rate (1.8%)
2000	$912	$896
2001	912	879
2002	912	864
2003	912	848
2004	912	833
2005	912	818
2006	912	803
2007	912	789
2008	912	774
2009	912	760
2010	912	747
2011	912	733
2012	912	720
2013	912	707
2014	912	694

| | Assumed Payment Rate | |
Year	Constant Amount	Declining Rate (1.8%)
2015	912	682
2016	786†	670
2017		658
2018		646
2019		634
2020		224†
Aggregate	$20,011	$20,011
Present value at 6.5%	**$10,515**	**$10,212**

---

†Residual to arrive at aggregate MLPs of $20,011.

Note that the two present value estimates of $10.5 billion and $10.2 billion are within 3% of each other.

C. Executory Costs

Reported MLPs include such executory costs as maintenance, taxes, and insurance on the leased assets. These costs are not financing costs and should be excluded from the calculation of the lease present value. However, because footnote disclosures generally do not reduce MLPs by executory costs, the present value calculation described above is biased.

In most cases that bias is small and can be ignored. However, the estimation method can be modified to adjust for this bias. When the firm discloses the total of the executory costs, we can assume that the pattern of the executory costs follows that of the MLPs. If we define p as the proportion of total executory costs to total MLPs,

$$p = \frac{\text{Total Executory Costs}}{\text{Total MLPs}}$$

then the procedures described above can be applied‡ to a pattern of *adjusted MLPs*, where the

$$\text{Adjusted MLP (for any year)} = (1 - p) \times \text{Unadjusted MLP (for that year)}$$

---

*From 1995 through 1999, the MLPs declined by about 3.6% or on average about 0.9% per year. In 1999 itself, the rate of decline was just over 2%. Thus, we decided on a rate between 0.9 and 2%, with a greater weighting given the last year, bringing us to a decline rate of 1.8%.

‡Alternatively, one can use the unadjusted MLPs and make the following two adjustments:
1. In calculating the implicit interest rate of the capital leases, "gross up" the present value of the capital leases by *dividing* by $(1 - p)$.
2. Using the interest rate calculated in step 1, find the present value of the unadjusted MLPs. *Multiply* that present value by $(1 - p)$.

Assets. Exhibit 11-1 reports total assets of $19.5 billion. Capitalization of the operating leases increases total assets by $10.5 billion. AMR is operating 50% more assets than reported on its balance sheet. Efficiency measures such as turnover or ROA use total assets in the denominator and are highly overstated; adjusted ratios more accurately portray AMR's asset efficiency.

Income and Cash Flow Effects. Adjustments for operating leases also affect the income and cash flow statement (as well as related ratios). These effects can be illustrated by using the 1995 MLP of $946 million as an example. Under the operating lease method, both rent expense and the CFO outflow equal $946 million. Capitalization results in allocation of that $946 million between interest expense and principal payments; in addition, the leased asset must be depreciated. These changes reduce reported income but increase CFO.

AMR: Effects of Operating Lease Adjustment, 1995 ($ in millions)

	As Reported	Adjusted
Income Statement		
Rent expense	$946	
Interest expense		$ 683*
Amortization expense		477†
		$1,160
Cash Flow Statement		
If interest payments are treated as CFO (per SFAS 95)		
CFO outflow	$946	$ 683
CFF outflow	0	$ 263
If interest payments are treated as CFF (per Chapter 3)		
CFO outflow	$946	0
CFF outflow	0	$ 946

*Interest Expense = Interest Rate × PV of Leases = 0.065 × $10.5 billion = $683
†Amortization Expense = PV of Lease Divided by Lease Term = $10.5/22 = $477

OFF-BALANCE-SHEET FINANCING ACTIVITIES

Leases are but one example of contractual arrangements that give rise to off-balance-sheet debt. In this section, we discuss other such arrangements and show how financial statements should be adjusted to reflect the underlying economic consequences. Like leases, some of these off-balance-sheet activities are commonplace and can be found in many firms and industries. Others tend to be industry-specific or are the product of specific market conditions.

Take-or-Pay and Throughput Arrangements

Firms use take-or-pay contracts to ensure the long-term availability of raw materials and other inputs necessary for operations.[10] These agreements are common in the natural gas, chemical, paper, and metal industries. Under these arrangements, the purchasing firm commits to buy a minimum quantity of an input over a specified time period. Input prices may be fixed by contract or may be related to market prices. Natural resource companies use throughput arrangements with pipelines or processors (such as refiners) to ensure future distribution or processing requirements.

These contracts are often used as collateral for bank or other financing by unrelated suppliers or by investors in joint ventures. The contract serves as an indirect guarantee of the related debt. However, neither the assets nor the debt incurred to obtain (or guarantee availability of) operating capacity are reflected on the balance sheet of the purchaser. SFAS 47 (1981) requires that, when a long-term commitment is used to obtain financing, the purchaser must disclose the nature of the commitment and the minimum required payments in its financial statement footnotes.

As take-or-pay contracts and throughput agreements effectively keep some operating assets and liabilities off the balance sheet, the analyst should add the present value of minimum future commitments to both property and debt.

Exhibit 11-2 contains the commitments and contingencies footnote from Alcan's *1994 Annual Report,* disclosing take-or-pay and similar obligations. Note that the disclosure is similar to that required for (capital and operating) leases. We can apply the method used earlier to compute the present value of the debt. The calculation is shown in panel B of the exhibit.

The take-or-pay contracts reported by Alcan represent $750 million of off-balance-sheet assets and debt. The impact of this adjustment on the leverage ratio is

Alcan Balance Sheet, at December 31, 1994 (Canadian $ in millions)

	Reported	Adjusted	Increase in Debt
Total debt	$2,471	$3,221	30%
Stockholders' equity	$4,308	$4,308	
Debt-to-equity ratio	0.57X	0.75X	

Sale of Receivables

Receivables are sometimes financed by their sale (or securitization) to unrelated parties. That is, the firm sells the receivables to a buyer (normally a financial institution or investor group).[11] The seller uses the proceeds from the sale for operations or to reduce existing or planned debt. The firm continues to service the original receivables; it receives payment from its customers but transfers those funds to the new owner of

[10]Inventories can also be financed through product financing arrangements under which inventories are sold and later repurchased. SFAS 49 (1981) requires that such arrangements that do not effectively transfer the risk of ownership to the buyer must be accounted for as debt financing rather than sale of inventory. In such cases, the cost of holding inventories (storage and insurance) and interest cost on the imputed debt must be recognized as incurred. Prior to SFAS 49, companies sometimes used these arrangements to defer these costs and accelerate the recognition of profit. Product financing arrangements are still accounted for as sales outside of the United States.

[11]Depending on the interest (if any) paid by customers and the effective interest rate on the sale transaction, the seller may recognize a gain or loss on the receivables sold.

EXHIBIT 11-2. ALCAN
Analysis of Take-or-Pay Contracts

A. Footnote: Commitments and Contingencies

To ensure long-term supplies of bauxite and access to alumina and fabricating facilities, Alcan participates in several long-term cost sharing arrangements with related companies. Alcan's fixed and determinable commitments, which comprise long-term debt service and "take-or-pay" obligations are estimated at $115 in 1995, $95 in 1996, $155 in 1997, $91 in 1998, $91 in 1999, and $222 thereafter. Total charges from these related companies were $132 in 1994, $280 in 1993, and $309 in 1992. In addition, there are guarantees for the repayment of approximately $23 of indebtedness by related companies. Alcan believes that none of these guarantees is likely to be invoked. Commitments with third parties for supplies of other inputs are estimated at $44 in 1995, $17 in 1996, $12 in 1997, $33 in 1998, $30 in 1999, and $189 thereafter. Total fixed charges from these third parties were $44 in 1994, $28 in 1993, and $35 in 1992.

Minimum rental obligations are estimated at $48 in 1995, $40 in 1996, $24 in 1997, $21 in 1998, $20 in 1999, and $57 thereafter. Total rental expenses amounted to $94 in 1994, $112 in 1993, and $114 in 1992.

B. Analysis: Fixed and Determinable Payments, 1995 to 1999 and Beyond
(in $ millions)

	Long-Term Debt Service and Take-or-Pay Obligations	To Third Parties
1995	$115	$ 44
1996	95	17
1997	155	12
1998	91	33
1999	91	30
Thereafter	222	189

Using the technique for capitalizing operating leases discussed earlier in the chapter, these payment streams can be discounted to their present value. Estimated payments continue after 1999 (using, for simplifying purposes, the constant rate assumption) for

$$\frac{\$222 \text{ million}}{\$91 \text{ million}} = 2.45 \text{ years}, \qquad \frac{\$189 \text{ million}}{\$30 \text{ million}} = 6.3 \text{ years}$$

Given these payment streams, the present values can be estimated using an estimated cost of debt (based on capitalized lease disclosures or other long-term debt). For Alcan, we estimate an interest rate of 9%. When applied to the minimum payments shown above, the resulting present value equals $553 million for long-term debt service and take-or-pay obligations and $197 million for the obligations to third parties. The total of $750 million should be used to adjust Alcan's property and total debt.

Source: Alcan, *1994 Annual Report.*

the receivables. Some arrangements are revolving in nature as collected receivables are periodically replaced by new ones.

Such transactions are generally recorded as sales under U.S. GAAP.[12] The sale

[12]SFAS 77, Reporting by Transferors for Transfers of Receivables with Recourse (1983), permits sales treatment when the risks and rewards have been substantially transferred to the buyer, even when the buyer has limited recourse to the seller for nonpayment. The primary requirement is that the recourse obligation (probability of nonpayment) can be estimated, permitting the seller to provide an adequate reserve for bad debts.

decreases accounts receivable, increasing cash from operations. However, most sales of receivables provide that the buyer has *limited recourse* in the event some customers do not pay. As the recourse provision is generally well above the expected loss ratio on the receivables, the seller retains the entire expected loss experience. These transactions are therefore effectively collateralized borrowings with the receivables serving as collateral. Sales of receivables are another form of off-balance-sheet financing and should be adjusted as follows:

- Both accounts receivable and current liabilities should be increased by the amount of receivables sold that have not yet been collected.

BOX 11-3
SFAS 125, Accounting for Transfers and Servicing of Financial Assets and Extinguishments of Liabilities

This statement contains accounting and reporting standards for transfers and servicing of financial assets and extinguishments of liabilities. It supersedes SFAS 77, Reporting by Transferors for Transfers of Receivables with Recourse (FASB, 1983), and SFAS 76, Extinguishment of Debt (FASB, 1983). It is effective for transactions occurring after December 31, 1996. It must be applied prospectively and early or retroactive application is prohibited.

SFAS 77 allowed sales treatment for transfers of receivables when the risks and rewards were substantially transferred to the buyer, even when the buyer retained "limited recourse" to the seller for noncollection.*

Transfers of financial assets have become considerably more complex since the issuance of SFAS 77. Sales treatment for transfers where the transferor has no continuing involvement with either the transferred asset or the transferee creates no accounting or analytic problems. However, SFAS 77 did not provide adequate guidance for transfers with continuing involvement (e.g., recourse, servicing, agreements to repurchase, options written or held, and pledges of collateral).

Under SFAS 125, transfers of financial assets (primarily securitizations) in which the transferor surrenders control† over the assets must be reported as sales to the extent that consideration other than beneficial interests in those assets is received in exchange. Transfers not meeting these criteria must be reported as secured borrowings with a pledge of collateral.

However, SFAS 125 does not continue the disclosure requirements of SFAS 77. As a result, some firms may no longer report data about receivables sold. Financial statement users will need to watch for clues regarding such sales and request the information needed for the required adjustments.

SFAS 125 also supersedes SFAS 76, allowing derecognition of liabilities only when the debtor pays the creditor and is legally released from being the primary obligor for the liability.

The standard also amends SFAS 115, Accounting for Certain Investments in Debt and Equity Securities, to prohibit the classification of debt securities in the held-to-maturity portfolio if it can be prepaid or settled in an amount less than the carrying amount of the investment. Reclassifications of qualifying held-to-maturity debt securities due to this amendment will not prejudice a company's intent to hold other debt securities to maturity. See Chapter 13 for a further discussion of SFAS 115.

---

*The primary requirement is the ability to estimate the recourse obligation, enabling the accrual of an adequate reserve for bad debts.
†Surrender of control criteria are very stringent and essentially legalistic. They are designed to ensure that the transferor is legally unable to benefit from the transferred assets. See para. 9(a)–(c).

- CFO must be adjusted; the increase in uncollected amount should be classified as cash from financing rather than CFO. SFAS 125, Accounting for Transfers and Servicing of Financial Assets and Extinguishment of Liabilities (1996), confirmed the current accounting treatment of receivable sales. Box 11-3 summarizes the financial reporting requirements of this standard.

■ Example: AMR and Delta Airlines

Exhibit 11-3 presents excerpts from the financial statements and footnotes of AMR and Delta Airlines describing their sales of receivables. AMR has engaged in sales of receivables since 1991 and reported a balance of $300 million of outstanding uncollected receivables in 1992 and 1993, with a decline to $112 million in 1994.

Delta sold $489 million of accounts receivable in 1994 and received two notes (one for $300 million and the other for $189 million) in return. The $300 million note was sold for cash; the $189 million note (the effective recourse obligation) remains on Delta's balance sheet as accounts receivable. The Delta sale is slightly more complex than AMR's as Delta sold receivables to one party and received cash from another. Nonetheless, the effects of the transaction and the required adjustments are similar.

Balance Sheet. Both companies report an allowance for doubtful accounts that includes estimated losses on the receivables sold. Delta states explicitly, "the Company has substantially the same credit risk as if the receivables had not been sold." The sale proceeds should therefore not be viewed as a reduction of accounts receivable, but rather as an increase in (short-term) borrowing. Delta's 1994 accounts receivable and current liabilities should both be increased by $300 million. AMR's 1994 (1993) accounts receivable and current liabilities should be increased by $112 ($300) million.

Adjustments to Balance Sheet for Sales of Receivables

	Increase Accounts Receivable and Current Liabilities by			
	AMR		DELTA	
	$112 in 1994 and $300 in 1993		*$300 in 1994*	
Adjusted Data	1994	1993	1994	1993
Cash and short-term investments	$ 777	$ 586	$1,710	$1,180
Accounts receivable, net of allowance	1,318	1,210	1,186	1,055
Quick assets	$2,095	$1,796	$2,896	$2,235
Current liabilities	$5,026	$4,717	$3,836	$3,019

Cash Flow Classification. Accounting for these transactions as sales distorts the amount and timing of CFO as the firm receives cash earlier than if the receiv-

392

EXHIBIT 11-3. AMR AND DELTA
Sale of Receivables

Excerpts from Footnotes and Balance Sheet

	AMR		DELTA	
	1994	1993	1994	1993
Cash and short-term investments	$ 777	$ 586	$1,710	$1,180
Accounts receivable, net	1,206	910	886	1,055
"Quick assets"	$1,983	$1,496	$2,596	$2,235
Current liabilities	4,914	4,417	3,536	3,019
Cash from operations	$1,609	$1,377	$1,324	$ 677

From AMR's 1994 Annual Report

Commitment and Contingencies Footnote

In July 1991, American entered into a five-year agreement whereby American transfers, on a continuing basis and with recourse to the receivables, an undivided interest in a designated pool of receivables. Undivided interests in new receivables are transferred daily as collections reduce previously transferred receivables. At December 1994 and 1993, receivables are presented net of approximately $112 million and $300 million, respectively, of such transferred receivables. American maintains an allowance for uncollectible receivables based upon expected collectability of all receivables, including the receivables transferred.

From AMR's 1993 Annual Report

Commitment and Contingencies Footnote

. . . At December 1993 and 1992, receivables are presented net of approximately $300 million of such transferred receivables. . . .

From Delta's 1994 Annual Report

Sale of Receivables Footnote

On June 24, 1994, Delta entered into a revolving accounts receivable facility (Facility) providing for the sale of $489 million of a defined pool of accounts receivable (Receivables) through a wholly-owned subsidiary to a trust in exchange for a senior certificate in the principal amount of $300 million (Senior Certificate) and a subordinate certificate in the principal amount of $189 million (Subordinate Certificate). The subsidiary retained the Subordinate Certificate and the Company received $300 million in cash from the sale of the Senior Certificate to a third party. The principal amount of the Subordinate Certificate fluctuates daily depending upon the volume of receivables sold, and is payable to the subsidiary only to the extent the collections received on the Receivables exceed amounts due on the Senior Certificate. The Facility, which replaced an interim facility established in March 1994, is scheduled to terminate in July 1995, subject to earlier termination in certain circumstances

At June 30, 1994, the $300 million net proceeds from the sale were reported as operating cash flows in the Company's Consolidated Statements of Cash Flows and as a reduction in accounts receivable on the Company's Consolidated Balance Sheets. The Subordinate Certificate is included in accounts receivable on the Company's Consolidated Balance Sheets. The full amount of the allowance for doubtful accounts related to the receivables sold has been retained, as the Company has substantially the same credit risk as if the receivables had not been sold.

Source: AMR and Delta, *1993–1994 Annual Reports.*

ables had been collected in due course. An adjustment is required that reclassifies *the change in the uncollected receivables sold*[13] from CFO to cash from financing.

If the balance of uncollected receivables stays the same each year, there is no distortion. Any variation, however, affects the year-to-year comparison of cash flows.

Delta's footnote points out the $300 million increase in cash from operations in 1994. This amount should be transferred from CFO to cash from financing. For AMR, there is no adjustment required for 1993 as the uncollected receivables were $300 million in both 1992 and 1993. In 1994, the uncollected receivables decreased by $188 million. Thus, *1994 CFO is understated* by this amount as AMR reported this cash as part of CFO in earlier years.

Adjusting CFO for Sale of Receivables

	Deduct (Add) Net Proceeds from (to) CFO			
	AMR		DELTA	
	$188 in 1994		*$300 in 1994*	
	1994	1993	1994	1993
Cash from operations	$1,797	$1,377	$1,024	$677

Effects of Adjustments. The effects of these adjustments can be demonstrated using selected data.

Comparison of Selected Data

| | As Reported (%) | | After Adjustment (%) | |
	AMR	DELTA	AMR	DELTA
% Change in receivables, 1994	32.3	(16.0)	8.9	12.4
Quick ratio (%)	40.3	73.4	41.7	75.5
% Change in CFO, 1994	16.8	95.6	30.5	51.2
CFO/current liabilities				
1994	32.7	37.4	35.8	26.7
1993	31.2	22.4	29.2	22.4

AMR's reported accounts receivable increased 32.3% in 1994 (from $910 to $1,206 million), whereas Delta's decreased by 16% (from $1,055 to $886 million). Given their similar revenue increase, the difference is notable. However, after adjustment for receivables sold, the percentage change in receivables is quite similar; Delta's receivables increased by approximately 12% and AMR's by 9%.

---

[13]In Chapter 3, it was shown that the change in accounts receivable is an adjustment to net income when deriving CFO. Because the uncollected balance of the receivables sold must be added to the reported balance of accounts receivable, calculation of the adjusted CFO requires exclusion of any change in the balance of uncollected receivables sold.

With respect to CFO, the adjustment procedure has a similar effect. For Delta, reported CFO nearly doubled, showing an increase of 95.6%, whereas AMR reported an increase of only 16.8%. When the effects of the transfers of receivables are removed, we find that the increase in CFO was a more modest 51% for Delta and a more comparable 30.5% for AMR.

Finally, Delta's reported CFO/current liabilities (liquidity) ratio improved by 50%, from 22.4% in 1993 to 37.4% in 1994; AMR's reported ratio remained basically unchanged at about 31 to 32%.[14] After adjustment for receivables sold, Delta's 1994 ratio of 26.7% was closer to its 1993 level; AMR's ratio also rose, from 29.2 to 35.8%.

The upward adjustment to receivables and short-term debt for receivables sold decreases the firm's accounts receivable turnover (increased A/R) and leverage ratios (increased debt). It may also reduce reported short-term liquidity. Similarly, when the level of sold receivables increases (the uncollected receivables rise), the adjustment reduces CFO and its related ratios. Interestingly, in this example, as the quick ratio is less than 1 for both companies, the adjustment increases that ratio as the same amount was added to both the numerator and denominator. ∎

Finance Subsidiaries

Many firms have long used legally separate (but wholly owned) finance subsidiaries to borrow funds to finance parent company receivables. Such debt is often lower-cost than general-purpose borrowings because of the well-defined collateral. Finance subsidiaries enable the parent to generate sales by granting credit to dealers and customers for purchases of its goods and services.

Until 1987, most firms used the equity method to account for finance subsidiaries; the consolidated balance sheet reported only the parent's net investment, suppressing the debt used to finance the receivables. As shown by Livnat and Sondhi (1986), the exclusion of subsidiary debt allowed firms to report higher coverage and lower leverage ratios, stabilized reported debt and debt ratios over time, and reduced the probability of a technical violation of bond covenants.

Heian and Thies (1989) identified 182 companies (in 35 industry groups) reporting unconsolidated finance subsidiaries in 1985. Supplementary disclosures provided by 140 of these companies indicated a total of $205 billion in subsidiary debt that had not been reported on the parent's balance sheet. The authors also computed debt-to-capital ratios on the basis of *pro forma* consolidation and compared them to the preconsolidation ratios; the average increase in the ratio for the sample was 34%, but nearly 90% for the firms with the 21 largest finance units.

The FASB eliminated the nonconsolidation option (SFAS 94)—and all firms must now consolidate the assets and liabilities of controlled financial subsidiaries. Some parent firms have reduced their ownership of finance subsidiaries below 50% and account for these units using the equity method (discussed in Chapter 13). The balance sheet reports the firm's net investment in the subsidiary and the parent's income (and equity) includes its proportionate share of the subsidiary's income (and equity).

Because the net investment in the finance subsidiary reflects the parent's proportionate share of the assets minus the liabilities of the subsidiary, the parent's financial statements do not report its share of the debt of its finance subsidiary. However, from

---

[14]The CFO/current liabilities ratio is affected by adjustments to both the numerator and denominator.

EXHIBIT 11-4. GEORGIA-PACIFIC
Joint Venture Financing

Note 11: Related Party Transactions

The Corporation is a 50% partner in a joint venture (GA-MET) with Metropolitan Life Insurance Company (Metropolitan). GA-MET owns and operates the Corporation's office headquarters complex in Atlanta, Georgia. The Corporation accounts for its investment in GA-MET under the equity method.

At December 31, 1994, GA-MET had an outstanding mortgage loan payable to Metropolitan in the amount of $158 million. The note bears interest at 9½%, requires monthly payments of principal and interest through 2011 and is secured by the land and building of the Atlanta headquarters complex. In the event of foreclosure, each partner has severally guaranteed payment of one-half of any shortfall of collateral value to the outstanding secured indebtedness. Based on the present market conditions and building occupancy, the likelihood of any obligation to the Corporation with respect to this guarantee is considered remote.

Source: Georgia-Pacific, *1994 Annual Report.*

an overall economic entity (parent firm plus share in the affiliate) perspective, the debt of finance subsidiaries should be considered explicitly because it is clearly required to maintain the parent's operations. Additionally, the parent firm generally supports finance subsidiary borrowings through extensive income maintenance agreements and direct or indirect guarantees of debt.

The analyst should compute (proportionately) consolidated debt-to-equity, receivables turnover, and interest coverage ratios. This requires the addition of the parent's proportionate share of the assets and liabilities of the finance subsidiary to the assets and liabilities of the parent.[15]

The information required for these adjustments to reported receivables and debt, and the turnover, interest coverage, and leverage ratios can be obtained from the footnotes, which may disclose the assets, liabilities, and results of operations of finance subsidiaries in a summarized format.[16]

Joint Ventures and Investment in Affiliates

Firms may acquire manufacturing and distribution capacity through investments in affiliated firms, including suppliers and end users. Joint ventures with other firms may offer economies of scale and provide opportunities to share operating, technological, and financial risks. To obtain financing for the venture, the investors often enter into take-or-pay or throughput contracts with minimum payments designed to meet the venture's debt service requirements. Direct or indirect guarantees of the joint venture debt may also be present.

Exhibit 11-4 contains an excerpt from the footnote on commitments and contingencies in the *1994 Annual Report* issued by Georgia Pacific (GP). It discloses a joint venture with Metropolitan Life. GP is clearly liable for one-half of this off-balance-sheet debt, and $79 million should be added to GP's (property and) debt.

[15]The net investment in affiliates must be eliminated against the equity accounts. See Chapter 13 for a discussion of the proportionate consolidation accounting method.

[16]When the finance subsidiary issues publicly traded debt, then full financial statements are available and can be used for more accurate adjustments.

In the GP example, the parent explicitly guaranteed the debt of the affiliate. Even in the absence of such guarantees, the proportionate share of the affiliate's debt should be added to the reported debt of the investor. Generally, firms account for their investments in joint ventures and affiliates (where they have 20 to 50% ownership) using the equity method. These adjustments will be illustrated shortly in the analysis of Ashland Oil and Exhibits 11-7 and 11-8. Case 11-1 examines Texaco and its 50% owned affiliate, Caltex, to explore the use of off-balance-sheet activities in a more complex setting.

Other Off-Balance-Sheet Activities

The activities discussed to this point are those most commonly found. However, given volatile economic conditions faced by some firms, other off-balance-sheet techniques are sometimes observed. Two such activities are illustrated in this section. They are reminders of the need to be alert when reviewing firm disclosures as new techniques are always being invented.

Commodity-Linked Bonds

Natural resource firms may finance operations with commodity-indexed debt, with interest and/or principal repayments that depend on the price of underlying commodities. Changing commodity prices should be monitored to determine their impact on the related debt and debt-to-equity ratios. Exhibit 11-5 contains one such disclosure.

The LAC bonds were denominated in Swiss francs and exchangeable for a specified amount of gold. As the firm is a gold producer, these bonds can be viewed as a hedge. If the price of gold rose, bondholders would take gold (which would have a higher value than the face amount of the bonds). This loss (LAC would have less gold to sell at higher prices) would partly offset the earnings gain from the higher gold price. If the price of gold remains low, LAC benefits from the low stated interest rate on the bonds (which investors accept because of the imbedded option to convert to gold). Issuing these bonds, therefore, reduces the sensitivity of reported earnings to the price of gold.

In 1991, LAC retired most of the bonds four years prior to maturity, taking advantage of the low price of gold at that time. The company recognized a small gain from that retirement and increased its sensitivity to future changes in the price of gold.

When the issuer can force conversion or redemption, or when economic conditions suggest that the holder would benefit from conversion or redemption, the analyst should compute the potential gain or loss to the issuer assuming conversion. If, for

---

EXHIBIT 11-5. LAC MINERALS
Commodity-Linked Bonds

Swiss franc 14,505,000 (1990—92,035,000) gold equivalent convertible bonds, due November 1995, bearing interest at 4 percent. Each Swiss franc 5,000 bond entitles the holder to exchange it at any time for the cash equivalent in U.S. dollars of 6.835 troy ounces of gold, based on the market price of gold on the day of the investor election. During the year, the Company made an offer to the bond holders to acquire all bonds outstanding at a discount to the par value of the bonds. Pursuant to this offer, the company retired Swiss franc 77,530,000 bonds for cash consideration totalling $44,685,000 and recorded a gain on retirement of $2.8 million.

Source: LAC Minerals, *1991 Annual Report.*

EXHIBIT 11-6. PANHANDLE EASTERN
Exchangeable Bonds

In May 1985, Panhandle issued $105,750,000 of 12% subordinated debentures due 2010 which were exchangeable for 3,000,000 shares of common stock of Quantum Chemical Corporation owned by Panhandle. At December 31, 1987, $104,623,000 principal amount of the debentures were outstanding and were exchangeable for 2,968,036 shares of the Quantum stock. Beginning May 1, 1988, these debentures are callable by Panhandle upon not less than thirty days' notice at 108.4% of face amount unless exchanged prior to the redemption date.

Source: Panhandle Eastern, *1987 Annual Report.*

example, the price of gold rises, Lac's debt should be valued at the conversion value and not its face.

Bonds Tied to Investments

Some firms issue long-term debt exchangeable (at the option of the bondholder) for the common stock of another publicly traded firm held as an investment. Motives for these transactions include lower borrowing costs, the deferral of capital gains tax liability, tax benefits related to the low corporate tax rates on dividends to corporations in the United States, and the desire to maintain an investment while having the use of cash. Exhibit 11-6 describes an exchangeable bond issued by Panhandle Eastern.

When the bonds were originally issued by Panhandle, it obtained $105 million of cash while maintaining its strategic investment in Quantum Chemical. Because of the low cost of the stock investment ($7.42 million), the bond sale allowed Panhandle to defer the capital gains tax on the unrealized gain of $98.33 million ($105.75 million − $7.42 million). In 1988, at the time of Panhandle's choosing, the bonds were called, forcing an exchange of the bonds for the Quantum Chemical shares. Possible reasons for the call were the desire to recognize the capital gain for both tax purposes (corporate capital gains taxes had been reduced) and financial reporting purposes. The decline in corporate tax rates had also made the tax deduction for interest expense less valuable.

As in the case of commodity-linked bonds, conversion should be assumed when it can be forced by the issuer or when it is advantageous to holders. The conversion assumption depends on the terms of the issue, as disclosed in the issuer's footnotes. Leverage, interest coverage, and profitability ratios should then be adjusted.

ANALYSIS OF OBS ACTIVITIES: ASHLAND OIL

Ashland Oil is a major refiner, marketer, and distributor of oil whose other interests include coal (through a 50% interest in Arch Mineral and a 39% ownership of Ashland Coal in 1994) and natural gas. Ashland Oil's distribution system includes interests of 18.6 to 20.4% in LOOP and LOCAP, joint ventures operating deepwater offshore port and pipeline facilities. Exhibit 11-7 contains excerpts from footnotes to Ashland Oil's 1994 financial statements. The footnotes disclose that firm's unconsolidated subsidiaries, leases, and commitments and contingencies.

Exhibit 11-8 provides an illustration of the adjustments for off-balance-sheet financing activities discussed in this chapter. Ashland's reported debt is adjusted for (the present value of) operating leases, debt of equity method subsidiaries, and its

EXHIBIT 11-7. ASHLAND OIL, INC.
Off-Balance-Sheet Activities

Excerpts from 1994 Notes to Financial Statements

Note D: Unconsolidated Affiliates

Affiliated companies accounted for under the equity method include: Arch Mineral Corporation (a 50% owned coal company); Ashland Coal, Inc. (a 39% owned publicly traded coal company); LOOP INC. and LOCAP INC. (18.6% and 21.4% owned corporate joint ventures operating a deepwater offshore port and related pipeline facilities in the Gulf of Mexico); and various other companies. Summarized financial information reported by these affiliates and a summary of the amounts recorded in Ashland's consolidated financial statements follow.

($ in millions)	Arch Mineral Corporation	Ashland Coal, Inc.	LOOP INC. and LOCAP INC.	Other	Total
September 30, 1994					
Financial position					
Current assets	$ 173	$ 119	$ 36	$ 204	
Current liabilities	(132)	(110)	(86)	(123)	
Working capital	41	9	(50)	81	
Noncurrent assets	797	721	638	203	
Noncurrent liabilities	(713)	(373)	(525)	(96)	
Stockholders' equity	$ 125	$ 357	$ 63	$ 188	
Results of operations					
Sales and operating revenues	$ 641	$ 561	$ 149	$ 701	
Gross profit	60	71	54	172	
Net income	14	17	15	14	
Amounts recorded by Ashland					
Investments and advances	70	138	12	71	$291
Equity income	7	6	3	6	22
Dividends received	—	3	—	5	8

Note G: Leases and Other Commitments

Leases

Ashland and its subsidiaries are lessees in noncancelable leasing agreements for office buildings, warehouses, pipelines, transportation and marine equipment, storage facilities, retail outlets, manufacturing facilities and other equipment and properties which expire at various dates. Capitalized lease obligations are not significant and are included in long-term debt. Future minimum rental payments at September 30, 1994, and rental expense under operating leases follow.

($ in millions)

Future Minimum Rental Payments		Rental Expense	1994	1993	1992
1995	$ 63				
1996	50	Minimum rentals			
1997	41	(including rentals under			
1998	40	short-term leases)	$113	$111	$104
1999	35	Contingent rentals	12	11	12
Later years	222	Sublease rental income	(12)	(17)	(13)
	$451		$113	$105	$103

EXHIBIT 11-7. (*continued*)

Other Commitments

Under agreements with LOOP and LOCAP (see Note D), Ashland is committed to advance funds against future transportation charges if these corporate joint ventures are unable to meet their cash requirements. Such advances are limited to Ashland's share, based on its equity interests, of the total debt service and defined operating and administrative costs of these companies. Such advances, however, are reduced by (1) transportation charges Ashland paid, (2) a pro rata portion of transportation charges paid by other equity participants in excess of their required amounts, and (3) a pro rata portion of transportation charges paid by third parties who are not equity participants. At September 30, 1994, all advances made to LOOP and LOCAP by Ashland had been applied against transportation charges. Transportation charges incurred amounted to $24 million in 1994, $22 million in 1993 and $25 million in 1992. At September 30, 1994, Ashland's contingent liability for its share of the indebtedness of LOOP and LOCAP secured by throughput and deficiency agreements amounted to approximately $100 million.

Ashland is contingently liable under guarantees of certain debt and lease obligations of Ashland Coal, Inc., an unconsolidated affiliate. At September 30, 1994, such obligations have a present value of approximately $16 million. Ashland is also contingently liable for up to $16 million of borrowings under a revolving credit agreement of AECOM Technology Corporation, an unconsolidated affiliate. Ashland's guaranteed portion of outstanding borrowings under this agreement amounted to $9 million at September 30, 1994.

Source: Ashland Oil, *1994 Annual Report.*

contingent obligation for the debt of these units. The result is a more comprehensive measure of the firm's leverage.

Also given in Exhibit 11-8 are the reported and adjusted leverage data for Ashland for the period 1990 to 1993, in addition to 1994. Data for previous years are provided for comparison purposes as the footnote disclosures in Exhibit 11-7 are insufficient to adjust for those years.

Adjustments to 1994 Debt. Since Ashland Oil owns 50% of Arch Minerals and 39% of Ashland Coal, proportionate amounts (0.50 × $713 and 0.39 × $373) of noncurrent liabilities of those two units were added to its reported debt. Current liabilities may include financing obligations, but they are excluded as no disclosures were provided. Similarly, we use 20% (the average percentage) of LOOP (18.6%) and LOCAP's (20.4%) noncurrent liabilities giving a share of debt of (0.2 × $525) $105. As the footnote does not disclose Ashland's percentage of ownership of its other affiliates, we have approximated the share using the ratio of $71 recorded as its investments and advances in these other affiliates to the reported total equity of $188, implying an average ownership of ($71/$188) 38% and a proportionate share of debt of (0.38 × $96) $36 million.

The contingent liability for the debt of LOOP, LOCAP, Ashland Coal, and AECOM Technology (discussed in the section entitled "Other Committments") is not added in separately because it has already been included in the adjustments made for Ashland's share of the debt of its affiliates.

The capitalization of operating leases is straightforward in 1990 to 1992. However, capital leases declined substantially in 1993 and are not separately reported in 1994. The implicit interest rate in the 1993 capital leases is 15.5%, significantly higher than the firm's indicated cost of debt (ranging from 7.7 to 8.4%) at any time over the 1990 to 1994 period. We have used 8.5%, the rate implicit in the 1992 disclosures.

Adjusted debt is 54% higher than reported debt in 1994 and 53% higher on average over the five-year period analyzed. Similar patterns emerge for the adjusted debt-to-

EXHIBIT 11-8. ASHLAND OIL, INC.
Adjusted Long-Term Debt and Solvency Analysis and Adjusted Capitalization

	($ in millions)					
	9/30/90	9/30/91	9/30/92	9/30/93	9/30/94	Average
Short-term debt	170	196	306	159	**133**	193
Long-term debt	1,180	1,289	1,403	1,398	**1,391**	1,332
Capitalized leases	55	48	41	1	—	29
Insurance reserves*	118	141	159	173	**173**	153
Total debt	1,523	1,673	1,910	1,731	**1,697**	1,707
Preferred Shares	—	—	—	293	**293**	117
Common equity†	1,364	1,515	1,137	1,211	**1,346**	1,315
Stockholders' equity (BV)	1,364	1,515	1,137	1,504	**1,639**	1,432
Total capital (BV)	2,886	3,188	3,047	3,235	**3,336**	3,139
Stockholders' equity (MV)‡	1,777	1,819	1,491	2,347	**2,504**	1,988
Total capital (MV)	3,300	3,492	3,401	4,079	**4,201**	3,694
Adjustments to debt						
50% of Arch Mineral's non-current liabilities	217	206	283	318	**357**	276
Ashland Coal's liabilities and redeemable preferred	124	132	264	177	**145**	168
LOOP and LOCAP debt	123	124	119	114	**105**	117
Other noncurrent liabilities	59	57	47	37	**36**	47
Capitalization of operating leases§	260	275	297	311	**296**	288
Adj. total debt	2,305	2,467	2,919	2,688	**2,636**	2,603
Adj. total capital (BV)	3,669	3,983	4,057	4,192	**4,275**	4,035
Adj. total capital (MV)	4,083	4,286	4,410	5,036	**5,140**	4,591
Debt						
To equity (BV)	1.12	1.10	1.68	1.15	**1.04**	1.19
To capital (BV)	0.53	0.52	0.63	0.54	**0.51**	0.54
Debt						
To equity (MV)	0.86	0.92	1.28	0.74	**0.68**	0.86
To capital (MV)	0.46	0.48	0.56	0.42	**0.40**	0.46
Adj. debt						
To equity (BV)	1.69	1.63	2.57	1.79	**1.61**	1.82
To adj. capital (BV)	0.63	0.62	0.72	0.64	**0.62**	0.65
Adj. debt						
To equity (MV)	1.30	1.36	1.96	1.15	**1.05**	1.31
To adj. capital (MV)	0.56	0.58	0.66	0.53	**0.51**	0.57

Footnotes (applicable to 1994 computations):

*Reflects obligations of captive insurance companies.

†Includes common stock, paid-in-capital, and retained earnings.

‡Includes equity at market value based on number of shares outstanding at year-end and market price on September 30, 1994 and the common stock equivalent (at market value) of the convertible preferred stock.

§From Note G, Present Value of Future Rental Payments Under Operating Lease. See text for an explanation of the discount rate used.

equity and debt-to-capital ratios (at both book and market values of equity) as they are significantly higher than reported ratios. Reported debt has declined relative to the level reached in 1992 and the average over time. Adjusted debt is also lower compared to the 1992 level but it is slightly higher than the average, although both have declined relative to the 1992 and five-year average ratios.

Exhibit 11-8 shows that both reported and adjusted leverage reached a peak in 1992 and since that time Ashland has been able to significantly reduce the amount of leverage in its capital structure. The 1993 improvement resulted from Ashland's issuance of preferred shares, which increased equity. Additionally, the issuance proceeds were used to reduce outstanding debt in 1993. The lower cost of the preferred issue was due to its conversion feature and the tax advantage (to corporate investors) of the 80% dividend exclusion.

Security Analysis: How to Analyze Accounting and Market Data to Value Securities

Robert W. Holthausen and Mark E. Zmijewski

Chapter 9

Price Multiple Valuation Techniques

---

1. **Valuation Models Using a Multiple of Some Firm Characteristic.**

Valuation models which use a price multiple may be used to assess the current value of the firm or its common equity, as well as to calculate the terminal value of the firm (or its common equity). Most price multiples only value the common equity directly, not the value of the firm (liabilities plus common equity), though there are some exceptions as we shall see.

In discussing the rationale underlying multiples, we will generally ignore the distinction between estimating terminal values and current values, but the application of multiple models is somewhat different depending on whether you are valuing a firm currently or valuing it at some future point in time as in a terminal value calculation. We discuss some additional points to consider when using price multiples to measure terminal values in a separate section of this chapter.

Price multiple valuation techniques are used extensively on the street. There is even evidence that suggests that if you want to mimic the valuations placed on "deals" by investment banking houses, you will come closer to those valuations using both price multiples and discounted cash flow forecasts.

Multiples are usually based on both publicly traded companies and on recent acquisitions. Using publicly traded companies gives one a sense for how a particular company is valued relative to its comparables. Using acquisition prices gives one a sense of what others have been willing to pay for a similar company in a control transaction.

A. The basic concept.

$$V_t = \text{Multiple}_t * \text{firm characteristic}_t.$$

(1)   where:

Multiple_t	=	a number by which a firm characteristic is multiplied, at time t, to measure the value of an asset (for example, the value of the common stock).

Security Analysis: How to Analyze Accounting and Market Data to Value Securities
Robert W. Holthausen and Mark E. Zmijewski
\CH9.W51

Do not reproduce without permission.
July 29, 1998

405

firm characteristic$_t$ =   a firm characteristic (for example, earnings) that is assumed to be useful for measuring firm value in conjunction with the price multiple.

B.   Comments.

    (1)   Used to measure the value of common equity.

        (a)   Most models using multiples, for example, the price to earnings (P/E) multiple model, value only the common equity of the firm, not the value of the firm.

        (b)   A few models using multiples can be used to measure the value of the firm, however, the market values of all of the securities (or all of the assets) are needed to estimate the appropriate multiple.

    (2)   How do you measure and use the multiple?

        (a)   First, define the numerator and denominator. For example, the P/E multiple could be defined by the current price per share divided by the most recent four quarters of primary earnings per share before extraordinary items and discontinued operations.

        (b)   Second, collect the multiple for a set of <u>comparable</u> firms which may include current as well as previous periods. This set of comparable firms provides a distribution of multiples. We discuss the selection of multiples later.

        (c)   Third, use the distribution of multiples to measure the multiple for the firm you are attempting to value.

        (d)   Fourth, multiply the appropriate firm characteristic by the multiple from step three.

    (3)   What is the relevant peer group to for the multiple?

        (a)   Firms in the same industry (as close as possible in products, operations, geographic regions, etc).

        (b)   Direct competitors.

        (c)   **Even if there is a group of firms in the same industry, it is important to control for other factors, for example, growth rates, that differ across the firms (more on this point later).** Some practitioners use all industry competitors and we shall see the flaws associated with that approach.

Security Analysis: How to Analyze Accounting and Market Data to Value Securities
Robert W. Holthausen and Mark E. Zmijewski
\CH9.W51

(d)   Firms which have recently been acquired or taken private in a management buyout (multiples based on recent transactions). This is a very common procedure for pricing control transactions.

(4)   Most multiples can be used to estimate either the per share value of the security or the total value of the security issue.

     (a)   Use a per share numerator and denominator and a per share firm characteristic to measure per share value (for example, use the price per share to earnings per share multiple multiplied by earnings per share).

     (b)   Use a total value numerator and denominator and total value for the firm characteristic to measure total value (for example, use the market value of common equity to total earnings multiple multiplied by total earnings).

C.   What are some potential multiples to examine?

     (1)   Market value to flow multiples.

          (a)   Market value of common equity to earnings (MVE/E or P/EPS).
          (b)   Market value of common equity to operating cash flow.
          (c)   Market value of common equity to free cash flow to common shareholders.
          (d)   Market value of common equity to sales, or MV Firm/Sales
          (e)   Market value of common equity to earnings before interest and taxes (MVE/EBIT), or MV Firm/EBIT
          (f)   Market value of common equity to earnings before depreciation, interest and taxes, or MV Firm/EBITD.
          (g)   Market value of firm to operating cash flows before interest and taxes (MV Firm/CFOIT).
          (h)   Market value of firm to free cash flows to unlevered firm (MV Firm/FCFUN).

Note that some of these commonly used multiples do not insure that the value of a claim and the flow to that claim are the same in the multiple calculation. For example, P/EBIT measures price per share (reflecting only common equity) to earnings before interest and taxes which represents flows to equityholders, debtholders and taxing authorities.

Mixing claimants in the numerator and denominator adds additional complexities.

Security Analysis: How to Analyze Accounting and Market Data to Value Securities
Robert W. Holthausen and Mark E. Zmijewski
\CH9.W51

(2)   Market value to stock multiples.

    (a)   Market value of equity to net book value (MVE/BV).
    (b)   Market value of equity to replacement cost of net book value (replacement cost of assets less market value of liabilities).
    (c)   Market value of assets to book value of total capital (total debt plus net book value).
    (d)   Market value of assets to replacement cost of total capital.

2.   The Price to Earnings Multiple.

A.   The price to earnings multiple model.

$$P_t = \text{"P/E Multiple"} * \text{"EARNINGS"}$$

where: P_t is the price per share at time t.

(1)   Data requirements.

    1)   "P/E."
    2)   "EARNINGS."

B.   Theoretical Basis for the P/E Multiple.

Where does the use of the P/E multiple come from? Can it be traced back to standard DCF models? Consider the following reconciliation of the P/E multiple with the DCF valuation model.

(1)   Recall the DCF valuation approach.

The value of a security is equal to the present value of the expected cash flows from that security, discounted at the appropriate risk adjusted discount rate.

(2)   The basic model.

$$V_{S,t} = \Sigma_{\tau=1}^{\infty} E_t(CF_{S,t+\tau})K_{S,t,t+\tau}$$

    (a)   where:

        1) $V_{S,t}$ =   the value of security S at time t.

        2) $E_t(*)$ =   the expectations operator; the expectation, at time t, of *, conditional on the information available at time t.

Security Analysis: How to Analyze Accounting and Market Data to Value Securities
Robert W. Holthausen and Mark E. Zmijewski
\CH9.W51

3) $CF_{S,t+\tau}$ =   the cash flow available for distribution to the owners of security S at time $t+\tau$.

4) $K_{S,t,\tau}$ =   the present value discount factor for security S, for period τ, to discount the period τ cash flow to period t.

(b)   Notes:

    1)   All expectations and discount factors are conditioned on all information available at time t.

    2)   If the appropriate risk adjusted discount rate for the expected cash flow in period $t+\tau$, $k_{S,t+\tau}$, is constant over time (i.e., $k_{S,t+1} = k_{S,t+2} = ... = k_{S,t+\infty}$), then $K_{S,t,t+\tau}$ is equal to $(1+k_s)^{-\tau}$.

    3)   Different securities, and, hence, cash flow streams, such as, cash flows from the security, interest and principal from debt, dividends, free cash flow to common shareholders, have different risk adjusted discount rates.

(3)   The DCF model with some simplifying assumptions (perpetuities).

    (a)   The simplest assumption.

       1)   Cash flows are expected to remain constant, i.e., the growth rate, g_S, is zero.

       2)   The appropriate risk adjusted discount rate for the cash flows is constant over time, k_S.

       3)   The simplest model, perpetuity with no growth, is

$$V_t = E_t(CF_{S,t+1})/(k_S).$$

    (b)   The constant growth assumption.

       1)   Cash flows are expected to grow at a constant rate, g_S, from period $t+1$ though ∞.

       2)   The appropriate risk adjusted discount rate for the cash flows is constant over time, k_S.

Security Analysis: How to Analyze Accounting and Market Data to Value Securities
Robert W. Holthausen and Mark E. Zmijewski
\CH9.W51

3)   The simple model, perpetuity with constant growth, is

$$V_t = E_t(CF_{S,t+1})/(k_S-g_S).$$

(4)   Make the following assumptions for a highly simplified example.

(a)   The firm has a perpetual life.
(b)   The firm is financed entirely with equity.
(c)   The cost of equity capital is k_E per year.
(d)   Annual free cash flow for the firm are identical each year.
(e)   The firm pays dividends equal to annual free cash flow each year.[1]
(f)   Cash capital expenditures equal depreciation charges.
(g)   Working capital does not change.

Given these assumptions, annual free cash flows of the unlevered firm equal accounting profit after taxes, and the DCF value of the equity ($P_{t,DCF}$) is equal to the expected annual accounting earnings for period $t+1$, divided by k_E, which is a no growth perpetuity. That is,

$P_t=E_t(Earnings_{t+1})/k_E$. Thus,

$P/E = 1/k_E$ and $E/P = k_E$.

Implication :   P/E multiples equal 1/cost of equity capital.

Riskier firms will have lower P/E multiples.

(5)   Adding growth to the simplified example.

If accounting earnings grow at g annually in the highly simplified example, the DCF value of the equity is equal to the expected annual accounting earnings divided by k_E-g, a perpetuity with constant growth model. That is,

$P_{t,}=E_t(Earnings_{t+1})/(k_E-g)$. Thus,

$P/E = 1/(k_E-g)$ and $E/P = k_E-g$.

Implication: P/E multiples equal 1/(cost of equity capital - constant % growth rate). Firms with greater growth will have higher P/E multiples.

---

[1]Recall that the free cash flows of the unlevered firm equal the free cash flows of the common equity if the firm is all equity financed.

Security Analysis: How to Analyze Accounting and Market Data to Value Securities
  Robert W. Holthausen and Mark E. Zmijewski
  \CH9.W51

What is growth in this model? Where does it come from? The above analysis assumes that growth results with no new investment. This assumption may be appropriate if growth is assumed to equal inflation and all cash flows grow with inflation.[2] Thus, there is no real growth, only nominal growth. The equity cost of capital in this case must be a nominal cost of capital.

An alternative assumption is to assume that growth results from additional investment. Thus, the firm grows (on a per share basis) by investing some of the free cash flows (before new investments) into new investments with identical risk and return characteristics as existing investments. We refer to the proportion of earnings reinvested in the firm as the reinvestment rate, X.[3] In this model, the growth rate is equal to the reinvestment rate multiplied by the rate of return on new investments, ROI, that is, $g = X*ROI$; and the dividend payment is equal to one minus the reinvestment rate multiplied by earnings, $E_t(Earnings_{t+1})*(1-X)$.

$$P_t = (E_t(Earnings_{t+1})*(1-X))/(k_E-g). \text{ Thus,}$$

$$P/E = (1-X)/(k_E-g) \text{ and}$$
$$E/P = (k_E-g)/(1-X).$$

Therefore P/E ratios are a function of reinvestment, growth, discount rate (risk).

Notice that since $g = X*ROI$, the above expression implies

$$P/E = (1-X)/(k_E-X*ROI)$$
$$P/E = (1-g/ROI)/(k_E-g)$$

Implication: real growth can only be attained if the firm invests some of its free cash flows in new investments, and these investments have a ROI that is in excess of the cost of capital. If the ROI is equal to the cost of capital, then there is no benefit to growth (i.e., there is no benefit to new investment).

[Note if this were not an all equity firm, we would use the ROE on new investment in place of ROI. We will continue to assume that this is an all equity firm.]

---

[2]Note, this assumption may not be reasonable because not all cash flow components would grow at the same rate, e.g., capital expenditures equal to depreciation may not be realistic because depreciation typically lags inflation.

[3]Although the reinvestment rate, X, is equal to one minus the dividend payout ratio, it is the reinvestment rate, in conjunction with the rate of return on investments, that drive value.

Security Analysis: How to Analyze Accounting and Market Data to Value Securities
Robert W. Holthausen and Mark E. Zmijewski
\CH9.W51

To see this more clearly, note that the above expression for P_t can be written in two components.

$$P_t = (E_t(Earnings_{t+1})/k_E +$$

$$[X(E_t(Earnings_{t+1})/k_E]*[(ROI-k_E)/(k_E-g)].$$

The first component is the value of the firm with no growth and the second component is the value of the firm's growth opportunities. This expression assumes that new investment will continue to earn a return in excess of the cost of equity capital and that return on new investment will not diminish, forever.

If one wanted to relax this valuation somewhat and allow for the profitable investment opportunity to exist for n years and then cease completely, the expression could be rewritten as

$$P_t = (E_t(Earnings_{t+1})/k_E +$$

$$[(E_t(Earnings_{t+1})/k_E]*\{[X(ROI-k_E)/(k_E-g)]*[1-((1+g)/(1+k_E))^n]\}$$

Figure 1 shows the P/E ratio for a firm with a 10% cost of equity capital, and varying ROIs and investment rates (X% of earnings). Note that for the case with ROI = 10% = k_E, the P/E ratio is equal to 10 and it is constant over reasonable values of investment percentage (X%). For the case with ROI = 8% < k_E, the P/E ratio is equal to 10 if the firm has no new investment (x% = 0), and it declines as the percent of earnings invested increases. Finally, for the case with ROI = 12% > k_E, the P/E ratio increases as the investment percentage (X%) increases to the point at which X*ROI=k_E. At that point, the model is undefined (denominator is equal to 0), and thereafter, when X*ROI>k_E, the P/E ratio is negative indicating that the model has no economic interpretation (since a basic assumption, g < k_E, is violated). **The message in this example is clear, do not invest in negative net present value projects, and maximize your investment in positive net present value projects.**

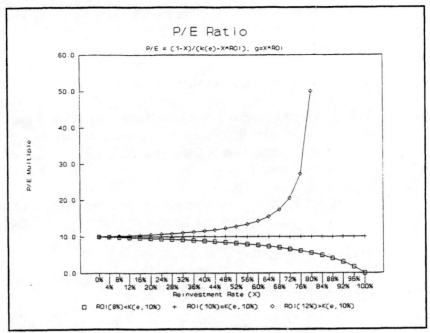

Figure 1

Overall:

P/E multiples do not have straight forward interpretations. A firm with pristine plant and equipment will have a higher P/E than a firm with poorer plant and equipment, even if they both face the same growth prospects, because one firm faces much lower reinvestment (capital expenditures) in the near term.

C.   How do you measure P/E multiples?

(1)   One obvious, but key point, is that you must use the same definition of earnings in calculating the multiple as you are using for measuring the firm characteristic.

(2)   The financial press typically reports current price divided by the sum of the last four quarter's earnings.

(3)   Different Definitions of P/E

(a)   FYE P/E Ratio - the price of the stock at the fiscal year divided by the earnings per share for the past fiscal year.

Security Analysis: How to Analyze Accounting and Market Data to Value Securities
Robert W. Holthausen and Mark E. Zmijewski
\CH9.W51

(b)   Projected P/E Ratio - the stock's current price divided by projected earnings per share (IBES, Zacks or other source).

(c)   LTM P/E Ratio - (last twelve months) the recent price divided by the sum of earnings per share reported during the last 12 months.

(d)   Average Annual P/E Ratio - the average price of the stock for the year divided by earnings per share as reported by the company for the year. In the case of fiscal year companies, all data are for the fiscal year.

(e)   Note, earnings are typically earnings before extraordinary items and Value Line provides a forecast of firms' P/E multiples.

(4)   What is "EARNINGS?"

(a)   Current accounting earnings?

If so, which accounting earnings? Primary, full-diluted, before extraordinary items and discontinued items, annual, quarterly, adjusted for specific accounting techniques (for example, pension accounting).

(b)   What about firms with negative earnings?

(c)   Trailing vs. future earnings? Often use estimates of future earnings.

(5)   What price do you use?

Price at a point in time or an average price over the period earnings are measured? Current price is appropriate if future earnings are used.

(6)   Best practice is to use current price and forecasted year ahead earnings per share for the comparable firms and then use forecasted earnings for your firm. This provides an assessment of current price.

D.   Practical Applications.

(1)   Widely used but we caution against using multiple models naively.

(2)   This method can be used to estimate the terminal value in a discounted cash flow model.

(3)   This method can also be used as a basic valuation model. Even if you believe more in the conceptual correctness of a DCF model, multiple valuation

Security Analysis: How to Analyze Accounting and Market Data to Value Securities
  Robert W. Holthausen and Mark E. Zmijewski
  \CH9.W51

Do not reproduce without permission.
July 29, 1998

414

models can serve as useful checks to see if your DCF calculation is within reasonable bounds of the so called multiple approaches.

(4)   If you use this method of valuation, know its limitations, which are many.

E.   How do analysts use P/E ratios?

Sell side analysts often base their recommendations to buy or not to buy a stock based on projected earnings figures and projected price-earnings multiples. For example, a recent report by Merrill Lynch on Schlumberger Ltd. (dated June 8, 1993), the analyst was predicting earnings per share for Schlumberger of $3.10 for 1994 and a P/E multiple of 26 yielding a price in the near term of $80.00 per share. Since the shares were selling at $67.00 at the time of the report, the analyst had a strong buy recommendation for Schlumberger. Often the P/E multiples used by the analysts are is the projected P/E for the S&P 500 in a six to twelve month time frame.

F.   Time-series variation in P/E ratios for all Compustat firms.

Figure 2 presents the distribution of quarterly P/E ratios (defined as price divided by 12 month trailing earnings) from March, 1986 to March 1990 for selected industry groups based on the COMPUSTAT database, and Table 1 presents the underlying numbers for Figure 2, and for some additional industries (see Table 1 at the end of these notes).

Industry 1 -- Compustat All Industrial Index
Industry 6 -- S&P 400
Industry 2834 -- Pharmaceuticals
Industry 4911 -- Electric Services
Industry 7372 -- Software

Security Analysis: How to Analyze Accounting and Market Data to Value Securities
Robert W. Holthausen and Mark E. Zmijewski
\CH9.W51

Do not reproduce without permission.
July 29, 1998

415

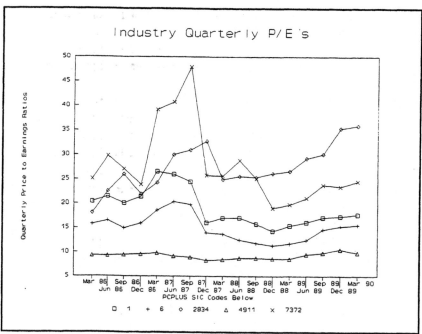

Figure 2

G. In addition, Table 2 (which is Panel A of Table 12.1 from George Foster's <u>Financial Statement Analysis</u>, provides information about the distribution of P/E ratios annually from 1964 to 1983 in the U.S. (uses Compustat firms).

Note the variation in P/E's through time.

H. Cross-sectional variation in P/E ratios for one year, by industry. (Foster - Table 12.1)

Table 1 also allows one to see the variation in Price/Earnings ratios across industries.

Panel B of Table 2 (which is Panel B of Table 12.1 from George Foster's <u>Financial Statement Analysis</u>, provides information about the cross-sectional distribution of P/E ratios in 1983 for U.S. firms across industries as well as providing information about the distribution of P/E ratios within an industry at a point in time. (uses Compustat firms).

Security Analysis: How to Analyze Accounting and Market Data to Value Securities
  Robert W. Holthausen and Mark E. Zmijewski
\CH9.W51

I.   Diversity in P/E ratios - Growth and Transitional Components

Panel A of Table 3, which is Table 12.2 of George Foster's <u>Financial Statement Analysis</u> provides information about the mean reversion in P/E ratios.

At time zero, portfolios of firms are formed on the basis of the ranking of P/E ratios. The average P/E ratio for those portfolios are reported for year 0 (the year of formation) and for the next 10 years. Note, the portfolios are held constant from year zero to year 10. The highest P/E's are in portfolio 1 and the lowest P/E's are in portfolio 25. Note two things, P/E's ratios quickly revert back towards the mean, but do not fully revert, and P/E ratios for the extreme portfolios are still very different ten years out.

Suppose earnings are composed of permanent earnings plus a transitory shock (a one-time shock to earnings which is not expected to persist). The reversion in P/E's reflects the fact that some things can affect earnings which don't affect prices (so called transitory components of earnings). For example, a firm could report poor earnings because of an accounting change or temporary phenomenon. If the market expected earnings to rebound immediately, current prices would hardly be affected. In that case, the observed P/E ratio would be very high, since earnings was temporarily low but price had not changed. The opposite would be true for positive transitory shocks to earnings. When we form portfolios on the basis of P/E ratios, we are sorting in part on the degree of transitory components.

Differences in P/E ratios continue to persist, in part because of differences in presumed growth rates and cost of capital.

Panel B of Table 3 provides information about differences in growth rates as a function of P/E ratios. At time zero, portfolios of firms are formed on the basis of the ranking of P/E ratios. The average growth rate in earnings for those portfolios are reported for year 0 (the year of formation) and for each of the next 10 years. Note, the portfolios are held constant from year zero to year 10. The highest P/E's are in portfolio 1 and the lowest P/E's are in portfolio 25. Note two things, growth rates for high P/E's ratio firms are negative in year 0 and high beyond year 0 whereas growth rates for low P/E's are high in year 0 and low in subsequent years. Even at year 7 there are noticeable differences in growth rates between portfolio 1 and 25.

The evidence in the table is consistent with a transitory component of earnings affecting the P/E ratio in year zero and with P/E ratios reflecting differences in annual earnings growth rates which persist for up to 5 years (at 5% significance levels) in the extreme portfolios and up to three years in the less extreme portfolios.

Security Analysis: How to Analyze Accounting and Market Data to Value Securities
   Robert W. Holthausen and Mark E. Zmijewski
\CH9.W51

J. Why do P/E multiples differ across firms or across time?

   (1) Differences in growth rates.

   (2) Differences in the time profile of earnings when growth rates are not constant. For example, if one firm is going to achieve growth in the next few years and another firm is going to experience similar growth but out several years, their time profiles of earnings would be different.

   (3) Differences in Risk (financial and business) which translate into different costs of capital.

   (4) Differences in reinvestment requirements (how much of cash flows before capital expenditures and working capital additions gets reinvested into the business).

   (5) Differences in return on investments.

   (6) Differences in the "Quality" or sustainability of earnings.

   (7) Different Accounting techniques. Differences in accounting techniques can obviously affect P/E ratios since two identical firms could report different earnings simply because of the choice of accounting techniques.

   (8) Under performing/idle assets. If a firm has a subset of its assets which are not earning as large a return as they could if properly deployed, then that firms P/E ratio will be affected. For example, suppose we have two firms with an identical set of assets and whose earnings are equivalent. Further assume that one firm also owns land (which the other does not) which is currently idle or underutilized. The value of the firm with the idle land should equal the value of the firm without the land plus the value of the land. Therefore, the P/E ratios of the two firms will differ. You could use the P/E multiple of the firm without the idle land to value the firm with the idle land, except the value of the land would have to be added to the P/E multiple valuation.

K. A spreadsheet for the VPMEG-ONE Company follows this discussion. This example examines the effect of financial leverage, growth, reinvestment requirements, risk, and profitability on various multiples.

The purpose of this example is to demonstrate how variation in certain parameters affects various price multiples. For example, with this example, one can see for a firm valued using a DCF approach, how changes in growth, risk, profitability, etc. affect P/E multiples, P/Sales multiples, MV/BV multiples etc. In every case, the example assumes that one factor is changed while all other factors are held constant.

Security Analysis: How to Analyze Accounting and Market Data to Value Securities
Robert W. Holthausen and Mark E. Zmijewski
\CH9.W51

While that approach is useful, it is also important to realize the potential flaws associated with some of the assumptions. For example, leverage ratios are changed without changing the cost of debt in the examples. How changes in leverage would actually affect variation in multiples would also be affected by how the cost of debt changes with leverage.

For each factor examined (leverage, growth rate, sales/net PPEQ, cost of capital, profitability as driven by SGA/Sales) there is a no tax and a tax panel.

(1)   Panel A shows the effect of leverage on multiples. Notice first of all that in the no tax panel, there is no variation in the value of the firm, the value of the equity declines (same firm value but there is less equity). In the tax panel, the value of the firm and the value of the equity increase with leverage. It should be noted that interest tax shields are being valued using Case II in this spreadsheet (see Chapter 2) as all interest tax shields are being discounted at the cost of debt. Case III would lead to slightly different results but the qualitative implications would not change.

(2)   Panel B shows the effect of growth rates on multiples. Notice the significant role that growth prospects play in determining multiples. Hence, it is critical that growth be considered when choosing comparable firms.

(3)   Panel C indicates what happens as sales to Net PPEQ increases, the sales driver in this example. This is essentially indicating what happens as ROA increases in that the firm is able to generate more sales for a given level of PPE as sales/PPE increases. As can be seen as ROE and ROA increase, multiple increase as well.

(4)   Panel D indicates how changes in the discount rate (risk) affect multiples. Again, it is obvious that increases in risk drive multiples down. Hence, it is important to control for differences in risk.

(5)   Panel E indicates how changes in profitability as proxied by variation in SGA/sales affect multiples. The effects here depend on the multiple considered. The multiples generally decrease as profitability worsen, but the effects are much more dramatic for multiples like price/sales than for price/earnings ratios. Why because as SG&A increases, earnings decrease, but sales is not changed. Hence as SG&A increase, price and earnings both decrease hence the P/E ratio does not change that much, whereas the price to sales ratio changes more.

Security Analysis: How to Analyze Accounting and Market Data to Value Securities
Robert W. Holthausen and Mark E. Zmijewski
\CH9.W51

HERE ARE THE BASIC DATA UNDERLYING THIS EXAMPLE.

3 Below is an example of a firm, VPMEG-ONE Company, with financial statement forecasts for six years.
4 Assume years seven through infinity will continue to grow at the growth rate.
5
6 Assumptions:
7
8 Income Tax Rate	0% or 40%	
9 Interest Rate (Cost of Debt)	15%	
10 Growth Rate	10%	
11		
12 Sales to Net PPEQ	1.250	
13 Straight Line Depreciation Rate	10.00%	
14 Sell, Gen & Admin % of Sales	40.00%	
15 Dividends		FCF to Common Equity
16 Required Cash Balance	9.50%	of net period's projected sales
17 Surplus Cash	0	Assume dividends equal FCF to common equity
18 Net Current Operating Assets	10.00%	of net period's projected sales
19 Net PPEQ - Starting Balance	40,000	
20 Net PPEQ - Subsequent Periods		Grow at growth rate in subsequent periods
21 Short Term Debt	0	
22 Initial $ of Long-Term Debt	10,000	Grow at growth rate in subsequent periods
23 Initial $ of Paid in Capital		Plug to balance initial balance sheet
24 Retained Earnings		Plug as per articulation of I/S and B/S
25
26

27 Various F/S Relations Given Assumptions		Year 1	Year 2	Year 3	Year 4	Year 5	Year 6
28							
29 ROA (ROI, Beginning Assets)	ROA	57.17%	57.17%	57.17%	57.17%	57.17%	57.17%
30 ROE (Beginning Equity)	ROE	67.53%	67.53%	67.53%	67.53%	67.53%	67.53%
31 % Earnings into New Investments	X	14.81%	14.81%	14.81%	14.81%	14.81%	14.81%
32 ROE * % Earnings Invested = Growth	ROE*X	10.00%	10.00%	10.00%	10.00%	10.00%	10.00%
33 Net Income to Sales	NIS	50.00%	50.00%	50.00%	50.00%	50.00%	50.00%
34 Total Debt to Total Assets	TDTA	19.71%	19.71%	19.71%	19.71%	19.71%	19.71%
35 Total Debt to Common Equity	TDCE	0.246	0.246	0.246	0.246	0.246	0.246
36 MV of Debt to MV of Firm	MVDMVF	4.18%	4.18%	4.18%	4.18%	4.18%	4.18%
37 MV of Debt to MV of Common Equity	MVDMVE	0.044	0.044	0.044	0.044	0.044	0.044
38 Investments to FCF-Unlevered+Investment	IFCFU	-27.49%	-27.49%	-27.49%	-27.49%	-27.49%	-27.49%
39 New Invest to FCF-Unlevered+New Invest	NIFCFU	-17.49%	-17.49%	-17.49%	-17.49%	-17.49%	-17.49%
40
41
42

43 Various Price Multiples given Assumptions at End of Year 0
44
45 Price to Earnings Ratio	P/E	8.337
46 Price to Sales	P/S	4.169
47 Price to FCF to CE	P/FCFCE	9.787
48 Price to Operating Income (EBIT)	P/OI	7.906
49 MV of Firm to Sales	MVF/S	4.350
50 MV of Firm to Operating Income	MVF/OI	8.251
51 MV of Firm to FCF of Unlevered Firm	MVF/FCFU	10.000
52 MV of Equity to BV of Equity	MVE/BVE	5.118
53 MV of Firm to BV of Firm	MVF/BVF	4.288
54

55	Year 0	Year 1	Year 2	Year 3	Year 4	Year 5	Year 6
57							
58 C of Cap for the Unlevered Firm (ku)		20.00%	20.00%	20.00%	20.00%	20.00%	20.00%
59 Weighted Average Cost of Capital (WACC) (if T=0%)		20.00%	20.00%	20.00%	20.00%	20.00%	20.00%
60 C of Cap for the common equity (ke)		20.22%	20.22%	20.22%	20.22%	20.22%	20.22%
61
62

Security Analysis: How to Analyze Accounting and Market Data to Value Securities
Robert W. Holthausen and Mark E. Zmijewski
\CH9.W51

Panel A

P/E Ratios and Financial Leverage Ratios

Income Tax Rate 40.00%

Initial $ of Long-Term Debt	P/E	P/S	P/FCFCE	P/OI	MVF/S	MVF/OI	MVF/FCFU	MVE/BVE	MVF/BVF	ROA	ROE	X	ROE*X	NIS	TDTA	TDCE	MVDHVF	MVDMVE	MVF	MVCE	IFCFU	NIFCFU
0	7.1	2.2	10.0	4.3	2.2	4.3	10.0	2.2	2.2	34.3%	34.3%	29.2%	10.0%	31.6%	0.0%	0.0	0.0%	0.0	123.275	123.275	-42.39%	-29.15%
5,000	7.3	2.2	10.0	4.3	2.4	4.5	10.5	2.5	2.3	34.3%	37.1%	27.0%	10.0%	30.8%	9.9%	0.1	3.9%	0.0	129.275	124.275	-42.39%	-29.15%
10,000	7.6	2.3	10.1	4.3	2.5	4.7	11.0	2.8	2.4	34.3%	40.5%	24.7%	10.0%	30.0%	19.7%	0.2	7.4%	0.1	135.275	125.275	-42.39%	-29.15%
15,000	7.9	2.3	10.2	4.4	2.6	4.9	11.5	3.2	2.5	34.3%	44.9%	22.3%	10.0%	29.2%	29.6%	0.4	10.6%	0.2	141.275	126.275	-42.39%	-29.15%
20,000	8.2	2.3	10.2	4.4	2.7	5.1	11.9	3.8	2.6	34.3%	50.8%	19.7%	10.0%	28.4%	39.4%	0.7	13.6%	0.2	147.275	127.275	-42.39%	-29.15%
25,000	8.5	2.3	10.2	4.4	2.8	5.3	12.4	4.5	2.7	34.3%	58.9%	17.0%	10.0%	27.5%	49.3%	1.0	16.3%	0.3	153.275	128.275	-42.39%	-29.15%
30,000	8.8	2.4	10.3	4.5	2.9	5.5	12.9	5.7	2.9	34.3%	70.9%	14.1%	10.0%	26.7%	59.1%	1.4	18.8%	0.3	159.275	129.275	-42.39%	-29.15%
35,000	9.1	2.4	10.3	4.5	3.0	5.7	13.4	7.5	3.0	34.3%	90.6%	11.0%	10.0%	25.9%	69.0%	2.2	21.2%	0.3	165.275	130.275	-42.39%	-29.15%
40,000	9.5	2.4	10.4	4.6	3.1	5.9	13.9	11.1	3.1	34.3%	128.7%	7.8%	10.0%	25.1%	78.9%	3.7	23.4%	0.4	171.275	131.275	-42.39%	-29.15%
45,000	9.9	2.4	10.4	4.6	3.2	6.1	14.4	21.0	3.3	34.3%	233.2%	4.3%	10.0%	24.3%	88.7%	7.9	25.4%	0.4	177.275	132.275	-42.39%	-29.15%
50,000	10.3	2.4	10.4	4.6	3.3	6.3	14.9	167.1	3.3	34.3%	1779.3%	0.6%	10.0%	23.5%	98.6%	69.0	27.3%	0.4	183.275	133.275	-42.39%	-29.15%
55,000	10.8	2.5	10.5	4.7	3.4	6.5	15.4	-28.6	3.5	34.3%	-291.2%	-3.4%	10.0%	22.6%	108.4%	-12.9	29.1%	0.5	189.275	134.275	-42.39%	-29.15%
60,000	11.3	2.5	10.5	4.7	3.6	6.7	15.8	-13.3	3.6	34.3%	-129.4%	-7.7%	10.0%	21.8%	118.3%	-6.5	30.7%	0.5	195.275	135.275	-42.39%	-29.15%
65,000	11.8	2.5	10.5	4.7	3.7	6.9	16.3	-8.7	3.6	34.3%	-80.9%	-12.4%	10.0%	21.0%	128.1%	-4.6	32.3%	0.5	201.275	136.275	-42.39%	-29.15%
70,000	12.4	2.5	10.5	4.7	3.8	7.1	16.8	-6.5	3.7	34.3%	-57.6%	-17.4%	10.0%	20.2%	138.0%	-3.6	33.8%	0.5	207.275	137.275	-42.39%	-29.15%
75,000	13.0	2.5	10.6	4.8	3.9	7.4	17.3	-5.2	3.8	34.3%	-43.9%	-22.8%	10.0%	19.4%	147.9%	-3.1	35.2%	0.5	213.275	138.275	-42.39%	-29.15%

Income Tax Rate 0.00%

Initial $ of Long-Term Debt	P/E	P/S	P/FCFCE	P/OI	MVF/S	MVF/OI	MVF/FCFU	MVE/BVE	MVF/BVF	ROA	ROE	X	ROE*X	NIS	TDTA	TDCE	MVDHVF	MVDMVE	MVF	MVCE	IFCFU	NIFCFU
0	8.3	4.4	10.0	8.3	4.4	8.3	10.0	4.3	4.3	57.2%	57.2%	17.5%	10.0%	52.7%	0.0%	0.0	0.0%	0.0	239.275	239.275	-27.49%	-17.49%
5,000	8.3	4.3	9.9	8.1	4.4	8.3	10.0	4.7	4.3	57.2%	61.8%	16.2%	10.0%	51.4%	9.9%	0.1	2.1%	0.0	239.275	234.275	-27.49%	-17.49%
10,000	8.3	4.1	9.8	7.9	4.4	8.3	10.0	5.1	4.3	57.2%	67.5%	14.8%	10.0%	50.0%	19.7%	0.2	4.2%	0.1	239.275	229.275	-27.49%	-17.49%
15,000	8.4	4.0	9.6	7.7	4.4	8.3	10.0	5.7	4.3	57.2%	74.9%	13.4%	10.0%	48.6%	29.6%	0.4	6.3%	0.1	239.275	224.275	-27.49%	-17.49%
20,000	8.4	3.9	9.4	7.4	4.4	8.3	10.0	6.5	4.3	57.2%	84.6%	11.8%	10.0%	47.3%	39.4%	0.7	8.4%	0.1	239.275	219.275	-27.49%	-17.49%
25,000	8.5	3.8	9.3	7.2	4.4	8.3	10.0	7.6	4.3	57.2%	98.2%	10.2%	10.0%	45.9%	49.3%	1.0	10.4%	0.2	239.275	214.275	-27.49%	-17.49%
30,000	8.6	3.7	9.2	7.0	4.4	8.3	10.0	9.2	4.3	57.2%	118.2%	8.5%	10.0%	44.5%	59.1%	1.4	12.5%	0.2	239.275	209.275	-27.49%	-17.49%
35,000	8.6	3.6	9.1	6.9	4.4	8.3	10.0	11.8	4.3	57.2%	151.0%	6.6%	10.0%	43.2%	69.0%	2.2	14.6%	0.2	239.275	204.275	-27.49%	-17.49%
40,000	8.7	3.5	9.0	6.7	4.4	8.3	10.0	16.9	4.3	57.2%	214.5%	4.7%	10.0%	41.8%	78.9%	3.7	16.7%	0.3	239.275	199.275	-27.49%	-17.49%
45,000	8.7	3.4	8.8	6.5	4.4	8.3	10.0	30.8	4.3	57.2%	388.6%	2.6%	10.0%	40.5%	88.7%	7.9	18.8%	0.3	239.275	194.275	-27.49%	-17.49%
50,000	8.8	3.4	8.7	6.4	4.4	8.3	10.0	237.3	4.3	57.2%	2965.5%	0.3%	10.0%	39.1%	98.6%	69.0	20.9%	0.3	239.275	189.275	-27.49%	-17.49%
55,000	8.9	3.3	8.6	6.2	4.4	8.3	10.0	-39.2	4.3	57.2%	-485.4%	-2.1%	10.0%	37.7%	108.4%	-12.9	23.0%	0.4	239.275	184.275	-27.49%	-17.49%
60,000	9.0	3.3	8.4	6.0	4.4	8.3	10.0	-17.6	4.3	57.2%	-215.6%	-4.6%	10.0%	36.4%	118.3%	-6.5	25.1%	0.4	239.275	179.275	-27.49%	-17.49%
65,000	9.1	3.2	8.3	5.8	4.4	8.3	10.0	-11.1	4.3	57.2%	-134.9%	-7.4%	10.0%	35.0%	128.1%	-4.6	27.2%	0.4	239.275	174.275	-27.49%	-17.49%
70,000	9.1	3.1	8.3	5.8	4.4	8.3	10.0	-8.0	4.3	57.2%	-96.0%	-10.4%	10.0%	33.6%	138.0%	-3.6	29.3%	0.5	239.275	169.275	-27.49%	-17.49%
75,000	9.3	3.0	8.1	5.7	4.4	8.3	10.0	-6.2	4.3	57.2%	-73.1%	-13.7%	10.0%	32.3%	147.9%	-3.1	31.3%	0.5	239.275	164.275	-27.49%	-17.49%

Security Analysis:: How to Analyze Accounting and Market Data to Value Securities
Robert W. Holthausen and Mark E. Zmijewski
\CH8.WS1

Price Multiple Valuation Techniques

Panel B

P/E Ratios and Growth Rates

Income Tax Rate 40.00%

Growth Rate	P/E	P/S	P/FCFCE	P/OI	HVF/S	HVF/OI	HVF/FCFU	HVE/BVE	HVF/BVF	ROA	ROE	X	ROE*X	NIS	TOTA	TDCE	HVDHVF	HVDHVE	HVF	HVCE	IFCFU	NIFCFU
-5.00%	4.5	1.3	3.9	2.5	1.5	2.9	4.2	1.7	1.5	29.8%	35.1%	-14.2%	-5.0%	29.1%	20.3%	0.3	14.0%	0.2	71.653	61.652	-8.22%	16.76%
-4.00%	4.5	1.3	4.1	2.6	1.5	3.0	4.4	1.7	1.5	30.1%	35.5%	-11.3%	-4.0%	29.1%	20.3%	0.3	13.6%	0.2	73.385	63.385	-10.73%	13.27%
-3.00%	4.6	1.3	4.3	2.6	1.6	3.0	4.5	1.7	1.6	30.5%	35.9%	-8.4%	-3.0%	29.2%	20.2%	0.3	13.3%	0.1	75.263	65.263	-13.20%	9.85%
-2.00%	4.7	1.4	4.4	2.7	1.6	3.1	4.8	1.8	1.6	30.8%	36.3%	-5.5%	-2.0%	29.3%	20.2%	0.3	12.9%	0.1	77.307	67.307	-15.64%	6.50%
-1.00%	4.8	1.4	4.7	2.7	1.6	3.1	5.0	1.8	1.6	31.1%	36.6%	-2.7%	-1.0%	29.3%	20.1%	0.3	12.6%	0.1	79.543	69.543	-18.04%	3.22%
-0.00%	4.9	1.4	4.9	2.8	1.7	3.2	5.3	1.9	1.7	31.4%	37.0%	0.0%	0.0%	29.4%	20.1%	0.3	12.2%	0.1	82.000	72.000	-20.41%	0.00%
1.00%	5.0	1.5	5.2	2.8	1.7	3.3	5.5	1.9	1.7	31.7%	37.3%	2.7%	1.0%	29.4%	20.1%	0.3	11.8%	0.1	84.715	74.715	-22.74%	-3.16%
2.00%	5.3	1.5	5.5	2.9	1.7	3.3	5.9	2.0	1.7	32.0%	37.7%	5.3%	2.0%	29.5%	20.1%	0.3	11.4%	0.1	87.733	77.733	-25.04%	-6.26%
3.00%	5.3	1.6	5.8	3.0	1.8	3.4	6.2	2.0	1.8	32.3%	38.1%	7.9%	3.0%	29.6%	20.0%	0.2	11.1%	0.1	91.110	81.110	-27.32%	-9.30%
4.00%	5.5	1.6	6.1	3.1	1.8	3.5	6.6	2.1	1.8	32.5%	38.4%	10.4%	4.0%	29.6%	20.0%	0.2	10.5%	0.1	94.920	84.920	-29.56%	-12.29%
5.00%	5.7	1.7	6.6	3.2	1.9	3.6	7.1	2.1	1.9	32.8%	38.8%	12.9%	5.0%	29.7%	19.9%	0.2	10.1%	0.1	99.254	89.254	-31.77%	-15.22%
6.00%	6.0	1.8	7.1	3.4	2.0	3.7	7.6	2.2	2.0	33.1%	39.1%	15.3%	6.0%	29.8%	19.9%	0.2	9.6%	0.1	104.237	94.237	-33.95%	-18.11%
7.00%	6.3	1.9	7.6	3.6	2.1	3.9	8.3	2.3	2.1	33.4%	39.5%	17.7%	7.0%	29.8%	19.8%	0.2	9.1%	0.1	110.036	100.036	-36.10%	-20.94%
8.00%	6.6	2.0	8.3	3.8	2.2	4.1	9.0	2.4	2.1	33.7%	39.8%	20.1%	8.0%	29.9%	19.8%	0.2	8.6%	0.1	116.885	106.885	-38.22%	-23.72%
9.00%	7.1	2.1	8.9	4.0	2.3	4.4	9.9	2.6	2.3	34.0%	40.2%	22.4%	9.0%	29.9%	19.8%	0.2	8.0%	0.1	125.123	115.123	-40.32%	-26.46%
10.00%	7.6	2.3	10.1	4.3	2.5	4.7	11.0	2.8	2.4	34.3%	40.5%	24.7%	10.0%	30.0%	19.7%	0.2	7.4%	0.1	135.275	125.275	-42.39%	-29.15%

Income Tax Rate 0.00%

Growth Rate	P/E	P/S	P/FCFCE	P/OI	HVF/S	HVF/OI	HVF/FCFU	HVE/BVE	HVF/BVF	ROA	ROE	X	ROE*X	NIS	TOTA	TDCE	HVDHVF	HVDHVE	HVF	HVCE	IFCFU	NIFCFU
-5.00%	4.3	2.1	3.9	4.0	2.3	4.4	4.0	2.6	2.3	49.7%	58.6%	-8.5%	-5.0%	48.4%	20.3%	0.3	9.3%	0.1	107.853	97.853	-5.39%	10.05%
-4.00%	4.4	2.1	4.1	4.1	2.3	4.5	4.2	2.7	2.4	50.2%	59.2%	-6.8%	-4.0%	48.5%	20.3%	0.3	9.0%	0.1	111.560	101.560	-7.03%	7.96%
-3.00%	4.4	2.2	4.3	4.2	2.4	4.6	4.3	2.8	2.4	50.8%	59.8%	-5.0%	-3.0%	48.7%	20.2%	0.3	8.7%	0.1	115.581	105.581	-8.65%	5.91%
-2.00%	4.6	2.2	4.5	4.3	2.4	4.7	4.5	2.8	2.5	51.3%	60.4%	-3.3%	-2.0%	48.8%	20.2%	0.3	8.3%	0.1	119.960	109.960	-10.23%	3.90%
-1.00%	4.7	2.3	4.7	4.5	2.5	4.9	4.8	2.9	2.5	51.8%	61.0%	-1.6%	-1.0%	48.9%	20.1%	0.3	8.0%	0.1	124.745	114.745	-11.80%	1.93%
-0.00%	4.9	2.4	4.9	4.6	2.6	5.0	5.0	3.0	2.6	52.3%	61.6%	0.0%	0.0%	49.0%	20.1%	0.3	7.7%	0.1	130.000	120.000	-13.33%	0.00%
1.00%	5.1	2.5	5.2	4.8	2.7	5.3	5.3	3.1	2.7	52.8%	62.2%	1.6%	1.0%	49.1%	20.1%	0.3	7.4%	0.1	135.798	125.798	-14.85%	-1.90%
2.00%	5.3	2.5	5.5	5.0	2.8	5.5	5.6	3.2	2.8	53.3%	62.8%	3.2%	2.0%	49.2%	20.1%	0.3	7.0%	0.1	142.228	132.228	-16.34%	-3.76%
3.00%	5.5	2.7	5.8	5.2	2.9	5.6	5.9	3.4	2.9	53.8%	63.4%	4.7%	3.0%	49.3%	20.0%	0.2	6.7%	0.1	149.404	139.404	-17.80%	-5.58%
4.00%	5.7	2.8	6.1	5.4	3.0	5.8	6.2	3.5	3.0	54.3%	64.0%	6.2%	4.0%	49.4%	20.0%	0.2	6.4%	0.1	157.465	147.465	-19.25%	-7.37%
5.00%	6.0	3.0	6.5	5.7	3.2	6.1	6.7	3.7	3.2	54.7%	64.6%	7.7%	5.0%	49.5%	19.9%	0.2	6.0%	0.1	166.588	156.587	-20.67%	-9.13%
6.00%	6.3	3.1	7.0	6.0	3.3	6.4	7.1	3.9	3.3	55.2%	65.2%	9.2%	6.0%	49.6%	19.9%	0.2	5.6%	0.1	176.999	166.999	-22.08%	-10.86%
7.00%	6.7	3.3	7.5	6.4	3.5	6.7	7.7	4.1	3.5	55.7%	65.8%	10.6%	7.0%	49.7%	19.8%	0.2	5.3%	0.1	188.998	178.998	-23.46%	-12.56%
8.00%	7.2	3.3	8.2	6.8	3.8	7.1	8.3	4.4	3.7	56.2%	66.4%	12.1%	8.0%	49.8%	19.8%	0.2	4.9%	0.0	202.980	192.980	-24.82%	-14.23%
9.00%	7.7	3.6	8.9	7.3	4.0	7.6	9.1	4.7	4.0	56.9%	66.9%	13.4%	9.0%	49.9%	19.8%	0.2	4.6%	0.0	219.487	209.487	-26.17%	-15.88%
10.00%	8.3	4.2	9.8	7.9	4.4	8.3	10.0	5.1	4.3	57.2%	67.5%	14.8%	10.0%	50.0%	19.7%	0.2	4.2%	0.0	239.275	229.275	-27.49%	-17.49%

Security Analysis: How to Analyze Accounting and Market Data to Value Securities
Robert W. Holthausen and Mark E. Zmijewski
\CH8.W51

Do not reproduce without permission.
July 29, 1998

Price Multiple Valuation Techniques

Panel C

P/E Ratios and Sales Driver Variation

Income Tax Rate 40.00%

Sales to Net PPEQ	P/E	P/S	P/FCFCE	P/OI	HVF/S	HVF/OI	HVF/FCFU	HVE/BVE	HVF/BVF	ROA	ROE	X	ROE*X	NIS	TDTA	TDCE	HVDHVF	HVDHVE	HVF	HVCE	IFCFU	NIFCFU
75.00%	5.9	1.5	9.5	3.2	1.8	3.8	12.5	1.3	1.2	20.4%	23.5%	42.5%	10.0%	26.0%	21.5%	0.3	16.6%	0.2	60.365	50.365	-64.12%	-48.98%
80.00%	6.2	1.6	10.2	3.4	1.9	4.0	12.1	1.4	1.3	21.9%	25.4%	39.3%	10.0%	26.6%	21.3%	0.3	14.7%	0.2	67.856	57.856	-60.86%	-45.62%
85.00%	6.4	1.7	10.2	3.5	2.0	4.1	11.9	1.6	1.4	23.4%	27.3%	36.9%	10.0%	27.2%	21.1%	0.3	13.3%	0.1	75.347	65.347	-57.95%	-42.74%
90.00%	6.6	1.8	10.1	3.7	2.1	4.2	11.7	1.6	1.4	24.8%	29.0%	34.4%	10.0%	27.7%	21.0%	0.3	12.1%	0.1	82.838	72.838	-55.32%	-40.25%
95.00%	6.8	1.9	10.1	3.8	2.2	4.4	11.5	1.7	1.6	26.3%	30.8%	32.5%	10.0%	28.1%	20.8%	0.3	11.1%	0.1	90.329	80.329	-52.95%	-38.07%
100.00%	7.0	2.0	10.1	3.9	2.2	4.4	11.4	1.8	1.7	27.7%	32.5%	30.8%	10.0%	28.5%	20.6%	0.3	10.2%	0.1	97.820	87.820	-50.79%	-36.15%
105.00%	7.1	2.1	10.1	4.0	2.3	4.5	11.3	2.0	1.8	29.0%	34.2%	29.3%	10.0%	28.9%	20.4%	0.3	9.5%	0.1	105.311	95.311	-48.82%	-34.44%
110.00%	7.3	2.1	10.1	4.1	2.3	4.6	11.2	2.1	2.0	30.4%	35.8%	27.9%	10.0%	29.2%	20.2%	0.2	8.9%	0.1	112.802	102.802	-47.01%	-32.91%
115.00%	7.4	2.2	10.1	4.2	2.4	4.6	11.1	2.2	2.1	31.7%	37.4%	26.7%	10.0%	29.5%	20.1%	0.2	8.3%	0.1	120.293	110.293	-45.35%	-31.53%
120.00%	7.5	2.2	10.1	4.3	2.4	4.7	11.1	2.4	2.2	33.0%	39.0%	25.7%	10.0%	29.8%	19.9%	0.2	7.8%	0.1	127.784	117.784	-43.82%	-30.28%
125.00%	7.6	2.3	10.1	4.3	2.5	4.7	11.0	2.5	2.3	34.3%	40.5%	24.7%	10.0%	30.0%	19.7%	0.2	7.4%	0.1	135.275	125.275	-42.39%	-29.15%
130.00%	7.7	2.4	10.1	4.4	2.5	4.7	11.0	2.7	2.4	35.6%	42.0%	23.8%	10.0%	30.2%	19.5%	0.2	7.0%	0.1	142.766	132.766	-41.08%	-28.12%
135.00%	7.8	2.4	10.1	4.4	2.5	4.8	10.9	2.8	2.5	36.8%	43.5%	23.0%	10.0%	30.4%	19.4%	0.2	6.7%	0.1	150.257	140.257	-39.85%	-27.17%
140.00%	7.8	2.4	10.1	4.5	2.6	4.8	10.8	2.9	2.6	38.0%	44.9%	22.3%	10.0%	30.6%	19.1%	0.2	6.3%	0.1	157.748	147.748	-38.70%	-26.30%
145.00%	7.9	2.4	10.1	4.5	2.6	4.8	10.8	3.3	2.9	39.2%	46.3%	21.6%	10.0%	30.8%	19.1%	0.2	6.1%	0.1	165.239	155.239	-37.63%	-25.50%
150.00%	8.0	2.5	10.1	4.6	2.6	4.9	10.7	3.5	3.0	40.4%	47.7%	21.0%	10.0%	31.0%	18.9%	0.2	5.8%	0.1	172.730	162.730	-36.62%	-24.75%

Income Tax Rate 0.00%

Sales to Net PPEQ	P/E	P/S	P/FCFCE	P/OI	HVF/S	HVF/OI	HVF/FCFU	HVE/BVE	HVF/BVF	ROA	ROE	X	ROE*X	NIS	TDTA	TDCE	HVDHVF	HVDHVE	HVF	HVCE	IFCFU	NIFCFU
75.00%	7.1	3.1	9.5	6.4	3.4	7.1	10.0	2.5	2.4	34.0%	39.2%	25.5%	10.0%	43.3%	21.5%	0.3	9.0%	0.1	111.565	101.565	43.65%	-29.39%
80.00%	7.3	3.2	9.6	6.7	3.5	7.3	10.0	2.6	2.6	36.5%	42.4%	23.6%	10.0%	44.4%	21.3%	0.3	8.0%	0.1	124.336	114.336	41.13%	-27.37%
85.00%	7.5	3.4	9.6	6.9	3.7	7.4	10.0	2.8	2.8	39.0%	45.4%	22.0%	10.0%	45.4%	21.1%	0.3	7.3%	0.1	137.107	127.107	38.90%	-25.65%
90.00%	7.7	3.5	9.7	7.1	3.8	7.6	10.0	2.9	2.9	41.4%	48.4%	20.7%	10.0%	46.1%	21.0%	0.3	6.7%	0.1	149.878	139.878	36.92%	-24.15%
95.00%	7.8	3.7	9.7	7.2	3.9	7.7	10.0	3.1	3.1	43.8%	51.3%	19.5%	10.0%	47.5%	20.8%	0.3	6.1%	0.1	162.649	152.649	35.15%	-22.84%
100.00%	7.9	3.8	9.7	7.4	4.0	7.8	10.0	3.3	3.3	46.1%	54.2%	18.5%	10.0%	48.1%	20.6%	0.3	5.7%	0.1	175.420	165.420	33.55%	-21.69%
105.00%	8.0	3.9	9.7	7.5	4.1	8.0	10.0	3.4	3.5	48.4%	57.0%	17.6%	10.0%	48.6%	20.4%	0.3	5.3%	0.1	188.191	178.191	32.11%	-20.66%
110.00%	8.1	3.9	9.8	7.6	4.1	8.0	10.0	3.5	3.7	50.6%	59.7%	16.8%	10.0%	48.6%	20.2%	0.3	5.0%	0.0	200.962	190.962	30.80%	-19.74%
115.00%	8.2	4.0	9.8	7.7	4.2	8.1	10.0	3.7	3.7	52.9%	62.4%	16.0%	10.0%	49.4%	20.1%	0.3	4.7%	0.0	213.733	203.733	29.60%	-18.92%
120.00%	8.3	4.1	9.8	7.8	4.3	8.3	10.0	3.8	4.1	55.1%	65.0%	15.4%	10.0%	49.6%	19.9%	0.2	4.4%	0.0	226.504	216.504	28.50%	-18.17%
125.00%	8.3	4.2	9.8	7.8	4.4	8.3	10.0	4.0	4.3	57.2%	67.5%	14.8%	10.0%	50.0%	19.7%	0.2	4.2%	0.0	239.275	229.275	27.49%	-17.49%
130.00%	8.4	4.2	9.8	7.9	4.4	8.4	10.0	4.2	4.5	59.3%	70.0%	14.3%	10.0%	50.4%	19.5%	0.2	4.0%	0.0	252.046	242.046	26.56%	-16.87%
135.00%	8.4	4.3	9.8	8.0	4.5	8.4	10.0	4.3	4.7	61.3%	72.5%	13.8%	10.0%	50.7%	19.4%	0.2	3.8%	0.0	264.817	254.817	25.70%	-16.30%
140.00%	8.5	4.3	9.8	8.1	4.5	8.5	10.0	4.5	4.9	63.4%	74.9%	13.4%	10.0%	51.1%	19.2%	0.2	3.6%	0.0	277.588	267.588	24.90%	-15.78%
145.00%	8.6	4.4	9.8	8.1	4.6	8.5	10.0	4.6	5.0	65.4%	77.2%	12.9%	10.0%	51.4%	19.1%	0.2	3.4%	0.0	290.359	280.359	24.15%	-15.30%
150.00%	8.6	4.4	9.8	8.2	4.6	8.5	10.0	4.8	5.2	67.3%	79.5%	12.6%	10.0%	51.7%	18.9%	0.2	3.3%	0.0	303.130	293.130	23.45%	-14.85%

Security Analysis: How to Analyze Accounting and Market Data to Value Securities
Robert W. Holthausen and Mark E. Zmijewski
\CH8.W51

Panel D

P/E Ratios and Unlevered Cost of Capital (Risk) Variation

Income Tax Rate 40.00%

Unlevered Cost of Capital	P/E	P/S	P/FCFCE	P/OI	MVF/S	MVF/OI	MVF/FCFU	MVE/BVE	MVF/BVF	ROA	ROE	X	ROE*X	NIS	TDTA	TDCE	MVDMVF	MVDMVE	MVF	MVCE	IFCFU	NIF
15.00%	15.1	4.5	20.0	8.6	4.7	8.9	21.0	5.5	4.6	34.3%	40.5%	24.7%	10.0%	30.0%	19.7%	0.2	3.9%	0.0	258.550	248.550	-42.39%	-29
16.00%	12.6	3.8	16.7	7.2	4.0	7.5	17.6	4.6	3.9	34.3%	40.5%	24.7%	10.0%	30.0%	19.7%	0.2	4.6%	0.0	217.458	207.458	-42.39%	-29
17.00%	10.8	3.2	14.3	6.1	3.4	6.5	15.3	4.0	3.4	34.3%	40.5%	24.7%	10.0%	30.0%	19.7%	0.2	5.3%	0.1	188.107	178.107	-42.39%	-29
18.00%	9.5	2.8	12.6	5.4	3.0	5.7	13.5	3.5	3.0	34.3%	40.5%	24.7%	10.0%	30.0%	19.7%	0.2	6.0%	0.1	166.094	156.094	-42.39%	-29
19.00%	8.4	2.5	11.2	4.8	2.7	5.1	12.1	3.1	2.7	34.3%	40.5%	24.7%	10.0%	30.0%	19.7%	0.2	6.7%	0.1	148.972	138.972	-42.39%	-29
20.00%	7.6	2.3	10.1	4.3	2.5	4.7	11.0	2.8	2.4	34.3%	40.5%	24.7%	10.0%	30.0%	19.7%	0.2	7.4%	0.1	135.275	125.275	-42.39%	-29
21.00%	6.9	2.1	9.2	3.9	2.3	4.3	10.1	2.5	2.2	34.3%	40.5%	24.7%	10.0%	30.0%	19.7%	0.2	8.1%	0.1	124.068	114.068	-42.39%	-29
22.00%	6.3	1.9	8.4	3.6	2.1	4.0	9.3	2.3	2.1	34.3%	40.5%	24.7%	10.0%	30.0%	19.7%	0.2	8.7%	0.1	114.729	104.729	-42.39%	-29
23.00%	5.8	1.8	7.8	3.3	2.1	3.7	8.7	2.3	1.9	34.3%	40.5%	24.7%	10.0%	30.0%	19.7%	0.2	9.4%	0.1	106.827	96.827	-42.39%	-29
24.00%	5.5	1.6	7.2	3.1	1.8	3.5	8.1	2.0	1.8	34.3%	40.5%	24.7%	10.0%	30.0%	19.7%	0.2	10.0%	0.1	100.054	90.054	-42.39%	-29
25.00%	5.1	1.5	6.8	2.9	1.8	3.2	7.6	1.9	1.7	34.3%	40.5%	24.7%	10.0%	30.0%	19.7%	0.2	10.6%	0.1	94.183	84.183	-42.39%	-29
26.00%	4.8	1.5	6.4	2.7	1.6	3.1	7.2	1.8	1.6	34.3%	40.5%	24.7%	10.0%	30.0%	19.7%	0.2	11.2%	0.1	89.047	79.047	-42.39%	-29
27.00%	4.5	1.4	6.0	2.6	1.5	2.9	6.9	1.7	1.5	34.3%	40.5%	24.7%	10.0%	30.0%	19.7%	0.2	11.8%	0.1	84.515	74.515	-42.39%	-29
28.00%	4.3	1.3	5.7	2.4	1.5	2.8	6.5	1.6	1.4	34.3%	40.5%	24.7%	10.0%	30.0%	19.7%	0.2	12.4%	0.1	80.486	70.486	-42.39%	-29
29.00%	4.1	1.2	5.4	2.3	1.4	2.7	6.2	1.5	1.4	34.3%	40.5%	24.7%	10.0%	30.0%	19.7%	0.2	13.0%	0.1	76.882	66.882	-42.39%	-29
30.00%	3.9	1.2	5.1	2.2	1.3	2.5	6.0	1.4	1.3	34.3%	40.5%	24.7%	10.0%	30.0%	19.7%	0.2	13.6%	0.2	73.637	63.637	-42.39%	-29

Income Tax Rate 0.00%

Unlevered Cost of Capital	P/E	P/S	P/FCFCE	P/OI	MVF/S	MVF/OI	MVF/FCFU	MVE/BVE	MVF/BVF	ROA	ROE	X	ROE*X	NIS	TDTA	TDCE	MVDMVF	MVDMVE	MVF	MVCE	IFCFU	NIF
15.00%	17.0	8.5	20.0	16.2	8.7	16.5	20.0	10.5	8.6	57.2%	67.5%	14.8%	10.0%	50.0%	19.7%	0.2	2.1%	0.0	478.550	468.550	27.49%	17
16.00%	14.1	7.1	16.6	13.4	7.3	13.8	16.7	8.7	7.1	57.2%	67.5%	14.8%	10.0%	50.0%	19.7%	0.2	2.5%	0.0	398.792	388.792	27.49%	17
17.00%	12.1	6.0	14.2	11.4	6.2	11.8	14.3	7.4	6.1	57.2%	67.5%	14.8%	10.0%	50.0%	19.7%	0.2	2.9%	0.0	341.821	331.821	27.49%	17
18.00%	10.5	5.3	12.3	10.0	5.4	10.3	12.5	6.5	5.4	57.2%	67.5%	14.8%	10.0%	50.0%	19.7%	0.2	3.3%	0.0	299.094	289.094	27.49%	17
19.00%	9.3	4.7	10.9	8.8	4.8	9.2	11.1	5.7	4.8	57.2%	67.5%	14.8%	10.0%	50.0%	19.7%	0.2	3.8%	0.0	265.861	255.861	27.49%	17
20.00%	8.3	4.2	9.8	7.9	4.4	8.3	10.0	5.1	4.3	57.2%	67.5%	14.8%	10.0%	50.0%	19.7%	0.2	4.2%	0.0	239.275	229.275	27.49%	17
21.00%	7.5	3.8	8.9	7.2	4.0	7.5	9.1	4.6	3.9	57.2%	67.5%	14.8%	10.0%	50.0%	19.7%	0.2	4.6%	0.1	217.523	207.523	27.49%	17
22.00%	6.9	3.4	8.1	6.5	3.6	6.9	8.3	4.2	3.6	57.2%	67.5%	14.8%	10.0%	50.0%	19.7%	0.2	5.0%	0.1	199.396	189.396	27.49%	17
23.00%	6.3	3.2	7.4	6.0	3.3	6.3	7.7	3.9	3.3	57.2%	67.5%	14.8%	10.0%	50.0%	19.7%	0.2	5.4%	0.1	184.058	174.058	27.49%	17
24.00%	5.9	2.9	6.9	5.5	3.1	5.9	7.1	3.6	3.1	57.2%	67.5%	14.8%	10.0%	50.0%	19.7%	0.2	5.9%	0.1	170.911	160.911	27.49%	17
25.00%	5.5	2.7	6.4	5.2	2.9	5.5	6.7	3.3	2.9	57.2%	67.5%	14.8%	10.0%	50.0%	19.7%	0.2	6.3%	0.1	159.517	149.517	27.49%	17
26.00%	5.1	2.5	6.0	4.8	2.7	5.2	6.2	3.1	2.7	57.2%	67.5%	14.8%	10.0%	50.0%	19.7%	0.2	6.7%	0.1	149.547	139.547	27.49%	17
27.00%	4.8	2.4	5.6	4.5	2.6	4.9	5.9	2.9	2.5	57.2%	67.5%	14.8%	10.0%	50.0%	19.7%	0.2	7.1%	0.1	140.750	130.750	27.49%	17
28.00%	4.5	2.2	5.2	4.2	2.4	4.6	5.6	2.7	2.4	57.2%	67.5%	14.8%	10.0%	50.0%	19.7%	0.2	7.5%	0.1	132.931	122.931	27.49%	17
29.00%	4.2	2.1	4.9	4.0	2.3	4.3	5.3	2.6	2.3	57.2%	67.5%	14.8%	10.0%	50.0%	19.7%	0.2	7.9%	0.1	125.934	115.934	27.49%	17
30.00%	4.0	2.0	4.7	3.8	2.2	4.1	5.0	2.4	2.1	57.2%	67.5%	14.8%	10.0%	50.0%	19.7%	0.2	8.4%	0.1	119.637	109.637	27.49%	17

Security Analysis:: How to Analyze Accounting and Market Data to Value Securities
Robert W. Holthausen and Mark E. Zmijewski
\CH8.W51

Panel E

P/E Ratios and Expenses as % Sales

Income Tax Rate 40.00%

Sell, Gen & Admin % of Sales	P/E	P/S	P/FCFCE	P/OI	MVF/S	MVF/OI	MVF/FCFU	MVE/BVE	MVF/BVF	ROA	ROE	X	ROE*X	NIS	TOTA	TDCE	HVDMVF	HVDHVE	MVF	MVCE	IFCFU	NIF
20.00%	8.3	3.5	10.1	4.8	3.7	5.0	10.6	4.3	3.6	47.3%	56.7%	17.6%	10.0%	42.0%	19.7%	0.2	5.0%	0.1	201.275	191.275	-32.40%	-21
22.00%	8.2	3.4	10.1	4.7	3.5	5.0	10.7	4.1	3.5	46.0%	55.1%	18.1%	10.0%	40.8%	19.7%	0.2	5.1%	0.1	194.675	184.675	-33.18%	-21
24.00%	8.2	3.2	10.1	4.7	3.4	5.0	10.7	4.0	3.4	44.7%	53.5%	18.7%	10.0%	39.6%	19.7%	0.2	5.3%	0.1	188.075	178.075	-34.00%	-22
26.00%	8.1	3.1	10.1	4.6	3.2	4.9	10.7	3.8	3.3	43.4%	51.9%	19.3%	10.0%	38.4%	19.7%	0.2	5.5%	0.1	181.475	171.475	-34.87%	-23
28.00%	8.1	3.0	10.1	4.6	3.1	4.9	10.8	3.7	3.1	42.1%	50.2%	19.9%	10.0%	37.2%	19.7%	0.2	5.7%	0.1	174.875	164.875	-35.77%	-23
30.00%	8.0	2.9	10.1	4.6	2.9	4.8	10.8	3.5	3.0	40.8%	48.6%	20.6%	10.0%	36.0%	19.7%	0.2	5.9%	0.1	168.275	158.275	-36.73%	-24
32.00%	7.9	2.8	10.1	4.5	2.8	4.8	10.9	3.4	2.9	39.5%	47.0%	21.3%	10.0%	34.8%	19.7%	0.2	6.2%	0.1	161.675	151.675	-37.74%	-25
34.00%	7.9	2.6	10.1	4.5	2.7	4.8	10.9	3.2	2.8	38.2%	45.4%	22.0%	10.0%	33.6%	19.7%	0.2	6.4%	0.1	155.075	145.075	-38.80%	-26
36.00%	7.8	2.5	10.1	4.4	2.6	4.7	11.0	3.1	2.7	36.9%	43.8%	22.9%	10.0%	32.4%	19.7%	0.2	6.7%	0.1	148.475	138.475	-39.93%	-27
38.00%	7.7	2.4	10.1	4.4	2.5	4.7	11.0	2.8	2.4	35.6%	42.1%	23.7%	10.0%	31.2%	19.7%	0.2	7.0%	0.1	141.875	131.875	-41.13%	-28
40.00%	7.6	2.3	10.1	4.4	2.3	4.7	11.0	2.6	2.3	34.3%	40.5%	24.7%	10.0%	30.0%	19.7%	0.2	7.4%	0.1	135.275	125.275	-42.39%	-29
42.00%	7.5	2.2	10.1	4.3	2.2	4.6	11.1	2.5	2.2	33.0%	38.9%	25.7%	10.0%	28.8%	19.7%	0.2	7.8%	0.1	128.675	118.675	-43.74%	-30
44.00%	7.4	2.0	10.1	4.1	2.1	4.6	11.1	2.4	2.2	31.7%	37.3%	26.8%	10.0%	27.6%	19.7%	0.2	8.2%	0.1	122.075	112.075	-45.18%	-31
46.00%	7.4	1.9	10.1	4.1	2.0	4.5	11.2	2.2	2.0	30.4%	35.7%	28.0%	10.0%	26.4%	19.7%	0.2	8.7%	0.1	115.475	105.475	-46.72%	-32
48.00%	7.3	1.8	10.1	4.1	2.0	4.4	11.2	2.1	1.8	29.1%	34.0%	29.4%	10.0%	25.2%	19.7%	0.2	9.2%	0.1	108.875	98.875	-48.36%	-34
50.00%	7.0	1.7	10.1	3.9	1.9	4.4	11.3	2.1	1.8	27.8%	32.4%	30.9%	10.0%	24.0%	19.7%	0.2	9.8%	0.1	102.275	92.275	-50.12%	-35

Income Tax Rate 0.00%

Sell, Gen & Admin % of Sales	P/E	P/S	P/FCFCE	P/OI	MVF/S	MVF/OI	MVF/FCFU	MVE/BVE	MVF/BVF	ROA	ROE	X	ROE*X	NIS	TOTA	TDCE	HVDMVF	HVDHVE	MVF	MVCE	IFCFU	NIF
20.00%	8.8	6.2	9.9	8.5	6.4	8.7	10.0	7.6	6.3	78.9%	94.5%	10.6%	10.0%	70.0%	19.7%	0.2	2.9%	0.0	349.275	339.275	20.62%	-12
22.00%	8.8	6.0	9.8	8.4	6.2	8.7	10.0	7.3	6.1	76.7%	91.8%	10.9%	10.0%	68.0%	19.7%	0.2	3.0%	0.0	338.275	328.275	21.15%	-13
24.00%	8.7	5.8	9.8	8.4	6.0	8.7	10.0	7.1	5.9	74.5%	89.1%	11.2%	10.0%	66.0%	19.7%	0.2	3.1%	0.0	327.275	317.275	21.70%	-13
26.00%	8.7	5.6	9.8	8.3	5.8	8.6	10.0	6.8	5.7	72.4%	86.4%	11.6%	10.0%	64.0%	19.7%	0.2	3.2%	0.0	316.275	306.275	22.29%	-13
28.00%	8.7	5.4	9.8	8.3	5.6	8.6	10.0	6.6	5.5	70.2%	83.7%	11.9%	10.0%	62.0%	19.7%	0.2	3.3%	0.0	305.275	295.275	22.91%	-14
30.00%	8.6	5.2	9.8	8.2	5.4	8.5	10.0	6.3	5.3	68.0%	81.0%	12.3%	10.0%	60.0%	19.7%	0.2	3.4%	0.0	294.275	284.275	23.56%	-14
32.00%	8.6	5.0	9.8	8.2	5.2	8.4	10.0	6.1	5.1	65.8%	78.3%	12.8%	10.0%	58.0%	19.7%	0.2	3.5%	0.0	283.275	273.275	24.26%	-15
34.00%	8.5	4.8	9.8	8.1	5.0	8.4	10.0	5.9	4.9	63.7%	75.6%	13.2%	10.0%	56.0%	19.7%	0.2	3.7%	0.0	272.275	262.275	24.99%	-15
36.00%	8.5	4.6	9.8	8.1	4.6	8.3	10.0	5.6	4.7	61.5%	72.9%	13.7%	10.0%	54.0%	19.7%	0.2	3.8%	0.0	261.275	251.275	25.77%	-16
38.00%	8.4	4.4	9.8	8.0	4.4	8.3	10.0	5.4	4.5	59.3%	70.2%	14.2%	10.0%	52.0%	19.7%	0.2	4.0%	0.0	250.275	240.275	26.61%	-16
40.00%	8.4	4.2	9.8	7.9	4.2	8.1	10.0	5.1	4.3	57.2%	67.5%	14.8%	10.0%	50.0%	19.7%	0.2	4.2%	0.0	239.275	229.275	27.49%	-17
42.00%	8.3	4.0	9.8	7.8	4.0	8.0	10.0	4.9	4.1	55.0%	64.8%	15.4%	10.0%	48.0%	19.7%	0.2	4.4%	0.0	228.275	218.275	28.44%	-18
44.00%	8.2	3.8	9.8	7.7	3.8	8.0	10.0	4.6	3.9	52.8%	62.1%	16.1%	10.0%	46.0%	19.7%	0.2	4.6%	0.0	217.275	207.275	29.46%	-18
46.00%	8.1	3.6	9.8	7.6	3.6	7.9	10.0	4.4	3.7	50.7%	59.4%	16.8%	10.0%	44.0%	19.7%	0.2	4.8%	0.0	206.275	196.275	30.55%	-19
48.00%	8.0	3.4	9.7	7.6	3.4	7.8	10.0	4.1	3.5	48.5%	56.7%	17.6%	10.0%	42.0%	19.7%	0.2	5.1%	0.0	195.275	185.275	31.72%	-20
50.00%	7.9	3.2	9.7	7.4	3.4	7.8	10.0	3.9	3.3	46.3%	54.0%	18.5%	10.0%	40.0%	19.7%	0.2	5.4%	0.0	184.275	174.275	32.99%	-21

Security Analysis: How to Analyze Accounting and Market Data to Value Securities
Robert W. Holthausen and Mark E. Zmijewski
\CH8.W51

3. Using the Comparables' Multiples

An important issue that we have not addressed is how best to use the distribution of comparable P/E ratios to value your company. An empirical study by Beatty, Riffe and Thompson (unpublished) provides some information about that issue.

They contrast a variety of different constructs. Average P/E, inverse average E/P, median P/E, sum of prices divided by sum of earnings (value weighted), sum of prices times earnings divided by sum of earnings squared, equally weighting inverse average E/P and the inverse average Book to Price, a multivariate linear weighting of earnings and book value of equity plus an intercept (obtained by regressing price on a constant, earnings and book value) and a linear weighting of earnings, book value of equity and dividends plus an intercept (obtained by regressing price on a constant, earnings, book value of equity and dividends).

Results indicate that average P/E is very poor and inverse average E/P is much better but not the best. Regression model of earnings and book value of earnings and regression model of earnings, book value of equity and dividends.

Results indicate that there is a size bias in most of these models (except the regression models with intercept). Models tend to overprice largest firms and underprice smallest firms. Thus, results suggest that matching on size is important if you are going to use something other than one of these regression models.

Results also indicate that industry models are better than non-industry models. There is no evidence in this study on whether to match companies on the items I have advocated (growth, etc.) Other studies have indicated that growth and risk are important determinants of P/E ratios however.

4. Market Value to Net Book Value (MV/BV) multiple model.

A.   The basic model.

$$CE_t = \text{"MV/BV Multiple"} * \text{"Net Book Value of Equity"}$$

where: CE_t is the value of the common equity.
         BV_t is the book value of the common equity.

B.   Requirements.

(1)   "MV/BV Multiple"
(2)   "Net Book Value of Equity"

C.   How do you measure MV/BV multiples?

(1)   Market value is the market value of the equity.

Security Analysis: How to Analyze Accounting and Market Data to Value Securities
Robert W. Holthausen and Mark E. Zmijewski
\CH8.W51

Do not reproduce without permission.
July 29, 1998

426

(2)   When is the market value measured? Since the book value is measured at one point in time, the market value should be measured at the same point in time.

(3)   What is book value (BV)?

(a)   Book value is conceptually the tangible net worth of the common shareholders' claims.

(4)   How to treat questionable items?

(a)   Minority interests?
(b)   Deferred taxes?
(c)   Goodwill?
(d)   Off balance sheet financing?

(5)   Do you use the difference between the book value and market value of debt to adjust the book value of common equity?

D.   Relation to the P/E multiple model.

(1)   Define A_t as accounting earnings (not earnings per share). Then, using accounting numbers, $P/E_t = CE_t/A_t$, and $MV/BV_t = CE_t/BV_t$.

(2) $MV/BV_t = P/E_t * ROE_t$, because $ROE_t = A_t/BV_t$

(a)   where:

ROE = rate of return on equity.

(3) $MV/BV_t = CE_t/A_t * A_t/S_t * S_t/TA_t * TA_t/BV_t$.

(a)   where:

S_t = sales for the firm at time t.
TA_t = total assets of the firm at firm t.
BV_t = the book value of common equity at time t.

(4)   Therefore:

$MV/BV = P/E * \text{Profit Margin} * \text{Asset Utilization} * \text{Financial Leverage}$

E.   Practical applications.

(1)   Same as the P/E multiple applications, although P/E multiples are more popular.

Security Analysis: How to Analyze Accounting and Market Data to Value Securities
Robert W. Holthausen and Mark E. Zmijewski
\CH8.W51

Do not reproduce without permission.
July 29, 1998

427

(2)   This approach is more useful than P/E multiples if the earnings series provides little information regarding the future (for example, a MV/BV multiple is more useful than a P/E multiple to value a mutual fund.)

F.   Variations on the theme.

(1)   Multiples of tangible net worth.
(2)   Multiples of total assets.
(3)   Multiples of replacement cost.

G.   Cross-sectional and time series variation in MV/BV multiples.

In Figure 3 we present the average market to book ratios for the years 1980 through 1989, partitioned by selected industry groups.

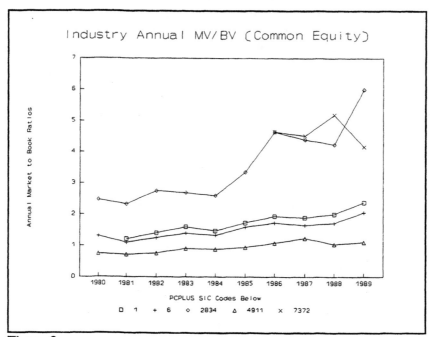

Figure 3

Table 2 presents the numbers underlying Figure 3, and some market to book ratios of other industry groups.

Security Analysis: How to Analyze Accounting and Market Data to Value Securities
Robert W. Holthausen and Mark E. Zmijewski
\CH8.W51

H.   Why do MV/BV multiples differ across firms or across time?

    (1)   MV/BV multiples differ across firms and across time for the same reasons as P/E multiples differ across time and across firms.

    (2)   Book value vs. market value of debt.

    (3)   Off-balance sheet financing such as under-funded pensions, leases, contingent liabilities (e.g. lawsuits).

    (4)   Off-balance sheet assets such as over-funded pensions, unrecorded goodwill, trademarks, unrecorded appreciation of assets.

    (5)   Treatment of deferred taxes, is it equity or debt? It likely varies across firms.

5.   **Choosing Comparable Firms.**

A.   Note, to implement the P/E, or other price multiple methods, it is important to identify firms that are comparable along the dimensions that affect the magnitude of the price multiple. For the P/E valuation approach, the following list indicates factors important to consider when identifying comparable firms.

    (1)   Differences in growth Rates.
    (2)   Differences in the time profile of earnings (growth rates not constant over time).
    (3)   Differences in risk (financial and business).
    (4)   Differences in reinvestment requirements (how much of cash flows before capital expenditures and working capital additions gets reinvested into the business)
    (5)   Differences in return on investments.
    (6)   Differences in the "Quality" or sustainability of earnings.
    (7)   Different accounting techniques.
    (8)   Under performing/idle assets.
    (9)   Leverage

B.   Other price multiples may require you to consider different factors when identifying comparable firms. Some examples follow.

    (1)   The P/EBIT (P/EBITD) approach requires that, in addition to the assumptions for implementing the price to earnings multiple, that the capital structures (capital structures and tax structures) are the same for the comparable firms and the firm being valued. Why? Because since the numerator and

Security Analysis: How to Analyze Accounting and Market Data to Value Securities
Robert W. Holthausen and Mark E. Zmijewski
\CH8.W51

denominator do not reflect the value and flows to the same claimants, the effect of the non-equity claims has to be constant across the firm being valued and the comparable firms.

(2) The price to gross margin approach requires that, in addition to the assumptions for implementing the P/EBITD multiple, that the effect of operating (selling, general, administrative, marketing, etc.) on the value of the common equity is the same for the comparable firms and the firm being valued.

(3) The price to sales approach requires that, in addition to the assumptions for implementing the price to gross margin approach, that the effect of cost of goods sold on the value of the common equity is the same for the comparable firms and the firm being valued.

C. The key is that when choosing the set of comparable companies to estimate the multiple, one must attempt to construct a set of firms where the factors that drive cross-sectional variation in multiples is similar between the firm being valued and the comparable firms. Thus, it would be important that growth, risk, reinvestment etc., be the same for the firm being valued and the set of comparable companies.

6. **The Use of Multiple Models in Terminal Value Calculations.**

A. Terminal values should be consistent with the cash flows that are being valued.

Example:

When valuing a firm, the terminal value should be the terminal value of the firm not the equity. Thus, a terminal value based on only a P/E multiple of earnings is inappropriate when valuing a firm. In this case, the value of any non-common equity claims would have to be added to the value of the equity derived from the P/E multiple.

B. In using multiples to value a firm's equity or the entire firm, be careful to avoid multiples based on high growth assumptions when you believe the firm will be in a low-growth phase at the time of the terminal value.

C. Current multiples are often inappropriate for terminal value calculations. One must use the estimated multiple appropriate at the date of the terminal value. For example, a company with large growth prospects currently will have a high price multiple ratio currently. But if you forecast year-by-year cash flows into the future beyond the high growth phase, the appropriate price multiple at that time will be lower than the current price multiple.

Security Analysis: How to Analyze Accounting and Market Data to Value Securities
Robert W. Holthausen and Mark E. Zmijewski
\CH8.W51

If you expect general discount rates to change, or risk changes, or reinvestment requirements to change, than current multiples will not be appropriate for a terminal value calculation. It is also true that price multiples are mean reverting. Thus, if current P/E's are extremely high or low in general, you would not want to use those price multiples as your best estimate of the appropriate price multiple at the time of your terminal value calculation.

D.   The terminal value should be consistent with the "strategy" implicit in the forecast up to the terminal value date.

Example:

If the cash flow forecasts include a generous allowance for replacements and maintenance, the terminal value should reflect the "pristine" value of the plant. On the other hand, if the strategy allows the plant to gradually run down, the terminal value should reflect the substantial reinvestment required to replace the plant.

Terminal value calculations based on multiples of cash flows or earnings should not be based on inconsistent assumptions regarding depreciation tax shields and the amount spent on capital expenditure.

E.   CAUTION: Be careful to use consistent assumptions about discount rates and cash flows in terminal value calculations. Assuming no growth in cash flows in conjunction with nominal discount rates based on some assumed inflation rate is likely inappropriate.

7.   **When to (not to) Use a Particular Price Multiple Approach.**

A.   A key to choosing a particular price multiple approach is to understand the underlying assumptions for each approach under consideration.

B.   The P/E approach is useful when the firm being valued appears to have an earnings series that is highly correlated with the underlying cash flow series and that is growing at a stable rate. That is, when earnings are sustainable. These comments are also relevant for the comparable firms. The P/E approach is not useful for a firm with volatile earnings, earnings that are negative, or earnings that are not sustainable.

C.   When faced with a firm with negative earnings, the price to operating income, price to gross margin, or price to sales approach may be considered. Keep in mind, however, that these approaches make additional assumptions regarding the comparability of the comparable firms (see our discussion of this issue above).

Security Analysis: How to Analyze Accounting and Market Data to Value Securities
Robert W. Holthausen and Mark E. Zmijewski
\CH8.W51

For example, the price to sales approach may be useful for valuing a firm with little or negative earnings. The price to sales approach may provide a more consistent valuation in this case. However, this approach does not provide a price for the firm under its current performance. This valuation approach assumes that the firm will immediately begin to operate (i.e., generate free cash flows) in a manner that is consistent with the comparable firms.

Note that multiples like price to gross margin, and price/sales as well as price to earnings before interest and taxes (or earnings before depreciation, interest and taxes) approach, "take out" the effect of financing flows in the denominator of the price multiples, but they do not adjust the numerator of the price multiples. That is the flows include the interest payments which are really not available to the equity holders.

These approaches are incorrect because they essentially assume that the firms have no debt financing. Thus, to use these approaches you must, at a minimum, match the comparable firms and the firm being valued on the basis of capital structure (e.g. cash interest payments required).

D.   The market value of the firm to pre-financing earnings approaches (i.e., market value of firm to earnings before interest and taxes, market value of firm to earnings before depreciation, interest and taxes and market value of firm to operating cash flows before interest) attempt to mitigate the above criticism. Note, that you could also use market value of firm to sales (or gross margin). These approaches do avoid the major error of the price to earnings before interest and taxes approaches of assuming no financial leverage, but they are incorrect if capital structure affects the value of the firm (i.e., the value of interest tax shields). Again, to use these approaches you must, at a minimum, match the comparable firms and the firm being valued on the basis of capital structure. Otherwise, the value of the tax shield, which affects the value of the firm, is based on the capital structure of the comparable firms chosen.

E.   Price to cash flow approaches may be more difficult to implement because cash flows from a single period tend to be more volatile than earnings, in large part because capital expenditures are often lumpy. Thus, you are more likely to observe free cash flows close to zero or negative, even though sustainable cash flows are positive and expected to have a stable growth. The benefits of this approach are that the effect of management's manipulation of the accruals affecting income (to the extent they exist), and the effect of different accounting principles across firms is mitigated. The price to free cash flow to common equity is an appropriate approach to use if the free cash flow series is sustainable and has stable growth. The lumpy capital expenditures problem can be circumvented by using an estimate of "normalized" capital expenditures (i.e., typical capital expenditures required to sustain growth) instead of actual capital expenditures.

Security Analysis: How to Analyze Accounting and Market Data to Value Securities
Robert W. Holthausen and Mark E. Zmijewski
\CH8.W51

8. Biggest Mistakes in Using Price Multiples

(1)   Pay multiple on earnings or EBIT or EBITDA on an asset that has been prepared for sale with no discounting for that factor.

(2)   If purchase an asset when price multiples for the overall market are quite high (relative to their long range mean), and then assume that you will be able to sell that asset at a similar multiple 5-10 years from now at the same multiple, you will significantly overpay for that asset. Similarly, if you use that multiple for a terminal value calculation.

Entry and exit multiples are often not the same. Ask some of the firms involved in LBO transactions in 1987, 1988 and 1989.

(3)   Same mistake as (2) except based on a cyclical business

(4)   Purchase a poorly performing company and assume that it will soon have multiples commensurate with the best performers in that industry.

(5)   Acquire a low multiple generic business (not a poor performer in a great industry, just a staid industry) and assume that it will soon be valued at the multiple of your core high-multiple business, simply because you own it.

9.   CONCLUSIONS: Price Multiple Valuation Techniques - PROS and CONS.

A.   DCF Models.

Pros: Based on well accepted corporate finance theory.
Flexibility to handle different patterns of cash inflows and outflows.
Recognize time value of money.
Allow explicit consideration of project risks.
Focus on future operations.

Cons: Demand extensive set of forecast data.
False precision attributed to sophisticated techniques.
Lack external reference to reconcile valuation differences.

Security Analysis: How to Analyze Accounting and Market Data to Value Securities
Robert W. Holthausen and Mark E. Zmijewski
\CH8.W51

B.   Price Multiple Models.

Pros: Ease of understanding and calculation ("back of the envelope").
         Commonly used yardstick/rule of thumb.

Cons: Absence of theoretical underpinning.
         Seductive simplicity.
         Many defects, in large part because of the typical reliance on accounting
         numbers.

C.   Combining the Two Approaches

Kaplan and Ruback [1996] indicate that one prediction transactions prices of highly
levered transactions more accurately using both DCF methods and multiple methods
than either alone.

Security Analysis: How to Analyze Accounting and Market Data to Value Securities
Robert W. Holthausen and Mark E. Zmijewski
\CH8.W51

Table 1

Distribution of Quarterly P/E Ratios Over Time (3/86- 3/90)
Partitioned by Selected Industry Groups

P/E by quarter	SIC	# firms	Mar 86	Jun 86	Sep 86	Dec 86	Mar 87	Jun 87	Sep 87	Dec 87	Mar 88	Jun 88	Sep 88	Dec 88	Mar 89	Jun 89	Sep 89	Dec 89	Mar 90
ALL INDUSTRIAL	1	2029	20.4	21.5	20.1	21.4	26.6	26.0	24.5	16.1	17.0	17.1	15.8	14.3	15.4	16.1	17.1	17.4	17.8
S & P 400	2	363	17.0	17.6	15.9	18.1	21.6	21.7	20.7	14.0	13.7	13.4	12.6	12.0	12.4	13.2	14.9	15.2	15.7
UTILITIES-COMPOSITE	3	43	11.0	11.6	11.4	10.9	11.2	10.9	11.3	9.8	10.0	10.6	10.7	11.2	11.6	13.1	14.0	14.8	13.5
FINANCIAL-COMPOSITE	4	53	16.4	15.7	14.0	10.2	11.2	40.3	35.3	32.4	32.5	8.6	9.0	7.5	8.4	8.7	14.0	16.5	17.1
TRANSPORTATION-COMPOSITE	5	15	16.4	43.3	48.9	86.8	73.0	23.4	27.1	17.3	17.1	18.1	13.1	12.1	10.7	10.1	13.9	16.8	20.9
S & P 500	6	474	15.8	16.5	15.0	15.9	18.6	20.4	19.8	14.0	13.7	12.5	11.9	11.4	11.7	12.5	14.6	15.3	15.6
DOW JONES INDUSTRIALS-30 STK	7	30	12.7	13.0	12.1	15.8	18.8	20.2	19.8	14.8	13.8	13.6	12.7	12.1	12.2	12.7	13.9	14.1	14.7
PAPER MILLS	2621	30	14.4	17.1	17.6	17.0	17.1	22.0	20.5	21.5	11.9	13.6	13.6	12.8	16.7	18.1	18.8	13.5	11.1
NEWSPAPER:PUBG, PUBG & PRINT	2711	23	22.7	21.4	18.0	19.0	23.5	24.7	26.1	16.7	16.7	15.7	15.2	15.6	16.7	18.1	18.8	15.7	13.8
PHARMACEUTICALS	2834	22	18.1	22.5	26.0	21.9	24.3	30.0	31.0	32.7	24.9	25.6	25.4	26.2	26.6	29.2	30.1	35.3	35.9
PETROLEUM REFINING	2911	34	9.3	9.9	10.9	11.5	14.4	16.0	16.3	13.1	14.4	14.1	13.7	14.1	15.2	14.8	15.9	14.5	13.0
ELECTRONIC COMPUTERS	3571	37	83.5	88.8	96.4	85.4	30.0	45.0	43.9	50.2	56.2	40.4	27.4	29.7	15.2	15.0	15.7	16.9	13.9
SEMICONDUCTOR.RELATED DEVICE	3674	30	32.0	38.1	39.2	34.5	30.4	31.1	43.1	46.4	13.2	9.0	10.2	10.8	10.6	10.2	10.4	10.5	25.6
MOTOR VEHICLE PART.ACCESSORY	3714	30	8.4	9.9	12.5	12.9	11.4	11.2	13.5	13.6	17.7	18.5	20.1	19.8	17.9	18.1	20.1	42.2	65.9
TRUCKING, EXCEPT LOCAL	4213	26				16.3	17.6	19.4	23.1	17.0	15.0	16.0	15.5	15.7	18.3	19.3	24.5	20.1	19.6
AIR TRANSPORT, SCHEDULED	4512	25	16.9	15.5	16.6	16.3	17.1	20.3	21.0	14.2	16.0	16.0	15.5	8.7	8.6	9.5	9.9	10.6	9.9
ELECTRIC SERVICES	4911	64	9.3	9.3	9.5	9.6	9.8	9.2	9.0	8.3	8.5	8.8	8.8	8.7	8.6	8.6	9.6	10.5	9.9
NATIONAL COMMERCIAL BANKS	6021	87	10.2	9.6	12.0	13.0	11.8	11.2	11.7	@NM	@NM	@NM	@NM	@NM	@NM	8.6	18.8	10.5	11.4
SAVINGS INSTN.FED CHARTERED	6035	30								7.9	6.0	6.0	6.4	8.1	7.5	8.6	8.8	@NM	@NM
FIRE, MARINE, CASUALTY INS	6331	26				12.6	13.9	10.9	10.3	7.9	7.6	8.5	9.5	9.0	9.9	9.3	11.1	11.1	10.5
PREPACKAGED SOFTWARE	7372	31	25.1	29.7	27.1	23.9	39.2	40.7	47.9	25.8	25.6	28.8	25.2	19.1	19.8	21.1	23.8	23.5	24.5

P/E = current price / 12 months trailing earnings (as per Compustat); @NM indicates not a meaningful number. @NA indicates not available.

Security Analysis: How to Analyze Accounting and Market Data to Value Securities
Robert W. Holthausen and Mark E. Zmijewski
\CH8.W51

Table 2

Distribution of P/E Ratios Over Time (1964-1983) and
Distribution of P/E Ratios Across Industries in 1983

Source: Financial Statement Analysis, George Foster, Prentice Hall, 1986, p. 440.

TABLE 12.1   PE Ratios of Compustat Firms: Time-Series and Cross-Sectional Differences

Panel A: Time-Series Data for 1964–1983					
Year	.1 Decile	.3 Decile	.5 Decile	.7 Decile	.9 Decile	No. of Firms
1964	8.2	11.6	14.8	18.3	24.9	1.227
1965	9.2	12.4	15.0	18.2	27.5	1.273
1966	6.6	9.1	11.6	14.8	22.7	1.357
1967	9.7	12.6	15.5	22.0	40.8	1.414
1968	12.4	15.6	19.5	26.8	51.2	1.537
1969	8.5	11.2	14.2	20.2	37.6	1.639
1970	6.5	11.2	13.8	18.6	31.2	1.710
1971	7.7	11.5	14.8	20.5	37.2	1.822
1972	7.8	10.5	13.2	18.2	35.1	1.930
1973	3.6	5.5	7.5	10.2	21.5	1.991
1974	1.6	3.6	4.9	6.5	12.5	2.035
1975	1.5	5.2	6.9	9.1	16.2	2.054
1976	3.7	6.4	8.0	9.8	15.5	2.087
1977	3.8	6.1	7.4	9.1	13.8	2.121
1978	3.8	5.5	6.8	8.4	13.5	2.163
1979	3.7	5.5	6.8	9.2	15.9	2.196
1980	4.0	6.1	7.8	11.5	22.6	2.242
1981	3.0	5.9	7.4	10.2	19.3	2.307
1982	−3.8	6.6	9.5	13.3	27.0	2.323
1983	−4.0	7.7	10.8	14.5	27.2	.2.140

Panel B: Cross-Sectional Data for 1983						
SIC Code	Short Industry Title	Deciles of Distribution					No. of Observations
		.1	.3	.5	.7	.9	
1311	Oil. crude producers	−13.18	.30	12.50	17.14	32.16	67
2300	Textile apparel manufacturing	−2.90	8.27	9.22	11.12	20.50	37
2600	Paper and allied products	−28.50	11.22	14.38	18.37	27.34	24
2830	Drugs	8.92	11.45	12.92	15.48	32.77	28
2911	Petroleum refining	−2.29	7.41	8.67	12.53	17.99	41
3310	Steel and blast furnaces	−41.38	−7.16	−3.49	2.81	28.92	29
3560	General industrial machinery	−30.34	−4.53	12.59	20.54	131.73	26
3662	Radio and T.V. transmitting equipment	−15.42	13.68	17.31	21.70	49.92	34
3679	Electronic components	−3.29	12.96	22.27	27.11	35.23	22
4511	Air transport	−16.98	−3.57	−.88	8.16	18.71	22
4924	Natural gas	6.13	6.99	7.38	8.23	11.13	42
4931	Electric and other services	4.73	5.97	6.58	7.24	8.10	48
5411	Retail food chains	7.45	9.56	10.27	12.62	19.09	30
6312	Life insurance	6.64	7.67	8.32	8.69	11.52	26
6798	Real estate investment trusts	−6.87	8.99	10.80	12.11	18.36	44

SOURCE: Computed from 1983 Compustat annual industrial file.

Table 3

Behavior of P/E Ratios for Fixed P/E Portfolios Over Time and Growth Rates of Fixed P/E Portfolios Over Time

Source: <u>Financial Statement Analysis</u>, George Foster, Prentice Hall, 1986, p. 441.

TABLE 12.2 Explaining Diversity in PE Ratios

Panel A. PE Ratios of Portfolios Subsequent to Year of Formation (year 0)											
	Years After Formation										
Portfolio	0	1	2	3	4	5	6	7	8	9	10
1 (high PE)	50.0	22.7	16.4	13.8	12.3	13.2	13.5	13.2	17.2	14.9	13.0
5	20.8	17.5	16.9	15.9	15.9	13.7	13.0	12.8	12.5	11.8	11.9
10	14.3	11.9	11.5	11.1	10.3	10.1	9.4	9.0	10.0	10.0	9.9
15	11.1	10.8	10.4	10.8	10.0	10.0	9.4	9.7	9.3	9.5	8.6
20	8.9	9.1	9.6	9.3	9.4	9.3	9.3	9.0	8.8	8.8	9.0
25 (low PE)	5.8	6.9	8.0	7.8	7.9	7.9	8.2	8.8	8.3	8.5	7.8
Panel B. Earnings Growth of PE Portfolios Subsequent to Year of Formation (year 0)											
	Years After Formation										
Portfolio	0	1	2	3	4	5	6	7	8	9	10
1 (high PE)	−4.1%	95.3%	37.2%	28.2%	16.4%	18.9%	18.1%	19.7%	13.1%	14.8%	15.3%
5	10.7	14.9	12.1	13.1	14.2	10.9	10.4	11.8	10.5	11.6	8.0
10	9.6	12.9	11.5	12.3	12.6	9.2	10.1	10.8	12.8	8.3	12.9
15	10.0	8.8	8.5	8.1	8.2	14.3	11.6	5.4	13.3	10.3	11.0
20	10.8	5.2	9.3	12.6	12.4	6.0	8.4	13.0	10.2	11.3	11.1
25 (low PE)	26.4	−3.3	7.5	10.8	8.3	12.9	17.1	13.6	18.0	12.8	16.7
SOURCE: Beaver and Morse (1978, Table 3, p. 68 and Table 5, p. 70).											

In both panels, portfolios are formed in year zero based on the magnitude of P/E ratios in that year. Portfolio 1 contains the highest P/E ratios and portfolio 25 contains the lowest P/E ratios. Panel A examines the behavior of P/E ratios for those 25 portfolios in the year subsequent to formation. Panel B examines the growth rates in earnings from year to year in years subsequent to the formation of the P/E portfolios.

Table 4

Distribution of Market to Book (MV/BV) Ratios Over Time (1980-1989) and Distribution of Market to Book Ratios Across Industries in 1983

Market to Book Value of Equity	SIC	# firms	1980	1981	1982	1983	1984	1985	1986	1987	1988	1989
ALL INDUSTRIAL	1	2029	1.4	1.2	1.4	1.6	1.5	1.7	1.9	1.9	2.0	2.4
S & P 400	2	363	0.9	1.2	1.3	1.5	1.5	1.7	1.9	1.9	1.9	2.3
UTILITIES-COMPOSITE	3	43	0.9	0.8	0.9	0.9	1.0	1.2	1.4	1.2	1.3	1.8
FINANCIAL-COMPOSITE	4	53	1.1	0.8	0.9	1.0	1.0	1.3	1.3	1.1	1.1	1.4
TRANSPORTATION-COMPOSITE	5	15	1.3	1.0	1.1	1.2	1.3	1.2	1.3	1.6	1.4	1.4
S & P 500	6	474	1.2	1.1	1.3	1.4	1.5	1.6	1.7	1.7	1.7	2.0
DOW JONES INDUSTRIALS-30 STK	7	30	0.9	1.0	1.2	1.0	1.4	1.6	1.7	1.8	1.8	2.1
PAPER MILLS	2621	23						1.2	1.6	1.8	1.7	1.5
NEWSPAPER:PUBG, PUBG & PRINT	2711	22	2.5	2.3	2.8	2.7	2.7	3.4	3.6	2.9	2.4	2.5
PHARMACEUTICALS	2834	34	1.4	0.9	0.8	0.9	2.6	3.4	4.6	4.4	4.2	6.0
PETROLEUM REFINING	2911	37					0.9	1.1	1.3	1.3	1.5	1.9
ELECTRONIC COMPUTERS	3571	30						2.5	3.3	3.2	3.2	2.6
SEMICONDUCTOR,RELATED DEVICE	3674	30				2.8	3.8	2.5	2.3	1.8	2.2	1.8
MOTOR VEHICLE,PART,ACCESSORY	3714	30	0.8	0.8	0.9	1.2	1.6	1.3	1.5	1.7	1.4	1.6
TRUCKING, EXCEPT LOCAL	4213	26						2.1	2.2	1.6	1.8	1.8
AIR TRANSPORT, SCHEDULED	4512	25				1.1	1.3	1.2	1.3	1.4	1.1	1.4
ELECTRIC SERVICES	4911	64	0.7	0.7	0.8	0.9	0.9	0.9	1.1	1.2	1.0	1.1
NATIONAL COMMERCIAL BANKS	6021	87	0.8	0.8	0.7	0.9	0.9	1.1	1.1	1.0	1.1	1.2
SAVINGS INSTN,FED CHARTERED	6035	30									0.6	0.6
FIRE, MARINE, CASUALTY INS	6331	26	0.9	1.0	1.0	1.1	1.2	1.7	1.5	1.2	1.1	1.4
PREPACKAGED SOFTWARE	7372	31							4.6	4.5	5.2	4.2

438

Security Analysis: How to Analyze Accounting and Market Data to Value Securities
© Robert W. Holthausen and Mark E. Zmijewski
\CHP09.W51

Table 5

Distribution of Market to Book (MV/BV) Ratios Over Time (1964-1983)

Source: Financial Statement Analysis, George Foster, Prentice Hall, 1986, p. 452.

TABLE 12.4 Price-to-Book Value Ratios of Compustat Firms, 1964–1983

Year	Deciles of the Distribution					Total Corporate Profits ($ billions)	Profit to Stockholders' Equity: Manufacturing	S&P 500 Composite Stock Index	U.S. Treasury Bill Rate (3-month)	Consumer Price Index (annual change)
	.1	.3	.5	.7	.9					
1964	.75	1.25	1.70	2.37	3.81	66.0	.116	81.37	.035	.012
1965	.94	1.43	1.93	2.53	4.21	76.0	.130	88.17	.040	.019
1966	.72	1.14	1.54	2.12	3.61	80.9	.134	85.26	.049	.033
1967	1.00	1.46	2.03	3.12	6.35	78.1	.117	91.93	.043	.030
1968	1.25	1.76	2.42	3.46	6.87	84.9	.121	98.70	.053	.047
1969	.83	1.23	1.65	2.46	5.08	80.8	.115	97.84	.067	.061
1970	.70	1.07	1.40	1.95	3.80	68.9	.093	83.22	.065	.055
1971	.74	1.14	1.51	2.20	4.50	82.0	.097	98.29	.043	.034
1972	.70	1.07	1.43	2.11	4.55	94.0	.106	109.20	.041	.034
1973	.36	.60	.84	1.24	2.77	105.6	.128	107.43	.070	.088
1974	.22	.39	.55	.77	1.61	96.7	.149	82.85	.079	.122
1975	.33	.54	.75	1.00	2.07	120.6	.116	86.16	.058	.070
1976	.46	.72	.94	1.25	2.19	151.6	.139	102.01	.050	.048
1977	.47	.71	.93	1.21	2.07	178.5	.142	98.20	.053	.068
1978	.48	.69	.89	1.19	2.07	205.1	.150	96.02	.072	.090
1979	.50	.74	.96	1.40	2.55	209.6	.164	103.01	.100	.133
1980	.51	.74	1.03	1.67	3.50	191.7	.139	118.78	.115	.124
1981	.50	.73	.98	1.43	2.55	197.6	.136	128.05	.140	.089
1982	.58	.83	1.09	1.57	2.86	156.0	.092	119.71	.107	.039
1983	.74	1.00	1.29	1.79	3.03	192.0	.106	160.41	.086	.038

SOURCES: Price-to-book value data computed from 1983 Compustat annual industrial file; macroeconomic data from *Economic Report of the President*, 1985.

Beatty, Riffe and Thompson Insert

The following three pages are Figure 1 and Table 2 Panel A from "The Method of Comparables in Tax Court Valuations of Privately-held Firms: An Empirical Investigation" by Randy Beatty, Susan Riffe and Rex Thompson of the Cox School of Business, Southern Methodist University (unpublished working paper).

Security Analysis: How to Analyze Accounting and Market Data to Value Securities
Robert W. Holthausen and Mark E. Zmijewski
\CHP09.W51

Figure 1
Model Summary

Definitions:　　x=earnings
　　　　　　　　B=book value
　　　　　　　　P=price
　　　　　　　　D=dividends

Univariate Proportional:

Average P/E

$$\hat{P}_i = \frac{1}{n}\sum_{i=1}^{n}(P_i/x_i)*x_i$$

Average P/B

$$\hat{P}_i = \frac{1}{n}\sum_{i=1}^{n}(P_i/B_i)*B_i$$

Inverse Average E/P

$$\hat{P}_i = \left[1/\left[\frac{1}{n}\sum_{i=1}^{n}(x_i/P_i)\right]\right]*x_i$$

Inverse Average B/P

$$\hat{P}_i = \left[1/\left[\frac{1}{n}\sum_{i=1}^{n}(B_i/P_i)\right]\right]*B_i$$

Median P/E

$$\hat{P}_i = Median(P_i/x_i)*x_i$$

Median P/B

$$\hat{P}_i = Median(P_i/B_i)*B_i$$

0 Mean Earnings

$$\hat{P}_i = \frac{\sum_{i=1}^{n}P_i}{\sum_{i=1}^{n}x_i}*x_i$$

0 Mean Book

$$\hat{P}_i = \frac{\sum_{i=1}^{n}P_i}{\sum_{i=1}^{n}B_i}*B_i$$

The 0 Mean Earnings and 0 Mean Book models result in the residuals having a mean of zero.

**Minimum Sum Squared
Errors Earnings**

$$\hat{P}_i = \frac{\sum_{i=1}^{n}P_ix_i}{\sum_{i=1}^{n}x_i^2}*x_i$$

**Minimum Sum Squared
Errors Book**

$$\hat{P}_i = \frac{\sum_{i=1}^{n}P_iB_i}{\sum_{i=1}^{n}B_i^2}*B_i$$

Multivariate Proportional:

Equal Weight

$$\hat{P}_i = .5\left(1/Avg(x/P)\right)*x_i + .5\left(1/Avg(B/P)\right)*B_i$$

Best Weight

$$\hat{P}_i = \omega_x\left(1/Avg(x/P)\right)x_i + (1-\omega_x)\left(1/Avg(B/P)\right)B_i$$

$$\omega_x = \sum(e_{B,i}^2 - e_{B,i}e_{x,i})/\sum(e_{B,i} - e_{x,i})$$

The Best Weight Model chooses the best weights subject to the constraint that the weights sum to 1.

Regression Weight

$$\hat{P}_i = \Gamma_1 x_i + \Gamma_2 B_i$$

$$\omega_x = \Gamma_1/\left(1/Avg(x/P)\right)$$

$$\omega_B = \Gamma_2/\left(1/Avg(B/P)\right)$$

The Regression Weight Model estimates the weights with regression without an intercept so there is no constraint that the weights sum to 1.

Univariate Linear:

Linear Earnings

$$\hat{P}_i = \Gamma_0 + \Gamma_1 x_i$$

Linear Book

$$\hat{P}_i = \Gamma_0 + \Gamma_1 B_i$$

Multivariate Linear:

Linear Earnings and Book

$$\hat{P}_i = \Gamma_0 + \Gamma_1 x_i + \Gamma_2 B_i$$

Linear Earnings, Book and Dividends

$$\hat{P}_i = \Gamma_0 + \Gamma_1 x_i + \Gamma_2 B_i + \Gamma_3 D_i$$

The coefficients on the Univariate and Multivariate Linear models are estimated using regression analysis.

Table 2
Panel A
Pricing Coefficients and Error Statistics
Per Share Estimation by SIC Code

	Inter	Earnings	Book	Dividend	Mean	Std. Dev.	Rho	RMSE	R Squared
Proportional:									
Earnings									
Average P/E					-10.04	15.37	-0.67	18.44	
1/Average E/P					1.00	7.47	-0.32	7.50	
Median P/E					-0.27	7.98	-0.42	7.93	
0 Mean					0.00	7.42	-0.42	7.20	
Minimum SSE					1.53	6.55	-0.29	6.67	
Book									
Average P/B			1.74		-2.64	9.66	-0.48	9.90	
1/Average B/P			1.27		1.83	7.94	-0.21	8.07	
Median P/B			1.45		0.19	8.39	-0.33	8.35	
0 Mean			1.48		0.00	8.03	-0.37	7.80	
Minimum SSE			1.33		1.49	7.25	-0.26	7.32	
Earnings & Book									
Equal Weight Const. to 1		0.50	0.50		1.41	6.54	-0.17	6.64	
Coefficient		5.69	0.64						
Best Weight Const. to 1		0.62	0.38		1.15	5.83	-0.14	5.88	
Coefficient		7.04	0.49						
Regression Weight Unconst.		0.63	0.41		0.75	5.34	-0.18	5.34	
Coefficient		7.18	0.52						
Linear:									
Earnings Model Coefficients	3.96	9.06			0.00	6.07	0.00	5.89	0.64
t statistics	35.21	136.46							
Book Model Coefficients	4.22		1.07		0.00	6.73	0.00	6.53	0.55
t statistics	30.75		117.61						
Earnings & Book Model Coefficients	2.48	6.80	0.40		0.00	5.01	0.00	4.87	0.75
t statistics	22.18	64.63	38.71						
Earn, Book, Div. Model Coefficients	2.40	6.78	0.36	0.51	0.00	4.53	0.00	4.40	0.79
t statistics	22.04	60.82	35.37	3.90					

Table 2 models are estimated by 3-digit SIC code industry subgroups by year for 1980, 1984, 1988, and 1992. The reported results are averaged across years and subgroups. The models are defined in Figure 1. The Inter column is the average estimated intercept from the linear regression equations. The Earnings, Book, and Dividend columns give the average estimated coefficients that would be multiplied by these variables to estimate price. The weights for the multivariate proportional models are the average amount multiplied by 1/Avg E/P or 1/Avg B/P to estimate the coefficients. The t-statistics for the linear regressions represent the number of standard deviations the average t-statistic is from zero. The prediction error is defined as actual price minus predicted price. The average of the mean prediction error, the standard deviation of the prediction error, and the root mean squared prediction error (RMSE) are reported. The rho is the average correlation between the prediction error and earnings per share for the univariate earnings models and book value per share for the other models. The R-squareds describe the average explanatory power of the regression models.

Chapter 9

Problems for Review

1. Valuing Privately Held Equity Securities for Buy-Out From Employees.

Part A.

Complete part A of this class discussion case before you read any of the materials for part B of this questions, and do not change your response to part A after reading the materials for part B.

1. Assume you are a consultant and have been hired by the board of directors of P. R. Value, Inc., a privately held firm, to develop a method of valuing the firm's common stock for the purpose of buying the shares of employees who retire, die or leave for any other reason. Employees receive shares of common stock as part of their bonus compensation arrangement and the firm repurchases the shares if the employee leaves the firm. Further, assume that you have identified five firms that have publicly traded stock, and they have growth rates, rates of return, capital structure, etc., which are similar to P. R. Value Inc.

2. Write the main ingredients of a contract that would be given to employees for the method of calculating the value of the common stock.

Part B.

Attached to these notes is a legal complaint regarding the valuation of a privately held common stock of a Public Broker. The plaintiff (an employee, now an ex-employee) states that he applied a straight-forward formula in the compensation contract to calculate the value of the plaintiff's privately held stock, but that the company refuses to pay that amount. The defendant (the company) states that the plaintiff incorrectly utilized the formula and that a correct application of the formula results in a much lower value for the security.

1. Review the formula in the contract and the application of the formula by the plaintiff.

    (a) Did the plaintiff, in your opinion, correctly utilize the formula? Discuss and defend your position. (Assume the timing of the figures for calculating average selling price and earnings is correct).

    (b) What components or terms of the formula are sufficiently unspecified such that alternative outcomes could result from the application of this formula using reasonable alternative specifications of these components or terms?

2. Suppose you had been hired as an expert witness for the defendant. How would you have defended yourself in this case? What alternative calculation would you have presented? Justify your alternative calculation.

Security Analysis: How to Analyze Accounting and Market Data to Value Securities
Robert W. Holthausen and Mark E. Zmijewski
\CHP09.W51

IN THE CIRCUIT COURT OF
    COUNTY, DEPARTMENT LAW DIVISION

Plaintiff   )
)
    v.   )
)
)
)
)
)
Defendant   )

AMENDED COMPLAINT FOR DECLARATORY JUDGMENT

NOW COMES the Plaintiff,   by his attorney,   ,complaining of the
defendant,   , a corporation, and requesting that this court enter judgment for the relief
hereinafter specified, states as follows:

1.   That the Plaintiff,   , is a citizen and resident of   and was at all
      times referred to herein a holder of stock in Defendant corporation.

2.   That Defendant,   , is a corporation organized and existing under the
      laws of

3.   That at various times and for a valuable consideration, Plaintiff purchased some 1,300 shares
      of stock in Defendant corporation; that as a result of stock splits issued by the corporation
      those shares increased in number to 26,000.

4.   That on October 29, 1982, Plaintiff terminated his full-time employment with Defendant
      corporation and resigned effective March 31, 1983.

5.   That there exists an agreement between Plaintiff and Defendant corporation dated January 15,
      1982. (Said agreement is hereinafter referred to as the "Agreement").

6.   That on April 1, 1984 and prior thereto, the Agreement was in full force and effect.

7.   That Paragraph 3(b) of said Agreement, entitled "Retirement or Termination", provides in
      part that the stockholder shall have the option to sell to the Defendant to the extent of a
      maximum of 25% of his shares on December 31, 1983 and April 1 and October 1, 1984 and
      April 1, 1985, respectively; that Paragraph 3(d) provides the manner in which the purchase
      price shall be determined is as specified in Paragraph 2(d) of the Agreement.

8.   That Paragraph 2(d) of the Agreement provides as follows:

Security Analysis: How to Analyze Accounting and Market Data to Value Securities
Robert W. Holthausen and Mark E. Zmijewski
\CHP09.W51

The price-earnings ratio for each of the Public Brokers (Carroon & Blank, Frank Hall, Marsh & McLennon and Alexander & Alexander) shall be determined by dividing (i) the average of the trading prices for that corporation's stock during the month of December next preceding the date of death or retirement (such average trading prices being the average of the closing quotations for such period on the New York Stock Exchange or the average of the bid prices per share for such period in the over-the-counter market, as may be applicable, all as reported in the Midwest Edition of the Wall Street Journal by (ii) such corporation's reported audited earnings per share for the fiscal year next preceding the date of death or retirement. To the extent such information is not available with respect to any of the Public Brokers because they have ceased existence as independent companies, such computations shall be made on the basis of the information for the remaining Public Brokers then available.

9. That Plaintiff caused to be delivered to Defendant on a timely basis a letter dated March 27, 1984 exercising the option provided in the Agreement to sell 6500 shares of stock to Defendant Corporation.

10. That in accordance with the terms of the Agreement, the calculation based upon the December, 1983 Midwest Editions of the Wall Street Journal, and the annual reports of the companies described in the contract, is as follows:

	Carroon & Black	Frank Hall	Marsh & McLennon	Alexander & Alexander
Average 12/83 Selling Price	24.286	24.73	47.74	20.64
1983 Earnings	2.22	1.02	3.49	0.03
Price/Earnings Ratios	10.94	24.25	13.68	688.00
Average Price/Earnings Ratio				184.22
Defendants 1983 Earnings per share				1.25
Defendant's Earnings per share times Average Price Earnings Multiple				230.27
Plaintiff's calculation of Price per share				230.27
Number of Shares being sold				6.500
Total Buyout Price				$1,496,755

11. That Plaintiff has fulfilled all of his obligations under the Agreement of February 15, 1982.

12. That there is an actual case in controversy. WHEREFORE, Plaintiff, requests the Court to enter judgment in his favor and against Defendant in the sum of $1,496,755.00 (ONE MILLION, FOUR HUNDRED NINETY-SIX THOUSAND SEVEN HUNDRED FIFTY-FIVE DOLLARS), together with interest and costs.

Security Analysis: How to Analyze Accounting and Market Data to Value Securities
Robert W. Holthausen and Mark E. Zmijewski
\CHP09.W51

2.   Here are data on TOYS "R" US and some firms in the toy industry and clothing industry from Value Line.

Item	TOYS	TOY A	TOY B	TOY C	GAP	OSHKOSH
Inventory	LIFO	LIFO	LIFO	FIFO	FIFO	LIFO
Debt (% of Cap) BV	9%	9%	28%	45%	5%	3%
Beta	1.30	1.00	1.15	1.45	1.35	1.10
Annual Growth - Past 5 Years						
Sales	22.5%	8.5%	17.5%	-5.5%	20.0%	22.5%
Cash Flow	23.5%	2.0%	2.5%	NMF	30.5%	25.5%
Earnings	23.5%	-0.5%	0.0%	NMF	34.5%	25.0%
Expected Growth - Next Year						
Sales	19.5%	4.7%	7.7%	5.4%	20.1%	11.1%
Cash Flow	20.7%	-3.7%	6.4%	-8.1%	21.0%	-1.0%
Earnings	22.0%	-21.5%	28.2%	233.3%	20.3%	-5.0%
Expected Total Growth - Next 5 Years						
Sales	94.5%	52.9%	50.2%	23.9%	78.4%	77.7%
Cash Flow	99.5%	124.6%	73.8%	2.0%	91.9%	63.2%
Earnings	101.1%	292.9%	233.3%	733.3%	91.5%	64.7%
Current NI/Sales	6.7%	0.7%	0.8%	0.1%	6.5%	11.9%
Current P/E	XXX	24.5[1]	12.3	132.9	16.9	15.9
Current P/Sales	XXX	0.2	0.1	0.1	1.0	1.9

[1] Earnings for TOY A dropped in half last year. In the year prior to that, TOY A's P/E ratio was equal to 12.

Required:

Suppose you were going to use two approaches to value the common stock of TOYS, P/E ratios and P/Sales ratios. What comparable firm(s) would you use for each. What is your estimate of the value per share of Toys R Us using each approach. TOYS most recent EPS were $1.64 and sales per share were $24.44.

Security Analysis: How to Analyze Accounting and Market Data to Value Securities
Robert W. Holthausen and Mark E. Zmijewski
\CH9.W51

19

VALUATION AND FORECASTING

INTRODUCTION

This chapter provides an overview of valuation models. In a perfect world, the models based on assets, dividends, cash flows, and earnings are identical. However, in the real world, this highly stylized environment does not exist and model results can differ. In such settings, the data used in valuation models are estimates of expected future values and their measurement is as important as their predictive ability.

The primary focus of the chapter, therefore, is not the theoretical underpinnings of these models, but rather the relationship of their parameters to information obtainable from the accounting system. In addition, consistent with forecasting requirements of valuation models, the chapter concludes with a discussion of forecasting and the time-series properties of earnings.

VALUATION MODELS

OVERVIEW OF MODELS

The valuation models most commonly used by analysts and investors generally fall into two classes:

1. Asset-based valuation models
2. Discounted cash flow (DCF) models

Additionally, we explore a third class, which has characteristics of the first two:

3. The abnormal earnings or Edwards–Bell–Ohlson (EBO) model.

Asset-based valuation models assign a value to the firm based on the current market value of the individual component assets. Liabilities (also at market value) are deducted to arrive at the (market) value of the firm's equity:

Value = Assets − Liabilities

In DCF models, value at time t is determined as the present value of future cash flows:

$$\text{Value}_t = \sum_i \frac{\text{CF}_{t+i}}{(1 + r)^i} \qquad (1)$$

where CF_{t+i} represents (expected[1]) cash flows i periods from time t and r is the discount factor (the firm's required rate of return). DCF models vary as to the appropriate measure of cash flow CF, defined variously as streams of future dividends, earnings, or free cash flows.

Conceptually, the DCF and asset-based approaches to valuation are related through the actual rate of return r^* earned by a firm on its equity investment. For an

---

[1]Technically, we should use the expectation operator $E(*)$ when discussing future period (as yet unknown) cash flows/earnings to differentiate from current period (known) earnings. This would, however, only add needlessly to the notation. From the context, it should be clear that when we speak of future earnings or cash flows, we are talking about their expected rather than actual values.

infinite (constant) cash flow stream, using the DCF model, we obtain

$$\text{Value} = \frac{\text{CF}}{r} \tag{2}$$

But the amount a firm earns, CF, is equal to

$$\text{CF} = r^*B$$

where B is the book value of the firm. If we assume that the firm earns the required rate of return r, $(r^* = r)$, then CF $= rB$ and

$$\text{Value} = \frac{\text{CF}}{r} = \frac{rB}{r} = B \tag{3}$$

This equation suggests that value can be equivalently defined as either a "stock" of assets or the flows those assets generate.

The EBO model, we shall see, determines value as a combination of the stock of assets representing the normal flow that assets generate and the discounted value of abnormal earnings generated by these assets.

The various approaches are equivalent in a highly stylized and perfect world. Such a world has no need for financial analysis as all is known. Analysis is challenging and rewarding, however, in real-world settings, with finite knowledge and horizons and costly information. In the real world, there is uncertainty with respect to both the definition and measurement of the model parameters and their actual outcomes. The equivalence of asset-based, DCF, and EBO models breaks down, and different valuations result. The uncertainties in these models include:

- Difficulties in forecasting over a finite horizon, let alone to infinity
- The random nature of cash flows and earnings and the difficulty in assessing whether reported amounts are *permanent* (will persist in the future) or *transitory* (nonrecurring)
- The measurement of assets, earnings, and cash flows, which can be influenced by the selection of accounting policies and by discretionary management policies

Analysts must be able to circumvent the pitfalls introduced by uncertainty and measurement problems. This chapter will discuss these problems further in the context of the valuation models themselves.

ASSET-BASED VALUATION MODELS

Asset-based models assign a value to the firm by aggregating the current market value of its individual component assets and liabilities. Chapter 17 discussed the steps required to develop an asset-based valuation. As derived in Exhibit 17-1, duPont's adjusted book value on December 31, 1994, was $18.7 billion, or $26.97 per share, approximately 46% higher than the reported book value of $13.0 billion, or $18.48 per share. Both amounts were considerably below the closing market price (at December 31, 1994) of $56.125. How should this discrepancy be interpreted? Should we expect to see the market price equal (the adjusted) book value?

451

One possibility is that the value of the firm exceeds the sum of its parts. Asset-based valuation calculates that sum; synergistic effects could then result in a premium (economic goodwill) for the going concern. Whether or not this is true depends on the firm's profitability. There may be other reasons for this discrepancy, including but not limited to the nature of the firm's assets, management's choice of financial reporting methods, mandatory and discretionary accounting changes, and other problems in the measurement of book value. We explore these causes to develop our understanding of the insights they provide and the pitfalls in the use of asset-based valuation models.

Market Price and Book Value: Theoretical Considerations

Earlier we showed that when the actual rate of return r^* equals the required rate of return r, then

$$\text{Value} = \frac{CF}{r} = \frac{rB}{r} = B$$

When r^* is not equal to r, then this equation can be transformed to

$$CF = r^*B = rB + (r^* - r)B$$

and, therefore, if

$$\text{Value} = \frac{CF}{r}$$

then

$$\text{Value} = \frac{rB + (r^* - r)B}{r}$$

$$= \left[1 + \frac{(r^* - r)}{r}\right]B \qquad (4)$$

$$= B + \left[\frac{(r^* - r)}{r}\right]B$$

Whether or not a firm's stock price is above or below book value depends on the intuitively appealing factor of how high the firm's expected rate of return is. As we shall see, $r^* > r$ is characteristic of a firm with positive growth opportunities, leading to market values greater than book value. Thus, the shares of a firm whose expected r^* is higher (lower) than the required r should sell at a price above (below) book value. The component

$$\left[\frac{(r^* - r)}{r}\right]B$$

is, in effect, a measure of the firm's economic goodwill, the excess of market over book value.[2]

---

[2] As we shall see, this relationship is basic to the EBO model.

Book Value: Measurement Issues

The calculation of duPont's adjusted book value, although detailed, was relatively straightforward for all liabilities and current assets as much of the required information was available. The major difficulty in applying asset-based valuation is the determination of the market (current) value of long-lived assets such as plant, machinery, and equipment. Because this is true for most companies, the relationship between (adjusted) book value and market price is affected by this measurement error.

For some analysts, reported book value is an "index" against which to compare the stock price. Under the assumption that the differential between market price and book value should be similar for firms in the same industry, the analysis turns on whether the relationship for a given firm is "in line" with a comparable population of firms.

When book value is used as an indicator, it is common practice to rely on unadjusted data that are simpler to obtain. These amounts do not measure value directly, but rather are viewed as benchmarks against which market value is compared. The focus is on how close market value is to book value. If it is very close to book value or below book value, then the stock is a "buy," as the downside risk is viewed as negligible.[3]

This comparison is generally conducted under the implicit or explicit assumption that historical cost-based book value reflects the minimum value of the firm. This minimum value assumption is justified by the fact that, since book value is based on historical cost, it does not reflect increases in value caused by inflation. Moreover, when there are adjustments to historical cost, only markdowns (such as impairment) not markups are permitted. (In some cases, such as marketable securities, markups are allowed.) Thus, book value is viewed as a conservative estimate of the firm's value.

Notwithstanding the foregoing, stocks do trade below the firm's book value. On an economy-wide level, Stober (1996) found the average price-to-book ratio to be less than 1 for every year in the 1973 to 1979 period; since that period, it has been greater than 1. Feltham and Ohlson (1995) noted that close to one-third of companies on the COMPUSTAT tape traded below their book values at some time. The relationship between price and book value depends to a great extent on the nature of the firm's assets, its reporting methods, its profitability, and the overall economy.

Firms reporting intangible assets such as goodwill can trade below reported book value. Relating this to the theoretical model earlier, we see that if the economic goodwill component $[(r^* - r)/r]\,B$ is less than the recorded goodwill, then a company can trade below its reported book value.[4] For a company that has no recorded goodwill, if its profitability is poor $(r^* < r)$, then it is possible for the firm's shares to trade below even its (historical) book value. Such a firm may have greater value broken up than as a going concern.

Book value is also a function of management's financial reporting choices that affect the allocations of revenues and expenses across time periods and as a result determine reported asset and liability balances. In some cases, these choices result in nonrecognition of economic obligations. These choices affect reported book value over time for a given firm, and at any given point in time, they affect comparisons of book value across firms.

---

[3]The results of Fama and French (1992), discussed in Chapters 5 and 18, imply that one of the variables that best explain differential market returns is the book value/price ratio. They suggest that this ratio may serve as a surrogate risk measure.

[4]This is true even if $r^* > r$.

A final point relates to restructurings and write-offs. It was indicated in Chapter 8 that the decision to write down long-lived tangible assets is somewhat subjective. Management determines the amount and may accelerate or delay the recognition of write-offs and restructurings affecting reported book value and earnings. Thus, if the market anticipates a write-off, the firm's shares could trade below book value.

Tobin's Q Ratio

The relationship between a company's market and book values can be measured by Tobin's q ratio,[5] defined as the market value of the firm divided by its book value on a replacement cost basis.[6] Q values below 1 (price less than replacement book value) imply that the firm earns less than the required rate of return; a (marginal) dollar invested in the firm's assets results in future cash flows whose present value is less than $1. Such firms are poor performers.

However (as discussed in Chapter 14), firms with low q ratios are often seen as prime takeover targets. Firms that want to expand find it cheaper to grow by acquiring an existing firm rather than constructing new production or marketing facilities. Implicit in such takeovers is the assumption that the acquired assets will perform better within the new firm due to diversification, synergistic effects, or better management.

The assumption of poor management can also motivate acquisitions even when the target firm is not in the same line of business. Low q ratios indicate poor firm performance. If this performance is due to poor management, bidders who believe they are better managers can buy the business at an attractive price.

Stability and Growth of Book Value

The growth of equity capital, the base on which shareholder returns are earned, is an important component of firm value. Even a constant return on equity, if applied to a growing capital base, will increase earnings. Thus, the trend of book value per share (BPS) is as important as its level; both are affected by operating, investing, and financing decisions, financial reporting choices, and discretionary or mandatory accounting changes. A brief discussion of factors which affect (and sometimes distort) BPS follows.

Earnings Retention

For most firms, retained earnings provide most of the growth in book value. That growth is affected by the firm's return on equity (ROE) and its dividend policy. If the payout ratio (dividends/net income) equals k, then the increase in book value B is

$$
\begin{aligned}
B_1 - B_0 &= \text{Income} - \text{Dividends} \\
&= (\text{ROE} \times B_0) - (k \times \text{ROE} \times B_0) \qquad (5) \\
&= (1 - k) \times \text{ROE} \times B_0
\end{aligned}
$$

where B_0 is the book value at the beginning of the period and $(1 - k)$ is the *earnings retention rate*. Thus, $(1 - k) \times \text{ROE}$ is the growth rate of book value per share due to earnings retention.[7]

---

[5]The ratio was developed by the Nobel prize-winning economist James Tobin.

[6]See Chapter 7 and Appendix 8-A for a discussion of the concepts of current cost and replacement cost.

[7]As we shall see in our discussion of DCF models, this is also one way of estimating earnings growth. We shall also indicate the problems in using these parameters to estimate growth.

Effect of New Equity Financing

Sales of new shares at prices above BPS increase book value per share, whereas sales below BPS result in dilution.[8] Similarly, repurchases of outstanding shares at prices below BPS increase it, whereas repurchases of shares above BPS dilute it.

Effect of Acquisitions

Acquisitions that are made for stock affect book value per share under either the purchase or pooling methods of acquisition accounting (see Chapter 14), although the impact differs.

When the pooling method is used, the newly issued shares are reflected at the book value of the acquired company:

$$\frac{\text{Book Value of Acquired Company}}{\text{Number of Shares Issued}}$$

If the BPS of the newly issued shares exceeds that of the acquirer, then BPS increases. If the BPS of the newly issued shares is lower, the acquirer's BPS is diluted.

Under the purchase method of accounting, the newly issued shares are recorded at market value. Thus, the effect on the acquirer's BPS depends on whether or not the market price of its shares is above or below its own BPS; it is as if the acquirer sold shares for cash and used that cash to purchase the acquired company.

Effect of Changing Exchange Rates

As discussed in Chapter 15, the equity of operations in functional currencies other than the reporting (parent) currency is translated at the exchange rate on the balance sheet date. As a result, when functional currencies appreciate, the firm's BPS rises. Similarly, the remeasurement of foreign operations and translation of foreign currency transactions affect the BPS and need careful evaluation.

Effect of Financial Reporting Choices and Accounting Changes

Much of this text has been devoted to analyses of the effects (including those on book value) of financial reporting choices such as inventory valuation, depreciation, employee benefits, leases, and other capitalization versus expensing decisions. Discretionary changes in these policies can also change the level and trend of growth (or decline) in BPS.

Finally, mandatory accounting changes can have a significant impact on reported book value. In recent years, new accounting standards have had significantly positive (income taxes and marketable securities) and negative (postemployment benefits and impairment) impacts on BPS. As noted in earlier chapters, long transition periods and alternative transition methods affect the level and trend of BPS of a given firm and comparisons across firms.

As a result of duPont's adoption of SFAS 106, Employers' Accounting for Postretirement Benefits Other Than Pensions, in 1992, for example, there was a cumulative negative effect of $4.8 billion ($7.18 per share). DuPont's book value was reduced by 30%!

---

[8]A mathematical formulation of this effect can be found in Cohen et al. (1987), p. 399.

Thus, although the trend of BPS is an important indicator of potential earnings growth, the analyst must discern whether or not BPS growth comes from operations (increases in retained earnings)[9] or the other factors discussed. To the extent that BPS growth evolves from nonoperating factors, that growth may be artificial or nonrecurring. Failure to consider the sources of BPS growth can result in erroneous conclusions regarding future earnings trends.

Restructuring Provisions

In recent years, many companies have reported large restructuring provisions that significantly reduced reported BPS. In the case of duPont, pretax restructuring charges were $828, $475, and $1,835 million in 1991 through 1993, followed by a $142 million reversal in 1994. In total, these charges (if we assume a 35% tax rate) reduced book value per share by approximately $2.90 per share, or 16%.

Although asset-based valuation can be a useful tool, because of the complexities and problems discussed above, analysts have sought to value companies using forecasts of future cash flows rather than the evaluation of the current stock of assets. We now turn to these models.

DISCOUNTED CASH FLOW VALUATION MODELS

The parameters that make up the DCF model

$$\text{Value} = \sum \frac{\text{CF}_{t+i}}{(1 + r)^i}$$

are related to risk (the required rate of return) and the return itself (CF). Chapter 18 dealt with the elements of risk and their impact on the required rate of return. This chapter focuses primarily on measurement of the return or CF measure.

These models (originating in the finance literature) use three alternative CF measures: dividends, accounting earnings, and free cash flows. Just as DCF and asset-based valuation models are equivalent under the assumptions of perfect markets, dividends, earnings, and free cash flow measures can be shown (theoretically) to yield equivalent results. Their implementation, however, is not straightforward.

First, there is inherent difficulty in defining the cash flows used in these models. Which cash flows and to whom do they flow? Conceptually, cash flows are defined differently depending on whether the valuation objective is the firm's equity (denoted as P), or the value of the firm's debt plus equity (V).

Assuming that we can define CF, we are left with another issue. The models need future cash flows as inputs. How is the cash flow stream estimated from present data? More important, are current and past dividends, earnings, or cash flows the best indicators of that stream? These (and other) pragmatic issues determine which model should be used. Before addressing these issues directly, we discuss various models based on these measures. Doing so will highlight some of the difficulties inherent in using them.

---

[9]This source of growth in BPS may also stem from financial reporting choices and the impact of such changes is not necessarily the same as real operating improvements.

Dividend-Based Models

The value of a firm's equity (P) equals the present value of all future dividends paid by the firm to its equity holders:

$$P_0 = \frac{D_1}{(1 + r)} + \frac{D_2}{(1 + r)^2} + \cdots$$
$$= \sum_{i=1}^{\infty} \frac{D_i}{(1 + r)^i} \qquad (6)$$

where

P_0 = the value of the firm's equity at the end of period 0

D_i = the dividend paid by the firm in period i

r = the firm's required rate of return based on the firm's risk class

This formulation requires forecasting dividends to infinity (see the discussion below), which is impossible. Thus, different patterns of future dividend payments must be assumed.

Growth Patterns

No-Growth–Constant Dividend Model. In its no-growth form, the dividend discount model assumes a constant dividend rate equal to the current dividend level, and Eq. (6) reduces to

$$P_0 = \frac{D_1}{r} \qquad (7)$$

In effect, dividends are capitalized at r to derive the value of the firm.

Constant Growth Model. For a firm with an expected (constant) growth rate g, dividends in the next period are expected to equal $(1 + g)$ times current dividends, $D_1 = D_0(1 + g)$, and the valuation model becomes

$$P_0 = \frac{D_0(1 + g)}{r - g} = \frac{D_1}{r - g} \qquad (8)$$

Explicit Forecasts with Terminal Value Assumptions. Equation (6) can be rewritten as

$$P_0 = \sum_{i=1}^{T} \frac{D_i}{(1 + r)^i} + \frac{P_T}{(1 + r)^T} \qquad (9)$$

where

$$P_T = \sum_{j=1}^{\infty} \frac{D_{T+j}}{(1 + r)^{T+j}}$$

Equation (9) states that firm value in period 0 equals the discounted value of a stream of dividends for T periods plus the (discounted) value of the firm at the end of T periods. Using this form of the model requires *explicit* forecasts of dividends for T

(usually three to five) years, plus a forecast of the terminal price (P_T) at the end of period T. This forecasted price usually incorporates (one of) the previously discussed growth assumptions.

Although the dividend model is easy to use, it presents a conceptual dilemma.[10] Finance theory[11] says that dividend policy does not matter; the pattern of dividends up to the terminal (liquidating) dividend is irrelevant. The model, however, requires forecasting dividends to infinity or making terminal value assumptions. Firms that presently do not pay any dividends are a case in point.[12] Such firms are not valueless. In fact, high-growth firms often pay no dividends, as they reinvest all funds available to them. When firm value is estimated using a dividend discount model, it depends on the dividend level of the firm after its growth stabilizes. *Future dividends depend on the earnings stream the firm will be able to generate.* Thus, the firm's expected future earnings are fundamental to such a valuation. Similarly, for a firm paying dividends, the level of dividends *may be* a discretionary choice of management that is restricted by available earnings.

When dividends are not paid out, value accumulates within the firm in the form of reinvested earnings. Alternatively, firms sometimes pay dividends right up to bankruptcy. Thus, dividends may say more about the allocation of earnings to different claimants than valuation.

Earnings-Based Models

The implementation problems with dividend-based models highlight the crucial role of earnings in valuation. We now proceed to a discussion of earnings-based valuation models by showing the relationship between dividends and earnings models. However, one caveat must be noted: The concept of earnings used in these models and accounting income are the same only under specific simplified assumptions. The notion of earnings in these theoretic models is closer to CFO or free cash flows. For the present, the term "earnings" should be viewed broadly. We shall expand and clarify this issue as we proceed.

Relationship Between Earnings-Based and Dividend-Based Models

An earnings-based model can be derived from the dividend-based model using k, the dividend payout ratio. If $D_i = kE_i$, then, for the *growth case,*

$$P_0 = \frac{kE_0(1 + g)}{r - g} = \frac{kE_1}{r - g} \tag{10}$$

As discussed shortly, a firm with no growth in dividends and earnings is (generally) not making *new* investments. Thus, all earnings are paid out as dividends. The payout ratio k equals 1, and the valuation model becomes

$$P_0 = \frac{E_0}{r}$$

[10]Penman labels this paradox the dividend conundrum.

[11]Miller and Modigliani's proposition. We ignore the potentially signaling aspect of dividends. (See footnote 20.)

[12]See Appendix 19-A for a discussion of such firms.

EXHIBIT 19-1
No-Growth Model

Income Statement

	All Years
Operating revenue	$ 350
Operating expense	(150)
	$ 200
Depreciation expense	(50)
Operating income before tax	$ 150
Tax @ 20%	(30)
Net operating income	**$ 120**
Interest expense (net of taxes)	(20)
Net income	**$ 100**

The Definition of Earnings and the Valuation Objective

Earnings-based models can be used to value either:

1. The equity of the firm (P), or
2. The firm as a whole (V), debt plus equity

The definition of earnings used depends on the valuation objective. To measure the value of the firm (V), earnings are defined *prior* to payment of interest, as net operating income. To value equity, earnings are measured *after* payment of interest, net income.[13] *The definition of such other parameters as the rate of return also differs for each case.*

No-Growth Model

For the no-growth case and a simplified income statement (Exhibit 19-1), the appropriate definitions for each case are:

Value	= Earnings	/ Rate of Return
Equity P =	Net income	/ Rate of return on equity [e.g., $r = r_f + \beta(r_m - r_f)$]
Firm V =	Net operating income	/ Rate of return on debt and equity (weighted-average cost of capital)

(1) Equity Valuation. When the valuation objective is the firm's equity, earnings are defined as net income, the amount available for distribution to equity shareholders. Similarly, the required rate of return is the *equity rate of return*. This rate of return is similar to that used for the dividend-based model and its estimation is discussed in

[13]This discussion assumes that there is no preferred stock. When preferred stock exists, a third possibility exists, the valuation of total (common and preferred) equity.

459

Chapter 18. By estimating the firm's beta,[14] the risk-free rate, and the (excess) market return, the CAPM can be used[15] to estimate r. If we assume r is 10%, the value of equity is

$$P = \frac{E}{r} = \frac{\$100}{0.10} = \$1,000$$

(2) Value of the Firm. Net operating income (before deducting interest), that is, the cash available to all providers of capital, is the appropriate measure of earnings when valuing the firm as a whole. Similarly, the rate of return is a weighted average of the required rates of return of all providers of capital: the weighted-average cost of capital (WACC). The weighting is based on the relative proportions of debt and equity.

In our example, if we assume that the firm has a debt-to-capital ratio of 20% (four-fifths equity and one-fifth debt) and further that the (after-tax) cost of debt is 8%, then the weighted-average cost of capital is

$$\textbf{WACC} = (0.8 \times 0.10) + (0.2 \times 0.08) = 0.096$$

and the value of the firm as a whole is

$$V = \frac{\textbf{Net Operating Income}}{\textbf{WACC}} = \frac{\$120}{0.096} = \$1,250$$

The value of the firm equals the value of its debt plus the value of its equity. The equity value P can be derived from the firm value V by deducting the value of debt. As we have assumed an (after-tax) cost of debt (interest rate) of 8% and the (after-tax) interest expense is $20, then the value of its debt must equal $250 ($20/8%). Thus, the equity value is $1,250 − $250 = $1,000, identical to the value for equity derived directly.[16]

Growth Model

For a growing firm, the relationships between earnings and the amounts flowing to the equity- and debtholders are somewhat more complex. We begin again with the valuation of equity followed by the valuation of the firm.

(1) Equity Valuation and Earnings. The firm's net income is assumed to be used either for (1) payment of dividends or (2) investment in new assets.

With k equal to the payout ratio, then $(1 - k)$ is the fraction of earnings reinvested in new assets. Exhibit 19-2A illustrates the allocation of net income between new investment and dividends given an assumed dividend payout ratio of 80%. If these

---

[14] In Chapter 18, we discuss alternative estimation procedures for beta.

[15] Additional adjustments may also be appropriate to control for such other risk factors as size.

[16] It should be noted that $1,000 equity and $250 debt are consistent with the debt-to-capital ratio of 20% based on the market values of the debt and equity.

EXHIBIT 19-2
Growth Model

A. *Derivation of Amount Available for Equityholders*
for Valuation of Equity

	Year 0
Operating revenue	$ 350
Operating expense	(150)
	$ 200
Depreciation expense	(50)
Operating income before tax	$ 150
Tax @ 20%	(30)
Net operating income	**$ 120**
Interest expense (net of taxes)	(20)
Net income	**$ 100**
New investment (equity)	(20)
Available for equityholders (dividends)	**$ 80**

B. *Derivation of Amount Available for Debt- and*
Equityholders for Valuation of Firm

	Year 0
Operating revenue	$ 350
Operating expense	(150)
	$ 200
Depreciation expense	(50)
Operating income before tax	$ 150
Tax @ 20%	(30)
Net operating income	**$ 120**
New investment	(30)
Available for debt- and equityholders	**$ 90**

Financing Distribution (Cash for Financing)

Dividends	$ 80
Interest expense (net of taxes)	20
New debt	(10)
	$ 90

new assets earn a rate of return $r^* = 20\%$, then the pattern of net income and its distribution between dividends and reinvestment, for $k = 0.80$, is:

Period	Earnings	= Dividend	+ New Investments
0	$E_0 = \$100$	$= 0.8E_0 = \$80$	$+ 0.2E_0 = \$20$
1	$E_1 = \$100 + (r^* \times \$20) = \$104$	$= 0.8E_1 = \$83.2$	$+ 0.2E_1 = \$20.8$
2	$E_2 = \$104 + (r^* \times \$20.8) = \$108.16$	$= 0.8E_2 = \$86.53$	$+ 0.2E_2 = \$21.63$

461

The firm's earnings, dividends, and investments all grow at a rate of 4%. As the next table indicates, this growth rate is the product of the fraction reinvested $(1 - k)$ times the rate of return the firm can earn on the reinvestment (r^*):

Period	Earnings	= Dividend	+ New Investments
0	E_0	$= kE_0$	$+ (1 - k) E_0$
1	$E_1 = E_0 + r^*(1 - k) E_0$ $= E_0[1 + r^*(1 - k)]$	$= kE_1$ $= kE_0[1 + r^*(1 - k)]$	$+ (1 - k) E_1$ $+ (1 - k) E_0[1 + r^*(1 - k)]$
2	$E_2 = E_1[1 + r^*(1 - k)]$ $= E_0[1 + r(1 - k)]^2$	$= kE_2$ $= kE_0[1 + r^*(1 - k)]^2$	$+ (1 - k) E_2$ $+ (1 - k) E_0[1 + r^*(1 - k)]^2$

Note that earnings, dividends, and new investment each grow at the rate $[r^*(1 - k)]$. The firm's growth rate g thus equals

$$g = r^*(1 - k) = 0.2 \times (1 - 0.8) = 0.04$$

This result is intuitively appealing: A firm's growth rate depends on the level of investment and the return on that investment. Thus, a no-growth company is one with no new investment: $k = 1$.

Using the growth formula to find the value of the firm's equity yields

$$P_0 = \frac{kE_0(1 + g)}{r - g} = \frac{kE_1}{r - r^*(1 - k)}$$

$$= \frac{0.8(\$104)}{0.10 - 0.04} = \$1,387$$

(2) Value of the Firm. We continue with our previous example. In the no-growth case, equity value was related to the earnings available to the equity shareholder, net income. To value the firm (total capital), we used the earnings available to the debt holders and shareholders, net operating income.

In the growth model, to value equity, net income is replaced by the amount available to the equity shareholder after new investment of equity (net income − reinvestment of equity). Similarly, to value the firm as a whole, we must determine the earnings available to all providers of capital: the debt- and equityholders. This amount equals net operating income minus *total* new investment. Total new investment is provided by both equity- and debtholders. Given the growth rate of 4% implied by the equity investment of $20, debt[17] must be increased[18] by $10 (4% of $250), making the total new investment equal to $30.

The two approaches are contrasted in Exhibit 19-2. We must carefully distinguish between total new investments and the reinvestment of equity referred to previously. The first is the actual investment in new assets made by the firm ($30, in the example).

[17]The debt-to-capital ratio of 20% developed for the no-growth case can no longer be maintained. That ratio was based on relative market values. Growth opportunities, however, are "captured" by equity shareholders, thereby altering the relative proportions of debt and equity. The new debt-to-capital ratio is 15.8% [$260/($1,387 + $260)], based on equity of $1,387 and debt of $260. This ratio will now be maintained as both the market value of debt and equity grow at a rate of 4%.

[18]The $10 of new debt is consistent with an assumed 4% growth in net income. For interest expense to increase by 4%, debt must increase by 4% from $250 to $260.

Financing for this investment is provided by debt ($10) and equity ($20). For equity valuation, reinvestment refers only to that amount (i.e., $20) provided by equityholders (net income − dividends).

With new debt of $10, total debt is now $260. The market value of equity, we have shown, is $1,387. Therefore, the firm's WACC equals 9.7%.[19]

Exhibit 19-2 provides year 0 data. All year 1 values are 4% higher. The value of the firm using this approach therefore equals

$$\frac{\textbf{(Operating Income − Total New Investment) (1 + g)}}{\textbf{WACC − g}} = \frac{(\$120 − \$30)(1.04)}{(0.097 − 0.04)}$$

$$= \frac{93.6}{0.057} = \$1,647$$

The $1,647 value of the firm is the sum of the value of the equity ($1,387) plus the value of the debt ($260).

Estimating Growth

The firm's growth rate can be estimated in one of two ways:

1. Estimating the individual components, k and r^*, that contribute to growth as $g = (1 − k)r^*$

2. Extrapolating the historical growth rate to the future

Defining and Estimating r*: *Return on New (Equity) Investment.* The terms r^* and r both represent rates of return for the equity investor. The former represents the actual return, whereas the latter refers to the required rate of return. *Growth opportunities exist only when expected returns* r^* *exceed the required rate of return* r *(i.e., $r^* > r$).* When $r^* = r$, then the growth model reduces to the no-growth case:

$$P = \frac{kE}{[r − r^*(1 − k)]}$$

$$= \frac{kE}{[r − r^* + r^*k]}$$

But $r = r^*$:

$$P = \frac{kE}{(r − r + rk)}$$

$$= \frac{E}{r}$$

[19]With debt of $260 and equity of $1,387, and the (after-tax) cost of debt and equity equal to 8% and 10%, respectively:

$$\textbf{WACC} = \frac{\$1,387}{\$1,387 + \$260} \times 10\% + \frac{\$260}{\$1,387 + \$260} \times 8\% = 9.7\%$$

463

This result does not imply that firms cannot make new investments and grow even when $r^* = r$. It does show that it does not make any difference whether or not the firm decides to grow. The value of the firm's equity is not affected whether the firm reinvests its net income or pays dividends. Recall our earlier example for the no-growth model in which we found the value of the equity equal to $100/0.10 = $1,000. That example assumed all income is paid out as dividends. The following table indicates the effect of alternative dividend payout ratios, beginning in period 1, when the remainder is reinvested at the rate $r^* = r = 0.10$:

Payout Ratio k	Reinvested Income $(1 - k) E_1$	Growth Rate $g = (1 - k) r$	Share Value $P_0 = kE_1/(r - g)$
0.75	25	$0.025 = (1 - 0.75) \times 0.1$	$1,000 = 75/(0.1 - 0.025)$
0.50	50	$0.050 = (1 - 0.50) \times 0.1$	$1,000 = 50/(0.1 - 0.050)$
0.25	75	$0.075 = (1 - 0.25) \times 0.1$	$1,000 = 25/(0.1 - 0.075)$

Shareholder's wealth is not affected by the firm's dividend policy.[20]

As r^* measures the actual return earned on (reinvested) equity, it is conceptually equivalent to the familiar ROE measure. Using ROE to measure r^* is reasonable if (along with the other assumptions of our simplified world) the firm's new investment opportunities are similar to past ones.

Estimating k: *The Dividend Payout Ratio.* The current dividend payout ratio is often used to estimate k. This gives us an estimate of the firm's earnings growth rate (often called the sustainable or implicit growth rate) in terms of the same ratios previously used to estimate growth in book value:

$$g = (1 - k) \times r^* = (1 - \textbf{Dividend Payout}) \times \textbf{ROE}$$

Using the dividend payout ratio and ROE to estimate future growth rates assumes constant levels for these parameters that can limit the usefulness of this technique. For stable growth companies, k and ROE are relatively constant. For cyclical companies, they are not. Exhibit 19-3 shows growth rate estimates for duPont derived from 1990 to 1994 data.

Given the volatility of these estimates, it is hard to use them with any confidence. Whenever dividends exceed EPS, the projected growth rate is negative. It should also be noted that it is theoretically incorrect to use the dividend payout ratio to estimate k. In the development of these models, no distinction is made among dividends paid

---

[20]We do not intend to review all the literature on dividend policy. Modigliani and Miller, in their famous proposition, note that, given a level of investment (growth opportunities), dividends are irrelevant as they are readily replaced by external financing. We address this issue in the next section by pointing out that dividend payout must be considered net of the raising of additional capital.

The issue of a firm's dividend policy remains controversial in the finance literature. There are those who argue that dividend policy is relevant because investors prefer the security of dividends; others view dividend policy in a "signaling" framework whereby management conveys its intentions and/or forecasts by its level of dividends. These issues are beyond the scope of our discussion. The foregoing argues only that in the context of this model, *ceteris paribus,* dividend policy is irrelevant.

EXHIBIT 19-3. DUPONT
Sustainable Growth Rate Estimates

Year	k	ROE	Growth Rate $(1 - k) \times$ ROE
1990	0.48	0.143	0.074
1991	0.81	0.083	0.016
1992	1.22	0.081	(0.018)
1993	2.22	0.048	(0.059)
1994	0.46	0.227	0.123

Note: Calculations are based on income before extraordinary charges and effects of changes in accounting policy.

out, stock repurchases, and issuance of new equity. That is,

$$kE = \text{Dividends} + \text{Share Repurchases} - \text{New Equity Issued}$$

should reflect net cash flows to and from equity shareholders; not just dividends.

Dividend payout measures only one portion of the total flow; it ignores new issues and repurchases and can distort the valuation model. A firm's choice of the form (the mix of dividends and the sale or repurchase of shares) of equity financing should not affect valuation. Thus, the more appropriate definition of k is

$$k = \frac{\text{Dividends} + \text{Share Repurchases} - \text{New Equity Issued}}{\text{Earnings}}$$

The potential instability of the individual growth rate components suggests that historical growth trends should not be used blindly to make growth projections. In a similar fashion, dividend policy affects the observed earnings trend.

Dividend Policy and EPS Growth. As stock values are expressed as price per share, many models that estimate earnings trends use earnings per share (EPS). The EPS growth rate can be distorted by a number of factors, not all of them value-related.

Dividend policy has an important impact on earnings growth. A firm with a low payout ratio grows faster than if it paid out most of its earnings, since reinvested earnings generate future earnings. This effect of dividend policy is meaningful. However, by choosing the mode of equity financing, that is, trading off dividends and the sale and repurchase of equity securities, the growth rate in EPS can be distorted. In Chapter 4 we discussed the adjustment of earnings per share for the effect of dividend policy. Exhibit 19-4 applies that methodology to duPont.

The adjustments shown for duPont are not very large for 1994. However, if the analysis is extended over a number of years, the effect is much greater. Dividend policy, by modifying the firm's need for external financing, ultimately affects the number of shares outstanding and, as a result, reported earnings per share. Firms with low dividend payouts should report faster EPS growth than firms with high payout policies.

465

EXHIBIT 19-4. DUPONT
Effect of Dividend Policy on Earnings per Share Growth

To show the effect of dividend policy on EPS growth, initially assume that duPont pays out earnings as dividends and sells new common shares equal to the increase in retained earnings. For 1994:

Net income	$ 2,727 million
Dividends	(1,237)
Increase in retained earnings	$ 1,490 million

If duPont distributed all its earnings as dividends, it would need to recover $1,490 million by selling new common shares. Using the 1994 mean price of $56 per share, duPont would have sold 26.6 million shares ($1,490/$56), increasing the number of shares outstanding by 4% and reducing EPS by 4%.

This analysis can be used in another way. If duPont paid no dividends in 1994, it would have had an additional $1,237 million of equity. If shares were repurchased (using the same price of $56), duPont would have repurchased 22 million shares ($1,237/$56), reducing the number of shares outstanding by 3% and increasing future EPS.

Alternative and Finite Growth Assumptions

We have demonstrated that the benefits from growth depend on the availability of investment opportunities earning a high rate of return, specifically, $r^* > r$. The valuation formula

$$P_0 = \frac{kE_0(1 + g)}{r - g} = \frac{kE_1}{r - g} \tag{10}$$

can be disaggregated into two components:

$$P_i = \frac{E_{i+1}}{r} + \frac{(1 - k) E_{i+1}}{r} \left[\frac{r^* - r}{r - (1 - k) r^*} \right]$$

The first component is the value of the firm in the absence of growth, the second component is the value of the firm's growth opportunities. Although the models assume infinite growth opportunities, high-return investment opportunities ($r^* > r$) do not exist forever in the real world. Appendix 19-A presents variations of (some of) these models using alternative growth assumptions.

Additionally, as discussed earlier, valuation models may use the following relationship:

$$P_0 = \frac{kE_1}{(1 + r)} + \frac{kE_2}{(1 + r)^2} \cdots \frac{kE_n}{(1 + r)^n} + \frac{P_n}{(1 + r)^n} \tag{11}$$

Explicit short-term horizon forecasts of earnings ($E_1, \ldots, E_n$) for a three-to-five-year period are made and then a terminal value (P_n) at the end of the period is estimated. This terminal value often incorporates the more general growth assumptions discussed. This valuation technique is especially useful under the more realistic assumption of growth opportunities with a finite horizon. We return to this issue later in the chapter.

Earnings Valuation and the Price/Earnings Ratio

The price/earnings (P/E) ratio is often used to compare firm valuations. This ratio is the multiple of earnings used by the market to value the firm. Its relationship to our valuation models is straightforward.

For the no-growth case,

$$P = \frac{E}{r}$$

becomes

$$\frac{P}{E} = \frac{1}{r} \tag{12}$$

The P/E ratio in this case equals the inverse of the firm's capitalization rate. For the growth case,

$$P_i = \frac{kE_i(1+g)}{r-g}$$

becomes

$$\frac{P_i}{E_i} = \frac{k(1+g)}{r-g} \tag{13}$$

Price/Earnings cum Dividend. Dividend irrelevancy implies that dividends and price are equivalent, dollar for dollar. Thus, from a pure theoretical perspective, P/E should be expressed as the ratio of *price plus dividends* to earnings. In practice, as dividends are small relative to price, modification does not affect the calculation materially. For discussion, however, we include this modification when necessary to show the development of these models.

Adding k to both sides of Eqs. (11) and (12) yields the *price/earnings cum dividend ratio.* For the no-growth case [Eq. (12)],

$$\frac{P}{E} + k = \frac{1}{r} + k$$

Since in the no-growth case, $k = 1$ and $D = E$:

$$\frac{P+D}{E} = \frac{1+r}{r} \tag{14}$$

In the growth case [Eq. (13)],

$$\frac{P_i}{E_i} + k = \frac{k(1+g)}{r-g} + k$$

$$\frac{P_i + D_i}{E_i} = \frac{k(1+r)}{r-g} \tag{15}$$

467

Earlier, we showed that, when a firm does not possess extraordinary growth opportunities (i.e., $r^* = r$), although it can still grow by reinvesting dividends, growth does not affect valuation. This can be illustrated with the price/earnings cum dividend ratio. When $r^* = r$, then $g = (1 - k) r$ and Eq. (15) reduces to

$$\frac{P_i + D_i}{E_i} = \frac{1 + r}{r} \tag{16}$$

which is identical to the no-growth relationship. *Thus, in the absence of (extraordinary) growth opportunities, $(1 + r)/r$ is the normal price/earnings relationship.*

Growth, Risk, and Valuation

The preceding discussions imply that the relationship between price and earnings is a function of the firm's growth rate and risk (as captured by r). Beaver and Morse (1978) compared the price/earnings ratios of a sample of firms to see whether growth and/or risk could explain differentials among firms. For 25 portfolios of firms ranked by P/E ratios, they compared the average portfolio P/E ratios over 15 years. Parts A and B of Exhibit 19-5 show P/E ratios and average earnings growth rates for different portfolios. Extreme P/E ratios revert to the mean over the period. Note the trend in the ratio of portfolio 1's P/E to that of portfolio 25.

Initially, at least, some of the differences in P/E ratios are due to the earnings growth rate. Portfolios with high P/E ratios have higher earnings growth in the first

EXHIBIT 19-5
Results of Beaver and Morse: P/E Ratio Patterns

A. Price/Earnings Ratio of Portfolio

Portfolio	Number of Years After Portfolio Formation						
	0	1	2	3	5	10	14
1	50.0	22.7	16.4	13.8	13.2	13.0	8.3
5	20.8	17.5	16.9	15.9	13.7	11.9	8.4
10	14.3	11.9	11.5	10.3	10.1	9.9	8.3
15	11.1	10.8	10.4	10.0	10.0	8.6	7.1
20	8.9	9.1	9.6	9.4	9.3	9.0	7.7
25	5.8	6.9	8.0	7.9	7.9	7.8	8.9
$\frac{\text{Portfolio 1}}{\text{Portfolio 25}}$	8.6	3.3	2.1	1.7	1.7	1.7	0.9

B. Cumulative Earnings Growth (%)

1	−4.1	9.53	37.2	28.2	18.9	15.3	11.8
5	10.7	14.9	12.1	13.1	10.9	8.0	18.1
10	9.6	12.9	11.5	12.3	9.2	12.9	29.6
15	10.0	8.8	8.5	8.1	14.3	11.0	33.4
20	10.8	5.2	9.3	12.6	6.0	11.1	18.0
25	26.4	−3.3	7.5	10.8	12.9	16.7	10.1

Source: William Beaver and Dale Morse, "What Determines Price-Earnings Ratios?," *Financial Analysts Journal*, July–August 1978, pp. 65–76. Adapted from Table 3 (p. 68) and Table 5 (p. 70).

few years. However, persistent differences in P/E ratios could not be explained by growth rate differentials (e.g., see year 10).

> Comparing the P/E analysis with the growth analysis, we conclude that some of the initial dissipation of the P/E ratio in the first three years after formation can be explained by differential growth in earnings. Beyond that, however, there clearly exists a P/E differential that cannot be explained by differential earnings growth.[21]

In addition to being unable to explain the long-run differentials using growth rates, Beaver and Morse could not explain variations in P/E ratios by differences in risk. They hypothesized that the long-run differential in P/E ratios was probably due to the effects of different accounting policies.[22]

Zarowin (1990) reexamined Beaver and Morse's findings and came to a different conclusion. Using a database in which earnings had been "normalized" in an effort to remove the effect of accounting differences,[23] Zarowin found[24] that the P/E ratio differences could not be explained (solely) by differing accounting policies. Even with normalized earnings, persistent differences remained among firms' P/E ratios.

To explain these differences, Zarowin used forecasted growth as a growth proxy. This contrasts with Beaver and Morse who used (*ex post*) actual growth. For *ex ante* valuation purposes, forecasted growth is more appropriate. As the model predicted, the differences in P/E ratios were attributable to differences in expected growth. Zarowin argued that Beaver and Morse's nonfindings resulted from using actual growth rather than expected growth rates.

Effects of Permanent and Transitory Earnings and Measurement Error

Beaver and Morse's findings with respect to short-term growth rates provide valuable insight into differential P/E ratios: the filtering of transitory earnings components by the market. In Exhibit 19-5, the high (low) P/E portfolios had low (high) earnings changes in the years that the portfolios were formed. Portfolio 1's earnings change in year 0 was −4%, whereas portfolio 25's exceeded 25%. The following year (year 1), the high- (low-) growth experienced was the opposite of the previous year. These observations indicate that reported earnings when the initial P/E portfolios were formed were abnormally low (high) for the high (low) P/E categories. The following year, earnings returned to their normal level. The market ignored the transitory component of earnings; it multiplied normal earnings by a constant. As a result, firms whose earnings were unusually low (high) appeared to have abnormally high (low) P/E ratios.

On a more general level, academic research has used the earnings response coefficient (ERC) to capture the relationship between prices and earnings. The ERC measures the price change that results from an earnings change. If the relationship between prices and earnings is exactly as the simple models suggest, then the ERC should

[21]William H. Beaver and Dale Morse, "What Determines Price-Earnings Ratios?," *Financial Analysts Journal*, July–August 1978, pp. 65–76.

[22]They did not test this hypothesis.

[23]The database used was from Cragg and Malkiel (1982).

[24]In his actual testing procedure, Zarowin used the earnings-to-price (E/P) ratio as the relationship between this ratio and risk and growth is hypothesized to be linear.

equal (or approximate) the P/E ratio. Although Collins and Kothari (1989) show that risk and growth explain some of the cross-sectional differences in ERCs, the ERCs generated are typically much lower than expected.

Explanations for these differences include the points we raised earlier. Collins and Kothari note that "persistence" (the extent to which earnings changes carry into the future) also affects the ERCs. That is, prices will not react as much to changes in earnings caused by transitory components. More specifically (as Box 19-1 indicates), transitory earnings components increase value on a dollar-for-dollar basis,[25] whereas permanent changes increase value by a multiplier (the P/E ratio).

This is consistent with Kormendi and Lipe's (1987) finding that higher persistence increases the ERC. Ryan and Zarowin (1995) demonstrate that measurement error also contributes to low ERCs.[26] The relationship between earnings and price (as Box 19-1 shows) is distorted by both transitory noise and measurement problems resulting from accounting choices. Thus, it is important, when using an earnings-based valuation model, to normalize earnings for nonrecurring items as well as to evaluate the impact of accounting choices, that is, the quality of earnings. Such an analysis and normalization of earnings for duPont are shown in Chapter 17.

Earnings or Cash Flows?

The concept of earnings used in these valuation models is closer to cash flow than GAAP net income. In the theoretical development of these models, earnings are generally defined as cash flow after the replacement of depreciated assets. Net income, as defined by GAAP, is not the appropriate input for these models. Only in a simplified world under stringent assumptions does net (operating) income under GAAP meet the foregoing definition of earnings.

The first assumption required is the equality of funds flow and cash flow. This holds only when working capital levels are kept (relatively) constant over time.[27] Generally, however, this assumption does not hold. Moreover, differences between cash flows and income are not due solely to working capital changes. The second required assumption is that depreciation expense approximates the replacement cost of depreciated assets. This also is generally true only by coincidence. Furthermore, the choice of accounting methods affects the calculation of income. Thus, as soon as we move away from a simplified world, the use of accounting income becomes problematic.

Using reported cash from operations (CFO) rather than income may solve some of the problems inherent in the first assumption. However, as has been shown throughout the book, reported CFO, cash for investments, and cash from financing are also affected by accounting choice. In addition, CFO does not provide for the replacement of depreciated assets. Finally, the classification of capital expenditures between investments made to maintain capacity and those made for growth is not directly available in most cases. Thus, the use of CFO in valuation models is also fraught with difficulties.

---

[25] An example of a transitory component is a holding gain such as an increase in the value of the firm's inventory. If such increases are not expected to be repeated in the future, then the effect on value should be dollar for dollar: A dollar increase in inventory value would result in a dollar increase in firm value.

[26] In the literature, the measurement error is referred to as the valuation-irrelevant component. See Ramakrishnan and Thomas (1991).

[27] Under this assumption, cash from operations and funds (working capital) from operations converge.

BOX 19-1
The Effects of Transitory Components and Measurement Error on Valuation

Permanent Versus Transitory Earnings and Valuation

The effects of the permanent/transitory dichotomy on the P/E ratio are described below. The P/E ratio, as we have shown, is consistent with some simplified valuation models. Use of the P/E ratio is meant to be illustrative of the general class of models discussed. The effects are more readily shown on the P/E ratio due to its simplicity.

A firm's permanent earnings are defined as the portion of the earnings stream that is to be carried into the future. For example, if we assume a constant dividend model where a firm pays out all earnings as dividends, the firm's expected earnings (dividends) are $5 per share, and $r = 10\%$, the value of the firm would be $5/0.1 = $50. The P/E ratio would be 10.

At the beginning of period 1, suppose it is known that due to some windfall the firm will actually earn $6.10 but after that the EPS will revert to $5. The value of the firm will be equal to $51 derived as

$$P_0 = \frac{E_1}{1.1} + \frac{P_1}{1.1} = \frac{\$6.10}{1.1} + \frac{\$50}{1.1} = \$51$$

The extra $1.10 earned in period 1 was not capitalized (i.e., the value of the firm did not go to $6.10/0.1 = $61). Only the permanent portion of $5.00 was capitalized. The one-shot or transitory portion of earnings entered into valuation only as a one-period adjustment (adding $\frac{\$1.10}{1.1} = \$1$ to value) without any carryover effects. The observed P/E ratio for this firm will be $51/$6.10 = 8.4 even though the firm's "true" capitalization rate is 10.

Would this low P/E ratio indicate that the firm is a buy?* It should not. The potential distortion in P/E ratios can be even greater if we consider measurement error inherent in accounting earnings.

Measurement Error and Its Effects on Valuation

Let E_a represent accounting earnings and E_e economic earnings. We will define the difference between them as measurement noise, $M = E_e - E_a$. Further, assume that economic earnings has a permanent and transitory component, that is,

$$E_e = E_{ep} + E_{et}$$

The true relationship between price and earnings will be $P = E_{ep}/r$, with an underlying "unobservable" P/E ratio of $1/r$. The market will fully capitalize only the permanent E_{ep}. Empirically, however, one observes P/E_a, which is equivalent to $P/(E_{ep} + E_{et} + M)$. This observable P/E ratio may be larger or smaller than the "true" P/E_{ep} capitalization rate, depending on the magnitudes and directions of the transitory component (E_{et}) and measurement error (M).

---

*In Chapter 5, we noted that one of the reported anomalies of efficient markets is the abnormal returns that seem to accrue to firms with low P/E ratios.

Free Cash Flow Approach to Valuation

The free cash flow (FCF) approach has been suggested by some as a potential solution to the problems just discussed. Free cash flow, *when the valuation objective is the firm,* is defined as the cash available to debt- and equityholders after investment.

Just as the dividend model is essentially equivalent to the earnings model, the FCF model that follows is equivalent to the earnings-based model of Exhibit 19-2B, where the valuation objective is the value of the firm. To illustrate the free cash flow approach, we return to that example. Free cash flow in that example is equal to $90, derived as follows:

Net operating income	$120
Total new investment	(30)
Free cash flow	$ 90

The problem with this definition in the general case is that, as previously noted, the breakdown between *new* and *replacement* investment is rarely provided. Only the total cash for investment is given in the statement of cash flows. Upon reflection, however, total investment is really the amount we want. There is no need to use depreciation expense, or any other surrogate for that matter, to estimate the cost of replacing depreciated assets. Our objective, in general, is the following calculation of free cash flow:

	Net operating income before replacement of depreciated assets
−	Replacement of depreciated assets
−	New investment
=	Free cash flow

This is equivalent to:

	Adjusted CFO (net operating income plus adjustments)
−	Cash for investment (new + replacement)
=	Free cash flow

Note that adjusted CFO is not the same CFO reported in the statement of cash flows. They differ with respect to the treatment of interest payments: CFO is reduced by interest payments as required by SFAS 95, whereas the adjusted measure is preinterest.

Exhibit 19-6 compares an SFAS 95 Statement of Cash Flows for our hypothetical company (column A) with free cash flow in the form used in this section (column B). The difference between them is the treatment of interest and the related income tax reduction. In column A, cash from operations is reduced by interest paid and income taxes include the related tax effect. In column B, interest paid and the associated tax deduction ($5 = 20% of $25) have been removed, increasing CFO by $20 ($25 − $5). After-tax interest paid is included in cash from financing.

Note that we have assumed no change in cash during the period. If a change had taken place, column B would include the change in cash from operations. By doing so, we explicitly assume that cash is an element of working capital, as is accounts receivable.

Column B calculates free cash flow, which, by definition, equals adjusted cash

EXHIBIT 19-6
Comparison of Statement of Cash Flows and Free Cash Flow

	A	B
	Cash Flow Statement (SFAS 95)	Free Cash Flow For Firm Valuation
Cash from customers	$ 350	$ 350
Cash for operating expenses	(150)	(150)
Cash for interest (pretax)	(25)	NA
Cash for taxes	(25)	(30)
Cash from operations	**$ 150**	**$ 170**
Cash for investment*	**(80)**	**(80)**
Free cash flow		**$ 90**
Interest (net of tax)	NA	(20)
Dividends	(80)	(80)
New debt	10	10
Cash for financing	**(70)**	**(90)**
Net change in cash	$ 0	$ 0

NA = not applicable.

*Cash from investment is equal to the $30 of total new investment plus the $50 of depreciation that in this simplified example is assumed to be equivalent to the replacement cost of depreciated assets.

from financing (CFF). This definition of CFF differs from CFF under SFAS 95 as it includes (after-tax) interest paid.

The free cash flow approach yields an estimated value for the firm. The appropriate discount rate is WACC. To derive the value of equity, subtract the value of debt from the firm value.

The advantage of the FCF approach is that many (but not all) of the issues relating to differences in accounting policies and of income versus cash flows disappear. Whether or not the accounting method defines something as CFO or cash from investment (e.g., capitalization versus expense issues) does not make any difference as the focus is on FCF (the net amount). Similarly, whether or not a cash flow is treated as principal or interest (see Chapter 10) also does not matter as all payments to creditors are excluded from free cash flow.

The remaining problems relate to whether or not to treat an item as operating/investment or financing. Some potential adjustments follow.

Adjustments to Reported Cash from Investment

- All leases should be capitalized and treated as a reduction in free cash flow at the time the lease is entered into even though no cash has yet changed hands.
- Capitalized interest expense should be removed from cash for investment and added to free cash flow.
- Assets acquired in exchange for debt or equity are presently not included in either cash from investment or financing. Such transactions are disclosed as "significant noncash investing and financing activities." The cost of the assets should be deducted from free cash flow.

473

The free cash flow approach, however, is not without problems. Valuation should not be affected by purely discretionary policies. The model assumes that any cash held within the firm is needed as operating working capital. But firms may decide to hold excess cash for other reasons.[28] Moreover, as shown, free cash flow is equal to financing cash flow. As Penman (1991) states:

> Thus the value increment under this accounting regime would represent (be manipulated by) stock and debt issues or repurchases, and, yes, dividends. This is venturing on the absurd. Free cash flow concerns *the distribution of wealth rather than the generation of wealth.*[29]

Dividends, Earnings, or Free Cash Flows?

All three DCF approaches rely on a measure of cash flows to the suppliers of capital (debt and equity) to the firm. They differ only in the choice of measurement, with the dividend approach measuring these cash flows directly and the others arriving at them in an indirect manner. The free cash flow approach arrives at the cash flow measure (if the firm is all-equity) by subtracting investment from operating cash flows, whereas the earnings approach expresses dividends indirectly as a fraction of earnings.

This begs the question: If the dividend approach can measure cash flows directly, why use a roundabout approach? The answer to this question brings us to the issues of uncertainty and forecasting.

Valuation depends on future CF, not current CF. The firm's future dividends depend on its future earnings. Thus, to forecast future dividends, it is first necessary to forecast future earnings. Similarly, the free cash flow model attempts to avoid the problem of estimating dividends from earnings, given the problems with earnings measurement. Nevertheless, free cash flow forecasts generally require[30] the analyst *to first forecast earnings and then adjust the forecasted earnings to generate free cash flow.* Additionally, in many applications of the free cash flow model, the following formulation is used:

$$V_0 = \sum_{i=1}^{n} \frac{\text{FCF}_i}{(1+r)^i} + \frac{V_n}{(1+r)^n} \tag{17}$$

As with earnings, free cash flows are forecast over a short horizon of n years (usually 5), and then a terminal value V_n is estimated. This terminal value, which can contribute over 60% of the total value, is often earnings-based.

Regardless of which valuation model is used, it relies on the ability to forecast future earnings. Analysts, as well as academics, often use accounting earnings for valuation purposes. The price/earnings ratio is the most widely used valuation measure and is calculated on the basis of accounting earnings. To a great extent, this is because reported earnings are readily available.

---

[28]See, for example, the discussion of financial slack in Box 12-2.

[29]Stephen H. Penman, "Return to Fundamentals," working paper, University of California at Berkeley, November 1991, pp. 29–30 (emphasis added).

[30]See, for example, Tom Copeland, Tim Koller, and Jack Murrin, *Valuation: Measuring and Managing the Value of Companies* (New York: John Wiley & Sons, 1990). They advocate the use of free cash flow for valuation, but arrive at that measure by first forecasting earnings.

Additionally, accounting earnings may yield better forecasts of future earning power or cash flows than historical cash flows. This should not come as a shock. After all, the underlying premise of accrual accounting is just that; recording a credit sale (but one example) provides useful information about future cash flows.

Another factor may make net income a better input for forecasting purposes than cash flows. Period-to-period changes in income and cash flows are random, with some portion transitory and the remainder permanent. For valuation, only permanent earnings are fully capitalized. If cash flow is more subject to random fluctuations due, for example, to the timing of payments, then income may produce better forecasts of permanent earnings than cash flows.

One final point must be reiterated before leaving this section. DCF models are all predicated on the dividend discount model. Finance theory, however, argues that dividends up to the terminal and liquidating dividend are irrelevant to valuation. Thus, applying these models requires growth assumptions to forecast past a finite horizon. As we cannot assume that dividends, earnings, and cash flows will converge (to zero or some steady state-value), the infinite horizon remains a problem. The next section introduces a valuation model that, although derivable from the dividend discount model, has a number of unique characteristics that warrant its own classification.

THE ABNORMAL EARNINGS OR EBO MODEL

The residual or abnormal earnings model, also referred to as the Edwards–Bell–Ohlson (EBO) model, is based on work by Ohlson (1991 and 1995) and Edwards and Bell (1961).[31] This model transforms the dividend discount model into a model based on book values and (abnormal) earnings and defines the value of equity as

$$P_0 = B_0 + \sum_{j=1}^{\infty} \frac{E_j - rB_{j-1}}{(1+r)^j} \qquad (18)$$

As $\text{ROE}_t = E_t/B_{t-1}$ the above is often expressed in its ROE form as

$$P_0 = B_0 + \sum_{j=1}^{\infty} \frac{(\text{ROE}_j - r)\, B_{j-1}}{(1+r)^j} \qquad (19)$$

The model is derived in Box 19-2. The link between book value, earnings, and dividends is based on the accounting identity

$$B_t = B_{t-1} + E_t - d_t$$

known as the *clean surplus relation*. Changes in book value are the result of income and dividends.[32]

---

[31]The origins of the residual income model can be traced to earlier work by Preinreich (1938), Edwards and Bell (1961), and Peasnell (1982). The model is also conceptually similar to the EVA model advocated by G. Bennett Stewart III, *The Quest for Value* (New York: Harper Business, 1991), Chapter 8. Stewart's EVA model is structured to value the firm; the model we discuss focuses on the value of equity. Feltham and Ohlson (1995) expand the EBO model to encompass the value of the firm.

[32]As in our previous discussion, dividends include share issues and repurchases.

BOX 19-2
Derivation of the EBO Model

Our derivation makes use of the following three relationships:

$$B_t = B_{t-1} + E_t - d_t \quad \text{or} \quad d_t = E_t - (B_t - B_{t-1}) \tag{1}$$

$$E_t = \text{ROE}_t B_{t-1} \tag{2}$$

$$\frac{B_t}{(1+r)} = B_t - \frac{rB_t}{(1+r)} \tag{3}$$

Relationships (1) and (2) are definitions: (1) is the clean surplus relationship and (2) defines income as ROE times opening book value. The dividend discount model is

$$P_0 = \sum_{j=1}^{\infty} \frac{d_j}{(1+r)^j}$$

Substituting the clean surplus relationship (1) yields

$$P_0 = \sum_{j=1}^{\infty} \frac{E_j - (B_j - B_{j-1})}{(1+r)^j}$$

For demonstration purposes, we expand the above expression for $j = 1$ and $j = 2$ and find that

$$P_0 = \frac{E_1 - (B_1 - B_0)}{(1+r)} + \frac{E_2 - (B_2 - B_0)}{(1+r)^2} + \sum_{j=3}^{\infty} \frac{E_j - (B_j - B_{j-1})}{(1+r)^j}$$

Using (3) yields

$$P_0 = \left[\frac{E_1}{(1+r)} - \frac{B_1}{(1+r)} + B_0 - \frac{rB_0}{(1+r)} \right] + \left[\frac{E_2}{(1+r)^2} - \frac{B_2}{(1+r)^2} + \frac{B_1}{(1+r)} - \frac{rB_1}{(1+r)^2} \right]$$
$$+ \sum_{j=3}^{\infty} \frac{E_j - (B_j - B_{j-1})}{(1+r)^j}$$

and

$$P_0 = B_0 + \left[\frac{E_1 - rB_0}{(1+r)} \right] + \left[\frac{E_2 - rB_1}{(1+r)^2} \right] - \frac{B_2}{(1+r)^2} + \sum_{j=3}^{\infty} \frac{E_j - (B_j - B_{j-1})}{(1+r)^j}$$

By similarly expanding the summation from $j = 3$ to ∞, we arrive at

$$P_0 = B_0 + \sum_{j=1}^{\infty} \frac{E_j - rB_{j-1}}{(1+r)^j}$$

Now from (2), since earnings in any period $E_t = \text{ROE}_t B_{t-1}$,

$$P_0 = B_0 + \sum_{j=1}^{\infty} \frac{(\text{ROE}_j - r) B_{j-1}}{(1+r)^j}$$

Thus, we have defined the value of the firm in terms of opening book value (B_0), ROE, and abnormal earnings [$(\text{ROE}_j - r) B_{j-1}$].

If we define rB_{t-1} as the required rate of return earned on the firm's (opening) book value in period t, residual or abnormal earnings can be defined as

$$E_t^a = E_t - rB_{t-1}$$

and we can express the valuation formulation as

$$P_0 = B_0 + \sum_{j=1}^{\infty} \frac{E_j^a}{(1+r)^j} \qquad (20)$$

The intuition behind the model is perhaps better understood if we consider a firm that only earns the required rate of return r (ROE $= r$) on its book value. Such a firm's shares will sell at a price equal to book value. If it earns more (less) than the required rate of return, the premium (discount) to book value is the present value of those abnormal earnings.[33]

The EBO valuation model can be applied to the example of Exhibits 19-1 and 19-2. Prior to the introduction of "growth," the firm earns a 10% return on its equity investment of $1,000. Using that as our starting point, we set the initial book value (B_{-1}) at the *beginning of period zero* at $1,000. During period zero, the firm's net income is $100 (see Exhibit 19-1). Because it now has growth opportunities, it pays a dividend of $80, leaving book value at the end of period 0; $B_0 = \$1,020$. Recall that net income grows at 4%.

Period i	Book Value Beginning B_{i-1}	Net Income E_i	Abnormal Earnings $E_i^a = E_i - (r \times B_{i-1})$	Dividend kE_i	Book Value End $B_i = B_{i-1} + (1-k) E_i$
0	$1,000	$100	0	$80	$1,020
1	1,020	104	$104 - (0.1)(1,020) = 2$	83.2	1,040.8
2	1,040.8	108.16	$108.16 - (0.1)(1,040.8) = 4.08$	86.528	1,062.432
3	1,062.432	112.4864	6.2432	. . .	. . .

Therefore, inserting the above into the EBO valuation (20), we obtain

$$P_0 = B_0 + \sum_{i=1}^{\infty} \frac{E_i^a}{(1+r)^i}$$

$$P_0 = 1,020 + \left[\frac{2}{(1.1)^1} + \frac{4.08}{(1.1)^2} + \frac{6.2432}{(1.1)^3} \cdots \right]$$

The series in the right bracket converges to $367, yielding, as before, the value of equity:

$$P_0 = 1,020 + 367 = \$1,387$$

---

[33]This is, of course, equivalent to our earlier formulation [Eq. (4)] for economic goodwill, albeit in a more rigorous fashion.

EBO Versus DCF Models

As the EBO model is essentially a variation of the DCF model, its result is identical. What then are its advantages? We consider both pragmatic and conceptual answers to this question.

Finite Horizons

In a nondeterministic world, where the future is unknown, valuation depends on forecasts of future dividends, earnings, or cash flows. As discussed earlier, it is not possible to make reliable forecasts to infinity. In practice, therefore, analysts make explicit forecasts for a few (usually five) years and then estimate a terminal value, based on simplifying assumptions, to capture the remaining value. In DCF models, the assumptions made to estimate the terminal value may be crucial, as it may constitute 70% of total value.

Proponents of the EBO model argue that terminal value estimates in that model are less troublesome. If we consider a finite horizon T, the valuation model (19) becomes[34]

$$P_0 = B_0 + \sum_{j=1}^{T} \frac{(\text{ROE}_j - r)\, B_{j-1}}{(1 + r)^j} + \frac{(P_T - B_T)}{(1 + r)^T} \qquad (21)$$

The last expression $(P_T - B_T)$ represents the premium over book value at the end of the finite horizon T. This premium is based on the abnormal earnings earned following period T. *Advocates of the EBO model argue that this premium should disappear as economic factors tend to drive abnormal earnings to zero within a relatively short time.*[35] More formally, as long as T is sufficiently large, $(P_T - B_T) \to 0$.

Recall that Figure 4-6 provides empirical evidence that ROEs converge from extreme positions toward an overall mean within approximately five years. As abnormal earnings are a function of the difference between ROE and the required rate of return r, this convergence in ROE is equivalent to abnormal earnings approaching zero.

Competitive forces are one reason for this convergence, as competitors enter business segments with abnormal profits, eventually reducing those profits to zero. *Even if a company could protect a particular source of abnormal profits indefinitely (through patents or copyrights), it is unlikely that it could find additional sources of abnormal profits indefinitely. Thus, reinvested profits would only earn a normal rate of return.* As reinvested profits increase book value, ROE (a weighted average of normal and abnormal profits) declines and the firm's abnormal earnings converge to a steady-state level.[36] That level can be used to estimate the terminal premium $(P_T - B_T)$.

---

[34]This expression can be derived by expansion of (19) to

$$P_0 = B_0 + \sum_{j=1}^{T} \frac{(\text{ROE}_j - r)\, B_{j-1}}{(1 + r)^j} + \sum_{k=T+1}^{\infty} \frac{(\text{ROE}_k - r)\, B_{k-1}}{(1 + r)^k}$$

and by using

$$P_T = B_T + (1 + r)^T \sum_{k=T+1}^{\infty} \frac{(\text{ROE}_k - r)\, B_{T-1}}{(1 + r)^k}$$

[35]Or, at the very least, their discounted values. Our example does not have this property as abnormal growth opportunities are considered to exist to infinity. However, $(\text{ROE} - r)$ does reach steady state at 10% as ROE approaches 20%.

[36]See the following section entitled, "Unbiased Versus Conservative Accounting."

Whatever the firm's current earnings, competitive forces are assumed to reduce the firm's abnormal earnings over time. At some point, the firm will have only zero net present value opportunities and zero abnormal earnings. Because of this convergence property, abnormal earnings play a central role in the valuation function . . .

. . . Although the valuation formula, like the Dividend Discount Model, incorporates the sum of an infinite series, its power derives from the fact that estimating abnormal earnings over a finite horizon can generate reasonable firm valuations.[37]

Simplified Assumptions for ROE, Book Values, and Terminal Value. The convergence of ROE, along with assumptions about the level and growth of ROE, leads to reasonably accurate and simplified valuation calculations. For example, assume $T = 3$ and ROE $= r$ after three periods. Then the valuation model reduces to estimates of ROE for the next three years and book values for the next two:

$$P_0 = B_0 + \frac{(\text{ROE}_1 - r)\, B_0}{(1 + r)} + \frac{(\text{ROE}_2 - r)\, B_1}{(1 + r)^2} + \frac{(\text{ROE}_3 - r)\, B_2}{(1 + r)^3}$$

This model is sometimes expressed in the form of the price/book value ratio, yielding

$$\frac{P_0}{B_0} = 1 + \frac{(\text{ROE}_1 - r)}{(1 + r)} + \frac{(\text{ROE}_2 - r)(1 + g_1)}{(1 + r)^2} + \frac{(\text{ROE}_3 - r)(1 + g_1)(1 + g_2)}{(1 + r)^3}$$

where g_i is the growth in book value in period i. Value equals current book value (B_0) multiplied by the price/book (P/B) ratio. This model requires an estimate of growth in book value. As noted earlier, the growth rate of book value equals $(1 - k)$ ROE; the exercise thus boils down to estimating ROEs and dividend payout ratios.

If we assume that abnormal earnings do not disappear, but reach steady state *after* period 3, then the above can be modified to incorporate the terminal value as

$$\frac{P_0}{B_0} = 1 + \frac{(\text{ROE}_1 - r)}{(1 + r)} + \frac{(\text{ROE}_2 - r)(1 + g_1)}{(1 + r)^2} + \frac{(\text{ROE}_3 - r)(1 + g_1)(1 + g_2)}{(1 + r)^3}$$
$$+ \frac{(\text{ROE}_4 - r)(1 + g_1)(1 + g_2)(1 + g_3)}{r(1 + r)^3}$$

where $(\text{ROE}_4 - r)$ is the terminal steady-state difference between the firm's ROE and its required rate of return r.

This formulation assumes that although the firm has abnormal earnings equal to $(\text{ROE}_4 - r)\, B_3$ after period 3, these abnormal earnings do not grow (although book value grows after period 3); similar reinvestment opportunities do not exist.

If, however, we assume that abnormal earnings do grow as book value grows at a rate equal to g_3, then the P/B ratio can be expressed as

$$\frac{P_0}{B_0} = 1 + \frac{(\text{ROE}_1 - r)}{(1 + r)} + \frac{(\text{ROE}_2 - r)(1 + g_1)}{(1 + r)^2} + \frac{(\text{ROE}_3 - r)(1 + g_1)(1 + g_2)}{(1 + r)^3}$$
$$+ \frac{(\text{ROE}_4 - r)(1 + g_1)(1 + g_2)(1 + g_3)}{(r - g_3)(1 + r)^3}$$

[37]Patricia M. Fairfield, "P/E, P/B and the Present Value of Future Dividends," *Financial Analysts Journal*, July–August 1994, p. 24.

Additional formulae for estimates of terminal values under differing growth assumptions and steady-state values are provided in Appendix 19-B.

Relative Importance of Terminal Value Calculations

The relative importance of terminal value calculations is a significant issue. In our previous example, the book value of $1,020 approximates 75% of the $1,387 firm value. *Book value, which often represents a sizable portion of firm value, is given and does not have to be estimated.* Further, when we consider the value derived from forecasts of the first few periods' abnormal earnings, the proportion of the terminal value to total value is small.

In DCF models, as noted, terminal values frequently constitute 60 to 70% of total value. All parameters must be estimated, and those that are most difficult to estimate play a large role in valuation.

The reason for the difference in the relative importance of terminal value relates to the accrual system of accounting. That system essentially quantifies (net) assets in terms of future benefits; that is, will they generate future cash flows? Those future benefits are, therefore, already quantified within the book value of the firm. The EBO model makes use of this quantification; it focuses on the difference between firm value and book value: abnormal earnings.

The DCF model, on the other hand, undoes the accrual process, forecasts future cash flows, and then rebundles them in the present value calculations. Everything must be reestimated. Put differently, DCF models estimate *firm value* itself; the EBO model estimates the *differential between firm value and book value,* a more manageable problem.

To be sure, when the models are applied in a consistent manner, they obtain the same result. The errors in DCF terminal value calculations are expected to appear in the shorter horizons of the EBO model. Pragmatically, however, forecasting is simpler for EBO models.

Effect of Accounting Policies

Both the EBO model and the earnings version of the dividend DCF models use accounting earnings as an input. There is, however, an important distinction between the two. In the DCF model, earnings (together with the payout ratio k) are a surrogate for dividends, and the efficacy of the model depends on the validity of that relationship.

Although the EBO model can be derived (as shown in Box 19-2) from the dividend discount model, it is not dependent on any set of accounting standards. Consistent with its accounting definition, earnings in the EBO model measure the creation of wealth, not as a surrogate for another parameter such as cash flows, dividends, or even economic earnings. As long as the *clean surplus* relationship is maintained, the model is applicable to any set of accounting rules.

At first glance, this may seem illogical. How can value be determined by a number (earnings) that can be manipulated by accounting choices? The answer lies in the *self-correcting* nature of accounting. Value under the EBO model is a function of current book value and (discounted) future abnormal earnings. If a given accounting method recognizes earnings in the current period, *the book value portion of the EBO valuation increases as current book value is higher.* However, in following periods, the higher book value increases the normal (required) earnings (rB). Consequently, *future abnormal earnings are lower (or negative), offsetting the higher book value in the valuation formula.* Thus, *over time,* different accounting choices catch up with each other.[38]

The foregoing does not mean that accounting is irrelevant. On the contrary, it creates an objective measure of "better" accounting policies. Our earlier discussion notes that the strength of the EBO model is its use of finite horizons, as abnormal earnings converge to zero as long as *T* is *sufficiently* large. The self-correcting process of differing accounting policies is another manifestation of this convergence process. Thus, a better accounting system is one in which this convergence takes place over a shorter horizon *T*. More important, in terms of adjusting reported financial data:

> . . . the accounting-based valuation methods *provide a motive for adjusting book values and earnings, much as analysts do*; with "better" accounting, value can be summarized with forecasts over shorter horizons.[39]

The Clean Surplus Relationship

The clean surplus relationship requires a definition of income similar to comprehensive income, discussed in Chapters 2 and 17. All changes in book value (other than transactions with stockholders) flow through the income statement without any direct charges to stockholders' equity.

U.S. GAAP is generally consistent with clean surplus accounting. There are exceptions, three of which are discussed in the book:

1. Adjustment for the minimum pension liability (Chapter 12)
2. Recognition of unrealized gains and losses on available-for-sale marketable securities (Chapter 13)
3. Exchange rate gains and losses under the all-current method (Chapter 15).

Thus, applying the EBO to U.S. firms requires adjustments to income for these items.

Unbiased Versus Conservative Accounting

The self-correcting process that drives abnormal earnings to zero and ROE to *r* is characterized by Ohlson as *unbiased* accounting. Not all accounting methods, however, possess this property.

For example, Chapter 7 compares capitalization versus expense accounting policies. Figure 7-3 shows that for a company that grows and then reaches steady state, ROE for the expensing firm is *higher and remains higher* relative to that of the capitalizing firm. *Conservative* accounting that expenses current expenditures *leads to higher abnormal earnings* (ROE > *r*) *indefinitely.* Thus, firms with high R&D expenditures (that must be expensed) report positive abnormal earnings indefinitely.[40] *The level of these abnormal earnings, however, reach steady state and the analysis discussed earlier and in Appendix 19-B must be adopted.*

---

[38] Problem 14 illustrates this property.

[39] Victor L. Bernard, "Accounting-Based Valuation Methods, Determinants of Market-to-Book Ratios and Implications for Financial Statement Analysis," working paper, University of Michigan, June 1993, p. 8 (emphasis added).

[40] See, for example, Exhibit 7-4, and the analysis of Merck's ROE from Lev and Sougiannis.

Value Drivers

The EBO model also has conceptual advantages. By focusing on earnings rather than dividends, *the model defines value in terms of wealth generation rather than wealth distribution.*

> Value is determined by the *creation* of wealth, measured by aggregate accounting earnings, rather than the *distribution* of wealth, measured as dividends.[41]

This argument can be extended to the valuation of firms that do not pay dividends. The valuation of these firms by EBO models is no different from that of any other firm, as value is determined by the generation of wealth (earnings), not its distribution as dividends.

The value drivers in the EBO model are precisely those attributes that analysts normally consider. Abnormal earnings depend on ROE, a ratio whose disaggregation and analysis are familiar (see Chapter 4). The various DCF models also use many of these drivers to estimate cash flows. However, as the EBO paradigm focuses on the attributes that are important for valuation, the impact of parameter and assumption changes can be seen *directly*. The valuation equation allows us to focus directly on price and its relationship to earnings, book value, ROE, and the growth and persistence of these components.

Price/Book Value and Price/Earnings Ratios Revisited

The EBO model provides a useful framework to revisit the questions addressed earlier: why companies sell at higher or lower price/book value and price/earnings ratios. The model allows us to reevaluate the parameters that are relevant to these ratios.

Price/Book Value Ratios. We begin with expression (19) evaluated at time t:

$$P_t = B_t + \sum_{j=1}^{\infty} \frac{(\text{ROE}_{j+t} - r)\, B_{j+t-1}}{(1 + r)^j}$$

Dividing by B_t yields

$$\frac{P_t}{B_t} = 1 + \sum_{j=1}^{\infty} \frac{(\text{ROE}_{j+t} - r)}{(1 + r)^j} \frac{B_{j+t-1}}{B_t}$$

This equation implies that the P/B ratio is related to future abnormal earnings (the difference between ROE and r*) and the growth of book value. If future abnormal earnings are zero, then the P/B ratio is "normal" (equal to 1). Note that current profitability is not relevant.*

Price/Earnings Ratios. We begin with expression (20) evaluated at time t:

$$P_t = B_t + \sum_{j=1}^{\infty} \frac{E_{j+t}^a}{(1 + r)^j}$$

[41]Bernard, op. cit.

482

Adding D_t to both sides and dividing by E_t and using the clean surplus relationship, we obtain

$$\frac{P_t + D_t}{E_t} = 1 + \frac{B_{t-1}}{E_t} + \sum_{j=1}^{\infty} \frac{E_{j+t}^a}{(1 + r)^j E_t} \tag{22}$$

B_{t-1}/E_t measures current year profitability, (the inverse of) ROE_t. The summation term reflects future (abnormal) earnings relative to current earnings. *Expression (22) states that the P/E ratio is related to both current and future profitability and the extent to which current profitability will persist.*

Since $E_t = E_t^a + rB_{t-1}$, after substituting for B_{t-1}, Eq. (22) reduces to

$$\frac{P_t + D_t}{E_t} = \left[\frac{1 + r}{r}\right] + \frac{1}{E_t}\left[\sum_{j=1}^{\infty} \frac{E_{j+t}^a}{(1 + r)^j} - \frac{E_t^a}{r}\right] \tag{23}$$

The term in the left bracket is the same one derived for "normal" P/E ratios (cum dividend) in the earnings DCF model. The term in the right bracket is the difference between the present value of *future abnormal* earnings and *current abnormal* earnings in perpetuity. That difference determines whether or not P/E ratios are high or low.

We first consider a situation where future abnormal earnings are equivalent to current abnormal earnings for all j; that is, $E_{j+t}^a = E_t^a$. Then

$$\sum_{j=1}^{\infty} \frac{1}{(1 + r)^j} = \frac{1}{r}$$

Equation (23) reduces to

$$\frac{P_t + D_t}{E_t} = \frac{1 + r}{r} \tag{24}$$

the expression for normal P/E ratios. *When future abnormal earnings are equivalent to current abnormal earnings, P/E ratios are normal.*[42]

High (low) P/E ratios are dependent on future abnormal earnings that are higher (lower) than current abnormal earnings. *The P/E ratio is a function of current abnormal earnings, their persistence, and the growth in future abnormal earnings.* Note that it is the *relative*, not absolute, levels of current and future abnormal earnings that matter. Growth affects P/E ratios only if future abnormal earnings exceed current abnormal earnings.

The relationship between P/B and P/E ratios and current and future (abnormal) earnings is illustrated in Figure 19-1.[43] The vertical axis plots future abnormal earnings (FE^a); the horizontal axis plots current abnormal earnings (CE^a).

Figure 19-1a shows that P/E ratios are a function of whether or not current levels of profitability persist in the future. The 45° line drawn in the graph represents

---

[42] In equation 16, we showed that P/E ratios are normal when there are no abnormal growth opportunities ($r^* = r$). Our EBO formulation shows that this restriction is too limiting. The important issue is the relative level of current and future abnormal earnings, not whether or not there are abnormal earnings at all.

[43] Figure 19-1 is similar to the analysis of Table 2 in Fairfield (1994) and the matrix of Penman (1996).

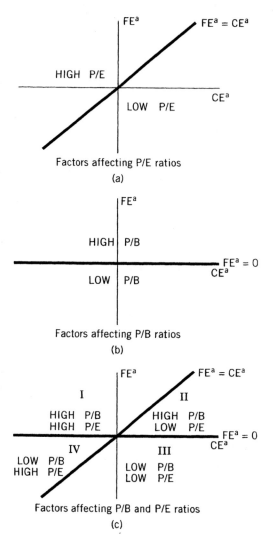

Factors affecting P/E ratios
(a)

Factors affecting P/B ratios
(b)

Factors affecting P/B and P/E ratios
(c)

FIGURE 19-1 Factors affecting price/earnings and price/book value ratios.

$CE^a = FE^a$. Along this line, current abnormal earnings are a good indicator of future abnormal earnings (earnings are persistent). The P/E ratio is normal and equal to $(1 + r)/r$.

On either side of this line, current profitability is not a good indicator of future profitability and P/E ratios are high or low. To the right and below the line, current profitability exceeds future profitability. Either current earnings have a transitory positive component or the high abnormal earnings are not sustainable in the future. The result is a low P/E ratio. To the left and above the 45° line, future profitability exceeds current profitability. Current earnings may have a transitory negative component. The P/E ratio is high.

Figure 19-1*b* shows that the P/B ratio is purely a function of future abnormal earnings. The horizontal axis is equivalent to $FE^a = 0$. When $FE^a = 0$, the P/B ratio is normal (equivalent to 1). When FE^a is positive, P/B ratios are high (exceed 1). When future abnormal earnings are negative, the P/B ratio is below 1.

Figure 19-1c combines Figures 19-1a and 19-1b, showing conditions for all possible combinations of (high or low) P/B and (high or low) P/E ratios. At the origin, the P/B and P/E ratios are normal.

- Region I represents companies with strong growth potential. FE^a is high and future profitability exceeds current levels. These companies have high P/E and P/B ratios.
- Region II contains mature companies in their harvesting years. Current and future E^a is positive; however, future profitability is below current profitability. These companies exhibit high P/B ratios and low P/E ratios.
- Region III represents poor performers. Future profitability is expected to be below normal (FE^a < 0) as well as below current levels. These companies exhibit low P/E and P/B ratios.
- Region IV shows distressed companies that are recovering. Future earnings are below normal (FE^a < 0); however, they are expected to rise from current levels. Companies that have had major restructurings (or a "big bath") would fall into this category, as current earnings are depressed. Although P/B ratios are low, P/E ratios are high.

The EBO Model: Concluding Comments

The efficacy of the EBO model has been tested in a number of studies. Bernard (1995) shows that a model using book values and forecasts of abnormal earnings for just three years explains variations in market prices far better than a comparable model based on discounted dividends. Penman and Sougiannis (1995) compare (variations of) the EBO model to a free cash flow and dividend discount model. They find the EBO model superior to the dividend model in all cases. Its performance vis-à-vis the free cash flow model depends on the assumption used to estimate terminal value. Only when the free cash flow model uses accrual earnings to calculate terminal value are the models comparable; otherwise, the EBO model dominates.

Frankel and Lee (1996) extend the EBO model to an international framework. They suggest that, since the EBO model is supposedly immune to accounting variations (see the earlier discussion), it can be used to compare firms across countries. To date, research results seem promising, with additional research underway.

VALUATION BY MULTIPLES

OVERVIEW

Although the bias of this book is very strongly tilted toward the use of discounted cash-flow (DCF) methods, it is impossible to ignore the fact that many analysts use other methods to value firms. The primary alternative valuation method is the use of multiples, in particular the Price/Earnings (P/E) ratio.

Valuation by multiples is quick and convenient. The simplicity and convenience of valuation by multiples constitute both the appeal of this valuation method and the problematics associated with its use: Simplicity means that too many facts are swept under the carpet and too many questions remain unasked. Multiples should never be your only valuation method and preferably not even your primary focus. When you have more than 5 minutes to value a firm, the DCF method, which *forces* you to consider the many aspects of an ongoing concern, is the preferred valuation method and the use of multiples should be secondary.

Having said this, multiple analysis can provide a valuable "sanity check." If we have done a thorough valuation, we can compare our predicted multiples, such as P/E and market to book (M/B), to representative multiples of similar firms. If our predicted multiples are comparable, we can, perhaps, feel more assured of the validity of our analysis. On the other hand, if our predicted multiples are out of line with the representative multiples of the market, then we have some explaining to do—first to ourselves, to convince us that our model is reasonable, and then to our clients and readers.

In valuation with multiples, we don't attempt to explain observed prices of firms. Instead, we use the *appropriately scaled average price of similar firms* to estimate values without specifying why prices are what they are. Hence, the trick in valuing with multiples is *selecting truly comparable firms* and *choosing the right scaling bases*—the right multiples.

We begin the discussion of valuation by multiples with a description of the method and some general principles and considerations in its application. We then focus on the P/E ratio. P/Es are the most useful and widely used of all valuation multiples. Nevertheless, the P/E ratio is often interpreted misleadingly and applied in a way which leads to ambiguous results. We will try to clear up some of these problems. We conclude the chapter with a discussion of other frequently used multiples.

10.1   PRINCIPLES OF VALUATION WITH MULTIPLES

To use the word "multiples" is to use a fancy name for market prices divided (or "scaled") by some measure of performance. In a typical valuation with multiples the average multiple—the average price scaled by some measure of performance—is applied to a performance measure of the firm that we value. For example, suppose we choose earnings as our scaling measure; that is, we choose earnings to be the performance measure by which prices of similar firms will be scaled. To scale the observed prices of firms by their earnings, we compute for each firm the ratio of its price to its earnings—its **P/E ratio** or its **earnings multiple.** We then average the individual P/E ratios to estimate a "representative" P/E ratio, or a representative earnings multiple. To value a firm, we multiply the projected profits of the firm that we value by the representative earnings multiple, the average P/E.

When we value with multiples, we are being agnostic about what determines prices. This means that we have no theory to guide us on how best to scale observed market prices: by Net Earnings, Earnings Before Interest and Taxes (EBIT), Sales, or Book Values. In practice, this means that valuation with multiples requires the use of *several scaling factors* or, in other words, several multiples. Often the best multiples for one industry may not be the preferred multiples in another industry. This implies, for example, that the practice of comparing P/E ratios of firms in different industries is problematic (and in many cases inappropriate altogether!). This further implies that when you do a multiple-based valuation, it is important first to find what the *industry* considers as the best measure of relative values: The square footage of the selling area may work with retail stores and the number of potential subscribers in the area may work for cellular telephone firms. These are often the best measures of relative values.

Although valuation by multiples differs from valuation by discounting cash flows, its application entails a similar procedure—first projecting performance, and then converting projected performance to values using market prices. This is done as follows:

• Project performance for the firm that you value, for example, by using proforma financial statements.

• Compute the average price per performance-measure dollar (i.e., the average multiple) by dividing observed prices of similar firms by the same performance measures you projected.

• Convert the projected performance to values by multiplying each projected performance measure by the relevant average multiple.

The detailed steps are described in the next subsection.

The Procedure of Valuation with Multiples

Valuation by multiples involves the following steps:

1 *Choose comparable firms.* Since we scale prices of *other* firms to value the firm being analyzed, we would like to use data of firms that are *as similar as possible to the firm that we value.* The flip side of this argument, however, is that by specifying too stringent criteria for similarity, we end up with too few firms to which we can compare. With a small sample of comparable firms, the idiosyncrasies of individual firms affect the average multiples too much so that the average multiple is no longer a representative multiple. In selecting the sample of comparable firms, you have to balance these two conflicting considerations. The idea is to obtain as large a sample as possible so that the idiosyncrasies of a single firm don't affect the valuation by much, yet not to choose so large a sample that the "comparable firms" are not comparable to the one that you value. (Some commonly used selection criteria are discussed in the following subsection.)

2 *Choose bases for multiples.* To convert market prices of comparable firms to a value for the firm being analyzed, you have to scale the valued firm relative to the comparable firms. This is typically done by using *several* bases of comparison. Some generic measures of relative size often used in multiple valuation are Sales, Gross Profits, Earnings, and Book Values. Often, however, industry-specific multiples are more suitable than generic multiples. Examples of industry-specific multiples are price per restaurant for fast-food chains and paid miles flown for airlines. In general, the higher-up that the scaling basis is in the income statement, the less it is subject to the vagaries of accounting principles. Thus, Sales is a scaling basis that is much less dependent on accounting methods than Earnings Per Share (EPS). Depreciation or treatment of convertible securities critically affect EPS calculations but hardly affect Sales. On the other hand, the higher-up that the scaling basis is in the income statement, the less it reflects differences in operating efficiency across firms—differences that critically affect the values of the comparable firms as well as the value of the firm being analyzed.

3 *Average across industry.* Once you have a sample of firms that you consider to be similar to the firm you value, you can average the prices that investors are willing to pay for *comparable* firms in order to obtain a price for your firm.

For example, after dividing each firm's share price by its EPS to get individual P/E ratios, you can average the P/E ratios of all comparable firms to estimate the earnings multiple that investors think is fair for firms with these characteristics. You do the same thing for *all* the scaling bases that you have chosen, calculating a "fair price" per dollar of Sales, per restaurant, per dollar of Book Value of Equity, and so on.

Note that we put "fair price" in quotation marks: Since there is no market for either EPS or Sales or any other scaling measure, the computation of average multiples is merely a scaling exercise and not an exercise in finding "how much the market is willing to pay for a dollar of earnings." Investors don't want to buy earnings; they only want cash flows (in the form of either dividends or capital gains). Earnings (or Sales) are paid for only to the extent that they generate cash. In computing average ratios for various bases, we implicitly assume that *the ability of firms to convert each basis (e.g., Sales, Book Value, and Earnings) to cash is the same.* Keep in mind that this assumption is more tenable in some cases than in others and for some scaling factors than for others.

4 *Project bases for the valued firm.* The average "prices per . . ." of comparable firms are applied to the projected performance of the firm being valued. Thus, we need to project the *same measures of the relative size* used in scaling the prices of the comparable firms for the firm being valued. For example:
  a To value a firm, we use Earnings as a scaling basis to determine the average earnings multiple (i.e., the average P/E ratio). Thus, we need to project the earnings of the firm being valued.
  b To use the average "price per restaurant" to value a fast-food chain, we need to project the number of restaurants the chain will have.
  c To use the average "price per dollar of book value" (the **market to book (M/B)** ratio), we need to project the Book Value of Equity.

The simplest application of valuation with multiples is by projecting the scaling bases 1 year forward and applying the average multiple of comparable firms to these projections. For example, we apply the comparable firms' average P/E ratio to the projected next year's earnings of the firm being valued. Clearly, by applying the average multiple to the next year's projections, we overemphasize the *immediate* prospects of the firm and *give no weight to more distant prospects.* To overcome this weakness of the one-step-ahead projections, we can use a more sophisticated approach, that is, apply the average multiples to "representative" projections—projections that better represent the long-term prospects of the firm. For example, instead of applying the average P/E ratio to *next year's* earnings, we can apply the comparable P/E ratio to the projected average EPS over the *next 5 years.* In this way the representative earnings' projections can also capture some of the long-term prospects of the firm, while next year's figures (with their idiosyncrasies) don't dominate valuations.

5 *Value the firm.* This is the final step—combining the average multiples of comparable firms to the projected parameters of the valued firm in order to obtain an estimated value. On the face of it, this is merely a simple technical step. Yet often it is not. The values that we obtain from various multiples (i.e., by using several scaling bases) are typically not the same; in fact, frequently they are quite different. This means that this step requires some analysis of its own—explaining why valuation by the average P/E ratio yields a lower value than the valuation by the Sales multiple (e.g., the valued firm has higher than normal Selling, General, and Administrative (SG&A) expenses) or why the M/B ratio yields a relatively low value.[1] The combination of several values into a final estimate of value, therefore, requires an economic analysis of both "appropriate" multiples and how multiple-based values should be adjusted to yield values that are economically reasonable. We consider these questions throughout the remainder of this chapter.

Selecting Comparable Firms to Estimate Average Multiples

Valuation with multiples doesn't begin with first principles. Rather, market prices of comparable firms are averaged under the assumption that they appropriately reflect all relevant determinants of value. Technically, we infer the value of the firm being analyzed by simply scaling the observed prices of similar firms to the size of the firm being valued. Thus, a crucial element in valuation with multiples is the exact definition of "similar" or, in other words, the criteria used in selecting a sample of comparable firms.

Selection criteria for comparable firms should give us tight enough restrictions so that firms whose market prices are averaged are indeed not too different from the firm being valued. On the other hand, since each firm has its own idiosyncrasies (which we don't want to take into account when valuing the firm analyzed), we need to obtain a large enough sample of comparable firms so that these idiosyncrasies are averaged out.

As an overall rule, we exclude "abnormal" firms—firms that experience unusual events such as business combinations or other major strategic alliances. There are two reasons for excluding such firms. First, the historic performance (measured by Sales, EPS, or any other potential scaling basis) of firms undergoing a strategic change is not indicative of future performance. However, the market prices of these firms reflect future performance, not historic performance. Second, firms in the midst of a strategic change are likely to undergo additional changes. Even if their current operations are comparable to those of the firm that we value, their future operations may be quite different. Thus, it is good practice to exclude such

---

[1]Here is a possible explanation. The firm being valued has issued equity long before the comparable firms have issued equity. Because accounting is in terms of historical costs, the valued firm's equity book value reflects "older" dollars than the book value of the comparable firms.

firms from the sample of comparable firms in order not to bias the computation of average multiples.

The following criteria are most often used for the selection of comparable firms:

- *Industry classification.* Include firms that produce or trade the same goods or services that the valued firm does. Preferably, although most often difficult to do, include only those firms with the same product characteristics. For example, although both weekly magazines and daily newspapers can be classified into a single "newspaper" industry, if it is possible to get separate multiples for weekly and daily publications, you would get more accurate valuation by separately averaging multiples than by pooling both industry segments together.

- *Technology.* When there are several possible ways of producing the same good or providing the same service, try to include only those firms that employ the same technology as the firm being valued. For example, although both railroad companies and trucking companies provide transportation services, it is difficult to compare the multiples of railroads to those of truckers because of differences in the cost structure.

- *Clientele.* Firms in the same industries may appeal to different clienteles. Clientele differences may be part of a deliberate strategic choice (e.g., the merchandise selection of a retailer depends on its positioning in the market), a matter of location (e.g., the location of a public utility), or any other physical constraint. Since different clienteles imply differences in product quality, markups, and so on, it is important to try to match clienteles in selecting comparable firms. For example, when you value public utilities, it makes sense to distinguish by geographical location since the price paid for a northeastern utility may be quite different (after scaling) from the price paid for a midwest utility.

- *Size.* Since there may be returns to scale in the production or in the marketing of the firm's product, it makes sense to try to select from the sample of comparable firms only those that sell about the same number of units. For example, when you value a hotel chain, it makes more sense to compare the Hilton to the Marriott, each of which has about 100,000 rooms, than to compare either company to La Quinta, which has fewer than 20,000 rooms.

- *Leverage.* In many valuations with multiples only the market price of the equity is included in the computation of average multiples. Yet leverage affects the risk of shareholders, and consequently the relation between market prices and the performance measure that is used for scaling these prices. For example, all other things being equal, the P/E ratio of a firm with high leverage should be lower (because its equity is riskier) than the P/E ratio of an otherwise similar firm with low leverage. Thus (unless you deal with leverage differences using whole-firm multiples, as described in the next subsection), match the leverage of the comparable firms to the leverage of the firm being valued.

Finally, keep in mind that there is no such thing as "a firm that is identical to the one that you value." Although the preceding selection criteria all make perfect sense, in practice you have to compromise or you will end up with no firm to which you can compare the firm of interest.

Valuation of Whole Firms versus Valuation of Shareholders' Equity

The most frequently used valuation multiple by far is the P/E ratio. In applying this ratio, we usually consider the EPS of comparable firms and the projected EPS of the firm being valued. It is possible that the leverage of the comparable firms and the leverage of the valued firm are quite different. Since leverage differences entail differences in the risk of the return to the shareholders, such leverage differences imply commensurate differences in multiples. We have suggested one way of dealing with leverage differences—selecting comparable firms with leverage similar to the leverage of the firm being valued. An alternative solution is to compute multiples for *whole firms* and, accordingly, to value the firm as a whole. The latter approach can also accommodate differential use of convertible securities, such as executive stock options or convertible bonds: Whenever convertible securities exist, their value is simply included in the total firm value. (To split the total value of the firm between the convertible and nonconvertible securities, we can use the Black and Scholes (B&S) or similar formulas. We discuss these issues in Chapter 12.)

Valuation of whole firms involves the same steps as the valuation of equities. The only difference is that both the values for the other firms and the bases for scaling these values are for the firm as a whole rather than for the shareholders' portion. For example, instead of using the P/E ratio, which is the ratio of the price of the *stock* and the earnings *per share,* we can compute the ratio of the *Total* Firm Value to *Operating Income*:

Total Value to Operating Income

$$= \frac{\text{value of Equity} + \text{value of Debt} + \text{value of all other Long-Term Securities}}{\text{Operating Income}}$$

In this multiple we scale the market value of *all* long-term securities by the *total* pre-tax income generated by *total* funds provided by *all* these securities. Similar multiples can be calculated by using Sales, FCF, or Total Assets as the scaling factors.

In estimating a total value multiple, we can easily find the market value of the firm's equity since it is mostly publicly traded. The market value of other long-term securities, such as debt, preferred stock, or convertible securities, however, may be harder to obtain if they are not traded. When we lack prices of fixed income securities, such as debt and preferred stock, it is common to calculate multiples using their book values, on the assumption (often correct) that for these securities book and market values are close. The problem is more severe when nontraded convertible securities exist. Here alternative proxies for nonexistent market values (based, for example, on the B&S formula and observed stock prices) can be used.

Beyond the effect that leverage may have on total firm value, total firm multiples are independent of the particular financing mix that the firm's management has chosen. Thus, using total firm multiples means that we don't have to be concerned about leverage differences among the comparable firms, or between the individual comparable firms and the firm being valued.

Total firm multiples allow us to value the firm as a whole. Often, however, we are interested only in the value of the equity of the firm. To get the equity value, we need to do an additional simple calculation—deducting the value of its debt obligations, the value of its preferred stock, or the value of its convertible securities from the total value of the firm. This is very similar to the procedure that we follow in estimating a value for the whole firm by discounting its Free Cash Flows (FCF) at a risk-adjusted weighted average cost of capital (WACC); only in the second stage do we divide this value among all its security holders.

10.2 EARNINGS MULTIPLES

The P/E ratio is one of the most widely used methods of valuation. Its simplicity—valuing a stock by multiplying its EPS by the industry's average earnings multiple—has made it an attractive method of valuing a company. This method of valuation has many obvious problems, however, which we discuss now.

There are two primary methods by which earnings multiples are calculated in practice: Either prices are normalized by *last year's* earnings or prices are normalizing by *next year's expected earnings.* The former are called **trailing earnings multiples** and the latter are called **leading earnings multiples.** Using "0" to denote last year's figures, "1" to denote this year's expected earnings, and P_0 to denote the current price of a stock, we express the formulas for these multiples as

$$\text{Trailing earnings multiple} = \text{AVG}\left[\frac{P_0}{E_0}\right]$$

$$\text{Leading earnings multiple} = \text{AVG}\left[\frac{P_0}{E_1}\right]$$

where the average is taken over all comparable firms. When earnings multiples are mentioned, the usual reference is to trailing multiples. However, since modern valuation techniques are applied to *future expected earnings,* leading multiples are more appropriate for valuation purposes.

The difficulty with leading earnings multiples is that to compute the average multiple, we need estimates of *all comparable firms' expected next year's earnings.* For an analyst following an industry this is no major problem: He or she routinely projects earnings for all the firms in the industry that they follow. Others who want to use leading earnings multiples but don't follow the whole industry can rely on commercially available services to obtain average analyst earnings projections for the comparable firms.

When using leading earnings multiples, you will find that the valuation of a firm based on the earnings you *project for next year* (e.g., the earnings' projections in the pro-forma statements of next year) is straightforward:

$$\text{Estimated value} = \text{average [leading earnings multiples]}$$

$$\cdot \text{ projected earnings of the firm}$$

$$= \text{AVG}\left[\frac{P_0}{E_1}\right] \cdot E_1^{\text{firm}}$$

Since both the earnings used to scale the prices of the comparable firm and the earnings used to value the firm are *next year's* earnings, E_1, the resulting value is indeed an appropriate estimate of the value of the firm *today*. This, however, is not the case when we use *trailing* earnings multiples to value the firm based on the *projected* earnings of the firm. Using the same notation, we have

$$\text{Estimated value} = \text{AVG}\left[\frac{P_0}{E_0}\right] \cdot E_1^{\text{firm}}$$

The equation shows that by using trailing earnings multiples, we would, for example, value a firm by multiplying the earnings projected for *1997* by employing the market's average multiple of *1996* earnings. An appropriate interpretation of the resulting value estimate is that this will be the value *next year,* the point in time when our *projected* earnings become *historical* earnings. In notation:

$$P_1^{\text{firm}} = \text{AVG}\left[\frac{P_0}{E_0}\right] \cdot E_1^{\text{firm}}$$

(Note the time subscripts!) To convert the projected P_1 to an equivalent price *today,* we need to discount P_1 for 1 year (at the equity RADR!):

$$P_0^{\text{firm}} = \frac{\text{AVG}\left[\dfrac{P_0}{E_0}\right] \cdot E_1^{\text{firm}}}{1 + \text{RADR}}$$

The application of a trailing earnings multiple in such a way, however, is problematic: When applying this method, we implicitly assume that the *current* earnings multiple will still apply 1 year from now.[2] The same problematic assumption underlies another use of multiples. Multiples are often used to estimate *terminal values* in valuations. For example, in a valuation of a leveraged buyout (LBO) it is common to assume that all the FCFs will be used to pay down the

---

[2]The use of multiples is often motivated by the analyst's desire to avoid the estimation of future cash flows and firm discount rates. Note that the use of trailing multiples implies the necessity of estimating such discount rates! As an alternative to the use of trailing multiples, you can use leading multiples, but in this case you have to estimate future earnings for all comparable firms.

debt issued at the time of the buyout. When debt reaches a "low enough" level, the LBO is expected to be sold back to the public. The selling price a few years down the road is often estimated by using earnings multiples for the projected earnings of the issue year. But is the implicit assumption—that the current multiples will still prevail in a few years when the issue is sold—in fact reasonable?

Valuation by earnings multiples has another major problem: It cannot be applied to firms with zero or negative current or expected earnings. This problem is not restricted only to firms with *current* negative earnings: A firm may well have projected earnings that are negative and positive projected FCFs (e.g., when projected depreciation charges greatly exceed projected capital investments). Such a firm should have a positive value, which cannot be computed by multiplying the projected negative earnings by the industry's average P/E ratio. One quick fix is to apply the average earnings multiple to the first year in which earnings are projected to be positive and to discount the resulting price back. Again, the implicit assumption underlying this solution is that current multiples will still prevail when the firm's earnings become positive, a nontrivial assumption.

The problem of negative earnings also plagues the calculation of *average* comparable earnings multiples. Since earnings multiples cannot be computed when earnings are negative, a common practice in calculating averages is to eliminate firms with negative earnings. This creates a subtle problem. We will use a simple example to illustrate how this practice affects valuations. Consider an industry with 10 firms. Each year each of the 10 firms has a 20 percent chance of losing $25,000 and an 80 percent chance of making a profit of $100,000. The expected earnings of a typical firm are

$$E(\text{earnings}) = 20\% \cdot \$(-25,000) + 80\% \cdot \$100,000 = \$75,000$$

We can consider the expected earnings as the "typical" earnings: Earnings fluctuate between $100,000 and $25,000, and on average are $75,000. Reflecting the possibility that earnings will be either negative or positive, we find that the price of each firm is $900,000. This implies an earnings multiple relative to the *representative* earnings of

$$P/E = \frac{\$900,000}{\$75,000} = 12$$

What would happen when only the *profitable* firms are included in the sample of comparable firms for the purpose of estimating the industry's earnings multiple? The prices in the numerator incorporate the possibility of a loss, but the earnings in the denominator are earnings of firms that are *selected because they had a profit*. This will create a *downward* bias in the calculated industry's average P/E ratio!

To see this, consider a typical year in which 8 out of the 10 firms had a profit of $100,000, whereas 2 firms lost $25,000. The P/E ratio calculated *by using only the prices and earnings of the profitable firms* will be

$$\text{AVG}\left[\frac{P}{E}\right] = \frac{1}{8}\sum_{i=1}^{8}\frac{\$900,000}{\$100,000} = 9$$

which is less than the true P/E ratio of 12.

The correct way to estimate the industry's earnings multiple in this case is to sum *separately* the values and earnings and to compute the ratio on the *aggregate* value and earnings:

$$\text{AVG}\left[\frac{P}{E}\right] = \frac{\displaystyle\sum_{i=1}^{10}\$900,000}{\displaystyle\sum_{i=1}^{8}\$100,000 + \sum_{i=1}^{2}\$(-25,000)} = \frac{\$9,000,000}{\$750,000} = 12$$

as it should be.

Last, but not least, there is our usual problem with earnings: Do earnings measure what they purport to measure? A wide body of evidence indicates that earnings—the denominator of the P/E ratio—are routinely manipulated.[3] Earnings reflect discretionary allocations of costs and revenues and are more easily manipulated than the firm's cash flows. Consequently, earnings-based valuations are unduly dependent on arbitrary accounting decisions. Although the use of several comparable firms reduces the impact of an individual firm's earnings manipulation on the estimated earnings multiple, remember to verify that the earnings that you use to scale the prices of the comparable firms don't include abnormal components.

Appropriate P/E Ratios

Despite the preceding qualifications and reservations about the use of P/E ratios as substitutes for full valuations of firms, P/E ratios are closely related to DCF-based values. In this section we will derive some simple relations, based on rather strong assumptions that buy us simplicity, between DCF-based values and P/E ratios. These relations help us to interpret some of the observed patterns in P/E ratios, such as why high-growth firms and industries have higher earnings multiples than stable firms and industries. By using these relations, we can also assess the validity of some interpretations and uses of P/E ratios and gain some theoretical foundation

[3]For example, there is an extensive accounting literature on the "smoothing" of earnings by firms and on the "management" of accruals (e.g., preceding initial public offerings or bankruptcies).

for estimating the appropriate P/E ratios from the fundamental determinants of value.

Our starting point is the Gordon formula that converts a constantly growing infinite stream of dividends to a price for the stock when the term structure of both interest rates and risk premiums is flat. We denote next year's expected dividend by Div_1 and the constant annual growth rate by g. The constant cost of equity capital, comprised of a constant risk-free rate and a constant risk premium, is denoted by r_e. Today's price of the stock, denoted by P_0, is given by

$$P_0 = \frac{\text{Div}_1}{r_e - g}$$

We can make a simple substitution into the Gordon model to find the P/E ratio. Assume that dividends are a fixed proportion b, the **payout ratio,** of EPS. Then next year's dividends are given by the relation

$$\text{Div}_1 = b \cdot \text{EPS}_1$$

Furthermore, next year's profits in the Gordon model are related to this year's earnings by the annual growth rate:

$$\text{EPS}_1 = \text{EPS}_0 \cdot (1 + g)$$

Thus,
$$\text{Div}_1 = b \cdot \text{EPS}_0 \cdot (1 + g)$$

Substituting into the Gordon model, we get

$$P_0 = \frac{b \cdot \text{EPS}_0 \cdot (1 + g)}{r_e - g}$$

By dividing both sides of the equation by EPS_0, we get the current appropriate P/E ratio:

$$\frac{P_0}{E_0} = \frac{P_0}{\text{EPS}_0} = \frac{b \cdot (1 + g)}{r_e - g}$$

This formula shows that even under strong simplifying assumptions—constant income growth, constant discount rate, and constant payout ratio—the appropriate P/E ratio depends on:

• The firm's equity discount rate, which incorporates both its basic business risk and the additional risk incurred by leverage
  • The growth rate of earnings
  • The firm's payout ratio

Nonetheless, as we will see, the preceding formula may be useful.

Here are some examples that illustrate both the use of the formula and some important properties of P/E ratios. As our starting point, let's assume that our analysis indicates that the long-term growth potential of firm A is 4 percent per year, that its equity RADR is 8 percent, and that we expect the firm to pay 50 percent of its annual income as dividends. These projections imply that the firm's P/E ratio (using *trailing* earnings) should be

$$\frac{P_0}{E_0} = \frac{b \cdot (1 + g)}{r_e - g} = \frac{50\% \cdot (1 + 4\%)}{8\% - 4\%} = 13$$

Thus, assuming that these determinants of value are forever fixed, we can compute the benchmark earnings multiple. This P/E ratio can help us to determine if firm A is over- or underpriced. Suppose we observe that firm A's *actual* P/E ratio is only 11. This means that firm A's stock price *is too low*—its price should be $13/11 - 1 = 18.2\%$ higher than it actually is.

Suppose now another firm, firm B, in the same industry uses a higher leverage than firm A. Since higher leverage means higher risk, the RADR of firm B is higher, say, 12 percent. Firm B, being in the same industry, has a growth potential that is similar to firm A, 4 percent a year. Further, firm B's dividend payout ratio is also 50 percent. This means that the appropriate P/E ratio for firm B is

$$\frac{P_0}{E_0} = \frac{b \cdot (1 + g)}{r_e - g} = \frac{50\% \cdot (1 + 4\%)}{12\% - 4\%} = 6.5$$

which is *one-half* the appropriate P/E ratio of firm A.

Suppose now the *actual* P/E ratio of firm B is 8, higher than its fundamentals indicate it should be. This means that the price of firm B is *too high*—firm B's stock is overpriced. We can use the example of firms A and B to illustrate a problematic aspect of the common use of P/E ratios. Someone analyzing the industry of firms A and B may look at the earnings multiples of the A and B stocks and say, "Stock B is a better stock to buy in the XXX industry than stock A since stock A sells for 11 times its earnings, whereas stock B sells for only 8 times its earnings." In this example the conclusion is obviously false: The undervalued stock is stock A (which has a high multiple), whereas stock B (which has a low multiple) is the overvalued one. The erroneous conclusion occurs because stock B, being more risky than stock A, should have a low multiple, even lower than the one for which it sells.

The preceding example highlights the difficulty of interpreting P/E ratios: P/E ratios reflect—besides the relative pricing of stocks—differences in risk, growth, and financial policies. Therefore, a low P/E by itself *doesn't* indicate a low stock price: A low P/E ratio may well equally indicate high-risk or low-growth potential!

Estimating Growth

As discussed in Chapter 9, the growth rate, g, can be estimated from the history of dividend payments, by simply averaging prior years' dividend growth rates. The key assumption underlying this procedure is that prior growth rates are indicative of future growth rates. To apply this method, we need to have a series of historical dividend payments that is long enough to estimate reliably the growth rate.

In many cases it is not reasonable to assume that past growth rates are indicative of future growth rates. In such cases we can use nondividend information to estimate future growth rates. In particular, we can estimate the growth rate of dividends by the product of the retention ratio and the return on equity (ROE):

$$g = \text{retention ratio} \cdot \text{ROE} = (1 - \text{dividend payout ratio}) \cdot \text{ROE}$$

The underlying assumption of this estimate of growth potential is that *growth is financed exclusively from internally generated funds*. The reasoning is that earnings (which drive dividends in the Gordon formula) grow because the firm invests a fraction of the earnings—the retained earnings—and earns a rate of ROE on these additional investments. Obviously, if the assumption that growth is exclusively financed by retaining some earnings is wrong, this way of estimating growth will not work.

Application of this method of estimating growth rates requires an estimate of the firm's ROE. One method that is often employed relies on accounting for the numbers used in estimating ROE:

$$\text{ROE} = \frac{\text{Profit after Tax}}{\text{Book Value of Equity}}$$

The intuition behind this equation is that the Book Value measures the *cost* of the investments and that the Profit after Tax measures the *return* on the investment.

Here is an illustration. Suppose the per-share equity book value (BV) of firm C is $10 and its EPS (earnings per share) are $0.80. The firm's dividend payout ratio is 25 percent. The growth rate implied by these numbers *and the assumption that Retained Earnings is the only source of growth* is

$$g = (1 - b) \cdot \text{ROE} = (1 - b) \cdot \frac{\text{EPS}}{\text{BV per share}}$$

$$= (1 - 25\%) \cdot \frac{\$0.80}{\$10.00} = 0.75 \cdot 8\% = 6\%$$

Suppose we estimate that the RADR of the stock is 9 percent. By using the estimated growth rate of 6 percent and RADR of 9 percent, we can determine the appropriate P/E ratio of the firm by using the previous formula:

$$\frac{P_0}{E_0} = \frac{b \cdot (1 + g)}{r_e - g} = \frac{25\% \cdot (1 + 6\%)}{9\% - 6\%} = 8.83$$

This illustrates one more important point about growth that is often overlooked. Growth by itself *doesn't create value.* Look back at the last example: The firm is growing by investing in projects that earn a rate of return (ROE) of 8 percent. The firm keeps holding on to cash (by paying out only 25 percent of the earnings as dividends) and reinvesting the remaining funds. But the ROE that the firm earns on its investments *is lower than the rate of return that investors demand given the firm's risk*: Given the firm's risk, investors demand a return of 9 percent. Thus, in this example growth *destroys* value.

10.3 THE RETAIL STORE INDUSTRY

We illustrate the use of multiples in valuation with the retail store industry. Exhibit 10.1 gives some initial facts about a sample of retail store companies taken from Value Line.

Exhibit 10.1

Retail Store Industry
Value Line Data, May 29, 1992

Retail Store		Share price	Trailing P/E*	Beta[†]	Market/ book,[‡] equity	Price/CF[¶] per share
Dillard Dept.	DDS	41	22.28	1.20	2.89	3.55
Dayton Hudson	DH	65	17.47	1.45	2.41	20.31
Dollar General	DOLR	20	24.39	1.00	3.38	14.29
Family Dollar	FDO	17	23.29	1.25	4.17	14.17
Jacobson Stores	JCBS	16	21.92	1.30	1.07	3.60
J. C. Penney	JCP	67	16.75	1.20	2.23	23.10
Kmart Corp.	KM	23	11.39	1.20	1.57	2.71
L. Luria & Son	LUR	6.6	30.00	1.10	0.46	1.83
May Dept. Stores	MA	55	13.68	1.35	2.83	44.00
Fred Meyer	MEYR	24	13.26	1.10	1.05	3.20
Nordstrom, Inc.	NOBE	33	19.88	1.25	2.87	10.31
Pic 'N' Save	PICN	16	14.29	1.15	2.51	8.21
Sears, Roebuck	S	45	12.13	1.10	1.12	5.96
Service Merchandise	SME	11	14.47	1.70	10.38	6.29
Venture Stores	VEN	30	12.10	nmf	4.05	6.82
Wal-Mart Stores	WMT	53	37.86	1.25	8.72	23.56
Woolworth Corp.	Z	28	18.54	1.25	1.80	6.36

*P/E is defined as the recent share price divided by EPS_{1991}.

[†]Beta is the stock's beta against the NYSE Composite Index.

[‡]Market/Book (M/B) is the ratio of the recent share price to the 1991 year-end per-share book value of equity.

[¶]Price/CF per share is the ratio of the recent share price to the 1991 per-share Cash Flows from Operations, defined by Value Line as PAT + Depreciation.

Source: Based on data from *Value Line Investment Survey,* May 29, 1992.

P/Es in the Retail Store Industry

Suppose we want to value Dayton Hudson (DH) based on our prediction of the EPS of DH. Assume that we agree with Value Line's projection that in 1992 DH's EPS will be $4.85, up $1.13 from its 1991 EPS. Obviously, underlying this EPS prediction is a complete analysis of DH's store distribution, market share, product mix, general and specific price trends, and the like about which we have little information. To simplify our illustration of the use of P/E ratios, we start the valuation of DH almost at its end, assuming that the end product of the detailed analysis of Value Line's analysts is a valid EPS prediction of $4.85.

The next step is to select from all the potential firms in DH's industry those firms that are most similar to DH. In other words, we want to select the set of firms that we consider comparable to DH. The basic consideration is the similarity of business—products, clients, location, and so on. DH operates 770 upscale department stores throughout the continental United States. The firms that are the closest to DH in terms of the type of business are Dillard Department Stores, May Department Stores, and Nordstrom, Inc. Allowing for some location or clientele differences, we can expand the sample of comparable firms to include Jacobson Stores, J. C. Penney, L. Luria & Son, and Sears. Next we want to compare these firms on the basis of their size and leverage. Exhibit 10.2 provides data for this comparison. Clearly, the firms that we consider potential candidates for our sample of comparable firms are of different sizes and use debt financing to differing degrees.

Exhibit 10.2

Retail store	Debt	Preferred stock	Equity (market value)	Total value	Leverage	Stores	Sales	Sales per store
	Book value							
Dayton Hudson	4,227	377	4,630	9,234	49.86%	770	16,115	21
Dillard Dept.	1,038	0	4,572	5,611	18.51%	198	4,036	20
Jacobson Stores	98	0	92	190	51.33%	24	396	16
J. C. Penney	3,354	684	7,816	11,854	34.07%	1,813	16,201	9
L. Luria & Son	2	0	35	38	6.38%	53	208	4
May Dept. Stores	3,918	394	6,790	11,102	38.84%	3,613	10,615	3
Nordstrom, Inc.	482	0	2,701	3,183	15.15%	63	3,180	50
Sears, Roebuck	19,200	325	15,486	35,011	55.77%	1,800	57,242	32

A key question in deciding whether to include or exclude firms on the basis of size differences depends on whether size itself is a potential determinant of value. If larger retailers can manage inventories more efficiently, deal with suppliers more skillfully, or train and manage employees better, the retail store industry will exhibit **returns to scale** and we should restrict our sample of comparable firms to firms with similar scales—similar annual Sales or a similar number of stores. On the other hand, if there are no returns to scale in the industry that we are analyzing, excluding firms just because they have a different size from the firm being valued is not justified. (Remember that before we apply the prices of the comparable firms to the firm being valued, we *scale* these prices—by earnings, Sales, or any other economically meaningful scaling basis in the industry.) Since in the retail store industry Sales is a good proxy for the width of the geographical distribution of the stores of the chain, we drop from the sample of comparable firms Jacobson Stores and L. Luria because they are too small and geographically concentrated, and drop Sears, which is 4 times as large as DH. This leaves us with a sample of four comparable retailers: Dillard Department Stores, J. C. Penney, May Department Stores, and Nordstrom, Inc.

The next point to consider is leverage. Exhibit 10.2 also presents data on the leverage of the sample of retail store firms. To calculate leverage, we first calculate the total value of the firm: We add the year-end 1991 book value of the fixed income securities (Debt and Preferred Stock) to the market value of the Equity—the recent price of the shares times the number of shares outstanding. Leverage is then calculated as the fraction of this total value financed by fixed income securities.

Two things should be mentioned concerning the leverage of the sample firms. First, the extent of debt financing ranges from 6 percent of the firm's value to 55 percent. Such a large difference within a rather homogeneous group of firms is hardly consistent with a capital structure theory of a trade-off between tax benefits and costs of financial distress. Apparently, neither tax benefits nor costs of financial distress are important determinants of capital structure in the retail store industry. On the other hand, the range of observed leverage figures is consistent with a Miller-type equilibrium, where $T \approx 0$.

The second point that emerges from the leverage data is that DH is one of the most levered retailers: It has a leverage of 50%. This means that we have to take into account explicitly the leverage differences in our valuation of DH's equity! Suppose we ignored the leverage information in valuing the shares of DH. Then we would simply average the P/E ratios of the four closest competitors of DH. This would give us an average P/E of 18.15 relative to which DH's *actual* P/E of 17.5 is low, suggesting that DH is a (weak?) "buy" opportunity. Alternatively, we can use the average P/E to multiply the projected EPS of $4.85 to obtain an estimated year-end ("target") share price of $88, which is equivalent to a return of 35% [= ($88 − $65)/65] on an investment in DH equity. But the simple analysis of the attractiveness of investing in DH stock is misleading: DH is much more levered than the comparable retailers. Since DH stock is more risky than the comparable stocks, investors require *higher rates of return* for investing in DH stock, which means that DH's P/E should be *lower* than the P/E of the other, less levered retailers.

The dependence of P/E ratios on leverage is a general result. Low-leverage firms are less risky than similar highly levered firms. Thus, all other things being equal, shares of low-leverage firms trade for higher prices than shares of high-leverage firms. This means that, within industries, we expect to observe a negative correlation between leverage and P/E ratios. As an illustration, in Figure 10.1 we plot

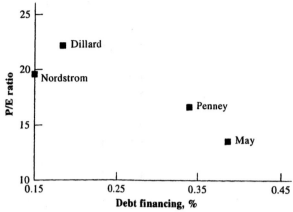

FIGURE 10.1 A plot of the Price/Earnings (P/E) ratios of four retailers in the retail store industry that are comparable to Dayton Hudson.

the P/E ratios of the four retailers that are comparable to DH. The negative correlation between leverage and P/E ratios is apparent.

Since we anticipate that the P/E ratios within the retail store industry will depend on leverage, our conclusion is that we cannot simply apply the average P/E ratio in the industry to DH's projected earnings because DH is more levered than comparable retailers. One quick fix for this problem is to value *whole firms* rather than just the equity of each firm. We can do this by computing ratios in which the total firm value is compared to some whole-firm scaling factor such as Operating Income or Sales. Exhibit 10.3 shows such ratios for the retailers that are comparable to DH.

Exhibit 10.3

Retail store	Total value	Leverage	EBIT	Value to EBIT	Sales	Value to sales
Dillard Dept. Stores	5,611	18.51%	412	13.625	4,184	1.341
J. C. Penney	11,854	34.07%	1050	11.285	17,295	0.685
May Dept. Stores	11,102	38.84%	1061	10.468	10,615	1.046
Nordstrom, Inc.	3,183	15.15%	263	12.086	3,170	1.004
Average				11.866		1.019

Note that the whole-firm multiples in Exhibit 10.3 show no leverage-related pattern: Neither Total Firm Value to EBIT nor Total Firm Value to Sales is related to leverage. Thus, whole-firm multiples appear to be, as they should if leverage doesn't affect the value of the firm, independent of the particular financing mix that the management of the comparable firms have chosen.

We can use the average whole-firm multiples to value DH. Suppose we follow Value Line in projecting that DH's 1992 Sales will be $18,000 million, up from its 1991 Sales of $16,115 million. If the EBIT/Sales ratio of DH stays at its current level of 4.78 percent, the expected Sales growth implies that DH's EBIT will grow from $770 million to $860 million. This means that based on the projected EBIT of DH and the average Value/EBIT ratio of the comparable firms, DH will be worth $860 · 11.866 = $10,210 million at the end of 1992. This value estimate of $10,210 million is based on the average *trailing* earnings multiple and DH's *leading* earnings. Hence, this is the value projected for DH *at the end of 1992*. To convert this value estimate to a value estimate in terms of *today's* dollars, we need to discount this value.

What is the appropriate discount rate? The value estimate is for the *whole firm*. Thus, the appropriate discount rate is the rate that reflects the risk of the whole firm, not just the risk of its equity. We can estimate this rate by estimating an industry's beta—the average asset beta of retail stores—and by using the CAPM. We can infer the beta of the asset of the industry from the beta estimates of the *equities* of the comparable firms and their leverage, using the following relation:

$$\beta_{assets} = \beta_{equity} \cdot \frac{E}{V} + \beta_{debt} \cdot (1 - t_c) \cdot \frac{D}{V}$$

where E = market value of the equity
D = market value of the fixed income securities
V = value of the whole firm—the sum of E and D

For low leverage levels $\beta_{debt} \approx 0$, so we can approximate the preceding relation by

$$\beta_{assets} \approx \beta_{equity} \cdot \frac{E}{V}$$

The following table is the basis for the estimation of the asset beta of retail stores that are similar to DH:

Retail store	E/V	β_{equity}	β_{debt}
Dillard	81.49%	1.20	0.98
Penney	65.93%	1.20	0.79
May	61.16%	1.35	0.83
Nordstrom	84.85%	1.25	1.06
Average			0.91

By using the average asset beta of comparable firms as our estimate of the asset beta of DH, we can estimate the RADR as

$$\text{RADR} = rf_{\text{debt}} \cdot (1 - t_c) + \beta_{\text{asset}} \cdot \pi_m$$

$$= 6\% \cdot (1 - 37\%) + 0.91 \cdot 8\% = 11.06\%$$

This estimate assumes a market-risk premium $\pi_m = 8\%$, the approximate value of the long-run historic average market-risk premium. By using the RADR of 11.48 percent, we can estimate the *current* value of DH as

$$\text{DH, total value} = \frac{\$10{,}210 \text{ million}}{(1 + 11.06\%)} = \$9{,}193 \text{ million}$$

To obtain an estimate of DH's *equity* value, we have to subtract the value of DH's fixed income securities from the value of *all* of DH's long-term securities. Specifically, the estimated equity value of DH is

DAYTON-HUDSON INC.
Using EBIT projections and whole-firm
multiples to estimate firm and equity values
($ millions)

Estimated firm value	$9,193
Value of debt	(4,227)
Value of preferred stock	(377)
Estimated equity value	$4,589

Note that this estimated value for DH's equity, unlike those obtained by applying average P/E ratios, takes into account the *specific* leverage of DH, which is different from the leverage of the other retailers to which we compare DH. The current market value of DH equity, $4,630 million, is only slightly above the estimated value based on Value Line's EBIT projections and our Value/EBIT multiple. This leads us to conclude that DH's equity is fairly priced.

As an alternative to using the whole-firm Value/EBIT ratio, we might also consider using the whole-firm Value/Sales ratio. The average of this value for the firms that are comparable to DH is 1.019. Using this ratio for DH's projected 1992 Sales of $16,115 million gives a projected year-end 1992 value of $19,962 for the firm. This is almost *twice* as large as the total-firm-value estimate that we arrived at by using the projected EBIT of DH for 1992! Is something wrong here? Some thoughts come to mind: Another look at the numbers show that historically DH's Value/Sales ratio has been very different from the rest of the sample. This suggests that this particular ratio is not appropriate despite the fact that we have decided that these firms are similar in many other respects to DH. In one sense, our disbelief in the valuation produced by the Value/Sales ratio is not that surprising: As we mentioned in Section 10.1, the *higher up* that the scaling basis is in the income statement, the less it reflects differences in strategies and operating efficiencies across firms. For example, DH may deliberately choose lower-profit margins than its competitors (possibly expecting a higher volume in return). Since such differences are critical in valuation, it is not surprising that the Value/Sales ratio doesn't produce a reliable estimate.

10.4 SOME OTHER MULTIPLES

Many other multiples are used by financial analysts to compare asset prices. Any or all of these multiples may prove to be useful as appropriate ways of measuring relative sizes and relative values for some industries. In this section we will describe some commonly used multiples and will present an illustration of some industry-specific multiples.

In general, any number in the income statement can be used as a measure of relative size: Sales, Gross Profits, Operating Profits, or Net Income. The lower you go in the income statement, the more firm-specific information is contained in the scaling measure:

- Using Sales as a scaling measure, you don't incorporate any firm-specific information about pricing policies, efficiency of production, or efficiency of selling.
- Using Gross Profits as a scaling measure, you incorporate information about the firm's pricing policies (i.e., average margin) and production efficiency (i.e., the relation between the Cost of Goods Sold (COGS) to Sales), but no information about marketing efficiency (i.e., Selling, General, and Administrative (SG&A) costs).
- Using Operating Profits to scale prices incorporates all operating aspects of the firm but doesn't incorporate any information about the firm's financial policies.
- Finally, using Net Income to scale prices incorporates both operating aspects and financial aspects of the firm. As the example in the subsection "Estimating Growth" illustrates, this may be *too much* information: You may want to scale comparable firms only on the basis of their common *operating* characteristics abstracting from *financial* differences, such as different leverages used by firms in the same industry.

The use of these increasingly informative measures of relative size is not without a cost: The lower in the income statement we go with our search for an appropriate scaling measure, the more the number depends on the vagaries of the accounting principles used by comparable firms. These accounting principles of firms in any given industry are far from being unique. Since income recognition criteria within an industry are likely to be similar, Sales is a measure of relative size that is virtually free of accounting differences, whereas Net Income is most affected by the firms' accounting policies. One remedy for this problem is to use *cash-flow-based multiples,* such as Price divided by CF to equity holders, and Price to FCF.

These ratios have the benefit of reflecting the information incorporated in the corresponding earnings numbers while being less affected by accounting principles.

Price/Sales Multiples

Dividing the price per share of a company by its Sales per share (the **Sales multiple**) is a common way of comparing firms in the same industry. The intuition underlying this ratio is that *within an industry* the gross margins and the operating efficiency are typically similar. Thus, using Sales to measure relative sizes is close to measuring relative sizes by profits and is *free of the accounting idiosyncrasies of individual firms*. To the extent that pricing policies and operating technologies of the sample of comparable firms that you use to estimate the average multiple are similar to the firm that you value, the Price/Sales ratio will do a good job even though it doesn't reflect any of the information in the firms' income statements other than Sales.

Consider the graph in Figure 10.2, which shows this ratio for the firms in the retail store industry. As the graph illustrates, there is a considerable variation in the Price/Sales ratios in the retail store industry, which is a fairly homogeneous industry in terms of product and operating methods. There seem to be a number of reasons that the Price/Sales ratio may not be accurate in valuing a company:

- The Price/Sales ratio doesn't reflect differences in *efficiency* between firms.
- It doesn't reflect differences in *capital investments*, which we know are a major component of many firms' FCFs.
- It doesn't reflect differences in *growth prospects*.

The problems with the Price/Sales ratio stem from the fact that when using this multiple, we scale the prices of comparable firms by the top number in a cash-flow

FIGURE 10.2   A graph of the Price/Sales ratio for firms in the retail store industry. (*Source: Value Line,* May 29, 1992.)

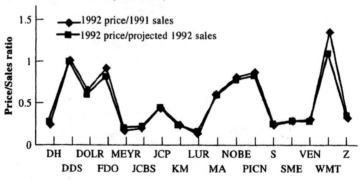

DDS = Dillard, DH = Dayton Hudson, DOLR = Dollar, FDO = Family Dollar, JCBS = Jacobson, JCP = Penney, KM = Kmart, LUR = Luria, MA = May, MEYR = Fred Meyer, NOBE = Nordstrom, S = Sears, SME = Service Merchandise, VEN = Venture, WMT = Wal-Mart, Z = Woolworth

statement. Such a scaling misses all the information contained in the numbers that follow Sales—COGS, SG&A, changes in working capital, and capital investments. By ignoring these numbers, we find that the Price/Sales ratio implicitly assumes that *within an industry all operating characteristics have the same relation to Sales for all firms.* If all the firms in an industry had the same operating efficiency and had no fixed costs, then their Price/Sales ratios would necessarily be equal. Under these assumptions earnings (and so EPS) would also be proportional to Sales, which means that

$$\frac{\text{Price}}{\text{Earnings}} = \frac{\text{Price}}{k \cdot \text{Sales}}$$

where k is a proportionality parameter that reflects the profit margins of the firm. This means that

$$\frac{\text{Price}}{\text{Sales}} = k \cdot \frac{\text{Price}}{\text{Earnings}}$$

Thus, if we think that the P/E ratio is meaningful, then the ratio of Price/Sales can be viewed as a backhanded way of getting at the firm's profit margin: Firms with a higher Price/Sales ratio can be taken, all other things being equal, to have a higher margin. We can check in our sample of retail stores if this is true.

As you can see in Figure 10.3, this premise appears to be largely true. The regression of Profit Margins on the Price/Sales ratio gives the following estimated relation for the department store industry:

$$\frac{\text{Price}}{\text{Sales}} = -0.0458 + 16.1622 \cdot \text{Profit Margin}, \qquad R^2 = 0.6074$$

This estimated relation can be used to value a retail store chain based on projected Sales and Gross Margins. If based on your analysis, you project 1992 Sales of

FIGURE 10.3   A comparison of the Price/Sales ratio with profit margin in the retail store industry. (*Source:* Based on *Value Line* predictions for 1992 Sales and profit margins, May 29, 1992.)

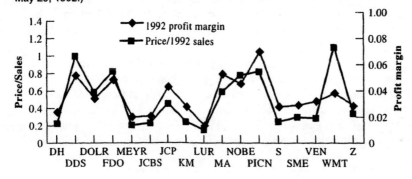

$250 million and a profit margin of 5 percent for the Goods "R" Us chain. First, by using the estimated relation between profit margins and Price/Sales ratios in the retail store industry, we can convert the projected profit margin of 5 percent to a projected Price/Sales multiple:

$$\frac{Price}{Sales} = -0.0458 + 16.1622 \cdot 0.05 = 0.762$$

Next the estimated "fair" Price/Sales ratio of 0.762 and the projected Sales of $250 million jointly imply a value of $250 million $\cdot$ 0.762 = $190 million.

Obviously, the simplicity of this valuation—all that it requires is the projection of Sales and Gross Margins—is both its advantage and a source of potential problems. The Sales-based valuation method will be valid only if Goods "R" Us is as efficient as the average (comparable) retailer: In applying the estimated relation, we implicitly assume that Goods "R" Us has similar SG&A and capital investments *per dollar of sales* as other retailers have. If this is a valid assumption, then the estimated value will be an accurate one. If Goods "R" Us is more efficient than its comparables, we will undervalue Goods "R" Us, whereas if Goods "R" Us is less efficient than its competitors, we will overvalue it.

Fixed Asset Multiples

There are many other multiples that are worth comparing for a given industry. In the next subsection we use data about the airline industry to examine some *fixed asset multiples.* In the airline industry the relevant fixed asset ratio is the ratio of **Market Value to Gross Equipment.** By *gross equipment* we mean the undepreciated equipment of each of the airlines. If the efficiency ratios, utilization rates, and growth prospects of any two airlines are roughly equal, then how much equipment an airline has will determine its *size* relative to other airlines in the industry as well as its *value* relative to the values of other airlines. This is also true of other industries: Fixed Assets at Cost will be a good measure of relative size if the industry's utilization rate is roughly the same; on the other hand, Fixed Assets will be a poor proxy for relative sizes if there are large intraindustry differences in efficiency and utilization.

A technical point discussed in relation to estimating capital expenditures of firms in Chapter 5 is worth repeating in the context of multiples valuation. When using Fixed Assets as a measure of relative size, you have to consider whether it is the *cost* of the fixed assets or the *net value*—cost less accumulated depreciation—that appropriately measures relative sizes. If production capacity deteriorates with the age of the fixed assets, *Net Fixed Assets* probably measures capacity better than Fixed Assets at Cost. If production capacity is little affected by the age of the machine (e.g., if an airplane can fly the same number of passengers for roughly the same cost in each year of its use until it is scrapped), capacity will be measured more accurately by the undepreciated cost of the Fixed Assets than by their net value. In our example we use the original cost of the airlines' equipment, implicitly assuming that airplanes' capacity to fly passengers doesn't deteriorate with age.

As with any fixed asset multiple, the use of the ratio of Value to Gross Equipment to compare airline values implicitly assumes that the *utilization rate* of the equipment is roughly the same across the industry. For airlines the actual utilization rate is called the **load factor**: An airline's *load factor* is the average percentage of occupied seats on its flights. Assuming that airlines don't own unused airplanes, the load factor can serve as a proxy for the *rate of utilization of fixed assets* of airlines. We use the load factor, which is reported by airlines, times the Gross Assets to measure the relative *effective* size of airlines. Figure 10.4 depicts both the ratios of **Market to Fixed Assets** and **Market to Load-Adjusted Fixed Assets.** The obvious pattern in the graph is that after adjusting the fixed assets by an estimate of their rate of utilization, the load factor, the cross-sectional dispersion of the ratio of market value to capacity is less widely spread than before the adjustment for the rate of utilization. This means that part of the intraindustry variation in the ratio of value to fixed assets is due to differences in the rate at which the fixed assets are utilized. Put differently, utilization-adjusted Fixed Assets is a better measure of relative size than Fixed Assets alone.

What does this result imply for the way that we use this ratio to value airlines? It means that to value an airline using Fixed Asset multiples, we need:

- To estimate the average ratio of Market to Fixed Assets adjusted by the utilization rate
- To project the Fixed Asset and the load factor for the airline being valued
- To apply the average utilization-adjusted Fixed Asset multiple to the projected Fixed Assets times the projected utilization rate of the airline that we want to value

These suggested steps are useful in other industries as well: It is better to compare firms on the basis of *utilization-adjusted* capacity than on the basis of *raw* capacity. The problem is that capacity utilization is not a readily available piece of data in most industries (the airline industry being a prominent exception). Nonetheless, if

FIGURE 10.4   The graph illustrates the Market to Fixed Asset ratios in the airline industry. (*Source: Value Line Investment Survey,* June 28, 1992.)

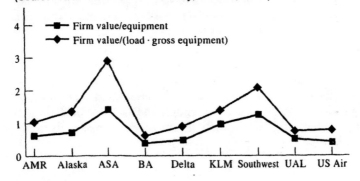

511

you want to use fixed asset multiples in valuation, you must get *some* estimate of the rate of capacity utilization.

SUMMARY

In this chapter we discussed the ''quick and dirty'' method of valuation—valuation with multiples. Valuation with multiples allows us to remain agnostic about the determinants of value. By using multiples, we *estimate values by appropriately scaling prices of similar firms.* Since the method is not based on an analysis of the determinants of value, it is important to select judiciously comparable firms and bases according to which the prices of these firms can be scaled to estimate values.

The process of valuation with multiples involves the following steps:

• Choosing comparable firms that are *as similar as possible to the firm that we value.*

• Choosing several bases to scale the prices of comparable firms, such as Sales, Gross Profits, Earnings, book values, and industry-specific measures.

• Averaging across industry the *scaled* prices of comparable firms—their prices divided by the various scales used to measure relative sizes

• Projecting bases for the valued firm to match the average ''prices per . . .'' of comparable firms

• Valuing the firm by multiplying the average multiples of comparable firms to the projected parameters of the valued firm

Since the values that we obtain from various multiples are typically different, the last step requires a careful examination of the differences in order to integrate them into a final value estimate. Since the selection of comparable firms has such a paramount role in valuation with multiples, special attention must be paid to selecting a true comparable sample of firms—firms that are in the same industry, employ the same technology, apply to similar clienteles, are of similar size, and so on. Inevitably, this selection will entail some compromises: Since there are no two identical firms, the selection of comparable firms should balance the desire to get as large a sample as possible so that idiosyncrasies of individual firms wash out against the desire to ensure a high degree of similarity of the sample to the firm being valued.

One potential source of cross-sectional differences is leverage: Even otherwise similar firms may choose quite different leverages. A possible solution is to use *whole-firm multiples*—multiples that compare total firm values to whole-firm measures of performance (Sales, EBIT, and the like)—rather than *equity multiples*—multiples that compare *equity* values to the measure of relative *equity* scale (most commonly, EPS). Whole-firm multiples can also be used when firms in the industry use a different mix of securities—some have issued preferred stocks, whereas others have not; some have given their employees stock options, whereas others have no warrants outstanding. When this is the case, simply add the value of all the securities of the firm to relate the value of the whole firm to the performance measure of the whole firm.

Finally, we return to the main message of this book: Athough we think that it is valuable to examine valuation ratios and multiples, we ultimately believe that you are better off concentrating your valuation efforts on a thorough analysis of the firm's cash flows. Valuation by multiples is subject to too many vagaries:

* It is too affected by transitory events.
* It hardly reflects future trends.
* It hardly reflects risk differences even when restricted to the same industry's comparisons.

EXERCISES

10.1 ABC Corp. has a Price/Earnings (P/E) ratio (defined as the ratio of the current price to last year's earnings, P_0/E_0) of 15. ABC's expected dividend payout ratio is 30 percent and its expected annual growth rate is 10 pecent.

    a What will be the cost of ABC's equity implied by its current P/E ratio if the assumptions of the Gordon formula are valid?

    b What would ABC's P/E ratio be if the cost of capital were 25 percent?

    c What would ABC's P/E ratio be if its cost of capital were 15 percent and its growth rate were 8 percent?

    d What do you learn from the relative P/E ratios about the appropriate use of P/E ratios?

10.2 The following 1994 information concerns the Grand-Widget industry's only two firms—LMN and QRS companies. The two companies face identical risks and are operated identically.

	LMN	QRS
Market value of debt	$200,000	$400,000
Market value of equity	$400,000	$100,000
Sales	$400,000	$200,000
Net income	$40,000	$12,000
After-tax interest expense	$10,000	$24,000

    a Based on their 1994 earnings, what are the *trailing earnings* multiples of LMN's and QRS's shares?

    b Based on their 1994 earnings and market prices, which of the two *firms* represents a better investment opportunity? Compare your answer in this part to your answer for part **a.** Is this reasonable? Given the relative *firm's* values, what would you expect the relative values of the stocks to be? Can you explain the difference?

    c If LMN's *total firm value* had the same relation to Sales as the relation of QRS's total value to Sales, what would be LMN's total firm value?

10

Price/Earnings Ratios

The Price/Earnings (P/E) multiple is the most widely used and misread of all multiples. Its simplicity makes it an attractive choice in applications ranging from pricing initial public offerings to making judgments on relative value, but its relationship to a firm's financial fundamentals is often ignored, leading to significant errors in applications. This chapter will try to provide some insight into the determinants of price/earnings ratios.

THE USE AND MISUSE OF P/E RATIOS

There are a number of reasons the P/E ratio is used so widely in valuation. First, it is an intuitively appealing statistic that relates the price paid to current earnings. Second, it is simple to compute for most stocks and is widely available, making comparisons across stocks simple. Third, P/E ratios are a proxy for a number of other characteristics of the firm, including risk and growth.

While there are good reasons for using a P/E ratio, there is wide potential for misuse. One reason given for using a P/E ratio is that it eliminates the need to make assumptions about risk, growth, and payout ratios, all of which have to be estimated for DCF valuation. This is disingenuous, because P/E ratios are ultimately determined by the very same parameters that determine value in DCF models. Thus, the use of P/E ratios is a way for some analysts to avoid having to be explicit about their assumptions on risk, growth, and payout ratios. This may be convenient, but it is certainly not a legitimate reason for using P/E ratios. Another reason for using the P/E ratios of comparable firms is that they are much more likely to reflect market moods and perceptions. Thus, if investors are upbeat about retail stocks, the P/E ratios of these stocks will be higher to reflect this optimism. Again, this can be viewed as a weakness, especially when markets make systematic errors in valuing entire sectors. If, for instance, investors have overvalued retail stocks, on average, using the average P/E ratio of these stocks will build in that error into the valuation.

ESTIMATING P/E RATIOS FROM FUNDAMENTALS

The P/E ratio can be related to the same fundamentals that determine value in DCF models: expected growth rates, payout ratios, and risk.

P/E Ratio for a Stable Firm

A stable firm is a firm growing at a rate comparable to the nominal-growth rate in the economy in which it operates. The value of equity for a stable firm, using the Gordon growth model described in Chapter 6, is:

$$P_0 = \frac{DPS_1}{r - g_n}$$

where P_0 = Value of equity
DPS_1 = Expected dividends per share next year
r = Required rate of return on equity
g_n = Growth rate in dividends (forever)

Substituting $EPS_0 \times$ Payout ratio $\times (1 + g_n)$ for DPS_1, the value of the equity can be written as:

$$P_0 = \frac{EPS_0 \times \text{Payout ratio} \times (1 + g_n)}{r - g_n}$$

Rewriting in terms of the PE ratio:

$$\frac{P_0}{EPS_0} = P/E = \frac{\text{Payout ratio} \times (1 + g_n)}{r - g_n}$$

If the P/E ratio is stated in terms of expected earnings in the next time period, this can be simplified to:

$$\frac{P_0}{EPS_1} = P/E_1 = \frac{\text{Payout ratio}}{r - g_n}$$

TABLE 10.1   P/E Ratios for Stable Firms

Multiply the firm's payout ratio by the appropriate number

Discount Rate	Expected Growth Rate								
	0.00%	1.00%	2.00%	3.00%	4.00%	5.00%	6.00%	7.00%	8.00%
12%	8.33	9.18	10.20	11.44	13.00	15.00	17.67	21.40	27.00
13%	7.69	8.42	9.27	10.30	11.56	13.13	15.14	17.83	21.60
14%	7.14	7.77	8.50	9.36	10.40	11.67	13.25	15.29	18.00
15%	6.67	7.21	7.85	8.58	9.45	10.50	11.78	13.38	15.43
16%	6.25	6.73	7.29	7.92	8.67	9.55	10.60	11.89	13.50
17%	5.88	6.31	6.80	7.36	8.00	8.75	9.64	10.70	12.00
18%	5.56	5.94	6.38	6.87	7.43	8.08	8.83	9.73	10.80
19%	5.26	5.61	6.00	6.44	6.93	7.50	8.15	8.92	9.82
20%	5.00	5.32	5.67	6.06	6.50	7.00	7.57	8.23	9.00

The P/E ratio is an increasing function of the payout ratio and the growth rate and a decreasing function of the riskiness of the firm.

Table 10.1 provides approximate P/E ratios for stable firms for a range of discount rates and growth rates.

Illustration 10.1   Estimating the P/E Ratio for a Stable Firm: Exxon

Exxon had EPS of $3.82 in 1992 and paid out 74% of its earnings as dividends that year. The growth rate in earnings and dividends, in the long term, was expected to be 6%. The beta for Exxon was 0.75 and the T.Bond rate was 7%.

Current dividend/payout ratio = 74%
Expected growth rate in earnings and dividends = 6%
Cost of equity = 7% + (0.75 × 5.5%) = 11.13%

P/E ratio based on fundamentals = 0.74 × 1.06/(0.1113 − 0.06) = 15.29

Exxon was selling at a P/E ratio of 17.02 at the time of this analysis, May 1993.

Illustration 10.2   Estimating the P/E Ratio for a Stable Firm: Royal Dutch Petroleum (Netherlands)

Royal Dutch Petroleum, one of the largest oil companies in the world, had EPS of 11.19 Dutch Guilders (NG) and dividends per share of 8.45 NG in 1992. The beta for the stock was 0.74. The 10-year bond rate in the

Netherlands in July 1993 was 6.24%, and the risk premium for stocks over bonds is assumed to be 4.50%.

Dividend payout ratio = 75.51%
Expected growth rate in earnings and dividends in long term = 5%
Cost of equity = 6.24% + 0.74(4.50%) = 9.57%

P/E ratio based upon fundamentals = $0.7551 \times 1.05/(0.0957 - 0.05)$
= 17.35

Royal Dutch Petroleum was selling at a P/E ratio of 16.19 in July 1993.

P/E Ratio for a High-Growth Firm

The P/E ratio for a high-growth firm can also be related to fundamentals. In the special case of the two-stage dividend-discount model, this relationship can be made explicit fairly simply. When the growth rate and payout ratios are known, the dividend-discount model can be written as follows:

$$P_0 = \frac{EPS_0 \times \text{Payout ratio} \times (1 + g) \times \left(1 - \frac{(1 + g)^n}{(1 + r)^n}\right)}{r - g}$$

$$+ \frac{EPS_0 \times \text{Payout ratio}_n \times (1 + g)^n \times (1 + g_n)}{(r - g_n)(1 + r)^n}$$

where EPS_0 = Earnings per share in year 0 (Current year)
g = Growth rate in the first n years
r = Required rate of return on equity
Payout = Payout ratio in the first n years
g_n = Growth rate after n years forever (stable-growth rate)
Payout_n = Payout ratio after n years for the stable firm

Bringing EPS_0 to the left-hand side of the equation,

$$\frac{P_0}{EPS_0} = \frac{\text{Payout ratio} \times (1 + g) \times \left(1 - \frac{(1 + g)^n}{(1 + r)^n}\right)}{r - g}$$

$$+ \frac{\text{Payout ratio}_n \times (1 + g)^n \times (1 + g_n)}{(r - g_n)(1 + r)^n}$$

The left-hand side of the equation is the P/E ratio. It is determined by the following:

1. *Payout ratio during the high-growth period and in the stable period:* The P/E ratio increases as the payout ratio increases.
2. *Riskiness (through the discount rate r):* The P/E ratio becomes lower as riskiness increases.
3. *Expected growth rate in earnings, in both the high-growth and stable phases:* The P/E increases as the growth rate increases, in either period.

This formula is general enough to be applied to any firm, even one that is not paying dividends currently. In fact, the ratio of FCF to earnings can be substituted for the payout ratio for firms that pay significantly less in dividends than they can afford to.

Illustration 10.3   Estimating the P/E Ratio for a High-Growth Firm in the Two-Stage Model

Assume that you have been asked to estimate the P/E ratio for a firm that has the following characteristics:

Growth rate in first five years = 25%	Payout ratio in first five years = 20%
Growth rate after five years = 8%	Payout ratio after five years = 50%
Beta = 1.0	Riskfree rate = T.Bond rate = 6%
Required rate of return = 6% + 1(5.5%) = 11.5%	

$$P/E = \frac{0.2 \times (1.25) \times \left(1 - \frac{(1.25)^5}{(1.115)^5}\right)}{(0.115 - 0.25)} + \frac{0.5 \times (1.25)^5 \times (1.08)}{(0.115 - 0.08)(1.115)^5} = 28.75$$

The estimated P/E ratio for this firm is 28.75.

Illustration 10.4   Estimating the P/E Ratio for Eli Lilly in May 1993

The following is an estimation of the appropriate P/E ratio for Eli Lilly in May 1993. The growth rate, estimated for the initial high-growth period from 1993 to 1997 of five years, was 9.81%, during which the payout ratio was expected to be 53.78%.

Growth rate in high-growth period = 9.81%
Length of high-growth period = 5 years
Payout ratio during high-growth period = 53.78% (equal to current payout ratio)

The beta of Eli Lilly was 1.05, and the T.Bond rate was 7%, yielding a cost of equity of 7% + (1.05 × 5.5%), or 12.78%. The expected growth rate in the stable phase is 6%, and the payout ratio during this phase is expected to be 67.44% (based upon fundamentals).

The P/E ratio can be estimated based upon these inputs:

$$P/E = \frac{0.5378 \times (1.0981) \times \left(1 - \frac{(1.0981)^5}{(1.1278)^5}\right)}{(0.1278 - 0.0981)}$$

$$+ \frac{0.6744 \times (1.0981)^5 \times (1.06)}{(0.1278 - 0.06)(1.1278)^5} = 11.72$$

Eli Lilly was trading at a P/E ratio of 10.67 in May 1993.

P/E Ratios and Expected Extraordinary Growth

The P/E ratio of a high-growth firm is a function of the expected extraordinary-growth rate—the higher the expected growth, the higher the P/E ratio for a firm. In Illustration 10.3, for instance, the P/E ratio can be graphed as a function of the extraordinary-growth rate. As the firm's anticipated extraordinary-growth rate in the first five years declines from 25% to 8%, the P/E ratio for the firm also decreases from 28.75 to 15.

Investment Strategies that Compare P/E to the Expected-Growth Rate

Portfolio managers and analysts sometimes compare P/E ratios to the expected-growth rate to identify undervalued and overvalued stocks. In the simplest form of this approach, firms with P/E ratios less than their expected-growth rate are viewed as undervalued. In its more general form, the ratio of P/E to growth is used as a measure of relative value, with lower values believed to indicate undervaluation relative to other firms. Peters (1991) provides a simple test of this proposition by classifying firms into deciles based upon the ratio of P/E to expected long term growth, for every quarter from January 1982 to June

FIGURE 10.1 P/E Ratios and Extraordinary Growth

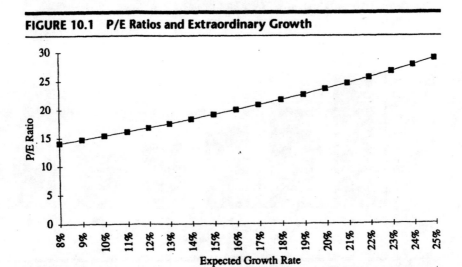

1989. The lowest P/E-growth decile outperformed the market in 26 out of the 30 quarters for which returns were measured and earned significantly higher returns than the S&P 500. The compounded return over the period was 1,536% for the lowest P/E-growth decile, while the return on the S&P 500 Index over the same period was 356%.

In its simple form, there is no basis for believing that a firm is undervalued just because it has a P/E ratio less than its expected-growth rate. This relationship may be consistent with a fairly valued or even an overvalued firm if interest rates are high or if a firm is of high risk. The following example expands on the firm described in Illustration 10.3, where under the initial assumptions about interest rates and risk, the firm had a P/E ratio of 28.75, which was greater than the expected-growth rate. It evaluates the P/E ratio as a function of the level of interest rates and of risk, as measured by betas.

Illustration 10.5 P/E Ratio versus Growth—The Effect of Interest Rates and Risk

In Illustration 10.3, the T.Bond rate used is 6%. The effects of increasing the T.Bond rate on P/E ratios is examined in Figure 10.2. As shown in the graph, the P/E ratio for this firm is lower than the expected-growth rate when the T.Bond rate is greater than 7%, though it is not undervalued. For instance, the P/E ratio will drop to 11.96 if the T.Bond rate

FIGURE 10.2 P/E Ratios and T.Bond Rates

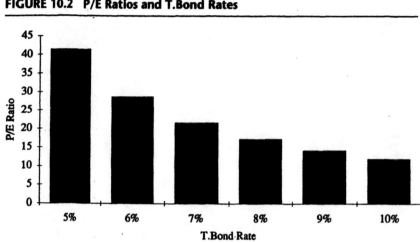

increases to 10%, well below the expected-growth rate of 25% in the first five years, but still correctly valued.

A similar analysis can be done relating the P/E ratio to the beta of the firm. In Illustration 10.3, the P/E ratio will decline as the beta is increased, and this relationship is summarized in the graph in Figure 10.3. In this graph as well, the P/E ratio for the firm will be lower than the expected growth rate if the beta of the firm exceeds 1.10, even though it is not undervalued.

FIGURE 10.3 P/E Ratios and Betas

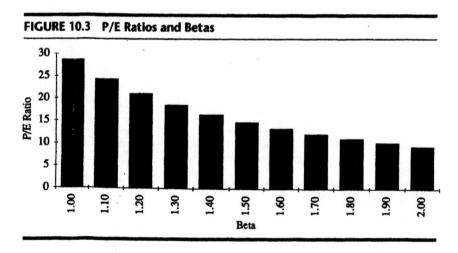

The danger of concluding that a firm is undervalued just because its P/E ratio is less than its expected-growth rate is that it may be the wrong conclusion for high-risk (beta) firms or when interest rates are high.

In its relative form, where firms are ranked on the basis of the ratio of P/E to expected growth, the rankings will provide a measure of relative value if (a) the length of the high-growth period is the same for all firms, and (b) all firms are of equivalent risk (if the model used is the CAPM, all firms have the same betas). If these assumptions are not fulfilled, however, a direct comparison of the ratio of P/E to expected growth may not be justified because a higher-risk firm should be expected to have a lower P/E ratio than another firm with the same expected-growth rate but much less risk. Similarly the P/E ratio for a firm for which high growth is expected to last 5 years will be lower than the P/E ratio for a firm for which the same high growth is expected to last 10 years.

Illustration 10.6 Comparing the P/E Ratios of Firms with Different Risk Levels

Consider two firms with the same expected-growth rates of 25% for the first five years and 8% after that and with the same payout policies (payout ratio in first five years = 20%; payout ratio after year 5 = 50%) but different levels of risk (beta of the first firm = 1.0; beta of the second firm = 1.5). The P/E ratio for the riskier firm will be lower than the P/E ratio for the safer firm.

P/E ratio of safer firm:

$$P/E = \frac{0.2 \times (1.25) \times \left(1 - \frac{(1.25)^5}{(1.115)^5}\right)}{(0.115 - 0.25)} + \frac{0.5 \times (1.25)^5 \times (1.08)}{(0.115 - 0.08)(1.115)^5} = 28.75$$

P/E ratio of riskier firm:

$$P/E = \frac{0.2 \times (1.25) \times \left(1 - \frac{(1.25)^5}{(1.1425)^5}\right)}{(0.425 - 0.25)} + \frac{0.5 \times (1.25)^5 \times (1.08)}{(0.1425 - 0.08)(1.1425)^5}$$

$$= 14.87$$

The P/E ratio of the safer firm will be higher than the P/E ratio of the riskier firm at every level of growth, as shown in Figure 10.4.

FIGURE 10.4   P/E Ratios and Expected Growth: High-Risk vs. Low-Risk

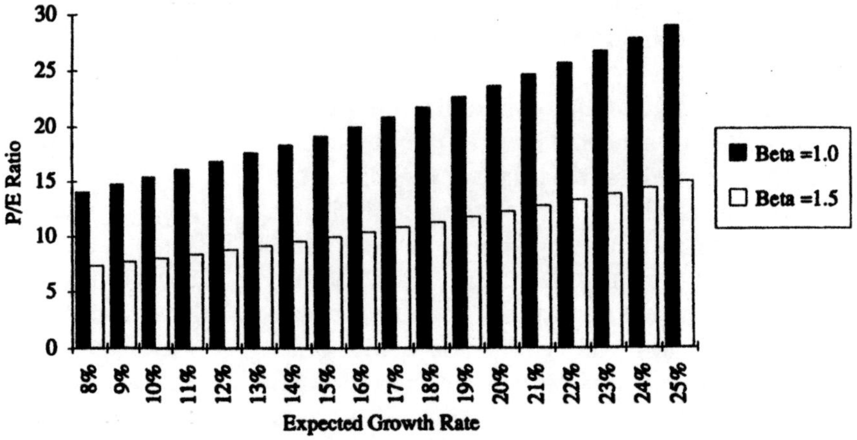

COMPARISONS OF P/E RATIOS

P/E ratios are often compared across countries, across companies, and across time. While these comparisons can yield valuable information, they often fail to control for changes in the fundamentals that affect these multiples.

Comparisons Across Countries

Comparisons are often made between P/E ratios in different countries with the intention of finding undervalued and overvalued markets. It is clearly misleading in these cases to compare P/E ratios across different markets without controlling for differences in the underlying variables. This is illustrated as follows:

Illustration 10.7   P/E Ratios in Markets with Different Fundamentals

The following table presents the summary economic statistics for stock markets in two different countries: Country 1 and Country 2. The key difference between the two countries is that interest rates are much higher in Country 1.

	Country 1	Country 2
T.Bond rate	10.00%	5.00%
Market premium	4.00%	5.50%
Expected market return	14.00%	10.50%
Expected inflation	4.00%	4.00%
Expected growth in real GNP	2.00%	3.00%
Expected nominal growth	6.00%	7.00%
Average payout ratio	50.00%	50.00%
Expected P/E ratio	$(0.5 \times 1.06)/(0.14 - 0.06)$ $= 6.625$	$(0.5 \times 1.07)/(0.105 - 0.07)$ $= 15.29$

In this case, the P/E ratio in Country 2 will be significantly higher than the P/E ratio in Country 1, but it can be justified on the basis of differences in financial fundamentals.

This principle can be extended to broader comparisons of P/E ratios across countries. The following table summarizes P/E ratios across different countries at the end of 1992, together with interest rates (short-term and long term) and expected growth in the GNP for 1993.

A naive comparison of P/E ratios would suggest that Japanese stocks, with a P/E ratio of 38.2, were overvalued, while Dutch stocks, with a P/E ratio of 12.8, were undervalued. There was, however, a strong positive correlation between P/E ratios and expected GNP growth, and a negative correlation between P/E ratios and interest rates.

TABLE 10.2   P/E Ratios, Interest Rates and Growth

Country	P/E Ratio	Interest Rate Short Term	Long Term	Expected Growth Rate in GNP-1993
Australia	20.1	5.65%	8.67%	3.0%
Canada	17.2	6.36%	8.69%	2.7%
France	14.9	12.31%	7.94%	0.6%
Germany	14.4	8.45%	7.01%	−0.8%
Great Britain	18.9	6.19%	8.54%	1.1%
Japan	38.2	3.46%	4.28%	1.7%
Netherlands	12.8	9.05%	8.55%	0.5%
Switzerland	15.2	5.75%	5.34%	0.4%
United States (S&P 500)	24.0	3.21%	7.25%	2.9%

Correlation between P/E ratio and short term interest
    rates = −0.883
Correlation between P/E ratio and long term interest
    rates = −0.183
Correlation between P/E ratio and expected growth rate in GNP
    = 0.767

A cross-sectional regression of P/E ratio on interest rates and expected-growth yields the following:

$$P/E \text{ ratio} = 41.85 - 0.20 \text{ Short term rate} - 3.44 \text{ Long term rate} + 3.21 \text{ Growth in GNP}$$

The three variables used in this regression explain a significant proportion (85%) of the differences in P/E ratios across countries. Based upon this regression, the predicted P/E ratios for the countries are as follows:

TABLE 10.3   Actual versus Predicted P/E Ratios

Country	Actual P/E	Predicted P/E	Over/Undervalued by
Australia	20.1	20.56	−0.46
Canada	17.2	19.38	−2.18
France	14.9	14.04	0.86
Germany	14.4	13.51	0.89
Great Britain	18.9	14.80	4.10
Japan	38.2	31.91	6.29
Netherlands	12.8	12.27	0.53
Switzerland	15.2	23.64	−8.44
United States (S&P 500)	24.0	25.60	−1.60

From this comparison, Dutch stocks, which had the lowest P/E ratio, would have been considered overvalued after controlling for differences in interest rates and GDP growth, while Canadian, Swiss, and U.S. stocks would have been considered undervalued.

Comparisons across Time

Another comparison that is often made is between P/E ratios across time. As the fundamentals (interest rates and expected growth) change over time, the P/E ratio will also change. A more appropriate comparison, therefore, is not between P/E ratios across time but between the actual

P/E ratio and the predicted P/E ratio based upon fundamentals existing at that time. This is shown in the following illustration:

Illustration 10.8   P/E Ratios across Time

The following table presents the summary economic statistics at two points in time for the same stock market. The interest rates in the first period were significantly higher than the interest rates in the second period.

	Period 1	Period 2
T.Bond rate	11.00%	6.00%
Market premium	5.50%	5.50%
Expected market return	16.50%	11.50%
Expected inflation	5.00%	4.00%
Expected growth in real GNP	3.00%	2.50%
Expected nominal growth	8.00%	6.50%
Average payout ratio	50.00%	50.00%
Expected P/E ratio	$(0.5 \times 1.08)/(0.165 - 0.08)$ = 6.35	$(0.5 \times 1.065)/(0.115 - 0.065)$ = 10.65

The P/E ratio in the second time period will be significantly higher than the P/E ratio in the first period, largely because of the drop in interest rates.

Figure 10.5 summarizes the Earnings/Price (E/P) ratios for the average stock in the market and the long term treasury bond rates in each year from 1960 to 1992. There is a strong positive relationship between E/P ratios and T.Bond rates, as evidenced by the correlation of 0.94 between the two variables. A regression of E/P ratios on short term and long term rates yields the following for U.S. stocks, using data from 1960 to 1992.

E/P = 3.35% − 0.1824 T.Bond Rate + 0.8942 T.Bill Rate
(3.52)   (0.67)   (3.43)

Based upon this regression, the predicted E/P ratio at the beginning of 1993, with the T.Bill rate at 3% and the T.Bond rate at 7%, would have been:

$E/P_{1993} = 3.35\% - 0.1824(7\%) + 0.8942(3\%) = 4.76\%$

which would have yielded a P/E ratio of:

$$P/E_{1993} = 1/E/P_{1993} = 1/0.0476 = 21.03$$

The actual P/E ratio in May 1993 was 22.50.

This regression can be enriched by adding other variables that should be correlated to the P/E ratio, such as expected growth in GNP and payout ratios, as independent variables.

Comparing P/E Ratios across Firms

P/E ratios vary across industries and across firms because of differences in fundamentals—higher growth generally translates into higher P/E ratios. When comparisons are made across firms, differences in risk, growth rates, and payout ratios have to be controlled for explicitly.

Using Comparable Firms—Pros and Cons

The most common approach to estimate the P/E ratio for a firm is to choose a group of comparable firms, to calculate the average P/E ratio

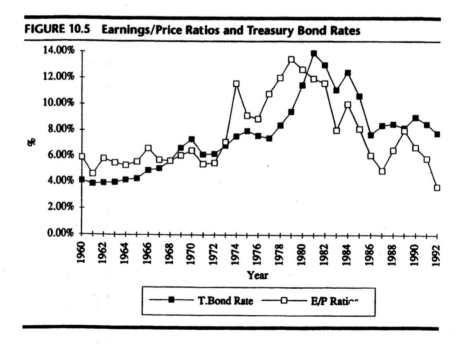

FIGURE 10.5   Earnings/Price Ratios and Treasury Bond Rates

for this group, and to subjectively adjust this average for differences between the firm being valued and the comparable firms.

There are several problems with this approach. First, the definition of a *comparable* firm is essentially a subjective one. The use of other firms in the industry as the control group is often not a solution because firms within the same industry can have very different business mixes and risk and growth profiles. There is also plenty of potential for bias. One clear example of this is in takeovers, where a high P/E ratio for the target firm is justified, using the P/E ratios of a control group of other firms that have been taken over. This group is designed to give an upward biased estimate of the P/E ratio and other multiples. Second, even when a legitimate group of comparable firms can be constructed, differences will continue to persist in fundamentals between the firm being valued and this group. Adjusting for differences subjectively does not provide a satisfactory solution to this problem.

Using the Entire Cross-section: A Regression Approach

In contrast to the comparable-firm approach, the regression approach uses the information in the entire cross-section of firms to predict P/E ratios. The simplest way of summarizing this information is with a multiple regression, with the P/E ratio as the dependent variable and proxies for risk, growth, and payout forming the independent variables.

1. Past studies. This approach is not new. One of the earliest studies was done by Kisor and Whitbeck (1963). Using data from the Bank of New York as of June 1962 for 135 stocks, they arrived at the following regression:

P/E = 8.2 + 1.5 (Growth rate in earnings) + 6.7 (Payout ratio)
        − 0.2 (Standard deviation in EPS changes)

Cragg and Malkiel (1968) followed up by estimating the coefficients for a regression of the P/E ratio on the growth rate, the payout ratio, and the beta for stocks for the time period from 1961 to 1965.

Year	Equation	R^2
1961	P/E = 4.73 + 3.28g + 2.05π − 0.85β	0.70
1962	P/E = 11.06 + 1.75g + 0.78π − 1.61β	0.70
1963	P/E = 2.94 + 2.55g + 7.62π − 0.27β	0.75
1964	P/E = 6.71 + 2.05g + 5.23π − 0.89β	0.75
1965	P/E = 0.96 + 2.74g + 5.01π − 0.35β	0.85

where P/E = Price/Earnings ratio at the start of the
year
g = Growth rate in earnings
π = Earnings payout ratio at the start of the
year
β = Beta of the stock

They concluded that while such models were useful in explaining P/E ratios, they were of little use in predicting performance.

Fuller, Huberts, and Levinson (1992) took a different tack and regressed E/P ratios of firms on the COMPUSTAT data bases against the growth rate in earnings in the subsequent eight years. They found that stocks with high E/P ratios (low P/E ratios) had significantly lower growth in the subsequent period than stocks with low E/P ratios (high P/E ratios), suggesting that E/P ratios do convey information about future earnings growth.

2. Updated regressions. These P/E ratio regressions have been updated in the following section using data from 1987 to 1991. The COMPUSTAT data base was used to extract information on P/E ratios, payout ratios, and earnings growth rates* (for the preceding five years) for all NYSE and AMEX firms with data available in each year. The betas were obtained from the CRSP tape for each year. All firms with negative earnings were eliminated from the sample, and the regression of P/E on the independent variable yielded the following for each year:

Year	Regression	R^2
1987	P/E = 7.1839 + 13.05 Payout − 0.6259 Beta + 6.5659 EGR	0.9287
1988	P/E = 2.5848 + 29.91 Payout − 4.5157 Beta + 19.9143 EGR	0.9465
1989	P/E = 4.6122 + 59.74 Payout − 0.7546 Beta + 9.0072 EGR	0.5613
1990	P/E = 3.5955 + 10.88 Payout − 0.2801 Beta + 5.4573 EGR	0.3497
1991	P/E = 2.7711 + 22.89 Payout − 0.1326 Beta + 13.8653 EGR	0.3217

where P/E = Price/Earnings ratio at the end of the year
Payout = Dividend/Payout ratio at the end of the year
Beta = Beta of the stock, using returns from prior five years
EGR = Earnings growth rate over the previous five years

* The use of past growth rates in the regression is not the preferred option. If projected growth rates had been available on the COMPUSTAT data base, as they are on the I/B/E/S tape, they would have been used instead.

3. Problems with the regression methodology.

The regression methodology is a convenient way of compressing large amounts of data into one equation that captures the relationship between P/E ratios and financial fundamentals. But it does have its limitations. First, the basic regression assumes a linear relationship between P/E ratios and the financial proxies, and that might not be appropriate. An analysis of the residuals from a regression may suggest transformations of the independent variables (squared, natural logs) that work better in explaining P/E ratios.

Second, the independent variables are correlated with each other; for example, high-growth firms tend to have high risk. This multicollinearity makes the coefficients of the regressions unreliable and may explain the "wrong" signs on the coefficients and the large changes in these coefficients from period to period.

Third, the basic relationship between P/E ratios and financial variables itself might not be stable, and if it shifts from year to year, the predictions from the model may not be reliable; for instance, the R^2 in the regressions reported from 1987 to 1991 declines from 0.93 in 1987 to 0.32 in 1991, and the coefficients change dramatically over time. Part of the reason for this is that earnings are volatile, and P/E ratios reflect this volatility. The low R^2 for the 1991 regression can be ascribed to the recession's effects on earnings in that year.

Illustration 10.9 Valuing a Private Firm Using the Cross-Sectional Regression

Assume that you had been asked to value a private firm early in 1992 and that you had obtained the following data on the company:

BV of Equity = $100 million
Net income in 1991 = $20 million
FCFE in 1991 = $8 million
Earnings growth rate over previous five years = 25%
Beta based upon comparable firms = 1.20

First compute the variables in the desired units,

Payout ratio = 8/20 = 0.40
Earnings growth rate = 25%
Beta = 1.20

Based upon the P/E ratio regression reported for the end of 1991,

$$\text{Predicted P/E Ratio} = 2.7711 + 22.89(0.40) - 0.1326(1.20)$$
$$+ 13.8653(0.25) = 15.23$$

$$\text{Predicted MV of equity} = \text{Net income} \times \text{P/E Ratio}$$
$$= 20 \times 15.23 = \$304.60 \text{ million}$$

PROBLEMS WITH P/E RATIOS

There are general problems associated with the estimation of P/E ratios that make its use troublesome. First, P/E ratios are not meaningful when the EPS is negative. While this can be partially overcome by using a normalized or average EPS, the problem cannot be eliminated. Second, the volatility of earnings can cause the P/E ratio to change dramatically from period to period. For a cyclical firm, earnings will follow the economy, whereas prices reflect expectations about the future. Thus, it is not uncommon for the P/E ratio of a cyclical firm to peak at the depths of a recession and bottom out at the peak of an economic boom.

Illustration 10.10 An Extended Application: Valuing an Initial Public Offering Using P/E Multiples

Consider the example of American Casinos, valued in Illustration 9.13 in the previous chapter using DCF valuation. American Casinos had current earnings of $37.20 million and was expected to register growth in earnings of 15% over the next five years. The P/E ratios for firms involved in gaming entertainment were as follows:

Firm	Beta	Debt/Equity	P/E Ratio	Payout Ratio	Expected Growth
Aztar Corporation	1.35	66.73%	14.70	5.00%	6.00%
Bally Manufacturing	1.60	349.87%	24.33	14.00%	20.00%
Caesar's World	1.35	29.75%	15.50	0.00%	14.50%
Circus Circus	1.35	11.17%	25.40	0.00%	16.50%
International Game Tech.	1.25	3.54%	52.90	0.00%	34.00%
Jackpot Enterprises	1.00	31.02%	22.30	58.00%	32.50%
Mirage Resorts	1.40	81.60%	30.40	0.00%	17.50%
Showboat Inc.	1.10	90.54%	16.10	7.00%	32.00%
Average	1.30	83.03%	25.20	10.50%	21.63%
American Casinos	1.19	50.00%	?	0.00%	15.00%

The average P/E ratio for firms in the gaming entertainment business was 25.20. Applying this P/E ratio to value the equity in American Casinos:

> Value of equity in American Casinos = $37.20 × 25.20
> = $937.58 million

This is much greater than the value of equity obtained from DCF valuation, which is $713.04 million.

One reason for the higher valuation, using the average P/E ratio from comparable firms, may be that publicly traded firms in gaming entertainment were overvalued. Another possible reason for the higher valuation may be that the public firms that form the comparable-firm sample had higher expected growth than American Casinos.

A regression of P/E ratios on fundamentals can also be done, using only the firms in the gaming entertainment business:

> P/E = −31.59 − 20.11 Payout ratio + 107.80 Expected growth
> + 27.38 Beta

Substituting the values for American Casinos,

> Predicted P/E = −31.59 − (20.11 × 0.00) + (107.80 × 0.15)
> + (27.38 × 1.19) = 17.16

Using this predicted P/E ratio yields a value of equity of:

> Value of equity = 37.20 million × 17.16 = $638.35 million

This value is much closer to the value obtained from DCF valuation.

VARIANTS OF THE P/E RATIO

There are several variants of earnings multiples in use—some use accounting earnings, while others use cash flows; some are based upon pretax earnings, while others use after-tax earnings. Most of these variants can be analyzed using the same framework used for analyzing the P/E ratio.

Price/FCFE Ratio

There are some analysts who prefer to use Price/FCFE ratios to value firms because of well-documented problems with accounting measures of earnings. In order to analyze the determinants of Price/FCFE ratios, consider the FCFE two-stage model:

$$P_0 = \frac{FCFE_0(1 + g)\left(1 - \dfrac{(1 + g)^n}{(1 + r)^n}\right)}{r - g} + \frac{FCFE_0(1 + g)^n(1 + g_n)}{(r - g_n)(1 + r)^n}$$

where P_0 = Value of the stock now

$FCFE_0$ = Free cash flow to equity in year 0

g = Expected growth rate during extraordinary-growth period (first n years)

r = Required rate of return on equity

g_n = Expected growth rate in stable period (after n years)

Rearranging terms:

$$\frac{P_0}{FCFE_0} = \frac{(1 + g)\left(1 - \dfrac{(1 + g)^n}{(1 + r)^n}\right)}{r - g} + \frac{(1 + g)^n(1 + g_n)}{(r - g_n)(1 + r)^n}$$

The determinants of Price/FCFE ratios are similar to the determinants of P/E ratios—they include expected-growth rate in the initial high-growth period, expected-growth rate during the stable period, and the relationship between capital spending and depreciation.

Note that a common variant of this multiple, which uses the cash flow prior to capital-spending and working-capital needs, overestimates the cash flow to equity investors in the firm and may lead to misleading estimates of value.

Illustration 10.11   Use of Price/FCFE Ratios: Intel Inc.

In 1993, Intel was expected to maintain a growth rate of 22.09%, from 1993 to 1997, in earnings. After 1998, the growth rate in earnings was expected to be 6%. The capital spending, depreciation, and revenue were expected to grow at the same rate as earnings, and the working capital as a percent of revenues was expected to remain unchanged at 40%. Intel had a beta of 1.30 in 1993, but was expected to have a beta of 1.1 in the stable period. The T.Bond rate was 7%.

The projected Price/FCFE ratio based upon these fundamentals is as follows:

$$\frac{P_0}{FCFE_0} = \frac{(1.2209)\left(1 - \frac{(1.2209)^5}{(1.1415)^n}\right)}{0.1415 - 0.2209} + \frac{(1.2209)^5(1.06)}{(0.1305 - 0.06)(1.1415)^5} = 27.19$$

Value of Firm/Free Cash Flow to the Firm

The multiples specified so far in this chapter relate specifically to valuing equity. An alternative ratio yields the value of the firm as a multiple of the FCFF, that is, the cash flows before debt payments. Again, the multiple can be written as follows:

$$V_0 = \frac{FCFF_0(1 + g)\left(1 - \frac{(1 + g)^n}{(1 + WACC)^n}\right)}{WACC - g} + \frac{FCFF_0(1 + g)^n(1 + g_n)}{(WACC - g_n)(1 + r)^n}$$

where V_0 = Value of the firm (today)

$FCFF_0$ = Free cash flow to the firm in current year

g = Expected growth rate in FCFF in extraordinary-growth period (first n years)

WACC = Weighted average cost of capital

g_n = Expected growth rate in FCFF in stable-growth period (after n years)

Rearranging terms:

$$\frac{V_0}{FCFF_0} = \frac{(1 + g)\left(1 - \frac{(1 + g)^n}{(1 + WACC)^n}\right)}{WACC - g} + \frac{(1 + g)^n(1 + g_n)}{(WACC - g_n)(1 + r)^n}$$

Again, this assumes that the FCFF is stated, after taxes, to the firm. Multiples of pretax FCFF (or earnings before interest, taxes, (EBIT)), can be similarly computed from the after-tax multiple:

$$\frac{V_0}{EBIT} = \frac{V_0}{FCFF_0}(1 - Tax\ Rate)$$

This assumes that capital spending is offset by depreciation. The advantage of using this approach for highly levered firms is that it examines the entire firm and may provide more reasonable estimates of value than looking at equity, which is only a small slice of the overall firm. The market value of the outstanding debt can be subtracted from the value of the firm to value equity.

A Note on Multiples of Pretax Cash Flows

Multiples of pretax cash flows will always be lower than multiples of after-tax cash flows. For a firm with a tax rate of 40%, the pretax multiple will be only 60% of the after-tax multiple (using the preceding equation for V_0/EBIT). For investors used to dealing with after-tax multiples, pretax multiples often seem low. This "illusory reasonableness" is part of the reason why they are used to justify large premiums in takeovers.

Illustration 10.12   Using Value/FCFF Approaches to Value a Firm: Time Warner Inc.

Time Warner Inc. had EBIT of $800 million in 1992. It expected FCFF to grow 8% a year for the next five years and 6% a year after that. The cost of capital was 10.43%. The predicted value/FCFF ratio for Time Warner was as follows:

$$\frac{V_0}{FCFF_0} = \frac{(1.08)\left(1 - \frac{(1.08)^5}{(1.1043)^5}\right)}{0.1043 - 0.08} + \frac{(1.08)^5(1.06)}{(0.1043 - 0.06)(1.1043)^5} = 26.09$$

The value/EBIT ratio for Time Warner can be estimated using the tax rate (36%):

$$\frac{V_0}{EBIT} = 26.09 \times (1 - 0.36) = 16.70$$

PRICE/DIVIDEND RATIOS AND DIVIDEND YIELDS

Investors have relied on the dividend yields of stocks, to varying degree, in constructing investment strategies. For value investors of the

Graham-Dodd school and to the Dow theorists,* a high-dividend yield has been a reliable indicator of undervaluation, both for the overall market and for individual stocks.

Determinants of Price/Dividend Ratios and Dividend Yields

The price/dividend ratio is the inverse of the dividend yield, and the determinants of this ratio can be obtained using the simple Gordon growth model:

$$\frac{P_0}{DPS_1} = \frac{1}{r - g_n}$$

where r = Required rate of return on equity

g_n = Expected growth rate in dividends (and earnings) in the long term

The dividend yield can then be written as:

Dividend yield = $r - g_n$ for a stable firm

Thus, the dividend yield for a stable firm should be the difference between the required rate of return on equity and the expected-growth rate in dividends in the long term.

Dividend Yields versus Treasury Rates

The Proposition

A common approach to finding under- or overvaluation in the market is to compare the dividend yield to the interest rate on T.Bonds, with high-dividend yields relative to T.Bond rates being considered a sign of undervaluation, and low-dividend yields a sign of overvaluation. The argument is generally couched in opportunity cost terms. Stocks, it is argued, become better bargains when their dividend yields are high, relative to the offerings on their prime competitors—bonds. Bonds become better investments as T.Bond rates rise relative to dividend yields.

---

* Charles H. Dow suggested that stocks selling at a dividend yield less than 3.5% were overvalued. Dow theorists have remained faithful to the founder's concept of value and argue that investors sell stocks when the dividend yield drops below 3.5% and buy stocks when the yield rises above 6%.

A Test of the Proposition

The graph in Figure 10.6 reports statistics on the dividend yield and T.Bond rates from 1960 to 1992. Does the difference between the average dividend yield on the market and the T.Bond rate have any power in predicting future stock returns? Does a low dividend yield, relative to the T.Bond rate, suggest that stocks are overvalued? To answer these questions, a regression of stock market returns, in annual periods from 1960 to 1992, against the difference between the dividend yield and the T.Bond rate was run. The result of the regression is reported below:

$$XRET_t = 0.0647 - 1.3662(DYLD_{t-1} - TBOND_{t-1})$$
$$(1.18)(1.06)$$

where $XRET_t$ = Stock market returns in period t
$DYLD_{t-1}$ = Dividend yield at the end of period $t-1$
$TBOND_{t-1}$ = Treasury bond rate at the end of period $t-1$

There is no evidence to suggest that the difference between the dividend yields and the T.Bond rates had any power in predicting stock returns in the next period. (The t statistics are insignificant, and the coefficient has the wrong sign.)

FIGURE 10.6   T.Bond Rates and Dividend Yields: 1960–1992

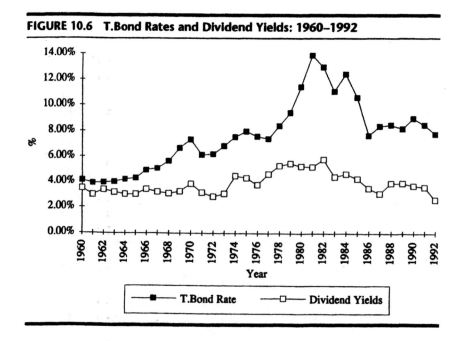

538

The Determinants

If the difference between the dividend yield and the T.Bond rate does not have any predictive power in explaining future stock returns, what, if anything, does it say about market conditions? The appropriate comparisons can be made by manipulating the equation for dividend yield:

$$\text{Dividend yield} = r - g_n$$
$$= (\text{T.Bond rate} + \text{Risk premium}) - g_n$$

$$\text{Dividend yield} - \text{T.Bond rate} = \text{Risk premium} - g_n$$

In general, the difference between the average dividend yield in the market and the T.Bond rate should be equal to the difference between the risk premium for investing in stocks and the expected-growth rate in corporate dividends (and earnings) in the long term. If the risk premium increases, either because investors become more risk averse or because the uncertainty in the underlying economy increases, dividend yields will increase relative to the T.Bond rate. Conversely, if the expected-growth rate increases or the risk premium decreases, T.Bond rates will increase relative to dividend yields.

P/E RATIOS AND STOCK RETURNS

One of the enduring irregularities that has been noted in tests of the CAPM is the tendency of low P/E ratio stocks to outperform the market and high P/E ratio stocks to underperform the market on a risk-adjusted basis. This has been established using a variety of different approaches. Basu (1977) uses the CAPM framework to show that low P/E ratio stocks earn positive excess returns relative to the market and that high P/E ratio stocks underperform the market. Goodman and Peavy (1983) use industry-relative P/E ratios and conclude that stocks with low P/E ratio stocks, relative to the industry in which they operate, earn excess returns. Levy and Lerman (1985) came to the same conclusions using stochastic dominance rather than the CAPM.

Practitioners recognized the value of low P/E ratios well before these academic studies were published. One of the key criteria used by Ben Graham (1962) to pick undervalued stocks was a low P/E ratio. Low P/E ratios also form an integral part of many contrarian strategies.

There are several competing rationale advanced for this phenomenon. One is that the CAPM does not adequately measure risk and that betas are underestimated for low P/E ratio stocks and overestimated for high P/E ratio stocks. Given that low P/E ratio stocks are usually large, stable firms with high dividends, there seems to be little basis for this argument. The second is that the model's focus on pretax returns obscures the higher tax liability that will be faced by the investor buying the low P/E stocks and getting higher dividends. While this critique may be justifiable when tax rates on dividends are significantly higher than capital gains tax rates, it becomes less sustainable when the tax rates on the two types of income are similar and when investors are tax-exempt. The third possibility is that investors consistently overestimate the value of growth and pay too much for high-growth firms and too little for stable firms. This would be a clear violation of market efficiency and could provide opportunities for excess returns for investors who go against the grain and buy portfolios of low P/E stocks.

CONCLUSION

The P/E ratio and other earnings multiples, which are widely used in valuation, have the potential to be misused. These multiples are ultimately determined by the same fundamentals that determine DCF value: expected growth, risk, and payout ratios. To the extent that there are differences in fundamentals across countries, across time, and across companies, the multiples will also be different. A failure to control for these differences in fundamentals can lead to erroneous conclusions based purely upon a direct comparison of multiples.

11

Price/Book Value Ratios

T he relationship between price and book value has always attracted the attention of investors. Stocks selling for well below the book value of equity have generally been considered good candidates for undervalued portfolios, while those selling for more than book value have been targets for overvalued portfolios. This chapter examines the price/book value ratio in more detail; it considers the determinants of this ratio and how best to evaluate or estimate the ratio.

GENERAL ISSUES IN ESTIMATING AND USING PRICE/BOOK VALUE RATIOS

Measurement

The *book value of equity* is the difference between the book value of assets and the book value of liabilities. The measurement of the book value of assets is largely determined by accounting convention. In the United States, it is the original price paid for the assets reduced by any allowable depreciation on the assets. Consequently, the book value of an asset decreases as it ages. The book value of liabilities similarly reflects the "at-issue" values of the liabilities.

Book Value versus Market Value

The market value of an asset reflects its earning power and expected cash flows. Since the book value of an asset reflects its original cost, it might deviate significantly from market value if the earning power of the asset has either increased or declined significantly since its acquisition.

Advantages of Using Price/Book Value Ratios

There are several reasons why investors find the price/book value ratio useful in investment analysis. The first is that the book value provides a relatively stable, intuitive measure of value that can be compared to the market price. For investors who instinctively mistrust DCF estimates of value, it is a much simpler benchmark for comparison. The second is that, given reasonably consistent accounting standards across firms, price/book value ratios can be compared across similar firms for signs of under- or overvaluation. Finally, even firms with negative earnings, which cannot be valued using price/earnings ratios, can be evaluated using price/book value ratios.

Disadvantages of Using Price/Book Value Ratios

There are several disadvantages associated with measuring and using price/book value ratios. First, book values, like earnings, are affected by accounting decisions on depreciation and other variables. When accounting standards vary widely across firms, the price/book value ratios may not be comparable across firms. A similar statement can be made about comparing price/book value ratios across countries with different accounting standards. Second, book value may not carry much meaning for service firms that do not have significant fixed assets. Third, the book value of equity can become negative if a firm has a sustained string of negative earnings reports, leading to a negative price/book value ratio.

ESTIMATING PRICE/BOOK VALUE RATIOS FROM FUNDAMENTALS

The price/book value (P/BV) ratio can be related to the same fundamentals that determine value in DCF models.

P/BV Ratio for a Stable Firm

A *stable firm* is a firm growing at a rate comparable to or lower than the nominal growth rate in the economy in which it operates. The value of equity for a stable firm, using the Gordon growth model, is:

$$P_0 = \frac{DPS_1}{r - g_n}$$

where P_0 = Value of equity
DPS_1 = Expected dividends per share next year
r = Required rate of return on equity
g_n = Growth rate in dividends (forever)

Substituting EPS_0 Payout ratio $(1 + g_n)$ for DPS_1, the value of the equity can be written as:

$$P_0 = \frac{EPS_0 \times \text{Payout ratio} \times (1 + g_n)}{r - g_n}$$

Defining the Return on Equity, or ROE as EPS_0/Book Value of Equity, or BV_0, EPS_0 can be written as $ROE \times BV_0$, and the value of equity, P_0, can be written as:

$$P_0 = \frac{BV_0 \times ROE \times \text{Payout ratio} \times (1 + g_n)}{r - g_n}$$

Rewriting in terms of the P/BV ratio:

$$\frac{P_0}{BV_0} = P/BV = \frac{ROE \times \text{Payout ratio} \times (1 + g_n)}{r - g_n}$$

If the ROE is based upon expected earnings in the next time period, this can be simplified to:

$$\frac{P_0}{BV_0} = P/BV = \frac{ROE \times \text{Payout ratio}}{r - g_n}$$

The P/BV ratio is an increasing function of the ROE, the payout ratio, and the growth rate, and a decreasing function of the riskiness of the firm.

This formulation can be simplified even further by relating growth to the ROE:

$$g = (1 - \text{Payout ratio}) \times ROE$$

Substituting back into the P/BV equation,

$$\frac{P_0}{BV_0} = P/BV = \frac{ROE - g_n}{r - g_n}$$

The P/BV ratio of a stable firm is determined by the differential between the ROE and the required rate of return on its projects. If the ROE exceeds the required rate of return, the price will exceed the book value of equity; if the ROE is lower than the required rate of return, it will be lower than the book value of equity. The advantage of this formulation is that it can be used to estimate P/BV ratios for firms that do not pay out dividends.

Illustration 11.1   Estimating the P/BV Ratio for a Stable Firm with Dividends: Exxon

Exxon had earnings per share of $3.82 in 1992 and paid out 74% of its earnings as dividends that year. The growth rate in earnings and dividends, in the long term, was expected to be 6%. The ROE at Exxon in 1992 was 15%. The beta for Exxon was 0.75 and the T. Bond rate was 7%.

Current dividend payout ratio = 74%
Expected growth rate in earnings and dividends = 6%
ROE = 15%
Cost of equity = 7% + (0.75 × 5.5%) = 11.13%

P/BV ratio based on fundamentals = 0.15 × 0.74 × 1.06/(0.1113 − 0.06)
= 2.29

Exxon was selling at a P/BV ratio of 2.44 on the day of this analysis, May 1993.

Illustration 11.2   Estimating the P/BV Ratio for a Privatization Candidate: Jenapharm (Germany)

One of the by-products of German reunification was the Treuhandanstalt, the German privatization agency set up to sell hundreds of formerly East German firms to other German companies, individual investors, and the public. One of the handful of firms that seemed to be a viable candidate for privatization was Jenapharm, the most respected pharmaceutical manufacturer in East Germany. Jenapharm, which was expected to have revenues of 230 million DM in 1991, also was expected to have EBIT of 30 million DM. The firm had a book value of assets of 110 million DM, and a book value of equity of 58 million DM. The interest expenses in 1991 amounted to 15 million DM.

544

The firm was expected to maintain sales in its niche product, a contraceptive pill, and grow at 5% a year in the long term, primarily by expanding into the generic drug market.

The average beta of pharmaceutical firms traded on the Frankfurt Stock Exchange was 1.05, though many of these firms had much more diversified product portfolios and less volatile cash flows. Allowing for the higher leverage and risk in Jenapharm, a beta of 1.25 was used for Jenapharm. The 10-year bond rate in Germany at the time of this valuation was 7%, and the risk premium for stocks over Government bonds is assumed to be 3.5%.

$$\text{Expected net income} = (\text{EBIT} - \text{Interest expense}) \times (1 - t)$$
$$= (30 - 15) \times (1 - 0.4) = 9 \text{ mil DM}$$
$$\text{ROE} = \text{Expected net income/Book value of equity} = 9/58$$
$$= 15.52\%$$
$$\text{Required Return} = 7\% + 1.25 \,(3.5\%) = 11.375\%$$
$$\text{P/BV ratio} = (\text{ROE} - g)/(r - g) = (0.1552 - 0.05)/(0.11375$$
$$-0.05) = 1.65$$
$$\text{Estimated MV of equity} = \text{BV of equity} \times \text{P/BV ratio} = 58 \times 1.65$$
$$= 95.70 \text{ mil DM}$$

P/BV Ratio for a High-Growth Firm

The P/BV ratio for a high-growth firm can also be related to fundamentals. In the special case of the two-stage dividend-discount model, this relationship can be made explicit fairly simply. The value of equity of a high-growth firm in the two-stage dividend-discount model can be written as:

$$\text{Value of equity} = \text{Present value of expected dividends} + \text{Present value of terminal price}$$

When the growth rate is assumed to be constant after the initial high-growth phase, the dividend-discount model can be written as follows:

$$P_0 = \frac{\text{EPS}_0 \times \text{Payout ratio} \times (1 + g) \times \left(1 - \frac{(1 + g)^n}{(1 + r)^n}\right)}{r - g}$$
$$+ \frac{\text{EPS}_0 \times \text{Payout ratio}_n \times (1 + g)^n \times (1 + g_n)}{(r - g_n)(1 + r)^n}$$

where   g = Growth rate in the first n years
   Payout ratio = Payout ratio in the first n years
              g_n = Growth rate after n years forever (stable-growth rate)
Payout ratio$_n$ = Payout ratio after n years for the stable firm

Rewriting EPS_0 in terms of the ROE yields $EPS_0 = BV_0 \times ROE$, and bringing BV_0 to the left-hand side of the equation yields:

$$\frac{P_0}{BV_0} = ROE \times \left[\frac{\text{Payout ratio} \times (1 + g) \times \left(1 - \frac{(1 + g)^n}{(1 + r)^n} \right)}{r - g} \right. $$

$$\left. + \frac{\text{Payout ratio}_n \times (1 + g)^n \times (1 + g_n)}{(r - g_n)(1 + r)^n} \right]$$

The left-hand side of the equation is the P/BV ratio. It is determined by:

   1. *ROE, or EPS/BV per share:* The P/BV ratio is an increasing function of the return on equity.
   2. *Payout ratio during the high-growth period and in the stable-growth period:* The P/BV ratio increases as the payout ratio increases.
   3. *Riskiness (through the discount rate r):* The P/BV ratio becomes lower as riskiness increases.
   4. *Growth rate in earnings, in both the high-growth and stable phases:* The P/BV increases as the growth rate increases, in either period.

This formula is general enough to be applied to any firm, even one that is not currently paying dividends.

Illustration 11.3   Estimating the P/BV Ratio for a High-Growth Firm in the Two-Stage Model

Assume that you have been asked to estimate the P/BV ratio for a firm that has the following characteristics:

   Growth rate in first five years = 20%
   Growth rate after five years = 8%
   Beta = 1.0

Return on equity = 25%
Required rate of return = 6% + 1(5.5%) = 11.5%
Payout ratio in first five years = 20%
Payout ratio after five years = 68%
Riskfree rate = T. Bond rate = 6%

$$P/BV = 0.25 \times \left[\frac{0.2 \times (1.20) \times \left(1 - \frac{(1.20)^5}{(1.115)^5}\right)}{(0.115 - 0.20)} \right.$$

$$\left. + \frac{0.68 \times (1.20)^5 \times (1.08)}{(0.115 - 0.08)(1.115)^5} \right] = 7.89$$

The estimated P/BV ratio for this firm is 7.89.

Illustration 11.4 Estimating the P/BV Ratio for a High-Growth Firm: Telefonos De Mexico

Telefonos De Mexico provides national and international long distance service in Mexico. The firm, which reported earnings growth of 49.53% between 1987 and 1992, was expected to maintain an average growth rate of 40% a year in earnings from 1993 to 2002. Beyond that point, the growth rate was expected to decline to 12%. (Note that these growth rates are high in nominal terms but are reasonable, given the higher inflation rate in Mexico.) The stock, which was traded on the Mexican Stock Exchange and as an ADR in the United States, had a beta of 1.11. The 10-year bond rate in Mexico was 12%, and the risk premium for stocks relative to bonds was 7.5%.

Telefonos De Mexico paid out 4% of its earnings as dividends in 1992, but it was expected to increase its payout ratio to 10% by 1993 and to 60% for the stable-growth period. The ROE in 1992 was 28.72% and was expected to decline to 15% in the stable-growth period.

High-Growth Period	*Stable-Growth Period*
Expected length = 10 years	Growth rate = 12%
Growth rate = 40%	Payout ratio = 60%
Payout ratio = 10%	ROE = 15%
ROE = 28.72%	
Cost of equity = 12% + (1.11 × 7.5%) = 20.325%	

The P/BV ratio, based upon these inputs, is calculated as:

$$P/BV = \left[0.2872 \times \frac{0.1 \times (1.40) \times \left(1 - \frac{(1.40)^{10}}{(1.2033)^{10}}\right)}{(0.2033 - 0.40)} + 0.15 \times \frac{0.60 \times (1.40)^{10} \times (1.12)}{(0.2033 - 0.12)(1.2033)^{10}} \right] = 6.22$$

Telefonos De Mexico traded at a P/BV ratio of 3.41 in July 1993.

Note that while this valuation has been done entirely in Mexican pesos, an equivalent analysis could have been done in U.S. dollars, as long as all the inputs were defined consistently. The cost of equity would have been much lower, since the riskfree rate and the risk premium would have been lower in dollar terms, but the expected-growth rates, in both the high-growth and the stable phases, would also have been lower because of expected currency depreciation (arising from differences in inflation in the two countries).

The contrast between Telefonos De Mexico and telecommunications firms in more stable, lower growth economies is clearly visible when P/BV ratios are compared across these firms.

Country	Firm	P/BV Ratio	Beta	Growth Rate	Payout Ratio
Canada	BCE	1.22	0.75	6%	62.00%
Italy	STET	1.57	1.00	8%	47.67%
Spain	Telefonica	0.96	0.98	10%	70.01%

The lower P/BV ratios can be attributed primarily to lower expected-growth rates in earnings.

The only other telecommunication firm with a comparable P/BV ratio is Nippon Telephone and Telegraph, which had a P/BV ratio of 3.35, with a ROE of only 3.76%. Given that the possibilities of extraordinary growth are limited in Japan, it is difficult to justify this P/BV ratio.

P/BV Ratios and Return on Equity

The P/BV ratio is strongly influenced by the ROE. A lower ROE affects the P/BV ratio directly through the formulation specified in the prior section and indirectly by lowering the expected growth or payout. A simple way of relating the ROE to growth is the following:

Expected-growth rate = Retention ratio × ROE

The effects of lower ROE on the P/BV ratio are shown in the following:

Illustration 11.5   ROE and P/BV

Assume that a firm has the following characteristics:

ROE = 25%   Payout ratio in first five years = 20%
Growth rate in first five years = 20%   Payout ratio after five years = 68%
Growth rate after five years = 8%   Required rate of return = 11.5%
Beta = 1.0

Note that the growth rate in first five years equals:

Retention ratio × ROE = 0.8 × 25% = 20%

and the growth rate after year 5 equals:

Retention ratio × ROE = 0.32 × 25% = 8%

$$
\text{P/BV} = 0.25 \times \left[\frac{0.2 \times (1.20) \times \left(1 - \dfrac{(1.20)^5}{(1.115)^5}\right)}{(0.115 - 0.20)} + \frac{0.68 \times (1.20)^5 \times (1.08)}{(0.115 - 0.08)(1.115)^5} \right] = 7.89
$$

If the firm's ROE drops to 12%, the P/BV will reflect the drop. The lower ROE will also lower expected growth in the initial high-growth period:

Expected-growth rate (first five years) = Retention ratio × ROE
= 0.80 × 12% = 9.6%

After year 5, either the retention ratio has to increase or the expected-growth rate has to be lower than 8%. If the retention ratio is adjusted, the following are true:

New retention ratio after year 5 = Expected growth/ROE = 8%/12%
$$= 66.67\%$$

New payout ratio after year 5 = 1 − Retention ratio = 33.33%

The new P/BV ratio can then be calculated as follows:

$$P/BV = 0.12 \times \left[\frac{0.2 \times (1.096) \times \left(1 - \frac{(1.096)^5}{(1.115)^5}\right)}{(0.115 - 0.096)} + \frac{0.333 \times (1.096)^5 \times (1.08)}{(0.115 - 0.08)(1.115)^5} \right] = 1.25$$

The drop in the ROE has a two-layered impact. First, it lowers the growth rate in earnings and/or the expected payout ratio, thus having an indirect effect on the P/BV ratio. Second, it reduces the P/BV ratio directly.

The P/BV ratio is also influenced by the required rate of return, with higher required rates of return leading to lower P/BV ratios. The influence of the ROE and the required rate of return can be consolidated in one measure by taking the difference between the two rates. The larger the ROE relative to the required rate of return, the greater is the P/BV ratio. In Illustration 11.5, for instance, the firm that had a required rate of return of 11.5% went from having a ROE that was 13.5% greater than the required rate of return to a ROE that barely broke even (0.5% greater than the required rate of return). Consequently, its P/BV ratio declined from 7.89 to 1.25. The graph in Figure 11.1 shows the P/BV as a function of the difference between the ROE and required rate of return.

Note that when the ROE is equal to the required return, the price is equal to the book value.

Illustration 11.6   ROE and P/BV Ratios—The Case of IBM

IBM provides a classic example of the effects of lower ROE on P/BV ratios. In 1983, IBM had a price that was three times its book value, one of the highest P/BV ratios among the Dow 30 stocks at that time. By 1992, the P/BV ratio for IBM had declined to one, significantly lower than the average ratio for the Dow 30 stocks. This decline in the P/BV ratio was triggered by the decline in ROE at IBM, from 25% in

FIGURE 11.1   P/BV Ratio as a Function of Return Differential

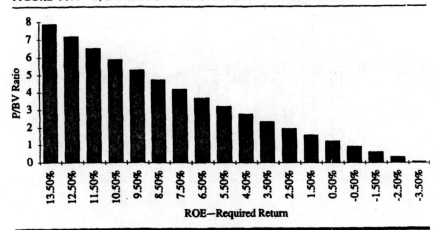

1983 and 1984 to about 5% in 1992. The graph in Figure 11.2 illustrates both variables between 1982 and 1992 for IBM.

Looking for Undervalued Securities—P/BV Ratios and ROE

Given the relationship between P/BV ratios and ROE, it is not surprising to see firms that have high returns on equity selling for well above book value and firms that have low returns on equity selling at or below book value. The firms that should draw attention from investors are those that provide mismatches of P/BV ratios and ROE: low P/BV ratios and high ROE, or high P/BV ratios and low ROE. This is illustrated in the matrix in Figure 11.3.

The table in Figure 11.4 graphs the Dow 30 stocks in March 1993 on this matrix, using P/BV ratios as of March 1993 and ROE in the latest financial year (1992–1993).

Coca-Cola, which had the highest P/BV ratio, also had the highest ROE. General Motors, which had the lowest P/BV ratio, had the lowest ROE. There was generally a positive relationship between the ROE and the P/BV ratio.

The Determinants of ROE

The emphasis placed on historical or current ROE in the analysis of the Dow 30 stocks should not obscure the fact that the price is determined by expectations of future ROE. To the extent that there is a

FIGURE 11.2 IBM: P/BV Ratios and ROE: 1982–1992

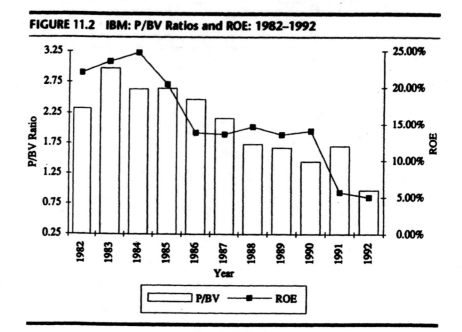

FIGURE 11.3 Undervalued and Overvalued Securities

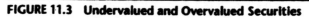
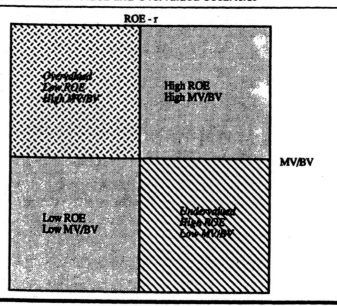

FIGURE 11.4   Dow 30: March 1993—P/BV Ratios and ROE

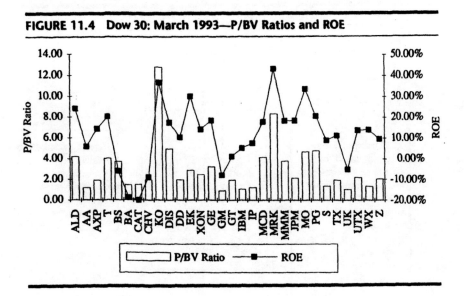

correlation between past ROE and future ROE, the historical measures matter. When the competitive environment is changing, however, focusing on the current ROE can be dangerous and can lead to significant errors in valuation (as evidenced in Illustration 11.6 concerning IBM).

The difference between ROE and the required rate of return is a measure of a firm's capacity to earn supernormal profits in the business in which it operates. Corporate strategists have examined the determinants of the size and expected duration of these excess profits (and high ROE) using a variety of frameworks. One of the better known is the "five forces of competition" framework developed by Porter (1980). In his approach, competition arises not only from established producers producing the same product but also from suppliers of substitutes and from potential new entrants into the market (see Figure 11.5).

In Porter's framework, firms are able to maintain a high ROE because there are significant barriers to entry by new firms or by competitors. The analysis of the ROE of a firm can be made richer and much more informative by examining the competitive environment in which it operates. There may also be clues in this analysis to the future direction of the ROE.

FIGURE 11.5   Five Forces of Competition

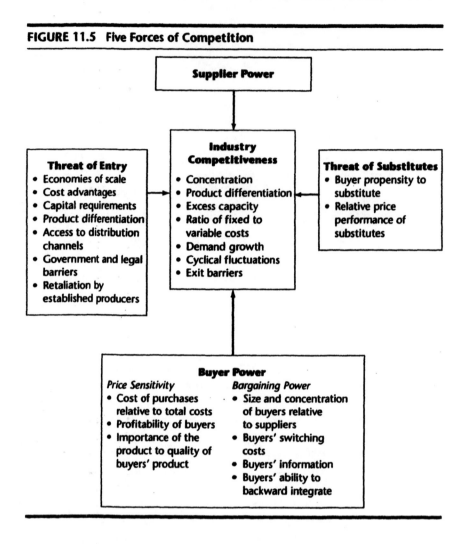

ESTIMATING P/BV RATIOS FROM COMPARABLES

P/BV ratios vary across firms for a number of reasons: different expected growth, different payout ratios, different risk levels, and, most importantly, different ROE. Comparisons of P/BV ratios across firms and/or across time that do not take into account these differences are likely to be flawed.

Using Comparable Firms: Pros and Cons

The most common approach to estimate the P/BV ratio for a firm is to choose a group of comparable firms, to calculate the average P/BV ratio for this group, and to base the P/BV ratio estimate for a firm on this average. The adjustments made to reflect differences in fundamentals between the firm being valued and the comparable group are usually subjective.

There are several problems with this approach. First, the definition of a *comparable* firm is essentially a subjective one. The use of other firms in the industry as the control group is often not a solution because firms within the same industry can have very different business mixes and risk-and-growth profiles. There is also plenty of potential for bias. Second, even when a legitimate group of comparable firms can be constructed, differences will continue to persist in fundamentals between the firm being valued and this group of comparable firms. Adjusting for differences subjectively does not provide a satisfactory solution to this problem, since these judgments are only as good as the analysts making them.

Using the Entire Cross-Section: A Cross-Sectional Regression

In contrast to the comparable-firm approach, the information in the entire cross-section of firms can be used to predict P/BV ratios. The simplest way of summarizing this information is with a multiple regression, with the P/BV ratio as the dependent variable and proxies for risk, growth, ROE, and payout forming the independent variables.

Past Studies

The relationship between P/BV ratios and the ROE has been highlighted in other studies. Wilcox (1984) posits a strong linear relationship between P/BV (plotted on a logarithmic scale) and ROE. Using data from 1981 for 949 Value Line stocks, he arrives at the following equation:

$$\log (P/BV) = -1.00 + 7.51 \ (ROE)$$

He also finds that this regression has much smaller mean squared error than competing models using P/E ratios and/or growth rates.

Updated Regressions

These P/BV ratio regressions have been updated in the following section using data from 1987 to 1991. The COMPUSTAT data base was used to extract information on P/BV ratios, ROE, payout ratios, and earnings growth rates (for the preceding five years) for all NYSE and AMEX firms with data available in each year. The betas were obtained from the CRSP tape for each year. All firms with negative book values were eliminated from the sample, and the regression of P/BV on the independent variables yielded the following for each year:

Year	Regression	R^2
1987	P/BV = 0.1841 + 0.00200 Payout − 0.3940 Beta +1.3389 EGR + 9.35 ROE	0.8617
1988	P/BV = 0.7113 + 0.00007 Payout − 0.5082 Beta +0.4605 EGR + 6.9374 ROE	0.8405
1989	P/BV = 0.4119 + 0.0063 Payout − 0.6406 Beta +1.0038 EGR + 9.55 ROE	0.8851
1990	P/BV = 0.8124 + 0.0099 Payout − 0.1857 Beta +1.1130 EGR + 6.61 ROE	0.8846
1991	P/BV = 1.1065 + 0.3505 Payout − 0.6471 Beta +1.0087 EGR + 10.51 ROE	0.8601

where P/BV = Price/Book value ratio at the end of the year
Payout = Dividend payout ratio at the end of the year
Beta = Beta of the stock
EGR = Growth rate in earnings over prior five years
ROE = Return on equity = Net income/Book value of equity

Illustration 11.7 Valuing a Private Firm Using the Cross-Sectional Regression

Assume that you had been asked to value a private firm early in 1992 and that you had obtained the following data on the company:

Book value of equity = $100 million
Net income in 1990 = $20 million
Beta based upon comparable firms = 1.20

First compute the variables in the desired units,

Payout = 8/20 = 40% (assuming FCFE is paid out as dividend)
Earnings growth rate = 25%
ROE = 20/100 = 20%
Beta = 1.20

$$\text{Predicted P/BV ratio} = 1.1065 + 0.3505\,(0.4) - 0.6471\,(1.20)$$
$$+ 1.0087\,(0.25) + 10.51\,(0.20) = 2.8245$$

$$\text{Predicted market value of equity} = 2.8245 \times 100 = 282.45 \text{ million}$$

P/BV RATIOS AND INVESTMENT STRATEGIES

Investors have used the relationship between price and book value in a number of investment strategies, ranging from the simple to the sophisticated. Some have used low P/BV ratios as a screen to pick undervalued stocks.

P/BV Ratios and Excess Returns

Several studies have established a relationship between P/BV ratios and excess returns. Rosenberg, Reid, and Lanstein (1985) found that the average returns on U.S. stocks were positively related to the ratio of a firm's book value to market value. Between 1973 and 1984, the strategy of picking stocks with high book value/price (BV/P) ratios (low P/BV ratios) yielded an excess return of 36 basis points a month. Fama and French (1992), in examining the cross-section of expected stock returns between 1963 and 1990, established that the positive relationship between BV/P ratios and average returns persists in both the univariate and multivariate tests and is even stronger than the size effect in explaining returns. When they classified firms on the basis of BV/P ratios into 12 portfolios, firms in the lowest BV/P (highest P/BV) class earned an average monthly return of 0.30%, while firms in the highest BV/P (lowest P/BV) class earned an average monthly return of 1.83% for the 1963–1990 period.

PRICE/BOOK VALUE RATIOS

Chan, Hamao, and Lakonishok (1991) found that the book/market
ratio has a strong role in explaining the cross-section of average returns
on Japanese stocks. Capaul, Rowley, and Sharpe (1993) extended the
analysis of P/BV ratios across other international markets and concluded that value stocks (stocks with low P/BV ratios) earned excess returns in every market that they analyzed between 1981 and 1992. Their
annualized estimates of the return differential earned by stocks with
low P/BV ratios, over the market index, were as follows:

Country	Added Return to Low P/BV Portfolio
France	3.26%
Germany	1.39%
Switzerland	1.17%
United Kingdom	1.09%
Japan	3.43%
United States	1.06%
Europe	1.30%
Global	1.88%

A caveat is in order. Fama and French pointed out that low P/BV
ratios may operate as a measure of risk, since firms with prices well below book value are more likely to be in trouble and go out of business.
Investors, therefore, have to evaluate for themselves whether the additional returns made by such firms justify the additional risk taken on by
investing in them.

Using P/BV Ratios as Investment Screens

The excess returns earned by firms with low P/BV ratios have been exploited by investment strategies that use P/BV ratios as a screen. Ben
Graham (1962) for instance, listed "price being less than two-thirds of
book value" as one of the criteria to be used to pick stocks.

The discussion earlier in this chapter emphasized the importance of
ROE in determining the P/BV ratio and noted that only firms with high
ROE and low P/BV ratio could be considered undervalued. This proposition was tested by screening all NYSE stocks from 1981 to 1990, on
the basis of both P/BV ratios and ROE, and creating two portfolios each
year—an undervalued portfolio with low P/BV ratios (in bottom 25% of

universe) and high ROE (in top 25% of universe) and an overvalued portfolio with high P/BV ratios (in top 25% of universe) and low ROE (in bottom 25% of universe)—and then estimating excess returns on each portfolio in the following year. The following table summarizes returns on those two portfolios for each year from 1982 to 1991.

Year	Undervalued Portfolio	Overvalued Portfolio	S&P 500
1982	37.64%	14.64%	40.35%
1983	34.89	3.07	0.68
1984	20.52	−28.82	15.43
1985	46.55	30.22	30.97
1986	33.61	0.60	24.44
1987	−8.80	−0.56	−2.69
1988	23.52	7.21	9.67
1989	37.50	16.55	⦁8.11
1990	−26.71	−10.98	6.18
1991	74.22	28.76	31.74
1982–1991	25.60%	10.61%	17.49%

The undervalued portfolios significantly outperformed the overvalued portfolios in eight out of ten years, earning an average of 14.99% more per year between 1982 and 1991, and also had an average return significantly higher than the S&P 500.

VARIANTS ON P/BV RATIOS

Tobin's Q: Market Value/Replacement Cost

Definition

Tobin's Q provides an alternative to the P/BV ratio, by relating the market value of the firm to the replacement value of the assets in place. In cases where inflation has pushed up the price of the assets or where technology has reduced the price of the assets, this measure may provide a better measure of undervaluation.

Tobin's Q = Market value of assets/Replacement value of assets in place

While this measure has some advantages in theory, it does have some practical problems. The first is that the replacement value of some assets may be difficult to estimate, largely because they are so firm-specific. The second is that, even where replacement values are available, substantially more information is needed to construct this measure than the traditional P/BV ratio.

In practice, analysts often use shortcuts to arrive at Tobin's Q, using book value of assets as a proxy for replacement value. In these cases, the only distinction between this measure and the P/BV ratio is that this ratio is stated in terms of the entire firm (rather than just the equity).

Determinants

The value obtained from Tobin's Q is determined by two variables: the market value of the firm and the replacement cost of assets in place. In inflationary times, when the cost of replacing assets increases significantly, Tobin's Q will generally be lower than the unadjusted P/BV ratio. Conversely, if the cost of replacing assets declines much faster than the book value (computers might be a good example), Tobin's Q will generally be higher than the unadjusted P/BV ratio.

Link to Takeovers

In recent years, many studies have suggested that a low Tobin's Q is indicative of an undervalued or a poorly managed firm, which is more likely to be taken over, and several have examined this relationship. Lang, Stulz, and Walkling (1989) concluded that firms with a low Tobin's Q are more likely to be taken over for purposes of restructuring and increasing value. They also found that shareholders of high Q bidders gain significantly more from successful tender offers than shareholders of low Q bidders.

The Estep T Score

The Estep T model takes into account three variables that have been emphasized in this chapter—return on equity, growth, and price/book value ratios—and consolidates them into one measure. Estep (1985, 1987) provides a simple derivation of this model, which yields the following:

$$T = g + \frac{(ROE - g)}{P/BV} + \frac{\Delta P/BV}{P/BV}(1 + g)$$

where T = Estep T = Total return
g = Growth of stockholders' book value of equity over period
ROE = Return on equity
PBV = Price/Book value of equity
Δ P/BV = Change in P/BV ratio over period

This approach can then be used to decompose actual returns from past periods into three components: growth, cash-flow yield, and valuation change. More importantly, this approach can also be used to predict future returns and to pick undervalued and overvalued securities. Estep tests out the performance of a portfolio, created on the basis of the highest expected return as measured by the T score, and concludes that, for the period 1982 to 1986, this portfolio would have earned an excess return of 5.2% over the S&P 500.

CONCLUSION

The relationship between price and book value is much more complex than most investors realize. The P/BV ratio of a firm is determined by its expected payout ratio, its expected growth rate in earnings, and its riskiness. The most important determinant, however, is the ROE earned by the firm: higher (lower) returns lead to higher (lower) P/BV ratios. The mismatch that should draw investor attention is the one between ROE and P/BV ratios: high P/BV ratios with low ROE (overvalued) and low P/BV ratios with high ROE (undervalued).

5

Estimation of Growth Rates

The value of a firm is ultimately determined not by current cash flows but by expected future cash flows. The estimation of growth rates in earnings and cash flows is, therefore, central to doing a reasonable valuation. Growth rates can be obtained in many ways: they can be based upon past growth, or they can be drawn from estimates made by other analysts who follow the firm, or they can be related to the firm's fundamentals. Since each of these approaches yields some valuable information, it makes sense to blend them to arrive at one composite growth rate to use in the valuation. This chapter examines different approaches to estimating future growth and discusses the determinants of growth.

THE USE OF HISTORICAL GROWTH RATES

There is a connection between past growth rates and expected future growth rates, but the reliability of this connection is open to question. This section explores various ways of using historical growth rates to predict future growth.

Using Average Growth Rates from the Past

This approach uses the average growth rate from the past as the predicted growth rate for the future. There are several estimation issues related to coming up with an average growth rate. Some of them are discussed here.

Arithmetic Average versus Geometric Average

The average growth rate can be very different depending upon whether it is an arithmetic average or a geometric average. The arithmetic average is the simple average of past growth rates, while the geometric mean takes into account the compounding effect. The latter is clearly a much more accurate measure of true growth in past earnings, especially when year-to-year growth has been erratic. This can be illustrated with a simple example.

Illustration 5.1   Using Arithmetic Average versus Geometric Average:
Autodesk Inc.

The following are the earnings per share at Autodesk Inc., a software firm that produces computer-aided design systems, starting in 1987 and ending in 1992:

Year	EPS	Growth Rate
1987	$0.89	
1988	$1.35	51.69%
1989	$1.91	41.48%
1990	$2.30	20.42%
1991	$2.31	0.43%
1992	$1.98	−14.29%

Arithmetic mean = (51.69% + 41.48% + 20.42% + 0.43% − 14.29%)/5
= 19.95%

Geometric mean = $(1.98/0.89)^{1/5} - 1 = 17.34\%$

An alternative to the standard calculation of the arithmetic mean is a weighted mean, with growth rates in more recent years being weighted more heavily than growth rates in earlier years. This would lead to a much lower estimate of the mean for Autodesk Inc.

Estimation Period

The average growth rate is sensitive to the starting and ending periods for the estimation. Thus, the growth rate in earnings over the last five years may be very different from the estimated growth rate over the last six years. The length of the estimation period is subject to the analyst's judgment, but the sensitivity of historical growth estimates to the length of the period should be a factor considered in deciding how much to weight these past growth rates in predictions.

Illustration 5.2 Sensitivity of Historical Growth Rates to the Length of the Estimation Period: Autodesk Inc.

The following provides earnings per share at Autodesk Inc., starting in 1986 instead of 1987, and uses six years of growth rather than five to estimate the arithmetic and geometric averages.

Year	EPS	Growth Rate
1986	$0.55	
1987	$0.89	61.82%
1988	$1.35	51.69%
1989	$1.91	41.48%
1990	$2.30	20.42%
1991	$2.31	0.43%
1992	$1.98	−14.29%

Arithmetic mean = (61.82% + 51.69% + 41.48% + 20.42% + 0.43% − 14.29%)/6 = 26.93%

Geometric mean = $(1.98/0.55)^{1/6} - 1 = 23.80\%$

The growth rates increase significantly if earnings per share starting in 1986 are used rather than earnings starting in 1987, with the arithmetic mean increasing from 19.95% to 26.93%.

Linear and Log-Linear Regression Models

The arithmetic mean weights percentage changes in earnings in each period equally and ignores compounding effects in earnings. The geometric mean considers compounding but focuses on the first and the last earnings observations in the series—it ignores the information in the intermediate observations and any trend in growth rates that may have developed over the period. These problems are at least partially overcome by using Ordinary Least Squares (OLS) regressions of Earnings Per Share (EPS) against time. (An OLS regression estimates regression coefficients by minimizing the squared differences of predicted from actual values.) The linear version of this model is:

$$EPS_t = a + bt$$

where EPS_t = Earnings per share in period t
t = Time period t

The slope coefficient on the time variable is a measure of earnings change per time period. The problem, however, with the linear model is that it specifies growth in terms of dollar EPS and is not appropriate for projecting future growth, given compounding.

The log-linear version of this model converts the coefficient into a percentage change:

$$\ln(EPS_t) = a + bt$$

where $\ln(EPS_t)$ = Natural logarithm of earnings per share in period t
t = Time period t

The coefficient b on the time variable becomes a measure of the percentage change in earnings per unit time.

Illustration 5.3   Linear and Log-Linear Models of Growth: Autodesk Inc.

The EPS from 1986 until 1992 is provided for Autodesk Inc., and the linear and log-linear regressions are done in the following table:

Time (t)	Year	EPS	ln(EPS)
1	1986	$0.55	−0.60
2	1987	$0.89	−0.12
3	1988	$1.35	0.30
4	1989	$1.91	0.65
5	1990	$2.30	0.83
6	1991	$2.31	0.84
7	1992	$1.98	0.68

Linear regression: EPS = 0.4586 + 0.2886t

Log-linear regression: ln(EPS) = −0.5282 + 0.2244t

The slope from the log-linear regression (0.2244) provides an estimate of growth rate of 22.44% in earnings. The slope from the linear regression is in dollar terms. The predictions for 1993 from each regression are as follows:

$$\text{Expected EPS (1993): linear regression} = 0.4586 + 0.2886(8)$$
$$= \$2.77$$

$$\text{Expected EPS (1993): log-linear regression} = e(-0.5282 + 0.2244(8))$$
$$= \$3.55$$

Dealing with Negative Earnings

Measures of historical growth are distorted by the presence of negative-earnings numbers. The percentage change in earnings on a year-by-year basis is defined as:

$$\% \text{ change in EPS in period } t = (EPS_t - EPS_{t-1})/EPS_{t-1}$$

If EPS_{t-1} is negative, this calculation yields a meaningless number. This extends into the calculation of the geometric mean. If the EPS in the initial time period is negative or zero, the geometric mean is not meaningful.

Similar problems arise in log-linear regressions, since the EPS has to be greater than zero for the log transformation to exist. There are at least two ways of trying to get meaningful estimates of earnings growth for firms with negative earnings. One is to run the linear regression of EPS against time specified in the previous regression:

$$EPS = a + bt$$

The growth rate can then be approximated as follows:

$$\frac{\text{Growth rate}}{\text{in EPS}} = b/\text{Average EPS over the time period of the regression}$$

This assumes that the average EPS over the time period is positive. Another approach to estimating growth for these firms, suggested by Arnott (1985), is as follows:

$$\% \text{ change in EPS} = (EPS_t - EPS_{t-1})/\text{Max}(EPS_t, EPS_{t-1})$$

Note that these approaches to estimating historical growth do not provide any information on whether these growth rates are useful in predicting future growth. It is not incorrect, and, in fact, it may be appropriate to conclude that the historical growth rate is "not meaningful" when earnings are negative and to ignore it in predicting future growth.

Illustration 5.4   Dealing with Negative Earnings: Oracle Inc.

The following series lists earnings per share from 1986 to 1992 for Oracle Inc., which had negative earnings per share in 1991.

Time (t)	Year	EPS	log (EPS)	Growth Rate	Modified Growth Rate (Arnott)
1	1986	$0.05	−3.00		
2	1987	$0.13	−2.04	160.00%	61.54%
3	1988	$0.33	−1.11	153.85%	60.61%
4	1989	$0.61	−0.49	84.85%	45.90%
5	1990	$0.86	−0.15	40.98%	29.07%
6	1991	($0.09)	NMF	−110.47%	−110.47%
7	1992	$0.43	−0.84	NMF	120.93%

Approach 1: Using the slope coefficient from the linear regression

$$EPS = 0.1557 + 0.0439t$$

Average EPS (1986–1992) = $0.33

Growth rate = 0.0439/0.33 = 13.25%

Approach 2: Using the minimum or maximum of earnings as the denominator

Arithmetic average, using modified growth rates = 34.60%

The geometric average can be computed in this case and is 43.14%.

Per Share versus Total Earnings

The growth rate in net income can be misleading for firms that have issued substantial amounts of new equity during the estimation time period. The funds raised from these equity issues will generate income that, in turn, will create growth in total net income. Hence, it makes sense to adjust income for the number of shares issued and to look at growth in earnings per share, rather than net income.

The number of shares to be used in calculating EPS is also an issue, since accountants measure EPS relative to both the actual number of shares outstanding (primary EPS) as well as in terms of the potential number of shares that could be outstanding, assuming conversion of warrants and convertible bonds (diluted EPS). The primary EPS, using the actual number of shares outstanding, is the appropriate number to use in calculating earnings growth. The potential dilution effects of convertible bonds and warrants on value can be better assessed using option-pricing models to value these securities.

Time-Series Models to Predict EPS

Time-series models use the same historical information as the simpler models described in the previous section. They attempt to extract better predictions from this data, however, through the use of sophisticated statistical techniques.

Box-Jenkins Models

Box and Jenkins developed a procedure for analyzing and forecasting univariate time-series data using an AutoRegressive Integrated Moving Average (ARIMA) model, which models a value in a time series as a linear combination of past values and past errors (shocks). Since historical data is used, these models are appropriate as long as the data does not show deterministic behavior, such as a time trend or a dependence on outside events or variables. ARIMA models are usually denoted by the notation:

ARIMA (p, d, q)

where p is the degree of the autoregressive part
    d is the degree of differencing
    q is the degree of the moving average process

The mathematical model can then be written as follows:

$$w_t = \phi_1 w_{t-1} + \phi_2 w_{t-2} + \ldots + \phi_p w_{t-p} + \theta_0 - \theta_1 a_{t-1} - \theta_2 a_{t-2} - \ldots - \theta_q a_{t-q} + \varepsilon_t$$

where w_t = Original data series or difference of degree d of the original data

$\phi_1, \phi_2, \ldots, \phi_p$ = Autoregressive parameters

θ_0 = Constant term

$\theta_1, \theta_2, \ldots, \theta_q$ = Moving average parameters

ε_t = Independent disturbances, random error

ARIMA models can also adjust for seasonality in the data, in which case the model is denoted by the notation:

SARIMA $(p, d, q) \times (p, d, q)_{s\,=\,n}$

where s = Seasonal parameter of length n

Time-Series Models in Earnings

Most time-series models used in forecasting earnings are built around quarterly EPS. In a survey paper, Bathke and Lorek (1984) point out that three time-series models have been shown to be useful in forecasting quarterly EPS. All three models are Seasonal AutoRegressive Integrated Moving Average (SARIMA) models, since quarterly EPS have a strong seasonal component. The first model, developed by Foster (1977), allows for seasonality in earnings and is as follows:

Model 1: SARIMA $(1, 0, 0) \times (0, 1, 0)_{s=4}$

$EPS_t = \phi_1 EPS_{t-1} + EPS_{t-4} - \phi_1 EPS_{t-5} + \theta_0 + \varepsilon_t$

This model was extended by Griffin and Watts to allow for a moving average parameter:

Model 2: SARIMA $(0,1,1) \times (0,1,1)_{s\,=\,4}$

$EPS_t = EPS_{t-1} + EPS_{t-4} - EPS_{t-5} - \theta_1\varepsilon_{t-1} - \Theta\varepsilon_{t-4} - \Theta\theta_1\varepsilon_{t-5} + \varepsilon_t$

where θ_1 = First-order moving average (MA(1)) parameter
Θ = First-order seasonal moving average parameter
ε_t = Disturbance realization at the end of quarter t

The third time-series model, developed by Brown and Rozeff (1979), is similar in its use of seasonal moving average parameter:

Model 3: SARIMA $(1,0,0) \times (0,1,1)_{s\,=\,4}$

$EPS_t = \phi_1 EPS_{t-1} + EPS_{t-4} - \phi_1 EPS_{t-5} + \theta_0 - \Theta\varepsilon_{t-4}$

How Good Are Time-Series Models at Predicting Earnings?

Time-series models do better than naive models (using past earnings) in predicting EPS in the next quarter. The forecast error (the difference between the actual EPS and forecasted EPS) from the time-series models is, on average, smaller than the forecast error from naive models (such as simple averages of past growth). The superiority of the models over naive estimates declines with longerterm forecasts, suggesting that the estimated time-series parameters are not stationary.

Among the time-series models themselves, there is no evidence that any one model is dominant, in terms of minimizing forecast error, for every firm in the sample. The gain from using the firm-specific best models, relative to using the same model for every firm, is relatively small.

Limitations in Using Time-Series Models in Valuation

In most studies, time-series models provide superior forecasts relative to naive models. There are several concerns, however, in using these models for forecasting earnings in valuation. First, time-series models require a lot of data, which is why most of them are built around quarterly EPS. In most valuation, the focus is on predicting annual EPS and not on quarterly earnings. Second, even with quarterly EPS, the number of observations is limited for most firms to 10 to 15 years of data (40 to 60 quarters of data), leading to large estimation errors* in time-series model parameters and in the forecasts. Third, the superiority of earnings forecasts from time-series models declines as the forecasting period is extended. Given that earnings forecasts in valuation have to be made for several years rather than a few quarters, the value of time-series models may be limited. Finally, studies indicate that analyst forecasts dominate even the best time-series models in forecasting earnings.

In conclusion, time-series models are likely to work best for firms that have a long history of earnings and for which the parameters of the models have not shifted significantly over time. For the most part, however, the cost of using these models is likely to exceed their benefits, at least in the context of valuation.

The Value of Past Growth in Predicting Future Growth

Past growth rates are useful in forecasting future growth but can seldom be considered sufficient information. In a study of the relationship between past growth rates and future growth rates, Little (1962) coined the term "Higgledy Piggledy Growth" because he found little evidence that firms that grew fast in one period continued to grow fast in the next period. In the process of running a series of correlations between

---

* Time-series models generally can be run as long as there are at least 30 observations, but the estimation error declines as the number of observations increases.

growth rates in consecutive periods of different length, he frequently found negative correlations between growth rates in the two periods, and the average correlation across the two periods was close to zero (0.02). His study was updated using growth rates in two more-recent five-year time periods—1981–1985 and 1986–1990—and the correlation coefficient in earnings growth, while positive, is still not significantly different from zero.

The value of past growth in predicting future growth is determined by a number of factors:

1. Variability in growth rates. The usefulness of past growth rates in predicting future growth is inversely related to the variability in these growth rates. This variability can be measured in a number of ways. A simple measure is the standard deviation in growth rates in past EPS:

$$\sigma_g = \frac{\sum_{t=1}^{n}(g_t - \bar{g})}{n - 1}$$

where σ_g = Standard deviation in growth rate in EPS
g_t = Growth rate in EPS in year t
$\bar{g}$ = Average growth rate in EPS over n periods
n = Number of periods of historical data

In the linear and log-linear regressions of EPS, described earlier, the variability can be measured by the standard error of the coefficient estimates as well as the R-squared of the regression. In general, analysts should be cautious about using past-growth rates in forecasting future-growth rates if there is significant volatility in these rates.

2. Size of the firm. Since the growth rate is stated in percentage terms, the role of size has to be weighed in the analysis. It is easier for a firm with $10 million in earnings to generate a 50% growth rate than it is for a firm with $500 million in earnings. Since it is more difficult for firms to sustain high growth rates as they become larger, past growth rates for firms that have grown dramatically in size and profits may be difficult to maintain in future periods.

Illustration 5.5   The Effect of Size on Growth: Microsoft

Microsoft was one of the biggest success stories of the 1980s, increasing its net income from $3.5 million in 1982 to $708 million in 1992. In the process, it posted growth rates that exceeded 50% on a regular basis.

The following shows the growth in net income (in millions) for Microsoft from 1987 to 1992, in both percentage and dollar terms.

Year	Net Income	% Growth Rate	Δ Net Income
1987	$ 78.10		
1988	$123.90	58.64%	$ 45.80
1989	$170.50	37.61%	$ 46.60
1990	$279.20	63.75%	$108.70
1991	$462.70	65.72%	$183.50
1992	$708.10	53.04%	$245.40

The geometric average growth rate in earnings from 1987 to 1992 was 55.41%. If Microsoft maintained this phenomenal growth rate for the 1993 to 1997 time period, the estimated net income for each of those years would be:

Year	Net Income	% Growth Rate	Δ Net Income
1993	$1,100.48	55.41%	$ 392.38
1994	$1,710.30	55.41%	$ 609.82
1995	$2,658.04	55.41%	$ 947.74
1996	$4,130.95	55.41%	$1,472.91
1997	$6,420.05	55.41%	$2,289.10

The dollar increase in net income needed each year to sustain a 55.41% growth rate becomes larger and larger and rises to $2.289 billion by 1997. Even if Microsoft remains a well-run and successful firm, it will become progressively more difficult over time to deliver these high growth rates.

3. *Cyclicality in economy.*   Historical growth rates for cyclical firms are stronger influenced by where in the business cycle the economy is at the time of the estimation. If historical growth rates are estimated for cyclical firms in the middle of a recession, the growth rates are likely to be very negative. The reverse is generally true if the estimation of historical growth is done at an economic peak. These growth rates are of little value, however, in predicting future growth.* It would be more useful to estimate growth across two or more economic cycles for these firms.

* The earnings of cyclical firms are likely to be depressed, relative to normal levels, during a recession. As the economy improves, these earnings can be expected to rebound strongly. Thus,

4. Changes in fundamentals. The observed growth rate is the result of fundamental decisions made by the firm on business mix, project choice, capital structure, and dividend policy. If a firm changes on any or all of these dimensions, the historical growth rate may not be a reliable indicator for future growth. For instance, the restructuring of a firm often changes both its asset and its liability mix, and makes past-growth rates fairly meaningless in predicting future growth.

The other problem with using past-growth rates arises when the business in which the firm is operating changes either as a result of market forces or government regulation. These changes in fundamentals may cause a shift upwards or downwards in growth for all companies in that business and have to be factored into predictions. Pharmaceutical companies, for instance, at the end of 1992 had enjoyed a decade of high growth as medical technology advanced and health-care costs surged. Looking into the future, however, market forces and the potential for health-care reform made it unlikely that these growth rates would continue.

5. Quality of earnings. All earnings growth is not equal. Earnings growth created by changes in accounting policy or acquisitions is inherently less reliable than growth created by increasing units sold and should be weighted less in forecasting future growth. Bernstein and Seigel (1979) present some guidelines for assessing earnings quality:

1. Earnings growth reported by firms with more liberal accounting policies* is less reliable (and of lower quality) than growth reported by firms with conservative accounting policies.

2. The integrity of the reporting period, that is, the extent to which current earnings benefit from past earnings or borrow from future earnings, is important for earnings quality. The earnings growth rates for firms that use accounting techniques to increase current earnings at the expense of future earnings should be used cautiously in analyses.

3. Earnings quality is also affected by whether proper provisions are made for discretionary costs needed to maintain assets and earnings power.

---

at the same time as historical growth is negative, the expected growth is likely to be strongly positive.

* In the aftermath of IBM's fall from grace, with the stock price dropping from $170 in 1986 to $50 in 1992, the *Wall Street Journal* revealed that accounting policies in the firm during the 1980s had been liberal in recognizing income (though the actions were not illegal).

THE USE OF ANALYSTS' FORECASTS OF EARNINGS

Few firms are valued in a vacuum. In most cases, an analyst valuing a firm has access to estimates of growth in earnings and cash flows made by other analysts who follow the same firm. Should the growth forecasts of other analysts be incorporated into the valuation? If so, how? The answers to these and other questions will be considered in this section.

What Information Do Analysts Use in Making Earnings Forecasts?

There is a simple reason why analyst forecasts should be better than mechanical models, which use only past earnings data. Analysts, in addition to using historical data, can avail themselves of other information that may be useful in predicting future growth.

1. Firm-specific information that has been made public since the last earnings report.   Analysts can use information that has come out about the firm since the last earnings report to make predictions about future growth. This information can sometimes lead to significant re-evaluation of the firm's expected cash flows. Leslie Fay, for instance, a leading women's apparel manufacturer, reported net income of $23.9 million in 1992. It revealed on January 29, 1993, that false entries had been made on the books and that it had really lost $13.7 million in 1992. Analysts following Leslie Fay proceeded to significantly lower expectations of future earnings, and this in turn led to a drop in the stock price from $12 on January 29 to $3.50 on April 8, 1993.

2. Macroeconomic information that may impact future growth.   The expected growth rates of all firms are affected by economic news on GNP growth, interest rates, and inflation. Analysts can update their projections of future growth as new information comes out about the overall economy and about changes in fiscal and monetary policy. Information, for instance, that shows the economy growing at a faster rate than forecast will result in analysts increasing their estimates of expected growth for cyclical firms.

3. Information revealed by competitors on future prospects.   Analysts can also condition their growth estimates for a firm on information revealed by competitors on pricing policy and future growth. Analysts following tobacco companies in March 1993 were forced to re-evaluate expectations of growth following the decision by Philip Morris to cut prices on its Marlboro brand and to, therefore, reduce profit margins. A similar action by American Airlines in the summer of 1992 on airline fares led to a re-estimation of growth and value for the airlines.

4. Private information about the firm. Analysts sometimes have access to private information about the firms they follow that may be relevant in forecasting future growth. This avoids answering the delicate question of when private information becomes illegal inside information. There is no doubt, however, that good private information can lead to significantly better estimates of future growth.

5. Public information other than earnings. Models for forecasting earnings that depend entirely upon past earnings data may ignore other publicly available information that is useful in forecasting future earnings. It has been shown, for instance, that other financial variables such as earnings retention, profit margins, and asset turnover are useful in predicting future growth. Analysts can incorporate information from these variables into their forecasts.

How Good Are Analysts at Forecasting Future Growth?

The ability of analysts to provide superior forecasts of future growth has been studied extensively. The results can be categorized on the basis of the time horizon for the forecasts—short term versus long term.

The Accuracy of Short Term Forecasts

The general consensus from studies that have looked at short term forecasts (one quarter ahead to four quarters ahead) of earnings is that analysts provide better forecasts of earnings than models that depend purely upon historical data. The following table summarizes the results from three studies of analysts' forecasts.

The mean relative absolute error measures the absolute difference between the actual earnings and the forecast for the next quarter, as a percent of the forecast. The mechanical models are all based upon historical data.

Two other studies shed further light on the value of analysts' forecasts. Crichfield, Dyckman, and Lakonishok (1978) examine the relative accuracy of forecasts in the *Earnings Forecaster,* a publication from

576

TABLE 5.1 Analyst Forecasts vs. Time Series Models

| Study | Analyst Group | Mean Relative Absolute Error | |
		Analyst Forecasts	Mechanical Models
Collins & Hopwood	Value Line Forecasts 1970–1974	31.7%	34.1%
Brown & Rozeff	Value Line Forecasts 1972–1975	28.4%	32.2%
Fried & Givoly	Earnings Forecaster 1969–1979	16.4%	19.8%

Standard and Poors that summarizes forecasts of earnings from more than 50 investment firms. They measure the squared-forecast errors by month of the year and compute the ratio of analyst-forecast error to the forecast error from time-series models of earnings. They find that the time-series models actually outperform analyst forecasts from April until August, but underperform them from September through January. They hypothesize that this is because there is more firm-specific information available to analysts during the latter part of the year. The other study by O'Brien (1988) compares consensus-analyst forecasts from the Institutions Brokers Estimate System (I/B/E/S) with time-series forecasts from one quarter ahead to four quarters ahead. The analyst forecasts outperform the time-series model for one-quarter-ahead and two-quarter-ahead forecasts, do as well as the time-series model for three-quarter-ahead forecasts, and worse than the time-series model for four-quarter-ahead forecasts. Thus, the advantage gained by analysts from firm-specific information seems to deteriorate as the time horizon for forecasting is extended.

The Accuracy of Long Term Forecasts

In valuation, the focus is more on longterm-growth rates in earnings than on next quarter's earnings. There is little evidence to suggest that analysts provide superior forecasts of earnings when the forecasts are over the long term. An early study by Cragg and Malkiel compared long term forecasts by five investment management firms in 1962 and 1963 with actual growth over the following three years to conclude that analysts were poor long term forecasters. This view is contested by Vander Weide and Carleton (1988), who find that the consensus prediction of

577

five-year growth in the I/B/E/S is superior to historically oriented growth measures in predicting future growth.

There is an intuitive basis for arguing that analyst predictions of growth rates must be better than time-series-based or other historical-data-based models simply because they use more information. The evidence indicates, however, that this superiority in forecasting is surprisingly small for long term forecasts and that past growth rates play a significant role in determining analyst forecasts.

Analyst Forecasts and Stock Prices

There is evidence from financial markets that analyst forecasts have informational value. Hawkins, Chamberlin, and Daniel (1984) find that revisions in forecasts seem to predict subsequent stock-price movements and that portfolios of stocks that had the largest upward revisions in consensus-earnings forecasts earned a risk-adjusted abnormal return of 14.2% in the following 12 months. Richards and Martin (1979) classify revisions by quarter of the year and find that revisions made in the first quarter contain more new information and lead to higher abnormal returns than revisions made later in the year. Other studies confirm the findings in those two that revisions in analyst forecasts contain new information and that financial markets do not impound this information in prices effectively.

How Do You Use Analyst Forecasts in Estimating Future Growth?

The information in the growth rates estimated by other analysts can and should be incorporated into the estimation of expected future growth. There are several factors that determine the weight assigned to analyst forecasts in predicting future growth.

1. Amount of recent firm-specific information. Analyst forecasts have an advantage over historical-data-based models because they incorporate more recent information about the firm and its future prospects. This advantage is likely to be greater for firms where there have been significant changes in management or business conditions in the recent past, for example, a restructuring or a shift in government policy relating to the firm's underlying business.

2. Number of analysts following the stock. Generally speaking, the larger the number of analysts following a stock, the more informative is their consensus forecast, and the greater should be the weight assigned to it in analysis. The informational gain from having more analysts is diminished somewhat by the well-established fact that most analysts do not act independently and that there is a high correlation across analysts' revisions of expected earnings.

3. Extent of disagreement between analysts. While consensus-earnings growth rates are useful in valuation, the extent of disagreement between analysts, measured by the standard deviation in growth predictions, is also a useful measure of the reliability of the consensus forecasts. Givoly and Lakonishok (1984) find that the dispersion of earnings is correlated with other measures of risk, such as beta, and is a good predictor of expected returns.

4. Quality of analysts following the stock. This is the hardest of the variables to quantify. One measure of quality is the size of the forecast error made by analysts following a stock, relative to models that use only historical data—the smaller this relative error, the larger the weight that should be attached to analyst forecasts. Another measure is the effect on stock prices of analyst revisions—the more informative the forecasts, the greater the effect on stock prices. There are some who argue that the focus on consensus forecasts misses the point that some analysts are better than others in predicting earnings and that their forecasts should be isolated from the rest and weighted more.

Analysts' forecasts may be useful in coming up with a predicted growth rate for a firm but there is a danger to blindly following consensus forecasts. Analysts often make significant errors in forecasting earnings, partly because they depend on the same data sources (which might have been erroneous or misleading) and partly because they sometimes overlook significant shifts in the fundamental characteristics of the firm. The secret to successful valuation often lies in discovering inconsistencies between analysts' forecasts of growth and a firm's fundamentals. The next section examines this relationship.

THE DETERMINANTS OF EARNINGS GROWTH

While growth in a firm may be measured using history or analyst forecasts, it is determined by fundamental decisions that a firm makes on product lines, profit margins, leverage, and dividend policy.

Retention Ratio and Return on Equity

The simplest relationship determining growth is one based upon the retention ratio (percentage of earnings retained in the firm) and the return on equity (ROE) on its projects (Return on equity = Net income/ Book value of equity). To establish this, note that:

$$g_t = (NI_t - NI_{t-1})/NI_{t-1}$$

where g_t = Growth rate in net income
NI_t = Net income in year t

Given the definition of return on equity, the net income in year $t-1$ can be written as:

$$NI_{t-1} = \text{Book value of equity}_{t-1} \times ROE_{t-1}$$

where ROE_{t-1} = Return on equity in year $t-1$

The net income in year t can be written as:

$$NI_t = (\text{Book value of equity}_{t-1} + \text{Retained earnings}_{t-1}) \times ROE_t$$

Assuming that the return on equity is unchanged, that is, $ROE_t = ROE_{t-1} = ROE$,

$$g_t = \text{Retained earnings}_{t-1}/NI_{t-1} \times ROE$$
$$= \text{Retention ratio} \times ROE$$
$$= b \times ROE$$

where b is the retention ratio.

In this relationship, growth in earnings is an increasing function of both the retention ratio and the ROE. The following table provides approximate growth rates for a firm given different retention ratios and ROE. This calculation of the growth rate assumes that the ROE is unchanged over time. If it changes over time, the growth rate in period t can be written as (BV is Book Value):

$$g_t = (\text{BV of equity}_t \times (ROE_t - ROE_{t-1})/NI_{t-1}) + b \times ROE$$

The first term captures the effect of changing ROE on the existing equity base—increases (decreases) in ROE make it more (less) profitable and create a higher (lower) growth rate.

TABLE 5.2 Growth Rate as a Function of Retention Ratios and ROE

ROE	0%	25%	50%	75%	100%
			Retention Ratio		
4%	0.00%	1.00%	2.00%	3.00%	4.00%
6%	0.00%	1.50%	3.00%	4.50%	6.00%
8%	0.00%	2.00%	4.00%	6.00%	8.00%
10%	0.00%	2.50%	5.00%	7.50%	10.00%
12%	0.00%	3.00%	6.00%	9.00%	12.00%
14%	0.00%	3.50%	7.00%	10.50%	14.00%
16%	0.00%	4.00%	8.00%	12.00%	16.00%
18%	0.00%	4.50%	9.00%	13.50%	18.00%
20%	0.00%	5.00%	10.00%	15.00%	20.00%

Illustration 5.6   Changes in ROE and Growth Rates: Coca-Cola Inc.

The following table provides information on the retention ratio and the ROE for Coca-Cola for 1992 and projections for 1993 and 1994.

	1992	1993	1994
BV of equity	$4,400		
Net income	$1,884		
Retention ratio	60%	60%	60%
ROE	43%	35%	35%
Growth rate	= 0.6 × 0.43 = 25.80%	= (4,400 × (0.35 − 0.43)/1,884) + 0.6 × 0.35 = 2.32%	= 0.6 × 0.35 = 19.5%

If the ROE after 1994 remained at 35%, the growth rate in earnings would also stay unchanged at 19.5% (assuming the retention ratio was 60%) after 1994. In 1993, however, when the ROE drops from 43% to 35%, the expected growth rate is only 2.32%.

ROE and Leverage

The ROE and, by implication, the growth rate are affected by the leverage decisions of the firm. In the broadest terms, increasing leverage will lead to a higher ROE if the preinterest, after-tax return on assets (ROA), or projects, exceeds the after-tax interest rate paid on debt. This is captured in the following formulation of ROE:

$$ROE = ROA + D/E(ROA - i(1 - t))$$

where ROA = (Net income + Interest$(1 - $tax rate$))/$BV of total assets
= EBIT$(1 - t)/$BV of total assets
D/E = BV of debt/BV of equity
i = Interest expense on debt/BV of debt
t = Tax rate on ordinary income

Note that BV of Total assets = BV of debt + BV of equity.

The derivation is simple and is provided in the footnote.[*] Using this expanded version of ROE, the growth rate can be written as:

$$g = b(ROA + D/E(ROA - i(1 - t)))$$

The advantage of this formulation is that it allows explicitly for changes in leverage and the consequent effects on growth. It is a useful way of analyzing the effects of restructuring on growth and value. There are generally three dimensions to restructuring:

1. Restructuring assets/projects. Asset restructuring generally takes the form of eliminating unprofitable projects and divisions and/or acquiring new assets. The objective in asset restructuring is to increase the firm's ROA, which in turn increases growth. The changing of a firm's asset mix also leads to a change in the riskiness of the firm, which causes discount rates to shift. The net effect of these changes in growth and risk will determine the change in firm value. The effect of changing ROA on growth can be obtained fairly simply using the growth formulation:

$$\delta g/\delta ROA = b(1 + D/E)$$

Thus, the effect of a change in the ROA on growth will depend upon the firm's retention ratio (b) and debt/equity ratio (D/E).

2. Changing capital structure. The other component in financial restructuring is a change in leverage—an increase or decrease in the debt financing in the firm. The effect on future growth can be captured by

---

[*] ROA + D/E(ROA − i(1 − t)) = (NI + Int(1 − t))/(D + E)
+ D/E{(NI + Int(1 − t))/(D + E) − Int(1 − t)/D}
= {(NI + Int(1 − t))/(D + E)}(1 + D/E) − Int(1 − t)/E
= NI/E + Int(1 − t)/E − Int(1 − t)/E = NI/E = ROE

changing the debt/equity ratio and interest rate in the growth rate formulation and recalculating the growth rate. The change in leverage will also lead to a change in risk (increases in leverage will increase risk while decreases in leverage will reduce risk) and in discount rates. Again, the net effect can be either positive or negative.

$$\delta g/\delta(D/E) = ROA - i(1 - t) - (\delta i/\delta D/E)(New\ D/E)(1 - t)$$

where $\delta i/\delta D/E$ = Change in interest rate as a result of the debt/equity change
New D/E = Debt/equity ratio after the change in leverage

3. Changing dividend policy.   The final aspect of financial restructuring is changing dividend policy. A decrease (increase) in dividends will lead to an increase (decrease) in the retention ratio and an increase in the expected growth rate. This has to be offset, however, by the effects of changing payout ratio on the expected dividends. The trade-off usually takes the form of higher growth for lower dividends, and the net effect on value can again be either positive or negative.

$$\delta g/\delta Payout = -(ROA + D/E(ROA - i(1 - t)))$$

In general terms, this formulation of expected growth rates ties value to corporate financial policy: capital budgeting, capital structure, and dividend-policy decisions.

Illustration 5.7   Effects of Restructuring on Expected Growth Rate and Risk: ARCO

Atlantic Richfield Co. (ARCO) went through a major restructuring in 1985, changing both their asset and liability mixes. The following table shows the effects of these changes on the growth rate and the beta.

Investment Policy. All of the company's refining and marketing operations east of the Mississippi River were sold. An $800-million reduction in capital outlays in areas where returns were low was also planned. All non-oil mineral operations were also sold. This was expected to increase the ROA from 12% to 16%.

	Before	*Planned Changes*	*After*
ROA	12.0%	Improve project choice. Eliminate unprofitable divisions.	16%

Financing Policy. ARCO planned to borrow $4 billion and repurchase $4 billion in equity.

	Before	Planned Changes	After
D/E	0.45%	Increase long term debt.	1.00%
Beta	0.60	Leverage increases β.	0.76
Interest rate	7.00%		8.00%

Dividend Policy. An increase in quarterly dividends to $1 per share from 75 cents per share was planned.

	Before	Planned Changes	After
Payout	0.50%	Reinvest less in company.	0.60%
Retention	0.50%	Reinvest less in company.	0.40%

Earnings Growth Rate. The growth rate in earnings can be expected to increase from 7.75% to 10.88% as a consequence of the restructuring. ARCO's stock price went up $5.25 to $58.25 after the restructuring was announced, representing a total gain of $1.3 billion to stockholders.

ROA, Profit Margin, and Asset Turnover

The analysis of ROA can be carried forward one step if it is related to profit margins and sales.

$$ROA = EBIT(1 - t)/\text{Total assets}$$
$$= (EBIT(1 - t)/\text{Sales}) \times (\text{Sales}/\text{Total assets})$$
$$= \text{Preinterest profit margin} \times \text{Asset turnover}$$

The ROA is an increasing function of both the preinterest profit margin and the asset turnover. The relationship is made more interesting, however, by the trade-off between the two variables—increasing profit margins will generally reduce asset turnover, and reducing profit margins will increase asset turnover. The net effect will depend upon the elasticity of demand for the product. Thus, the effects on ROA of the decision by Philip Morris to reduce prices (and, hence, profit margins) on its Marlboro brand of cigarettes cannot be evaluated without making some assumptions about the effect of lower prices on sales.

This extension of the growth formulation allows for the linkage of value to corporate strategy. Sears, for instance, in 1991, decided that it was going to reduce prices and profit margins on products to increase sales. The effects of this lower-margin, higher-turnover strategy on value could have been analyzed by estimating the effects of the shift on growth and, consequently, on value.

Illustration 5.8 Evaluating the Effects of Corporate Strategy on Growth Rate and Value: Procter & Gamble

Procter & Gamble decided to reduce prices on their disposable diapers in April 1993 to compete better with low-price private-label brands. The preinterest, after-tax profit margin was expected to drop from 7.43% to 7% as a consequence, and the asset turnover was expected to increase from 1.6851 to 1.80. The following table provides projections in profit margins, asset turnover, and growth rates after the shift in corporate strategy:

	1992	After Shift in Strategy
EBIT (1 − tax rate)	$ 2,181	
Sales	$29,362	
Preinterest, after-tax profit margin	7.43%	7.00%
Total assets	$17,424	
Asset turnover	1.6851	1.80
Return on assets	12.52%	12.60%
Retention ratio	58.00%	58.00%
Debt/Equity (book value)	0.7108	0.7108
Interest rate on debt (1 − tax rate)	4.27%	4.27%
Growth rate	10.66%	10.74%

(All $ figures in millions)

The shift in corporate strategy increases the expected growth rate in earnings marginally. This is conditioned, of course, on the assumption that sales would increase enough to cause the asset turnover to increase to 1.8.

Product-Line Analysis

One criticism that is often leveled at analysts is that by focusing on aggregates at the firm level, they might be missing significant trends in the profitability of individual product lines. Thus, a firm with an aging product-line mix may look healthy in terms of historical growth and current profitability, but it is not likely to sustain this growth into the future. The analysis of growth for a firm can be made more complete by looking at its individual product lines and examining where they stand in terms of the product life cycle. The classical analysis of the product life cycle suggests that as products go through the different growth phases from high growth to decline, the profit margins vary systematically with each phase. The growth rates across time for individual product lines can then be estimated as follows:

$$g_{jt} = b(\pi_{jt} \times \tau_{jt} - D/E(\pi_{jt} \times \tau_{jt} - i(1 - t)))$$

where g_{jt} = Growth rate in year t for product line j
   π_{jt} = Preinterest, after-tax profit margin in year t for product line j
   τ_{jt} = Asset turnover in year t for product line j
   D/E = Debt/Equity ratio for the firm
   i = Interest rate on debt
   t = Tax rate on ordinary income

Figure 5.1 adapts a classical life-cycle chart to growth analysis, with profit margins and revenues in each stage.

Some General Issues Relating to Fundamental Models

There are clearly benefits to examining the determinants of growth and estimating growth rates in terms of financial fundamentals. There are issues, however, in their usage that need to be considered:

1. Estimation of inputs

One of the costs of using fundamental models of growth is the increase in the number of inputs needed to estimate growth and value a firm. There are several estimation issues that arise in this context.

a. Current versus projected values. The current values of most of the inputs used in these models are generally easily available. Given that the objective in valuation is the forecasting of future growth rates, the real inputs that are needed are projected values for these variables. The current values may be a useful starting point, but they seldom provide sufficient information for making good predictions.

FIGURE 5.1   Product-Line Analysis

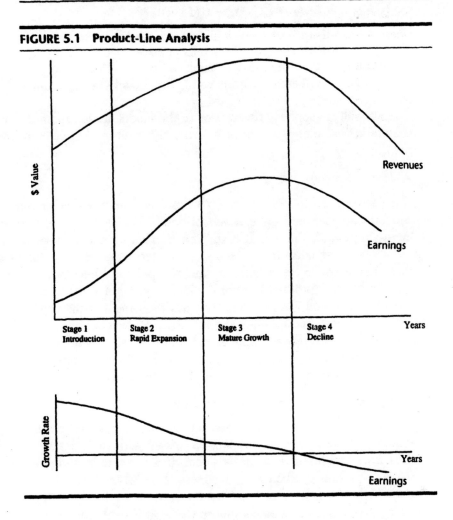

b. Emphasis on book value.   The emphasis placed on book value in all these models is troublesome, though it is much less of a factor for future projections than it is for current values for the variables. If, for instance, a firm has a current debt/equity ratio of 50% in book-value terms and target debt/equity ratio of 100% in market-value terms, the use of the latter may provide a better estimate of future growth in earnings. For those who are still squeamish about the use of book value, the growth rate can be stated entirely in Market-Value (MV) terms:

$$g_t = b(ROA_m + (D/E)_m(ROA_m - i_m(1 - t)))$$

where ROA_m = Return on assets in place (in market-value terms)

$\qquad$ = $EBIT(1 - t)/MV$ of assets in place

$\qquad (D/E)_m$ = MV of debt/(MV of assets in place − MV of debt)

$\qquad i_m$ = Market interest rate on the firm's debt

The difficulty in applying this version of the model lies in separating out the market value of assets in place from the total market value of the firm.

2. Level of detail

The fundamental models for growth described in this section can be carried to higher and higher levels of detail. While there are gains to increasing detail, there is a cost. The number of inputs needed increases, and the noise in the valuation created by errors in estimating these inputs has to be weighed against the potential benefits. In some cases, where the product lines of the firm are distinct and in different growth phases and where the analyst has the time and the experience to analyze these product lines, the estimates of growth are likely to become more accurate with more detail. In other cases, where any or all of these conditions do not apply, additional detail may actually result in inferior estimates of growth and less accurate valuation.

3. Consistency of inputs with firm type

It is important that analysts, when forecasting inputs to these models, ensure that the values they use are consistent with their description of the firm. If, for instance, an analyst considers a firm to be a high-growth firm in a profitable, albeit risky, business, it is likely to have a low payout ratio, high return on assets, and low leverage during the growth period. As it grows larger and becomes more stable, it is likely to increase dividend payout, its projects will no longer be generating supernormal returns, and it will generally increase leverage. Though individual firms may deviate from these generalities, a good reason has to be provided for these deviations.

Illustration 5.9 Adjusting Inputs for Firm Type: Neutrogena Inc.

The following table provides estimates of ROA, retention ratio, and interest rates for Neutrogena, a cosmetics manufacturer. Neutrogena is expected to grow at an extraordinary rate in the first five years (growth phase) and at a stable rate after that (steady state).

	Growth Phase	Steady State
Retention ratio	76%	50%
ROA	19.5%	15%
Debt/Equity	0%	25%
Interest rate on debt	10%	8.00%
Growth rate	14.82%	8.375%

Note that the retention ratio decreases, the ROA decreases, and the debt/equity ratio increases after the firm enters steady state. The firm is also expected to have lower default risk and to pay a lower interest rate on borrowing. The steady-state values for inputs were obtained from the cross-sectional averages for larger (and presumably more stable) firms in the cosmetic industry.

The questions of what is reasonable for a firm in the long term will in large part be determined by the cross-section not only in the firm's industry but across all industries. Thus, a firm that has a profit margin of 22% in an industry in which the average profit margin is 10% is unlikely to maintain that margin after it reaches stable growth, by which point it has presumably exhausted some or all of the differential advantage that gave it the high margin in the first place. In forecasting values for fundamental variables, it is useful to know where other firms stand in terms of the same inputs. The following table gives the average values for the retention ratio (b), ROA, and debt/equity ratios for large manufacturing firms between 1987 and 1991 (from COMPUSTAT).

TABLE 5.3 Cross-Sectional Averages: Financial Fundamentals

Year	Retention Ratio	ROA	Debt/Equity Ratio
1987	72.49%	10.41%	25.68%
1988	70.95%	9.93%	21.84%
1989	68.38%	9.23%	25.62%
1990	68.70%	9.22%	24.48%
1991	68.84%	5.96%	25.85%

GENERAL ISSUES IN ESTIMATING GROWTH

There are several approaches to estimating growth, and the analyst should exploit the information in each approach. This section examines two issues: the weighting of the growth rates from historical data, analyst forecasts, and fundamentals; and the smoothing of future growth for firms that have had volatile earnings in the past.

Weighting Different Estimates of Growth

There are three possible ways to estimate growth: use historical data in either naive or time-series models, use the consensus forecasts made by other analysts, or use growth rates estimated from the firm's fundamentals. From a practical standpoint, the three approaches often overlap. Analysts use historical data in forecasting earnings, and analyst estimates of fundamentals (such as profit margins) as well as historical data drive many fundamental models of growth. This does not imply, however, that the approaches always yield similar values. On the contrary, they often provide very different estimates of growth, leaving the analyst with the difficult decision of which growth rate or which combination of growth rates to use in valuation.

If only one of these three growth rates is to be used, the appropriate growth rate to use will depend upon the firm being analyzed. If the firm is going through a complex restructuring, the growth rate from fundamentals is the best choice because it can be conditioned on the planned changes in the asset and liability mix. If the firm is relatively stable in terms of its fundamentals, and is heavily followed by analysts, their long term forecasts are likely to dominate forecasts from the other approaches. If a firm has established a stable pattern of historical growth and the fundamentals of the business have not changed, the time-series models based upon historical data will provide accurate forecasts of future growth.

There is no reason, however, to use only one of these growth rates. Each approach provides a forecast of future growth and is informative. A weighted average of these growth rates, with the weight based upon the informativeness of each growth rate, may provide a superior estimate of future growth than any one of the three. The tricky part is measuring the informativeness of each growth rate. One approach is to calculate the standard errors for each of the estimates and to weight them based upon these errors—the larger the error, the smaller the weight. For models based upon historical data, this will be measured by the standard error in data-series or in the time-series models. For analyst forecasts, it will be determined by the extent of disagreement between analysts and measured by the standard deviation across their forecasts. For fundamental models, it will be driven by standard errors in the inputs to the model. Illustration 5.10 provides an example of "weighted" growth rates.

Illustration 5.10 Weighting Based upon Standard Deviations: Autodesk Inc.

Consider again the example of Autodesk Inc., from Illustration 5.1, with EPS available from 1987 to 1992. The following also provides analyst forecasts of expected growth from 1993–1997 from nine analysts following Autodesk.

	Historical EPS		Analyst Estimates	
Year	EPS	Growth Rate	Analyst Number	Estimated Growth
1987	$0.89		1	10.00%
1988	$1.35	51.69%	2	10.50%
1989	$1.91	41.48%	3	12.00%
1990	$2.30	20.42%	4	12.50%
1991	$2.31	0.43%	5	13.00%
1992	$1.98	−14.29%	6	16.00%
Arithmetic mean = 19.95%			7	16.00%
Standard deviation = 27.49%			8	18.00%
			9	20.00%
			Consensus forecast = 14%	
			Standard deviation = 3.45%	

The analyst forecast will be weighted more, because of its lower standard deviation.

The problem with this approach is that it assumes that the standard errors in the different estimates are comparable and provide good measures of the informativeness of the estimates. Consider, for instance, a firm that has been in a regulated business in which its earnings have grown at 10% a year for the last decade, with very low variability (assume that the standard error is 2%). Now, assume that this firm has just announced its entry into an unregulated risky business for which analysts forecast that they will grow much faster but disagree on how fast (consensus forecast of growth = 25%; standard error = 20%). A weighting based purely upon standard error would weight the historical growth rate more and the analyst forecast less. Common sense suggests that the analyst forecasts should be weighted more because they impound valuable information on changes in the underlying business of the firm.

The more satisfactory, though subjective, way of dealing with the weighting is to assign weights based upon both the standard errors and other factors. Since it is subjective, there will be room for reasonable analysts to disagree and for biased analysts to build in their bias. Table 5.4 lists some of the factors that should be considered in coming up with a weighting.

Smoothing Future Growth

Analysts often use smoothed forecasts of earnings, even for firms that have had volatile earnings in the past. This is often criticized as unrealistic. It is true that forecasts of earnings that incorporate future

TABLE 5.4 Factors Determining Weights for Different Forecasts

Growth Rate	Factors to Consider	Weight Assigned Higher ←→ Lower
Historical	1. How much history is available?	More ←→ Less
	2. How variable are past earnings?	Less ←→ More
	3. How cyclical is the firm?	Less ←→ More
	4. Has the firm made any fundamental changes in business or leverage?	No ←→ Yes
	5. Has the firm's size changed much over time	No ←→ Yes
Analysts	1. How much firm-specific information has come out since the last earnings report?	Less ←→ More
	2. How many analysts follow the stock?	Many ←→ Few
	3. How much agreement is there between analysts?	More ←→ Less
	4. How good are the analysts?	Good ←→ Poor
Fundamental	1. How much change has there been in firm fundamentals?	More ←→ Less
	2. How well can the inputs to the model be estimated?	Well ←→ Poorly

business cycles accurately are more realistic than those that use smoothed growth rates (and, hence, do not attempt to forecast either the timing or the effects of future recessions or recoveries). It is also true, however, that analysts who try to predict cyclical movements in the economy three or four years into the future are unlikely to succeed in making accurate predictions. Thus, it might be prudent to accept the less realistic approach of smoothing earnings rather than expose the analysis to the error inherent in forecasting economic cycles. While the smoothed earnings will not reflect the volatility of the firm's income stream, the discount rate will. Firms with variable earnings will, in general, have higher discount rates. (There is a high correlation between variance in earnings and betas of stocks—firms with more variable earnings generally tend to have higher betas and, therefore, higher expected returns.)

CONCLUSION

The estimation of future growth rates plays a key role in valuation. This chapter looked at three approaches to estimate these growth rates: the first uses past earnings, the second is built on forecasts made by other analysts who follow the same firm, and the third relates growth rates to fundamentals. Each approach has some informational value, and the estimates from all three can be incorporated into the final analysis, with the weights attached to each a function of its informativeness. This informativeness can be measured using both statistical measures (such as standard error) and subjective factors.